Concurrences Books

Tributes

Eleanor M. Fox – Antitrust Ambassador to the World, *2021*

Herbert Hovenkamp – The Dean of American Antitrust Law, *2021*

Frédéric Jenny – Standing Up for Convergence and Relevance in Antitrust, (Vol. I & II), *2019 & 2021*

Albert Foer – A Consumer Voice in the Antitrust Arena, *2020*

Richard Whish – Taking Competition Law Outside the Box, *2020*

Douglas H. Ginsburg – An Antitrust Professor on the Bench (Vol. I & II), *2018 & 2020*

Wang Xiaoye – The Pioneer of Competition Law in China, *A. Emch, W. Ng (eds.), 2019*

Ian S. Forrester – A Scot without Borders (Vol. I & II), *A. Komninos (eds.), 2015*

William E. Kovacic – An Antitrust Tribute (Vol. I & II), *2013 & 2014*

Practical Books

Global Dictionary of Competition Law, *D. Healey, W. Kovacic, P. Trevisan, R. Whish, Forthcoming 2022*

Antitrust in the Pharmaceutical Sector, *M. Cowie, G. Gordon M. Thill-Tayara, Forthcoming 2022*

Competition Law Treatment of Joint Ventures, *B. Bleicher, N. Campbell, A. Hamilton, N. Hukkinen, P. Khan, Forthcoming 2022 (in collaboration with the IBA)*

State Aid & National Enforcement, *J. Derenne, D. Jouve, C. Lemaire, F. Martucci (eds.), Forthcoming 2022*

Competition Digest – A Synthesis of EU and National Leading Cases, 5th edition, *F. Jenny N. Charbit, (eds.) Forthcoming 2022*

Information Exchange and Related Risks – A Practical Guide, *Z. Marosi & M. Soares (eds.), Forthcoming 2021 (in collaboration with the IBA)*

Perspectives on Antitrust Compliance, *A. Riley, A. Stephan, A. Tubbs (eds.), Forthcoming 2021 (in collaboration with the ICC)*

Turkish Competition Law, *G. Gürkaynak, Forthcoming 2021*

Competition Law – Climate Change & Environmental Sustainability, *S. Holmes, D. Middelschulte, M. Snoep (eds.), 2021*

Merger Control in Latin America – A Jurisdictional Guide, *P. Burnier da Silveira, P. Sittenfeld, 2020*

Competition Inspections under EU Law – A Practitioner's Guide, *N. Jalabert-Doury, 2020*

Gun Jumping in Merger Control – A Jurisdictional Guide, *C. Hatton, Y. Comtois, A. Hamilton (eds.), 2019 (in collaboration with the IBA)*

Choice – A New Standard for Competition Analysis? *P. Nihoul, 2016*

PhD Theses

Essays in Competition Economics, *T. Klein Forthcoming 2022*

Competition & Regulation in Network Industries – Essays in Industrial Organization, *J-M. Zogheib, 2021*

The Role of Media Pluralism in the Enforcement of EU Competition Law, *K. Bania, 2019*

Buyer Power, *I. Herrera Anchustegui, 2017*

General Interest

Women and Antitrust – Voices from the Field (Vol I & II), *E. Kurgonaite & K. Nordlander, 2020*

Conference Proceedings

Antitrust in Emerging and Developing Countries – (Vol I & II), *E. Fox, H. First, 2015 & 2016*

Global Antitrust Law – Current Issues in Antitrust Law and Economics, *D. Ginsburg, J. Wright, (eds.) 2015*

Competition Law on the Global Stage – David Gerber's Global Competition Law in Perspective, *D. Gerber, 2014*

e-Book versions available for **Concurrences+** subscribers

Turkish Competition Law

Gönenç Gürkaynak

Foreword by Richard Whish
Introduction by Eleanor M. Fox

Copyright © 2021 by Institute of Competition Law
106 West 32nd Street, Suite 144 New York, NY, 10001, USA
www.concurrences.com
book@concurrences.com

First Printing, November 2021
978-1-954750-00-5

Cover: Yves Buliard, www.yvesbuliard.fr
Book Design and Layout implementation: Nordcompo

Dedicated with love to my pride and joy, my son, Mehmet.

AUTHOR BIOGRAPHY

Mr. Gönenç Gürkaynak is the founding partner of ELIG Gürkaynak Attorneys-at-Law, a leading law firm of 80 lawyers based in Istanbul, Turkey. He is also an academician, teaching law & economics and competition law at undergraduate and graduate levels at two universities in Turkey.

Mr. Gürkaynak graduated from Ankara University, Faculty of Law in 1997, and was called to the Istanbul Bar in 1998. He then received his LL.M. degree from Harvard Law School, and he is qualified to practice in Istanbul, New York, Brussels and England and Wales. Before founding ELIG Gürkaynak Attorneys-at-Law in 2005, Mr. Gürkaynak worked as an attorney at the Istanbul, New York and Brussels offices of a global law firm for more than eight years. He has been practicing law in multiple jurisdictions as an attorney for more than 25 years, with Turkey being the center of gravity of his practice particularly for the last 15 years.

Mr. Gürkaynak heads the competition law and regulatory department of ELIG Gürkaynak Attorneys-at-Law, which currently consists of 52 lawyers. He has unparalleled experience in Turkish competition law counseling through more than 500 files before the Turkish Competition Authority in more than 25 years of competition law experience, since the establishment of the Turkish Competition Authority. Every year Mr. Gürkaynak represents multinational companies and large domestic clients in more than 30 written and oral defenses in investigations of the Turkish Competition Authority, about 20 antitrust appeal cases in the high administrative courts, and over 90 merger control clearances of the Turkish Competition Authority, in addition to coordinating various worldwide merger notifications, drafting non-compete agreements and clauses, and preparing hundreds of legal memoranda concerning a wide array of Turkish and EU competition law topics.

Mr. Gürkaynak has authored five books: "A Discussion on the Prime Objective of the Turkish Competition Law From a Law & Economics Perspective" published by the Turkish Competition Authority; "Fundamental Concepts of Anglo-American Law", "The Academic Gift Book of ELIG Gürkaynak Attorneys-at-Law in Honor of the 20th Anniversary of Competition Law Practice in Turkey" and "The Second Academic Gift Book of ELIG Gürkaynak Attorneys-at-Law on Selected Contemporary Competition Law Matters" published by Legal Publishing; and this treatise on Turkish Competition Law published by Concurrences. Mr. Gürkaynak has also published more than 200 academic articles in English and in Turkish by various international and local publishers.

FOREWORD

RICHARD WHISH, QC (HON)
King's College London

I was delighted to be asked by Gönenç Gürkaynak to write a Foreword to this excellent new book on Turkish Competition Law.

I have watched the development of Turkish Competition Law with great interest over many years. I remember the discussions around the adoption of Law No. 4054 of 1994 on the Protection of Competition, and have had the pleasure of visiting Turkey on numerous occasions since then to participate in competition law conferences and to provide lectures and training on aspects of the law; some of those visits were in the early years after Law No. 4054 was adopted, when competition law was a little-known subject in the country. It was an extremely interesting time, when lawyers, economists and other interested stakeholders were having to come to terms with the new concepts and processes that competition law entails. It has also been a great pleasure to have taught a significant number of excellent Turkish students at King's College London over many years, whose career developments I have followed with great interest.

Turkish competition law is unusual in that it is rooted in Article 16 of the Turkish Constitution, which places a duty and responsibility on the state to take measures 'to ensure and promote the sound, orderly functioning of the money, credit, goods and services markets' and to prevent 'the formation, in practice or by agreement, of monopolies and cartels in the market'. Of course there has been another powerful influence on the development of Turkish competition law, that is to say Turkey's relationship with the European Union. Whether and when accession to the EU might occur is of course very much in doubt; as I write this Foreword in October of 2021 it seems to be a remote possibility in the foreseeable future. However, insofar as Turkey is required by the Ankara Agreement of 1963 and the Customs Union of Agreement of 1995 to align its competition law with that of the EU, much of the necessary groundwork has been done, with the exception of the creation of a regime for the scrutiny of state aid to match Articles 107 to 109 TFEU.

Various amendments to the Law of 1994 have been proposed and made over the intervening years. Of particular importance is Law No. 7246 of 16 June 2020. The 2020 Law introduces a de minimis principle into Article of the legislation, which prohibits anti-competitive agreements; this will enable the Competition Authority to make better use of its resources, as it will be able to exercise its prosecutorial discretion not to take action in cases where any harm to competition would be insignificant in its effect. The changes to the law introduce two useful new possibilities for the Authority. The first is the possibility for the Turkish Authority to accept legally-binding commitments from undertakings under investigation that they will change their market behaviour in the future; in return the case will be closed, without a formal finding of infringement (or non-infringement). The introduction of a commitments procedure in Article 9

Foreword

of EU Regulation 1/2003 has proved to be a very useful tool for the European Commission, and the Turkish Authority will no doubt draw upon the Commission's experience to date when deciding how and when to use its new power. It is important to note that the commitments procedure will not be available for 'hard-core' infringements of Turkish Competition Law, mirroring the position in the EU. Commitments were accepted in a decision involving Coca-Cola Satış ve Dağıtım A.Ş in September 2021.

A second new possibility for the Authority is the introduction of a settlement procedure (not to be confused with commitments), whereby the parties to an investigation can admit their infringement of the prohibitions in the Competition Act and waive the formalities of a full-contested procedure in return for a reduction of the fine(s) they would otherwise have paid. In the Turkish system the 'discount' will be higher (up to 25%) than in the EU (10%). Unlike in the EU settling parties in Turkey will have to agree that they will not appeal against the Authority's final decision. I note with interest that the first case was decided under the settlement procedure in August of 2021 in a case involving Türk Philips Ticaret A.Ş. and various other undertakings found to have infringed Article 4 of the Competition Act. It will be interesting to see in the future how many cases will be settled: in the EU it is now clear that a majority of cartel cases tend to be settled rather than being taken through the fully contentious procedure.

The Law of 2020 introduces other significant amendments to the original law of 1994, for example in relation to on-site inspections and the system of merger control. Various Communiqués from the Competition Authority supplement these amendments. The Turkish Authority has been and remains an active one, and has not shied away from major investigations of significant international firms; apart from Coca-Cola and Philips, already referred to, the Authority has been investigating Google and the practices of concern to the European Commission in its Google Shopping and Google Android decisions. The recent changes to Turkish Competition Law equip the Competition Authority with much the same toolkit as the European Commission's. This excellent, comprehensive and timely book will be invaluable to anyone interested in the future of Turkish Competition Law. The authors (and publishers) are to be congratulated on bringing this book to the market as quickly as they have done.

INTRODUCTION

ELEANOR M. FOX
New York University School of Law

It is my great pleasure to write the introduction to this monumental new book by Gönenç Gürkaynak. It is a special pleasure not only because the book is an extraordinary, incomparable treatise that is sure to make its mark in explaining and even guiding the competition law of Turkey and beyond, but because this is the twentieth anniversary of my meeting its remarkable author, Gonenc Gurkaynak.

I first met Gönenç when he was a dripping wet young Harvard graduate student arriving at my house in a sudden downpour accompanying his wife-to-be Serra, who was my student at New York University School of Law. Since then, I have watched Gönenç's illustrious career begin and blossom. I observed his contributions to and influence on the competition community around the world. I watched and admired his forming his own competition law firm and building it into one of the finest in Turkey and a player in the world. I admire his being not only a practitioner and advisor but a scholar and teacher, and certainly not a technocratic competition-law-only expert but a constitutional and civil rights expert concerned with human rights and free speech.

The publication of Gönenç's *Turkish Competition Law* is an event of moment. The book is an all-encompassing treatise. It is the first treatise of its kind on the entirety of Turkish competition law. It spans all matters of Turkish competition law, from practical details and procedures to institutions, to all aspects of substantive competition law with nuances of analysis, to guidelines and other guidance as well as the cases that light the path.

The book is beautifully conceived, organized, and written, and had to be a long and hard labor of love. Despite aspects of the subject matter that you might think tedious and dull, reading the book is never tedious and dull. The book is essentially interesting and engaging, no doubt due to the master intellect, filled with experience, behind the words.

The competition law of the European Union was the model for Turkish competition law. Therefore, not surprisingly, frequent reference is made to the competition law of the EU. Occasional reference and comparisons are made with the antitrust law of the United States. Accordingly, the Treatise is not just a one-nation work; it is also a comparative work. It promises to be indispensable to practitioners, advisors, and teachers of Turkish competition law and practitioners and advisors everywhere in the world whose transactions have effects in Turkey. It is of important interest to everyone in the competition law/policy community for its insightful exposition and analysis, including comparative analysis, of competition law and its institutions.

TABLE OF CONTENTS

Chapter 2 – Article 4 and Article 5 of the Competition Law: Basic Principles

Gönenç Gürkaynak, Esq., Fırat Eğrilmez and Aybüke Akdağ

Chapter 3 – Cartels and Tacit Collusion

Gönenç Gürkaynak, Esq., Hilal Özçelik Güldeste and Sinan Haluk Tandoğan

Chapter 4 – Other Horizontal Agreements 97
Gönenç Gürkaynak, Esq., Sinem Uğur and Aydeniz Baytaş

Table of Contents

Chapter 8 – Abuse of Dominance – Exploitative and Discriminatory Practices

Chapter 9 – Merger Control: Procedural Aspects

Chapter 11 – Public Enforcement and Procedures 357
Gönenç Gürkaynak, Esq. and Naz Altınsoy Uçar

Chapter 12 – Sanctions and the Termination of Infringements 395

Gönenç Gürkaynak, Esq., Hakan Demirkan, Esma Aktaş and Uzay Görkem Yıldız

ACKNOWLEDGEMENTS

I had different levels and forms of assistance from different colleagues while writing this book. While we display, both in the table of contents and at the top of each chapter, the names of those that consistently contributed to research work and initial drafting, we hereby recognise the names of some others that had a more intermittent contribution to this work product, with thanks, in alphabetical order: Aslı Su Çoruk, Aysu Tanoğlu, Barış Yüksel, Ebru İnce, Ece Cebecioğlu, Göktuğ Selvitopu, Helin Yüksel, Kansu Aydoğan Yeşilaltay, Melih Yağcı, Merve Öner, Oğuz Erkan, Orçun Horozoğlu, Uygar Yetkiner, Sıla Coşkunoğlu, Ulya Tan, Yasemin Işık, Yeşim Yargıcı, Zeynep Özgültekin.

ACKNOWLEDGEMENTS

LIST OF ABBREVIATIONS

AAC	Average Avoidable Cost
Additional Protocol	Additional Protocol of 1970
AECT	As Efficient Competitor Test
Amendment Law	Law No. 7246 on Amendments to the Law on the Protection of Competition
Ankara Agreement	Agreement Establishing an Association between the EEC and Turkey (signed in Ankara on 12 September 1963)
Authority	Turkish Competition Authority
AVC	Average Variable Cost
ATC	Average Total Cost
Banking Law	Banking Law No. 5411
Board	Turkish Competition Board
CJN	Commission's Consolidated Jurisdictional Notice under Council Regulation (EC) No. 139/2004
CJEU	Court of Justice of the European Union
Code of Obligations	Code of Obligations (Law No. 6098)
Commission	The European Commission
Communiqué No. 2002/2	Block Exemption Communiqué No. 2002/2 on Vertical Agreements
Communiqué No. 2005/4	Block Exemption Communiqué No. 2005/4 on Vertical Agreements and Concerted Practices in the Motor Vehicles Sector
Communiqué No. 2008/2	Block Exemption Communiqué No. 2008/2 on Technology Transfer Agreements
Communiqué No. 2008/3	Block Exemption Communiqué No. 2008/3 in Relation to the Insurance Sector
Communiqué No. 2010/2	Communiqué No. 2010/2 on Oral Hearings Made Before the Competition Board
Communiqué No. 2010/3	Communiqué No. 2010/3 on the Right of Access to the File and Protection of Trade Secrets
Communiqué No. 2010/4	Communiqué No. 2010/4 on Mergers and Acquisitions Subject to the Approval of the Turkish Competition Board
Communiqué No. 2012/2	Communiqué No. 2012/2 on the Application Procedure for Infringements of Competition
Communiqué No. 2013/3	Block Exemption Communiqué No. 2013/3 on Specialisation Agreements
Communiqué No. 2016/5	Block Exemption Communiqué No. 2016/5 on Research and Development Agreements
Communiqué No. 2017/2	Communiqué No. 2017/2 Amending Communiqué No. 2010/4 on Mergers and Acquisitions Requiring the Approval of the Competition Board
Communiqué No. 2017/3	Block Exemption Communiqué No. 2017/3 on Vertical Agreements in the Motor Vehicles Sector

List of Abbreviations

Communiqué No. 2021/2	Communiqué No. 2021/2 on the Commitments to be proposed in Preliminary Investigations and Investigations with respect to Anticompetitive Agreements, Concerted Practices and Decisions and Abuse of Dominance
Communiqué No. 2021/3	Communiqué No. 2021/3 on the Agreements, Concerted Practices and Decision and Practices of Associations of Undertakings which Do Not Appreciably Restrict Competition
Constitution	Constitution of the Republic of Turkey (Law No. 2709)
Decision No. 1/95	Decision No. 1/95 of the EC-Turkey Association Council of 22 December 1995
Directive 2014/104	Directive 2014/104/EU of the European Parliament and of the Council of 26 November 2014 on certain rules governing actions for damages under national law for infringements of the competition law provisions of the Member States and of the European Union
EC Dominance Guidance	Guidance on the Commission's Enforcement Priorities in Applying Article 82 of the European Commission Treaty to Abusive Exclusionary Conduct by Dominant Undertakings
EC Horizontal Guidelines	Guidelines on the applicability of Article 101 of the Treaty on the Functioning of the European Union to horizontal co-operation agreements (2011/C 11/01)
EC Merger Regulation or ECMR	Council Regulation (EC) No. 139/2004 of 20 January 2004 on the control of concentrations between undertakings
ECHR	The European Convention on Human Rights
EEC	The European Economic Community
EU	The European Union
EU De Minimis Notice	Notice on agreements of minor importance which do not appreciably restrict competition under Article 101(1) of the Treaty on the Functioning of the European Union (2014/C 291/01)
EU Guidelines on Horizontal Mergers	EU Commission's Guidelines on the assessment of horizontal mergers under the Council Regulation on the control of concentrations between undertakings (2004/C 31/03)
EVT	Economic Value Test
FMCG	Fast-Moving Consumer Goods
Guidelines on Abuse of Dominance	Guidelines on the Assessment of Exclusionary Abusive Conduct by Dominant Undertakings
Guidelines on Certain Subcontracting Agreements	Guidelines on Certain Subcontracting Agreements Between Non-Competitors
Guidelines on Examination of Digital Data	Guidelines on Examination of Digital Data during On-site Inspections
Guidelines on Horizontal Agreements	Guidelines on Horizontal Cooperation Agreements
Guidelines on Horizontal Mergers	Guidelines on the Assessment of Horizontal Mergers and Acquisitions
Guidelines on Non-Horizontal Mergers	Guidelines on the Assessment of Non-Horizontal Mergers and Acquisitions
Guidelines on Remedies	Guidelines on Remedies that are Acceptable by the Turkish Competition Authority in Merger/Acquisition Transactions

Guidelines on Active Cooperation	Guidelines on the Explanation of the Regulation on Active Cooperation for Detecting Cartels
Guidelines on the Block Exemption in the Motor Vehicles Sector	Guidelines Explaining the Block Exemption Communiqué on Vertical Agreements in the Motor Vehicles Sector, No. 2017/3
Guidelines on the Concept of Control	Guidelines on Cases Considered as a Merger or an Acquisition and the Concept of Control
Guidelines on Exemptions	Guidelines on the General Principles of Exemption
Guidelines on the Relevant Market	Guidelines on the Definition of Relevant Market
Guidelines on Technology Transfer Agreements	Guidelines on the Application of Articles 4 and 5 of the Act No. 4054 on the Protection of Competition to Technology Transfer Agreements
Guidelines on Voluntary Notifications	Guidelines on the Voluntary Notification of Agreements, Concerted Practices and Decisions of Associations of Undertakings
Guidelines on Undertakings Concerned, Turnover and Ancillary Restraints	Guidelines on Undertakings Concerned, Turnover and Ancillary Restraints in Mergers and Acquisitions
Guidelines on Vertical Agreements	Guidelines on Vertical Agreements
HHI	Herfindahl-Hirschman Index
IP Rights	Intellectual property rights
Law No. 1136	Attorneyship Law No. 1136
Law No. 2575	Law No. 2575 on the Council of State
Law No. 2576	Law No. 2576 on the Establishment and Duties of Regional Administrative Courts, Administrative Courts and Tax Courts
Law No. 2577	Law No. 2577 on Administrative Procedure
Law No. 4054	Law No. 4054 on the Protection of Competition
Law No. 4734	Law No. 4734 on Public Procurement
Law No. 4982	Law No. 4982 on Right to Information
Law No. 5271	Law No. 5271 on Turkish Criminal Procedure
Law No. 5326	Law No. 5326 on Misdemeanours
Law No. 5718	Law No. 5718 on International Private and Procedure Law
Law No. 5809	Law No. 5809 on Electronic Communications
Law No. 6098	Code of Obligations
Law No. 6100	Code of Civil Procedure
Law No. 6102	Code of Commerce
Law No. 6545	Law No. 6545 Amending the Turkish Penal Code and Other Codes
Law No. 6741	Law No. 6741 on Establishment of the Turkey Wealth Fund Management Company and Amendments in Certain Laws
Law No. 7246	Law No. 7246 on Amendments to the Law on the Protection of Competition (also Amendment Law)
LRAIC	Long-run average incremental cost
MFN	Most-favoured nation (customer)
OECD	Organisation for Economic Co-operation and Development
Presidential Decree No. 3	Presidential Decree No. 3 on the Appointment Procedures Concerning Top Level Government Executives and State Institutions and Organisations

List of Abbreviations

Procurement Authority	The Public Procurement Authority
R&D	Research and Development
Regulation on Fines	Regulation on Fines to Apply in Cases of Agreements, Concerted Practices and Decisions Limiting Competition, and Abuse of Dominant Position
Regulation on Leniency	Regulation on Active Cooperation for Detecting Cartels (Active Cooperation/Leniency Regulation)
Regulation on Settlement Procedure	Regulation on the Settlement Procedure for Investigations on Anticompetitive Agreements, Concerted Practices, Decisions and Abuse of Dominant Position
Regulation on the Authority	Regulation on Working Procedures and Principles of the Competition Authority
SEP	Standard Essential Patent
SIEC	Significant impediment of effective competition
TFEU	Treaty on the Functioning of the European Union
UNCTAD	United Nations Conference on Trade and Development
WB	World Bank
WTO	World Trade Organization

Chapter 1
An Overview of Competition Law Enforcement

GÖNENÇ GÜRKAYNAK, ESQ., EFE OKER[*]

Turkish competition law is an approximately three decade-old doctrine, which has quickly grown and developed in substance since Law No. 4054 was first introduced in 1994. Rooted in the Constitution, the protection of consumer welfare in the face of anti-competitive mergers and market behaviour has been the focal point of Turkish competition law through its sentinel, the Authority, and its enforcement body, the Board. The Board's practice and the legislative framework have been shaped similar to if not the same as the EU's competition law framework, moving forwards as the relationship between Turkey and the EU continues to make progress.

Turkey's primary piece of competition legislation is Law No. 4054, which governs, among others, (i) agreements and concerted practices restricting competition (Article 4); (ii) individual exemption to the agreements and concerted practices (Article 5); (iii) abuse of dominance (Article 6); and (iv) merger control (Article 7). As such, Law No. 4054 scopes every major aspect of the competition legislation of Turkey.

This chapter aims to give a historical perspective on the development of competition law in Turkey. In this respect, this section provides a historical background of the introduction of Law No. 4054, whose first steps date back to the 1970s in conjunction with the association and accession processes between Turkey and the EU, the requirements under the Constitution, as well as an elaborate overview of the recent amendments to Law No. 4054 and the secondary legislation, in order to establish a bridge between the past and the present of Turkish competition law. The structure, composition and powers of the Authority and Board, as well as the judicial review process of the Board's decisions, will be set out in brief. Finally, the legal and geographic scopes of Turkish competition law are discussed in order to provide preliminary guidance for the application and interpretation of certain substantive competition law concepts under the Turkish competition law regime.

---

[*] Associate, ELIG Gürkaynak Attorneys-at-Law, Istanbul <efe.oker@elig.com>.

1.1 The Roots and Historical Progression of Turkish Competition Law

1.1.1 Constitutional Basis for Competition Law in Turkey (Article 167)

The Constitution requires the state to maintain and protect the functioning of the markets and competition, and to draft the necessary legislation for this purpose, which provides the basis for competition enforcement at the top of the legislative ladder. Accordingly, Article 167 of the Constitution titled "Supervision of Markets and Regulation of Foreign Trade" stipulates in the first paragraph that, "the State shall take measures to ensure and promote the sound and orderly functioning of markets for money, credit, capital, goods and services; and prevent the formation of monopolies and cartels in the markets, which may emerge through practice or by agreement". In this respect, the Constitution sustains the Turkish competition law regime and constitutes the root of the entire legislation aimed at the protection of competition in the markets.

As explained in its preamble, Article 167 assigns the state three duties in the above paragraph. The first one is that the state shall help private enterprises to develop for the better, within the requirements of competition. The second duty on this front obliges the state to prevent de facto monopolies or those that emerge by way of agreements. Lastly, although falling short of monopolies, any cartels formed by manufacturers and service providers via price agreements, manufacturing activities, market allocation or other means are also prohibited. The purpose of these duties is indicated as the prevention of any disadvantages that could arise from a society where competition is eliminated, and prices are determined by monopolies and cartels.

Until the adoption of Law No. 4054, Article 167 of the Constitution was the only legislation that stipulated the prohibition of cartels; however, there was no enforcement due to the lack of an enforcement agency. Apart from targeting the prohibition of cartels, Article 167 of the Constitution also aims to eliminate monopolisation, itself.[1] In this respect, the relevant provision of Article 167 of the Constitution regarding monopolisation was the result of a more rigid approach, compared to the one adopted within the scope of Law No. 4054, since Law No. 4054 does not prohibit "monopolisation" per se, but the abuse of a dominant position in that context.[2]

---

[1] K. C. Sanlı, *Rekabetin Korunması Hakkındaki Kanun'da Öngörülen Yasaklayıcı Hükümler ve Bu Hükümlere Aykırı Sözleşme ve Teşebbüs Birliği Kararlarının Geçersizliği* (Ankara: Rekabet Kurumu, 2000), p. 19.

[2] Ibid.

1.1.2 EU Membership and Shaping the Legislative Framework

Turkish competition law is largely influenced by the EU legislative framework. The development of the Turkish legislation goes hand in hand with Turkey's membership journey to the EU and Turkey's accession to the Customs Union in between. Therefore, Turkish competition law is akin to its European counterpart in very significant aspects. Yet, considering that competition law development is fast-paced and case-law driven, differences may arise between the applications of the legislative framework for the two competition law enforcers in question: the Board and the Commission.

Since the inception of Turkey's adventure for membership to the EU and the accompanying association relationship, competition law has been a field that was borne and shaped in light of the principles under Articles 101 and 102 TFEU, as well as the secondary legislation, almost mimicking their counterparts in the EU. Therefore, observing the interplay between the two doctrines plays a significant role in understanding the field in Turkey; as such, we will examine below how the Turkish doctrine was influenced and shaped by the accession talks. It is important to highlight that the legislation changes in Law No. 4054 in June 2020 brought the Turkish framework closer to the EU legislation. Having said this, as of 24 June 2020, Turkey is still lacking the legislation and a policy stance on State aid.

The EU's 2020 report on Turkey currently defines Turkey's progress on the matter as:

> Turkey has *some level of preparation* in the area of competition policy. There was *backsliding*, on account of an increase in [S]tate aid and its lack of transparency. Long awaited amendments were made to the Law on the Protection of Competition. Concerns remain in the enforcement capacity in the field of State aid. Legislation on anti-trust and mergers is largely aligned with the EU *acquis*.[3]

As such, we will also touch upon the European perspective regarding the progress of Turkish competition law, below.

1.1.3 Ankara Agreement and EC-Turkey Association Council Decisions

The relationship between Turkey and the EU, for the purpose of Turkey's integration into the EU, is based on three principal international agreements: (i) the Ankara Agreement,[4] which established an association between the EEC and the Republic of Turkey;

---

[3]   European Commission, Commission Staff Working Document, "Turkey 2020 Report", SWD(2020) 355 final, 6.10.2020, p. 75.
[4]   Available at <https://eur-lex.europa.eu/resource.html?uri=cellar:f8e2f9f4-75c8-4f62-ae3f-b86ca5842eee.0008.02/DOC_2&format=PDF>.

(ii) the Additional Protocol,[5] which was executed based on the Ankara Agreement; and (iii) Decision No. 1/95.[6]

In all three documents, Turkey undertook to align its competition law legislation with the EU competition law regime. For instance, Article 16 of the Ankara Agreement stipulates that the principles laid down in the provisions on competition, taxation and the approximation of laws contained in Title I of Part III of the Treaty establishing the Community must be made applicable to the contracting parties' relations within the Association.

These steps are put in for the sake of Turkey's membership process, as well as the association relationship, building up to the possibility of a membership. To elaborate, upon Turkey's application for membership to the EU, it was agreed that, in order to bring the Turkish economy to a level where it can be a competitive force in the internal market of the EU, the parties were initiating the association relationship with the end goal of Turkey's eventual membership.

The most prominent step of the association relationship between Turkey and the EU was the foundation of the Customs Union, under which the parties removed tariffs, quotas, and measures of equivalent effect. In this respect, Decision No. 1/95, finalising the Customs Union, includes extensive and highly detailed articles regarding the harmonisation of the Turkish competition law with the EU competition law regime. Section II of Chapter IV of Decision No. 1/95 is divided into two subheadings–namely, "Competition rules of the Customs Union" and "Approximation of legislation".

The relevant articles under the "Competition rules of the Customs Union" subheading are aimed at prohibiting all agreements between undertakings, decisions by associations of undertakings, and concerted practices that have, as their object or effect, the prevention, restriction, or distortion of competition. These articles also prohibit any abuse by one or more undertakings of a dominant position in the territories of the EEC and/or of Turkey, as a whole or in a substantial part, as incompatible with the proper functioning of the Customs Union, in so far as they may affect trade between the EEC and Turkey.

On the other hand, the articles under the "Approximation of legislation" subheading obligate Turkey to, inter alia, (i) ensure that its legislation in the field of competition rules is made compatible with that of the EU and applied effectively; (ii) adopt a law which shall prohibit behaviours of undertakings under the conditions laid down in Articles 85 and 86 of the Treaty of Rome[7] and ensure that the principles contained in block exemption regulations in force in the EEC, as well as in the case law developed by EC authorities,

---

5   Available at <https://eur-lex.europa.eu/legal-content/EN/ALL/?uri=CELEX%3A21970A1123%2801%29>.
6   Available at <https://eur-lex.europa.eu/legal-content/EN/TXT/?uri=uriserv:OJ.L_.1996.035.01.0001.01. ENG&toc=OJ:L:1996:035:TOC>.
7   The Treaty of Rome (officially the Treaty establishing the European Economic Community), which entered into force on 1 January 1958, has been amended and renamed on several occasions. The Treaty of Lisbon, which entered into force on 1 December 2009, renamed it the Treaty on the Functioning of the European Union. Notwithstanding the amendments, Articles 85 and 86 of the Treaty of Rome are similar to Articles 101 and 102 TFEU in the sense that they prohibit anti-competitive agreements, decisions and concerted practices (i.e., Articles 85 and 101), as well as abuse of dominance (i.e., Articles 86 and 102), with only very minor differences between their respective wording.

shall be applied in Turkey; and (iii) establish a competition authority which shall apply these rules and principles effectively.

Indeed, today the EU accepts that Turkish competition law legislation has "some level of preparation" for harmonisation with its European counterpart.[8] Indeed the competition law secondary legislation, as well as enforcement, follows suit. However, it is considered that, so long as there are no regulations towards State aid, the competition policy chapter would remain incomplete for Turkey.

1.1.4 The Introduction of Law No. 4054 and the Founding of the Authority

Before the adoption of Law No. 4054, there was a legislative gap in Turkish law with respect to the protection of free market and competition, regardless of the constitutional basis and the developments on the EU front. While there had been a number of attempts to fill this legal gap in Turkey since the 1970s, none of these efforts reached a successful outcome. The first attempt was the draft Law on the Regulation of Trade and Protection of Consumers, which was prepared in 1975, followed by other draft laws such as Law on the Regulation of Domestic and Foreign Trade in 1978 and Law on the Regulation of Commercial Activities and Protection of Consumers in 1981. None of these draft laws was enacted by the Turkish Parliament.

In the 1980s and early 1990s, there were more attempts at preparing systematic regulations aimed at the protection of competition, such as the draft Law on Anti-Competitive Agreements and Practices (1984) and the draft Law on the Restrictions of Competition (1990). However, similar to the earlier attempts, these draft laws were not enacted, either.

In this respect, Turkey was the only OECD member without a legislation on competition law at the beginning of the 1990s.[9] Although there were several provisions that protected competition within the scope of unfair competition, criminal law and civil law regulations, these provisions were dispersed among different laws, were not directly aimed at the comprehensive protection of competition in all markets and had limited enforceability in terms of preventing restrictive practices.[10]

Eventually, a commission was established within the body of the Ministry of Industry and Trade in 1992 and put in charge of preparing a draft competition law. The commission took into account the competition law regimes of the EU, the United States of America and the United Kingdom when preparing the draft law.[11] The commission completed the preparation of the draft competition law within two years and submitted the draft to the Grand National Assembly. Eventually, Law No. 4054 was finally

---

[8]   Turkey 2020 Report (n. 3)
[9]   M. T. Müftüoğlu, "Rekabet Kanunu ve İki Yıllık Uygulaması", *Rekabet Dergisi*, 2000, No. 1, p. 5.
[10]   Sanlı (n. 1), pp. 22–23.
[11]   Müftüoğlu (n. 9), p. 10.

approved by the Turkish Parliament on 7 December 1994 and entered into force on 13 December 1994.[12]

Approximately twenty-seven months after the adoption of Law No. 4054, the Board–which is the decisional body of the Authority and responsible for enforcing Law No. 4054–was established following the appointment of its members on 27 February 1997 by the decision of the Council of Ministers.[13] At the time of its establishment, the Board comprised of eleven members, including its first president, Prof. Dr Aydın Ayaydın. On 5 March 1997, the Board members took their oaths in the presence of the First Presidency Council of the High Court of Appeals, and the Board officially became active on that same day.[14] The Board completed the establishment of the Authority within eight months, which was announced on 4 November 1997[15] pursuant to Communiqué No. 1997/5 Concerning the Establishment of the Competition Authority, and started evaluating case applications as of that date.[16] During this period, the Board not only completed its institutional establishment and internal organisation but also published the relevant regulations and communiqués regarding the implementation of Law No. 4054.

1.1.5 Summary of Significant Changes in Legislation and Competition Policy

The Authority has been involved in constant legislative efforts to amend Law No. 4054 since 2003.[17] In this respect, there have been amendments to Law No. 4054 in 2003, 2004, 2005, 2008 and 2012, as well as amendments through statutory decrees in 2011 and 2018. That being said, most of these amendments were aimed at resolving certain significant and urgent problems, rather than amending the more policy-relevant and substantial aspects of Law No. 4054 as a whole.[18] For instance, the purpose of the amendment in 2003 was to increase the effectiveness and deterrence of administrative monetary fines, while the 2005 amendment was aimed at resolving the setbacks caused by the notification-based exemption regime. In 2007, an extensive draft proposal for the amendment of Law No. 4054 was prepared. The draft proposal in 2007 stipulated certain amendments regarding the administrative establishment of the Authority and the procedural provisions of Law No. 4054 (e.g., preliminary investigation, on-site inspections, fully-fledged investigations) as well as amendments to substantive competition law rules such as the

---

[12]   Law No. 4054 was published in the Official Gazette dated 13 December 1994 and numbered 22140.
[13]   8. Five Year Development Plan, Competition Law and Politics Specialisation Commission Report, Ankara 2000, p. 11.
[14]   A. Eğerci, *Rekabet Kurulu Kararlarının Hukuki Niteliği ve Yargısal Denetimi* (Ankara: Rekabet Kurumu, 2005), p. 81.
[15]   As a result, the Authority became active as of 5 November 1997.
[16]   Eğerci (n. 14), p. 81.
[17]   K. C. Sanlı, "Rekabetin Korunması Hakkında Kanun'da Değişiklik Yapılmasına Dair Kanun Tasarısı Taslağı'nın Özel Hukuk Alanında Getirdiği Değişikliklerinin Değerlendirilmesi", *Rekabet Dergisi*, No. 30, 2008, p. 5.
[18]   Ibid., p. 5.

adoption of *de minimis* principle in terms of anti-competitive agreements.[19] However, the draft proposal in 2007 was not promulgated. The amendments in 2008 related to the provisions regarding the administrative monetary fines that could be imposed by the Board. Furthermore, in 2012, the provision regarding the judicial review of the Board's decisions was amended and the first instance court was made the administrative courts instead of the Council of State.

In the following years, there were further attempts to make comprehensive amendments to Law No. 4054. The long-awaited amendments became a hot topic when the Grand National Assembly of Turkey announced that the draft law was officially added to the statutory drafts and proposals list in 2014. The Ministry of Customs and Trade prepared the draft proposal, and it was submitted to the Grand National Assembly of Turkey on 23 January 2014, pursuant to the Council of Ministers' decision of 2 January 2014. The Prime Ministry sent the draft law to the Presidency of the Grand National Assembly of Turkey on 23 January 2014. The draft law was discussed in the Industry, Trade, Energy, Natural Sources, and Information Technologies Commission during the first half of February 2014.

The draft law in 2014 was designed to be more compatible with the EU competition law. The proposed amendments to Law No. 4054 included topics that had been subject to discussions for years in Turkey and contained important reforms (e.g., the adoption of *de minimis* principle, SIEC test, settlement, and commitment mechanisms).

However, in 2015, the draft law became obsolete again owing to the Turkish general elections taking place in June and November 2015, which reset the legislative agenda. The Authority then announced that it has requested the re-initiation of the legislative procedure concerning the draft law. The Authority further noted that it might also consider taking steps toward making the relevant changes by way of issuing secondary legislation if the Grand National Assembly of Turkey did not pass the draft law.

1.1.5.1 Law No. 4054 Is Finally Revised

After rounds of failed attempts over a span of almost two decades, the proposal for an amendment to Law No. 4054 was finally approved in 2020 by the Grand National Assembly of Turkey. This was the most comprehensive set of amendments that Law No. 4054 has gone through since its initial adoption back in 1994. The Amendment Law,[20] which entered into force on 24 June 2020, introduced several new mechanisms for the Authority to focus on and streamline certain of its processes, such as the use of the *de minimis* principle in its selection of cases, a new substantive test for merger control, behavioural and structural remedies for anti-competitive conduct, and procedural tools including commitments and settlement mechanism.

1.1.5.1.1 *De Minimis* Principle

The Amendment Law is aimed at the efficient utilisation of public resources. The most important amendment on this front is the introduction of the *de minimis* principle, which

---

[19]   Ibid., p. 6.
[20]   The Amendment Law was published in the Official Gazette dated 24 June 2020 and numbered 31165.

had its initial legislative background under the draft law back in 2007. Furthermore, it had been indicated within the "Competition Policy" chapters of the EU reports on Turkey between 2005 and 2019 that Turkey was expected to align its legislation with that of the EU in terms of agreements that have no appreciable effect on competition. Approximately nine months after the Amendment Law entered into force, in March 2021, Communiqué No. 2021/3 was promulgated.[21] It is closely modelled after the Commission's De Minimis Notice, which provides a "safe harbour" for companies whose market shares do not exceed 10% for agreements between competitors, or 15% for agreements between non-competitors, except for agreements that have an anti-competitive object. With this amendment, the Board will be able to decide not to launch a fully-fledged investigation for agreements, concerted practices and/or decisions of associations of undertakings that do not exceed the relevant market share thresholds, which are set at the same level as in the EU. This principle will not be applicable to hard-core violations such as price-fixing, territory and/or customer sharing, and restriction of supply or resale price maintenance. With this new mechanism, the Authority's aim appears to be to steer its direction, as well as public resources, towards more significant and effect-bearing violations.

1.1.5.1.2 Commitment and Settlement Mechanisms

The other two mechanisms aimed at efficient utilisation of public resources and enabling the Board to end investigations without going through the entire pre-investigation and investigation procedures are the commitment and settlement mechanisms, which are again inspired by the EU law. Both of these mechanisms had been stipulated within the scope of the draft law proposal in 2014, and the Authority had indicated in its Strategic Plan for 2014–2018 that it would be beneficial to introduce settlement and commitment mechanisms into the Turkish competition law regime.[22] In general, a commitment mechanism mitigates the harm that may arise due to a competition law violation, meanwhile the settlement mechanism benefits public interest through reducing the public expense of conducting investigations regarding competition law violations by terminating the violation and the process in a timely manner. Thus, both mechanisms are aimed at efficiently concluding investigations and reducing the workload of the Authority.

The commitment mechanism allows undertakings or associations of undertakings to voluntarily offer commitments during a preliminary investigation or fully-fledged investigation, in order to eliminate the Authority's competitive concerns in terms of Articles 4 and 6 of Law No. 4054, which prohibit restrictive agreements and abuse of dominance, respectively. Depending on the timing and sufficiency of the commitments offered, the Board can now decide not to launch a fully-fledged investigation following the preliminary investigation or to end an ongoing investigation without completing the entire investigation procedure. However, commitments will not be accepted for hard-core violations such as price-fixing between competitors, territory or customer sharing, the restriction of supply or resale price maintenance. The commitment will help a competition law violation to be brought to an end in a very short timeframe, which would otherwise persist for the duration of a detailed examination and investigation process. This would allow

---

[21]   Communiqué No. 2021/3 was published in the Official Gazette dated 16 March 2021 and numbered 31425.
[22]   Competition Authority Strategic Plan for 2014–2018, p. 52.

limiting any damages that could arise and using public resources more effectively. The relevant Communiqué No. 2021/2 was also promulgated in March 2021[23] and sets out the principles and rules regarding the commitment process, as well as the assessment of commitments to be proposed by the undertakings.

Article 43 of Law No. 4054, as amended, sets out the primary rules governing the settlement mechanism and provides that the Board, *ex officio* or upon the investigated parties' request, can initiate the settlement procedure during fully-fledged investigations. Accordingly, the Board is capable of settling with those parties that concede the existence and scope of an infringement, before the date the investigation report is officially served on them. In order for the parties to benefit from the settlement procedure, they must submit a settlement letter to the Authority within the peremptory time period determined by the Board. Subsequently, the investigation will be ended with a final decision, which will comprise the finding of a violation and the imposing of an administrative monetary fine. Should the investigation end with a settlement, the Board can reduce the administrative monetary fine amount by up to 25%. Finally, the administrative monetary fine and the matters under the settlement letter cannot be made subject to an appeal before the court. The settlement mechanism will allow the Board to swiftly conclude an ongoing investigation and shorten the investigation process as well as reduce the public expenses for a potential litigation process regarding such investigations.

Although the Amendment Law is an attempt for further alignment with the EU competition law in general, there are certain crucial differences in terms of the settlement procedure. The first notable difference is that while the settlement before the Commission is only applicable to cartel cases, the process described under the amended Article 43 of Law No. 4054 can be applied to all infringement types. Secondly, the applicable reduction of the monetary fine amount in case of settlement differs significantly. The Commission offers a reduction of 10% of the fine for settling a case, for each settling party. Meanwhile, the rate of reduction of the administrative monetary fine can be as high as 25%. The third substantial distinction relates to the right to bring administrative proceedings against the settlement decisions issued, before the relevant courts. The settlement procedure before the Commission does not prejudice the parties' right to appeal after the settlement. On the other hand, Article 43(8) of Law No. 4054 explicitly stipulates that the settling parties cannot appeal the Board's decisions in the aftermath of the settlement.

1.1.5.1.3 The SIEC Test

The Amendment Law also introduces significant changes in terms of the Turkish merger control regime. In line with the EU law, the Amendment Law replaces the dominance test, which was the previous substantial merger control test, with the SIEC test. This is also a long-awaited change as it was included within the scope of the draft proposal in 2014, as well. This amendment aims to allow a more reliable assessment of the unilateral and coordinated effects that might arise as a result of mergers or acquisitions. The Amendment Law also provides legal certainty and enables the utilisation of the Board's past experience regarding mergers and acquisitions by indicating that

---

[23] Communiqué No. 2021/2 was published in the Official Gazette dated 16 March 2021 and numbered 31425.

a significant impediment of effective competition essentially occurs through the creation or strengthening of a dominant position. With this new test, the Board will be able to prohibit not only transactions that may result in creating a dominant position or strengthening an existing dominant position, but also those that can significantly impede competition. On the other hand, one can expect that in practice, the Board's assessment of concentrations would not materially change given that the Authority's guidelines regarding the merger control regime are already aligned with and closely modelled after the relevant notices and guidelines in the EU, which were based on the SIEC test.

1.1.5.1.4 Behavioural and Structural Remedies

One of the other amendments concerns the structural remedies which are already stipulated under the EU competition law. The Amendment Law aims to grant the Board the power to order structural remedies for anti-competitive conduct infringing Articles 4, 6 and 7 of Law No. 4054, provided that first the behavioural remedies were applied but failed. Further, if the Board determines with a final decision that behavioural remedies have failed, undertakings or associations of undertakings will be granted at least six months to comply with structural remedies. Both behavioural and structural remedies should be proportionate and necessary to end the infringement effectively. This amendment is in line with the EC Regulation No. 1/2003 on the implementation of the rules on competition laid down in Articles 81 and 82 of the Treaty but takes a step further to provide assurance to the companies that structural remedies for competition law infringements will only be applied when behavioural remedies have first been tried but proved to be ineffective. The Amendment Law provides that the Authority is equipped with significant instruments for the purposes of effectively fighting competition law violations.

1.1.5.1.5 On-Site Inspections

The Amendment Law also clarifies the extent of the Authority's powers during on-site inspections, which are particularly important in terms of uncovering cartels. In this respect, the Amendment Law includes an explicit provision that during on-site inspections, the Authority can inspect and make copies of all information and documents in companies' physical records as well as those in electronic media and IT systems, which the Authority was already doing in practice.

1.1.5.1.6 Self-Assessment Principle

The "self-assessment" principle was initially adopted with the amendments to Law No. 4054 in 2005, following the legal reform in EU law in 2003. The Amendment Law now aims to provide legal certainty as to the individual exemption regime, by clarifying that the "self-assessment" principle applies to agreements (as well as concerted practices and decisions of associations of undertakings) that may potentially restrict competition. "Self-assessment" allows undertakings to evaluate on their own whether an agreement benefits from the protective cloak of a block exemption communiqué and, if not, whether it satisfies the conditions for individual exemption, without requiring them to notify the relevant undertaking to the Authority. That being said, the option to apply to the Board for individual exemption is still available.

1.1.5.2 Recent Changes in Secondary Legislation

Secondary legislation of the Authority includes the guidelines, communiqués, and regulations drafted by the Authority for the purpose of facilitating and supporting the implementation and enforcement of Law No. 4054, as well as clarifying the rules and principles regarding certain competition law matters. According to Article 27 of Law No. 4054, the Board is authorised to (i) issue communiqués and make the necessary regulations in relation to the implementation of Law No. 4054 and (ii) opine, directly or upon the request of the Ministry of Trade, concerning the amendments to be made to the legislation with regard to the competition law.

Between 2015 and 2021, the Board made significant changes in the secondary legislation including the (i) amendments to Communiqué No. 2010/4; (ii) introduction of Communiqué No. 2017/3; (iii) amendments to the Guidelines on Vertical Agreements; (iv) introduction of the Guidelines on Examination of Digital Data; (v) introduction of Communiqué No. 2021/2; (vi) introduction of Communiqué No. 2021/3; and (vii) introduction of the Regulation on Settlement Procedure.

1.1.5.2.1 Amendments to Communiqué No. 2010/4

The Board also improved its secondary legislation in terms of the Turkish merger control regime. While Communiqué No. 2010/4 was already closely modelled after and akin to EC Merger Regulation, the Authority introduced Communiqué No. 2017/2 on 24 February 2017 in order to further harmonise the Turkish merger control regime with the EC Merger Regulation. Article 8(5) of Communiqué No. 2010/4, as amended by Article 2 of Communiqué No. 2017/2, paragraph 38 of the Guidelines on Undertakings Concerned, Turnover and Ancillary Restraints and paragraph 37 of the Guidelines on the Concept of Control, which are modelled after Article 5(2) second subparagraph of the EC Merger Regulation and paragraph 50 of the CJN, provide that (i) two or more transactions realised between the same persons or parties within three years or (ii) two or more transactions realised by the same undertaking within the same relevant product market within three years are to be considered as a single transaction in terms of the calculation of the turnover that would be used to compare against the turnover thresholds. Although the exception under Article 8(5) of Communiqué No. 2010/4 resembles its counterpart in the EU, Article 5(2) of EC Merger Regulation does not include any references to transactions realised by the same undertaking within the same relevant product market.

Additionally, Article 3 of Communiqué No. 2017/2 introduced a new paragraph to be included in Article 10 of Communiqué No. 2010/4 which is similar to Article 7(2) of the EC Merger Regulation and provides that if the control is acquired from various sellers by way of a series of transactions in terms of securities within the stock exchange, the concentration could be notified to the Board after the transactions were realised, provided that (i) the concentration is notified to the Board without delay and (ii) the voting rights attached to the acquired securities are not exercised, or exercised solely to maintain the full value of its investments, in accordance with an exception to be granted by a decision of the Board. On the other hand, even before the derogation under Article 10(6) of Communiqué No. 2010/4 was introduced, in its *Camargo/ Cimpor* decision, the Board recognised that it was possible for the parties to purchase shares via a public bid on a listed company before notifying the Board and obtaining approval, provided that (i) the transaction is notified to the Board without any delay and (ii) the acquirer does not exercise its control over the target pending the Board's approval decision.[24] In this respect, as Article 10(6) of Communiqué No. 2010/4 was not introduced at the time of the decision, the Board referred to Article 7(2) of the EC Merger Regulation.

1.1.5.2.2 Introduction of Communiqué No. 2017/3

The Authority also introduced Communiqué No. 2017/3, which replaced Communiqué No. 2005/4, and published the Guidelines on the Block Exemption in the Motor Vehicles Sector on its website on 7 March 2017. The Guidelines on the Block Exemption in the Motor Vehicles Sector aim to provide certainty in the interpretation of Communiqué No. 2017/3, as well as to clarify matters that the Board would take into consideration in terms of the application of Communiqué No. 2017/3. In general, the Board took into account the competitive landscape of the motor vehicle sector, as well as the difficulties in implementing Communiqué No. 2005/4, and in particular, the competitive concerns that have been continuing with regard to the provision of maintenance and repair services and distribution of spare parts during the preparation of Communiqué No. 2017/3.

1.1.5.2.3 Amendments to the Guidelines on Vertical Agreements

The Authority published the final version of the Guidelines on Vertical Agreements on its official website on 30 March 2018. The Guidelines on Vertical Agreements include newly introduced regulations and/or amendments with regard to (i) online sales and (ii) MFN (most-favoured nation) clauses in order to eliminate inconsistencies in the existing legislative framework and to meet the needs of the evolving market conditions in the digital economy. In terms of online sales, the new articles added to the Guidelines on Vertical Agreements point out the necessity of providing specific provisions regarding online sales under the Turkish competition law regime and aim to harmonise the current legislative framework with the approach adopted by the Commission's Guidelines on Vertical Restraints.

In sum, the amendments provide the following: (i) restrictions with regard to online sales that exclude the relevant agreement from the block exemption (i.e., hard-core restrictions for online sales); (ii) conditions that may be stipulated for websites to be utilised as sales channels; and (iii) provisions regarding online sales in the selective distribution systems. The amendments provide that suppliers can only stipulate conditions for website sales channels, with respect to fair, objective, and standardised justifications. The suppliers are now also allowed to require the distributors within selective distribution systems to have at least one physical store. The Guidelines on Vertical Agreements also introduce provisions with regard to MFN clauses. In general, the Guidelines on Vertical Agreements evaluate MFN clauses under the "rule of reason" approach. As MFN clauses do not give rise to the same consequences in each case, the Guidelines on Vertical Agreements indicate that such clauses should be evaluated on a case-by-case basis by thoroughly analysing various factors such as (i) the position of the parties and their competitors within the relevant market;

---

[24]   *Camargo/Cimpor* (3 May 2012, 12-24/665-187).

(ii) the purpose of the MFN clause placed in the relevant agreement; (iii) the specific characteristics of the relevant market and the MFN clause in question. On the other hand, the Guidelines also underline the fact that MFN clauses may not result in a competition concern but rather have pro-competitive effects under certain circumstances.

1.1.5.2.4 Introduction of the Guidelines on Examination of Digital Data

Meanwhile, the Board has also been attempting to eliminate the questions regarding the Authority's powers in terms of on-site inspections and examination of certain data. Following the Amendment Law, which stipulated that the Authority can inspect and make copies of all information and documents in electronic media and IT systems during on-site inspections, the Authority published its Guidelines on Examination of Digital Data, which set forth the general principles with respect to the examination, processing and storage of data and documents held in the electronic media and information systems during the on-site inspections to be conducted by the Authority. The Guidelines on Examination of Digital Data essentially (i) clarify the procedures to be abided by when the data on the electronic media or information systems are required to be examined by the case handlers during on-site inspections, in a way that relatively echoes the recent enforcement practices of the Authority, and (ii) introduce a new method for the examination of digital data, which is akin to the methodology and principles set forth within the Commission's Explanatory note on Commission inspections pursuant to Article 20(4) of Council Regulation (EC) No. 1/2003. In this respect, the Guidelines on Examination of Digital Data are expected to bring the Authority's on-site inspection practices closer to the Commission's practices.

1.1.5.2.5 Introduction of Communiqué No. 2021/2

Communiqué No. 2021/2 entered into force on 16 March 2021. According to Article 2 of Communiqué No. 2021/2, undertakings cannot submit commitments for hard-core violations such as horizontal price-fixing, allocation of customers, suppliers, regions or trade channels, restriction of supply, bid rigging, exchange of competitively sensitive information and resale price maintenance. Article 5 of Communiqué No. 2021/2 provides that undertakings could request to submit commitments during a preliminary investigation or a fully-fledged investigation. Meanwhile, undertakings are only able to submit commitments within three months following the service of the investigation notice.

After the commitment procedure is initiated, if the parties decide to submit commitments, they must send a copy of the commitment text along with the non-confidential version, and a summary thereof to the Authority. Following that, the Board will evaluate whether the commitment eliminates the competition problems and other issues deemed necessary, by assessing the commitment letter in substance. In case the Board finds the commitment appropriate, it may either (i) render a commitment decision which would be binding for the party concerned or (ii) request the opinions of third parties. Should the Board render a commitment decision binding, the Board will also decide not to initiate an investigation, or as the case may be, discontinue the ongoing investigation. However, if after the first round of the commitment discussions or after evaluating the opinions of the third parties, the Board does not find the commitment acceptable, then the Board may decide to allow the parties to make amendments to the commitment text.

Articles 8 and 9 of Communiqué No. 2021/2 provide details on the main points that must be incorporated within the commitment text. According to Article 8 of Communiqué

No. 2021/2, the commitment text must include (i) the competition problems to be resolved by the commitment; (ii) what the commitment is; (iii) the start date, duration and method of implementation of the commitment; (iv) any time periods to be complied with during the implementation; (v) under what conditions such periods can be expanded; (vi) the effect of the commitment to the market; (vii) how the commitment will meet the competition concern; (viii) how their compliance with the commitment can be monitored and other issues deemed necessary. Moreover, Article 9 states that behavioural or structural commitments can be offered individually or jointly. The offered commitment must be (i) proportional with respect to the competition concerns; (ii) adequate to address them; (iii) executable in the short term; and (iv) conducive to efficient implementation.

1.1.5.2.6 Introduction of Communiqué No. 2021/3

By virtue of Communiqué No. 2021/3, undertakings will have legal certainty as to which actions fall within the scope of the *de minimis* principle. According to Article 1 of Communiqué No. 2021/3, the main goal of the relevant legislation is to identify agreements, concerted practices and decisions of associations of undertakings that do not significantly restrict competition in the market, so that they can be excluded from an investigation, with the exception of evident and hard-core violations. In line with this, Communiqué No. 2021/3 aims to direct the resources and time of the Authority towards the resolution of more critical competition law issues and to introduce a "procedural economy" tool for certain violations.

According to Article 4 of Communiqué No. 2021/3, "evident and hard-core" violations include horizontal price-fixing, allocation of customers, suppliers, regions or trade channels, restriction of supply, bid rigging, exchange of competitively sensitive information and resale price maintenance. Article 5 of Communiqué No. 2021/3 stipulates the following categorisation and thresholds to describe which agreements/decisions would be deemed not to appreciably restrict competition:

– Agreements between competitors: cases where the combined market share of the parties to the agreement does not exceed 10% in any of the relevant markets affected by the agreement.

– Agreements between non-competing undertakings: cases where the market share of each of the parties does not exceed 15% in any of the relevant markets affected by the agreement.

– Decisions of associations of undertakings: cases where the combined market share of the members of an association of undertakings does not exceed 10% in any of the relevant markets affected by the decision.

1.1.5.2.7 Introduction of the Regulation on Settlement Procedure

The Regulation on Settlement Procedure, which entered into force on 15 July 2021, determines the other procedures and fundamentals of the settlement process which are not covered in Law No. 4054. As regards the applicability of the settlement mechanism, Law No. 4054 imposes no restrictions in terms of the nature of the violation. According to the Regulation on Settlement Procedure, if the Authority *ex officio* invites the investigation parties to settlement negotiations, the parties should declare whether they accept the invitation to initiate settlement negotiations with the Authority within fifteen days.

Article 4(4) of the Regulation on Settlement Procedure provides that the Board has the discretion to grant a settlement reduction between 10% and 25%, indicating that the actual reduction of fine due to settlement would not be less than 10%.

Article 6(5) of the Regulation on Settlement Procedure stipulates that the Authority would inform the settling party regarding the (i) content of the allegations; (ii) nature and scope of the alleged violation; (iii) main pieces of evidence that constitute a basis for the allegations; (iv) potential reduction rate to be applied in case of settlement; and (v) range of potential administrative monetary fine which might be imposed against the settling party. Following the settlement negotiations, the Board would adopt an interim decision, which would inter alia include the nature and scope of the alleged violation, the maximum rate for the administrative monetary fine in accordance with the Regulation on Fines, and the reduction rate to be applied at the end of the settlement procedure. Subsequently, if the settling party agrees on the matters set forth therein, it will submit a settlement letter which shall include inter alia an express declaration of admission as to the existence and scope of the violation. Article 9(1) of the Regulation on Settlement Procedure provides that the Board shall adopt its final decision to end the investigation within fifteen days following the submission of the settlement letter. The Board's final decision shall include the finding of the violation and the administrative monetary fine to be imposed against the settling undertaking.

1.1.5.3 The Authority's Competition Policy in Recent Years

As indicated within the scope of its 2020 Annual Report, the Authority's priorities for the upcoming years include (i) drafting the necessary regulations in the secondary legislation further to the amendments to Law No. 4054; (ii) developing evidence-gathering mechanisms in order to fight against the competition law violations with greater success; and (iii) closely following the markets that change with digitalisation in order to develop more effective competition law policies and practices in terms of these markets. The Authority has more or less achieved its goals of making the necessary amendments in secondary legislation, developing evidence-gathering mechanisms, and monitoring digital markets.

The Authority is also diligently pursuing its target of following the digital markets very closely. In this respect, the Authority launched a study for its Digitalisation and Competition Policy Report in January 2020, which foreshadows its intention to put the digital economy, including big tech platforms, under scrutiny in the near future. Additionally, the Authority also launched a sector inquiry with respect to Online Marketplace Platforms in July 2020 and published its preliminary report on its website on 7 May 2021.[25] In January 2021, the Authority initiated a sector inquiry regarding online advertising services, in conjunction with its efforts aimed at determining the competition issues in digital markets, and the regulatory preparations to be made in order to intervene effectively with these issues. Indications of the Authority's intention can also be observed from

---

[25]   The preliminary report is available at <https://www.rekabet.gov.tr/Dosya/geneldosya/e-pazaryeri-si-on-rapor-teslim-tsi_son-pdf>.

its enforcement track record in between 2018 and 2020 concerning platforms, which include its *Hepsiburada*,[26] *Kitapyurdu*,[27] *Google Shopping*,[28] *Google Android*,[29] *Çiçek Sepeti*,[30] and *Yemek Sepeti*[31] decisions.

The Authority has also closely followed the market developments during the COVID-19 pandemic. In the early stages of the pandemic, on 23 March 2020, the Authority made a public announcement where it indicated that there were excessive price increases in the food industry and in particular in the fresh fruit and vegetable market, and the most severe administrative monetary fines would be imposed against undertakings that restricted competition in this industry. Following the announcement, the Authority initiated a fully-fledged investigation against 29 undertakings including chain stores and stated that especially price increases of some of the undertakings active in terms of production and sale of food and cleaning/hygiene products might constitute a violation of competition law. On 9 January 2021, the president of the Board expressed that there was an increase in the complaints regarding pricing behaviours, particularly in the health, hygiene, and food industries, and the investigation against food stores was about to be concluded. On the other hand, the Board completed its investigation regarding the allegations that undertakings active in sales of masks agreed to increase their prices during the COVID-19 pandemic, on 30 December 2020. The Board decided that the relevant undertakings did not violate Law No. 4054 and, furthermore, also decided to send its opinions to the Ministry of Treasury and Finance and the Unfair Price Evaluation Board to share the findings of the investigation.[32] The communication between the Board and the Unfair Price Evaluation Board also bears some significance given that there is an alleged conflict of authority between the two bodies. While the Board is entitled to impose administrative monetary fines in case of excessive pricing only by a dominant undertaking, the Unfair Price Evaluation Board could prevent excessive pricing and impose monetary fines against the relevant undertakings irrespective of whether these enjoy a dominant position in the market.

Between 2018 and 2020, the Authority strengthened its enforcement record, especially in energy and telecommunications. In fact, the Board's *Fuel Companies* decision[33] in 2020 involved four of the highest ever administrative monetary fines imposed by the Authority in its history. In the relevant decision, the Board imposed administrative monetary fines of TL 1,502,778,821.56 (approx. EUR 215,606,717 at the time of the decision) in total, to four undertakings on resale price maintenance claims.

In general, the total administrative monetary fines imposed by the Board have been consistently increasing for the last five years, with the exception of a slight decrease in 2019. Similarly, while the Board handled approximately 85 investigation/preliminary

---

[26]   *Hepsiburada* (15 April 2021, 21-22/266-116).
[27]   *Kitapyurdu* (5 November 2020, 20-48/658-289).
[28]   *Google Shopping* (13 February 2020, 20-10/119-69).
[29]   *Google Android* (19 September 2018, 18-33/555-273).
[30]   *Çiçek Sepeti* (8 March 2018, 18-07/111-58).
[31]   *Yemek Sepeti* (9 June 2016, 16-20/347-156).
[32]   Available at <https://www.rekabet.gov.tr/Dosya/geneldosya/maske-nihai-karar-internet-duyurusu-pdf>.
[33]   *Fuel Companies* (12 March 2020, 20-14/192-98).

investigation cases per year between 2015 and 2018, this number was reduced to 69 in 2019.[34] That being said, the fall in the figures is very likely attributable to the considerable delay in the appointment of some of Board members in 2019. Furthermore, although there is a big gap between the number of the Board's decisions regarding competition law violations in 2013 (i.e., 191 decisions) and 2020 (i.e., 65 decisions), the number of infringement decisions actually increased from 14 to 16 together with an increase of the total administrative monetary fines imposed.[35] It seems that the Authority has reduced its workload throughout the years, meanwhile increasing the efficiency of its enforcement capacity by deploying its resources to the more significant cases, which could be interpreted as a direct result of its competition policies. From a merger control standpoint, the Board has been consistently dealing with over 200 transactions per year for the last couple of years.

1.2 The Institutional Structure of Turkish Competition Law

The Authority and the Board were founded and are governed by Law No. 4054 and the secondary legislation on a regulation level. The general preamble of Law No. 4054 explains the independent role of the Authority by also associating it with the democratisation process and free trade:

> It is possible to guarantee the rights of actors in commercial life only with the help of organs that are able to operate and take decisions independently. Our country, where democratization process still continues, needs independent administration agents operating in such a manner. The Competition Authority with such characteristics will develop and maintain free competition in the country and free trade and freedom of enterprise will be guaranteed in this way.

In view of the foregoing aim and principles, the Authority and the Board will be examined separately in the following section, along with their position within the structure of public administration in Turkey.

1.2.1 The Authority

Article 20 of Law No. 4054 establishes the Authority as an institution with "an administrative and financial autonomy", with the purpose of implementing Law No. 4054. Therefore, as an enforcer of economic law, the Authority uses its powers to take measures, regulate and audit, to ensure the protection of competition.

---

[34] <https://www.rekabet.gov.tr/Dosya/guncel-karar-istatistikleri/2019-yillik-web-20200110120424416-pdf>.
[35] The 2020 statistics are available at <https://www.rekabet.gov.tr/Dosya/guncel-karar-istatistikleri/2020-yillik-20210115105059951-pdf>.

In 2020, within the amendments made to Law No. 4054, the Authority was described as being "affiliated" to the Ministry of Trade[36] in the preamble, and considered to be administratively linked or related to the Ministry of Trade. Nevertheless, Article 20 explicitly provides that the Authority is independent in fulfilling its duties from any influence, commands, or instructions. Indeed, Article 20 establishes the Authority as a legal entity. Having financial and administrative autonomy, the Authority is not organically linked to any other institution, and the "affiliation" to the Ministry of Trade should not be construed that way. In other words, the Authority is not in a "hierarchical relationship" with the Ministry of Trade; the relationship between the two mostly relies on budgetary matters, as well as the Authority providing opinions to the Ministry.[37]

The Authority is located in the capital city of Ankara. Article 21 of Law No. 4054 explains that the Authority is made up of the Board, the Presidency, and Service Units. The Board, explained separately below, is the competent decision-making body of the Authority and responsible for, inter alia, reviewing cases of dominance, agreements, and concerted practices, as well as mergers and acquisitions under Law No. 4054. The Presidency, according to the Regulation on the Authority, consists of the president of the Board, the deputy president, and the vice presidents.

The Service Units consist of six supervision and enforcement departments: department of decisions, economic analyses and research department, information management department, external relations, training and competition advocacy department, strategy development, regulation and budget department, and cartel on-the-spot inspections support division. Each supervision and enforcement department focuses on a few select "sector(s)" under its job definition.

The Authority's personnel include senior competition experts, competition experts and assistant competition experts, which are assigned by the chairperson of the Board as case handlers during preliminary investigations, fully-fledged investigations and merger control reviews.

The Strategic Plan of the Authority pertaining to the 2019–2023 period explains the primary fields of work of the Authority as:

- The application of Law No. 4054: This includes not only the enforcement powers, but also the power to legislate based on Articles 5, 7, 16, 27 and 62 of Law No. 4054.

- Competition advocacy: The primary aim herein is to create public knowledge and awareness of competition policies. The Authority notes that the advocacy activities are different for public authorities, private sector, consumers, and civil society.

- Policy-making: This aspect of the Authority's duties is both legislative and strategic. From a legislative perspective, this goal encompasses not just competition law legislation, but any other legislation that could restrict competition and result in the decrease of consumer welfare. From a strategic perspective,

---

[36] Formerly named the Ministry of Industry and Trade.
[37] E. Öztürk, *Türk İdare Sisteminde Rekabet Kurumunun Yeri ve Diğer Bağımsız İdari Otoritelerle Karşılaştırılması* (Ankara: Rekabet Kurumu, 2003).

the policies aim to develop concrete application strategies and principles that guide the Authority and embody the work to be done.[38]

In view of the foregoing, it is important to highlight that the Authority embraces a hybrid role, similar to the Commission, when it comes to legislation, enforcement, and advocacy.

1.2.1.1 Relationships with Other Competition Authorities

The Authority has multilateral and bilateral relationships with international organisations, other states, and the EU in the face of the globalised world economy and how this affects the markets in each individual state.

According to official sources, the Authority works with OECD, UNCTAD, WTO and the WB. The Authority also has cooperation agreements with Albania, Austria, Azerbaijan, Bulgaria, Bosnia-Herzegovina, Croatia, Egypt, Georgia, Kazakhstan, Kosovo, Kyrgyzstan, Macedonia, Mongolia, Morocco, Portugal, Romania, Russian Federation, Serbia, South Korea, Tunisia, Turkish Republic of Northern Cyprus, and Ukraine.

It is not an exaggeration to say that the most significant bilateral relationship the Authority has is with the Commission. Considering the geographic and commercial proximity resulting from the Customs Union, the Turkish markets and the European markets do enjoy similarities. Further, Turkish competition enforcement is largely based and influenced by the EU practices. Indeed, Turkey has a positive duty, in the scope of its accession process, to unify and harmonise its competition law legislation. The Authority, according to the Strategic Plan for 2019–2023, continues to attend the EU-Turkey Association Committee meetings and participates in the debates.

The Commission's influence is not limited to legislation. Indeed, the Authority follows the Commission's practices in case law and other elements as well. For example, there are multiple investigations in digital markets, which are given specific attention by competition authorities around the world, where the Authority followed suit and examined the same predominant undertakings with similar claims as the Commission. Furthermore, in 2020 the Authority initiated a market inquiry which will ultimately result in a "Digitalisation and Competition Policy Report". The Authority also initiated legislation/regulation efforts to effectively fight against competition concerns in digital markets. This specific focus mirrors the 2019 report of the Commission on the same subject. Similar influences are seen on how certain fundamental competition law concepts are perceived, such as the relevant market or the concept of an undertaking.

The influence of the Commission is also apparent in a number of merger control decisions, where the commitments submitted to the Commission were taken as a basis to render a decision in Turkey. Having said that, these decisions mainly concerned transactions where the overlaps or the competition law concerns in Turkey were also removed by the commitments provided to the Commission.[39]

---

[38]   Competition Authority, Strategic Plan 2019–2023, p. 19.
[39]   E.g., *Bayer/Monsanto Company* (8 May 2018, 18-14/261-126); *Nidec/Whirlpool* (18 April 2019, 19-16/231-103).

1.2.1.2 Other Work: Publications, Conferences, Sector Inquiries

In the scope of its advocacy mission, the Authority is a very active administrative body, especially when it comes to publications and events that have the potential to raise awareness about competition law and enforcement.

The most prominent of these are the expert theses, published by the Authority's case handlers. These are 70–200 page, in-depth analyses of contemporary Turkish competition law topics. Further, the Authority publishes sector reports of the most prominent and competition-law relevant sectors. The most recent of these were trade fair/exhibition organisation, hazelnut production, digitalisation and television broadcasting, cement, cinema, wholesale and retail sale of electricity, motor vehicles and pharma. As of June 2021, it is known that the examination of digital markets and fast-moving consumer goods is underway.[40] The Authority also organises the Competition Forum, an annual event that includes speeches and debates with other competition law authorities and practitioners worldwide.

1.2.2 The Board

The constitution and duties of the Board, the conditions for the appointment of its members, as well as their terms of service, are set out in Articles 22 to 28 of Law No. 4054 and the Presidential Decree No. 3.

To that end, the Board, which is the decision-making body of the Authority, is composed of a total of seven members appointed by the president of the Republic of Turkey, including a chairperson and a deputy chairperson. According to Article 23 of Law No. 4054, the members of the Board shall be appointed from among those with a four-year higher education degree and who bear the qualifications specified in Article 48, paragraph (A), subparagraphs 1, 4, 5, 6 and 7 of the Civil Servants Law No. 657.[41]

Until the Statutory Decree dated 2 July 2018 and numbered 703 repealed the relevant provision of Article 24 of Law No. 4054, the term of service for the chairperson, the deputy chairperson and the members of the Board was six years. That being said, currently, Law No. 4054 has no rules regarding the term of service of the chairperson, the deputy chairperson and the members of the Board. In the absence of explicit rules governing the term of service stipulated by Law No. 4054, the provisions of the Presidential Decree No. 3 would be applicable, which sets the terms of service of the chairpersons and the members of the regulatory and supervisory authorities (with the exception of the

---

[40] The Authority's preliminary reports regarding online marketplace platforms and fast-moving consumer goods are published on its website, available at <https://www.rekabet.gov.tr/Dosya/geneldosya/e-pazaryeri-si-on-rapor-teslim-tsi_son-pdf> and <https://www.rekabet.gov.tr/Dosya/geneldosya/htmperakendeciligisektorincelemesionraporu-pdf>.

[41] Accordingly, the members (i) must be Turkish citizens, (ii) must not have been deprived of public rights, (iii) must not have been sentenced for certain offences (including offences against state security, offences against the constitutional order and its functioning, etc.), (iv) must not be under military duty, and (v) must not have a mental illness which would prevent him or her from doing his or her duty.

Radio and Television Supreme Council) at four years under its Schedule 3. Accordingly, the term of service for the chairperson, the deputy chairperson and the members of the Board is also deemed to be four years.

According to Article 24 of Law No. 4054, should the chairperson's position and memberships be vacated before the expiration of their term of office, the selection and appointment for the vacated seats are carried out within one month. In this case, the appointee completes the term of the person he or she replaces. Furthermore, the offices of the chairperson and Board members cannot be terminated prior to the completion of their term except where, by the decision of the Board, they are found to have lost the qualifications required for their appointment or their position is found to be contrary to Article 25 of Law No. 4054, or where their offence(s) with regard to abuse of the duties vested in them by Law No. 4054 is proven by a court decision.

The duties and powers of the Board are listed under Article 27 of Law No. 4054. The main duties of the Board are (i) to carry out, pursuant to an application or *ex officio*, examinations, inquiries and investigations concerning the activities and legal transactions which are prohibited by Law No. 4054; (ii) to take the necessary measures for terminating the infringements of the provisions stipulated under Law No. 4054; and (iii) to impose administrative monetary fines against those responsible for the infringements. The Board is also in charge of and authorised to evaluate the exemption and negative clearance requests of the relevant parties, and to grant exemption or negative clearances to those agreements that qualify, as well as to approve merger and acquisition transactions. With respect to its decisions regarding exemption and negative clearances, the Board is also commissioned to constantly monitor the markets that are related to its exemption and negative clearance decisions, and to re-evaluate the exemption and negative clearance applications in case of changes in the markets, or the positions of the relevant parties.

The Board is also authorised with respect to the legislative and statutory instruments of competition law in Turkey. In this respect, the Board can (i) issue communiqués and make the necessary regulations for the implementation of Law No. 4054; (ii) opine, directly or upon the request of the Ministry of Trade, concerning the amendments to be made to the legislation with regard to competition law; and (iii) monitor legislations, practices, policies and measures of other jurisdictions with respect to agreements and decisions that restrict competition.

Other duties and powers of the Board that are listed under Article 27 of Law No. 4054 include: (i) appointment of the vice presidents and the chief legal counsel upon the proposal of the president; (ii) determination of the personnel policies of the Authority and monitoring their implementation, processing personnel appointments, approval of the annual budget, final account of revenues and expenses, and annual work schedules of the Authority which are prepared by the Presidency and deciding on the transfers between the accounts in the budget if necessary; (iii) issuing annual reports on its works, and the situation and developments in its scope of duty; (iv) negotiating and resolving proposals concerning purchases, sales and leasing such as the procurement of movable and real property and fixtures, and to make the necessary arrangements on this front; (v) deciding on any kind of transactions about receivables, rights and obligations of the Authority with regard to third parties; and (vi) fulfilment of other duties assigned by Law No. 4054.

1.3 Scope of Turkish Competition Law

1.3.1 Legal Scope

1.3.1.1 Legal Scope According to Legislation: What Can the Authority Act on?

As a legal entity with administrative and financial autonomy, the Authority has an exclusive authority to enforce Law No. 4054. The Authority's powers include regulation, imposing sanctions and monitoring market activities, and presenting opinions.[42]

Sanctions available under Law No. 4054 are administrative in nature. Therefore, the Board could impose administrative monetary fines (and civil liability) pursuant to Law No. 4054, but not criminal sanctions. In this respect, for instance, cartel conduct would not result in imprisonment against the implicated individuals. That being said, there have been certain cases where the matter had to be referred to a public prosecutor before or after the competition law investigation was completed. One example would be bid-rigging activities, which may be criminally prosecutable under Articles 235 *et seq.* of the Turkish Criminal Code. Illegal price manipulation (manipulation through disinformation or other fraudulent means) may also be penalised with up to two years of imprisonment and a judicial monetary fine be imposed under Article 237 of the Turkish Criminal Code. In this respect, if a cartel activity amounts to a criminal act such as bid rigging in public tenders, it may be adjudicated separately and prosecuted before the Turkish criminal courts by public prosecutors.

According to Article 2 of Law No. 5326, a misdemeanour is a wrongdoing against which an administrative sanction would be imposed. Given that competition law violations are subject to administrative sanctions, competition law violations also constitute misdemeanours and fall within the scope of Law No. 5326. The Council of State and the administrative courts also refer to and apply the provisions under Law No. 5326 in cases where there are no specific regulations under Law No. 4054. The fact that competition law violations qualify as misdemeanours results in these violations being subject to the same principles as misdemeanours.[43] These principles include the principle of legality, the principle of *lex mitior*, culpability, individual criminal responsibility and *non bis in idem*.

1.3.1.2 Competence and Other Relevant Administrative Authorities

There are some sector-specific rules and regulations on competition, which were brought by and overseen by the respective authorities of regulated industries–such as the Information and Communication Technologies Authority, the Energy Market Regulatory

---

[42]   Öztürk, (n. 37).
[43]   B. Arı, *Karşılaştırmalı Hukukta Rekabet İhlallerine Verilen Cezalar* (Ankara: Rekabet Kurumu, 2020), pp. 13–14.

Authority, and the Banking Regulation and Supervision Authority. That being said, these regulatory authorities do not assume any control mechanisms over competition. The Authority is the only regulatory body that investigates and condemns competition law issues in Turkey. In fact, the Authority indicated in its *Syndicated Loans* decision that although there was no doubt that the Banking Regulation and Supervision Authority was the regulatory authority for the banking and finance industry, these regulatory powers did not prevent the Authority from conducting investigations in terms of practices which fell within the scope of the Authority's powers.[44]

However, in terms of its investigations involving regulated industries such as banking, energy or telecommunications, the Authority does consult the relevant regulatory authorities. In this respect, Article 7(2) of Law No. 5809 requires the Authority to seek the opinion of the Information and Communication Technologies Authority with regard to its decisions concerning the electronic communications industry. The Authority has also entered into cooperation protocols with the Information and Communication Technologies Authority in 2011, with the Banking Regulation and Supervision Agency in 2012 and with the Energy Market Regulatory Authority in 2015. Most recent examples on this front include the Board's *Syndicated Loans*,[45] *Fuel Companies*[46] and *Türk Telekom*[47] decisions. Within the scope of these cases, the Authority collaborated with the Banking Regulation and Supervision Authority, the Energy Market Regulatory Authority and the Information and Communication Technologies Authority respectively, in order to receive their opinions and responses with respect to the regulatory frameworks of the relevant industries, as well as the facts of each case.

1.3.2 Geographic Scope

1.3.2.1 Geographic Scope in Legislation

Turkey is one of the "effects theory" jurisdictions, where what matters is whether an activity or practice has produced effects on the Turkish markets, regardless of the nationality of the relevant undertakings, where the activity or practice in question took place or whether the relevant undertakings have subsidiaries or presence in Turkey. The purpose of the "effects theory" is to make it clear for the undertakings which provisions set out in Law No. 4054 are applicable.

Under the Turkish competition law regime, the use of "effects theory" derives from Article 2 of Law No. 4054, which sets forth the following:

> This Act covers all agreements, decisions and practices which prevent, distort or restrict competition between any undertakings operating in or affecting markets for goods and services within the borders of the Republic of Turkey; abuse

[44] *Syndicated Loans* (28 November 2017, 17-39/636-276), para. 306.
[45] *Syndicated Loans* (n. 44)
[46] *Fuel Companies* (n. 33).
[47] *Türk Telekom* (27 February 2020, 20-12/153-83).

of dominance by dominant undertakings in the market; any kind of legal transactions and behaviour having the nature of mergers and acquisitions which may significantly decrease competition; and transactions concerning the measures, observations, regulations and supervisions aimed at the protection of competition.

The preamble of Law No. 4054 for Article 2 explains that the "effects theory" requires the application of the provisions of Law No. 4054 to the undertakings whose economic activities affect the Turkish markets, regardless of where such undertakings are headquartered.

Accordingly, the preambles provide that:

> It is normal to expect the benefits of competition from all areas of the economy as a whole. For this reason, competition rules must be applied to all undertakings which have economic operations. It is not important whether the undertakings belong to public institutions or to private persons. Even though the goals of protecting the public interest and public order come to the forefront in the competition law, the fulfilment of the duties of the undertakings charged with serving the general economic interests should not conflict with the competition rules. The system called 'effect theory' in competition law literature is also adopted in this act. In other words, those undertakings whose headquarters are out of the borders of the Republic of Turkey but who operate in Turkey also fall within the scope of this act.

In this respect, an anti-competitive practice could be evaluated under Law No. 4054 provided that the practice in question has any effect within the markets for goods and services in Turkey, irrespective of where the relevant undertakings are headquartered or whether the relevant foreign undertakings have any subsidiaries or branches in Turkey.

There are no specific rules regarding the criteria in determining whether the anti-competitive practices of the relevant foreign undertakings have any effects on the Turkish markets. That being said, the Board has acknowledged in its *Railroad Cargo* decision[48] that the criteria under the US antitrust law which provides that the effect must be "direct", "significant" and "foreseeable" could be taken into account in cases where "effects theory" is discussed, to the extent these criteria are applicable to the specific case at hand.

That being said, from a merger control standpoint, so long as there is a change in control on a lasting basis involving a full-function joint venture and one of the applicable jurisdictional turnover thresholds is met, a joint venture transaction will require a mandatory merger control filing before the Authority. The relevant legislation does not seek the existence of affected markets/overlaps in assessing whether a transaction triggers a notification requirement, and there are no exceptions to avoid the filing requirement. In this respect, the regulatory framework on this front has been clear since the promulgation of Communiqué No. 2010/4 in October 2010.

1.3.2.2 Geographic Scope in Case Law

In terms of competition law infringements, the Board has refrained from declining jurisdiction over non-Turkish cartels or cartel members in the past, as long as there has

---

[48] *Rail Cargo Logistics* (16 December 2015, 15-44/740-267).

been an effect on the Turkish markets. For instance, in its *Şişecam/Yioula* decision,[49] the Board concluded that there was no evidence which proved that the investigated parties agreed to allocate the market which would affect the Turkish market for glass containers. Similarly in *Railroad Cargo Logistics*,[50] the Board decided that the allegations could not be evaluated within the scope of Law No. 4054, given that within the framework of Article 2 of Law No. 4054, it was understood that (i) the market allocation agreement under the Balkan Train cooperation did not have any effect on the Turkish markets between 2005 and 2006 and it was not possible to determine whether it had any effects on the Turkish markets between 1999–2004 and 2007–2011, and (ii) the market allocation agreement under the Soptrain cooperation did not have any effect on the Turkish markets.

In terms of the Turkish merger control regime, the Board's settled case law explicitly and consistently indicates that a joint venture transaction would be subject to a mandatory merger control filing whenever the jurisdictional turnover thresholds are exceeded, even in cases where the joint venture is not or will not be active in Turkey and will not have any effects in the near future (or perhaps ever) in Turkish markets. If and to the extent the jurisdictional turnover thresholds are exceeded, the approval of the Board will be required before closing the joint venture transaction.

Some of the most recent precedents of the Board that explicitly set forth this settled position on this front include the following: *Generali/Union-Zaragoza Properties*,[51] *Alpla Holding/PTT Global*,[52] *HSI/Hilton Sao Paulo Morumbi*,[53] *FSI/Snam-OLT Offshore*,[54] *Faurecia/Michelin-SymbioFCell*,[55] *Bamesa/Steel Center*,[56] *Engie/EDF/CDC/La Poste*,[57] *CDC/Total*,[58] *Astorg/eResearch Technology*,[59] *Mitsubishi/Wallenius Wilhelmsen*,[60] *Leoni/ Hengtong*,[61] *Daimler/Volkswagen-MT Holding*,[62] and *DENSO/Aisin Seiki*.[63]

The consistent track record of the Board explicitly demonstrates that there are no exceptions on this front and particularly illustrates the irrelevance of the absence of (i) any current/future Turkey-related activities of the JV and/or (ii) any affected markets/overlaps among the parties within the scope of the notifiability analysis. In this respect, the Board is adamant on deeming such transactions notifiable and it does not have any discretion other than following the procedural steps to enforce the legal sanctions, once the violation of the suspension requirement is detected.

---

[49] *Şişecam/Yioula* (28 February 2007, 07-17/155-50).
[50] *Railroad Cargo Logistics* (n. 48).
[51] *Generali/Union-Zaragoza Properties* (6 February 2020, 20-08/73-41).
[52] *Alpla Holding/PTT Global* (16 January 2020, 20-04/37-19).
[53] *HSI/Hilton Sao Paulo Morumbi* (16 January 2020, 20-04/33-16).
[54] *FSI/Snam-OLT Offshore* (9 January 2020, 20-03/18-8).
[55] *Faurecia/Michelin-SymbioFCell* (26 September 2019, 19-33/491-211).
[56] *Bamesa/Steel Center* (12 December 2019, 19-44/739-316).
[57] *Engie/EDF/CDC/La Poste* (19 December 2019, 19-45/747-321).
[58] *CDC/Total* (29 November 2019, 19-42/700-299).
[59] *Astorg/eResearch Technology* (12 December 2019, 19-44/730-310).
[60] *Mitsubishi/Wallenius Wilhelmsen* (16 January 2020, 20-04/35-18).
[61] *Leoni/Hengtong* (21 February 2019, 19-08/93-38).
[62] *Daimler/Volkswagen-MT Holding* (7 February 2019, 19-06/61-25).
[63] *DENSO/Aisin Seiki* (17 January 2019, 19-04/32-13).

Chapter 2
Article 4 and Article 5
of the Competition Law: Basic Principles

GÖNENÇ GÜRKAYNAK, ESQ., FIRAT EĞRILMEZ[*]
AND AYBÜKE AKDAĞ[**]

Article 4 of Law No. 4054 prohibits agreements and concerted practices between different undertakings as well as the decisions of associations of undertakings that have as their object or effect or potential effect of restricting competition and deems such agreements and concerted practices as unlawful. This provision outlines the constituent elements of conducts falling within the scope of Article 4 as follows: (i) there should be two or more undertakings engaging in a certain conduct; (ii) this conduct should be an agreement, a decision (of association of undertakings) or a concerted practice; and (iii) the conduct in question should have as its object or effect (including potential effect) of restricting competition.

Before delving into the details of implementation of Article 4 of Law No. 4054 under chapters 3, 4 and 5 of this book, the sections below will focus on the basic principles of Article 4, in order to lay out the fundamental dynamics that are needed to explore the more complex matters. These dynamics revolve around the following concepts: "undertaking", "agreement", "decision", "concerted practice", "horizontal agreement", "vertical agreement", "inter-brand competition", "intra-brand competition", and "appreciability".

2.1 Undertakings and Associations of Undertakings

The concept of "undertaking" is essential from a competition law standpoint as it establishes the focal point in terms of implementing the substantive rules of competition law set out in Article 4, Article 6, and Article 7 of Law No. 4054. Indeed, undertakings are regarded as the subjects of competition law.[64] Similarly, the concept of "association of undertakings" also has a particular significance in terms of competition law; however, when compared with

---

[*]   Associate, ELIG Gürkaynak Attorneys-at-Law, Istanbul <firat.egilmez@elig.com>.
[**]   Associate, ELIG Gürkaynak Attorneys-at-Law, Istanbul <aybuke.akdag@elig.com>.

[64]   H. Tamer, "Rekabet Hukukunda Ekonomik Bütünlük Kavramı ve Hukuki Sonuçları", Marmara University, 2017 <https://tez.yok.gov.tr/UlusalTezMerkezi/tezDetay.jsp?id=vgS15QTODAu9XUQE0MeR8w&no=qFD_aZESAy-pExtKr1gg8wQ> (last accessed on 11 June 2021), p. 114.

the term "undertaking", the function of the latter is predominantly related to Article 4 of Law No. 4054, which prohibits "undertakings" from partaking in agreements or concerted practices that have the object or effect of preventing, distorting or restricting competition, as well as the decisions of the "association of undertakings" to the same effect.

Furthermore, the concept of undertaking has a specific significance in terms of Article 7 of Law No. 4054, which enables the Board to prohibit concentrations that would result in a significant lessening of effective competition (the so-called SIEC test) within a market for goods or services in the entirety or a portion of the country, particularly in the form of creating or strengthening a dominant position. That is because the Board takes the concept of "undertaking" into account when conducting a merger control analysis under Article 7 of Law No. 4054 rather than the concepts of "legal person" or "legal entity".

Against the foregoing, this subsection will first explain the concept of "undertaking" in general terms, and then, provide explanations on the status of state-owned entities in terms of this concept, and finally, explain the concept of "association of undertakings".

2.1.1 The Concept of Undertaking

The term "undertaking" in competition law refers to a unique concept that is independent of the other law disciplines. Similar to the enforcement practices in other jurisdictions, Turkish competition law is concerned predominantly with the practices of "undertakings". Article 3 of Law No. 4054 defines the term as those natural and legal persons forming a unit that can decide independently and constituting an economic whole, producing, marketing and selling goods and services in the market. Therefore, the concept of "undertaking" is mainly composed of two main elements: (i) economic activity and (ii) economic independence.[65,66] There are also Board decisions that consider the "economic entity" as an element that is separate from the elements of "economic activity" and "economic independence".[67]

Turkish competition law does not embrace a formalistic approach towards the concept of "undertaking". To that end, it is not required for an economic unit to be a legal entity for it to be deemed an "undertaking". Furthermore, it is also not a prerequisite for an economic unit to be registered in any chamber of commerce. In a similar way, there is also no need for legal persons to be private entities. Following this exact line of reasoning, in *TMMOB*, the Board arrives at the conclusion that self-employed architects and engineers who provide paid services will be deemed undertakings within Law No. 4054 since self-employment is (i) based on personal work and scientific/professional knowledge or expertise, and (ii) provided independently and under personal responsibility.[68]

---

[65] Please see *İzmir Municipality* (11 February 2010, 10-16/183-70), para. 200 and *Meat and Fish Authority* (25 November 2010, 10-73/1509-577), paras. 340–350. In these decisions, the Board underscores that the criteria for being deemed to be an "undertaking" are "conducting economic activity" and "undertaking such economic activity in an independent manner".

[66] O. Güzel, *Rekabet Hukukunda Teşebbüs ve Teşebbüs Birlikleri* (Ankara: Rekabet Kurumu, 2003), p. 59.

[67] *TFF* (27 October 2011, 11-54/1385-495), p. 6.

[68] *TMMOB* (22 January 2002, 02-04/40-21).

In certain instances, the same entity might be acting as an "undertaking" within the meaning of competition law for some of its activities, and not for others, simultaneously. In such borderline cases, it might be necessary to adopt a functional approach for evaluating whether a particular entity constitutes an undertaking.[69] The Board's decisional practice makes references to the functional approach in the EU competition law practice and also implements the said approach itself.[70] Therefore, one should consider how the relevant entity functions separately for each of its activities when evaluating whether the relevant entity constitutes an "undertaking" vis-à-vis the competition laws.

2.1.1.1 Economic Activity

In order for an entity to be considered as an undertaking, it should first be engaged in an economic activity. For satisfying the "economic activity" criteria, an entity should offer a good or service in a particular market.

The Board's approach on "economic activity" is manifested in its decision concerning the TFF (Turkish Football Federation). In *TFF*, the Board resolved that although it could be accepted that the success or failure of sports clubs in their field has somehow affected their economic activities (such as ticket sales, player transfers, advertisement and sponsorship rights), this relationship between sportive performance and economic performance is not a direct relation but an indirect one, where attributing some economic consequences to any sporting event is not enough to qualify that event as an economic activity in itself.[71]

The criterion of undertaking an "economic activity" was further elaborated by the Board in *TSSF* (Turkish Underwater Sports Federation).[72] In *TSSF*, the Board distinguishes the activities of public authorities by categorising them as "economic" and "non-economic". To that end, the Board underlines that the first criterion for a public authority to be deemed as an "undertaking" is conducting "economic activity".[73] The Board remarked that "economic activity" was defined by the European Court of Justice as "production or provision of goods and services within a particular market"[74] and that the first parameter in terms of defining whether an activity is economic or not concerns whether the relevant entity supplies goods or services to the market. Additionally, the Board underlined that it was not important for an undertaking to profit from the activity, but it was important that an entity could potentially earn profits as a result. Accordingly, the Board found that even if TSSF is a public authority and conducted its activities of provision of diver and instructor certification without seeking to make profits, since third parties could earn profit from such activities, these could thereby be deemed as "economic activities".

Medical Consumables provides further insight on the criteria of "economic activity".[75] In the relevant decision, the Board assessed whether SSK (Social Security Institution)

---

[69]   R. Whish and D. Bailey, *Competition Law* (7th ed., Oxford University Press, 2012), pp. 84–85.
[70]   *TSSF* (7 August 2014, 14-26/530-235), pp. 64–69; *TCDD* (3 March 2005, 05-12/145-52) p. 4.
[71]   *TFF* (n. 67), p. 5.
[72]   *TSSF* (n. 70).
[73]   Ibid., p. 66.
[74]   Ibid., p. 77 and Case 118/85 *Commission v. Italian Republic* [1987] ECR 2599.
[75]   *Medical Consumables* (7 October 2010, 10-63/1325-497).

could be deemed as an "undertaking", particularly in consideration of its activities that fall within the scope of the investigation. The particular focus concerned SSK's purchases of goods and services from private entities, for the national insurance and healthcare services that it provides for social security purposes. To that end, the Board underscored that SSK is a public authority that is autonomous in administrative and financial terms and has been providing insurance and healthcare services for social security purposes since 2002. The Board characterised the healthcare services provided by SSK to be "its statutory duty to provide, non-profit and wholly for social purposes, and moreover, where the cost of services is incomparably higher than the premiums charged to the insurance holders". To that end, the Board determined that the healthcare and insurance services provided by SSK for the insurance holders within the healthcare system did not hold the characteristics of a normal economic activity and thereby SSK could not be deemed as an "undertaking".

Following from *Medical Consumables*, the Board's viewpoint on which activities could be characterised as "economic activities" is further crystallised in *Devlet Malzeme Ofisi* and *SSK-I*, with a particular focus on the activities of the public authorities.[76] In *SSK-I*, the Board assessed that SSK's purchases of pharmaceuticals could not be deemed as economic activity due to the fact that such purchases were made for providing public healthcare and insurance services. Following that, the Board remarked that purchases made for non-economic activities also could not be deemed as economic activities. Within that context, the Board emphasised that the national insurance system that SSK managed was mandatory for its members and SSK's offerings related to insurance and healthcare services were subsidised and pursued for public benefit. Accordingly, the Board assessed that the SSK's pharmaceutical purchases made within the scope of its public healthcare and insurance services could not be deemed as economic activity.

Similarly, in *Devlet Malzeme Ofisi* the Board remarked that the procurement activities of the State Supply Office, which is a public establishment, could not be deemed as economic activity, due to the fact that such purchases were not made for the purpose of resale in the market but to supply low-cost goods for other public bodies. Consequently, the Board concluded that the State Supply Office procurements could not be deemed as economic activity, as these did not pursue such an aim and instead were conducted for budget-saving.

Furthermore, in *Beylikdüzü Municipality*,[77] the Board's evaluation regarding the allegation of discrimination asserted against Beylikdüzü Municipality regarding its tenders for private security service procurement boiled down to the assessment on whether the respective municipality could be deemed as an undertaking or not. Accordingly, the Board noted that the relevant allegations could be deemed admissible if Beylikdüzü Municipality could qualify as an undertaking. To that end, the Board reiterated that the two essential elements of being qualified as an undertaking are "economic activity" and "being able to make independent decisions". Within that scope, the Board noted that rather than pursuing an economic aim, the tender that the municipality organised

---

[76] *Devlet Malzeme Ofisi* (10 October 2017, 17-31/522-226) p. 9; *SSK-I* (27 May 2003, 03-35/416-182).
[77] *Beylikdüzü Municipality* (26 November 2014, 14-46/847-386).

was aimed to better achieve the primary duties and authority vested in it by the laws, and such service procurement was of an ancillary nature. In light of the foregoing, the Board remarked that Beylikdüzü Municipality could not be deemed as an undertaking.

There are also Board decisions that do not consider social insurance activities as economic activities since the insurance and health services that public institutions provide (i) have mandatory membership; (ii) the relevant activities are social in nature; and (iii) the insured party does not receive a service that is proportional to the premiums paid.[78]

Lastly, the decisional practice of the Board also brings another micro dimension to the element of "economic activity" based on the criterion of "individual needs". Within that scope, in an instance where the Board evaluated whether the employers' payment of meal expenses, based on invoices declared by employees, could be considered as an economic activity, the Board relied on the respective criterion. To that end, the Board stated that the practices, which cannot be extended to third parties or to the market–or put differently, could not be offered within a market–cannot be qualified as "economic activities" within the framework of competition law, since their nature does not meet the requirement that an economic activity should exceed the individual needs.[79]

2.1.1.2 Economic Independence

The concept of independence refers to circumstances where the relevant economic unit is able to determine its economic and commercial policies without intervention.[80] According to the Guidelines on the Concept of Control, the concept of control could be defined as having the ability to exercise decisive influence over another undertaking.[81] To that end, if an undertaking enjoys the right to determine the strategic commercial decisions of other undertakings, it is deemed to have a decisive influence over them. The Guidelines on the Concept of Control do not require an actual exercise of decisive influence or an anticipated exercise thereof at a given future date and deem having the ability to exercise such influence sufficient for having control. According to Communiqué No. 2010/4, the possibility of exercising decisive influence on an undertaking can be obtained through rights, contracts or other means, individually or in combination, and can exist on a legal and de facto basis. In addition, control may take the form of sole or joint control, and extend to the whole or parts of one or more undertakings. The Guidelines on the Concept of Control remark that a right to determine the strategic commercial decisions is usually achieved by the acquisition of the majority voting rights in a company or having the ability to veto strategic decisions. Accordingly, for a legal entity to be deemed economically independent, such an entity should not be under the control or decisive influence of another legal and/or natural person.

In *TSSF*, the Board assessed whether TSSF, which is a public authority, is an "undertaking" and elaborated on the "economic independence" criterion. To that end, the Board

---

[78]   *State Retirement Fund* (19 June 2003, 03-44/501-221), p. 7; *Social Security Institution* (13 July 2017, 17-22/362-158), pp. 56–58.

[79]   *Sodexho* (28 September 2006, 06-67/905-262), para. 210.

[80]   *Government of Singapore Investment/Citigroup* (6 January 2010, 10-01/17-10). Also see Tamer, 2017, p. 8.

[81]   Guidelines on the Concept of Control, https://www.rekabet.gov.tr/Dosya/guidelines/10-pdf ,para. 40.

remarked that in order for an entity to be considered as an "undertaking", it is sufficient for it to produce or sell goods or services in a given market in an independent manner.[82] Delving into the independency criterion, the Board further remarked that this refers to "not being subject to the approval of any superior authority in terms of making decisions regarding economic activities and also implementing them" and implies "a situation where the control is not in the hands of another undertaking".[83]

A noteworthy example in this regard is *ASKİ*,[84] where the Board decided that ASKİ's activity subject to complaint should be reviewed under the functional criterion defined as producing, marketing, selling goods and services in the market–in other words, operating in the market. The Board evaluated ASKİ on the basis of two criteria: independent decision-making and the form of economic integrity. The Board noted with certainty that the sale of water meters is a commercial activity, where there are many undertakings with similar operations in the market. Also considering that ASKİ has an independent budget, a separate source of income from the municipality and a separate administration, the Board concluded that ASKİ could make its own independent decisions. Therefore, the Board decided that the functional and formal criteria are both met, allowing ASKİ to be considered as an undertaking.

In many instances, the Board decided that what were separate legal entities should not be considered as separate undertakings and should be deemed as being in a single economic unit, due to the "family ties" between them.[85] At that point, the "economic entity" is, indeed, the result of economic dependence and the two elements are highly interrelated.

2.1.1.3 Economic Entity

The Board makes it clear that an undertaking, as the subject of the competition law, does not necessarily have to be a legal entity, but there should, instead, be an "economic entity".[86] Based on the notion of "economic entity",[87] a company will be considered as belonging to the same economic integrity/whole as the other companies that are within the same group. While a company may seem to make its daily business decisions by itself, it might belong to a much larger group, which is led by a legal entity or a natural person that is entitled to make strategic decisions on behalf of the undertakings belonging to that group.

Where separate undertakings are considered to be part of a single economic entity/whole: (i) the agreements concluded between these undertakings are not caught by Article 4 of Law No. 4054 prohibitions[88] and (ii) there is no need to make a notification as per Article 7 of Law No. 4054 for a transaction which merely involves the entities belonging to such single economic entity.[89] Overall, Law No. 4054 does not apply to the interplay

---

[82] *TSSF* (n. 70), p. 74.
[83] Ibid., p. 76.
[84] *ASKİ* (8 August 2002, 02-47/587-240).
[85] *Bayburt İnşaat* (3 May 2012, 12-24/666-188).
[86] *TFF* (n. 67), p. 6.
[87] N. Kocadağ, *Rekabet Hukuku Kapsamında Ana Şirketin Yavru Şirket İhlallerinden Doğan Sorumluluğu* (Ankara: Rekabet Kurumu, 2015), p. 48; Güzel, 2003, p. 59.
[88] *Bayburt İnşaat* (n. 85).
[89] *Alstom Power* (4 March 2010, 10-21/264-97).

between undertakings stemming from a single economic entity. Likewise, an abuse of dominant position analysis also involves an assessment that would take into consideration the whole economic entity, instead of the single business unit or firm that the conduct under scrutiny is directly attributable to, and such analysis would be inclusive of the respective business unit or the firm together with its parent companies and subsidiaries.

The important question here is, what brings two different legal entities under a single economic integrity/whole? The Board remarks that in assessing whether different natural and/or legal persons belong to a single economic integrity/whole, the following are taken into account: (i) whether there are economic and familial ties between persons and/or groups; (ii) the foundations, nature, scale of such economic ties and the comparison of dependent activities with independent activities, if any; and (iii) whether there is a unity of interest between persons and/or groups.[90]

The concept of control is not applicable in terms of the relationships between natural persons, so the concept of "unity of interest" is employed as the main criterion for determining whether two legal entities controlled by two natural persons belong to a single economic entity.[91] If the Board determines that there exists a "unity of interest" between two natural persons and/or groups, it is assumed that there is no motive for competition between such persons and/or groups and the legal entities controlled by them. In *Yıldızlar*,[92] the Board remarked that the assessment as to whether there is a unity of interest between two or more natural persons involves the query of whether these persons could be considered a singular economic decision-making mechanism.

The Board puts forth that familial ties are an essential element in terms of the assessment of the relationship between natural persons from an economic integrity standpoint.[93] In *Bilkom*, the Board considered different legal entities held by different natural persons, who were siblings, as a single economic entity due to familial ties.[94] Similarly, in *Altıparmak Gıda*,[95] the Board deemed different companies controlled by siblings to be within a single economic entity and remarked that the familial ties between the controlling persons affected its assessment on economic integrity to a great extent. Additionally, the Board put a particular emphasis on the fact that these companies controlled by different siblings were active in the same relevant product market and this contributed to the Board's assessment that there was a unity of interest between these companies. In *Misbis*,[96] the Board determined that the legal entity that was jointly controlled by five family members by means of equal shares was within the same economic entity as the company controlled by only one of these family members.

That being said, the familial ties between two or more natural persons controlling different legal entities would not necessarily result in a "unity of interest" between these

[90] *MGS/Gıdasa* (7 February 2008, 08-12/130-46), para. 310.
[91] *Bilkom* (9 January 2001, 01-03/10-3); *Volkan Metro* (2 December 2013, 13-67/928-390); *LMC Gıda* (1 June 2016, 16-19/313-142); *Çimentas* (7 August 2001, 01-39/391-100); *ParıltıSofra* (4 October 2002, 02-61/759-307); *Misbis* (8 November 2007, 07-85/1039-401).
[92] *Yıldızlar* (13 August 2020, 20-37/525-233), para. 10.
[93] *Mosaş* (12 March 2020, 20-14/191-97), para. 30.
[94] *Bilkom* (n. 91).
[95] *Altıparmak Gıda* (31 March 2010, 10-27/393-146).
[96] *Misbis* (n. 91).

entities. For instance, in *Parrafin and Vaselin*[97] the Board inquired whether AGS and Mercan Kimya, which were active in the same relevant market, could be deemed to be within a single economic entity due to familial ties, as the natural persons controlling the respective entities were siblings. The Board considered that AGS and Mercan Kimya were two different undertakings based on the evidence that these entities compete with each other and that there were no indicators that these entities shared common shareholders or managers.

Furthermore, there are other factors that would be taken into account in the assessment as to whether multiple legal entities form an economic entity, besides the familial ties. That being said, these are predominantly considered as complementary factors that would bolster the Board's assessment that familial ties result in "unity of interest". For instance, in *Mosaş*[98] the Board regarded factors such as purchaser-customer relations between different legal entities, as well as joint utilisation of certain employees, as factors that would manifest the unity of interest. Similarly, in *Ajans Press/Pr Net*,[99] the Board determined that the sharing of digital formats being used as inputs, between Ajans Press and Interpress, which are two different legal entities active in the same relevant product market, and the protocol between them that aimed at cooperation in terms of marketing and sales, as well as their strategies against other players in the relevant market, were factors signifying the unity of interest between these entities, along with the familial ties.

Lastly, *Ülker/Şok* sets an important precedent in terms of the "unity of interest" concept. In the relevant decision, the Board highlighted the significance of the relevant market in terms of determining whether two or more economic entities form a single economic unity or not.[100] In that, the Board remarked that two different entities could be deemed as being in a single economic unit within a specific relevant market, while these entities could be considered as separate undertakings in another.[101] Within that scope, the Board's economic integrity assessment was based on the factors of whether there is an "economic union/conflict of interest", "economic dependence", and "competitive motivation" between Ülker Group and Topbaş Group in terms of economic activities in the market.[102]

The Board's assessment revolved around the market levels that the economic groups under scrutiny were operating at. To that end, the Board highlighted that Ülker Group and Topbaş Group were active at different levels of the market, in terms of fast-moving consumer goods retailing. Accordingly, it was highlighted that the former was predominantly active at the production level (upstream), having minor activities at the retail level in partnership with the latter (via minority shareholding), while the latter was active at the retail level.

In light of the foregoing, the Board pointed to the competitive pressure that retail level undertakings started to exert on the production level. In that, the Board explained that

---

[97]   *Parrafin and Vaselin* (28 October 2009, 09-49/1220-308), para. 290.
[98]   *Mosaş* (n. 93), paras. 41–43.
[99]   *Ajans Press/PR Net* (21 October 2010, 10-66/1402-523), para. 560.
[100]   *Ülker/Şok* (17 August 2011, 11-45/1044-357).
[101]   Ibid., para. 990.
[102]   See the Authority's public announcement regarding the transfer of Şok Stores to Ülker Group dated 27 December 2012 <https://www.rekabet.gov.tr/en/Guncel/statement-concerning-the-transfer-of-sok-01afdd1d66654b2f9af-1249ce49213e0> (last accessed on 29 June 2021).

private label products (such as those offered by Topbaş Group's retail chain, BİM) were becoming considered as a viable alternative to the branded products (as offered by Ülker Group) by consumers, and such a competitive pressure would alter the unity of interest that the two groups had in the production level and could result in a conflict of interest at the retail level. Accordingly, the Board remarked that such a conflict of interest would steer these two economic groups towards making independent decisions at the retail level.

Additionally, the Board assessed the level of turnover that Ülker Group generates from its partnership with Topbaş Group, and its proportion to Ülker Group's business activities in general; concluding that the particular turnover amount could not be considered to result in dependence to Topbaş Group.

Lastly, the Board assessed whether the unity of interest was viable between Ülker Group and Topbaş Group at the retail level. To that end, the Board considered a hypothetical scenario where Ülker Group implemented discriminatory terms in favour of BİM (the majority shares of which was held by Topbaş Group and the minority shares of which was held by Ülker Group) and concluded such a strategy would undermine the continuity of Ülker's activities, as Ülker generated most of its turnover from its activities at the production level, as well as its sales from the retailers competing with BİM. In light of the foregoing, the Board remarked that Ülker and Topbaş groups were not in an economic integrity/whole.

2.1.1.4 Status of State-Owned Entities

Publicly owned entities can also be qualified as undertakings and are subject to competition law rules. The preamble of Article 2 of Law No. 4054 explicitly states that "competition rules must be applied to all undertakings which have economic operations. It is not important whether the undertakings belong to public institutions or to private persons. Even though the goals of protecting the public interest and public order come to the forefront in competition law, the fulfilment of the duties of the undertakings charged with serving the general economic interests should not conflict with the competition rules". Therefore, it is clear that state-owned entities might be subject to competition law reviews and investigations, as well.

Still, when state-owned entities were alleged to have engaged in certain anti-competitive behaviours, a number of cases before the Board dealt with the question of the status of state entities within the meaning of the term "undertaking" under competition law. In essence, the Board decided that the concept of undertaking should include all the actors of all sectors that meet the economic activity criteria within the scope of the law, by broadening the scope to encompass every undertaking that performs an economic activity, regardless of (i) how the activity is pursued; (ii) whether the entity is public or private; or (iii) whether it serves private or general economic interests.[103] In other words, the Board principally approaches the issue of state-owned entities by disregarding the specific legal nature of the entity conducting the activity: whether they are natural or legal, public or private, all actors engaged in economic activity are undertakings.[104]

---

[103]   *TFF* (n. 67), p. 6.
[104]   *TCDD* (n. 70) p. 4.

However, the Board also draws the line by stating that those activities carried out by a public authority which must be done by the state provide social benefits and are among the fundamental duties of the state; thus, these cannot be deemed as economic activities.[105] *Government of Singapore Investment/Citigroup*[106] might provide further guidance in terms of the Board's viewpoint on the status of state-owned enterprises from a competition law standpoint. In the relevant decision, the Board found that the sole purpose of Government of Singapore Investment was to manage the country's foreign reserves, and it invested with these reserves to provide a reasonable return on inflation, within acceptable risk limits. Additionally, it was determined that Government of Singapore Investment passed on the revenue from its investments to the government and the Central Bank, and furthermore, Government of Singapore Investment was established in accordance with the laws granting it a special constitutional status. Against the foregoing, the Board concluded that Government of Singapore Investment could not be qualified as an undertaking according to Article 3 of Law No. 4054 as its area of responsibility was limited to the management of the country's resources and it did not engage in any commercial activity independently.

Another important point to address concerning the state-owned entities was explored in *12 Banks*.[107] In the relevant case, the Board examined whether the three state-owned banks–namely, T.C. Ziraat Bankası A.Ş., Türkiye Vakıflar Bankası T.A.O and Türkiye Halk Bankası A.Ş. – could be deemed to be a single economic entity due to the fact that their majority shares are state-owned. That being said, the Board concluded that these undertakings did not form a single economic unit on the grounds that the strategic decisions of these state-owned banks were not being taken by the state, and the role of the state was limited to supervising and monitoring their activities. To that end, it is apparent that the Board primarily considers the strategic decision-making structure, rather than the ownership structure, when determining the control structure of the state-owned entities.

In the more recent *Güneş Sigorta*,[108] the Board followed a similar line of reasoning but adopted an outcome that was distinctly different from *12 Banks* due to the changed circumstances. In *Güneş Sigorta*, the Board elaborated on its assessment, which had led it to consider T.C. Ziraat Bank A.Ş., Türkiye Vakıflar Bankası T.A.O. and Türkiye Halk Bankası A.Ş. under a single economic entity, and emphasised that the respective assessment was based on the fact that public authorities' majority shareholding in these banks were exercised in a way that was limited to general monitoring and supervision, and the public authorities did not interfere in the strategic decisions of these banks. Following from the respective assessment in *12 Banks*, the Board assessed whether TVF's (Turkish Wealth Fund) majority shareholding since February 2017 consisted of a mere "monitoring and supervision" authority over the respective state-owned banks and concluded that Turkish Wealth Fund could actually exercise decisive influence over the business plan, capital increase and strategic decisions of T.C. Ziraat Bank A.Ş., Türkiye Vakıflar Bankası T.A.O. and Türkiye Halk Bankası A.Ş. Consequently, the Board remarked that

---

[105]   *Citigroup/US Treasure* (6 January 2010, 10-01/18-11), p. 4.
[106]   *Government of Singapore Investment/Citigroup* (n. 80).
[107]   *12 Banks* (8 March 2013, 13-13/198-100).
[108]   *Güneş Sigorta* (27 August 2020, 20-39/539-240).

TVF's control over T.C. Ziraat Bank A.Ş., Türkiye Vakıflar Bankası T.A.O. and Türkiye Halk Bankası A.Ş. should be interpreted in a way that the respective state-owned banks belong to a single economic unit which is under control of Turkish Wealth Fund.

Chinese National Nuclear Corporation/Tsinghua Tongfang[109] is also a noteworthy example that might shed light on the status of the state-owned entities. In the relevant decision, the Board first recognised that both Chinese National Nuclear Corporation (CNNC) and Tsinghua Tongfang were ultimately under the control of the Chinese government. Similar to the line of reasoning in *12 Banks*, the Board once again established that state ownership does not necessarily mean that all legal entities, which are owned or whose majority shares are owned by the state, form an economic entity/integrity. Accordingly, in *Chinese National Nuclear Corporation/Tsinghua Tongfang*, the Board assessed whether CNNC and Tsinghua Holdings, which were both in state ownership, were actually controlled by the Chinese state or not. The Board found that the Chinese state does not interfere in strategic decisions of the relevant state-owned entities, such as strategic planning, daily operations, personnel assignment, significant financial matters, development plans, annual investment plans and designation of the management team. Furthermore, the Board determined that the Chinese state did not have the authority to designate the board of directors of the respective entities and the state's authority was limited to supervisory matters. Consequently, the Board concluded that the respective entities could not be deemed as a single undertaking as they were not controlled by the state.

2.1.2 Association of Undertakings

Article 3 of Law No. 4054 defines the term "association of undertakings" as follows: "Any kind of associations with or without a legal personality, which are formed by undertakings to accomplish particular goals." This term, which differs from the term "undertaking", is only important for the implementation of Article 4 of Law No. 4054.

Pursuant to Article 16 of Law No. 4054, the associations of undertakings might be held responsible for competition law violations. Indeed, there are many decisions of the Board that recognise the association of undertakings as a subject of competition law and fine the associations of undertakings for competition law violations and other breaches of Law No. 4054.[110]

The Board also noted that the association of undertakings does not necessarily have to be a legal entity as per the definition of "association of undertakings" in Article 3 of Law No. 4054. Therefore, even if an entity were composed of the undertakings that met the criteria listed above, an association of undertakings that was not a legal entity in itself could still be considered as an association of undertakings and its decisions could

---

[109]   *Chinese National Nuclear Corporation/Tsinghua Tongfang* (31 October 2019, 19-37/550-226).
[110]   *Van Natural Gas and Mechanical Installation Companies Professional Solidarity Association* (19 November 2020, 20-50/694-305); *Konya Exchangers and Goldsmiths Association* (14 February 2013, 13-10/152-75); *Biletix* (9 August 2012, 12-41/1159-376).

still be assessed as a decision of an association of undertakings within the meaning of Article 4 of Law No. 4054.[111]

In a remarkable decision of the Board examining the status of the Union of Chambers of Turkish Engineers and Architects, *TMMOB*,[112] the Board first states that self-employed engineers, architects, and urban planners who supply and sell services are undertakings, as explained above. Secondly, the Board goes on to analyse the status of the Union of Chambers of Turkish Engineers and Architects and concludes that both the individual chambers which these self-employed engineers, architects and urban planners are members of and the Union of Chambers of Turkish Engineers and Architects should be regarded as associations of undertakings. Before drawing this conclusion, the Board also provides important commentary on the general status of the association of undertakings, emphasising that there is no doubt such chambers serve to "achieve certain purposes" and establishing these entities voluntarily or by law does not change the nature of the work, as long as the said entity could take decisions that might affect its members.

2.2 Agreements, Decisions and Concerted Practices

Article 4 of Law No. 4054 aims to prohibit and illegalise the agreements and concerted practices, as well as the decisions of the associations of undertakings, which prevent, distort or restrict competition by object or by effect, directly or indirectly in a particular market for goods or services. Although the primary objective of Article 4 is to prevent and prohibit cartel agreements and other anti-competitive horizontal concurrences between competitors, one should bear in mind that it also applies to vertical agreements (i.e., the agreements between undertakings operating at different levels of the production or distribution chain).

The lawmakers intended the term "agreement" to be overarching with a view to preventing any circumvention of the rules set out in Law No. 4054. To that end, the application of Article 4 of Law No. 4054 is not limited to legal contracts. As set out in the preamble of Article 4, the term agreement "is used to refer to all kinds of compromise or accord to which the parties feel bound, even if these do not meet the conditions for validity as regards the Civil Law". Accordingly, the lawmakers indicated that for the purposes of Article 4 of Law No. 4054, it is not important whether the agreement is written or verbal. In the preamble, the lawmakers explicated their intention to prevent the undertakings from legitimising their acts or conducts limiting competition, via an evasion of the law (*fraude à la loi*).

Additionally, the lawmakers' intention of formulating an overarching rule covering all kinds of concurrences that have the object or effect of preventing, distorting or restricting

---

[111] *Gas Stations* (13 December 2007, 07-90/1162-454); *Konya Mechanical Engineers* (15 December 2005, 05-84/1150-330); *Motor Renewal Firms* (27 February 2001, 01-10/100-24); *Water Distributors* (22 January 2002, 02-04/39-20).

[112] *TMMOB* (n. 68).

competition, regardless of their form, also shows itself in the remarks set out in the preamble of Article 4 in relation to the concerted practices. In that context, if the existence of an agreement could not be established, "direct or indirect relations between the undertakings that replace their own independent activities and ensure a coordination and practical cooperation" would be treated as an agreement, provided that it leads to the same result.[113] In certain cases where such concurrences, which replace competing undertakings' independent activities and ensure coordination and practical cooperation, are present, but an explicit agreement could not be evidenced by the competition authority, the concept of "concerted practice" comes into play. A vertical restraint that falls within the scope of Article 4 of Law No. 4054 could also be considered as a concerted practice.[114]

Thus, the decisional practice of the Board, as well as the primary and the secondary legislation on that front, has allowed for a broad interpretation of the terms "agreement", "concerted practice" and "decision". The following section will explore these terms in light of the primary and the secondary legislation concerning competition law in Turkey and the landmark cases of the Board.

2.2.1 Agreements

Law No. 4054 does not define the term "agreement".[115] Yet, the preamble of Article 4 describes an agreement as "all kinds of compromise or accord to which the parties feel bound, even if these do not meet the conditions for validity as regards the Civil Law". Thus, although a legal contract is certainly considered as an "agreement" within the meaning of Turkish competition law, this is not limited to the term "contracts" under the general framework of the Code of Obligations.

In keeping with the preamble of Article 4, the Board's decisional practice also clearly provides that it is not mandatory to point to a consensus or decision that the parties have expressly agreed to, in order to put forward that an agreement exists within the scope of Law No. 4054; an agreement of the wills of the parties is considered sufficient.[116]

Similarly, the Board determined that "putting into practice all kinds of relations that distort the competitive environment without a contract is also an agreement".[117] In another decision, the concept of agreement in competition law legislation is used to describe all kinds of meetings of the minds between the relevant parties.[118] Another assessment of the Board also confirms that agreement in competition law practices is interpreted

---

[113] The preamble of Article 4 of Law No. 4054.
[114] *KWS* (25 November 2009, 09-57/1365-357).
[115] There are definitions for particular types of vertical agreements that are subject to vertical exemption communiqués. See Communiqué No. 2002/2. Communiqué No. 2008/2, Communiqué No. 2013/3, Communiqué No. 2016/5, Communiqué No. 2017/3.
[116] *Consumer Electronics* (7 November 2016, 16-37/628-279).
[117] *Fertilizers* (19 January 2011, 11-04/64-26).
[118] *White Meat* (25 November 2009, 09-57/1393-362).

more broadly than the contracts that constitute the subject of the law of obligations. The practices of competitors may constitute an agreement even in the absence of what could constitute formal requirements of the law of obligations. As such, even non-binding or verbal agreements may be scrutinized within the scope of the competition law.[119] Thus, it is also clear that there is no form required or sought as proof in order for an agreement to be considered as an "agreement" within the meaning of competition law.

Indeed, the Board's decisions emphasise that in accordance with the purpose of Article 4 of Law No. 4054, an "agreement" means any compromise or agreement that the parties feel bound with, even if the validity requirements of the Civil Law are not fulfilled. It does not matter whether the agreement is written or verbal. Indeed, even if the Board does not find an agreement between the undertakings, the decisional practice of the Board prohibits direct or indirect relations that allow coordination or practical work between undertakings as a substitute for their own independent behaviour, in case that they produce the same results as agreements.[120]

The Board's decisional practice makes references to the *Polypropylene*[121] decision of the Commission that establishes the concept of "single, overall agreement".[122] In this context, the Council of State has evaluated the Board's decisions in this regard and concluded that the Board clearly adopts the "single, overall agreement" doctrine in its evaluations concerning Article 4 of Law No. 4054.[123] The Board's own explanations of *Polypropylene* is as follows: Instead of a static approach that defines the moment when the compromise is reached, the concept of "a single continuous agreement-complex arrangements"[124] has been developed, which covers the entire process in which competition is violated.[125] Thus, in Turkish competition law as well, an undertaking can be held responsible for an overall cartel, even though it participated in only one or some of its constituent elements, "if it is shown that it knew, or must have known, that the collusion in which it participated... was part of an overall plan intended to distort competition and that the overall plan included all the constituent elements of the cartel".[126]

This understanding of the Board is repeated in various European courts judgments as well. In the *Limburgse Vinyl Maatschappij*[127] of the Court of First Instance, the "single, overall agreement" doctrine was depicted as the following:

> An undertaking may be held responsible for an overall cartel even though it is shown to have participated directly only in one or some of its constituent elements if it is shown that it knew, or must have known, that the collusion in which

---

[119] *Automotive Market* (18 April 2011, 11-24/464-139).
[120] *LPG* (26 November 1998, 93/750-159).
[121] Commission Decision 86/398/EEC OJ [1986] L 230/1, [1988] 4 CMLR 347.
[122] *Ceramic* (2 February 2006, 06-08/121-30).
[123] 13th Chamber of the Council of State (21 May 2019, E. 2016/4058, K. 2019/1782).
[124] See Chapter 12.
[125] *Ceramic* (n. 122).
[126] Whish and Bailey, 2012, pp. 84–85.
[127] Joined Cases T-305/94, T-306/94, T-307/94, T-313/94 to T-316/94, T-318/94, T-325/94, T-328/94, T-329/94 and T-335/94 *Limburgse Vinyl Maatschappij and others v. Commission of the European Communities* [1999] ECR II-931, para. 773.

it participated, especially by means of regular meetings organised over several years, was part of an overall plan intended to distort competition and that the overall plan included all the constituent elements of the cartel.

Similarly, in *Total Raffinage Marketing*[128] and in *JFE Engineering*[129] a similar approach was adopted.

On the other side, the administrative courts approach with great caution the single ongoing infringement concept in their decisions and emphasise that it requires determining the scope and boundaries of the framework agreement or joint plan accurately, revealing the connection and coordination between agreements or concerted practices between more than one undertaking, demonstrating that the undertakings participating in the breach know or are in a position to know the framework agreement.[130] It may be the case that a particular undertaking was not aware of nor a participant in all aspects of the single ongoing infringement, which could limit its liability to only the part of the breach that it was involved in. The administrative courts, therefore, state that an error by the Board in the determining of the specified issues could greatly expand the liability of the undertakings in terms of administrative fines, statute of limitations and especially private law liability, thus causing the undertakings to face situations that are incompatible with the material reality.[131]

2.2.2 Decisions of Associations of Undertakings

Article 4 of Law No. 4054 also prohibits decisions of associations of undertakings in cases where they restrict competition. This is because independent undertakings might easily coordinate their activities under a trade association. Indeed, there are many decisions of the Board where certain decisions of associations of undertakings are found to be anti-competitive. In one of its latest decisions, which concerns the Union of Chambers of Turkish Engineers and Architects (*Chamber of Electrical Engineers*),[132] the Authority carried out the entire investigation process vis-à-vis the relevant association of undertakings,

---

[128] Case T-566/08 *Total Raffinage Marketing v. European Commission*, EU:T:2013:423. The relevant remarks in the decision are as follows: "The fact that the applicant did not participate in that meeting cannot prevent the Commission from concluding, generally, that it had participated in the price-fixing agreements and from taking into account in that regard the evidence relating to that meeting. An undertaking may be held liable for an overall cartel even though it is shown to have participated directly in only one or some of its constituent elements, if it knew, or must necessarily have known, that the collusion in which it participated, especially by means of regular meetings organised over several years, was part of an overall plan intended to distort normal competition and that that overall plan included all the constituent elements of the cartel", para 108.

[129] Joined Cases T-67/00, T-68/00, T-71/00 and T-78/00 *JFE Engineering Corp and others v. Commission of the European Communities* [2004] ECR II-2501. The relevant remarks in the decision are as follows: "As the Commission correctly points out, an undertaking may be held responsible for an overall cartel even though it is shown to have participated directly only in one or some of its constituent elements if it is shown that it knew, or must have known, that the collusion in which it participated, especially by means of regular meetings organised over several years, was part of an overall plan intended to distort competition and that the overall plan included all the constituent elements of the cartel" (para. 370).

[130] 13th Chamber of the Council of State (n. 123).

[131] Ibid.

[132] *Chamber of Electrical Engineers* (26 December 2019, 19-46/791-345).

instead of the individual undertakings forming it. At the end of the investigation, the Board decided that the Chamber of Electrical Engineers violated Law No. 4054 due to its decisions and practices concerning the minimum wage practice and imposed an administrative monetary fine against the relevant association of undertakings.[133,134]

There are many similar decisions of the Board where it evaluated whether an association of undertakings had violated Article 4 of Law No. 4054. Recent examples include *TÜKEBİR*,[135] *Pharmacists Association II*,[136] and *Automotive Distributors' Association.*[137]

Even though some decisions of the associations of undertakings would constitute a competition law violation in and of themselves, there may be barriers that prevent them from being subject to competition laws. This is possible when the legislator provides explicit statutory powers to that association of undertakings to act in a manner that would be in contradiction with Law No. 4054, which is also recognised by the Board in its decisional practice.[138] The most well-known example is the minimum fee tariffs that the Turkish Bar Association sets out for various services rendered by attorneys. These minimum fee tariffs would easily constitute a violation of Article 4 of Law No. 4054, as such conduct imposes a uniform minimum price for a specific type of service affecting an entire relevant market. Yet, Law No. 1136 legitimises this practice, by authorising the Turkish Bar Association to determine the minimum fees for services provided by attorneys.[139] Very similar examples can also be provided for the monopoly rights, minimum education requirements, membership requirements and minimum/maximum/guiding price tariffs within the association of undertakings for other professions such as medical doctors, pharmacists, engineers, architects, independent accountants and financial advisors.[140]

2.2.3 Concerted Practices

The "concerted practice" tool is aimed to address the problem, for the competition authorities, to prove the existence of a cartel due to the fact that a cartel would likely try to destroy evidence of meetings, e-mail messages, fax messages and other similar correspondences, "in which case the temptation of the competition authority may be to infer the existence of an agreement or concerted practice from circumstantial evidence such as parallel conduct on the market".[141] While the decisional practice of the Board predominantly utilises the concept of "concerted practice" for tackling horizontal concurrences, the concerted practice tool could also be utilised for vertical restraints.

---

[133]   Ibid.
[134]   See other decisions: *Van Natural Gas and Mechanical Installation Companies Professional Solidarity Association* (n. 110); *Konya Exchangers and Goldsmiths Association* (n. 110); *Chamber of Electrical Engineers* (n. 132); *Turkish Pharmacists' Association I* (7 July 2015, 15-28/336-108).
[135]   *TÜKEBİR* (27 February 2020, 20-12/145-80).
[136]   *Turkish Pharmacists' Association II* (14 November 2019, 19-40/643-271).
[137]   *Automotive Distributors' Association* (28 February 2019, 19-10/115-46).
[138]   *Burdur Mechanical Engineers* (14 December 2017, 17-41/640-279), p. 28.
[139]   See, e.g., Article 164 of Law No. 1136.
[140]   *Burdur Mechanical Engineers* (14 December 2017, 17-41/640-279).
[141]   Whish and Bailey, 2012 (p. 117 in the 8th edition, 2015).

To that end, Law No. 4054 also introduces a presumption of concerted practice, which reads as the following:

> In cases where the existence of an agreement cannot be proved, a similarity of price changes in the market, or the balance of demand and supply, or the operational regions of undertakings to those markets where competition is prevented, distorted or restricted, constitutes a presumption that the undertakings are engaged in concerted practice.[142]

To that end, the wording of Law No. 4054 enables the Authority to benefit from a shift in the burden of proof if the market parameters show resemblance to the markets where competition is prevented, distorted or restricted. In such condition, the Authority releases itself from the burden of proving that there is an agreement or concerted practice between the undertakings that are being scrutinised, and conversely the respective undertakings are expected to show that they were not involved in any anti-competitive agreement or concerted practice. However, as will be elaborated thoroughly in Chapter 3, while the presumption of concerted practice set out in Law No. 4054 may have significantly affected the enforcement practice of the Board, the cases where the Board actually resorted to a naked application of the presumption of concerted practice are rather scarce.

To depict a clearer picture, the presumption of concerted practice set out in Article 4 of Law No. 4054 enables the Board to decide that Article 4 of Law No. 4054 had been violated based on mere economic evidence, without having to show any other circumstantial basis, especially evidence of communication. Accordingly, the presumption paves the way for determining that there had been a concerted practice based on the undertakings' parallel market behaviour that could not be justified with economic and rational reasons. In that sense, the presumption of concerted practice set out in Law No. 4054 grants the Board a broader framework to interfere in the market behaviour of undertakings, in comparison to the legal framework applicable in the EU.[143] However, the Board has rarely resorted to the naked application of the presumption of concerted practice, i.e., there are few cases where it relied solely on economic evidence to establish the existence of a concerted practice.[144] As also acknowledged by the Board,[145] evidencing a direct or indirect communication or contact between competitors becomes a prominent element in terms of achieving the standard of proof when establishing the existence of a concerted practice. To that end, the Board underscores that in cases where there is no evidence of communication that would prove the existence of an agreement or a concerted practice between competitors, the economic evidence that would enable the Board to apply the presumption of concerted practice should be advanced and concrete.

Following from the Board's above line of reasoning, giving too much weight to the presumption of concerted practice might have negative effects. This is put further into context within the concept of tacit collusion. Tacit collusion arises where firms coordinate their behaviour by means of intelligently adapting to the market behaviours of

---

[142] Article 4(3) of Law No. 4054.
[143] *Şanlıurfa Autogas* (28 July 2020, 20-36/505-223).
[144] Ibid., para. 34.
[145] Ibid., para. 38.

their competitors, without entering into an agreement or partaking in a concerted practice within the meaning of Article 4 of Law No. 4054.[146] To that end, aggressive implementation of the presumption of concerted practice or naked application of the presumption might undermine the instances where competitors indeed did not partake in any collusive contact, but merely adapted their competitive behaviour by means of the market intelligence that they gathered by virtue of the market characteristics. This is likely to happen in markets where the market structure is transparent by its nature (e.g., in markets where the cost structure of the competitors does not differ for different competitors or the competing firms can easily find out about each other's pricing decisions from the market without resorting to direct contact). Within that context, if the Board were to aggressively implement the presumption of concerted practice, without having to rely on additional communication evidence, that enforcement practice would be prone to Type I errors,[147] where a competition authority incorrectly concludes that pro-competitive behaviour is anti-competitive.[148]

The rare instances where the Board opted for a naked application of the presumption of concerted practice are *Yeast*[149] and *Göltaş Çimento*.[150] In *Yeast* the Board put forth its concluding remarks on whether the parallel behaviour of undertakings stems from the oligopolistic market structure or an anti-competitive agreement/concerted practice, as follows:

> Although by definition, price movements would show resemblance in the oligopolistic markets, [in this case] there is no economic reason other than concerted practice for the fact that all four firms increased their prices higher than their cost of production and the rate of inflation, in the absence of any objective change in the market conditions, and the fact that they were able to keep raising prices at the outset for two months running, with high rates of increase and also sustain the increasing price trends subsequently.[151]

Additionally in *Göltaş Çimento* the Board's approach on the naked application of the presumption of concerted practice was depicted as follows:

> If an undertaking, along with other undertakings does not act in a way that would benefit its interests under normal market conditions; or for example, the movement of certain parameters such as prices differs from what is expected to be under normal circumstances, it could be said that the undertakings active in such market had violated Article 4 of the Law by means of concerted practice.[152]

---

[146]   Whish and Bailey, 2012, p. 562.
[147]   Within the context of competition law, a Type I error, also known as a false positive, refers to the finding of a violation when in fact the conduct under analysis is pro-competitive. Whereas a Type II error, also known as a false negative, occurs when an anti-competitive conduct is found to be pro-competitive. In short, Type I errors refer to "false convictions", Type II errors refer to "false acquittals" (see J. D. Wright and M. C. Mungan, "The Easterbrook Theorem: An Application to Digital Markets", *The Yale Law Journal*, Vol. 130, 2021, p. 623).
[148]   İ. Atiyas and G. Gürkaynak, "'Presumption of Concerted Practice': A Legal and Economic Analysis", 4th Symposium on Recent Developments in Competition Law, Erciyes University, 7 April 2006, p. 15.
[149]   *Yeast* (12 November 2008, 08-63/1050-409).
[150]   *Göltaş Çimento* (20 September 2007, 07-76/908-346).
[151]   *Yeast* (n. 149), para. 1100.
[152]   *Göltaş Çimento* (n. 150), paras. 1300–1310. For more detailed information, see Chapter 3.

However, when it comes to the standard of proof regarding concerted practices, the case law of the Board[153] is more inclined to resemble the remarks set out in *Newspaper Publishers*[154] and requires evidencing of contact or communication between the parties regarding the alleged conduct:

> The subject matter of the investigation is fixing the sales prices through concerted practice. A behaviour can only be defined as concerted practice under the following conditions:
>
> - there must have been affirming contacts between the parties such as meetings, discussions, exchanges of information, which are generally expressed orally or in writing,
> - such contact must be aimed at influencing the market behaviour and especially eliminating the uncertainty of an undertaking's future competitive behaviour in advance,
> - they must have influenced or changed the commercial behaviour of the concerned undertaking in a manner that cannot fully be explained with reference to competitive effects.
>
> The crucial issue here is the information obtained by the undertakings about the future behaviour of their competitors and the elimination of market uncertainties.
>
> An important problem in concerted practice cases is finding and proving the fact that undertakings were engaged in concerted practice. Law No. 4054 stipulates that a presumption for a concerted practice can arise when the price changes or the supply-demand equilibrium or the territories of undertakings become similar to markets where competition is prevented, hindered or restricted, and imposes on the parties the burden to prove the non-existence of concerted practice through economic and rational grounds. However, as is the case in the present investigation, it is not sufficient to claim that the way the prices were determined resembles the price-fixing in markets where competition is restricted. In addition to this, it is necessary to prove the existence of a relationship between the undertakings that would not have existed under competitive conditions and that prevented them from acting independently.
>
> The following three basic findings are sufficient to establish the existence of concerted practice:
>
> - the existence of a relationship between competing undertakings,
> - the existence of actions among the competing undertakings which result in a joint stance and influence the actions of other competing undertakings;
> - the existence of a situation where competing undertakings are no longer able to act independently.

---

[153]   In *Ambarlı Ro-Ro* (18 April 2019, 19-16/229-101) and *Ready-Mixed Concrete* (22 August 2017, 17-27/452-194), the Board sought the existence of finding(s) that would evidence contact/communication between the undertakings under investigation to establish that such undertakings were involved in concerted practice.

[154]   *Newspapers Publishers* (26 July 2007, 07-62/742-269), paras. 710–740. Similar criteria in terms of establishing the existence of a concerted practice were reiterated by the Board in *Göltaş* (31 March 2011, 11-20/378-117) and *Automotive* (24 June 2009, 09-30/637-150).

One of the very well-known defences against the allegations developed on the presumption of concerted practice causes is the "oligopolistic interdependence" defences.[155] For this and other similar economically rational explanations to parallel behaviours, Law No. 4054 also provides as a remedy that "Each of the parties may relieve itself of the responsibility by proving, on the basis of economic and rational facts, that it has not engaged in concerted practices".[156]

In *Aegean Cement*,[157] the Board adopted a rather high standard of proof for the investigated parties in terms of their arguments based on oligopolistic interdependence:

> The situation mentioned in the Report goes beyond oligopolistic interdependence. That is, if there is a downwards trend in prices, then all the undertakings in the market should comply with such trend, or else there would be major problems in terms of sales. However, in terms of upwards movement of prices, the situation is slightly different than the former. Increasing prices should be a behaviour that would not be preferred by undertakings under normal circumstances. That is because the sales amount of the undertaking that does not follow the price increases would significantly increase. Again, under normal circumstances, an undertaking anticipating to increase its prices bears the risk of not being followed by other undertakings. Therefore, unless it is compulsory, it would not prefer to increase prices. However, if all undertakings in the market are sure that a price increase by an individual firm would be followed by the others, then significant price increases could easily be observed. On the other hand, if there is a common increase in the costs, the reflection of such increase in the prices could be deemed natural to a certain extent. That being said, in terms of the case at hand, as is explained in detail in the Report, the abnormal price increases in 2002 and 2003 were made independent of the costs. Besides, both the two documents listed above and the comparison with Ankara cement market, as well as the endeavour to standardise the payment terms for sales, support the relevant presumption of the concerted practice.

To that end, in *Aegean Cement*, the Board apparently did not consider that the sole defence arguing that the parallel pricing behaviour of the competing firms stemmed from the oligopolistic structure of the market was credible and required further reasoning that would justify price increases in the market, such as increased costs.

That being said, not in all cases does the Board set such a high standard of proof for the undertakings that endeavour to utilise the oligopolistic interdependence defences.

---

[155] The Turkish Competition Authority's *Competition Law Dictionary* explains oligopolistic independence as follows: "Undertakings operating in oligopoly markets with a small number of other undertakings feel the need to closely monitor the market conditions they are in, and the decisions and actions of their competitors operating in the same market, while making strategic decisions such as price level or production plan. This is due to the fact that undertakings operating in the market in oligopolies are aware that their decisions affect the decisions of their competitors and that the profit of an undertaking depends not only on their own behaviour but on the reactions of their competitors to this behaviour. Because the reactions of competitors trigger an ongoing process, the process may result in the undertaking being deprived of the profit they plan to achieve. This situation, which is expressed as 'oligopolistic interdependence' in the literature, causes prices to converge in 'transparent' markets where the activity and price movements of competitors can be observed" (see *Oligopoly* (11 September 2008, 08-52/783-312). See Chapter 3 for detailed analysis.

[156] Article 4(4) of Law No. 4054.

[157] *Aegean Cement* (19 October 2006, 06-77/992-287), lines 1660–1670.

For instance, in *Philip Morris/JTI*,[158] the Board concluded that the "follow-the-leader" pricing stemmed from the market's oligopolistic structure and that this did not constitute a sufficient ground to establish that the parties were involved in a concerted practice:

> With due consideration to the special features of the relevant market, where the existence and activities of the state-controlled 'TEKEL' Administration (General Directorate of Tobacco Products, Salt and Alcohol Operations) result in the undertakings display a parallel behaviour of price following, we hereby decide by a MAJORITY VOTE that there is no sufficient evidence to prove that the price parallelisms established during the investigation are the result of concerted practice by the investigated undertakings and not due to economic and rational reasons, in a manner that would violate Law No. 4054, and that there is no need to impose an administrative fine.

2.3 Horizontal and Vertical Agreements

The term "anti-competitive agreements" refers to horizontal and vertical agreements. In case that a vertical agreement restricts competition, the concept that addresses this situation is "vertical restraints". Similarly, when a horizontal agreement between the competitors restricts competition, we are talking about "horizontal restraints".

Due to the nature of the vertical agreements, their anti-competitive effects are ambiguous as they might also bring significant efficiencies. On the other hand, vertical restraints such as resale price maintenance, exclusivity requirements and loyalty discounts might have negative impacts on inter-brand and intra-brand competition, as will be explained below.[159]

2.4 Inter-Brand and Intra-Brand Competition

Inter-brand competition is the competition between undertakings either producing the same product or obtaining it through commercial means, which is then put on the market directly or through resellers and dealers.[160] Intra-brand competition, on the other hand, is the competition between resellers and distributors which are conducting their sales regarding the same branded products.[161] The Board's Guidelines on Vertical Agreements provide that both "inter-brand competition" and "intra-brand competition" concepts gain importance when the subject undertaking has significant market power.[162]

---

[158]   *Philip Morris/JTI* (24 December 2002, 02-80/937-385).

[159]   M. Tokgöz, *Münhasır Dikey Anlaşmaların 4054 sayılı Kanun'un 4. veya 6. Maddesi Kapsamında Değerlendirilmesi Sorunu* (Ankara: Rekabet Kurumu, 2017).

[160]   Grounds for Articles for Law No. 4054 on the Protection of Competition at <https://www.rekabet.gov.tr/en/Sayfa/Legislation/act-no-4054/grounds-for-the-articles> (last accessed on 19 April 2021),.

[161]   Ibid.

[162]   Guidelines on Vertical Agreements, para. 77. Following this, the Guidelines also provide information on the importance of intra-brand competition via arbitrage, provision of efficiency, innovation in distribution and positive contribution to competition in the upstream market. Throughout the Guidelines on Vertical Agreements,

Inter-brand competition can be categorised under five competitive powers, which are (i) new entries to the market; (ii) substitutable products; (iii) market power of sellers; (iv) market power of buyers; and (v) the existing competition.[163] Intra-brand competition, on the other hand, differs from inter-brand competition on several distinct aspects. The relevant product subject to the sale is largely homogenous in nature, thus narrowing the area of competition.[164]

Inter-brand and intra-brand competition are frequently assessed in the decisions adopted by the Board. The dynamics of both types of brand competition in the market are evaluated in the assessment of restrictions.

The reduction of intra-brand competition may also reduce inter-brand competition as it leads to less downward pressure on the price for particular goods. Turkish competition laws consider resale price maintenance to have the unintended effect of reducing, or even eliminating, intra-brand competition. In *Vira Kozmetik*[165] and many subsequent decisions, the Board adopted an effects-based approach in terms of its assessment regarding the allegations of resale price maintenance.[166] The Board analysed the alleged resale price maintenance practice's positive and negative effects on customers and consumers. The negative effects identified by the Board were the restriction of intra-brand competition and horizontal cooperation in the downstream market by increasing transparency. These decisions also discussed the positive effects of resale price maintenance practices. Resolving free-riding and double-profit marginalisation problems, increasing inter-brand competition and consumer accessibility to products with different price and quality levels are examples of positive effects.

In many instances, the Board opted for an effects-based analysis as long as the alleged practices did not result in cartels between suppliers or resellers, in inter-brand restrictions and in a reduction of consumer welfare.[167] The Board discussed the competitiveness, concentration levels, the market power and share of the alleged violator and its competitors, buying power, the effects of the alleged resale price maintenance practice and potential consumer benefits in these decisions. For instance, in *UFO*, the Board assessed the market structure for electric heaters, the market shares of UFO and its competitors, and their market power. It did not ultimately find a resale price maintenance practice. The Board concluded that UFO did not have high market shares in the upstream and downstream markets and that there were many high profile brands in the market. Moreover, it analysed the entry barriers and found that the initial investments to enter the market were not high and that there were no barriers to entry. Additionally, the Board pointed out that the negative effects of vertical restraints would be lessened in the growing and dynamic market where horizontal competition is high. Finally, the Board indicated that there were many options in the market that would enable consumers to benchmark and choose the cheapest one and that would increase the competition in the market.

---

the Board discusses the relationship between the vertical agreements and inter and intra-brand competition.
[163]   M. Ayber, *Markaiçi ve Markalararası Rekabetin Dengelenmesi Gereken Hallerde Rekabet Otoritelerinin Yaklaşımı* (Ankara: Rekabet Kurumu, 2003), p. 18.
[164]   Ibid., p. 25.
[165]   *Vira Kozmetik* (2 August 2007, 07-63/767-275).
[166]   *Yatsan* (23 September 2010, 10-60/1251-469); *UFO* (27 October 2011, 11-54/1380-490); *KWS* (n. 114).
[167]   *Vira Kozmetik* (n. 165); *UFO* (n. 166); *Yatsan* (n. 166); *Dagi* (15 July 2009, 09-33/725-165).

Undertakings may implement certain practices to create brand loyalty, such as rebates. Loyalty-inducing rebates would normally raise issues for undertakings with a dominant position. However, Article 4 of Law No. 4054 applies to those rebate schemes that affect not only inter-brand but also intra-brand competition. These cases are clear examples where the Board found exclusionary conduct and restriction of intra-brand competition and imposed administrative monetary fines on the suppliers holding no dominant position for the restriction of intra-brand competition through anti-competitive agreements.

It is also important to keep the relationship with the wholesalers transparent, as there are decisions where discrimination against the wholesalers is condemned given that it hinders intra-brand competition. Market foreclosure of competing wholesalers will not be a concern where those competitors have similar market power and can offer similar sales possibilities.[168] Market share indicates market power to a certain degree; however, it is not the only conclusive factor. After the establishment of the undertakings' market power in the relevant product market, other relevant factors such as behaving independently from competitors, the degree of vertical integration, the existence of the entry barriers and intellectual property rights are taken into consideration.

2.5 *De Minimis* Concept

As amended by Law No. 7246, Article 41(2) of Law No. 4054 will now allow the Authority to forgo investigating certain agreements, concerted practices and decisions of associations of undertakings that do not significantly restrict competition in the market under certain conditions (i.e., the *de minimis* application). This will enable the Authority to allocate its resources to more critical and severe violations, such as fighting against cartels and monopolies.

Article 41(2) of Law No. 4054 stipulates that the procedures and principles regarding the implementation of *de minimis* will be determined by the communiqué issued by the Board. The Communiqué No. 2021/3, in other words, the *De Minimis* Communiqué–was drafted for this purpose and came into force upon its publication on 16 March 2021.

The *de minimis* concept brought to Article 41(2) of Law No. 4054 in line with the European Union *acquis*[169] aims to devote the resources and time of the Competition Authority to the resolution of more critical competition law issues and introduces a "procedural efficiency" tool for certain violations that may be caused by agreements with relatively limited effects on competition. This way, without being subject to the investigation phase that lasts about one and a half years due to the demanding and time-consuming work such as on-site inspections, written and oral defences, the Authority will now be able to

---

[168]   The Guidelines on Vertical Agreements, p. 192.
[169]   Communication from the Commission, Notice on agreements of minor importance which do not appreciably restrict competition under Article 101(1) of the Treaty on the Functioning of the European Union (2014/C 291/01) (EU *De Minimis* Notice).

decide that the relevant agreements, concerted practices or decisions do not significantly restrict competition, and thus undertakings will have legal certainty as to which actions fall within the scope of *de minimis* practice.

However, as a side issue, there is no clarification as to which communiqué will prevail for an agreement within the scope of the *De Minimis* Communiqué, in the event that other communiqués of the Competition Authority on block exemptions are also applicable. In other words, it is not yet apparent which communiqué will prevail for agreements which fall within the scope of both (i) the market share thresholds provided under the *De Minimis* Communiqué and (ii) the block exemption communiqués, e.g., Communiqué No. 2002/2, Communiqué No. 2008/2 or Communiqué No. 2016/5. The EU *De Minimis* Notice explicitly states in paragraph 14 that the *de minimis* protection is particularly applicable to categories of agreements that are not covered by any block exemption regulations of the Commission. Accordingly, the *de minimis* protection is applied to agreements that do not constitute hard-core restriction and which do not fall within the scope of the Commission's block exemptions. Yet, the *De Minimis* Communiqué remains silent in case of a similar scenario in the Turkish competition law practice. Therefore, there is a need for clarification in terms of practice regarding this issue.

In any event, the *De Minimis* Communiqué serves to grant the Board the opportunity to focus on more significant competition law matters, as well as bringing the Turkish competition law closer to the standards in EU competition law on which it is modelled.

According to Article 5 of the *De Minimis* Communiqué, the following agreements/decisions do not significantly restrict competition:

- If the agreement is signed between competing undertakings: if the total market share of the parties to the agreement does not exceed 10% in any of the relevant markets affected by the agreement, then the agreement in question will be deemed not to significantly restrict the competition in the market.

- If the agreement is signed between non-competing undertakings: if the market share of each of the parties does not exceed 15% in any of the relevant markets affected by the agreement, then the agreement in question will be deemed not to significantly restrict competition in the market.

- If the agreement cannot be classified as being between competing or non-competing undertakings: in this case, the provision for the agreements signed between competing undertakings would be applicable.

- Decisions of associations of undertakings: if the total share of the members of an association of undertakings does not exceed 10% in any of the relevant markets affected by the decision, then the decisions in question will be deemed not to significantly restrict competition in the market.

- If the agreement is signed between competing and non-competing undertakings, as well as decisions, which includes vertical restrictions: if parallel networks created by similar vertical restrictions cover more than 50% of the relevant market, the thresholds set out under Article 5 of the Communiqué are applied as 5%.

2.6 Concepts of Restriction "By Object" and Restriction "By Effect"

In order to talk about a competition law violation within the context Article 4, Law No. 4054 clearly states that there must either be (i) an agreement between the parties; (ii) a concerted practice; or (iii) an undertaking association decision present. Without mutual declaration and alignment of intent, it is not possible to violate Article 4 of Law No. 4054. In this regard, unilateral actions such as recommendations, warnings or instructions would not constitute an agreement, so long as these do not represent a meeting of minds between the competing parties.[170,171]

Article 4 prohibits all agreements between undertakings, decisions by associations of undertakings, and concerted practices that have (or may have) as their object or effect the prevention, restriction or distortion of competition; including any form of agreement that has the "potential" to prevent, restrict or distort competition. Thereby, Article 4 grants a broad discretion to the Board. Additionally, the examples of possible restrictive agreements set out in Article 4 are not exhaustive: For example, similar to Article 101(1) TFEU, the provision does not explicitly refer to or define the terms "cartel" or "resale price maintenance".

Aside from the presence of an agreement or concerted practice, the said agreement or practice should bear the object to restrict competition or affect the restriction of competition. Without it, every concerted action between competitors–including pro-competitive ones such as a joint venture or risk pool–would be deemed illegal. That is precisely why competition laws impose this requirement: i.e. so that the prohibition only affects those agreements and concerted practices whose object or effect is anti-competitive.

---

[170] H. Karakılıç, "Avrupa Birliği Rekabet Hukukunda Hakim Durumda Olmayan Teşebbüslerin Tek Yanlı Uygulamaları", *Rekabet Dergisi*, Vol. 14, No. 4, October 2013, pp. 3–48, esp. p. 12.

[171] In paras. 46 and 47 of the Guidelines on Horizontal Agreements, the risk that certain unilateral conducts of competing undertakings, particularly unilateral disclosures of information entail in terms of violating Article 4 of Law No. 4054, is explained as follows: "There is no difference between an undertaking unilaterally disclosing its competition-sensitive information via various means such as e-mail, phone calls, meetings, etc. to its competitors who then explicitly or implicitly accepting such information, and many undertakings sharing information concerning their goals and plans among themselves. For example, mere attendance at a meeting where an undertaking discloses its pricing policy to its competitors may be caught by Article 4 of the Act, even in the absence of an explicit agreement to raise prices. When an undertaking is sent competition-sensitive information by a competitor, the relevant undertaking will be presumed to have accepted the information and adapted its market conduct accordingly, unless it responds with a clear statement that it does not wish to receive such information.

In general, if an undertaking makes a unilateral disclosure concerning its competition-sensitive information in a genuinely public manner, for example through a newspaper, this does not constitute a violation. However, the characteristics underlying the case at hand will be decisive in terms of the assessment to be conducted under Article 4. For example, competitors following such a disclosure with similar disclosures concerning their own competition-sensitive information may indicate cooperation."

2.6.1 By Object Restrictions and Their Evolution in the Case Law

Agreements that have restriction of competition as their object are prohibited both under the EU and Turkish competition law legislation. When the existence of such an agreement is detected, the Authority is authorised to conclude directly that the agreement infringes competition law, relieving itself of the burden to assess and prove the actual anti-competitive effects of the agreement. This way, while the object restriction emerges as a handy tool for competition authorities, it also creates great risks for undertakings. The importance of correctly determining the scope of this mechanism carries particular importance as undertakings taking part in agreements that have anti-competitive objectives may also come face-to-face with significant monetary fines.

Pursuant to the Turkish and EU Guidelines on Horizontal Agreements, in order to assess whether a "by object" violation has occurred, the contents of any agreement/concerted practice, the objectives it is seeking to attain, and the economic and legal framework in which it takes place must be properly analysed and taken into account. In order to establish the anti-competitive object of an infringement, the objective of the alleged agreement should be identified, and it should be assessed whether the agreement, by its very nature, can be regarded as being harmful to the proper functioning of normal competition.[172]

The fact that Article 4 of Law No. 4054 adopts a similar approach to Article 101(1) TFEU has resulted in the agreements that restrict competition by object to be deemed as violations, regardless of the effect they have on the competitive landscape (if they are not able to benefit from an exemption). Within the Competition Board's earlier decisions, it can be seen that the Board has adopted a per se approach on violations regarding agreements restricting competition by object. For example, in *Ege Bölgesi Çimento*,[173] it has been stated that "if the object of restricting competition in an agreement is evident, the agreement itself or at least the anti-competitive provisions constitute a 'per se' competition violation". Upon the annulment of this decision by the Council of State due to procedural issues, the term "per se" was altered by the Board in the reissued decision, which instead stated, "if the object of restricting competition in an agreement is evident, the agreement itself or at least the anti-competitive provisions constitute an evident competition violation".[174] That said, even though the wording "per se" was omitted in practice, the Board seems to still keep in mind the approach of per se violations.

A manifestation of this approach can be seen from the assessment of the Board in *Steel Ring Manufacturers*: "it is evident that all agreements that aim to eliminate or restrict competition is automatically [per se] prohibited and would constitute a violation".[175] Though the relevant decision is pertaining to cartels which entail one of the most serious violations, the above statement tars all such agreements with the same brush. Even still, the Board adopts this

---

[172] Guidelines on Horizontal Agreements, p. 56, and EC Horizontal Guidelines, p. 72.
[173] *Ege Bölgesi Çimento* (17 June 1999, 99-30/276-166).
[174] *Çimento* (26 July 2007, 07-62/740-268); *Çimento* (13 September 2005, 05-57/850-230).
[175] *Steel Ring Manufacturers* (30 October 2012, 12-52/1479-508).

not only for serious competition law violations, but also for less severe practices. In its *Doğan/Feza*, where exclusivity agreements were assessed, the Board has also differentiated between by object and by effect restrictions, by stating the following:

> When a correlation is established between the approaches regarding agreements within the doctrine, it is possible to differentiate the agreements as agreements prohibited in terms of object under the directly [per se] prohibited category and the agreements prohibited in terms of effect within agreements subject to rule of reason assessment.[176]

However, it is not possible to assess all agreements restricting competition by object as per se violations, since per se violations are categorically prohibited, whereas those agreements restricting competition by object may theoretically benefit from exemption provided under Article 5 of Law No. 4054, given that the agreement meets the conditions therein.[177] The relationship between by object restrictions and exemption will be further analysed under the relevant Section.

2.6.2 Economic-Based Approach and Effects-Based Analysis

Article 101(1) TFEU and Article 4 of Law No. 4054 are similar in the sense of implementation. If an agreement, decision or concerted practice is proved to have the purpose of restricting competition in and of itself, it would be categorised as a by-object approach, as the object of the agreement, decision or concerted practice is sufficient in reaching a conclusion on the said conduct.[178]

With regard to the effects-based approach, if the agreement, decision or concerted practice of an undertaking cannot be proved to have an anti-competitive object by itself, the competition authorities would then conduct an effects-based analysis, where any anti-competitive effects or potential effects would be sought.

For instance, in terms of resale price maintenance, the enforcement practice of the Board through time is a noteworthy subject to elaborate on, in terms of effects-based analysis. Before delving into the decisional practice of the Board, it would be beneficial to put resale price maintenance into further context based on the applicable rules. According to the EU legislation, vertical restraints do not restrict competition if sufficient interbrand competition exists. The Commission's Guidelines on Vertical Restraints state that:

> For most vertical restraints, competition concerns can only arise if there is insufficient competition at one or more levels of trade, that is, if there is some degree of market power at the level of the supplier or the buyer or at both levels.[179]

---

[176]   *Doğan Yayın* (1 July 2010, 10-47/858-296).

[177]   *Anadolu Elektronik* (23 June 2011, 11-39/838-262).

[178]   G. Gürkaynak and A. G. Yaşar, "Re-Assessing Object Restrictions: A New Day in Light of the 'Groupement des cartes bancaires v Commission' Decision", *Rekabet Dergisi*, Vol. 16, No. 1, January 2015.

[179]   European Commission, Guidelines on Vertical Restraints (2010/C 130/01), para. 23.

The market position of the supplier and its competitors is of major importance, as the loss of intra-brand competition can only be problematic if inter-brand competition is limited.[180]

The Authority's Guidelines on Vertical Agreements provide almost identical explanations.[181]

While its recent decisional practice shows that the Board is more inclined to opt for a conclusion that resale price maintenance violates Article 4 of Law No. 4054 by object,[182] this has not always been the case. In its earlier decisions, such as *Vira Kozmetik, Şölen Çikolata, UFO, Yatsan* and *Kuralkan*, the Board examined the positive and negative impact of the resale price maintenance on the market and consumers and carried out an effects-based analysis.[183] In these decisions, it was stated that the negative effects would occur in case the supplier prevents intra-brand competition by determining the resale price of the seller; thereby leading to horizontal cooperation among competitors in the downstream market by increasing price transparency. . In the effects-based analyses, it has been examined whether these violations impede competition significantly and also to what extent the competition violations realised within the scope of vertical agreements affect the competition in the market.

According to the Board's previous approach, resale price maintenance does not necessarily restrict competition in each and every case. In many subsequent decisions, the Board analysed the alleged resale price maintenance practice's positive effects on customers and consumers.[184] The Board stated that resolving free-riding and double-marginalisation problems, increasing inter-brand competition and consumer accessibility to products with different price and quality levels are examples of positive effects of resale price maintenance.[185]

Although the position of the Board in the decisions where it carried out an effects-based analysis refers to different parameters, the nature of these parameters and the consequences that they give rise to are essentially related to whether or not the competition is restricted, or to what extent it is restricted and the ultimate impacts of the foregoing on consumers. Indeed, though resale price maintenance is deemed to be a hard-core vertical competition law violation, the Board opted to inform the undertakings concerned of its opinions in writing and merely ordering the termination of the infringement based on Article 9(3) of Law No. 4054[186] rather than imposing monetary fines, particularly in cases where the conduct does not give rise to significant anti-competitive effects.

---

[180]   Ibid., para. 153.

[181]   Guidelines on Vertical Agreements, p. 168.

[182]   *Baymak* (26 March 2020, 20-16/232-113); *Henkel* (19 September 2018, 18-33/556-274); *Sony Eurasia* (22 November 2018, 18-44/703-345); *Consumer Electronics* (n. 116).

[183]   *Vira Kozmetik* (n. 165); *Şölen Çikolata* (16 January 2014, 14-02/35-14); *UFO* (n. 166); *Yatsan* (n. 166); *Kuralkan* (27 May 2008, 08-35/462-162).

[184]   *Yatsan* (23 September 2010, 10-60/1251-469), paras. 670–880.

[185]   Ibid.

[186]   *İstikbal* (16 December 2010, 10-78/1624-624); *Frito-Lay* (11 January 2007, 07-01/12-7); *Kütaş Teekanne* (24 August 2006, 06-59/773-226); *Fuel Oil* (15 November 2006, 06-84/1059-306); *Dagi* (n. 167); *KWS* (n. 114); *Aygaz* (13 March 2013, 13-14/204-105); *Yatsan* (n. 166); *Kuralkan* (n. 183); *Çağdaş* (24 October 2013, 13-59/825-350); *Reckitt Benckiser I* (13 June 2013, 13-36/468-204); *Çilek* (20 August 2014, 14-29/597-263); *Dogati* (22 October 2014, 14-42/764-340).

Vertical restraints other than resale price maintenance that also fall within the scope of Article 4 of Law No. 4054 may also benefit from an effects-based analysis. For instance, in *Red Bull*[187] the Board examined Red Bull's discount/rebate scheme as well as Red Bull's other conducts that might induce exclusivity on the sales points such as providing the coolers free of charge, by way of utilising an effects-based analysis. To that end, the Board concluded that neither the discount/rebate scheme nor free of charge cooler campaigns of Red Bull give rise to an exclusive effect in the relevant market.

Furthermore, in *Abalıoğlu*,[188] the Council of State required the Board to make an effects-based assessment regarding the dealership agreement between Abalıoğlu (a poultry producer) and its dealers, which the Council of State assumed might give rise to de facto exclusivity. In the relevant decision of the Council of State, the necessity of an effects-based analysis is emphasised in those cases where the Board determines that the relevant agreement had no object of violating competition rules:

> It is understood that article 46 of the dealership agreement has aspects that might give rise to a de facto exclusivity in practice (given the difficulties that non-exclusive may face), and any analysis that fails to take this into consideration will be lacking. Furthermore, the letter that was sent to the dealers demonstrates an intention to take up exclusive dealership, and in any case, the focus should be on the actual status quo rather than the statements of the undertaking that is subject to the complaint; and [therefore] the effects of the dealership agreements within the context of competition law should be demonstrated.[189]

2.7 Criteria for Individual Exemption

Even if an agreement falls within the ambit of Article 4 of Law No. 4054, it is not necessarily illegal. Article 5 of Law No. 4054, which mirrors Article 101(3) TFEU, provides an "individual exemption mechanism" that constitutes a legal exception for the implementation of Article 4 of Law No. 4054.

In order for an agreement, decision or concerted practice to be granted an individual exemption, it should meet all of the following four criteria (cumulative conditions):

- "They must ensure new developments or improvements or economic or technical improvement in the production or distribution of goods, and in the provision of services" (Article 5(1)(a) of Law No. 4054).

- "The consumer must benefit from the above-mentioned" (Article 5(1)(b) of Law No. 4054).

- "They must not eliminate competition in a significant part of the relevant market" (Article 5(1)(c) of Law No. 4054).

---

[187] *Red Bull* (19 December 2019, 19-45/767-329).
[188] *Abalıoğlu* (13 March 2019, 19-12/156-71).
[189] 13th Chamber of the Council of State (27 December 2017; E. 2011/3511, K. 2017/4404).

- They must not restrict competition more than necessary to achieve the goals set out in sub-paragraphs (a) and (b)" (Article 5(1)(d) of Law No. 4054).

Before the amendments of Law No. 7246,[190] Law No. 4054 stipulated that the Board may individually exempt certain agreements, concerted practices and decisions of associations of undertakings, which left it somewhat unclear whether "self-assessment" could be applicable. The amendments aim to provide legal certainty as to the individual exemption regime by clarifying that the "self-assessment" principle applies to agreements (as well as concerted practices and decisions of associations of undertakings) that may potentially restrict competition. Applying to the Board for individual exemption is also still an available option, as per the new Article 5(2) of Law No. 4054:

> Relevant undertakings or associations of undertakings may make an application to the Competition Authority in order to have the Board confirm that the agreements, concerted practices or decisions of associations of undertakings falling under Article 4 meet the requirements of the exemption.

In case that the undertakings concerned apply for a negative clearance, there is a burden of proof to show that the relevant agreement is not violating Article 4 of Law No. 4054 and that it satisfies all four requirements, as in the EU law. In case of individual exemption, the undertakings applying for exemption are required to demonstrate the grounds regarding why they should be deemed exempt from the implementation of Law No. 4054.[191] After evaluating the cumulative criteria under Article 5(1) of Law No. 4054, the Board may grant a negative clearance,[192] an unconditional[193] or conditional[194] exemption for the relevant agreement, or it may reject the individual exemption application in its entirety.[195] Besides, there are many decisions where the Board re-evaluated the individual exemptions previously granted to the applicants and revoked them due to the changes in the market structure.[196]

For certain agreements that meet the above criteria, the Board issued block exemption communiqués[197] so that particular types of agreements will be considered exempt from the prohibition in Article 4 of Law No. 4054, provided they fall under the conditions laid out in these communiqués.[198] Agreements between undertakings that do not meet the requirements set forth in the block exemption communiqués might result in a restriction of competition within the meaning of Article 4 of Law No. 4054, unless the agreement

---

[190] Law No. 7246 was published in the Official Gazette on 24 June 2020 and numbered 31165.
[191] Whish and Bailey, 2012, p. 152.
[192] See, for example, *Güneş Sigorta* (n. 108); *Construction Equipment* (7 May 2020, 20-23/293-141).
[193] See, for example, *Zurich Sigorta/TEB* (3 December 2020, 20-52/735-326); *BNP Paribas* (4 February 2021, 21-06/73-33); *2021 Turkcell* (3 December 2020, 20-52/723-320); *Reckitt Benckiser II* (19 November 2020, 20-50/684-299); *Bayer* (28 July 2020, 20-36/488-214); *Financial Institutions Union* (7 May 2020, 20-23/296-143).
[194] See, for example, *2020 Efes* (26 November 2020, 20-51/701-310); *Casting Agencies* (24 September 2020, 20-43/588-262); *Novo Nordisk* (28 July 2020, 20-36/493-218); *Air France* (4 June 2020, 20-27/329-154); *Turkish Bankers' Union* (30 April 2020, 20-21/280-134).
[195] See, for example, *İSDER II* (19 November 2020, 20-50/688-302); *Insurance Information and Supervision Center* (12 November 2020, 20-49/672-294); *Turkish Ceramic Federation* (20 August 2020, 20-38/526-234); *İSDER* (19 November 2020, 20-50/687-301); *Johnson & Johnson* (3 September 2020, 20-40/553-249).
[196] See, for example, *Tuborg* (20 June 2019, 19-22/335-152); *Yemek Sepeti* (20 September 2004, 04-60/869-206).
[197] Communiqué No. 2002/2, Communiqué No. 2008/2, Communiqué No. 2008/3, Communiqué No. 2013/3, Communiqué No. 2016/5, Communiqué No. 2017/3.
[198] For detailed explanations on the block exemption regime for vertical agreements, see Chapter 5.

qualifies for an individual exemption under Article 5 of Law No. 4054.[199] In this regard, one has to evaluate whether the practices based on the agreements within the scope of Article 4 of Law No. 4054 would qualify for an individual exemption.

Below we will examine all of these criteria one by one, along with how the Board's approach on the implementation of Article 5 of Law No. 4054 shapes the Turkish competition law practice.

2.7.1 Improving the Production or Distribution of Goods or Promoting Technical or Economic Progress

In the Guidelines on the Exemption, efficiency gains are the first of the cumulative conditions, i.e., failure of one condition makes an analysis of the others unnecessary.[200] The Guidelines on the Exemption provide detailed explanations on the different types of efficiency under (i) cost efficiencies and (ii) qualitative (dynamic) efficiencies.[201] According to the Board, the gains from efficiency should be objective and the competition law assessments on that front should not rely on the subjective point of view of the parties.[202] As a prominent example, in Yataş,[203] the Board concluded that bringing a restriction to online (passive) sales would not satisfy the condition in Article 5(1)(a) of Law No. 4054.

The Guidelines on the Exemption state that if the relevant agreement, decision or concerted practice is not exempted via a block exemption, the Board should consider while granting individual exemption: (i) "the nature of the claimed efficiencies"; (ii) "the causal link between the agreement and the efficiencies"; (iii) "the likelihood and magnitude of each claimed efficiency"; and (iv) "how and when each claimed efficiency would be achieved".[204]

Not surprisingly, the analyses on this first condition mainly revolve around the term "efficiency". The Authority's understanding of the term "efficiency" is also laid down under the Guidelines on the Exemption. Starting with "cost efficiencies", the Guidelines on the Exemption state that there are multiple ways to achieve cost efficiencies, including: (i) the "development of new production technologies and methods"; (ii) combination of the existing assets that have complementary strengths; (iii) economies of scale[205] where

---

[199]   For example, if the market share of an undertaking exceeds the 40% threshold, its vertical agreements automatically fall outside the scope of the block exemption under Communiqué No. 2002/2.
[200]   Guidelines on the Exemption, paras. 21–22.
[201]   Ibid., paras. 32–41.
[202]   *Trakya Cam/Düzcam Exemption* (25 June 2020, 20-31/382-171).
[203]   *Yataş* (6 February 2020, 20-08/83-50).
[204]   Guidelines on the Exemption para. 24.
[205]   An economy of scale is "the theory of the relationship between the scale of use of a properly chosen combination of all productive services and the rate of output of the enterprise". G. J. Stigler, "The Economies of Scale", *The Journal of Law & Economics*, Vol. 1, 1958, pp. 54–71.

the cost per unit is reduced and undertakings share the work; (iv) economies of scope[206] that may arise when undertakings supplying related goods come together to reduce their costs; and (v) "agreements that allow for better planning of production, reducing the costs of inventory and for better capacity utilisation".[207]

The burden of proof to show that the agreement in question fulfils the exemption requirements rests with the parties to the agreement. In addition, in case that there is not enough data for calculation of the cost efficiencies, the Guidelines on the Exemption explicitly require the parties to provide their own estimations along with how the relevant cost efficiencies will be gained, along with their extent.[208] A noteworthy decision on that note is *Trakya Cam/Düzcam Exemption*,[209] where the Board provides detailed assessments on the fulfilment of the first two conditions of exemption. In that case, the agreement that is subject to the exemption review authorises the dealers of Trakya Cam to sell Trakya Cam's sheet glass to the "sheet glass" market.[210] The agreement could not benefit from an individual exemption since the Board arrived at the conclusion that the parties failed to provide sufficient explanations and concrete data to show the efficiency gains arising from the agreement and their impact on consumers.[211]

As well as the cost efficiencies, the Authority also considers the "qualitative efficiencies", which may bring new and advanced products, product variety and increased quality. Indeed, the cooperation of the undertakings might create efficiencies that "would not have been possible without the restrictive agreement or would have been possible only with substantial delay or at higher cost".[212] The other examples that the Guidelines on the Exemption give for the agreements increasing qualitative efficiencies are as follows: (i) the combination of complementary assets, like in licence agreements; (ii) joint production agreements; and (iii) distribution agreements.[213]

---

[206] Economies of scope is defined as "cost savings which result from the scope (rather than the scale) of the enterprise. There are economies of scope where it is less costly to combine two or more product lines in one firm than to produce them separately". J. C. Panzar and R. D. Willig, "Sustainability Analysis: Economies of Scope", *The American Economic Review*, Vol. 71, No. 2, 1981, pp. 268–272.

[207] Guidelines on the Exemption, paras. 32–36.

[208] Guidelines on the Exemption, para. 37.

[209] *Trakya Cam/Düzcam Exemption* (n. 202).

[210] For the Board's established precedents defining the market for "sheet glass", see *Trakya Cam* (17 November 2011, 11-57/1477-533); *Trakya Cam/Isıcam Exemption* (24 January 2013, 13-07/73-42); *Trakya Cam/Düzcam Exemption* (2 December 2015, 15-42/704-258); *Trakya Cam/Düzcam Exemption* (21 December 2017, 17-42/670-298).

[211] The conclusion of the dissenting opinion of the *Trakya Cam/Düzcam Exemption* is that the agreement in question should have been granted an exemption. With respect to the first condition, it states that the relevant agreement would have provided Trakya Cam with the opportunity to (i) better evaluate demand, (ii) get better feedback on the market, (iii) formulate a more efficient plan, (iv) ensure product range as well as the continuation of supply, and (v) reduce its logistic and stock costs. Therefore, the dissenting opinion is also worth mentioning for its evaluations of the elements of the individual exemption.

[212] Guidelines on the Exemption, paras. 38–39. The Guidelines on the Exemption especially point out instances from research and development agreements to exemplify this: "For instance, firms A and B establish a joint venture for product development to produce a tire that can be used after it is punctured. This new technology aims to remove the risk of collapse of the tire in case of puncture. The tire is thus safer than a traditional tire, there is no need for immediate action in case of puncture and thus to carry a spare. Those constitute efficiency gains that can be considered under the first condition of exemption."

[213] Ibid., paras. 40–41.

While evaluating the "magnitude of each claimed efficiency", the grounds for Article 5 of Law No. 4054 provide that: "agreements restricting competition must be exempted from the prohibition of Article 4", if the beneficial effects they give rise to "are greater than [their] harmful effects".[214] The Board's decisions also implement this approach by explicitly referring to this phenomenon.[215]

2.7.2 Consumers Must Benefit From the Efficiency Gains

The second condition among the cumulative exemption conditions is the "consumer benefit". By referring to the positive effects garnered from the efficiencies explained above, the grounds for Article 5 of Law No. 4054 explain the place of consumer benefit condition specifically within the exemption mechanism, as well as within the competition law in general:

> In case these positive effects are not reflected on the consumer and stay as firm profits, the exemption will not be implemented. The fact that the consumer receives a just share of the benefit created also reveals the social side of the competition law.[216]

To that end, the Guidelines on the Exemption also delve into the details of the concepts of "consumer" and "consumer benefit". The term "consumer" is defined to be encompassing all direct or indirect users of the products or services in the relevant market covered by the agreement.[217] Therefore the entities that are considered within the concept of "consumers" include end-users, as well as those legal or real persons who purchase the products for resale purposes.

Vodafone/Superonline provides substantive remarks regarding the Board's understanding of "consumer benefit".[218] The Board firstly recognises that fibre-optic broadband provides a better quality of service to consumers even at long distances compared to copper phone line services.[219] The Board mentions that parties having access to each other's infrastructure would enable them to supply consumers with faster internet and better quality access. It also adds that the agreement would contribute to consumer choice when Superonline and Vodafone grant each other access to their infrastructure since the consumers would have the opportunity to purchase the services of different providers.

---

[214] Grounds for Articles for Law No. 4054 (n. 160)

[215] *Turkish Football Federation* (26 November 2014, 14-46/834-375), p. 13; *Tofaş* (5 October 2011, 11-51/1288-453), p. 6; *Arcon Cosmetics* (9 September 2009, 09-41/987-249).

[216] Grounds for Articles for Law No. 4054 (n. 160)

[217] Guidelines on the Exemption, para. 43; G. Gürkaynak., *Türk Rekabet Hukuku Uygulaması İçin "Hukuk ve İktisat" Perspektifinden "Amaç" Tartışması*, Rekabet Kurumu, 2003, p. 29.

[218] *Vodafone/Superonline* (8 August 2018, 18-27/438-208).

[219] G. Gürkaynak, "The Turkish Competition Authority publishes a decision regarding an agreement granting access to infrastructure and support services between two telecom companies (*Vodafone / Superonline*)", *e-Competitions* August 2018, art. No. 88979 <https://www.concurrences.com/en/bulletin/news-issues/august-2018/the-turkish-competition-board-publishes-a-decision-regarding-an-agreement> (last accessed 30 June 2021).

The decision also mentions further benefits for consumers including support services that Superonline and Vodafone were planning to provide together and cost benefits due to the possibility of lower prices at the retail channel.[220]

Above we explained that the efficiencies gained from the relevant agreement should exceed the harm caused by the competition law restrictions. In a similar vein, this second condition echoes the first one, to require that "the resulting efficiency gains must compensate the consumers for any actual or potential negative impact of the agreement on competition or consumers".[221] Thus, as a rule, the Board seeks at least a neutral net effect of the agreement on consumers, where worsening the conditions for consumers would leave the agreement out of the exemption mechanism. To that end, the greater the restriction of competition, the greater the efficiencies and the pass-on to consumers must be. In a case where the competition restrictions arising from the agreement are significant when compared with the efficiency gains to be reflected on consumers, it would not be likely for the agreement to be granted an exemption as per Article 5 of Law No. 4054.

On the other hand, this does not mean that the Turkish competition law requires all of the efficiency gains from the subject agreement to be passed on to consumers. As the Guidelines on the Exemption also make clear: "It is important that sufficient benefits be passed on to compensate for the negative effects of the agreement."[222]

As the Guidelines on the Exemption acknowledge, assessing the qualitative efficiencies is subjective in its very nature. Thus, it is harder to show qualitative efficiencies than the cost efficiencies explained above. Yet, the significant issue to assess in the fulfilment of this second condition is "whether the efficiencies are passed on to the extent that the negative effects borne by the consumers due to the restriction of competition are compensated".[223] Under such conditions, the consumers will be better off than without the agreement and, this way, the consumer benefit requirement will also be met.

2.7.3 Should Not Eliminate Competition in a Significant Part of the Relevant Market

The third condition for granting an exemption as per Article 5 of Law No. 4054 requires that "with these limitations, competition must not be eliminated in a significant part of the relevant product market", as stated in the grounds of the article.

---

[220] Ibid.
[221] Guidelines on the Exemption, para. 44.
[222] Guidelines on the Exemption, paras. 46–47: "The resulting efficiency gains may be in the form of not only cost efficiencies but also qualitative efficiencies such as the introduction of new products and technological progress. For instance, a producer of drinks whose distribution network is relatively smaller may make a distribution agreement with another one that has a country-wide distribution network and reduce its distribution costs. An example of qualitative efficiency is the case where two pharmaceutical firms make joint research and development activities and consequently introduce a new medicine more quickly."
[223] Ibid., para. 52.

The main principle for assessing the exemption requirements focuses on whether the competitive process in the market is maintained. In this regard, the Guidelines on the Exemption state that:

> When competition is eliminated in the relevant market, even if short-term efficiency gains are created, they will not be able to outweigh longer-term negative effects such as higher prices, reduced innovation and misallocation of resources.[224]

For analysing this, the main parameter that the Guidelines on the Exemption take into consideration is the "restrictive impact of the agreement on competition". Increased restrictive impacts would reduce the possibility of meeting the third condition of the exemption. Evaluating these issues necessitates considering (i) the position of the competitors in the market by assessing the market shares and the capacity and incentive for competition and (ii) how the agreement would impact the actual and potential competition by assessing the barriers to entry.[225,226]

The Board's *Tuborg*[227] is a noteworthy example showing a dynamic interpretation of the issue on the "restrictive impact of the agreement on competition" in line with Article 13(1) (a) of Law No. 4054.[228] In this decision rendered in 2019, the Board withdrew Tuborg's individual exemption that had been granted to its agreements with on-trade sales points including exclusivity clauses, back in 2010.[229] Upon a complaint by Efes, a competing undertaking, the Board found that Tuborg's market share, sales amount, availability and financial strength had increased and, therefore, the Board concluded that, in the previous nine years, market conditions had significantly changed in favour of Tuborg. A parameter that the Board considered before withdrawing the exemption was that Efes continuously lost market share, while Tuborg gained some market power. Considering all these, the Board decided that Tuborg's exclusive agreements would restrict competition in a significant part of the market so they would no longer satisfy the requirement under Article 5(1)(c) of Law No. 4054.

The barriers to entry in a market might be determinative for the assessment of the exemption criteria. For this reason, the Guidelines on the Exemption set out the following points that may be considered while evaluating the market entry restrictions and the probability of new entrants into the market:[230]

- impact of legal regulations

- costs of entry, including any sunk costs

- minimum efficient scale

- characteristics of undertakings that are potential entrants

---

[224] Ibid., para. 54.
[225] Guidelines on the Exemption, paras. 55, 57 and 62.
[226] See *Vodafone/Superonline* (n. 218), where the Board also evaluated the retail-level entry barriers.
[227] *Tuborg* (n. 196).
[228] Article 13(1)(a) of Law No. 4054 provides that exemption may be revoked in case of a change in any of the circumstances constituting the basis of the decision.
[229] *Tuborg* (18 March 2010, 10-24/331-119).
[230] Guidelines on the Exemption, para. 63.

- position of buyers in the market and their ability to compete
- likely competitive response of the incumbents to entrants
- structure and the development of the market
- previous entries of a significant scale, and their success.

A noteworthy example on that front is the Board's decision[231] reviewing Roche's request for a negative clearance or an exemption, with respect to its planned distribution system where Roche would minimise the number of its warehouses to be no more than ten and no less than five. In its analysis regarding whether the proposed distribution system would pass the exemption criteria, the Board firstly analysed the third condition requiring that the agreement should not eliminate competition in a significant part of the relevant market. The Board decided that an individual exemption could not be granted since the intended system might especially preclude small and medium-sized warehouse activities in the market. The Board added that the proposed distribution system would raise the concentration in the market, as small and medium-sized warehouses might even exit the market or new entries might be blocked. The Board also adopted a similar approach in its decision[232] to fine the Customs Brokers Association, concerning one of its decisions which brought certain restrictions for brokers. Before arriving at the conclusion that the relevant decision violated Article 4 of Law No. 4054, the Board analysed the association's decision through the framework of individual exemption requirements and stated that it is not possible to grant an individual exemption as the said decision restricted the activities of member brokers, as well as preventing new entries to the market.

The Guidelines on the Exemption also provide explanations relating to the grounds for rejection of the exemption request when the third condition is not met. The first of these requires that the relevant agreement do not entirely eliminate "the basic parameters of competition such as price competition, innovation and development of new products".[233] In a similar vein, in case that there are "substantial price increases or engag[ing] in other conduct indicating the existence of a considerable degree of market power", or "an important source of competition" might have been removed from the market, these might be considered as a sign that the competition has been eliminated in a substantial part of the market.[234] In addition, the Guidelines on the Exemption explicitly provide that "the more substitutable the products offered by the parties to the agreement are, the more restrictive the effects of the agreement will be".[235] However, the *GlaxoSmithKline/Pfizer* is a notable example showing that this rule is not written in stone, as it shows that it is possible to grant exemptions even when such agreements are between direct competitors, as long as sufficient benefits for competition or promotion of consumer choice could be demonstrated.[236]

---

[231] *Roche Exemption* (12 December 2019, 19-44/732-312).
[232] *Customs Brokers Association* (20 June 2019, 19-22/352-158).
[233] Guidelines on the Exemption, para. 58.
[234] Ibid., paras. 59–60.
[235] See *Vodafone* (11 April 2019, 19-15/203-90) and Guidelines on the Exemption, para. 61.
[236] *GlaxoSmithKline/Pfizer* (20 June 2008, 08-40/535-201).

2.7.4 Should Not Limit Competition More Than What is Necessary

The grounds for Article 5 of Law No. 4054 explain the fourth and final condition for exemption by stating that "where less limitation on competition can be sufficient to achieve these beneficial effects, the agreements will not be granted exemption". Thus, in order for an agreement to benefit from exemption, it cannot restrict competition more than necessary to achieve the efficiencies aimed by the agreement.[237]

For assessing this final condition, the Guidelines on the Exemption set forth a two-stage test: (i) the necessity and indispensability of the agreement for achieving the efficiencies and (ii) individual assessment of each restriction to see if it is necessary.[238]

While evaluating the first condition on necessity and indispensability, the Guidelines on the Exemption provide that the agreements might be deemed as indispensable as long as there are no less restrictive alternative means for achieving the alleged efficiency gains.[239] Even though the undertakings are not expected to speculate on hypothetical alternatives, they are expected to "demonstrate why less restrictive, economically rational and practical alternatives would be significantly less efficient".[240] While analysing this, the Guidelines on the Exemption also underline the importance of considering the minimum efficient scale:[241]

> The larger the minimum efficient scale compared to the size of the parties, the more likely it is that the efficiencies will be attained due to the agreement. The agreement is necessary for efficiency gains, to the extent that it produces synergies through the combination of complementary assets and capabilities.[242]

Considering the second stage, the Board goes on to examine the indispensability of each restriction to achieve the efficiency gains.[243] The actual and potential impacts of the agreement are examined. According to the Guidelines on the Exemption, "a restriction can be deemed indispensable for the claimed efficiencies if its absence would significantly reduce the efficiencies that follow from the agreement or make it significantly less likely that they will materialise".[244] Yet, the Guidelines on the Exemption also makes clear that it is less likely for blacklisted or hard-core restrictions to pass this test and be deemed as indispensable. In these analyses, the market conditions and the time period where the restrictions would still remain indispensable should also be taken into consideration.[245]

---

[237]   Guidelines on the Exemption, para. 65.
[238]   Ibid.
[239]   *THY* (14 November 2019, 19-40/653-279); *Insurance* (24 December 2020, 20-55/769-341); *BKM* (30 May 2019, 19-20/291-126). Also see, Guidelines on the Exemption, para. 67.
[240]   Guidelines on the Exemption, para. 68.
[241]   See *TTNET* (13 August 2014, 14-28/558-241) for the evaluations on the assessments of the synergy created by the union of undertakings and its relation with satisfying the condition under Article 5(1)(d).
[242]   Guidelines on the Exemption, para. 70.
[243]   See *Garanti/THY* (7 September 2017, 17-28/465-204); Guidelines on the Exemption, para. 71.
[244]   Guidelines on the Exemption, para. 72.
[245]   Ibid., paras. 73–74.

For instance, in *Say Reklamcılık*, where the Board examined the contractor agreement between Say Reklamcılık and Tekyapı,[246] the Board rejected the individual exemption request since the agreement did not meet the condition specified in subparagraph (d) of Article 5(1) of Law No. 4054. That is because, the Board found that the agreement obliges Tekyapı with a non-compete clause for an indefinite duration, even though the parties claimed that the contract would only eliminate competition in a limited part of the outdoor advertising or corporate identity markets, and the scope of non-compete obligation is limited to certain dealers. Although the said obligation is for a small part of the relevant market, due to its indefinite duration, it has been concluded that it fails to comply with the requisite conditions under Law No. 4054 and that no individual exemption can be granted to the contract.

As to the time period of the restrictions, the *Vodafone/Superonline* is a fine example of how the Board might shorten the duration of the agreements when it deems that it is the only possible way to meet the last criterion.[247] In this decision, even though the agreement's original duration as proposed by the parties was five years, after analysing the potential for developments in global, regional and national scales, the Board arrived at the conclusion that it could be granted only a three-year exemption. The Board decision also provided that this last criterion is satisfied because: (i) the agreement does not include an exclusivity clause; (ii) the cooperation would only be among the parties of the agreement; and (iii) the parties will continue to compete for each other's customers through active and passive marketing.[248]

An agreement may fulfil all the other three criteria, yet the failure to meet this final condition among the cumulative criteria leads to the rejection of the individual exemption request. For example, in *İSDER* (Materials Handling, Storage & Industrial Equipment Association), the Board analysed the reports that İSDER shared or would share with its members and concluded that despite having met all the other three criteria, these reports fell short of the condition in subparagraph (d) of Article 5(1) of Law No. 4054 considering (i) the undertaking-based data sharing; (ii) the limits of the data to be shared and the purpose for which it is collected; (iii) the fact that it is not possible to describe the data to be shared as actual publicly available data; (iv) the frequency of information exchange; and (v) the fact that the data was being compiled by the employees of the association, not by an independent research company.[249] Therefore, the Board rejected both of İSDER's requests for negative clearance and individual exemption.

---

[246]   *Say Reklamcılık* (15 January 2015, 15-03/25-11).
[247]   *Vodafone/Superonline* (n. 218).
[248]   Ibid.
[249]   *İSDER* (n. 195). Also see *İSDER II* (n. 195).

Chapter 3
Cartels and Tacit Collusion

GÖNENÇ GÜRKAYNAK, ESQ., HILAL ÖZÇELIK GÜLDESTE[*]
AND SINAN HALUK TANDOĞAN[**]

Participants active in the same market might tend to communicate and interact with each other in order to limit or eliminate competition, reduce risks and increase profitability, which could ultimately result in collusion. The legal treatment of collusion depends on the form it takes: explicit, tacit, or any combination of the two.[250]

Explicit collusion is where a group of undertakings directly communicate with each other, usually with the intention of coordinating and/or monitoring their actions to raise profits above competitive levels, and such agreements are prohibited by competition law.[251] Tacit collusion, on the other hand, is not a "collusion" in the legal sense because it does not involve any communication between undertakings, and is therefore considered to be unilateral. That said, tacit collusion could yield a similar outcome to explicit collusion. Thereby, evaluation of tacit collusion from a competition law perspective is trickier compared to explicit collusion. Concerted practices reside between these two extremes and refer to instances where supra-competitive prices are achieved with communication–such as about intentions–but firms do not expressly propose and reach an agreement.[252] Therefore, it is not possible to prove concerted practices via an explicit agreement. That said concerted practices are also prohibited in order to prevent collusion between the market players. From a Turkish competition law perspective, explicit collusion and concerted practices are prohibited by Law No. 4054 as they constitute "restrictive agreements".

The most straightforward, harmful, and severely sanctioned type of restrictive agreement between competitors is cartels. Pursuant to Article 4 of Law No. 4054, cartels include restrictive agreements between competitors created by way of (i) fixing the purchase or sale price of goods or services, elements such as cost and profit which form the price, and any condition of purchase or sale; (ii) allocation of markets for goods or services, and sharing or controlling all kinds of market resources or elements;

---

[*]   Associate, ELIG Gürkaynak Attorneys-at-Law, Istanbul <hilal.ozcelik@elig.com>.
[**]   Associate, ELIG Gürkaynak Attorneys-at-Law, Istanbul <sinan.tandogan@elig.com>.
[250]   M. Ivaldi, B. Jullien, P. Rey, P. Seabright, and J. Tirole, "The Economics of Tacit Collusion: Implications for Merger Control", in *The Political Economy of Antitrust*, V. Ghosal and J. Stennek, eds. (Bingley: Emerald Group Publishing Limited, 2007), p. 217
[251]   L. Garrod and M. Olczak, "Explicit vs tacit collusion: The effects of firm numbers and asymmetries", *International Journal of Industrial Organization*, Vol. 56, Issue C, 2018, p. 2.
[252]   J. E. Harrington, "A Theory of Tacit Collusion", *Working Paper* No. 588, The Johns Hopkins University, Department of Economics, 2012, p. 3.

and (iii) controlling the amount of supply or demand for goods or services, or determining them outside the market. Cartels may be created by way of explicit collusion, as well as by concerted practices. However, as tacit collusion is not considered to be a violation of competition law and thus generally not punishable, it is not considered to constitute a cartel. Cartels are usually illegal and prohibited under competition law in almost all jurisdictions of the developed and emerging countries. The Turkish antitrust regime also strictly prohibits cartels and deems them to be unlawful. Hence, detected cartels usually face hefty sanctions to punish and deter such conduct, and undetected cartels are incentivised to reveal themselves through leniency programmes that grant immunity to the first cartel member to turn itself in.[253] As the Turkish cartel legislation is administrative and civil in nature, not criminal, cartels are subject to administrative fines.

This chapter will focus on cartels and tacit collusion cases, following a brief discussion of Turkish competition law's restrictive agreements regime.

3.1 A General Overview of Restrictive Agreements Regime

The relevant legislation for the prohibition of restrictive agreements (including cartels) and for enforcement regime in Turkey is Law No. 4054, and the applicable provision is again Article 4. It lays down the basic principles of the cartel regulation and is applicable to both undertakings and associations of undertakings, as well as individuals, corporations and any other forms of entities that act as an undertaking.

Article 4 sets out a non-exhaustive list of restrictive agreements that is, to a large extent, identical to Article 101(1) TFEU. Particular examples of such prohibited conducts can be listed as:

- Fixing the purchase or sale price of goods or services, elements such as cost and profit which form the price, and any condition of purchase or sale.

- Allocation of markets for goods or services, and sharing or controlling all kinds of market resources or elements.

- Controlling the amount of supply or demand for goods or services, or determining them outside the market.

- Obstructing and restricting the activities of competing undertakings, or excluding undertakings operating in the market by boycotts or other behaviour, or foreclosing the market to potential new entrants.

- Except for exclusive dealing, applying different terms to persons with equal status for equal rights, obligations and acts.

---

[253] Garrod and Olczak, (n. 251), p. 2.

–   Contrary to the nature of the agreement or commercial practices, requiring the purchase of other goods or services together with a good or service, or tying a good or service demanded by purchasers acting as intermediary undertakings to the condition of displaying another good or service by the purchaser, or putting forward terms as to the resupply of a good or service supplied.

The list is not exhaustive; it intends to comprise other examples of restrictive agreements as well. In other words, the Board is entitled to investigate any other matter which it finds questionable within the scope of Law No. 4054.

As explained earlier in Chapter 2, Law No. 4054 does not provide any definition for agreement, concerted practice, decisions by associations of undertakings; however, the preamble of the law reveals that all these terms are interpreted in a broader scope. The preamble of Article 4 indicated that it is sufficient that there is an agreement which the parties feel bound by for an agreement to exist within the scope of Turkish competition law. In this context, the term "agreement" within the scope of Law No. 4054 refers to an implicit or explicit consensus or concerted practice which has the purpose and/or effect of restricting competition for mutual benefit.[254]

Moreover, in terms of Turkish competition law, there is no difference between a written or verbal agreement as long as mutual consent exists. Thus, it can be inferred that the Board defines the fundamental condition of an agreement in terms of competition law as an agreement of the wills of the parties.[255] In that sense, the Turkish competition law regime does not differentiate between concerted practices and agreements, and prohibits concerted practices as well, although there is no explicit agreement between the competitors. That being said, tacit collusion does not fall within the scope of the restrictive agreements regime in Turkish competition law in principle, since the communication condition required for the existence of a restrictive agreement is not present there. There is still a risk for the Board to intervene in tacit collusion because the presumption of concerted practice set out in Law No. 4054 grants the Board a broader framework to interfere in the market behaviour of undertakings, as explained in Section 2.2.3 above.

Anti-competitive restrictions including price-fixing, market or customer allocation, output restriction and bid rigging are the categories of conduct defined as cartels. The agreements which contain such restrictions are highly likely to restrict competition and therefore have consistently been considered to restrict competition by object, and prohibited without examining their actual or potential effects on the market.[256] Accordingly, as opposed to the other types of restrictive agreements included within Article 4 of Law No. 4054, cartels, by their nature, do not benefit from a block exemption, nor are they eligible for an individual exemption issued pursuant to paragraph 18 of the Guidelines on the Exemption.

---

[254]   *12 Banks* (n. 254).
[255]   *Consumer Electronics* (7 November 2016, 16-37/628-279).
[256]   *Adıyaman Autogas* (29 March 2018, 18-09/180-85); *8 Banks* (7 March 2011, 11-13/243-78); *Automotive Market* (18 April 2011, 11-24/464-139); *12 Banks* (n. 254); *Sinop Ready-Mixed Concrete* (18 February 2016, 16-05/117-520); *Antalya Tour Operators* (21 November 2016, 16-40/662-296).

3.2 Cartels

Similar to the TFEU, Article 4 itself does not set out a definition of "cartel"; instead, the Authority has defined it under Article 3(1)(c) of the Regulation on Leniency and Article 3 of the Regulation on Fines. According to these regulations, cartels are described as agreements (i) restricting competition and/or concerted practices between competitors for price-fixing; (ii) allocating customers, providers, territories or trade channels; (iii) restricting the amount of supply or imposing quotas, and bid rigging. In this respect, within the non-exhaustive list of restrictive agreements included under Article 4 of Law No. 4054, examples that are directly related to cartels are as follows: (i) fixing the purchase or sale price of goods or services, the elements which form the price, such as cost and profit, and any condition of purchase or sale; (ii) allocation of markets for goods or services, and sharing or controlling all kinds of market resources or elements; and (iii) controlling the amount of supply or demand for goods or services, or determining them outside the market.

Moreover, the *De Minimis* Communiqué also provides content on the types of cartel agreements. In fact, Article 4 of the *De Minimis* Communiqué defines the naked and hard-core violations as agreements and/or concerted practices, as well as decisions and practices of associations of undertakings, with the aim of directly or indirectly preventing, distorting or restricting competition in the market for a good or service, or those which have led or may lead to such effects. Article 4 of the *De Minimis* Communiqué specifically refers to two main categories of agreements that constitute naked and hard-core violations:

– price-fixing, allocation of customers/suppliers/regions/trade channels, restriction of supply amounts or imposing quotas, collusive bidding in tenders, sharing competitively sensitive information including future prices, output or sales amounts among competing undertakings;

– fixing the buyer's flat or minimum sale prices in a relationship between undertakings operating at different levels of a production or distribution chain.

By definition, all cartel agreements can be classified within the first category.

As a consequence, cartels, which are included within the restrictive agreements, hinder competition and do not create any tangible benefit in the form of compensation. On the contrary, cartels harm consumers and society since they cause prices to rise above the competitive level. As a result of the price increase, consumers cannot buy the service at all or they buy the same goods or services at a higher price. In this manner, while there is a decrease in consumer welfare and therefore social welfare, there is only an increase in the welfare of cartel members.[257] In fact, Recital 5 of the Guidelines on Active Cooperation describes them as "the most egregious infringements of competition". In this sense, like all other competition authorities, the Board is also extremely strict regarding the assessment and penalisation of cartels.

---

[257] *Adıyaman Autogas* (n. 256).

3.2.1 Overview of the Cartel Enforcement Regime

The Turkish national authority for investigating competition law matters, including cartel investigations, is the Authority, with the Board as its competent body for enforcement. The Turkish cartel regime is principally administrative and civil in nature, not criminal. Having said that, if a cartel activity amounts to a criminally prosecutable act, it may be separately adjudicated and prosecuted by Turkish criminal courts and public prosecutors, by reason of the Board not having any criminal competence. Thus, the Board's investigation of cartel conduct will not result in imprisonment of the individuals involved within the scope of competition law. However, there have been cases where the matter was referred to a public prosecutor before or after the competition law investigation was completed. For example, bid rigging can be prosecuted criminally under Article 235 *et seq.* of the Turkish Criminal Code. Additionally, illegal price manipulation can also be punished by up to two years' imprisonment and subjected to a judicial monetary fine under Article 237 of the Turkish Criminal Code.

As explained thoroughly in Chapter 2, Turkey is one of the "effect theory" jurisdictions[258] where what matters is whether the cartel activity has produced any effects on Turkish markets, regardless of (i) the nationality of the cartel members; (ii) where the cartel activity took place; or (iii) whether the members have a subsidiary in Turkey. In the past, the Board refrained from declining jurisdiction over non-Turkish cartels or cartel members,[259] as long as there was an effect on the Turkish markets.[260] In more recent years, the Board concluded an investigation in relation to the allegation that nine international companies active in the railway freight forwarding services market have restricted competition by sharing customers.[261] The Board explained that the practices of foreign undertakings may be subject to Law No. 4054 if they have any effect on the Turkish markets within the meaning of Article 2, regardless of whether these undertakings have any subsidiaries or affiliated entities in Turkey; and that the criteria for measuring such anti-competitive activities of foreign undertakings should be whether they have "direct", "significant" and "intended/foreseeable" effects on the Turkish markets. The Board concluded that the agreements have not produced effects on the Turkish markets within the meaning of Article 2 and, therefore, the allegations in question did not fall within the scope of Law No. 4054. The decision establishes that the Authority's jurisdiction is limited to conducts that create an effect on any given product market in Turkey, notwithstanding whether the agreement, decision or practice takes place in or outside of Turkey. It should be noted, however, that the Board is yet to enforce monetary or other sanctions against firms located abroad and without any local presence in Turkey, mostly due to enforcement handicaps (such as difficulties of formal service to foreign entities).[262]

[258] *Isdemir/Odak* (15 December 1999, 99-59/639-406); *ČEZ Bohunice* (15 July 2009, 09-33/763-183); *Ter-Tuz/ Alkan* (24 April 2009, 09-20/404-99).

[259] *Şişecam/Yioula* (n. 49); *Gas Insulated Switchgears* (24 June 2004, 04-43/538-133); *Refrigerator Compressor* (1 July 2009, 09-31/668-156).

[260] *Rail Cargo Logistics* (n. 48); *Güneş Ekspres/Condor* (27 October 2011, 11-54/1431-507); *Imported Coal* (2 September 2010, 10-57/1141-430); *Refrigerator Compressors* (n. 259); *Şişecam/Yioula* (n. 259); *Gas Insulated Switchgears* (n. 259).

[261] *Rail Cargo Logistics* (n. 48).

[262] G. Gürkaynak and Ö. İnanılır, in *Global Legal Insights – Cartels: Enforcement, Appeals & Damages Actions* (9th edition, London: Global Legal Group, 2021).

In the event that the Board evaluates that there is a violation of competition law by cartel activity, the following measures can and will be taken by the Board:

- Pursuant to Article 16 of Law No. 4504, up to 10% of the Turkish turnover generated in the financial year preceding the date of the fining decision will be imposed as an administrative fine to the offending undertakings. It should be noted that individuals such as employees of the undertakings may be subject to administrative fines as well, on the condition that they have a decisive influence on creating the violation. This fine may be up to 5% of the fine that has been imposed upon the offending undertaking.

- The Board is also entitled to take all measures to put an end to the violation and the consequences that have arisen from the said illegal agreement pursuant to Article 9(3) of Law No. 4504.

- Pursuant to Article 9(4) of Law No. 4504, the Board may take interim measures if it deems necessary, more specifically to prevent any likely, serious and irreparable harm.

- Pursuant to Article 56 of Law No. 4504, the cartel agreement will be deemed null and void *ex officio*.

- With the introduction of the commitment mechanism into Law No. 4054, pursuant to Article 43, undertakings accused of cartel activity now have the option to submit commitments to the Authority until the end of the preliminary or fully-fledged investigation period.

Enforcement is supplemented with private lawsuits as well, as explained in detail under Chapter 14 below. Private suits against cartel members are tried before civil courts, as opposed to administrative or criminal ones.[263] Owing to a treble-damage clause allowing litigants to obtain three times their loss as compensation, private antitrust litigations increasingly make their presence felt in the cartel enforcement arena. Most courts wait for the decision of the Authority and build their own rulings on that decision.

3.2.2 Different Variations of Cartel Agreements

As explained above, Article 4 of Law No. 4054 prohibits all forms of anti-competitive agreements, irrespective of whether they are horizontal or vertical and whether they have the effect or object of restricting competition. Cartels are also prohibited as they are agreements and/or concerted practices between competitors that are restricting competition by object. That is, no effect analysis is required as cartels restrict competition by their very nature.

The assessment of whether an agreement restricts competition by object is based on the content of the agreement, the objectives it attains and the economic and legal context.

---

[263] E.g., Istanbul 6th Commercial Court of First Instance (21 October 2018, E. 2017/33, K. 2018/1153); 11th Civil Chamber of the High Court of Appeals (5 October 2009, E. 2008/5575, K. 2009/10045).

The parties' intention is irrelevant to the finding of liability, but it may operate as an aggravating or mitigating factor, depending on the circumstances.[264] Article 4 also prohibits any form of agreement that has the potential to prevent, restrict or distort competition. Again, this is a specific feature of the Turkish cartel regulation system, recognising a broad discretionary power to the Board.

Pursuant to the Guidelines on Horizontal Cooperation Agreements ("Guidelines on Horizontal Agreements"), the restrictive effects are assessed on the basis of their adverse impact on at least one of the parameters of the competition in the market, such as price, output, quality, product variety or innovation. As explained above, Article 4 brings a non-exhaustive list of restrictive agreements that is almost identical to Article 101(1) TFEU. A number of the restrictive horizontal agreement types listed, such as price-fixing, market allocation, collective refusals to deal (group boycotts) and bid rigging, constitute cartel activities and have consistently been deemed restrictions by object–in other words, per se illegal. Certain other types of competitor agreements such as purchasing cartels are generally subject to a "competitive effects" test.[265] The details of other horizontal agreements are explained under Chapter 4.

Restrictions of competition "by object" are those that by their very nature have the potential to restrict competition (see Chapter 2). The types of restrictions that are considered to constitute restrictions "by object" differ depending on whether the agreements are entered into between actual or potential competitors, or between non-competitors (for example, between a supplier and a distributor). In the case of agreements between competitors (horizontal agreements), restrictions of competition by object include, in particular, price-fixing, output limitation and sharing of markets and customers, all of which constitute cartel activities. All in all, cartel activity amounts to agreements that restrict competition by object and no effect analysis is required as these agreements restrict competition by their very nature.

Accordingly, the subsections below will discuss certain types of cartel agreements and address the principles in evaluating such agreements through the precedents of the Board.

3.2.2.1 Price-Fixing

At the top of the non-exhaustive list of prohibited restrictive agreements under Article 4 of Law No. 4054, paragraph (a) prohibits price-fixing, stipulating that agreements "fixing the purchase or sale price of goods or services, elements such as cost and profit which form the price, and any conditions of purchase or sale" are illegal, which applies both for buying and selling prices. This provision reveals that price-fixing is strictly prohibited by law.[266] Price-fixing is one of the most common forms of cartel agreements, and as stated in the Board's *Ginnery* decision,[267] it is deemed to be one of the most serious violations of competition law, as price competition is one of the core pillars of competition.

---

[264]   G. Gürkaynak and A. G. Yaşar, "Re-Assessing Object Restrictions: A New Day in Light of the 'Groupement des cartes bancaires v Commission' Decision", *Rekabet Dergisi*, Vol. 16, No. 1, January 2015, p. 41.

[265]   G. Gürkaynak and K. Yıldırım, in *Cartel Regulation 2021*, Lexology Getting The Deal Through in association with Dechert LLP (London: Law Business Research Ltd, 2020).

[266]   *Adıyaman Autogas* (n. 256).

[267]   *Ginnery* (27 June 2008, 08-41/567-215), p. 180.

Considering that price is the most strategic parameter in competition,[268] those agreements, concerted practices and decisions of associations of undertakings that would coordinate the prices of competitors are always scrutinised by the Authority. Price-fixing between competitors is thus set out as one of the primary agreements that distort competition under Article 4 of Law No. 4054. So-called "hard-core" restrictions are generally restrictions "by object" when assessed in an individual case, and agreements containing one or more "by object" or hard-core restrictions cannot benefit from the safe harbour of the *de minimis* principle.[269] Thus, as cartel agreements constitute agreements that restrict competition by object, it is a crucial fact that any agreement involving cartel activity will not be able to benefit from the *de minimis* principle.

Prices may be fixed by determining maximum or minimum prices. Therefore, aside from those agreements that directly fix prices, practices that induce price control mechanisms in an indirect manner may also fall under price-fixing prohibition and thereby constitute a competition law violation. Another important point is that it does not matter whether the fixed price is above or below the market price. In both situations, it will still be a violation of competition law and considered price-fixing. Moreover, in its *Esgaz* decision,[270] the Board states that any plea by an undertaking pertaining to statements that point towards the fixed price being reasonable for the relevant market will not be taken into consideration, as the determination regarding the reasonable price which reflects the true economic value of a product or service is only possible by way of evaluating all the elements pertaining to supply and demand, all together.

In addition to the agreements/concerted practices between the competitors, price-fixing may also occur through decisions of trade associations and members of trade associations. To provide an example of enforcement against a price-fixing arrangement conducted by members of trade associations, in its *Peugeot*[271] decision, the Board fined several Peugeot dealers 0.5% of their turnover for engaging in concerted determination of prices and allocation of territories. This decision came as a result of an investigation which spun off from an earlier investigation, where a large group of Peugeot's dealers had been fined between 1% and 4% of their turnovers.[272] In its above-mentioned *Peugeot*[273] decision, the administrative fine was only imposed on the members of the trade association and not on the trade association itself. However, as stated above, it is also possible for the Board to impose an administrative fine on the trade association itself. In fact, in its *Van Natural Gas Association* decision,[274] the Board assessed whether the Van Natural Gas Association had been conducting any acts of price-fixing. Upon evaluating the information and evidence, the Board ultimately concluded that the Van Natural Gas Association had indeed engaged in price-fixing by way of decisions made during association meetings. The Board ultimately imposed an administrative fine on the Van Natural Gas Association,

---

[268]   *Cargo* (3 September 2010, 10-58/1193-449), p. 25.
[269]   Guidance on restrictions of competition "by object" for the purpose of defining which agreements may benefit from the *De Minimis* Notice.
[270]   *Esgaz* (9 August 2012, 12-41/1171-384).
[271]   *Peugeot* (12 April 2012, 12-20/557-141).
[272]   *Peugeot* (6 August 2010, 10-53/1057-391).
[273]   *Peugeot* (n. 271).
[274]   *Van Natural Gas Association* (19 November 2020, 20-50/694-305).

but not on its members. The Board is entitled to impose administrative fines on either the trade association or its members or both

Particularly, a regular exchange of information, which can be a restrictive agreement in and of itself (see Chapter 4), may also be seen by the Board as a facilitating practice for price-fixing activity, and therefore result in a competition law violation. Exchange of commercially sensitive information could constitute a violation of competition law as one of the core pillars of competition in a market is "not knowing how your competitors will act". If undertakings have information related to how their competitors will act, they will be able to prepare their strategies accordingly, which will eliminate competition. This is especially valid for prices, terms of sale and market policies of competitors. Information exchange pertaining to how the prices will be determined for a product is treated in the same way with direct price-fixing. This can be done by exchange of information regarding price lists, rebates to be applied, sale terms, proportional changes in discounts, and the time frame these changes are planned to be made–all are issues related to pricing policies.[275] As stated in its *Leasing*[276] decision, information regarding future-oriented price changes resulting in the elimination of strategic uncertainty and information that will turn a market more transparent than necessary may lead to coordination between undertakings and eliminate competition in markets. Therefore, if the information exchange leads to collusion on future prices and the amount of supply, it would be considered as a cartel and prohibited under Law No. 4054. Similarly, information exchange that is used to monitor whether competitors comply with the cartel arrangement–in other words, those facilitating cartels–are also assessed as a part of the cartel arrangement. Direct information exchanges between competitors relating to future pricing and output decisions are usually considered to be risky.

Exchange of commercially sensitive information among competitors can result in an agreement pertaining to price-fixing. Moreover, this exchange of information does not have to be in written form–that is, just a verbal exchange of information can also constitute price-fixing. An example regarding the implications of such verbal exchange of information would be the *White Meat* decision,[277] where the Board stated that it has concluded that the white meat producers have exchanged information during Besd-Bir meetings and that this exchange of information led to the creation of a platform that facilitates the violation of Law No. 4054 by way of price-fixing and restrictions of production in the market. As for the exchange of written information pertaining to price-fixing, in its *Yozgat Ready-Mixed Concrete Manufacturers*[278] decision, the Board proceeded to impose an administrative fine on the accused undertakings due to their price-fixing acts, as a result of their exchange of information in written form. Thus, the Board clearly indicated that, whether oral or written, an exchange of information that leads to price-fixing is a violation of Law No. 4054.

---

[275]   BSH (12 June 2012, 12-32/916-275), p. 137; *Turkish Ceramics Federation* (20 August 2020, 20-38/526-234), p. 31.

[276]   *Leasing, Factoring and Financing Companies Union* (15 February 2018, 18-05/79-43).

[277]   *White Meat* (25 November 2019, 09-57/1393-362), pp. 39–40.

[278]   *Yozgat Ready-Mixed Concrete Manufacturers* (19 March 2020, 20-15/215-107).

Finally, it should be noted that price-fixing practices are not eligible for any kind of exemption. In its *Doğan Yayın* decision,[279] the Board has stated that "agreements which do not even require an evaluation of the impact they have on the market are those that restrict competition by object, such as price-fixing, restriction of production and market-sharing agreements"; thus, as price-fixing agreements fall within the scope of the per se illegal category, there is no exemption for such restrictive agreements within the scope of Turkish competition law. Furthermore, the Board has confirmed its approach in its *Casting Agencies Association* decision,[280] where it has evaluated the exemption application of the Casting Agencies Association. The Board has stated that "the agreement at hand may benefit from individual exemption, on the condition that the terms leading to price-fixing are removed", clearly precluding price-fixing from benefits of exemptions in any way.

3.2.2.2 Market Sharing

Market sharing is prohibited under paragraph (b) of Article 4 of Law No. 4054, which stipulates that agreements pertaining to "allocation of markets for goods or services, and sharing or controlling all kinds of market resources or elements" are illegal. With this provision, market sharing is strictly prohibited by law.

Market sharing refers to an agreement regarding the division and allocation of customers and geographic areas between competitors instead of trading freely at their sole discretion. Market sharing restricts competition, increases the prices in the market and reduces choices available on price and quality for consumers and other businesses. Accordingly, partitioning markets for goods or services and sharing or controlling all kinds of market resources or elements are considered per se illegal pursuant to Article 4 of Law No. 4054. In other words, such agreements are considered inherently anti-competitive. As market-sharing agreements fall within the scope of the per se illegal category, there is no exemption for such restrictive agreements within the scope of Turkish competition law.

Market sharing may take the form of (i) allocating customers by contracts dividing geographic area/territory and (ii) agreeing not to compete for established customers or produce each other's products or services or expand into a competitor's market.[281]

Agreements that allocate customers by geographic area. In the event that two or more competing undertakings agree to divide the country or a region in which they operate into separate regions/areas and also not to operate in one another's regions/areas, this situation will constitute a classic example of market sharing. This will enable the undertakings to eliminate all competition in their own regions contrary to the nature of business, as seen in the Board's *Aegean Cement Producers* decision[282] and thus depriving the consumers in the allocated regions of their freedom to choose.[283]

---

[279]   *Doğan Yayın* (1 July 2010, 10-47/858-296), p. 4.
[280]   *Casting Agencies* (n. 194), p. 7.
[281]   Mondaq, Turkey: Competition and Antitrust, "Turkey: Market Sharing Practice Guide", ELIG Gürkaynak Attorneys-at-Law.
[282]   *Aegean Cement Producers* (14 January 2016, 16-02/44-14), p. 177.
[283]   O. Can, "4054 Sayılı Rekabet Kanunu'na Göre Rekabeti Sınırlandıran Anlaşmalar ve Uygulamada Sıkça Rastlanan Anlaşma Örnekleri", Kırıkkale Üniversitesi, 2004

The evaluation of agreements that involve allocating customers by geographic areas should always be done once the relevant market is determined. In the event that there is an allegation regarding such an agreement, it is critical to see if the undertakings that are subject to the market allocation allegations operate in the same product and service market, and that the products and services provided by the undertakings that are subject to the allegations are in the same product market as well. This is because different product markets cannot be evaluated within the scope of geographic allocation, pursuant to Article 4 of Law No. 4054. The relevant product market can be defined as a district, a city or a whole country.[284]

In its *Bread Market* decision,[285] where the Board has evaluated the allegations that some undertakings have violated Law No. 4054 by market allocation, the Board took into consideration the fact that the transport of bread between different locations is difficult, as bread gets stale very quickly. However, the Board observed that the trade of bread between districts of Istanbul is indeed possible. As for the relevant product market, the Board took into consideration the fact that bread is a staple and has no substitutability with other food products, thus defining the relevant product market as "the bread market". Ultimately the Board defined the geographic market as Istanbul, based on the fact that the transportation of bread is possible between the districts of Istanbul before it gets stale, and not much farther. Subsequently, it found that some associations which operated in the aforementioned relevant geographic and product markets have been allocating customers by geographic area dividing agreements.

In its *Yozgat Ready-Mixed Concrete Manufacturers* decision,[286] the Board launched a fully-fledged investigation against seven ready-mixed concrete manufacturers operating in the province of Yozgat, Turkey. The allegations against the ready-mixed concrete manufacturers contained acts of market sharing and price-fixing. All of the evidence gathered during on-site inspections made the assessment very straightforward for the Board, as it ultimately imposed an administrative fine on the accused undertakings for violating Law No. 4054 by allocating customers through geographic area dividing agreements.

Similarly, in its *Sakarya Bus Firms* decision,[287] where the Board ultimately imposed an administrative fine on three bus firms due to market sharing by allocating customers through geographic area dividing agreements, the Board evaluated allegations pertaining to acts of market sharing by bus firms operating in the Sakarya district of Turkey. Upon its investigation, the Board came across a notarised protocol signed between the three bus firms which clearly demonstrated that there was an act of market sharing by allocating customers by geographic area dividing agreements between the three bus firms.

Non-compete agreements regarding established customers, producing each other's products or services or expanding into a competitor's market. In the event that undertakings predetermine the conditions and/or restrictions where a product can be sold only to certain distributors and/or to whom the distributors can or cannot sell the product to, this will

---

[284]   Ibid.
[285]   *Istanbul Bread* (27 October 1999, 99-49/536-337 (a)).
[286]   *Yozgat Ready-Mixed Concrete Manufacturers* (n. 278).
[287]   *Sakarya Bus Firms* (25 July 2006, 06-55/713-203).

result in an allocation of customers between undertakings, which will ultimately lead to market sharing. For example, if the undertakings predetermine that a certain product will only be sold to hotels and restaurants, this will ultimately result in market sharing.

3.2.2.3 Output Restrictions

Continuing on from the (non-exhaustive) list of prohibited restrictive agreements under Article 4 of Law No. 4054, we note that output restrictions are strictly prohibited under paragraph (c), which stipulates that agreements pertaining to "controlling the amount of supply or demand for goods or services, or determining them outside the market" are illegal.

Controlling the amount of supply for goods or services directly affects pricing, considering the fact that in normal circumstances, prices are determined in accordance with supply and demand. Normally, when supply increases, prices decrease and vice versa, thus fixing or controlling the supply or demand for goods or services is a violation of competition law. This is, interestingly, different from Article 101 TFEU, which states that the limitation or control of production, markets, technical development, or investment is prohibited and is a restriction of competition. Article 4 of Law No. 4054 does not include the phrase "technical development, or investment". However, if two undertakings would agree not to make any investments for ten years, or only to use technology that is already present without working on new technological developments, these would regardless constitute a restriction of competition under Turkish competition law. Since the list of examples of anti-competitive agreements is not exhaustive, the two aforementioned instances would be considered as a restriction of competition even though Article 4 of Law No. 4054 does not expressly refer to "technical development, or investment".

The *Suction Glass Tubes* decision might be instructive in providing an example of the criteria used by the Board while evaluating the existence of an output restriction allegation.[288] In this decision, the Board evaluated the correspondence between Aslanlar, Solar-San and other undertakings, and found that Aslanlar and Solar-San were making proposals to other undertakings regarding the restriction of supply of suction glass tubes. However, the Board stated that the evidence was not sufficient to conclude that Aslanlar and Solar-San had entered into an agreement pertaining to the restriction of supply. Therefore, the Board proceeded to examine the market behaviour of the accused undertakings in order to determine whether an output restriction was in existence between the accused undertakings. The Board evaluated the accused undertakings' (i) established capacity; (ii) rate of capacity utilisation; (iii) current output; (iv) end product stock; (v) sales amount of the products subject to the investigation; (vi) sale price of the products; and (vii) the price-cost trend of the products subject to the investigation. Ultimately, the Board came to the conclusion that the acts of the accused undertakings could be reasonably justified, thus the Board decided that there was no need to impose an administrative fine on Aslanlar and Solar-San.

Furthermore, in its *Tera* decision,[289] the Board launched a fully-fledged investigation against Tera and other undertakings operating in the medical consumables market, upon

---

[288]   *Suction Glass Tubes* (2 February 2017, 17-08/100-43).
[289]   *Medical Devices* (1 September 2015, 15-34/514-162).

allegations pertaining to cartel agreements regarding output restrictions and other viola-tions of Article 4 of Law No. 4054. The allegations pertaining to restriction of production consisted of supply boycotts, withdrawal of consignments from hospitals and refusing to participate in tenders by the accused undertakings operating in the medical consumables market. Upon evaluating the evidence, the Board ultimately concluded that Tera had engaged in supply boycotts, withdrawal of consignments from hospitals and refusing to participate in tenders and thus Tera had determined the amount of supply or demand for goods or services outside the market.

In its *TEB* decision,[290] the Board launched a fully-fledged investigation against TEB, an association of undertakings, which invited member pharmacists through its website to boycott some of the pharmaceutical product manufacturers and importers on the grounds that they reduced the trade discounts and fixed dates they were offering to pharmacies. In its assessment, the Board evaluated the gathered evidence and it stated that "TEB clearly has the intention to determine the terms of supply or demand for goods or ser-vices outside the market". The Board also put great emphasis on the term "collective boycott" in its assessment. The Board defined the term as follows:

> Collective boycott refers to the act of refusal to contract with one or more customers, suppliers or competitors by two or more undertakings acting together. The purpose of the boycott may be to punish a customer, supplier or competitor who has been creating problems, or to force them to act in a certain way. A collective boycott may constitute a violation on its own, or it may serve as a gateway for another violation.

Therefore, it clearly pointed out that "collective boycotting" is a form of restriction of competition. Moreover, the Board stated that:

> It is clear that acts such as 'Providing the equivalent products, if any, [instead of] the products of companies that do not accept TEB's demands' are included in the term 'collective boycott'. With these acts, the goal is to create the desired purchasing conditions by putting pressure on the suppliers.

Ultimately, it came to the conclusion that TEB had violated Article 4 of Law No. 4504 by controlling the amount of supply or demand for goods or services, or determining them outside the market.

3.2.2.4 Bid Rigging (Collusive Tendering)

Even though bid rigging is not explicitly included within the non-exhaustive list of prohibited restrictive agreements set forth by Article 4 of Law No. 4054, Article 3 of the Regulation on Fines states that cartel activity corresponds to "agreements restricting competition and/or concerted practices between competitors for fixing prices; allocation of customers, providers, territories or trade channels; restricting the amount of supply or imposing quotas, and bid rigging". Similarly, Article 3 of the Regulation on Leniency also includes the very same explanation and therefore lists bid rigging as a type of cartel. Consequently, bid rigging is also prohibited by the law.

---

[290]   *TEB* (8 July 2010, 10-49/912-321).

Collusive tendering emerges in cases where undertakings, which would be expected to compete under normal circumstances, proceed to take a different route and instead act with the intention to fix prices, reduce the quality of goods and services and/or engage in other types of anti-competitive behaviour within the scope of Law No. 4054. Most of the time, the successful tenderer will be pre-determined beforehand between the so-called "competitors" of the tender. The reasoning behind collusive tendering may vary, however, usually, the idea behind it is to ultimately split the earned profit which has been gained as a result of collusive tendering, or to share tenders between the market participants, or to simply hinder other honest competitors partaking in the tender. Another important point is the fact that bid-rigging in public tenders or price manipulation is also criminally prosecutable under Article 235 of the Turkish Criminal Code, and perpetrators of this offence face imprisonment.[291]

The definition of tendering within the scope of Law No. 4054 may be handled in two separate categories: (i) tenders issued by private undertakings and (ii) public tenders which are issued by public institutions. It should be noted that there is no legislation that prohibits private undertakings from tendering a product and/or service, hence undertakings are eligible to issue tenders themselves as long as the tender does not involve any anti-competitive conduct; meaning that Law No. 4054 will still be applicable in the case of a tender conducted in the absence of a legal mandate. The public tenders, however, are to be conducted in accordance with the Public Procurement Law ("Law No. 4734"). The responsible authority for monitoring public tenders is the Public Procurement Authority ("Procurement Authority"), an independent public body that is also the competent authority for the implementation of the public tender legislation. Law No. 4734 contains a competition principle regarding the tenders (in line with Law No. 4054, which contains two provisions–namely, Articles 17 and 58) that prohibits anti-competitive acts. This situation leads to a dichotomy, as the Procurement Authority and the Authority are simultaneously empowered to monitor public tenders within the meaning of competition law.

Collusive tendering may emerge in forms of (i) negotiation with competitors pertaining to the tender or the elements of the tender, before or during the tender process; (ii) reaching an agreement with competitors regarding price, quantity, etc., of the product/service subject to the tender; (iii) in the event of multiple tenders, acting in a way that results in sharing tenders with competitors; and (iv) agreeing with competitors so they are withdrawing from the tender in favour of one or more competitors.[292] Some examples and types of collusive tendering are as follows:[293]

- Bid suppression: This type of collusive tendering emerges when undertakings who compete for a tender refrain from making any bids and/or withdraw their bids in order to ensure that the undertaking that has been picked/determined beforehand will be the successful tenderer.

---

[291] G. Gürkaynak et al. Chambers Global Practice Guides: "Cartels 2020", 2020.

[292] "Competition Law Handbook for small and medium-sized enterprises (SMEs)", External Affairs, Department of Education Competition Advocacy, Ankara, February 2016 ("KOBİ'ler için Rekabet Hukuku El Kitabı", Dış ilişkiler, Eğitim ve Rekabet Savunuculuğu Dairesi Ankara, Şubat 2016).

[293] E. Yaldızlı, *Kamu İhale Hukukunda Düzenlenen İş Ortaklıkları ve Konsorsiyumların Rekabet Hukuku Kapsamında Değerlendirilmesi* (Ankara: Rekabet Kurumu, 2020), pp. 39-40.

- Complementary bidding (also known as protective bidding and shadow bidding): In order to ensure that a specific, predetermined undertaking will be the successful tenderer, undertakings participating in a tender withdraw from the tender either by submitting an offer with unacceptable conditions or by bidding extremely low in order to stay below the figure the predetermined successful tenderer has bid. The intention here is to give the impression of "competition" in the tender.

- Bid rotation: Each competitor submits its bid to the tender; however, the bids are discussed and agreed upon between the cartel members before submission, in order to ensure that the predetermined bid will stand out among the other bids as the most advantageous one.

- Subcontracting agreements: The successful tenderer subcontracts the bid to those undertakings which are ineligible to place bids in a public tender, or to the undertakings that placed bids with no intention of being the successful tenderer. These can be considered as a reward for placing bids that are not competitive and/or for not partaking in the tender.

- Market sharing: This type of collusive tendering emerges when undertakings that operate in the same market agree, in favour of one specific undertaking which operates in the same product market, that the rest of them will not participate in certain geographical market tenders.

In its *Traffic Signalisation Market* decision,[294] the Board launched a fully-fledged investigation against undertakings operating in the traffic signalisation market, where it ultimately came to the conclusion that the acts in the case at hand were clear indications of collusive tendering. The Board proceeded to impose administrative fines on the accused undertakings based on the grounds that they had violated Article 4 of Law No. 4054. The Board collected evidence during its on-site investigation and subsequently stated that the evidence indicated that, in many of the tenders held by the General Directorate of Highways (KGM) as well as municipalities regarding the purchase of traffic signalisation systems and led systems, competing undertakings were sharing their unit price offers with each other before the tender, preparing the required documents for the tender jointly, as well as submitting the tender documents to the administration issuing the tender on behalf of other cartel members.

In its *12 Banks* decision,[295] the Board launched a fully-fledged investigation against twelve of the biggest banks operating in Turkey, in an effort to address the allegations pertaining to collusive tendering. The allegations concerned whether the accused twelve banks violated Article 4 of Law No. 4054 by way of agreement and/or concerted practice regarding deposits, bank loans and credit card services. The Board stated that upon evaluating the information and documents received from the municipality and from the aforementioned banks, and upon assessing the tender offers submitted by the accused banks as a whole, in the tender regarding banking services and interest rates offered for the municipality's public funds deposits, three banks agreed to

[294]   *Mosaş* (12 March 2020, 20-14/191-97).
[295]   *12 Banks* (n. 254).

tender in a collusive manner by way of offering a pre-agreed interest rate. However, it is understood that Halkbank and Ziraat Bank offered higher interest rates than the concerted interest rate, going against the agreement, which led to Ziraat winning the tender. Thus, it is evident that Ziraat, Halkbank and Vakıfbank were involved in collusive tendering. Another piece of evidence clearly indicated that, in a tender held by the municipality, Vakıfbank ensured that Halkbank would be the successful tenderer by keeping its own bid marginally lower. The following day, the accused banks requested each other's help in three other tenders and submitted bids collectively in the said tenders. The said evidence led the Board to ultimately conclude that there were clear indications of collusive tendering, thus the Board proceeded to impose administrative fines on the accused undertakings based on the grounds that they had violated Article 4 of Law No. 4054.

In its *Chemotherapy Medicine Bids* decision,[296] the Board assessed whether the accused undertakings have been conducting collusive tendering in the chemotherapy drug preparation systems market. The Board expressed that each tender process consists of many steps that should be competitive by nature and that, in order for the tender to result in a competitive equilibrium, the tenderers should be competing with each other in every step of the tender. Therefore, the determination of whether the parties have conducted collusive tendering covers not only the actual bidding stage of the tender but also its preparation stages. Moreover, the Board stated that the act of collusive tendering by the parties during the tender process eliminated the uncertainty by way of making the tender process transparent, and it caused loss of public funds and harm to social welfare due to a low number of participants and high tender prices. The Board ultimately stated that allocating hospitals or manipulating the approximate cost calculation process during the tender preparation phase hinder development and any improvement of production or distribution of goods and the provision of services in the market, and ultimately encumber consumer benefit. It was concluded that the parties subject to the allegations had indeed violated Article 4 of Law No. 4054, and as a result, administrative fines were imposed on the parties.

3.2.3 Leniency Applications in Cartel Agreements

While the statutory basis for cartel regulation in Turkey is Law No. 4054, the details of the cartel leniency mechanism and principles of immunity are set out under the secondary legislation, i.e., the Leniency Regulation and the Guidelines on Clarification of Regulation on Leniency ("Guidelines on Leniency").[297] The undertakings that benefit from the Regulation on Leniency will be immune from sanctions and administrative fines they would have faced under normal circumstances. Parallel to the primary and secondary legislation, the Authority also issued the Leniency Guidelines to (i) provide certainty in the interpretation of the statutory provisions; (ii) reduce uncertainty in practice; and

---

[296] *Chemotherapy Medicine Bids* (2 January 2020, 20-01/14-06).
[297] See Chapter 12 of this book for further information on leniency applications.

(iii) provide guidance to undertakings as per the transparency principle, and enable them to benefit from the leniency programme more efficiently.[298]

Under the Regulation on Leniency, parties that actively cooperate with the Authority regarding a cartel may be granted full immunity or a discount on their fines, depending on the timing of their leniency application. Pursuant to Article 6(1) of the Regulation on Leniency, the leniency programme is only applicable for cartel cases.[299] It does not apply to other forms of antitrust violations. Furthermore, the Turkish cartel leniency regime does not require the evidence submitted within the scope of leniency applications to have significant added value,[300] unlike the leniency practices of the Commission.[301]

A cartelist can apply for leniency until the investigation report is officially served pursuant to Article 4(2) of the Regulation on Leniency. Depending on the order that the leniency application was submitted, there may be full immunity or a reduction in the fine.[302] The first undertaking to file a complete application for leniency before the opening of a preliminary investigation may benefit from full immunity. In general, if the leniency application is made after the initiation of the preliminary investigation up until the date that the "investigation report" is officially served, the applicant can only benefit from full immunity provided the Authority had no evidence on the cartel infringement at the time when the application is made. That being said, the case law shows that there are some instances where the Board does not apply this principle in practice–e.g., in its *Yeast Producers* decision,[303] even though the Authority had information and evidence pertaining to cartel activity, the Board decided to grant full immunity to the leniency applicant. Employees/managers of the first applicant will also be fully immune. However, the applicant must not be the "ringleader" in order to be eligible for full immunity.[304] If that is the case (for example, where the applicant has forced the other cartelists to participate in the cartel), there may only be a reduction of fine between 33% and 50% for the undertaking and between 33% and 100% for the employees/managers.

The second applicant to file a correctly prepared application will receive a 33% to 50% reduction of the fine. Employees/managers of the second applicant who actively co-operate with the Authority will benefit from a reduction of 33% to 100%. The third applicant will receive a 25% to 33% reduction. Employees/managers of the third applicant who actively co-operate with the Authority will benefit from a reduction of 25% to

---

[298]   G. Gürkaynak and B. Yüksel, Practical Law Cartel Leniency Global Guide, "Cartel Leniency in Turkey", Thomson Reuters, 2020.

[299]   *Chemotherapy Medicine Bids* (n. 296); *Sodaş Sodyum* (3 May 2012, 12-24/711-199); *Yeast Producers* (22 October 2014, 14-42/783-346); *Rail Cargo Logistics* (n. 48); *Burdur Mechanical Engineers* (14 December 2017, 17-41/640-279); *Syndicated Loans* (n. 44); *Ambarlı Ro-Ro* (18 April 2019, 19-16/229-101); *Arçelik/Vestel* (2 January 2020, 20-01/13-5).

[300]   D. Toprak, *Avrupa Birliği Uygulamaları Işığında Türk Rekabet Hukukunda Pişmanlık Programının Değerlendirilmesi* (Ankara: Rekabet Kurumu, 2020), p. 40.

[301]   European Commission, Commission Notice on Immunity from fines and reduction of fines in cartel cases (2006/C 298/11), p. 4.

[302]   Article 4 and Article 5 of the Regulation on Leniency.

[303]   *Yeast Producers* (n. 299), pp. 41–42.

[304]   Gürkaynak and Yüksel (n. 298)2020.

100%. Subsequent applicants will receive a 16% to 25% reduction. Employees/managers of subsequent applicants will benefit from a reduction of 16% to 100%.

The main goal of the Regulation on Leniency is to prevent cartel activity *ab initio*. Pursuant to Article 6(1) of the Regulation on Leniency, the conditions for benefiting from the immunity/reduction are as follows:

- The applicant must submit:

    (a) information on the products affected by the cartel

    (b) information on the duration of the cartel

    (c) names of the cartelists

    (d) dates, locations, and participants of the cartel meetings

    (e) other information or documents about the cartel activity.

- The required information can be submitted verbally.

- The applicant must avoid concealing/destroying the information/documents on the cartel activity.

- Unless the authorised division of the Authority decides otherwise, the applicant must stop taking part in the cartel.

- Unless the authorised division of the Authority instructs otherwise, the application must be kept confidential until the investigation report has been served.

- The applicant must continue to actively cooperate with the Authority until the final decision on the case has been rendered.[305]

In principle, the leniency protection is limited to the specific investigation that the undertaking is part of. If the Authority discovers further evidence of the investigated act, this does not deprive the applicant of the benefits of the leniency protection, to the extent the applicant continues to comply with the Regulation on Leniency. The leniency protection in a specific investigation does not spill over to other violations that are or may be investigated in other proceedings.[306]

The Board's evaluation of leniency applications can be exemplified in its *Ambarlı Ro-Ro* decision.[307] In this case, the Board had initiated an investigation against undertakings active in the Ambarlı-Bandırma and Ambarlı-Topçular Ro-Ro transportation lines– namely, Tramola Gemi İşletmeciliği ve Ticaret AŞ (Tramola), Kale Nakliyat Seyahat ve Turizm AŞ (Kale), İstanbullines Denizcilik Yatırım AŞ (İstanbullines), Kabotaj Hattı Ro-Ro ve Feribot İşletmecileri Derneği (Association), İstanbul Deniz Nakliyat Gıda İnşaat Sanayi Ticaret Şti (İDN) and İstanbul Deniz Otobüsleri Sanayi ve Ticaret AŞ (İDO). The Board found that Tramola, Kale Nakliyat and İstanbullines (operating in the Ambarlı-Bandırma Ro-Ro line) and İDN and İDO (both active in the Ambarlı-Topçular Ro-Ro line) violated Article 4 of Law No. 4054 by collectively fixing the prices. The Board imposed administrative fines on the undertakings, ranging from 0.8% to 4% of their

---

[305] Ibid.

[306] Ibid.

[307] *Ambarlı Ro-Ro* (n. 153).

annual turnover. However, the administrative fine imposed on Kale was reduced by 50%, as Kale had sought a leniency application after receiving the investigation notice. Nevertheless, Kale did not benefit from full immunity and had to settle for merely a reduction to its fine, as its leniency application was not made prior to the initiation of the preliminary investigation and the Board already possessed evidence of cartel infringement at the time of the application. It is important to note, however, that the evidence submitted by Kale in its leniency application led the Board to conclude that the violation lasted longer than what had been anticipated based on the evidence collected by the Board prior to the leniency application. As a result, while the Board, therefore, extended the duration of the violation to match the full (previously unknown) period of the cartel for the other investigated parties, the evidence presented in the leniency application was not taken into consideration when determining the duration of Kale's violation.

Moreover, in its *Burdur Mechanical Engineering* decision,[308] the Board initiated an investigation against sixteen freelance mechanical engineers to determine whether they violated Article 4 of Law No. 4054 by forming a profit-sharing cartel. One of the investigated undertakings applied for leniency during the course of the preliminary examination. The Board concluded that the freelance mechanical engineers were parties to a cartel arrangement, but the leniency applicant received full immunity from fines.

Similarly, in its *Steel Ring Manufacturers* decision,[309] the Board stated that the undertakings, MPS and BEKAP, fixed the prices of steel strapping materials and were acting in collusion regarding certain tenders, and decided that both undertakings had violated Article 4 of Law No. 4054. The Board considered the leniency application of MPS and imposed a fine equal to 1% of its annual gross income in 2011. The reason for granting only partial immunity was that the documents previously gathered during the on-site inspection allegedly already proved a cartel. However, it could be said that in this case, the Board set a high standard for cooperation within the context of the leniency programme.[310]

On an important note, although a potential leniency application could increase the risk profile regarding the violation type as well as the ultimate decision of the Board, the Board is not bound by the statements of a leniency applicant and will conduct its own assessment based on the evidence gathered during the preliminary investigation and investigation phases, rather than fully relying on the leniency applicant's acknowledgement of the existence of a cartel.[311] In other words, a leniency application would not automatically result in the finding of the existence of a cartel by the Board.

In fact, there are previous cases where the Board launched fully-fledged investigations pursuant to leniency applications and eventually defined the violations as "other violations" rather than "cartels", or even not found any violation of competition law at all.

---

[308] *Burdur Mechanical Engineers* (n. 299).
[309] *Steel Ring Manufacturers* (30 October 2012, 12-52/1479-508).
[310] G. Gürkaynak and Ö. İnanılır, in *Global Legal Insights – Cartels: Enforcement, Appeals & Damages Actions* (8th edition, London: Global Legal Group, 2020).
[311] *Sodaş Sodyum* (n. 299); *Yeast Producers* (n. 299); *Rail Cargo Logistics* (n. 48); *Burdur Mechanical Engineers*; *Syndicated Loans* (n. 44); *Ambarlı Ro-Ro*; *Arçelik/Vestel* (n. 299).

For instance, in the *Syndicated Loans* decision,[312] where Bank of Tokyo-Mitsubishi UFJ Turkey (BTMU) filed for a leniency application, the Board found that there was a concerted practice/agreement between three of the investigated banks and imposed separate administrative monetary fines against them. However, it also decided that other investigated banks did not violate Law No. 4054. Accordingly, when determining the amount of the administrative monetary fines, the Board considered the concerted practice/agreement in question to be an "other type of violation". At this point, we should point out that only cartelists can benefit from the leniency application. However, in the above-mentioned decision, although the Board decided that the violation should be characterised as an anti-competitive information exchange rather than a cartel, the BTMU (leniency applicant) was granted full immunity from fines. In this case, however, the Board grounded its decision on its authority to grant full immunity under Article 16(6) of Law No. 4054 and did not apply the Regulation on Leniency. Two of the investigated banks were subjected to fines, whereas the remaining eight investigated undertakings were not found to be in violation of Law No. 4054.

This decision should not, however, be interpreted to mean that leniency applicants can always benefit from full immunity, even when the relevant violation does not constitute a cartel. In fact, in its *Hyundai Dealers* decision,[313] the Board clearly stated that the leniency applicant would not benefit from the Regulation on Leniency, as the violation in question was characterised as an anti-competitive information exchange and not a cartel.

3.3 Tacit Collusion

Tacit collusion refers to market players' ability to coordinate, even in the absence of an express agreement, to raise prices or, more generally, to increase their profits to the detriment of consumers.[314] Although the concept of tacit collusion refers to a collusive outcome, it does not constitute a punishable "explicit collusion" in the context of current competition law practice. In fact, in tacit collusion, there is no communication between competitors, and tacit collusion is a state of coordination that emerges through the discovery of the interdependence of companies as a result of the ongoing competition in the market, and a unilateral compliance with the tacit order that limits competition by deliberately avoiding competition. Therefore, although the market behaviour of the companies depends on the competitors' behaviour and ultimately leads to the restriction of competition by way of coordination, it does not contain direct or indirect communication that will lead to an agreement within the scope of competition law. Thus, tacit collusion is not included in the scope of restrictive agreements regime as it is essentially unilateral (i.e., independent).[315]

---

[312]   *Syndicated Loans* (n. 44).
[313]   *Hyundai Dealers* (16 December 2013, 13-70/952-403).
[314]   M. Ivaldi et al., (n. 250), p. 217.
[315]   OECD, Policy Roundtables, "Unilateral Disclosure of Information with Anticompetitive Effects", DAF/COMP(2012)17, 11 October 2012, p. 29.

Under certain market conditions (i.e., markets with few sellers and homogenous products), supra-competitive price strategies may be the normal outcome of rational economic behaviour of each firm on the market. It is for this reason that tacit collusion or conscious parallelism falls outside the reach of competition laws on cartels.[316] It results in an apparent coordination between companies and allows them to set prices above the competitive level without violating the competition rules. It is referred to as tacit collusion only because the outcome (in terms of prices set or quantities produced, for example) may very well resemble that of explicit collusion, or even of an official cartel.[317]

The more customer-tailored products are offered with customer-specific prices, the less attainable tacit collusion will become, in light of the companies' cost structures and their differentiated products. The General Court of the European Union clearly set forth in its *Bayer* judgment that an agreement within the meaning of Article 101 TFEU requires the existence of a meeting of minds, or a concurrence of wills between competitors, with the intention to restrict competition, and that the parties need to feel bound by the said agreement.[318] Furthermore, the concept of "concerted practice" has been defined by the CJEU as "a form of coordination between undertakings, which, without having been taken to the stage where an agreement properly so-called has been concluded, knowingly substitutes for the risks of competition", through any direct or indirect contact which may influence market conduct of an undertaking's competitors or disclose its own prospective market conduct.[319] However, the CJEU also recognises that Article 101 TFEU does not outlaw firms' parallel behaviour that might be the result of their individual and *intelligent* adaptation to the existing and anticipated market conditions–namely, tacit collusion.[320] A similar judgement exists in the Turkish antitrust precedents, as well. As discussed in detail below, the Board's past interpretation of the issue demonstrated that it required the existence of a direct link between the undertakings in question in order to make a finding of a violation.

Accordingly, in order to constitute tacit collusion, the behaviour of undertakings in a given market must satisfy four main criteria, as follows: (i) sharing a common understanding; (ii) detecting deviations; (iii) credible threat of retaliation; and (iv) high entry barriers.[321] If all of these conditions are met, then the existence of tacit collusion may be considered. Such conscious parallel behaviour or tacit collusion generally has the same economic

---

[316]   Ibid.
[317]   M. Ivaldi, B. Jullien, P. Rey, P. Seabright, and J. Tirole, "The Economics of Tacit Collusion", IDEI Toulouse, Final Report for DG Competition, European Commission, 2003.
[318]   Case T-41/96 *Bayer AG v. Commission of the European Communities* [2000] ECR II-3383, para. 69: "The concept of an agreement within the meaning of Article 85(1) of the Treaty [now Article 101(1) TFEU], as interpreted by the case-law, centres around the existence of a concurrence of wills between at least two parties, the form in which it is manifested being unimportant so long as it constitutes the faithful expression of the parties' intention."
[319]   Case C-48/69 *Imperial Chemical Industries Ltd. v. Commission of the European Communities* [1972] 619, para. 69 and Joined Cases 40 to 48, 50, 54 to 56, 111, 113 and 114-73 *Coöperatieve Vereniging "Suiker Unie" UA and others v. Commission of the European Communities* [1975] ECR 1663, paras. 26 and 174.
[320]   *Imperial Chemical Industries Ltd. v. Commission of the European Communities* (n. 319), para. 174 and *Coöperatieve Vereniging "Suiker Unie" UA and others v. Commission of the European Communities* (n. 319), paras. 26 and 174.
[321]   G. J. Stigler, "Theory of Oligopoly", (1964) 72 *Journal of Political Economy*, 44; D. K. Osborne, "Cartel Problems", (1976) 66(5) *American Economic Review*, 835, p. 838; D. A. Yao and S. S. Desanti, Game Theory and the legal Analysis of Tacit Collusion, (1993) *The Antitrust Bulletin*, 113 (as cited in N. Petit, "The Oligopoly Problem in EU Competition Law" (2012), pp. 6–7).

effects as collusive actions, such as combination, conspiracy or price-fixing agreement.[322] That being said, whether or not conscious parallel behaviour constitutes an illegal action that restricts competition is a controversial subject in both competition law and economics. The difference between concerted practice and tacit collusion (i.e., conscious parallelism) arises from the fact that the undertakings do not make their decisions independently, in concerted practices.[323] Conscious parallelism and tacit collusion are used interchangeably.

The economic theory of collusion focuses on what outcomes are sustainable and the strategy profiles that sustain them; and therefore sees no difference between explicit and tacit collusion. However, the primary focus of competition law is not on the outcome nor the strategies that sustain an outcome but rather the means by which a collusive arrangement is achieved (i.e., what mutual understanding exists among firms and how it was arrived at).[324] Tacit collusion is not accepted as punishable explicit collusion by the current competition law practice, although it includes a kind of coordination between competitors.

Although the US and the EU, without dispute, accept that tacit collusion does not constitute a violation of competition, Law No. 4054 does not explicitly refer to the doctrine known as tacit collusion or conscious parallelism. Tacit collusion, which leads to the same market outcome as explicit collusion, does not fall within the scope of Article 4 of Law No. 4054in principle, since it lacks the communication condition required for the existence of a restrictive agreement. In other words, while competition law prohibits and imposes penalties on explicit collusion based on communication, as a rule it cannot directly intervene in and impose penalties on tacit collusion, where coordination occurs as a result of parallel market conduct stemming from repeated interaction with competitors, without any direct or indirect communication or contact.

However, Article 4(3) of Law No. 4054 introduces a presumption of concerted practice, which reads as follows:

> In cases where the existence of an agreement cannot be proved, a similarity of price changes in the market, or the balance of demand and supply, or the operational regions of undertakings to those markets where competition is prevented, distorted or restricted, constitutes a presumption that the undertakings are engaged in concerted practice.

Therefore, the wording of Article 4 of Law No. 4054 points out that concerted practice can be presumed without any communication evidence but in the presence of purely economic evidence showing parallel behaviour. Accordingly, Article 4 creates a possible intervention area that can also include "tacit collusion".[325] (See Section 3.3.2 below on "Presumption of Concerted Practices" for further details on the mentioned area of intervention.)

---

[322] OECD, "Glossary of Industrial Organisation Economics and Competition Law", compiled by R. S. Khemani and D. M. Shapiro, commissioned by the Directorate for Financial, Fiscal and Enterprise Affairs, 1993, p. 26 <https://www.oecd.org/regreform/sectors/2376087.pdf> (last accessed on 24 June 2021).
[323] White Cement (25 June 2014, 14-22/460-202), p. 5.
[324] Harrington, (n. 252), p. 2.
[325] E. Ince, "Gizli Anlaşma: İktisadi Temelleri ve Rekabeti Kısıtlayıcı Anlaşmalar Rejimi İçin Çıkarımlar" ("Tacit Collusion: Economics and Implications for Anti-Competitive Agreements Regime"), Rekabet Dergisi, Vol. 20, Issue 2, December 2019, p. 50.

In terms of establishing and maintaining the tacit collusion balance, the market should be structurally suitable for providing and maintaining coordination without the need for communication. In this context, market parameters such as low number of competitors, high barriers to entry, frequency of interaction/competition, multi-market interaction, market transparency, and being a growing market facilitate tacit collusion; while parameters such as innovative markets, asymmetry, buyer power, and fluctuating demand make it more difficult.[326]

These market parameters are also important with respect to the evaluation of tacit collusion in the merger control regime. In terms of the current legal framework, it is generally accepted by the competition authorities that tacit collusion will not be penalised under the regime of restrictive agreements. However, there might be an intervention in terms of merger control regime in order to prevent the formation of market structures that will give rise to tacit collusion within the scope of "collective dominance" and "coordination effects". On that note, these market parameters are imperative in order to be able to (i) determine the potential of markets in terms of establishing and maintaining restrictive agreements between competitors; (ii) investigate possible agreements and concerted practices in these markets; and (iii) prevent markets from becoming open to coordination within the scope of "collective dominance" and "coordination effects" and thus maintain the competitive balance in markets.

In most jurisdictions, rational unilateral reactions to market dynamics are permitted. Given that tacit collusion does not amount to concerted practice, it escapes from the prohibition set out in Article 101 TFEU, as is the case with Article 4 of Law No. 4054. As such, pure forms of tacit collusion that result only from a unilateral reaction to market dynamics do not usually trigger competition law liability. On the other hand, similar to tacit collusion that may serve to establish collective dominance under Article 102 TFEU, companies can be deemed to hold collective dominance as per Article 6 of Law No. 4054. However, precedents concerning collective dominance are not abundant and mature enough to allow for a clear inference of a set of minimum conditions under which collective dominance can be alleged. That said, the Board has considered it necessary to establish an economic link for a finding of abuse of collective dominance.[327]

3.3.1 Oligopolistic Interdependency

Oligopolistic interdependency is accepted as the basis of tacit collusion.[328] In fact, tacit collusion results from an interdependency situation, in other words, from an apparent effect of an undertaking's behaviour on its competitor, which signals that there are only a few undertakings active in the market. Therefore, tacit collusion is generally discussed within the scope of oligopolistic markets. Tacit collusion continues to remain on the

---

[326] Ibid., p. 64.
[327] *Biryay* (17 July 2000, 00-26/292-162); *National Roaming* (9 June 2003, 03-40/432-186).
[328] Europe Economics, "Study on Assessment Criteria for Distinguishing between Competitive and Dominant Oligopolies in Merger Control", 2001, p. 21.

agenda, especially as a reason for the weak competitive functioning of oligopolistic markets, and forms the basis of discussions on this subject.[329]

In oligopolistic markets, the pricing and output actions of one firm have a significant impact upon those of its competitors.[330] Therefore, in oligopolistic markets and sectors, players tend to be interdependent in their pricing and output decisions, so that the actions of each competitor impact on and result in a counter-response from the other competitor(s). In such instances, oligopolistic undertakings may take their competitors' actions into account, and the result could be the coordination of their actions as if they were in a cartel, without an explicit or overt agreement.[331] This effect is due to the particular characteristics of these markets, in which companies are aware of their competitors' presence and are thus compelled to coordinate their market strategies involving production, capacity or prices, with one another.[332] The fear of deviating from such behaviour may lead to costly price-cutting, lower profits and market share instability, which may further incentivise undertakings to maintain such an implicit arrangement between themselves. This creates an interdependency of undertakings in their decision-making processes, called "oligopolistic interdependency". These behaviours showing interdependency are deemed to be rational within the scope of the relevant oligopolistic market structure.

Every oligopolistic undertaking can take its economic decision by considering the possible reactions of its competitors, and this type of interdependency in an oligopolistic market cannot, absent concrete evidence of violation, be punished by competition law. The same, however, cannot be said outside the scope of oligopolies as the very nature of oligopolies deems such behaviour of undertakings a pillar of these sectors and markets.

In line with that, the case law of the Board shows that defences on the oligopolistic interdependency are, to a very large extent, accepted by the Board. The precedents support the thesis that Turkish competition law practice seeks evidence of communication to be able to conclude that a conscious parallelism (in other words, tacit collusion) constitutes a violation. In many of its decisions,[333] the Board accepts the defence of oligopolistic dependency since the low number of undertakings and the transparency of oligopolistic markets enable the undertakings to easily follow the decisions of other undertakings, and to make decisions accordingly, which creates a conscious parallelism (i.e., tacit collusion).

This can be observed in the *Yeast* decision,[334] where the Board investigated allegations of price-fixing as a result of collusion on the part of yeast producers, by way of raising prices at the same rate. Within the scope of its investigation, the Board failed to find

---

[329] OECD, (n. 315).
[330] OECD, (n. 322), p. 21.
[331] Ibid.
[332] Ibid.
[333] *Pamukkale Taşımacılık* (1 October 2014, 14-37/713-318); *Gürsel Turizm* (16 January 2014, 14-02/40-18); *Ankara-Adana Highway* (20 February 2013, 13-11/165-87); *Şırnak Bus Companies* (29 December 2011, 11-64/1666-596); *İzmir-Konya Bus Companies* (24 November 2011, 11-59/1521-546); *Konya-Akşehir Bus Companies* (17 November 2011, 11-57/1461-519); *Anamur-Ankara Bus Companies* (4 November 2010, 10-69/1466-564); *White Cement* (n. 323); *Astur* (17 July 2008, 08-45/626-238).
[334] *Yeast* (27 June 2000, 00-24/255-138), pp. 13–14.

any direct or indirect communication among the yeast producers, which could be classified as a concerted practice aimed at eliminating any irregularities within the market pertaining to sale prices. Furthermore, the Board concluded that the yeast producers increased their prices in very close proximity to one another in terms of timing and rates and that no similarities with respect to the cost structures of the undertakings were discovered which could lead to such similar increases in prices. In the end, the Board determined that such parallel price movements resulted from the homogenous and oligopolistic nature of the baker's yeast market rather than a collusive behaviour of the players active in it.

Similarly, within its *White Cement* decision,[335] the Board stated the criteria for evaluating parallel behaviours of competitors from a collusion standpoint as (i) the need for communication between competitors aiming to impede competition, and (ii) the necessity of being able to find and present such collusion via clear and consistent evidence. Subsequently, the Board proceeded not to issue administrative monetary fines to the undertakings active in the market as it stated that any evidence of communication between oligopolists failed to meet the criteria set out. Moreover, within the scope of other decisions of the Board such as the *Advertising Space*,[336] it was stated that (i) the argument of oligopolistic interdependency would be a sufficient defence on the instance of the presence of economic indicators alone, and (ii) the communication evidence would be prioritised.

In its *Milk* decision,[337] the Board examined the behaviours of the undertakings which accounted for more than 60% of the milk market in Turkey and concluded that (i) the undertakings never raised their respective prices concurrently, with the exception of a single instance; (ii) the increase rates of the undertakings' prices did not fall within a pattern; and (iii) the eventual prices of the products were determined through the adding of the dealership profit margins and the subsequent subtraction of differing dealership abatements from the factory price. Thus, the Board concluded that within the aforementioned scheme, prices could not be fixed through a collusive effort and that the behaviour of the market was found to be resulting from its oligopolistic nature rather than from collusion on the part of the undertakings active in such market.

Moreover, within the scope of the Board's decision[338] investigating insurance companies' alleged collusion within the market for traffic insurance, (i) the lack of a high number of competitors; (ii) high levels of concentration; (iii) presence of barriers to entry; (iv) frequent communication among the undertakings; and (v) transparency of the market were stated as the criteria which enabled the existence of conscious parallel movements in this market with oligopolistic characteristics.

Contradicting such precedents, the Board settled upon a different approach within the scope of its *Yeast* decision.[339] Upon evaluating the increases in the prices of wet or

---

[335] *White Cement* (n. 323), p. 5.
[336] *Advertising Space* (1 February 2000, 00-4/41-19), p. 21.
[337] *Milk* (23 March 2000, 00-11/109-54), pp. 5–6.
[338] *Traffic Insurance* (19 July 2017, 17-23/383-166), p. 147.
[339] *Yeast* (23 September 2005, 05-60/896-241), p. 40.

fresh baker's yeast, despite not finding any concrete evidence of a concerted practice, the Board concluded that while the nature of oligopolistic markets allowed for similar price movements in the market, the fact that four different players raised their prices considerably higher than the actual increases to their costs or the inflation, despite the lack of an objective change within the market dynamics, as well as the fact that they were able to raise their prices two months running, with high rates even at the start, and to keep such trend afloat in the subsequent months, could not reasonably be the result of any economic phenomenon but rather the result of concerted practices. Similarly, in its *Özgür Çimento/Göltaş-Denizli Çimento* decision,[340] the Board did not go to the trouble of seeking communication evidence along with conscious parallelism, since naked parallel behaviour and economic evidence were established.

Therefore, although fewer in number, there are some exceptional instances where the Board reaches the violation conclusion based merely on the economic evidence showing the parallel conducts (by using the presumption of concerted practices) and therefore does not credit the oligopolistic interdependency defence. Such exceptional cases support the discussions that there is an intervention area for tacit collusion in the Turkish competition law regime, as the Board has decided on violation without having any concrete direct or indirect communication evidence in these cases. The difference between the Board's two approaches in these cases came down, in essence, to the question of whether or not economic indicators are sufficient to establish and evidence a violation on a standalone basis, or is the presence of communication between the undertakings also needed to deem undertakings' behaviour as a violation per se. Besides, the Board shifts the burden of proof in connection with concerted practice allegations by rejecting the defences on oligopolistic interdependency and concluding that the parallel conduct in the market results from a restrictive agreement. This mechanism is called "the presumption of concerted practice" and will be further explained in the following section.

Owing to the "presumption of concerted practice", oligopolistic markets for the supply of homogeneous products (e.g., meal coupon/card market,[341] the market for wet/fresh baker's yeast,[342] the market for ready-mixed concrete,[343] the market for white cement,[344] and the market for milk[345]) have constantly been under investigation for tacit collusion and/or concerted practices.

3.3.2 Presumption of Concerted Practice

The definition of concerted practice in Turkey does not fall far from the definition used in EU competition law, as already explained in detail under Chapters 2 and 3. A concerted practice is defined as a form of coordination between undertakings, who (without reaching

[340] *Göltaş Çimento* (20 September 2007, 07-76/908-346), pp. 38–40.
[341] *Meal Coupons/Cards* (15 November 2018, 18-43/694-339).
[342] *Yeast* (12 November 2008, 08-63/1050-409).
[343] *Ready-Mixed Concrete* (25 June 2014, 14-22/441-199).
[344] *White Cement* (n. 323).
[345] *Milk* (n. 337).

the stage where an agreement has been properly concluded) knowingly substituted practical cooperation with each other, for the risks of competition. The coordination does not need to be in writing; it is sufficient if the parties have expressed their joint intention to behave in a particular way, perhaps in a meeting, via a telephone call or through exchange of letters.

Concerted practices occur when the undertakings establish direct or indirect contact with one another in one way or the other, reach or seek to reach a consensus as to what sort of strategies they will adopt in this regard.[346] Therefore, the Authority has the burden of deciding whether the evidence available to it suffices to prove the presence of any communication and contact. As we have seen, in the absence of communication and contact, the Authority might end up with tacit collusion (or conscious parallelism) resulting from the oligopolistic interdependency, which is not actually illegal, contrary to concerted practices.

In this respect, discussions regarding the various underlying criteria and those surrounding a so-called "presumption of concerted practice" exist within the context of the sort of evidence competition authorities from jurisdictions around the globe shall muster to prove that the competitive landscape of a given market is disrupted by way of concerted practices, beyond the limits of the natural behaviour that can be expected from players active in oligopolistic markets, as well as the evidence that must be put forth by the undertakings to overcome the criteria of the presumption of concerted practice and overturn the allegations of concerted practice. As discussed in detail below, certain forms and levels of communication and contact between competitors active within the same product market may, in some instances, be deemed sufficient to constitute a concerted practice under this presumption.[347]

While the definition of concerted practice in Turkey does not differ significantly from the definition used in the EU, the same cannot be said with respect to "the presumption of concerted practice". In fact, unlike the Turkish antitrust regime, the naked application of the logic of "presumption of concerted practice" does not exist in the current implementations of the respective competition law regimes in the US and the EU.

According to Article 4 of Law No. 4054, the price changes in the market, or the balance of demand and supply, or the operational areas of undertakings, which are similar to those markets where competition is prevented, distorted or restricted, constitute a presumption that the undertakings are engaged in concerted practices, even if the existence of an agreement cannot be proven.[348] The Turkish antitrust regime, therefore, condemns concerted practices and the Authority easily shifts the burden of proof in connection with concerted practice allegations through a mechanism called "the presumption of concerted practice". The lack of such a mechanism within the US and EU antitrust regimes is not the result of an unconscious deficiency, but rather a conscious choice largely due to the possible harm posed by such a mechanism, in light of the universal principles and norms of law.[349]

[346] İ. Atiyas and G. Gürkaynak, "'Presumption of Concerted Practice': A Legal and Economic Analysis", 4th Symposium on Recent Developments in Competition Law, Erciyes University, 7 April 2006, p. 11.
[347] Ibid., p. 4.
[348] OECD, (n. 315), p. 153.
[349] G. Gürkaynak, K. Yıldırımet, H. Özgökçen, and B. Aydın, "A Discussion on Proof Matters in Turkish Competition Law Focusing on Proof of Concerted Practices", Rekabet Dergisi, Vol. 12, No. 4, October 2011, pp. 75–125, at p. 94.

The material issue specific to Turkey is the very low standard of proof adopted by the Board. The participation of an undertaking in a cartel activity requires proof that there was such a cartel activity or, in the case of multilateral discussions or cooperation, that the particular undertaking was a participant.[350] With a broadening interpretation of Law No. 4054, and especially of the "object or effect of which..." wording, the Board has established an extremely low standard of proof concerning cartel activity. The standard of proof is even lower as far as concerted practices are concerned; in practice, if a parallel behaviour is established, a concerted practice might readily be inferred and the undertakings concerned might be required to prove that the parallel behaviour was not the result of a concerted practice, but that it was based on economic and rational business decisions.

At the background of "the presumption of concerted practice" within the scope of the Turkish antitrust regime lies Articles 4 and 59 of Law No. 4054, which define the presumption of concerted practice as follows:

> In cases where the existence of an agreement cannot be proved, a similarity of price changes in the market, or the balance of demand and supply, or the operational regions of undertakings to those markets where competition is prevented, distorted or restricted, constitutes a presumption that the undertakings are engaged in concerted practice.

And reverses the burden of proof with the following: "Each of the parties may relieve itself of the responsibility by proving, on the basis of economic and rational facts that it has not engaged in concerted practices."

The reasoning of the relevant articles of Law No. 4054 points to the fact that concerted practices, and more specifically agreements aimed at distorting competition, are usually conducted in secret and therefore it is very hard or almost impossible to prove the existence of such agreements; thus in such cases the burden of proof shall reverse in order to prevent the relevant articles of Law No. 4054 from becoming obsolete.

Accordingly, the relevant article of Law No. 4054 provides for a "presumption of concerted practice", which enables the Board to bring an Article 4 case where price changes in the market, supply-demand equilibrium or fields of activity of enterprises resemble those in markets where competition is obstructed, disrupted or restricted. While explicit collusion (such as cartels and concerted practices) is viewed by most competition authorities as one of the most serious violations of competition law, tacit collusion or conscious parallel behaviour is, on the contrary, not considered as illegal, despite the fact that the outcome can be the same as in explicit collusion cases: prices jointly rise to the supra-competitive levels and possibly to the monopoly level.[351] This raises an enforcement dilemma on how to deal with those practices which do not amount to explicit collusion but favour tacit collusion.

Turkish antitrust precedents recognise that conscious parallelism (i.e., tacit collusion) is rebuttable evidence of forbidden behaviour and constitutes sufficient grounds to

[350] G. Gürkaynak, in *The Cartels and Leniency Review*, C. A. Varney, ed. (2d edition, London: Law Business Research, 2014), Chapter 30 (Turkey), p. 360.
[351] OECD, (n. 315), p. 20.

impose fines on the undertakings concerned. Therefore, the burden of proof is very easily switched, and it becomes incumbent upon the defendants to demonstrate that the parallelism in question is not based on concerted practice but has economic and rational reasons behind it.

Within the scope of a decision in 2017, the Board reviewed allegations that ten undertakings that were active in producing ready-mix concrete in Turkey's İzmir region planned to artificially increase the prices of ready-mix concrete by entering into an anti-competitive agreement or concerted practice.[352] The Board took into account the fact that economic evidence demonstrated that the relevant undertakings had not been involved in an anti-competitive agreement or concerted practice, and it is understood that the Board took the defendants' view that it was implausible that they reached an arrangement within the alleged duration of the anti-competitive agreement, which was only three months. The Board's decision constitutes a good example that the undertakings subject to an investigation based on allegations of anti-competitive agreements or concerted practices can defend themselves using economic and legal evidence, even when they are under the presumption of concerted practice of Article 4 of Law No. 4054, and so proves the importance of economic evidence in such instances.

Additionally, in most decisions,[353] the Board recognises that undertakings active in a given product market may consciously follow the commercial strategies of their competitors and, in the absence of any communication between competitors regarding collusion or exchange of commercially sensitive information, parallel conduct alone would not be sufficient to meet the standard of proof for a cartel or the existence of concerted practices.

In light of the Board's approach on the subject, it is pointed out that in the application of this presumption, "more rigorous practices that increase the standards of proof should be preferred, especially avoiding the 'naked use of the presumption of concerted practice'".[354] This is viewed as a condition for legal compliance with the presumption of innocence protected by constitutional law. In other words, the existence of a presumption of concerted practices on a stand-alone basis, without evidence proving the existence of any concerted practices between the parties, is not considered sufficient. Moreover, even the Board has accepted that bringing forth clear and consistent additional evidence demonstrating the communication between the parties, as well as the parallel behaviour within the context set out by the law, is necessary when applying the presumption.[355]

In its above-mentioned *Ready-Mixed Concrete II* decision,[356] even though some internal correspondence obtained during the on-site investigations conducted within the scope

352   *Ready-Mixed Concrete* (n. 153), p. 44.
353   *Cement* (26 June 2013, 13-40/528-235); *Mixed Feed* (27 October 2016, 16-35/596-264); *Newspaper* (17 July 2000, 00-26/291-161); *Aegean Cement* (19 October 2006, 06-77/992-287).
354   G. Gürkaynak et al., "Naked Application of the Presumption of Concerted Practices in Turkish Law: *Baker's Yeast* Decision", Symposium on Board and Judiciary Decisions Regarding Competition Law, 15–16 October 2010, p. 115.
355   *Şanlıurfa Autogas* (28 July 2020, 20-36/505-223), para. 38; *Fuel Sector Preliminary Investigation* (4 July 2012, 12-36/1040-328), pp. 3–5; *White Cement* (n. 323), pp. 5–9.
356   *Ready-Mix Concrete* (n. 352), p. 44.

of the investigation created the impression that some of the investigated parties had communicated with the aim of restricting competition after December 2015, since no further evidence was found to show that the parties were in such communication or consultations, the Board concluded that the undertakings under investigation did not violate Article 4 of Law No. 4054 considering the internal nature of the correspondence and the lack of economic findings. As can be seen, despite the existence of a statutory presumption, the quality of the evidence related to available communication evidence was examined and in order to achieve a high and consistent standard, further evidence was sought to show that the issues mentioned in the internal correspondence were true. Since this could not be achieved, the investigation regarding the claim could not go beyond mere suspicion and was concluded without penalty.

At the core of the discussions and the debate pertaining to the presumption of concerted practices in the Turkish antitrust regime lies the idea that the reversing of the burden of proof via the presumption of concerted practices, from the prosecution to the respondent, contradicts the *in dubio pro reo* principle, which represents one of the pillars of administrative law ensuring a fair trial of the respondent.[357] This school of thought further argues that the Board cannot possibly rule in favour of a violation in cases where the Authority, as the plaintiff, is not able to show sufficient evidence which points to a violation.[358] Behind this stance is the argument that "burden of proof" in Turkish law is a concept which is specific to civil law, and cannot simply be utilised within the scope of administrative investigations in which the administration stands as both the plaintiff and the judicial authority.[359]

As a matter of fact, within the dissenting opinion of the 13th Chamber of the Council of State's *Batısöke* decision,[360] it was argued that (i) the communication evidence in the case was related to exports and did not include any data regarding the domestic market, and that (ii) the meeting minutes used as evidence did not explicitly demonstrate undertakings' object to restrict competition. Furthermore, it was also stated that the Board could not detect any other communication evidence and did not examine any other factor in the cement market that could lead to price increases, such as changes in the capacity usage rates due to seasonality in the cement sector, infrastructure or superstructure projects in the region, etc. It was concluded that the causal relation between both the beginning and the end of the violation and the conduct allegedly leading to the violation was not demonstrated by solid, explicit and convincing evidence. Moreover, it was indicated that cartels cannot be proven based on merely economic evidence in the absence of material evidence; thus imposing a monetary fine based on mere presumptions violates the *in dubio pro reo* principle. Therefore, the dissenting opinion argued that the appeal request should be accepted and that the Board's decision should be annulled. Given that price uniformity may be a natural outcome of rational economic behaviour in oligopolistic markets with few sellers and homogenous products, arguments have been advanced that

---

[357] D. Cengiz, "Uyumlu Eylem Karinesinin ve Rekabet Kurulu'nun Bu Karineye İlişkin Uygulamalarının Değerlendirilmesi", *Rekabet Dergisi*, Vol. 35, 2008, p. 18.
[358] Ibid., p. 20.
[359] Ibid., p. 21.
[360] *Batısöke* (13th Chamber of the Council of State, 11 December 2019, E. 2019/1035, K. 2019/4253).

the burden of proof must be higher than circumstantial evidence of concerted or parallel behaviour and uniform pricing and output policies. In other words, it has been a topic of discussion that tacit collusion in and of itself should not necessarily be construed as evidence of concerted practices.

Moreover, within the scope of the Board's *Aegean Cement* decision,[361] the defendants argued that the presumption of concerted practices, as defined within Articles 4 and 59 of Law No. 4054, is, in fact, unconstitutional. However, within the scope of its reasoned decision, the Board refrained from entertaining such an argument and stated that the Board was not the competent authority to evaluate such an argument regarding Law No. 4054.

In a similar vein, within the scope of its *Mixed Feed* decision,[362] the Board concluded that a broad interpretation of the presumption of concerted practices might give way to the inclusion of unprohibited actions such as "oligopolistic dependence" and "parallel behaviourism" within the scope of the prohibited actions under Law No. 4054. Furthermore, it was stated that the model of repeated games proved that parallel behaviour could exist, even in cases where certain conditions would make it difficult for interdependence to exist. Thus it was concluded that the ability of parallel behaviours to prove concerted practices weakened in time, and as such "additional factors" shall be set forth alongside parallel behaviour by the Authority, during the course of investigations of alleged concerted practices, similar to the practices in place in the US and the EU. Such "additional factors" were non-exhaustively stated as proof of communication between the undertakings and the suitability of the market to such concerted practices.

In line with the explanations above, aggressive implementation of the presumption of concerted practice, or naked application of the presumption, might undermine the instances where competitors indeed did not partake in any collusive contact but merely adapted their competitive behaviour by means of the market intelligence that they gathered by virtue of the market characteristics (i.e., tacit collusion). Within that context, the possibility of aggressively implementing the presumption of concerted practice, without having to rely on additional communication evidence, might create an intervention area for tacit collusion in the Turkish competition law regime as the Board might decide on violation without having any concrete direct or indirect communication evidence. In fact, there are some exceptional decisions, as explained above, where the Board rejects the defence of oligopolistic interdependency and therefore decides on violation based merely on economic evidence.

The rare instances where the Board opted for a naked application of the presumption of concerted practice are *Yeast*[363] and *Göltaş Cement.*[364] In *Yeast* the Board put forth its concluding remarks on whether the parallel behaviour of undertakings stems from oligopolistic market structure or an anti-competitive agreement/concerted practice by stating that, in most cases, the price movements would follow a similar trend in oligopolistic

---

[361] *Aegean Cement* (n. 353), p. 31.
[362] *Mixed Feed* (n. 353), p. 7.
[363] *Yeast* (n. 342).
[364] *Göltaş Çimento* (n. 340).

markets. However, the Board found, in this particular case, that the economic reason behind such a trend was, without doubt, a concerted practice, mainly due to the facts that the rate of the said price increase was groundlessly high and there was no significant change in the market conditions that would lead to such an increase.[365] Additionally, in *Göltaş Cement*, the Board's approach on the naked application of the presumption of concerted practice was depicted as:

> If an undertaking, along with other undertakings does not act in a way that would coincide with its interests under normal market conditions or for example, the movement of certain parameters such as price differs from what is expected to be under normal circumstances, it could be said that the undertakings active in such market had violated Article 4 of Law by means of concerted practice.[366]

However, when it comes to the standard of proof regarding concerted practices, the case law of the Board[367] is more inclined to resemble the remarks set out in *Newspaper Publishers*[368] and require evidence of a contact/communication between the parties subject to the alleged conduct. As discussed, one of the very well-known defences against the allegations developed on the presumption of concerted practice is the "oligopolistic interdependence" defences,[369] based on the causes of interdependence.

In light of the foregoing, while Article 4 of Law No. 4054 equips the Board with a tool that is not available to its European counterpart to the same extent and simply not available to its American counterpart at all, the primary responsibility of the Board shall be to "ensure that the presumption of concerted practice is used in moderation and in harmony with the specific conditions of each investigation, and that this presumption is abandoned in cases where it may pose a threat of diminishing welfare in the long run, rather than serving the purpose of the investigation".[370]

---

[365] *Yeast* (n. 342), para. 1100.
[366] *Göltaş Çimento* (n. 340), paras. 1300–1310.
[367] In *Ambarlı Ro-Ro* (n. 299) and *İzmir Ready-Mixed Concrete* (n. 153), the Board sought the existence of finding(s) that would evidence contact/communication between the undertakings under investigation to establish that such undertakings were involved in concerted practice.
[368] *Newspapers Publishers* (n. 154), para. 710–740. Similar criteria in terms of establishing the existence of a concerted practice were reiterated by the Board in *Göltaş* (n. 154) and *Automotive* (n. 154).
[369] *Pamukkale Taşımacılık* (n. 333); *Gürsel Turizm* (n. 333); *Ankara-Adana Highway* (n. 333); *Şırnak Bus Companies* (n. 333); *İzmir-Konya Bus Companies* (n. 333); *Konya-Akşehir Bus Companies* (n. 333); *Anamur-Ankara Bus Companies* (4 November 2010, 10-69/1466-564); *White Cement* (n. 323); *Astur* (n. 333).
[370] Atiyas and Gürkaynak, (n. 346), p. 25.

Chapter 4
Other Horizontal Agreements

GÖNENÇ GÜRKAYNAK, ESQ., SINEM UĞUR*
AND AYDENIZ BAYTAŞ**

Horizontal agreements are regulated under Article 4 of Law No. 4054,[371] which prohibits all agreements between undertakings, decisions by associations of undertakings and concerted practices that have (or may have) as their object or effect the prevention, restriction or distortion of competition within a Turkish product or services market or a part thereof. As discussed above, Article 4 provides a non-exhaustive list of conducts that are deemed as agreements, concerted practices and/or decisions restricting competition.

However, the said anti-competitive conducts could also benefit from exemption if they meet the conditions for block exemption or individual exemption set out under Article 5. The secondary legislation that provides general guidance on "other horizontal agreements" is the Guidelines on Horizontal Agreements published in 2013, which set out the principles to be considered in the assessment of agreements between undertakings, decisions of associations of undertakings and concerted practices with the nature of horizontal cooperation, within the framework of Article 4 and Article 5.

The Guidelines on Horizontal Agreements cover not only the horizontal agreements between existing or potential competitors[372] but also those between undertakings (which are neither existing nor potential competitors) that are, for instance, active in different geographic markets. The Guidelines on Horizontal Agreements shed light on the competitive analysis with respect to (i) information exchanges; (ii) R&D agreements; (iii) joint production agreements; (iv) joint purchasing agreements; (v) commercialisation agreements; and (vi) standardisation agreements.

In addition, various types of horizontal agreements are regulated by block exemption communiqués: Communiqué No. 2016/5, Communiqué No. 2013/3 or the sector-specific Communiqué No. 2008/3.

Against this background, this chapter will address the above principles in evaluating the various horizontal agreements under Article 4 and Article 5, along with recent and

---

*   Associate, ELIG Gürkaynak Attorneys-at-Law, Istanbul <sinem.ugur@elig.com>.
**   Associate, ELIG Gürkaynak Attorneys-at-Law, Istanbul <aydeniz.baytas@elig.com>.
371   Unless stated otherwise, all references to Article 4 and Article 5 herein refer to Law No. 4054.
372   Agreements between companies under the same economic entity (in accordance with the definition of undertaking in Article 3 of Law No. 4054) are not considered as horizontal agreements, as these companies are not considered as independent competitors but instead as part of an economic whole (see Chapter 2).

landmark cases on the matter. In addition, this chapter will also focus on labour markets considering the increasing significance attributed to them in Turkey as well as in leading antitrust jurisdictions such as the US.[373]

4.1 Cooperation Agreements and their Assessment

The Guidelines on Horizontal Agreements confirm that a case-by-case analysis is necessary in each instance of horizontal cooperation, which depends on the dynamics of the relevant market as well as the characteristics of the parties involved in the horizontal cooperation (mostly, the parties' respective market powers).[374]

In assessing horizontal cooperation agreements, the first step is the determination of whether the cooperation is subject to Article 4, i.e., whether the horizontal agreement leads to restriction of competition by object and/or effect. Pursuant to Communiqué No. 2021/3, agreements between competitors with a combined market share of less than 10% and those between non-competitors whose aggregate market share does not exceed 15% can benefit from the safe harbour, except in cases of hard-core restrictions (such as price-fixing, territory or customer sharing and restriction of supply).[375] The second step involves conducting an exemption assessment, i.e., the determination on whether the horizontal agreement benefits from a block exemption or meets the cumulative conditions for individual exemption under Article 5. If an agreement does not meet the requirements and cannot benefit from the protective cloak of the block exemption, the relevant parties are entitled to make a self-assessment to check whether their agreement fulfils the conditions of the individual exemption, or to apply to the Authority, as set out under Article 5. Thus, if an arrangement cannot benefit from a block exemption, but satisfies the two positive and two negative conditions in Article 5, it can benefit from an individual exemption.

Article 5 allows an individual exemption for agreements and concerted practices that meet the four conditions outlined below:

- The agreement must contribute to improving the production or distribution of goods or to promoting technical or economic progress (efficiency gains).

- The agreement must allow consumers a fair share of the resulting benefit (passing on to consumers).

---

[373]   The Federal Trade Commission published specific guidance for human resources: US Department of Justice, Federal Trade Commission, Antitrust Guidance for Human Resource Professionals (October 2016) <https://www.justice.gov/atr/file/903511/download> (last accessed on 29 March 2021).

[374]   Market power is the ability to profitably maintain prices above competitive levels for a certain period of time or to profitably maintain certain elements such as output, product quality and variety or innovation below competitive levels for a certain period of time. See the Guidelines on Horizontal Agreements, para. 25.

[375]   On 16 March 2021, the Board published Communiqué No. 2021/3, which provides the principles and scope of the *de minimis* standard. The communiqué sets forth market share thresholds which are closely modelled on the Notice on agreements of minor importance which do not appreciably restrict competition under Article 101(1) of the Treaty on the Functioning of the European Union (2014/C 291/01) (*De Minimis* Notice).

- The agreement should not afford the parties the possibility of eliminating competition in respect of a substantial part of the products in question (non-elimination of competition).

- The agreement should not restrict the competition beyond what is strictly necessary to get the aforementioned positive effects (indispensability).

The foregoing is not an alternative test; all conditions must be met cumulatively for the individual exemption to be granted.

Horizontal cooperation agreements may lead to both (i) economic benefits, such as sharing risks, saving costs, increasing investments, pooling know-how, improving quality and range of products and increasing innovation, and (ii) various competition concerns if the agreement serves the purpose of acquiring, protecting or increasing market power and thus leading to negative effects in the market in terms of prices, production amounts, product quality, product variety or innovation. Each type of horizontal agreement may have different outcomes in this context, and cause different effects under different market conditions. Thus, a variety of horizontal cooperation agreements has been discussed separately, below.

4.1.1   Information Exchange[376]

4.1.1.1   Definition and Scope

When two or more competing entities exchange commercially sensitive information with each other, this can affect their decisions regarding competition. Information exchange can be an anti-competitive agreement in and of itself,[377] but also a facilitator of other anti-competitive agreements as it makes it easier to determine whether collusion between competitors is complied with or not. Such information exchange increases the chances of detection as competitors cannot know whether their sales dropped due to competitors' competitive conduct, or a decrease in demand in its absence.[378]

Exchange of information between competitors is among the most common types of horizontal relations in practice. Both direct and indirect information exchange among competitors can lead to competition law concerns. Information may be directly

---

[376]   If the information exchange leads to collusion on future prices and the amount of supply, it would be considered as a cartel and prohibited under Law No. 4054, e.g., *Adıyaman Autogas* (29 March 2018, 18-09/180-85); *Aegean Cement Producers* (n. 282). However, the precedent of the Board suggests that the exchange of competitively sensitive information may be an infringement in and of itself, without being necessarily categorised as a cartel (*Automotive Market* (18 April 2011, 11-24/464-139)). As Chapter 3 has presented a detailed discussion on cartels, this section focuses on other types of horizontal agreements.

[377]   The Board considered the exchange of competitively sensitive information as an infringement in and of itself and decided that sharing information with competitors on pricing strategy reduces the uncertainty regarding competitors' future behaviour and provides a basis for future cooperation (*Syndicated Loans* (n. 44); *12 Banks* (8 March 2013, 13-13/198-100)).

[378]   Turkish Competition Authority, "Rekabet Terimleri Sözlüğü" (Glossary of Competition Definitions), 5th edition, April 2014.

exchanged among undertakings, or indirectly via associations of undertakings such as trade associations, research companies and other third parties (including publicly available platforms)[379] or via the supply or distribution network of undertakings.[380] In *Ambarlı Ro-Ro*, the Board explained the criterion for assessing information exchanges between companies which are both customers/suppliers and competitors of one another.[381] The Board held that to the extent the information exchange was necessary for and limited to the purposes of the customer-supplier relationship, and the parties took the necessary steps to prevent potential anti-competitive effects, such exchange may not infringe Article 4 of Law No. 4054. The Board, however, underlined the risk of price-related information exchanges between competitors. In the relevant case, the Board found the price-related information exchange among the parties went beyond the customer-supplier relationship, on the basis of the communications between these companies seen in evidence.

Information exchange may lead to efficiencies such as helping competitors reduce their inventories, ensure quicker delivery of perishable products to consumers, or lower their costs caused by unstable demand. On the other hand, it may also restrict competition when it enables undertakings to be aware of their competitors' market strategies and may even lead to cartel allegations if the aim of information exchange is fixing prices or quantities. Therefore, the Board takes into account the nature of the information exchanged and whether it leads to coordinated effects in the market, conducting a case-by-case analysis in the information exchange cases.[382]

4.1.1.2 Assessment under Article 4 of Law No. 4054

Pursuant to the Guidelines on Horizontal Agreements, the restrictive effects of information exchange are assessed on the basis of their adverse impact on at least one of the parameters of competition in the market, such as price, output, quality, product variety or innovation.[383]

As noted above, an exchange of information may lead to restriction of competition, in particular in situations where it enables undertakings to be aware of their competitors' market strategies.[384] The competitive analysis of information exchange depends mainly on the structure of the market, such as the degree of concentration, transparency and stability of the market, and the similarity of the undertakings in it, as well as the nature of the information exchanged. These factors are taken into account in the assessment of whether such information exchange may easily enable the competitors to collude.

---

[379]   *Petder* (22 September 2011, 11-48/1215-428). The Board granted negative clearance for information exchange through Oil Industry Association.

[380]   The Guidelines on Horizontal Agreements, para. 40.

[381]   *Ambarlı Ro-Ro* (18 April 2019, 19-16/229-101).

[382]   *International Transporter's Association* (28 January 2010, 10-10/94-42); *ODD* (9 September 2009, 09-41/998-255); OECD, Policy Roundtables, "Information Exchanges Between Competitors under Competition Law", DAF/COMP(2010)37, 11 July 2011 <http://www.oecd.org/competition/cartels/48379006.pdf> (last accessed on 29 March 2021).

[383]   The Guidelines on Horizontal Agreements, para. 19.

[384]   Ibid., para. 43.

Markets' characteristics[385] and in particular the market structure[386] are also considered in assessing whether information exchange leads to restrictive effects or is exempted from Article 4.

Information exchange can facilitate a collusive outcome by increasing transparency in the market, reducing market complexity and asymmetry, and by stabilising the market. In line with the Guidelines on Horizontal Agreements, the Board evaluates the market for (i) transparency; (ii) degree of concentration; (iii) complexity; (iv) stability; (v) similarity of the firms; and also (vii) other factors. For instance, an oligopolistic market with high levels of transparency invokes different competition law concerns than a highly competitive market with low entry barriers.[387]

The Board takes into account the following criteria to analyse information exchanges: whether the information is (i) strategic; (ii) aggregated or individualised; (iii) historical or related to current or future strategies; (iv) frequent or sporadic; (v) public; and (vi) whether the total share of competitors exchanging information amounts to a majority of the market. For example, in *Leasing, Factoring and Financing Companies Union*,[388] concerning an exchange of retrospective data, the Board conducted a rule of reason analysis and decided that (i) exchange of retrospective information such as the data on the turnover reports or accounts receivable reports for the past financial periods would not infringe Article 4, however, (ii) exchange of current information such as the data on the turnover reports or accounts receivable reports for recent financial periods, the number of the existing customers or contracts, would constitute competition law violation. Similarly, in *Diye Danışmanlık*,[389] the Board considered, inter alia, the date, nature and frequency of the exchanged information in its assessment of the anti-competitive nature of the information. A similar assessment could be found in the *Keşan Cement* decision.[390]

---

[385] For example, code-sharing agreements in air transport are allowed to a certain extent due to the characteristics of the market. Banks are capable of exchanging customer credit risk information as long as they adhere to the specifications in Article 73 of the Banking Law No. 5411. The insurance sector was assigned specific competition rules based on the nature of the service offered and the structuring of the sector. The Block Exemption Communiqué No. 2008/3 Concerning Insurance sets the prerequisite conditions for the exemption of certain agreements in the insurance sector, such as pooling insurance-related risk information into databases or exchanging the same information between different players in the insurance market. Moreover, the cement market and recently the energy market are also examined carefully in terms of sharing information (*Akdeniz Elektrik* (20 February 2018, 18-06/101-52); *İzmir Ready-Mixed Concrete* (n. 153); *Aegean Cement Producers* (n. 282).

[386] For example, *Forex* (24 November 2016, 16-41/667-300). The Board launched a preliminary investigation against several banks in order to determine whether traders of competing banks who are responsible for buying and selling foreign currencies exchanged commercially sensitive information in Bloomberg and Reuters chat rooms. Due to the nature of the market, the traders could be each other's competitors and customers at the same time, and thus constantly exchanged information. Although most of the exchanges could be considered as common business practice, the Board identified twenty-four documents that included confidential information on the customers' purchase and sales amounts, as well as traders' positions on certain currencies. The Board decided not to initiate a fully-fledged investigation on the grounds that, despite being commercially sensitive, the information exchange was isolated, sporadic, and unable to restrict competition. The Board further held that the purpose of the information exchange was essentially to increase the profit from a specific customer, and thus it was more of a manipulation than a competition infringement.

[387] *Automotive Market* (n. 376).

[388] *Leasing, Factoring and Financing Companies Union* (15 February 2018, 18-05/79-43).

[389] *Diye Danışmanlık* (12 December 2014, 14-51/900-410). While this decision is annulled by the administrative courts, it still reflects the Board's evaluation criteria regarding the date, nature and frequency of the exchanged information.

[390] *Keşan Cement* (19 December 2019, 19-45/758-327).

In general, exchanges of public information are not expected to constitute an infringement under Article 4 of Law No. 4054.[391] Public information is defined in paragraph 72 of the Guidelines on Horizontal Agreements as information that is equally accessible to all competitors and customers in terms of the cost of access. Some markets such as banking, insurance and advertisement rely greatly on the availability of reliable and accurate data. The data cannot be considered public if the cost of collecting the relevant data that is frequently exchanged among competitors is deterring new players from entering the market. The insurance sector especially differs from other sectors due to its nature. Communiqué No. 2008/3 establishes the conditions for certain agreement categories within the insurance sector to benefit from the block exemption regime; and allows competing insurance companies to share certain calculations, tables and research, as well as to establish co-insurance and co-reinsurance groups under certain conditions. The Board has many precedents where it evaluated the exchange of various data in the insurance sector; however, since Communiqué No. 2008/3 has a specific scope, many cases were subject to general principles that were not covered by Communiqué No. 2008/3.[392]

However, the fact that information is exchanged publicly would not mean that the possibility of a collusive outcome in the market is completely eliminated, as noted in paragraph 74 of the Guidelines on Horizontal Agreements. Accordingly, in *Petroleum Industry Association*,[393] the Board decided that circulating price lists on a monthly basis among petroleum industry members would likely raise competition law concerns as it would greatly increase the price transparency in the market, whereas in *Turkey Construction Industrialists Employers Union*,[394] the Board decided not to grant an individual exemption to a survey as the Board found no causal link between the alleged cost efficiency and sharing aggregated input prices, and concluded that the information exchange would facilitate coordination among Union members.

4.1.1.3 Assessment Under Article 5 of Law No. 4054

As noted above, information exchange may also lead to various efficiencies, e.g., by eliminating information asymmetries between the parties. Certain information exchanges between market players may offer them reliable benchmarks against which they can compare their productivity.

Sharing information may also help undertakings to better micromanage their inventories, ensure quicker delivery of products to consumers, or lower their perception of market

---

[391] For example, *IQVIA Health* (12 June 2018, 18-19/330-164). The Board decided that exchanging information regarding the prices of pharmaceuticals is not strategic, given that IQVIA Health calculates the prices in accordance with the profit margins determined by the Council of Ministers. Thus, the Board did not launch a fully-fledged investigation since the information was publicly available. Similarly, in *EBS Automotive* (n. 391), EBS Automotive shared new and second-hand vehicle sales data with the market and third parties through its website. The Board decided that the data to be shared was already public and easily accessible from public records and thus, granted negative clearance to EBS Automotive.

[392] *Insurance Sector* (23 January 2020, 20-06/61-33); *Neova* (30 May 2019, 19-20/290-125); *Bereket* (21 February 2019, 19-08/100-40); *Traffic Insurance* (27 September 2017, 17-30/500-219).

[393] *Petroleum Industry Association* (21 November 2013, 13-64/904-384).

[394] *Turkey Construction Industrialists Employers Union* (18 January 2018, 18-03/31-18).

volatility. This may result in direct benefits for consumers, who would, in turn, benefit from reduced search costs, increased choice and better overall quality of service.

These potential efficiencies depend on the nature of the information and market conditions.[395] For instance, aggregated and historical data are more likely to be considered pro-competitive relative to individualised and future data, in particular those related to prices and trade strategies.[396] In *Philips/Group SEB*, the Board indicated that (i) the file alleged to be evidence of information exchange contained retrospective information which does not reflect continuously collected data that is spread over a large time period; (ii) competitors following each other's actions and taking position accordingly is an ordinary event; (iii) collecting information from the market through their own means is not deemed as anti-competitive conduct; (iv) no information, document and communication towards information exchange were found at the investigated undertakings.[397] Therefore, the Board decided not to initiate a fully-fledged investigation since it was concluded that the undertakings did not breach competition law via an exchange of competition sensitive information.

Furthermore, the Board has consistently distinguished current information from historical data.[398] The Guidelines on Horizontal Agreements confirm that historical data is less likely to restrict competition compared to current or future data and that the older the data is, the less likely it is for competitors to detect deviations and retaliate by relying on it. Under Communiqué No. 2021/3, information exchange related to future prices, future production or sales amounts are considered as hard-core restrictions, and these kinds of information exchanges are not within the scope of Communiqué No. 2021/3; accordingly, they do not benefit from the "*de minimis*" principle. Similarly, the Board[399] takes the approach that information exchange related to future prices restricts competition by object without considering its effect on the market and is a per se violation of competition law. In the same vein, in *White Meat Producers*, the Board held that nine poultry producers violated Article 4 by exchanging information on future prices and by supply restrictions.[400] The Board considered the fact that competitors could calculate each other's production amounts and unit costs by means of commercially sensitive information they exchanged, such as broiler chicken production and slaughtering numbers, and the fact that they had access to current and future price lists. Accordingly, the Board concluded that there was no remaining information that could create competitive uncertainty among the relevant companies. The Board ultimately decided that this conduct infringed Article 4 of Law No. 4054. That said, there is no predetermined threshold for how old the data must be in order not to create any risk of distorting competition.

---

[395] Examples of such efficiencies are found in the banking and insurance sectors, where there are frequent exchanges of information about consumer risks and their defaults. For example, the Block Exemption Communiqué No. 2008/3 Concerning the Insurance Sector also allows insurance-related databases pooling risk information of multiple insurers. These databases are exempted from the general rule even though they may contain strategic and valuable information considering that they contribute to the public welfare.

[396] *EBS Automotive* (n. 391); *Automotive Distributors Association* (15 April 2004, 04-26/287-65).

[397] *Philips/Group SEB* (13 February 2020, 20-10/109-65).

[398] *Automotive Distributors Association* (n. 396); *Turkey Construction Industrialists Employers Union* (n. 394); *EBS Automotive* (n. 391).

[399] *Automotive Market* (n. 376).

[400] *White Meat* (13 March 2019, 19-12/155-70).

Below are some examples of the Board's decisions that show that some information exchanges may generate efficiency gains and, therefore, do not fall within the scope of Article 4 of Law No. 4054.

In *Migros/Boyner/BNR*, the Board granted an individual exemption to an agreement on information exchange on the grounds that this information exchange would decrease the operational costs of the parties, increase the quality of their services, and lead to a more comprehensive understanding of the consumer needs, which could make better consumer campaigns possible.[401]

In *Başkent Gaz*, the Board granted negative clearance to Başkent Gaz since the concerned information exchanged was a list that contained objective data related to the service quality of the undertakings active in the natural gas sector, which would eliminate the problem of information asymmetry between customers and undertakings active in the sector, and thereby lead to pro-competitive effects in the market.[402]

In *Turkey Port Managers Association*, the Board (i) analysed whether the subject information had anti-competitive purpose; (ii) granted negative clearance to the vessel acceptance and personnel numbers which were publicly available; and (iii) determined that individualised sales amounts (the handling quantities per load) were strategic, would create coordination risks among competitors and potentially help to control deviations from a possible agreement on quantity or customer sharing.[403] However, by taking into consideration, among others, (i) the efficiencies, including eliminating idle capacity, decreasing costs, contribution to incentives for service quality improvement; (ii) the increase of consumers' bargaining power; (iii) the fact that the data will be published quarterly and yearly, the Board granted an individual exemption for the publication of the relevant data by the Port Managers Association for five years.

4.1.2 R&D Agreements and Communiqué No. 2016/5

4.1.2.1 Definition and Scope

There are various scopes of R&D agreements, such as (i) outsourcing R&D activities to third parties; (ii) joint improvement of existing technologies; and (iii) cooperation concerning the research, development and marketing of completely new products.[404] R&D agreements may also take different forms, for instance like signing a cooperation agreement or establishing an undertaking under joint control.[405] R&D agreements aim to bring to life those projects which undertakings could not carry out alone due to issues

---

[401] *Hopi/Migros* (3 May 2018, 18-13/238-111).
[402] *Başkent Gaz* (5 July 2018, 18-22/374-182).
[403] *Turkey Port Managers Association* (14 November 2019, 19-40/655-280).
[404] The Guidelines on Horizontal Agreements, para. 91.
[405] Ibid.

of finance, technology and risks, etc.[406] They are sometimes conducted between undertakings to share the cost of R&D, in the narrow market of the product which will be produced as a result.[407]

4.1.2.2 Communiqué No. 2016/5

Pursuant to the definition of R&D agreements under Article 4 of Communiqué No. 2016/5, agreements for the purposes of paid R&D of products, or technologies subject to the agreement and joint exploitation from the results of the R&D, are deemed to be R&D agreements. On the other hand, agreements that have another basic goal such as joint production, resale and transfer of intellectual rights, and which involve merely subsidiary provisions concerning joint R&D, fall outside the scope of the block exemption provided by Communiqué No. 2016/5.[408]

R&D agreements between competitors can benefit from the block exemption under Communiqué No. 2016/5, provided that the combined market share of the parties does not exceed the market share thresholds specified in Communiqué No. 2016/5 and the other conditions are fulfilled. Accordingly, if the agreement includes joint exploitation from the results and the parties to the R&D agreement are competitors in the relevant market, Communiqué No. 2016/5 could be applicable so long as the parties' aggregate market share does not exceed 40% in the relevant market.[409] In the case of paid-for R&D, where the same party is the financing party in multiple R&D agreements regarding the same contract products or contract technologies, the above market share threshold of 40% is sought for the combined market share of the financing party and all the relevant parties. However, the R&D agreements including an exclusive distribution mechanism are an exception to the above and require a market share threshold of 20%. This threshold narrows down the scope of Communiqué No. 2016/5 substantially since the combined market share of the parties can easily reach such a low threshold.

Additionally, Article 7 provides the general conditions of exemption and the market share threshold condition is one of the said general conditions. Article 7(3) of Communiqué No. 2016/5 clearly states that R&D agreements between the undertakings that are not competitors in the relevant market are not subject to the threshold conditions specified in Article 7.

As per Article 8 of Communiqué No. 2016/5, the block exemption is applicable during the term of the agreement if the agreement solely relates to R&D; and where the results are jointly exploited, the exemption continues to apply for seven years after the contract products or contract technologies are first put on the Turkish market. Since the period of benefit is

---

[406]   A. Ö. Uzun, *Stratejik İşbirlikleri ve Rekabet* (Strategic Alliances and Competition), (Ankara: Rekabet Kurumu), p. 55.

[407]   Ibid.

[408]   Article 2 of Communiqué No. 2016/5.

[409]   *Association of Steel Guard Rails and Road Safety Systems* (22 November 2018, 18-44/702-344). The Board decided that although the cooperation, which concerned the product design within joint product development, their documentation and use of their results, was considered as an R&D agreement, the cooperation was not within the scope of Communiqué No. 2016/5 since the parties' aggregate market share which was calculated based on agreement price exceeded 40%.

crucial and the R&D activities require a significant investment cost, the parties enjoy the results of their investment in the long term. In this respect, the revision of the exemption period as seven years can be evaluated as a positive outcome and incentive for R&D activities.

Communiqué No. 2016/5 divides the restrictions falling outside the scope of the exemption into two:

- "hard-core restrictions" (which would result in the agreement not benefiting from the block exemption, as a whole)

- "excluded restrictions" (only the problematic parts of the agreement would be excluded from the scope of the block exemption). Unlike hard-core restrictions, if an R&D agreement includes excluded restrictions, the block exemption may still be applied to the rest of the agreement. Excluded restrictions include:

  a) restricting the right to challenge the validity of the related intellectual property rights after completion of the R&D;

  b) restricting the right to grant licences to third parties to manufacture the contract products or to apply the contract technologies (where the agreement does not provide for the joint exploitation of R&D results, or such exploitation does not, in fact, take place).

4.1.2.3 Determination of Relevant Markets

The main point in defining the relevant market is to identify those products, technologies or R&D efforts that will comprise the main competitive pressure on the parties.[410] This analysis may require the examination of both the existing markets and the impact of the agreement on innovation.[411]

In terms of existing products, if the R&D efforts are aimed at significantly changing the existing products or creating new products to replace the existing ones, it may be concluded that the old and the potentially new products do not belong to the same relevant market, since it may be impossible to fully substitute these with other products already in the market or substitute them in the short term.[412] If the R&D concerns an important component of a final product, not only the market for that component, but also the market for the final product may be taken into consideration in the assessment.[413] In terms of existing technology markets, technology markets consist of the intellectual property rights that are licensed, and other technologies which may be used as close substitutes thereof.[414]

R&D cooperation may affect competition not only in existing markets but also in innovation and new product markets.[415] Where the R&D agreement only aims at improving or refining existing products, that market will include products directly concerned by

---

[410] The Guidelines on Horizontal Agreements, para. 92.
[411] Ibid.
[412] Ibid., para. 94.
[413] Ibid., para. 95.
[414] Ibid., para. 96.
[415] Ibid., para. 99.

the R&D effort.[416] If the R&D cooperation aims at developing a new product to replace existing products, it is again possible to calculate market shares on the basis of the sales value of the existing products.[417]

4.1.2.4 Assessment Under Article 4 of Law No. 4054

R&D cooperation can restrict competition in various ways. First, it may reduce or slow down innovation, leading to fewer or lower quality products entering the market.[418] Secondly, R&D cooperation may lead to increasing prices, by significantly reducing competition between the undertakings which are not parties to the agreement in product or technology markets, or by making coordination of competitive conduct in those markets possible.[419]

R&D cooperation between non-competing undertakings would not generally give rise to restrictive effects on competition.[420] However, if there is exclusive exploitation of the results obtained from the cooperation and if one of the parties to the agreement holds significant market power related to a key technology, then R&D cooperation between non-competing undertakings may result in market foreclosure.[421]

4.1.2.5 Assessment Under Article 5 of Law No. 4054

Many R&D agreements can provide efficiency gains by ensuring more rapid development and marketing of new or improved products and technologies.[422] They can also ensure further innovation by allowing wider dissemination of knowledge and lead to cost reductions.[423]

Efficiency gains attained must be passed on to consumers in a way that compensates for the restrictive effects of the R&D agreement on competition. If competition is eliminated in a significant part of the relevant product or technology markets, and if the restrictions under the agreement go beyond what is necessary to achieve the efficiency gains, the agreement may not benefit from exemption under Article 5 of Law No. 4054.

The Board's below decisions on R&D agreements might provide guidance for companies on enforcement.

In the *Association of Steel Guard Rails and Road Safety Systems*, the Board evaluated the horizontal cooperation agreements executed among the members of the Association of Steel Guard Rails and Road Safety Systems within the scope of Article 4 of Law No. 4054 due to the coordination risks.[424] The Board decided that the cooperation, which

---

[416]   Ibid., para. 103.
[417]   Ibid.
[418]   Ibid., para. 106.
[419]   Ibid.
[420]   Ibid., para. 109.
[421]   Ibid.
[422]   Ibid., para. 121.
[423]   Ibid.
[424]   *Association of Steel Guard Rails and Road Safety Systems* (n. 409).

concerned (i) the product design within the joint product development; (ii) their documentation; and (iii) use of their results, constituted an R&D agreement.[425] In the assessment of the parties' market shares, the Board considered that the market solely consisted of tenders, there was a high level of cooperation due to joint participation in the tenders in the form of joint ventures/business partnerships, and the cooperation among competitors fell outside the scope of Communiqué No. 2016/5 since the parties' aggregate market share, which was calculated based on agreement price, exceeded 40%.[426]

Further to its assessments, the Board ruled that cooperation on R&D would lead to product innovation and cost reduction resulting in consumer benefit, and would not eliminate competition in a significant part of the relevant market, as the agreements would not prevent undertakings from acting independently, especially in terms of price-setting and tender participation processes.

The Board further noted that the agreements did not include any non-compete or exclusivity clauses. The Board also held that horizontal cooperation agreements allow undertakings to perform activities that would cost considerably more, if carried out individually by the undertakings due to limited technical means, and concluded that the said agreements would not restrict competition more than necessary. In light of the foregoing, the Board granted these agreements an individual exemption under Article 5 of Law No. 4054.

In *Tofaş – Fiat – Peugeot*,[427] the Board assessed the exemption request for the "Product Development and Manufacturing Agreement" between Tofaş Türk Otomobil Fabrikası A.Ş. ("Tofaş"), Fiat Auto S.p.A. ("Fiat") and Peugeot Citroën Automobiles SA ("Peugeot"). The relevant product market was defined as light commercial vehicles market. The Board stated that the agreement consisted of two stages, consisting of the development and the production of a vehicle, since the aim of the cooperation between the undertakings was to develop a light commercial vehicle and produce it at Tofaş facilities for seven years. The vehicles produced at Tofaş facilities were sold to Fiat and Peugeot with transfer prices, and the undertakings distributed the vehicles independently from each other.

The Board defined the agreement as a "horizontal cooperation agreement" since the parties to the agreement–Fiat, Peugeot and Tofaş – are in competition with each other in several product markets. The Board first assessed the agreement under Article 4 of Law No. 4054 and stated that (i) in terms of R&D activity, there was no exclusivity or provision on price or supply restriction, and thus there was no violation of Article 4 of Law No. 4054; (ii) in terms of the joint production as a result of R&D activity, which is the second stage of the agreement, the market share and partnership of the cost should be assessed to see whether the joint production restricts competition. In the particular case, each undertaking determined its own sales price of the vehicles, and thus there was no partnership between the parties in terms of distribution and marketing and the profit share; and the market share of the parties to the agreement was sufficient to affect the

---

[425] Ibid., para. 395.
[426] Ibid.
[427] *Tofaş – Fiat – Peugeot* (8 July 2005, 05-44/628-161).

competition in the market as a result of the joint production. Consequently, the Board decided that the agreement was within the scope of Article 4 of Law No. 4054. In this regard, the Board evaluated the agreement under Communiqué No. 2003/2 and decided that the agreement fulfilled the conditions stated thereunder, save for the duration of the agreement, which was seven years. The Board decided that the duration of seven years was reasonable for the production of light commercial vehicles, although normally there should be an individual exemption analysis if the conditions of block exemptions are not satisfied.

Consequently, the Board decided that (i) the agreement can benefit from the block exemption for five years following the date of the first product launch; and (ii) in the case that the parties do not terminate the agreement after five years, the agreement will be effective, and the parties should apply for an individual exemption for the duration of the the joint production.

Indeed, the parties applied for an individual exemption after the expiration of the five-year period, and the Board granted it.[428] As a result, the agreement was in force for seven years due to the fact that it benefited from both the block exemption and the individual exemption.

4.1.3 Production Agreements and Communiqué No. 2013/3

4.1.3.1 Definition and Scope

Production agreements may allow the parties to achieve economies of scale or scope that they could not achieve individually.[429] Undertakings can engage in joint production by way of a joint venture company under their shared control, operating one or more production facilities,[430] or via looser forms of cooperation such as toll manufacturing agreements[431] where one party (the contractor) entrusts to another party (subcontractor) the production of a good.[432]

---

[428] *Tofaş – Fiat – Peugeot* (31 January 2013, 13-08/93-54).
[429] The Guidelines on Horizontal Agreements, para. 38; *Association of Steel Guard Rails and Road Safety Systems* (n. 409), para. 396.
[430] Transactions aimed at the establishment of a joint venture which will permanently perform all functions of an independent economic entity are primarily addressed under Law No. 4054 in Article 7 on Mergers and Acquisitions and Communiqué No. 2010/4 on Mergers and Acquisitions Subject to the Approval of the Turkish Competition Board. However, Articles 4 and 5 are still applicable if the establishment of the joint venture restricts competition by object and/or effect.
[431] In *Sanofi* (31 May 2018, 18-17/299-149), the Board examined a toll manufacturing agreement between Sanofi and Abdi İbrahim concerning the manufacturing of certain insulin products by Abdi İbrahim for Sanofi. Similarly, in *Novo Nordisk* (28 July 2020, 20-36/493-218), the Board assessed a production agreement in which Novo Nordisk provided the necessary know-how, production equipment and devices, and raw materials to Abdi İbrahim for the production of the medicines by Abdi İbrahim. Similarly, in its *Automobile Project* (26 September 2018, 18-34/566-279), the Board evaluated a joint production agreement, which is also explained in this chapter.
[432] The Guidelines on Horizontal Agreements, para. 129.

For instance, in *ArcelorMittal*,[433] the Board evaluated the individual exemption request regarding the agreement concerning the production of welding plates used in the automobile industry. The Board decided that as the main purpose of the agreement is the joint production of welding plates, the transfer of certain know-how and technology being solely an ancillary element of the agreement, the agreement can be considered as a production agreement.[434]

4.1.3.2 Communiqué No. 2013/3

Communiqué No. 2013/3 establishes the conditions for granting block exemptions to specialisation agreements between undertakings and extends this exemption to licensing or intellectual property transfer agreements that are directly related to, or necessary for, the functioning of the exempted specialisation agreements.

Unilateral specialisation agreements are agreements between two parties that operate in the same product market, wherein one party agrees to cease production of certain products fully or partly, or to purchase them from the other party, and the other party agrees to produce and supply the products in question. In order to benefit from the block exemption provided by Communiqué No. 2013/3, the combined market share of the parties must be below 25%.

In any event, unilateral or reciprocal specialisation agreements, as well as joint production agreements that include certain commercialisation activities such as joint distribution, are covered by Communiqué No. 2013/3, provided that the combined market share of the parties in the relevant market or markets does not exceed 25% and that the other conditions listed in Communiqué No. 2013/3 are fulfilled. However, if the combined market share of the parties exceeds 25%, the restrictive effects on competition would have to be analysed, since the agreement would not be covered by Communiqué No. 2013/3.

The exemption also extends to the licensing or intellectual property transfer agreements that are directly related to or necessary for the functioning of the relevant specialisation agreements. Furthermore, the exemption remains in effect even where the relevant agreements contain exclusive sale or exclusive purchase obligations, or when the parties also agree upon the joint distribution of the relevant products. On the other hand, the presence of the following elements causes the relevant agreements to fall outside the coverage of the block exemption according to Article 6 of Communiqué No. 2013/3: (i) maintenance of the sale price to third parties, with the exception of direct purchasers, in the case of joint production agreements; (ii) any sharing of territories or customers; or (iii) the limitation of production or sale amounts. That being said, mutual or one-sided specialisation agreements may contain provisions regarding the relevant product volume, and for joint production agreements to set the production capacity or volume, or sale targets in the case of joint distribution.

---

[433] *ArcelorMittal* (21 January 2016, 16-03/54-19).
[434] Ibid., para. 66.

4.1.3.3 Determination of Relevant Markets

It is necessary first to define the relevant market to which the products manufactured under the production agreement belong.[435] The spillover markets will be taken into consideration in the assessment to be conducted as well, if the markets are interdependent and the parties are in a strong position in the spillover markets.[436]

4.1.3.4 Assessment Under Article 4 of Law No. 4054

Production agreements may lead to higher prices or reduced output, product quality, product variety or innovation.[437] Production agreements may also lead to the foreclosure of related markets to other undertakings.[438] For instance, by gaining enough market power, parties engaging in joint production activities in the upstream market may be able to raise the price of a key component for a downstream market, and thus they could use the joint production activity to raise the costs of their downstream competitors and, ultimately, force these competitors off the market.[439]

Generally, agreements that involve price-fixing, limiting output or allocating markets or customers restrict competition by object.[440] However, in the context of production agreements, this does not apply under the following circumstances:

– where the parties agree on the elements directly concerned by the production agreement (for example, the capacity and production volume of a joint venture or the percentage of products to be outsourced to third parties), provided that the other parameters of competition are not eliminated;

– where a production agreement that provides for the joint distribution of the products manufactured as a result of the cooperation also jointly determines the sales prices for the products manufactured, provided that this is absolutely necessary for the parties to come to an agreement concerning joint production.

In these two cases, an assessment is required as to whether the agreement gives rise to restrictive effects on competition within the scope of Article 4 of Law No. 4054.[441]

In the Board's *Automobile Project*,[442] the Board examined whether the transaction concerning designing, developing, producing, and marketing electrically powered and new generation cars, along with the production of their spare parts and the provision of maintenance and repair services within the scope of "Turkey's Automobile" project, violates Article 4 of Law No. 4054. The Board first noted that the parties agree on matters directly concerning production agreements (such as the capacity and production

---

[435] The Guidelines on Horizontal Agreements, para. 134.
[436] Ibid., para. 135.
[437] Ibid., para. 136.
[438] Ibid., para. 138.
[439] Ibid.
[440] Ibid., para. 139.
[441] Ibid., para. 140.
[442] *Automobile Project* (n. 431).

volumes of a joint venture or the percentageof products that would be outsourced to third parties, etc.) and that the agreements are within the scope of Article 5(1) of Communiqué No. 2013/3. The Board considered that the company would determine (i) the number of cars which will be produced and sold; (ii) the sales regions; and (iii) price. The Board referred to paragraph 139 of the Guidelines on Horizontal Agreements and stated that determination of capacity, production volume and sales price in joint production agreements cannot restrict competition by object. In light of this principle, the Board decided that the project did not have the object of restricting competition, despite the fact that the JV's activity would not be limited to the production of electrically powered cars.

If a new market is created as a result of production agreements, the agreement is not likely to give rise to restrictive effects on competition.[443] Also, in the Board's *Automobile Project* decision, the Board decided that joint production agreement might not restrict competition by effect since the parties can produce products which they cannot achieve individually due to objective reasons (such as high investment amount, developed distribution network, technical expertise requirements).[444] Consequently, the Board granted negative clearance for the agreements.

On the other hand, a production agreement can lead to a collusive outcome in the market or foreclose the market to competitors if it increases the undertakings' market power or their commonality of costs, or if it involves the exchange of competitively sensitive information.[445] In terms of market power and exchange of information, when the Board assessed a production agreement between Akçansa and Saros, in *Keşan Cement*, where the Board did not launch a fully-fledged investigation,[446] the Board primarily examined the market powers of the parties. The Board decided, by taking into account the existence of competitors, surplus capacity and homogeneous nature of the products, that the agreement would not change the specific structure of the market although the parties' total market share exceeds 25%.[447] Then, the Board examined the information exchange and concluded that there was no need to share the strategic information in the case considering the nature of the production agreement.[448]

Additionally, in terms of commonality of costs, in the Board's *Automobile Project*, the Board decided that since the parties did not produce a product which they used for their input, the production agreement did not lead to a commonality of costs.[449]

4.1.3.5 Assessment Under Article 5 of Law No. 4054

Production agreements can provide efficiency gains such as cost savings or improvement in production technologies.[450] By producing together, undertakings can save costs by avoiding cost duplication. If, as a result of the cooperation, marginal costs decrease in line with the

---

443   The Guidelines on Horizontal Agreements, para. 143.
444   *Automobile Project* (n. 431).
445   The Guidelines on Horizontal Agreements, para. 145.
446   *Keşan Cement* (n. 390).
447   Ibid., para. 60.
448   Ibid., para. 63.
449   *Automobile Project* (n. 431), para. 33.
450   The Guidelines on Horizontal Agreements, para. 162.

increase in the output, that is to say, if economies of scale are utilised, then the production costs of the undertakings would also decline. Joint production can also help undertakings to improve product quality if they put together their complementary skills and know-how. Cooperation can also enable an increase in product variety, which the undertakings could not have financed or achieved otherwise. If joint production allows an increase in product variety, it can also provide cost savings by means of economies of scope.

In *Novo Nordisk*, the Board assessed the exemption request for the "Toll Manufacturing Agreements" between Novo Nordisk Sağlık Ürünleri Tic. Ltd. Şti. ("Novo Nordisk") and Abdi İbrahim İlaç San. ve Tic. A.Ş. ("Abdi İbrahim").[451] The agreement concerned the transfer of know-how from Novo Nordisk to Abdi İbrahim to produce medical products. Abdi İbrahim was a competitor of Novo Nordisk in terms of distribution. The Board stated that the agreement contained provisions to restrict competition.

The Board assessed the agreement under Communiqué No. 2013/3 and evaluated Novo Nordisk's products turnover in insulin and Novo Nordisk's market share in ATC-3. As Novo Nordisk's market share exceeds 25%, it was decided that the agreement cannot benefit from the block exemption. In its subsequent assessment for individual exemption, the Board considered that the production agreement improved both production and distribution of the product and promoted economic and technical progress. The Board also decided that the production agreement allowed consumers to access low-cost products, and the agreement was also expected to give a fair share of the resulting benefit to consumers. Accordingly, the Board granted an individual exemption for the said agreement.

In *Kamrusepa*, the Board assessed the exemption request for the "Distribution Agreement" between Kamrusepa-Samyoung Nükleer Ürünler Medikal Sanayi ve Ticaret A.Ş. ("Kamrusepa-Samyoung") and Up Nükleer Medikal Danışmanlık İnşaat Turizm Eğitim Sağlık Tic. İthalat İhracat Ltd. Şti. ("Up") and IBA Molecular Turkey İlaç Sanayi ve Ticaret Ltd. Şti ("IBA"), which were undertakings active in the same market.[452] In this agreement, IBA is an exclusive distributor of Kamrusepa-Samyoung's products and non-exclusive supplier of raw materials; and undertakes not to sell or distribute competitor products. Thus, the Board considered that the agreement was a unilateral specialisation agreement. The Board then stated that as the combined market share of the parties does not exceed 25%, the agreement can benefit from Communiqué No. 2013/3.

In *Steel Plate*, the Board assessed the exemption request for the "Consensus Agreement" concerning the production of steel plates between undertakings that are competitors to each other. As the agreement contained transfer of know-how, the Board discussed which block exemption communiqués would be applicable in the case.[453] The Board decided that (i) know-how transfer was not the main aim of the agreement; (ii) the main aim of the agreement was joint production of steel plates in Turkey; (iii) know-how transfer was only necessary for the production. Thus, the Board stated

451   *Novo Nordisk* (n. 431).
452   *Kamrusepa* (1 June 2016, 16-19/312-141).
453   *ArcelorMittal* (n. 433).

that the agreement was a joint production agreement and decided that the agreement could not benefit from Communiqué No. 2013/3 since the market shares of the parties exceeded 25%.

4.1.4 Joint Purchasing Agreements

4.1.4.1 Definition and Scope

Joint purchasing can be carried out by a company controlled jointly by more than one undertaking, by a company in which many other undertakings hold non-controlling stakes, by a contractual arrangement or by looser forms of cooperation.[454] Joint purchasing arrangements aim at the creation of buying power, thereby usually ensuring lower prices or better quality products or services for consumers.[455] However, buying power may, under certain circumstances, also give rise to competition problems.[456]

Joint purchasing agreements are generally observed in the form of associations of undertakings formed by a group of retailers for the joint purchasing of products.[457]

4.1.4.2 Determination of Relevant Markets

There are two markets that might be affected by a joint purchasing agreement.[458] One of them is the purchasing market that is directly relevant to the joint purchasing agreement.[459] The other one is the selling market, which is the downstream market(s) where the parties are active as sellers.[460]

The definition of relevant purchasing markets is based generally on the concept of substitutability.[461] The only difference between the definition of purchasing markets and the definition of selling markets is that substitutability has to be defined from the point of supply instead of demand.[462]

4.1.4.3 Assessment Under Article 4 of Law No. 4054

Guidelines on Horizontal Agreements set out the following possible competition law concerns that might arise from a joint purchasing agreement:

- Joint purchasing agreements may lead to restrictive effects on competition in the purchasing and/or downstream selling market or markets, such as increased

---

[454] The Guidelines on Horizontal Agreements, para. 171.
[455] Ibid.
[456] Ibid.
[457] Ibid., para. 173.
[458] Ibid., para. 174.
[459] Ibid.
[460] Ibid.
[461] Ibid., para. 175.
[462] Ibid.

prices, reduced output, product quality or variety, or innovation, market allocation, or anti-competitive foreclosure of other possible purchasers.[463]

–   If downstream competitors purchase a significant part of their products together,
    their incentives for price competition in the selling market or markets may be
    considerably reduced. If the parties have a significant degree of market power
    (which does not necessarily amount to dominance) in the selling market or
    markets, the lower purchase prices achieved by the joint purchasing arrangement
    are likely not to be passed on to consumers.[464]

–   If the parties have a significant degree of market power in the purchasing market
    (buying power), there is a risk that they may force suppliers to reduce the range
    or quality of products they produce, which may bring about restrictive effects
    on competition such as quality reductions, lessening of innovation efforts, or
    ultimately suboptimal supply.[465]

–   The buying power of the parties to the joint purchasing arrangement could be
    used to foreclose competing purchasers by limiting their access to efficient
    suppliers. This is most likely if there are a limited number of suppliers and
    there are barriers to entry on the supply side of the upstream market.[466]

4.1.4.4 Assessment Under Article 5 of Law No. 4054

Joint purchasing arrangements can give rise to significant efficiency gains. In particular,
economies of scale may be realised by ensuring savings in cost items by various means
such as lower purchase prices or reducing transaction, transportation and storage costs.[467]
Moreover, joint purchasing arrangements may give rise to qualitative efficiency gains by
leading suppliers to innovate and introduce new or improved products in the markets.[468]

On the other hand, if the combined market share of the parties does not exceed 15% on
both the purchasing and the selling markets, it is likely that the conditions of Article 5
of Law No. 4054 are fulfilled.[469] In other words, it is unlikely that market power exists
if the combined market share of the parties to the joint purchasing arrangement does not
exceed 15% in the purchasing markets and 15% in the selling markets.[470]

In *Ceramic*,[471] the Board assessed whether the agreement concluded between members
of the Eskişehir Bilecik Kütahya Ceramics Business Cluster Association to purchase
certain raw materials from suppliers can benefit from the exemption. The members of
the association were able to negotiate with the supplier and determine the buying price
independently from each other.[472]

---

[463]   Ibid., para. 177.
[464]   Ibid., para. 178.
[465]   Ibid., para. 179.
[466]   Ibid., para. 180.
[467]   Ibid., para. 194.
[468]   Ibid.
[469]   Ibid., para. 185.
[470]   Ibid.
[471]   *Ceramic* (13 March 2013, 13-14/201-103).
[472]   Ibid., para. 8.

The Board defined the purchasing market as "zircon, kaolin, rheotane and medium raw materials markets" and the selling market as "ceramic coating materials" and "ceramic sanitary ware".[473] The Board defined the relevant agreement as a joint purchasing agreement since there will be joint action between member undertakings.[474] In the assessment under Article 4, the Board decided that (i) there is no cartel in the case since the agreement does not determine buying price, and each member conducts their own negotiations with the supplier;[475] (ii) the agreement might restrict competition by effect by considering the high market power of the undertakings in the selling market, the concentration of cooperation in the sector, the nature of the ceramic market, as well as the previous competition law analysis on the ceramic market.[476]

Thus, the Board determined that the horizontal cooperation agreement falls within the scope of Article 4, necessitating an individual exemption assessment. In the assessment of Article 5 of Law No. 4054, the Board considered that (i) the agreement will ensure the importation of kaolin material, which is a vital raw material for Turkey; (ii) the cost advantage that the undertakings benefit as a result of the joint purchasing agreement would cause competitive pressure on the powerful competitors in the sector, which are not parties to the joint purchasing agreement. Accordingly, the Board granted an individual exemption to the joint purchasing agreement and decided to monitor the relevant market in case the parties' market power within the joint purchasing agreement increases, which then could restrict competition.[477]

In the *Fayda Mağazacılık* case, Fayda A.Ş. was established as a joint venture in order to provide products to the local retailers that are its shareholders.[478] Thus, the Board considered this joint venture as a joint purchasing agreement and decided that Fayda A.Ş. is not an independent economic entity. This meant that the Board examined Fayda A.Ş. as a horizontal cooperation agreement under Article 4 of Law No. 4054. The agreement did not impose responsibility regarding the amount of purchasing products or the placement of the products in markets but recommended sales prices.[479] The Board decided that the relevant agreement could increase the competition of local retailers and ensure buying power against the producers, and that local retailers might be able to compete against supermarkets through this agreement. Thus, the Board decided that the Fayda A.Ş. horizontal cooperation agreement could change the power balance in the upstream market on behalf of retailers.

The Board then examined the agreement under Article 5 of Law No. 4054 and decided that the agreement (i) could lead to cost savings; (ii) did not adversely affect the downstream market; and (iii) did not restrict competition in the supply market. As a result, the Board granted the agreement an individual exemption for three years since the shareholders of Fayda A.Ş. have high market potential, and the agreement might restrict competition in the future.

---

[473]   Ibid., paras. 20–21.
[474]   Ibid., para. 25.
[475]   Ibid., para. 32.
[476]   Ibid., para. 60.
[477]   Ibid., para. 89.
[478]   *Fayda Mağazacılık* (11 November 2009, 09-54/1291-325).
[479]   Ibid., para. 570.

In *Goodyear*, the Board examined Premio Franchise Agreement, which aimed to establish a network of independent service providers that would operate under uniform quality standards (Premio).[480] Apart from the vertical relationship between the producers and the distributors under the agreement, there was also a vertical relationship between the undertakings, which purchased certain branded products under the agreement.[481] Thus, the Board decided that the agreement included a joint purchasing arrangement since it was mandatory to purchase certain products for the undertakings within the agreement, and this could provide financial benefit through bargaining power as a result of the agreement. Consequently, the Board granted an individual exemption to the agreement for three years.

4.1.5 Commercialisation Agreements

4.1.5.1 Definition and Scope

Commercialisation agreements may involve cooperation between competitors with regard to the sales, distribution or promotion of substitute products.[482] Agreements of this type can take widely varying forms, depending on the commercialisation functions covered by the cooperation. Therefore, such agreements may lead to a joint determination of all commercial aspects related to the sale of the product, including the price, and may also take a more limited form, in which the agreement would only concern/cover a specific commercialisation function, such as distribution, after-sales services, or advertising.

4.1.5.2 Determination of Relevant Markets

Since a commercialisation agreement in one market may also affect the competitive behaviour of the undertakings in a neighbouring market with close ties to the relevant market, any such neighbouring markets must also be defined.[483] The neighbouring market in question may be horizontally or vertically related to the market where the cooperation takes place.

4.1.5.3 Assessment Under Article 4 of Law No. 4054

Commercialisation agreements are capable of leading to restrictions on competition in several different ways. For instance, commercialisation agreements may lead to price-fixing or cause supply restriction through the determination of production volumes, or result in the allocation of markets or customers. Moreover, commercialisation agreements could also result in collusive outcomes by leading to an exchange of competitively sensitive information related to subjects falling within or outside the scope of the cooperation, as well as by leading to a commonality of costs.[484]

---

[480] *Goodyear* (25 July 2007, 07-61/716-248).
[481] Ibid., para. 340.
[482] The Guidelines on Horizontal Agreements, para. 202.
[483] Ibid., para. 206.
[484] Ibid., para. 207.

The Guidelines on Horizontal Agreements designate "price-fixing" as one of the major competition law problems arising from commercialisation agreements between competitors. Indeed, agreements limited to joint selling generally aim to coordinate the pricing policies of competitors. Along with eliminating price competition between the parties in terms of substitute products, such agreements can also restrict the total volume of products to be offered by the parties in the relevant market through a system for allocating orders. Based on the foregoing considerations, the Guidelines on Horizontal Agreements set forth that such agreements are likely to restrict competition by object.[485]

Moreover, in cases where the parties to a commercialisation agreement possess a certain degree of market power, such agreements can have restrictive effects on competition. If the combined market share of the parties to the agreement does not exceed 15%, it is unlikely that market power will be deemed to exist in most cases, and it is likely that the conditions for receiving an individual exemption will be fulfilled.[486] On the other hand, the fact that the parties possess a combined market share above 15% does not necessarily mean that such an agreement would lead to restrictive effects on competition. In such cases, the likely impact of that joint commercialisation agreement on the market must be assessed.[487] For example, it could be stated that the safe harbour could be narrowed by an approach that focuses on consumers.

4.1.5.4 Assessment Under Article 5 of Law No. 4054

Commercialisation agreements can lead to significant efficiencies, especially for smaller producers, stemming from economies of scale and scope. The efficiencies depend on the nature of the activity and of the parties to the cooperation. In this respect, it is important for the parties to make significant contributions to capital, technology, or other assets within the framework of the cooperation. Cost savings through a reduction in the number of resources and facilities used for the same job will also be deemed as acceptable gains. On the other hand, a joint commercialisation agreement that lacks any investments and is no different than a sales department is considered likely to be a disguised cartel and is unlikely to fulfil the conditions of Article 5 of Law No. 4054.[488]

When the parties to a joint commercialisation agreement have a combined market share above 15%, the Board is compelled to assess the likely impact of such an agreement on the relevant market.[489] In fact, a commercialisation agreement is not likely to give rise to competitive problems in cases where (i) such an agreement is deemed to be objectively necessary for one of the parties' entry to the relevant market, and when (ii) this party would not have been able to enter the market individually due to entry costs or other similar barriers.[490] As explained below, the key factor taken into account in the Board's decisions relating to commercialisation agreements is the opportunity for the party in question to reach the points of sale that would have been otherwise inaccessible to it

---

[485]   Ibid., para. 208.
[486]   Ibid., para. 214.
[487]   Ibid., para. 215.
[488]   See, e.g., *Yozgat Ready-Mixed Concrete* (19 March 2020, 20-15/215-107), para. 192.
[489]   The Guidelines on Horizontal Agreements, para. 215.
[490]   Ibid., para. 211.

without the commercialisation agreement, which, in turn, provides consumers with the opportunity to gain access to more products.

The Board precedents assessing commercialisation agreements concept are outlined below.

In *BKM*, the Board considered the cooperation between BKM and DFS to be aimed at the joint use of the infrastructures of the DFS and BKM systems, and emphasised in its decision that (i) DFS would benefit from BKM's facilities for the promotion of its own payment system by entering into a commercialisation agreement; (ii) the cooperation agreement should create efficiency gains stemming from the integration of economic activities beyond the reduced costs resulting from the elimination of competition; (iii) the parties would contribute significantly with respect to capital, technology or other assets within the framework of cooperation; and (iv) the competitive levels in the market would not be reduced, since consumers would benefit from the relevant agreement.[491] In this regard, the Board ultimately held that the cooperation agreement between BKM and DFS, which had a commercialisation nature, would benefit from the individual exemption.

Moreover, in *Reckitt Benckiser*, the agreement concluded between Reckitt Benckiser and Drogsan, which regulated the exclusive granting of joint marketing rights to RB by Drogsan with respect to a certain product, was considered and treated as a typical example of commercialisation.[492] Even though the combined market share of the transaction parties exceeded 15%, the Board nevertheless granted an individual exemption to the relevant agreement since it satisfied the necessary conditions.

In *Arçelik-Sony Eurasia*, the Board chose to grant an individual exemption to a distribution agreement executed between competitors.[493] The Board emphasised that the distribution agreement carried the risk of allowing and enabling the parties to regularly exchange information regarding Sony Eurasia's sales prices, campaign or promotions, which could lead Arçelik to adjust or determine its business activities on the basis of such information concerning its competitor's pricing and marketing strategies. Nevertheless, the Board decided to grant an individual exemption to the agreement by reasoning that:

- Sony products would be distributed more efficiently to customers through an increased number of sales points, in addition to the growth of product variety at Arçelik's sales points;

- customers would be able to access Sony products more easily through the support of Arçelik's distribution/service systems, which would be beneficial to consumers;

- Arçelik would only distribute a certain segment of Sony products (i.e., not all Sony products);

- Arçelik's market share in the relevant market was not significantly high (17%), even with the distribution of Sony products;

- the relevant market was competitive and dynamic.

[491]   *BKM* (18 February 2016, 16-05/106-47).
[492]   *Reckitt Benckiser* (7 July 2015, 15-28/344-114), para. 28.
[493]   *Arçelik-Sony Eurasia* (4 February 2010, 10-13/145-61).

Accordingly, the foregoing case confirms the approach in the Guidelines on Horizontal Agreements, which deems that non-reciprocal distribution agreements are less likely to result in market allocation concerns compared to reciprocal distribution agreements executed between competitors.[494]

In *Biovesta/Abdi İbrahim*, the Board determined that the agreement concerning the distribution of a medicine by an incumbent firm in Turkey fulfilled the conditions for receiving an individual exemption, on the grounds that (i) the production and distribution costs of the parties would be optimized as a result of more efficient distribution and marketing activities relating to the product; (ii) the product would enter into the Turkish market; (iii) there were several players in the relevant market; and (iv) the business partner's market share was low.[495]

In *Merck Sharp & Dohme*, the Board assessed a hybrid cooperation agreement concerning the joint marketing and toll manufacturing of a specific medicine and granted an individual exemption to the relevant agreement.[496] In its decision, the Board considered that (i) the relevant product had been offered efficiently to the market through the agreement, which was achieved by using the distribution channel of the distributor firm, and (ii) the number of products offered to the end-consumers in the relevant market had increased.

In light of the foregoing, the precedents of the Board confirm that commercialisation agreements executed between competitors frequently benefit from the individual exemption, provided that the agreement yields efficiencies and is deemed to be essential for reaching a pro-competitive outcome.

4.1.6 Standardisation Agreements

4.1.6.1 Definition and Scope

The main objective of standardisation agreements is to determine the technical requirements or quality standards for the harmonisation of existing products or future products, production processes, services or methods.[497] Different issues could fall within the scope of the standardisation agreements, such as standardisation of different classes or dimensions of a particular product or standardisation of technical specifications in product or service markets where compliance and interoperability with other products and services are essential.[498]

The necessary conditions for access to a specific quality standard or for the approval of a regulatory authority may also be considered as a standard.[499] This includes agreements setting standards for the environmental performance of a product or for production

---

[494] Paragraph 212 of the Guidelines on Horizontal Agreements also adopts the view that the risk of restrictive effects on competition is less pronounced in the case of non-reciprocal agreements.

[495] *Biovesta* (27 November 2012, 12-60/1597-581).

[496] *MSD* (18 July 2012, 12-38/1086-345).

[497] The Guidelines on Horizontal Agreements, para. 229.

[498] Ibid.

[499] Ibid.

processes.[500] The standard terms that determine the standard purchase or sale terms for substitute products between competitors and consumers are also considered to be covered by the Guidelines on Horizontal Agreements; however, the standard terms of purchase and sale conditions among competitors are not. Where standard terms find a wide range of areas of use in a specific sector, the purchase or sale terms used in this sector may be compatible without being subject to an agreement. However, the standard conditions prepared by an undertaking for its own use in agreements executed with its suppliers or customers are not covered by the Guidelines on Horizontal Agreements, as there is no horizontal agreement.

In certain sectors, standard purchase or sale terms (standard terms) which have been prepared by the association of undertakings, or by direct competitors are put in use. For instance, standard conditions play an important role in the banking and insurance sectors.[501]

4.1.6.2 Assessment Under Article 4 of Law No. 4054

Standardisation agreements usually produce significant positive economic effects through various means such as creating new and improved products or markets and promoting the improvement of supply conditions.[502] Normally, standards benefit economies as a whole by increasing competition and lowering production and sales costs. Standards can maintain and enhance quality, provide information, ensure interoperability and compatibility and thus increase benefits for consumers.[503]

Standard setting can, however, in certain circumstances, also give rise to restrictive effects on competition by potentially restricting price competition and limiting or controlling production, market, innovation or technical development.[504] This can occur in three ways:

- Reduction in price competition: If undertakings were to engage in anti-competitive discussions in the context of standard setting, this could reduce or eliminate price competition in the markets concerned, thereby facilitating a collusive outcome in the market.[505]

- Foreclosure of the market to innovative technologies: Standards that set detailed technical specifications for a product or service may limit technical development and innovation. Once a specific technology has been chosen and the standard has been set, competing technologies and undertakings may face a barrier to entry and may potentially be excluded from the market. In addition, standards that require the exclusive use of a particular technology or which force the members of the standard-setting organisation to exclusively use a particular standard may lead to the

---

[500] Ibid.
[501] Ibid., para. 231.
[502] Ibid., para. 235.
[503] Ibid.
[504] Ibid., para. 236.
[505] Ibid., para. 237.

same effect. The risk of limiting innovation is increased if one or more undertakings are excluded from the standard-setting process without an objective reason.[506]

– Exclusion of, or discrimination against, certain undertakings by prevention of effective access to the standard: Where standardisation leads to restrictive effects on competition by preventing certain undertakings from obtaining effective access to the results of the standard-setting process, that is to say, to the technical specifications and/or to the intellectual property rights essential for the implementation of the standard.[507]

4.1.6.3 Assessment Under Article 5 of Law No. 4054

Standardisation agreements generally give rise to significant efficiency gains. For example, standards that establish technical interoperability and compatibility often encourage performance-based competition between technologies from different undertakings, thereby preventing dependency on a single supplier.[508] To achieve those efficiency gains in the case of standardisation agreements, the information necessary to apply the standard must be accessible to those wishing to enter the market.[509]

The Board provided its first approach on standardisation agreements in *Yonga Levha*, where it evaluated the application of a negative clearance in regard to the standardisation decision made by the Turkish Particle Board Industrialists Association, concerning setting a standard for particle boards which are subject to numerous patents registered before the Turkish Patent Institute.[510] The Board considered the agreement as standardisation agreement and evaluated the application pursuant to Article 4, and decided to grant negative clearance to the association's decision.

In *Construction Equipment*, the Turkish Construction Equipment Industrialists Association requested negative clearance for a protocol that aimed to control whether the products in the sector comply with the legislation and documentation.[511] The Board first made its assessment of whether the protocol can be considered as a standardisation agreement. The Board decided that the protocol cannot be considered as a standardisation agreement, since (i) the protocol does not aim to determine a quality standard and (ii) the protocol is only a control mechanism to control whether the undertakings comply with the quality standards regulated in the legislations. On this basis, the Board found that the protocol does not constitute a competition law violation and granted negative clearance.

In *Turkish Insurance, Reinsurance and Retirement Companies Associations*, the association requested an individual exemption for its project concerning the mandatory request of quality standard documents from service points.[512] The Board decided that this project

---

[506]   Ibid., para. 238.
[507]   Ibid., para. 239.
[508]   Ibid., para. 278.
[509]   Ibid., para. 279.
[510]   *Yonga Levha* (14 August 2003, 03-56/650-298).
[511]   *Construction Equipment* (n. 192).
[512]   *Turkish Insurance, Reinsurance and Retirement Companies Associations* (20 December 2018, 18-48/751-364).

can be considered as a type of standardisation agreement. However, the Board did not grant an individual exemption for the project since the Board decided that the mandatory documentation process for all players in the market can restrict competition.

4.2 Horizontal Agreements in Labour Markets[513]

4.2.1 Labour Markets and Competition Law

Labour market can be considered as an input market where employees provide the workforce.[514] Under the Turkish competition law regime, there are no specific guidelines on horizontal agreements that address competition in labour markets; however, case law confirms that factors regarding workforce or labour such as wages and salaries are subject to antitrust scrutiny.

In recent years, the Board scrutinised labour markets in terms of no-poaching[515] and wage-fixing agreements[516] in Turkey. For instance, in *Izmir Container Transporters*, the Board clearly acknowledged[517] that agreements and conducts in the labour market could indirectly prevent competition in markets for goods and services; therefore, agreements in the labour market can fall within the scope of Law No. 4054. The Board further acknowledged that wage-fixing or no-poaching agreements are not different from buying cartels.[518]

4.2.2 No-Poaching Agreements

Employees are vital assets for the undertakings. It could be stated that especially when a productive employee switches to a competitor, this could cause serious harm to employers. One of the recruiting methods is to contact successful employees of competitors in order to poach them. At this point, offering higher wages would be among the determining factors affecting employees' decision to switch or not.[519] However, firms might not wish to lose their experienced and productive employees and certainly do not want their rivals to recruit them. Thus, firms can choose to restrict competition in the labour market

---

[513] As this section concerns horizontal agreements in labour markets, vertical agreements in labour markets are not evaluated under this section.

[514] G. Gürkaynak, B. Aktüre and D. Benli, "What Standard of Competition Law Review to Ensure Healthy Competition for Talent?" *The Academic Gift Book of ELIG, Attorneys-at-Law in Honor of the 20th Anniversary of Competition Law Practice in Turkey*, 2018.

[515] *BFIT* (7 February 2019, 19-06/64-27).

[516] *Izmir Container Transporters* (2 January 2020, 20-01/3-2).

[517] Ibid., para. 29.

[518] Ibid., para. 32.

[519] Ibid., para. 28.

by no-poaching agreements or wage-fixing agreements.[520] The Board provided in *Izmir Container Transporters* that no-poaching agreements have no fundamental difference from customer or market allocation, with the exception that the former is on the buyer side and the latter on the seller side, as also confirmed in the literature.[521]

4.2.3 Wage-Fixing Agreements

High wages offered by competitor firms can attract employees and incentivise them to decide to switch; thus, the differences between wages among firms enhance competition in labour markets.[522] Accordingly, besides no-poaching agreements,[523] undertakings might enter into a wage-fixing arrangement to eliminate such competition in the labour market.

In *TV Series Producers*, the Board determined that a wage-fixing agreement could be defined as an agreement for fixing purchasing prices considering the features of the sector and thus might have the object of restricting competition.[524]

In terms of exchange of human resources information, in *Private Schools*, the Board considered that information on wages were competitively sensitive information, and thus the exchange of such information might violate competition law.[525]

The Board has been recently focusing on the competition law issues in labour markets, as seen from the Authority's announcement regarding the labour market[526] and the new investigation against thirty-two undertakings active in the digital market, for gentlemen's agreements in labour markets.[527] The Authority states in its announcement that:

> In particular, the prevention of employee transfers [poaching] between undertakings through direct/indirect agreements by employers competing for labour in the labour market, deprive the employees of job opportunities with higher wages and better conditions. Thus, the competitive structure in the labour market can be harmed by reducing the mobility of the labour factor among the undertakings, and/or the wages determined for the labour may not reflect their real value of

---

[520]   Ibid.

[521]   Ibid., para. 32.

[522]   H. Hovenkamp, "Competition Policy for Labour Markets", OECD, DAF/COMP/WD(2019)67, 17 September 2020.

[523]   Other typical forms of relevant anticompetitive practices among competitors in labour markets include fixing working conditions or exchanging sensitive information, which are also referred to by the Board via the OECD paper "Competition Concerns in Labour Markets – Background Note", DAF/COMP(2019)2, 13 May 2019, pp. 19–21.

[524]   *Television Series Producers* (28 July 2005, 05-49/710-195).

[525]   *Private Schools* (3 March 2011, 11-12/226-76).

[526]   See <https://www.rekabet.gov.tr/tr/Guncel/rekabet-kurumu-baskani-birol-kule-isgucu-704d8ab983ade-b11812e00505694b4c6> (last accessed on 22 May 2021).

[527]   See <https://www.rekabet.gov.tr/tr/Guncel/isgucu-piyasasina-yonelik-centilmenlik-a-d8bc3379-bea1eb11812e00505694b4c6> (last accessed on 4 September 2021).

work. This may lead the undervalued labour force to shift towards other markets or abroad where their labour can be rewarded.[528]

The Board's below precedents on the issue show that it adopts the same approach.

In *Izmir Container Transporters*, the Board found that the undertakings aimed to fix the wages and prevent employee mobility.[529] The Board noted that undertakings were reacting to the wage levels and employee transfers to competitors, which could infringe competition under Law No. 4054[530] and focused its assessment on whether the anti-competitive conducts in the case constituted wage-fixing or no-poaching agreements. The Board reached the conclusion that wage-fixing prevents employee mobility, accordingly the results of wage-fixing are similar to the results of a no-poaching agreement.[531] But, taking into account the facts of the specific case, the Board noted that the mutual understanding among the container transporters seemed to be on fixing wages–although no-poaching agreements can be a part of or an intended outcome of the wage-fixing.[532] Nevertheless, the Board refrained from initiating a fully-fledged investigation as the agreement did not create an appreciable effect in the market in this case. Instead, it decided to issue an opinion letter to each of the undertakings, ordering them to cease the behaviours that could constitute an anti-competitive agreement as per Article 4 of Law No. 4054. However, three Board members issued a dissenting opinion and stated that the violation should be investigated in the current investigation (No. 2018-4-036), which was launched against the same undertakings subject to *Izmir Container Transporters* decision, since the subject of the *Izmir Container Transporters* decision overlapped with the subject of the relevant investigation (No. 2018-4-036).

In *Private Schools*, the Board examined whether the private schools and school associations in question reached agreements or engaged in concerted practices to fix their prices and coordinate their personnel policy through the Private Schools Association's policies and thus breached competition law rules.[533] The ethics policy of the schools contained a no-poaching agreement clause among the private schools that restricted teachers' ability to switch from one school to another rival school. The Board decided that such no-poaching agreement among the private schools violated competition law, although the Private Schools Association provided that the concerned agreement was non-binding.[534] As a result, the Board did not launch a fully-fledged investigation but stated that the violation should be terminated. Contrary to *Private Schools*, the Board decided in its *Henkel* decision that companies have a legitimate interest to prohibit the transfer of employees for a certain period, in the sectors where know-how and innovation are important.[535]

---

[528]   Ibid.
[529]   *Izmir Container Transporters* (n. 516).
[530]   Ibid., para. 59.
[531]   Ibid., para. 60.
[532]   Ibid.
[533]   *Private Schools* (3 March 2011, 11-12/226-76).
[534]   Ibid., para. 560.
[535]   *Henkel* (26 May 2011, 11-32/650-201), para. 80.

In *BFIT*, BFIT imposed non-compete obligation and no-poaching obligation on the franchisee and franchisee's employees, and required seeking its approval before a franchisee could employ previous or current employees from other franchisees, BFIT's or competitors.[536] After considering the guidelines of the Federal Trade Commission and the US Department of Justice, which state that no-poaching terms or wage-fixing agreements are considered per se illegal, the Board concluded that the non-compete and no-poaching clauses should be modified to comply with the conditions of individual exemption, which resulted in limiting the relevant clauses to the duration of the agreement and BFIT providing a clear reasoning when its prior written approval is required.

---

[536]   *BFIT* (n. 515).

Chapter 5
Vertical Agreements

GÖNENÇ GÜRKAYNAK, ESQ., DILARA YEŞILYAPRAK[*]
AND ASLI SU ÇORUK[**]

The main provision governing vertical restraints is Article 4 of Law No. 4054, which, as detailed in the above chapters, prohibits agreements that have or may have the object or effect of prevention, restriction or distortion of competition in a product or services market affecting Turkey or a part thereof. Even though Law No. 4054 does not attribute a specific objective to vertical restraints, as a general rule, Turkish competition law aims to protect competition by way of eliminating entry barriers, encouraging innovation, creating efficiencies and increasing consumer benefits. More specifically, as explained in Article 1 of Law No. 4054, the main purpose of the law is to prevent agreements, decisions and practices precluding, distorting or restricting competition in markets for products or services, and the abuse of dominance by the undertakings dominant in the market, and to ensure the protection of competition by performing the necessary regulations and supervision to this end.

Law No. 4054 does not provide a detailed definition of vertical restraints; however, Communiqué No. 2002/2 and the Guidelines on Vertical Agreements outline the principles to be adopted in the assessment of vertical agreements. Vertical restraints may have negative effects especially in terms of decreasing intra-brand and inter-brand competition and they may lead to foreclosure and restriction of consumer choice. However, there may also be positive effects that justify the implementation of vertical restraints–namely, they may serve as a solution for free-riding and hold-up problems, facilitate entry into new markets, and address problems on matters such as uniformity and access to quality.

In terms of the general rules regarding the assessment of vertical restraints, resale price maintenance is one of the most common vertical restraints prohibited under the legislation and setting fixed or minimum sales prices for the buyer is prohibited; however, the supplier may set maximum sales prices for the buyer or offer recommended sales prices to the buyer, provided that these do not transform into fixed or minimum sales prices. On this note, MFN clauses are considered as tools that may facilitate resale price maintenance and thus must be carefully analysed vis-à-vis the dynamics of the relevant vertical relationship, the relevant market, as well as the market share of the relevant undertakings (especially the entity benefiting from the MFN clause). Furthermore, the legislation prohibits imposing restrictions on buyers of the products or services, with

---

[*] Associate, ELIG Gürkaynak Attorneys-at-Law, Istanbul <dilara.yesilyaprak@elig.com>.
[**] Associate, ELIG Gürkaynak Attorneys-at-Law, Istanbul <asli.coruk@elig.com>.

certain exceptions. Generally speaking, a supplier is allowed to impose certain distribution restrictions on the buyers of its products, provided that the parties (especially the supplier) do not hold a significant market share (i.e., less than 40%) in the relevant market subject to the distribution relationship. Some restrictions may still be allowed even if the parties' market share is above 40%. By way of an example, so long as there is a relationship of territory and/or customer exclusivity, the suppliers are generally allowed to prevent the buyer from engaging in active sales of products or services towards the exclusive territory or customer groups, provided that this restriction does not cover resale by the buyer's customer. As another example, in selective distribution systems, an authorised distributor may be generally prevented from selling products to unauthorised distributors. Moreover, the supplier may also require single branding and obligation to supply a single buyer. Rules may be implemented in varying ways in different sectors such as the motor vehicle sector or across different business models such as the franchising and technology transfer arrangements.

5.1 Types of Vertical Restrictions

5.1.1 Resale Price Maintenance

Article 4 of Law No. 4054 lists certain restrictions which are prohibited under Turkish competition law. Fixing the purchase or sale price of products or services, or those elements such as cost and profit which form the price, and any terms of purchase or sale, fall within the prohibition set out in Article 4(1)(a) of Law No. 4054.

In order for a restriction on competition falling under Article 4 of Law No. 4054 to be in compliance with the law, the restriction should either benefit from a block exemption or an individual exemption pursuant to Article 5 of Law No. 4054. On this note, Communiqué No. 2002/2 provides a non-exhaustive list of vertical restraints and sets forth that, even if the market share of the undertakings parties to the vertical agreement is less than 40%, vertical agreements including any one of the relevant restraints that have the object or effect to hinder competition directly or indirectly cannot benefit from the protective cloak of the block exemption granted by the relevant communiqué. The non-exhaustive list, inter alia, includes "preventing the purchaser from determining its own selling price" by way of fixing the resale price or setting the minimum resale price, and indeed, pursuant to Article 4(1)(a) of Communiqué No. 2002/2 resale price maintenance is considered to be a hard-core violation that cannot benefit from the block exemption. Indeed, Communiqué No. 2021/2 and Communiqué No. 2021/3 also regard resale price maintenance practices as hard-core violations.

Accordingly, inter alia, instructing dealers and/or customers not to sell below a certain price level or at a certain profit margin; or monitoring the resale prices and taking actions for the implementation of such prices through monitoring practices would be considered as resale price maintenance and thus would violate competition law. Indeed, the Guidelines on Vertical Agreements explicitly provide that besides having an explicit resale price maintenance term in a vertical agreement, setting the profit margin of the buyer, setting the maximum rate of discount that may be implemented by the buyer over a recommended price level, providing discounts to the buyer to the extent that the buyer complies with recommended prices, or threatening the buyer with delaying and suspending deliveries, or terminating the agreement in case the buyer does not comply with those recommended prices or the actual implementation of such penalties are accepted as examples of indirect resale price maintenance practices.[537]

Overall, resale price maintenance is prohibited since it may have the direct effect of reducing, or even eliminating, intra-brand competition. Furthermore, it can also facilitate horizontal price-fixing cartels since the increased transparency of prices makes price cuts at the retail level easier to detect. The reduction in intra-brand competition would typically lead to less downward pressure on the price of a particular product or service and this may also have an indirect effect of a reduced level of inter-brand competition. Therefore, if resale price maintenance results in price collusion between distributors, it could be considered as an agreement or concerted practice violating Article 4 of Law No. 4054.[538] In such a case, the supplier that conducts resale price maintenance could also be considered as the facilitator of collusion between resellers and thus such action could be considered a violation of competition law. Indeed, the determination of resale prices by the suppliers may lead to a highly transparent market in terms of product prices and the solidification of the prices by means of eliminating the downward pressure that can be observed in prices as a result of intra-brand competition.[539]

Accordingly, resale price maintenance practices are considered as practices that may create or strengthen cartel agreements or collusion at production and distribution levels, lead to increased prices, hinder new entries to markets or lead to foreclosure of the markets to competitors and overall become far from creating efficiencies for the consumers.

While restricting a reseller's discretion and ability to determine its own prices is prohibited, both Communiqué No. 2002/2 and the Guidelines on Vertical Agreements[540] set forth that a supplier can determine maximum resale prices or recommend resale prices provided that they do not transform into fixed or minimum sales prices–especially through pressure or encouragement of a supplier. Recommended resale price is generally considered to provide reference selling points for buyers and reference selling points for the consumers. On the other hand, maximum resale price is generally considered to help keep prices reach excessive levels. Indeed in *Mercedes-Benz*,[541] an individual exemption analysis is carried out for the authorised dealership agreement, which includes both recommended resale prices and maximum resale prices, and it is evaluated that both practices seek to reflect Mercedes's long-lasting experience in the relevant market and serve as reference points for the authorised dealers whilst also ensuring that the authorised dealers are free to determine their resale prices.

---

[537]   Guidelines on Vertical Agreements, para. 18.
[538]   *Consumer Electronics* (7 November 2016, 16-37/628-279).
[539]   *Baymak* (26 March 2020, 20-16/232-113).
[540]   The Guidelines on Vertical Agreements issued by the Board's decision dated 30 June 2003 set forth the principles to be taken into account in terms of the implementation of Communiqué No. 2002/2. The Board has updated the Guidelines on Vertical Agreements with its decision dated 29 March 2018.
[541]   *Mercedes-Benz* (13 August 2013, 13-47/644-282).

The Guidelines on Vertical Agreements provide that in order to ensure that maximum or recommended resale prices do not become minimum or fixed resale prices, price lists set by the suppliers for the relevant product or service must clearly communicate the maximum or recommended nature of the resale prices. By way of an example, if a producer/supplier of a bag of potato chips would like to print its recommended or maximum resale price on the packaging, the packaging is advised to clearly indicate that the price printed by the producer/supplier is recommended or maximum.

As provided under Communiqué No. 2002/2 and the Guidelines on Vertical Agreements, undertakings with less than 40% share in the relevant market(s) for contracted products or services subject to the vertical relationship may recommend resale prices to their dealers and customers or determine maximum resale prices. Taking into consideration the wording of Communiqué No. 2002/2 and the Guidelines on Vertical Agreements, a safe harbour is not provided if the undertakings parties to the vertical agreement have more than 40% market share in the relevant market(s). Accordingly, if such undertakings wish to recommend a resale price or set a maximum resale price, a balancing activity must be carried out to weigh the pro-competitive and anti-competitive effects of the terms, and it must be assessed whether the agreement meets all of the conditions provided under Article 5 of Law No. 4054 and benefits from an individual exemption.

When evaluating the anti-competitive effects of the maximum or recommended resale prices, first and foremost, the supplier's position in the relevant market should be taken into consideration. If the supplier has a strong position in the relevant market, the risk of maximum or recommended prices being used as reference (focal point) by the resellers would be higher. By way of example, the resellers may find it difficult to deviate from the price recommended by such a strong supplier and comply with the relevant prices. For instance, in *Trakya Cam/Düzcam Exemption*,[542] the Board stated that due to Trakya Cam's high market power in the flat glass market, the recommended resale prices imposed on the authorised dealers by means of the agreements had significant anti-competitive effects as they were deprived of defining their own resale prices. As another example, if maximum prices, which should have been essentially set to prevent excessive pricing of the products or services, are set at a level that is almost always adopted by the resellers, such maximum prices may serve as resale prices in practice. On this note, if most or all of the resellers comply with the recommended or maximum prices, determining maximum resale prices or recommending resale prices may lead to uniformity of price levels.

In addition to the supplier's position, competitors' positions and the level of competition in the relevant product market should also be taken into account. Especially in tight oligopolistic markets, publishing and using maximum or recommended prices may increase price transparency at the price level and decrease the possibility of applying lower prices in the market, and thus may facilitate collusion amongst suppliers.

Moreover, in the assessment of resale price maintenance practice, the efficiencies created and their benefit on the consumers are also analysed.

---

[542]   *Trakya Cam/Düzcam Exemption* (n. 210).

On this note, in some of its decisions, the Board recognises that intervention to resale prices may be considered to have competitive effects such as eliminating free riding and increasing efficiency in distribution.[543] The free-riding problem mainly arises in products where consumers' knowledge concerning the product is limited (e.g., due to its new launch, no investment in its marketing and advertisement, etc.).

Another competitive effect of vertical resale price maintenance is eliminating the double marginalisation problem in the market. The double marginalisation problem usually arises when the buyer with high market power is able to sell the products purchased from the seller by adding margins close to monopolistic profit margins. In such a case, vertical resale price maintenance may prevent excessive price increases by fixing the buyer's margin.

Resale price maintenance may be deemed necessary in a franchise system or distribution network to carry out short-term (2–6 weeks) campaigns organised for the benefit of the customer. Indeed, although there are yet no decisions that focus on this directly, the Board generally recognises that resale price maintenance may be used in launching new products or services in order to facilitate marketing and sales, increase demand for established products or services, and support the market presence of the newly launched products or services.

For instance, in *Besler Gıda*,[544] while evaluating the conditions for an individual exemption, the Board took into consideration whether the provisions of the agreement leading to resale price maintenance were essential for improving Besler Gıda's distribution system. The Board stated that in the case at hand, resale price maintenance was not necessary as it restricted the competition based on prices between the dealers and also the trade between different areas, which is contrary to the consumers' benefit.

Furthermore, in *Mars Cinema*,[545] the Board examined the possible positive effects of vertical resale price maintenance and made an individual exemption analysis. In the relevant decision, it has been detected that the agreements with certain shopping malls included provisions indicating that Mars would determine the prices and promotions of the tickets and snack bar, and the franchisee could not change the prices. Mars asserted that the relevant cinemas were established with Mars' consultancy and management, in compliance with its corporate standards, and within this context, the relevant agreements enabled new cinemas to start operating, while consumers were provided with the opportunity to watch cinemas in more locations, increasing efficiency and enhancing consumer benefit in the relevant market. However, the Board found that the relevant consumer benefit and efficiencies may not be associated with vertical price maintenance and can be achieved without it. The Board also indicated that it was possible to see positive effects with competitive market structure, a new product entering the market, or short-term discounts within a franchise system. However, the Board found that Mars' right to determine the price was not limited to short term discounts, and vertical price determination did not serve the purpose of increasing the demand for the product by encouraging the efforts

---

[543]   *Frito-Lay* (12 June 2018, 18-19/329-163) and *Yataş* (27 September 2017, 17-30/487-211).
[544]   *Besler Gıda* (22 November 1999, 99-53/575-364).
[545]   *Mars Cinema* (20 November 2015, 15-41/682-243).

of the distributors to promote and sell the product, as the agreements did not concern new geographic markets but rather those in which Mars was already operating. Thus, the Board concluded that the agreements could not be granted an individual exemption.

On the other hand, in *Dogati*,[546] considering the high level of intra-brand competition competitive structure in the fast food market and Dogati's negligible market share, the Board stated that although there were indications that Dogati restricted the franchisees' freedom to determine their own prices, it had tried to keep the prices at a certain level rather than dictating a fixed price. Furthermore, Dogati's practices were deemed to be significant for efficiency gains such as quality-price balance, brand image and customer satisfaction within a franchise system. Thus, the Board concluded that there was not a competitive concern in terms of inter-brand competition.

Against this background, some of the cornerstone decisions and recent cases of the Board on the different types of resale price maintenance practices are discussed below.

5.1.1.1 Direct Resale Price Maintenance Practices

The suppliers may directly determine resale prices through explicit contractual obligations to observe the supplier's price policy.[547] By way of example, in *Baymak*,[548] the dealership agreements of Baymak included provisions stating that the dealers could only make sales based on the list prices provided by Baymak and that they could not sell products at prices lower than the list prices. The Board further noted that Baymak actively monitored its dealers' resale prices and even intervened if the prices were lower than the list prices and, inter alia, concluded a violation for resale price maintenance. Similarly, in *Okan Okandan*,[549] the Board held that the agreements set forth that the discounts and prices to be applied to the customer by the dealers were determined by the supplier, and the relevant conducts resulted in resale price maintenance.

5.1.1.2 Indirect Resale Price Maintenance Practices

Resale price maintenance does not only occur through the explicit provisions of vertical agreements; it may also be generated indirectly by means of miscellaneous practices. Most common indirect resale price maintenance practices include withdrawing incentives, determining the buyer's profit margin, sanctioning the distributors that are not applying the prices recommended by the suppliers, sending out price lists without noting their recommended nature, as well as price monitoring through hand terminals and invoice controls, which strengthen the effectiveness of the aforementioned measures.[550]

In practice, there are various ways for sanctioning distributors that do not comply with the suppliers' instructions regarding the resale prices of the products. For instance, warning,

---

[546] *Dogati* (22 October 2014, 14-42/764-340).
[547] *KWS* (25 November 2009, 09-57/1365-357); *Dagi* (15 July 2009, 09-33/725-165); *Akmaya* (20 May 2009, 09-23/491-117).
[548] *Baymak* (n. 539).
[549] *Okan Okandan* (7 March 2019, 19-11/129-56).
[550] Guidelines on Vertical Agreements, para. 18.

threatening, imposing penal sanctions, terminating the contracts, putting the shipping of the orders on hold or cancelling orders can be considered among these sanctions. By way of example, in *Sony Eurasia*,[551] the Board stated that monitoring resale prices on online platforms and threatening to cease the financial support provided to the resellers that do not comply with the recommended prices were considered to amount to resale price maintenance. Whereas, in *BSH*,[552] the Board examined whether BSH (i) terminated its contracts with dealers as they did not comply with the recommended resale prices and (ii) monitored its dealers' retail prices through the system, which allows entering the product codes and recommended resale prices. However, the Board did not find any indication of indirect resale price maintenance, as the price lists concerned merely recommended resale prices and the system used by BSH did not allow monitoring retail prices.

Overall, monitoring and control of buyer prices and/or other price-related conditions by the suppliers are considered to facilitate indirect resale price maintenance.[553] However pure monitoring of the resale prices does not constitute any violation. Indeed, in *Henkel*,[554] the Board notes that the sole fact that Henkel collects data on its products' resale prices on the market and that it uses this information in its own planning of commercial and promotional activities cannot be considered as a violation. However, intervening directly to the resale prices, which should be freely determined within the scope of the independent commercial decisions of the buyers, and preventing the buyers from setting the resale prices constitute a violation. Indeed, in the relevant decision, the Board concluded that Henkel's conduct went beyond talking to the customer and monitoring the sales prices of the reseller; instead, Henkel intervened in its customers' independent decision-making by applying measures in order to determine the resale prices of its products within a certain programme, and thus prevented its customers from freely determining their prices.

Increasingly, hand terminals, an electronic system used for storing the products' data, including their resale prices, sales volumes, customers or other information, are used in distribution agreements for manufacturing, supply, logistics planning and commercial arrangement reasons. From a competition law perspective, hand terminals are also considered as tools for monitoring and potentially controlling the resale prices of products and services. Overall, the mere use of hand terminals does not amount to an infringement and an evaluation must be made on whether the use of this system leads to resale price maintenance by restricting the distributors' ability to set their own resale prices.[555]

Historically, there have been cases whereby the Board has found that hand terminal practices have led to resale price maintenance. For example, in the *Frito-Lay*,[556] the Board examined the independence of the distributors with respect to the adoption of resale prices entered into the hand terminals by Frito-Lay. Distributors were evaluated to have the ability to amend prices through hand terminals by inserting discounts, yet in practice, the distributors were too reluctant to implement such discounts in order not to sacrifice

---

[551]   *Sony Eurasia* (n. 182).
[552]   *BSH* (14 July 2011, 11-43/941-305).
[553]   Guidelines on Vertical Agreements, para. 19.
[554]   *Henkel* (19 September 2018, 18-33/556-274).
[555]   *Gillette* (20 March 2008, 08-25/261-88).
[556]   *Frito-Lay* (11 January 2007, 07-01/12-7).

their profits. Moreover, it was observed that any price or discount-related insertion of the distributors to the system was subject to the prior approval of Frito-Lay employees. In the relevant decision, the Board also examined the employment status of people conducting the sales and inserting price data through the hand terminals, and found that the relevant employees, who also met with distributor customers in sales arrangements and inserted new orders through hand terminals, were on Frito-Lay's payroll. Accordingly, the Board concluded that hand terminals actually restricted distributors' ability to set their resale prices and, besides, the involvement of Frito-Lay employees in distributor sales resulted in resale price maintenance. Having said that, as also laid out in the Board's *Frito-Lay*,[557] *Mey İçki*,[558] *Reckitt Benckiser*,[559] in general the distributors having the discretion to determine discounts, promotions or prices that they will be applying to the resellers, and their ability to revise the recommended sales prices, indicate that the use of hand terminals does not amount to resale price maintenance.

Recently, in *Red Bull*,[560] the Board, inter alia, evaluated the recommended price practice of Red Bull and looked into whether it interfered with its distributors' minimum resale prices and discount rates. Overall, Red Bull adopted a "perfect store" measurement system in order to improve its marketing and sales operations. Within the scope of the said system, Red Bull set out various criteria, one of which was compliance with the recommended resale prices. The Board analysed whether compliance to the recommended price criteria in the respective system indirectly resulted in resale price maintenance. Accordingly, the Board found that the weight attributed to the recommended price criteria was relatively low in consideration of the overall score for "perfect store", meaning the said criterion was not determinative for qualifying as a "perfect store". In this regard, the Board concluded that the said practice did not result in resale price maintenance. Furthermore, the Board examined the handheld terminal system adopted by Red Bull and evaluated that both Red Bull and its distributors (via their operators) had the authority to set and change both prices and discounts. To that end, the Board concluded that Red Bull did not interfere with the resale prices through the said system.

Invoice controlling also stands out as a practice used for monitoring resale prices in vertical arrangements. In *Şölen*,[561] the Board evaluated whether there was an intervention regarding the resale prices of Şölen's Octavia branded chocolates, by means of a price difference invoice sent to the seller by the markets where the products were sold. In the said decision, Şölen was alleged to maintain resale prices by applying pressure on markets buying the Octavia branded chocolates through price difference invoices. The Board examined the allegations and stated that Şölen's practice might not be considered as an indication of pressure on the undertakings in order to ensure resale price maintenance, and noted that the markets were able to freely determine their prices with regard to the product in question. In *Benckiser*,[562] in case the chain markets selling the products of Benckiser did not comply with the recommended sales prices, the difference

---

[557] *Frito-Lay* (n. 543).
[558] *Mey İçki* (19 September 2018, 18-33/547-270).
[559] *Reckitt Benckiser* (13 June 2013, 13-36/468-204).
[560] *Red Bull* (19 December 2019, 19-45/767-329).
[561] *Şölen* (16 January 2014, 14-02/35-14).
[562] *Benckiser* (3 July 2008, 08-43/591-223).

Vertical Agreements

between the listed recommended sales prices and the actual resale prices was invoiced to the chain markets as "service fee" and the Board evaluated that the sole fact that the supplier controlled the prices applied by the distributor undertakings by means of a supplementary invoice did not constitute a violation. However, the Board opined that the fact that the supplier determined the discounts to be applied by the distributors to customers and accordingly controlled whether these were complied with by means of invoices constituted a violation. In the case at hand, Benckiser had terminated one of its agreements with a distributor due to non-compliance with the discount percentages imposed by Benckiser. Overall, the relevant invoicing mechanism was considered to prevent the distributor from freely determining its prices, and accordingly, an administrative fine was imposed on the relevant undertaking.

On the other hand, even though it is possible to determine maximum resale prices or recommend resale prices, in order to ensure that maximum or recommended sales prices notified to the reseller do not transform into minimum or fixed prices, price lists or packaging of the product are recommended to explicitly indicate that the relevant prices are maximum or recommended prices. Otherwise, sending out price lists without noting their nature as recommended or maximum prices may be considered to amount to resale price maintenance practices and thus constitute a competition law violation.[563] The Board's *Yataş II*,[564] *KWS*[565] and *Boyner*[566] decisions confirm this finding. More specifically, in *Yataş II*, the dealers were aware of the recommended nature of the listed prices, and they had the possibility to freely determine their sales prices without being obliged to apply the listed prices. They also had the possibility to apply different percentages of discounts and offer various payment methods to customers. On the other hand, in *KWS*, as the annual price lists sent to the dealers did not contain any provision indicating that these were recommended sales prices, the Board decided that this practice constituted resale price maintenance. Finally, in *Boyner*, the Board confirmed that the price lists or the tags on the products must indicate the recommended nature of these prices in order to prevent them from transforming into minimum or fixed sales prices. Having said that, in *Setre*,[567] even though the price tags on the products did not mention that these were recommended prices, the Board evaluated whether the distributor had the possibility to set its own resale prices and concluded that the sole fact that the prices were not explicitly labelled as recommended prices did not amount to resale price maintenance, since it was possible for the distributor to amend those prices or apply discounts without any pressure or encouragement.

On the other hand, the Board's precedents demonstrate that if an undertaking's behaviour amounts to resale price maintenance, the mere usage of "recommended prices" terminology would not be sufficient to determine whether the undertaking's actions are in violation of competition law.[568] In *Unilever*,[569] the Board examined the provisions in the distributor contracts, which set forth the distributors' obligation to ensure that the sales prices to the

---

[563] Guidelines on Vertical Agreements, para. 17.
[564] *Yataş* (6 February 2020, 20-08/83-50).
[565] *KWS* (25 November 2009, 09-57/1365-357).
[566] *Boyner* (27 October 2011, 11-54/1379-489).
[567] *Setre* (9 February 2012, 12-06/191-53).
[568] *Doğuş Otomotiv* (28 January 2010, 10-10/90-40).
[569] *Unilever* (18 February 2009, 09-07/129-40).

end customers will be in accordance with the recommended sales prices in the price lists sent to the distributors. In this respect, the Board concluded that the provisions in question put pressure on the distributors for applying the recommended prices, which resulted in resale price maintenance. Despite the fact that they were called "recommended" sales prices, the distributors were forced to comply with them. Overall, the Board is not bound with the terminology of these prices and, therefore, the essence of its analysis is based on the distributors having the discretion to freely determine their own prices.

In conclusion, while defining indirect resale price maintenance, the key factor taken into consideration is the distributor's ability to freely determine the resale prices of the products without any type of intervention by the supplier. If the buyer is somehow deprived of its right to determine resale prices, discount amounts, margins or promotions for the product or services, such practices may be considered as indirect resale price maintenance practices.

5.1.1.3 By Object Restriction vs. Effects-Based Analysis

Generally speaking, the Authority has focused its attention towards vertical agreements, especially on resale price maintenance practices over the last two years.[570] Moreover, the recently enacted legislation, Communiqué No. 2021/2 and Communiqué No. 2021/3, also regard resale price maintenance practices as hard-core violations. However, decisional practice shows that resale price arrangements are not scrutinised on their own but under certain restrictive approach models.

While evaluating resale price maintenance practices, the Board is observed to adopt two different approaches. In certain (and more recent) cases, the Board concludes that resale price maintenance practices constitute by object restrictions; whereas, in other cases, it may choose to conduct an effects-based analysis to reach its conclusion. Effects-based analysis takes into consideration the pro-competitive and the anti-competitive effects of the resale price maintenance in the market. It is primarily based on the examination of the under-taking's position in the market, its market share, the level of competition in the market and the consumers' benefit. Despite certain decisions where the Board somehow signals "rule of reason" analysis by considering the market structure, competition level and effect on consumers,[571] the Board's established precedent clearly points towards viewing resale price maintenance as a per se violation.[572]

In *Fuel Companies*,[573] the Board stated that in light of its recent precedents including *Sony*,[574] *Henkel*,[575] *Turkcell*,[576] and *Maysan*[577] decisions, resale price maintenance constitutes a by object restriction.

---

[570]   *Yataş II* (n. 564); *Kubota* (9 January 2020, 20-03/21-11); *Red Bull* (n. 560); *Maysan* (20 June 2019, 19-22/353-159).

[571]   *Çilek* (20 August 2014, 14-29/597-263); *Dogati* (n. 546); *Yataş* (n. 543).

[572]   *Samsung* (23 June 2011, 11-39/838-262); *Akmaya* (n. 547); *Kuralkan* (27 May 2008, 08-35/462-16).

[573]   *Fuel Companies* (n. 33). Ankara 7th Administrative Court suspended the execution of monetary fine against Opet Petrolcülük A.Ş. (14 January 2021, E. 2021/60).

[574]   *Sony Eurasia* (n. 182).

[575]   *Henkel* (n. 554).

[576]   *Turkcell* (10 January 2019, 19-03/23-10).

[577]   *Maysan* (n. 570).

On the other hand, in its previous decisions, the Board adopted a different approach and conducted an effects analysis while evaluating violations related to resale price maintenance. In *Duru Bulgur*,[578] within the scope of its effects analysis, the Board examined the possible positive and negative impacts of resale price maintenance. *Mars Cinema*[579] was also a significant decision where an effects-based analysis was conducted by the Board in relation to Mars's agreements included provisions that constituted resale price maintenance. Mars stated that the provisions in question led to benefit consumers. Overall, the Board concluded that without any resale price maintenance, the same result could have been achieved based on a competitive effects-based analysis of the practice as well as the position of the buyers and the sellers in the relevant market.

In *Vira Kozmetik*,[580] the Board referred to the rule of reason analysis and stated that in order for any vertical restriction to be considered as a per se prohibition, it should have anti-competitive effect in almost every case when examined in the light of the rule of reason approach. In this respect, it was opined that the rule of reason approach should be applied if the vertical agreement does not limit the competition between brands, reduce the benefit of consumers or enable the formation of cartels for the purposes of increasing competitive level in the market.

To sum up, it is sufficient for either the effect or the object to exist in order for there to be a violation. In its later dated decisions, the Board typically conducted an effects analysis in order to evaluate whether positive effects outweighed restrictive effects. However, the Board considered resale price maintenance as a by object restriction in its recent decisions. Therefore, it can be said that the Board's current approach to resale price maintenance is closer to considering such practices as a per se prohibition rather than conducting a rule of reason analysis for the said practices.

5.1.2 Exclusive Distribution

Exclusivity arrangements are entered between undertakings that operate in different levels of the production or distribution chain, and they include the obligation to collaborate solely among party/parties to the arrangement. Under an exclusive distribution agreement, a supplier may grant an exclusive purchase, sale or resale right of a specific product or service to a distributor, and exclusivity may be granted to the distributor for a specific geographic territory and/or to a specific customer group.

Exclusive distribution may arise in various forms. Exclusivity can be ensured by including a provision in the agreement executed between the supplier and the buyer or it can be realised de facto through the adoption of certain incentives such as rebates or promo-

---

[578]   *Duru Bulgur* (8 March 2018, 18-07/112-59). This decision has been annulled by Ankara 13th Administrative Court's decision (17 September 2020, E. 2020/315, K. 2020/1569). In this respect, by means of its decision (20-54/754-M), the Board decided to launch a fully-fledged investigation against Duru Bulgur Gıda San. ve Tic. A.Ş. in order to determine whether it has violated Article 41 of Law No. 4054.

[579]   *Mars Cinema* (n. 545).

[580]   *Vira Kozmetik* (2 August 2007, 07-63/767-275).

tions (e.g., *Red Bull*)[581] or through the implementation of sanctioning mechanisms (e.g., *BASF Coatings-Riwax*).[582]

The main purpose for the supplier to grant exclusivity is to provide the distributor with incentives to promote the product and provide better service to customers. In this respect, exclusive distribution may contribute to inter-brand competition by means of boosting the quality standards in the market. On the other hand, exclusive distribution may also lead to the decrease of intra-brand competition as undertakings with high market power in the upstream market may strengthen their position in the downstream market as well and lead to market allocation at both the supply and the distribution levels. Also, it may prevent other distributors from accessing the market and thus reduce the competition. Generally speaking, when inter-brand competition is high, reduction of the intra-brand competition does not negatively impact the consumer as inter-brand competition forces undertakings to innovate and, therefore, leads to technical and economic improvement in the market.

Exclusive distribution agreements fall within the scope of Article 4 of Law No. 4054. However, according to Article 5 of Law No. 4054, these agreements may also benefit from the exemptions set forth in Communiqué No. 2002/2 if the conditions laid out in the relevant communiqué are fulfilled. According to Article 2 of Communiqué No. 2002/2, if the market share of the buyer party to an exclusive distribution agreement is above 40% in the relevant product market in which it provides the products or services that are subject to the vertical agreement, the agreement cannot benefit from the block exemption. However, the agreement may benefit from an individual exemption if it cumulatively fulfils the conditions set forth under Article 5 of Law No. 4054 (e.g., *IGA/THY*).[583]

Pursuant to Article 4 of Communiqué No. 2002/2, restrictions requiring the buyer not to sell the products or services in certain geographic territories or to certain customers may be considered as a violation by object of Article 4 of Law No. 4054. There are, however, a number of exceptions to this rule. Indeed, Article 4(b)(1) of Communiqué No. 2002/2 allows the supplier to prevent the buyer from active sales of contracted products or services to an exclusive territory or customers allocated to a supplier or another buyer, provided that this restriction does not cover any resale by the buyer's customer. Communiqué No. 2002/2 grants block exemption to the practices listed above. Provisions extending beyond what is permissible under an appropriately defined exclusive distribution system, such as restriction of passive sales, which consist of restriction of resale of a product or a service by the buyer's customer, cannot benefit from the block exemption and may exclude the vertical agreement from the application of Communiqué No. 2002/2 (e.g., *Cargo*).[584]

5.1.2.1 Active Sales Bans

"Active sales" can be defined as sales realised by targeting a specific region or a group of customers and that are made by directly reaching the customers by means of opening a physical store or targeting the consumer directly via marketing and advertisements. Sales

---

[581]   *Red Bull* (n. 560).
[582]   *BASF Coatings-Riwax* (27 September 2012, 12-46/1396-469).
[583]   *IGA/THY* (26 December 2019, 19-46/786-343).
[584]   *Cargo* (16 January 2020, 20-04/47-25).

to individual customers in the exclusive region or exclusive customer group of another buyer through e-mails, mailing catalogues, letters or visits, creating advertisements or promotions that directly target customers in a region or customer group assigned to another buyer, establishing a point of sales or distribution warehouse in the region of another buyer are listed among active sales methods.[585]

In active sales, a direct link is established in order to influence the target audience. As mentioned above, active sales bans are possible under the conditions set forth under Communiqué No. 2002/2 provided that an exclusive territory or a customer group is determined within the scope of the distribution agreement. For example, in *Cargo*,[586] the investigation mainly involved the integrator companies, which are service providers that collect overseas shipments sent from Turkey and deliver them to the recipients abroad through their own international distribution networks, and various reseller cargo companies that essentially purchased overseas distribution services from the integrator companies for their international cargo transport services. Although the integrator companies and resellers appear to compete at the distribution level, there is actually a vertical relationship between these companies, as a result of which the agreements between integrator companies and resellers are considered as dual distribution agreements. Against this background, upon its examinations, the Board found that the integrators, which did not determine exclusive customers or regions and yet imposed active, and in some cases passive, sales restrictions on resellers without any objective justifications, did not benefit from a block exemption. Moreover, an individual exemption could not be provided, especially considering that the integrators ultimately engaged in customer allocation practices without any objective justifications for gains at the distribution level and in any case, the resellers did not require any transfer of know-how or expert assistance for relevant services; such practices restricted consumer choices and access, and restricted competition. Overall, the practices of the integrator companies against the resellers were seen as distortions of the competitive structure of the market. In conclusion, the Board held that DHL Express, TNT, UPS and Yurtiçi Kargo, as the integrator companies, violated Article 4 of Law No. 4054 by way of imposing a restriction on resellers' customers that (i) created no efficiency gain in the market; (ii) restricted consumer preferences within the brand; (iii) caused a decrease in consumer welfare; and (iv) was likely to adversely affect inter-brand competition when used by most of the providers in the market.

5.1.2.1.1 Territorial/Geographical Exclusivity

In an agreement comprising territorial exclusivity, the supplier agrees to sell its products or to provide its services to a single buyer or a distributor in a specific area. In such agreements, the distributor's active sales outside the relevant territory may be, and generally are, restricted. By way of example, in *Mutlu Akü*,[587] the distribution agreement executed between Mutlu and Alacakaya Petrol contained a provision that restricted Alacakaya's active sales outside the allocated territory.

---

[585] Guidelines on Vertical Agreements, paras. 23–24.
[586] *Cargo* (n. 584).
[587] *Mutlu Akü* (8 August 2018, 18-27/446-216).

If the number of undertakings actively making sales in a specific territory is two or more, the relevant geographic territory cannot be defined as an exclusive territory. In that case, any buyer would be able to actively sell products to the relevant "free" area, which is not exclusive to a single buyer or a distributor. In such case, prevention of active or passive sales in a "free" area constitutes a competition law violation. In *Trakya Cam*[588] it was alleged that Trakya Cam prevented dealers from selling to customers outside their territories. The Board assessed that Trakya Cam de facto implemented distribution agreements in 2016 that had been determined to be in violation of Articles 4 and 6 of Law No. 4054 through *Trakya Cam/Düzcam Exemption*[589] and revoked the individual exemption granted to Trakya Cam's industrial customer purchasing agreement that was signed with its industrialist customers. Upon complaints, the Board examined the dealers' sales to customers outside their territories before and after Trakya Cam's territorial exclusivity system and found that their sales decreased dramatically due to territorial exclusivity. The Board held that Trakya Cam's territorial exclusivity violated Article 4 of Law No. 4054. Trakya Cam was imposed an administrative monetary fine and was ordered to provide eighteen of its distributors with written notices declaring that there is no regional exclusivity and acknowledging that they may carry out sales activities throughout Turkey.

Within the scope of the territorial/geographical exclusivity, parallel imports should also be evaluated. Although Law No. 4054 does not contain any direct regulation with regard to the parallel imports, the Board's precedents[590] and doctrine shed light on the subject. Accordingly, even though restrictions of parallel import are not specifically regulated under Law No. 4054, the Board has taken the position that any kind of arrangement/conduct, with the aim of restricting parallel import activities in Turkey, should be deemed as falling within the scope of either (i) Article 4 of Law No. 4054 (as restriction on parallel import is an arrangement with the aim of prevention, restriction or distortion of competition within a Turkish product or services market or a part thereof, within the meaning of Article 4), or (ii) Article 6 of Law No. 4054 (as restriction on parallel import is an arrangement that may result in directly or indirectly preventing entries into the market or hindering competitor activity in the market within the meaning of Article 6). Although in the relevant decisions, the Board did not conclude that the investigated undertakings violated Law No. 4054, it further indicated that prevention of imports conducted legally–in other words, parallel import restrictions–would violate Law No. 4054. That being said, in *Mastervolt/Artı Marin*,[591] the Board re-evaluated its assessments on parallel import restrictions. In its first assessment, the Board found that parallel import restriction falls outside of the scope of Law No. 4054. However, in accordance with the decision of the 13th Chamber of the Council of State,[592] the Board's decision has been annulled. In its re-evaluation, the Board referred to the decisional practice of the Commission and CJEU, and although the Board held that the findings were not sufficient

---

[588]   *Trakya Cam* (14 December 2017, 17-41/641-280).
[589]   *Trakya Cam/Düzcam Exemption* (n. 210).
[590]   *Sesa* (6 November 2000, 00-44/472-257), *Vira Kozmetik* (n. 580) and *Armada Bilgisayar* (18 September 2008, 08-54/852-340).
[591]   *Mastervolt/Artı Marin*,(11 May 2016, 16-16/278-122).
[592]   13th Chamber of the Council of State (12 November 2014; E. 2010/4464, K. 2014/3480).

to demonstrate that there was a restrictive agreement and that it affected the relevant product market, it acknowledged that agreements aimed at preventing parallel import would violate Law No. 4054.

In *Glaxo Wellcome-PNG*,[593] the Board evaluated PNG's exclusivity set forth for Glaxo Wellcome's products' production, sales, distribution and marketing in Turkey within the scope of the licence agreement. The Board evaluated that such agreements that give exclusive rights to the licensee are deemed necessary in order to implement the licence agreement effectively and for the licensee to get returns for its investments, and assessed whether the exclusivity for Turkey was absolute or not. Glaxo Welcome did not have a commitment that set forth that the medicines produced outside of the contract territory would not be shipped to Turkey; in other words, the agreement did not comprise a parallel import restriction. On the other hand, the agreement included a provision preventing the licensee from using Glaxo Wellcome's trademark outside the defined territory without Glaxo Wellcome's prior consent. Consequently, the Board also evaluated the parallel export restrictions and indicated that the relevant provision concerned the sales outside Turkey and would bear its effects in foreign countries. Accordingly, restriction on parallel export has been considered to fall out of the scope of Article 2 of Law No. 4054.

5.1.2.1.2 Customer Exclusivity

In an agreement comprising customer exclusivity, the distributor agrees to sell its products or to provide its services to a specified group of customers. In such agreements, the distributor's active sales outside the specified group of customers may be, and generally are, restricted. By way of example, in *SMC/Entek*,[594] the agreement executed between the parties included a provision that set forth the obligation for Entek, SMC's dealer, not to sell any products to SMC's allocated customer group. If the number of undertakings active in sales to a specific group of customers is two or more, the territory or the customer group cannot be defined as exclusive. In that case, any buyer would be able to actively sell products to the relevant "free" customers who are not exclusive to a single buyer or distributor.

In Paşabahçe,[595] authorised dealers were not allowed to make active sales to certain customer groups of Paşabahçe, which were exclusive to Paşabahçe, and to selected resellers exclusive to certain regions and customer groups, in relation to the wholesale channel concerning houseware products. However, no passive sales restrictions were imposed on the authorised dealers. The Board evaluated that the relevant arrangement was beneficial in order to promote customer-specific investments and to increase interbrand competition. As a side note, the agreement concerning glassware products has been evaluated within the scope of individual exemption due to the fact that Paşabahçe's market share in the glassware market exceeded 40%. On the other hand, the agreement involving porcelain houseware products was evaluated within the scope of the exemption set forth under Communiqué No. 2002/2, as Paşabahçe's market share in this particular market did not exceed 40%.

[593] *Glaxo Wellcome-PNG* (26 September 2002, 02-57/727-289).
[594] *SMC/Entek* (10 October 2012, 12-49/1439-490).
[595] *Paşabahçe* (12 December 2019, 19-44/737-314).

In *Industrial Gas*,[596] the Board confirmed that in order to define a customer group as exclusive, only a single buyer or a provider should actively sell products to that specific group of customers. In this decision, the Board stated that despite the active and passive sales customer restrictions between Linde and Yalız and Orsez, no exclusive territory or customer group was defined. The Board decided that the agreements leading to customer restriction in the case at hand aimed to reduce competition rather than contribute to the effectiveness of the distribution system. In this respect, the Board decided that these agreements did not benefit from the block exemption within the scope of Communiqué No. 2002/2. The Board also evaluated the conditions for an individual exemption within the scope of Article 5 of Law No. 4054. However, the Board did not grant the individual exemption, as Linde's conduct did not lead to any economic improvement and, therefore, it was contrary to the customers' benefit. Indeed, the Board imposed an administrative fine on Linde as its practices were in violation of Article 4 of Law No. 4054.

5.1.2.2 Passive Sales Ban

"Passive sales" can be defined as sales that do not include an active effort by the distributor, even if the buyer carries out deliveries or advertises the product to a reasonable degree. Advertisements or promotions of a general nature in the media through online channels or similar methods are generally classified as passive sales.[597]

As explained above, Communiqué No. 2002/2 provides a block exemption to suppliers adopting a distribution system where distributors are allocated exclusive territories or customer groups. That being said, under such a distribution system, a supplier can only limit active sales to a customer group or territory, and only if such group or territory has already been allocated exclusively to a particular reseller. On the other hand, restrictions on passive sales should be categorically avoided, since the restriction of passive sales is evaluated as a hard-core restriction and condemned by the Board in a variety of decisions.[598] In other words, restrictions on the exclusive distributor's passive sales do not benefit from the block exemption under any circumstance, and interference in the passive sales of the exclusive distributor is evaluated under Article 4 of Law No. 4054.

As explained in *Hayal Seramik*,[599] restrictions on passive sales are unlikely to also benefit from an individual exemption. More specifically, in its *Hayal Seramik* decision, the Board stated that not fulfilling the demands of customers from a specific territory that has been previously allocated to another dealer may constitute passive sales restrictions and may not benefit from an individual exemption. Although there are numerous decisions in which the Board has not made an individual exemption analysis regarding restriction on passive sales,[600] in certain decisions, without conducting a detailed individual exemption analysis, the Board indicated that individual exemption can be granted to agreements that

---

[596]   *Industrial Gas* (29 August 2013, 13-49/710-297).
[597]   Guidelines on Vertical Agreements, para. 24.
[598]   *Hayal Seramik* (26 December 2019, 19-46/772-333); *Çaykur II* (14 November 2019, 19-40/645-272); *Mates-Atek* (4 January 2018, 18-01/1-1); *Altınbaş Petrol* (6 November 2012, 12-54/1517-535); *Doğuş Otomotiv* (n. 568).
[599]   *Hayal Seramik* (n. 598), pp. 12–13.
[600]   *Xerox* (4 December 2008, 08-69/1121-437 and 2 May 2013, 13-25/331-150); *Karadeniz Tüpgaz* (14 July 2011, 11-43/953-307); *Koçaklar* (9 June 2011, 11-36/757-234); *Kuralkan* (27 May 2008, 08-35/462-162).

include such restrictions, only in exceptional cases.[601] Within this context, for instance, undertakings that are suppliers of certain hazardous substances may prevent their buyers from selling such products to certain customers due to reasons such as safety and health, or in cases where a new market is established, the supplier may prevent active or passive sales to the new market for a certain period of time.[602] Moreover, in *Mates-Atek*,[603] it is observed that the Board does not prefer to launch an investigation regarding conducts concerning restriction on passive sales. Instead, the Board sends an opinion to the undertakings concerned as per Article 9(3) of Law No. 4054, which requires parties to stop any direct or indirect passive sales practices and ensure no passive sales restriction is imposed.[604] On this note, the passive sales restriction in the decision concerned an obligation imposed by Corghi towards Mates requiring them to direct any demand made by the automotive stores to Atek and, in return, obligation imposed by Corghi towards Atek in order to direct the demands made by the tire stores to Mates.

Overall, while analysing restrictions on passive sales, the Board takes into consideration different factors such as the vertical nature of the violation, the competitive structure of the market, the violation's effects on the potential and actual competition, the market positions of the supplier and the buyers, and the entry barriers to the market.

5.1.2.2.1 Export Bans

The ban on parallel exports is a significant issue with regard to territorial exclusivity. Turkish competition law evaluates restrictions on export sales on two fronts: (i) the direct restrictions imposed by the supplier to the export sales of the buyer, and (ii) the indirect restrictions imposed by the seller on the buyer's customers.

As Article 2 of Law No. 4054 limits the jurisdiction of the Authority to Turkey, a restriction that will bear no effect in Turkey would not be considered within the scope of Law No. 4054.[605] In other words, a supplier can restrict the direct export sales of the buyer due to the jurisdictional limits of Law No. 4054, as this would bear no effect within the Turkish market. A number of precedents of the Board indicate that an export ban placed on the distributors, under which the distributors' sales are limited to within Turkey, would not be in violation of Turkish competition law. The reasoning of the Board in the said decisions is that the effect of the export ban is felt outside of Turkey rather than within Turkey, and thus would not violate Turkish competition law.

In *Levi's*, the Board held that the anti-competitive effects of such restriction on export would affect the targeted country and not Turkey. A similar approach was also adopted in *Glaxo Wellcome*,[606] as explained above, where direct restrictions on export were regarded out of the scope of Law No. 4054 as per Article 2.

---

[601]   *KWS* (n. 547); *Yatsan* (n. 166).

[602]   Guidelines on Vertical Agreements, paras. 20 and 99.

[603]   *Mates-Atek* (n. 598).

[604]   *KWS* (n. 547); *Kuralkan* (n. 600); *Yatsan* (n. 166); *Alarko* (21 February 2007, 07-15/142-45); *Philip Morris* (11 March 2005, 05-14/170-62).

[605]   *Levi's* (27 June 2008, 08-41/565-213); *Hyundai* (11 July 2007, 07-59/684-240); *Sodima* (8 June 2004, 04-46/597-145); *Glaxo Wellcome-PNG* (n. 593).

[606]   *Glaxo Wellcome-PNG* (n. 593).

Having stated the general rule in terms of indirect restrictions of export, however, it should be underlined that a supplier cannot restrict a distributor's sale within Turkey, knowing that the distributor will sell to a customer in Turkey, who will then re-sell the products abroad. In other words, there is an exception to the jurisdictional limits of Law No. 4054 when the restriction directed towards sales out of Turkey also has an effect on the Turkish markets, since the effects of such a restriction could be felt within Turkey as the initial sale (sale from the distributor to the customer) is made in Turkey.[607] This would be deemed as a vertical restriction in violation of Article 4 of Law No. 4054 as it is an indirect attempt to ban exports where the effects are felt within Turkey.

Pfizer/Dilek[608] shows that when a restriction is imposed by the seller, in order to interfere in the possible sales of the buyer's customers that intend to conduct sales outside of Turkey, anti-competitive effects could arise in Turkey, and such arrangement would, therefore, fall within the scope of Law No. 4054. In this context, as the agreement between Pfizer and Dilek included a clause that prohibited Dilek to sell products to customers who were either known or reasonably assumed to conduct sales outside of Turkey, subsequent to its assessment of the relevant contractual obligation under Communiqué No. 2002/2, the Board concluded that such a restriction would be regarded as interfering in third parties' sales and third parties were free to sell (actively/passively) as they wished. As a result, the indirect export prohibition was concluded not to benefit from Communiqué No. 2002/2, since, pursuant to Article 4(b)(1), restrictions on the sales made by the customers of the purchaser were deemed to fall outside the protective cloak of the block exemption regime. The Board decided that individual exemption could be granted to the agreement on the condition that the relevant restrictions were removed from the agreement. Accordingly, this approach places indirect restrictions of export under the scope of Law No. 4054 and, as can be seen from the *Pfizer/Dilek* decision, would require an individual exemption assessment under Article 5 of Law No. 4054. Indeed, a similar approach was also adopted in *Johnson & Johnson.*[609]

As a recent development, the Council of State has annulled[610] the Board's *Roche-Corena I*[611] decision, where the Board concluded that a direct export ban fell out of the scope of Law No. 4054, as the export ban would not bear any effect on the market for medicines for human use in Turkey and decided not to launch an investigation against Roche. As a result of its assessment of the export ban in the vertical agreement between Corena and Roche, the Board concluded that the restrictions imposed by a supplier that may restrict the territory or customer groups would be considered within Article 4 of Law No. 4054. With that in mind, the Board also stated that restrictions to the sales territory outside Turkey would not be considered within the meaning of Article 2, which determines the territorial scope of Law No. 4054. That being said, the Council of State decided that, since the plaintiff claimed that such restriction also created effects on Turkish markets, the Board should have also assessed these claims and ascertained whether this export

---

[607] *Marble-Cutters* (24 February 2005, 05-11/114-44).
[608] *Pfizer-Dilek* (2 August 2007, 07-63/774-281).
[609] *Johnson & Johnson* (14 November 2019, 19-40/642-270).
[610] 13th Chamber of the Council of State (16 December 2016, E. 2010/4617, K. 2016/4241).
[611] *Roche-Corena I* (17 June 2010, 10-44/785-262).

ban created any effects on Turkish markets. Pursuant to the annulment decision, the Board initiated a fully-fledged investigation against Roche. In the reasoned decision[612] of the long-standing process, the Board evaluated the plaintiff's allegation that direct and indirect export bans in the agreements restricted active and passive sales of warehouses; therefore, constituted a hard-core violation under Article 4. The Board concluded that the agreements did not adopt an allocation of territories or customer groups within the borders of Turkey; therefore, it was not possible to evaluate the direct and indirect export ban as restriction on active and passive sales. Consequently, the Board held that the export ban had no anti-competitive effect on the markets in Turkey, and the direct and indirect export bans could not be evaluated as a hard-core restriction under Article 4 of Communiqué No. 2002/2 nor a violation of Article 4 of Law No. 4054.

Also in *Novo Nordisk*,[613] *Novartis*[614] and *Server-Zirve*,[615] the Board concluded that prevention of warehouses' sales to third-party warehouses that were either known or reasonably assumed to conduct sales outside of Turkey cannot be evaluated within the scope of Law No. 4054, since export bans do not bear any effect on the market for medicines for human use in Turkey. The Board justified its decisions by deeming these restrictions to be crucial (i) to ensure the availability of the medicines in Turkey, and (ii) to prevent medicines from being exported abroad without meeting the necessary technical requirements, risking assets and damage to people's health.

5.1.2.2.2 Online Sales

Generally speaking, online sales constitute passive sales, and as explained in the previous sections, passive sales are restricted under Turkish competition rules. The revised Guidelines on Vertical Agreements published on 30 March 2018 provide detailed insight on what constitutes passive online sales and restrictions acceptable under Turkish competition law.

Overall, as the Guidelines on Vertical Agreements also states, "in principle, every distributor must be allowed to use the internet to sell products". Accordingly, a supplier imposing restrictions on sales through distributors'/dealers'/buyers' websites will be regarded as a restriction on passive sales. Within this context, purchases made through consumers' (i) visits to resellers' websites; (ii) contacts with resellers; or (iii) requests to be informed by resellers automatically are considered to be passive sales. Having said that, the different/multiple language options offered on the resellers' websites do not affect the passive nature of the sales. Accordingly, inter alia, the following restrictions on internet sales are considered to be hard-core restrictions and will not benefit from the block exemption under Communiqué No. 2002/2:

– restriction on an (exclusive) reseller's website to consumers located in another (exclusive) reseller's region or diverting such consumers' access to the supplier's or the other (exclusive) resellers' websites;

---

[612] *Roche* (26 September 2018, 18-34/577-283).
[613] *Novo Nordisk* (5 February 2015; 15-06/71-29).
[614] *Novartis* (11 April 2019; 19-15/215-95).
[615] Server-Zirve (23 June 2016; 16-21/363-169).

- (exclusive) reseller's termination of transaction after realising the customer is not located in its (exclusive) region through the customer's delivery, mail, credit card, address information;

- setting a maximum sales limit for internet sales (certain exceptions apply);

- imposing conditions requiring a reseller to pay more to the suppliers for the products sold online when compared to products sold in physical brick-and-mortar stores .[616]

Generally speaking, requirements imposed with regard to brick-and-mortar store sales and internet sales do not have to be identical, yet any requirement as such must (i) serve the same purpose, (ii) ensure comparable outcomes, and (iii) be able to verify the intrinsic differences adopted for the two sales channels based on the equivalence principle, and in this regard, (iv) discouraging the use of the internet as a sales channel is also regarded to amount to a violation.[617]

Moreover, restrictions on the internet sales made to a particular exclusive region or a particular exclusive customer group of another distributor through promotion or similar methods or advertisements directed to a specific group of customers and/or a specific geographical region and (unsolicited) e-mails are considered to constitute active sale restrictions and may benefit from the protective cloak provided under Communiqué No. 2002/2 and Article 5 of Law No. 4054.[618]

In *BSH*,[619] the practices of directing the online sales tabs of BSH's dealers' websites to the main website of BSH and the pre-2015 internet sales ban clause in the contacts have been evaluated as restrictions on passive sales. BSH was alleged to restrict online sales of Bosch branded products by way of certain terms that required BSH's distributors to obtain BSH's prior authorisation before making any online sales and adopting certain repressive practices towards the restriction of online sales by way of warning distributors on online sales prices and refusing to supply in case of incompliance. The Board assessed that the relevant clauses in the distribution agreement and BSH's "warning practices" as such may lead to potential restrictions of online sales and carried out an individual exemption analysis which concluded that the relevant practices hindered new developments and improvements, or economic or technical development of production or distribution of products.

In *Baymak*,[620] the Board confirmed that internet sales (unless they are made as a result of an active action of the seller) are considered passive sales and that the restriction of internet sales cannot benefit from a block exemption and that there should be a legitimate reason in order for the restriction to be granted an individual exemption.

That being said, imposing restrictions deemed proportionated by the Board (for instance, restrictions on the customers' purchase amount via internet sales, which can also be imposed towards physical sales points under certain conditions) may avoid competition law concerns, in line with the new amendments to the Guidelines on Vertical Agreements.

---

[616] Guidelines on Vertical Agreements, para. 25.
[617] Ibid., para. 29.
[618] Ibid., para. 26.
[619] *BSH* (22 August 2017, 17-27/454-195).
[620] *Baymak* (n. 539).

5.1.3 Selective Distribution

As per the definition of "selective distribution system" within the scope of Turkish competition law, a supplier that establishes such distribution system undertakes to sell the contract products or services, either directly or indirectly, only to resellers selected on the basis of specified criteria. On the other hand, authorised resellers within such selective distribution system undertake not to sell contracted products or services to unauthorised resellers.[621]

Selective distribution agreements, like exclusive distribution agreements, restrict the number of authorised resellers as well as the possibilities of resale. The difference between selective and exclusive distribution is that the restriction of the number of resellers within the selective distribution system does not depend on the number of territories but on the selection criteria based on the nature of the product. Also, another difference is that the restriction on resale is not a restriction on active selling to a territory but a restriction on any sales to unauthorised resellers, leaving only the appointed resellers and end-users as potential buyers.

As the selective distribution systems limit the number of authorised resellers and certain resale practices, such distribution systems may restrict competition due to their nature. To be more specific, selective distribution systems may result in competitive restrictions as they could (i) reduce the intra-brand competition; (ii) lead to foreclosure of certain types of resellers; and (iii) facilitate collusion between suppliers or resellers.[622] That being said, selective distribution systems may be significant especially in certain sectors where the presale services could play an important role for branded products such as jewellery and fragrance. Moreover, the marketing of such branded products may require the adoption of specific physical features at sale points and competent sales personnel.

Overall, the Guidelines on Vertical Agreements make a distinction between (i) purely qualitative selective distribution systems and (ii) quantitative selective distribution systems. Within the purely qualitative selective distribution systems, the supplier authorises the resellers only on the basis of objective criteria required by the nature of the product, such as training of sales personnel, the service provided at the point of sale, a certain range of products being sold. In this respect, if the following three conditions are met, it is assumed that the purely qualitative selective distribution systems are not restrictive: (i) the nature of the product must necessitate a selective distribution system to preserve its quality and ensure its proper use (a legitimate requirement); (ii) resellers must be chosen on the basis of objective criteria of a qualitative nature which are laid down uniformly for all and made available to all potential resellers and are not applied in a discriminatory manner; and (iii) the criteria laid down should not go beyond what is necessary. On the other hand, the quantitative selective distribution systems add further criteria for selection which rather more directly limits the potential number of dealers by, for instance, requiring minimum or maximum sales, by fixing the number of dealers.

---

[621]   Article 3(g) of Communiqué No. 2002/2.
[622]   Guidelines on Vertical Agreements, para. 171.

As indicated in *Antis*,[623] there may be reasons such as protecting the brand image and ensuring the correct and healthy use of the product, especially for a manufacturer of advanced technology and/or luxury products, in order to establish a distribution system that will ensure that its product can only be found at selected sales points that meet certain criteria. Examples of such criteria may be qualifications of the sellers and personnel, the location, appearance and size of the point of sale, minimum turnover capacity, pre-sales and after-sales service and repair services, participation in some promotional activities.

Similarly, in *Teknosa*,[624] the Board examined the selective distribution system including non-compete obligation between Teknosa and İklimsa and indicated that in case the products are sold by unauthorised distributors, there may be risks of fire and gas leaks due to the inappropriate and low-quality parts. Therefore, the Board concluded that the restrictions are within the scope of Communiqué No. 2002/2 and further added that there is no indication that Teknosa restricts the distributors' physical or online sales. Also, in *Arçelik*,[625] whereby the Board evaluated the agreements concerning electrical and electronic household items such as refrigerators, washing machines, dishwashers, microwave ovens and tube televisions, the Board concluded that the selective distribution system is necessary in order to protect the quality of product's features which are subject to high technology and constantly evolving research and development activities.

In *Jotun*,[626] the Board indicated that although Jotun established a selective distribution system, a provision restricting online sales of authorised dealers would cause the vertical agreement to fall outside the scope of Communiqué No. 2002/2. The Board further added that prohibiting online sales as a whole with the purpose of restricting the sales to unauthorised dealers would be disproportionate and would not benefit from an individual exemption. In *Jotun*, the Board underlined that the restriction of dealers' online sales as a whole could not be justified merely with the nature of the selective distribution system and the purpose of restricting sales to unauthorised dealers. In its decision, the Board decided that there is no need for launching a fully-fledged investigation against Jotun. However, the Board also decided that Jotun must terminate all practices related to the restriction of passive sales, including online sales, and accordingly revise the existing provisions in the agreements.

Communiqué No. 2002/2 sets forth certain conditions that are required for the selective distribution system to benefit from the block exemption. First of all, the supplier's Turkey-specific market share within the preceding calendar year for the relevant product market in which it supplies the contract products or services should not exceed 40%. Moreover, even if the supplier's market share does not exceed the relevant threshold, an agreement should not contain any restrictions that are listed within Communiqué No. 2002/2.

In *Johnson & Johnson*,[627] the Board took into consideration the nature of the products in determining whether the relevant distribution system could be characterised as a selective

---

[623] *Antis* (8 May 2008, 08-32/401-136).
[624] *Teknosa* (9 November 2017, 17-36/578-252).
[625] *Arçelik* (18 October 2011, 11-53/1353-479).
[626] *Jotun* (15 February 2018, 18-05/74-40).
[627] *Johnson & Johnson* (3 September 2020, 20-40/553-249).

distribution system within the meaning of Communiqué No. 2002/2, even though the market share of the supplier was below the 40% threshold.

Even though the Guidelines on Vertical Agreements[628] unequivocally state that the characteristics of the products must be disregarded when determining whether a selective distribution system will benefit from the block exemption in case the 40% market share threshold is not exceeded, the relevant agreement was evaluated "based on the nature of the product". The agreement subject to the decision sought to establish a quantitative selective distribution system whereby nine pharmaceutical warehouses that satisfy certain criteria determined by Johnson & Johnson would be appointed as the authorised distributors of four pharmaceuticals to pharmacies. The relevant agreement prevented the authorised distributors from selling the relevant pharmaceuticals to any unauthorised resellers. Finally, the agreement imposed direct and indirect export bans on the authorised distributors, prohibiting them from selling those pharmaceuticals outside Turkey. In light of the relevant restrictions, the Board found that the agreement did not satisfy the conditions of the block exemption set forth under Communiqué No. 2002/2 and also refused to grant an individual exemption.

Both active and passive sales of authorised resellers to the unauthorised resellers may be restricted by the supplier within the scope of the selective distribution system. That being said, the sales and purchases between the members of a selective distribution system (cross-supply) may not be restricted and such practice would be considered as a hard-core restriction.[629] Accordingly, the members of a selective distribution system cannot be forced to purchase the contracted products or services exclusively from the supplier or a given source.

In *Arcon Cosmetics*,[630] the Board found that Arcon (i) restricted the members of its selective distribution system from selling the products by any means except at their sale point (e.g., prohibition of sales through mail, catalogue, etc.); (ii) required that the members of the selective distribution system exclusively supply the products from Arcon (i.e., restriction of cross-supply); and (iii) intervened in the resale prices of the members of the selective distribution system. In this respect, the Board concluded that Arcon's selective distribution agreement would not benefit from the block exemption. The Board further added that although the contact between the end-users and sales personnel could be important with regard to skincare products, as the end-users would be guided to appropriate products, prohibiting the authorised resellers from selling any Christian Dior branded products outside of sale points would reduce consumer welfare. Moreover, the Board indicated that due to the restriction of cross-supply, the members of the selective distribution systems would have to purchase the products exclusively from Arcon. The Board stated that this restriction was against the nature of the selective distribution system and that it could not be objectively justified to adopt such restriction for the purposes of Arcon's selective distribution system. To that end, the Board stated that Arcon's selective distribution system could not be granted with an individual exemption.

---

[628]   Guidelines on Vertical Agreements, para. 172.
[629]   Article 4(d) of Communiqué No. 2002/2.
[630]   *Arcon Cosmetics* (9 September 2009, 09-41/987-249).

Active and passive sales to the end-users by the members of a selective distribution system should not be restricted.[631] This means that within the scope of passive sales, online sales to end-users should not be prohibited.

Moreover, customer exclusivity may not be imposed within a selective distribution system. In other words, within a selective distribution system, the supplier may not allocate certain customers to the specific resellers.

That being said, the selective distribution systems may be combined with the exclusive territory allocation as long as the supplier's relevant market share does not exceed the 40% threshold and the agreement does not include any hard-core restrictions. To that end, although Communiqué No. 2002/2 allows restriction of active sales made to an exclusive territory reserved for the other reseller(s) within the exclusive distribution system,[632] when the selective distribution is combined with the exclusive territory allocation, such active sales could not be restricted.

Overall, given that the physical characteristics of the stores are important for a selective distribution system, the supplier may prevent a reseller from (i) changing the location of its store where it conducts its activities or (ii) establishing a new sale point. Nevertheless, if a member of the selective distribution system would launch a website to conduct their sales through the internet, such activity would not be deemed as the establishment of a new physical sale point, and thus the supplier could not prevent such reseller on this front.

On this note, under certain conditions, suppliers may impose restrictions on the internet sales of their resellers within selective distribution systems. For example, suppliers may require quality standards for the website or may require provision of certain services to the end-users for their purchases through the internet. Although there is no exhaustive list of those conditions, as per Guidelines on Vertical Agreements and the precedents of the Board, these conditions could be identified as follows: (i) restrictions imposed by the supplier should not aim to directly or indirectly restrict resellers' online sales and price competition; (ii) justifications for the restrictions imposed by the supplier on online sales should be objective, reasonable and acceptable with respect to the aspects that enhance the distribution system's qualifications and quality, brand image and/or potential efficiencies; (iii) requirements imposed on physical sales and internet sales should not be identical due to the differences in sales conditions.

That being said, any requirements brought for both online sales channels and brick-and-mortar shops should (i) serve the same purpose; (ii) ensure comparable outcomes; and (iii) be able to verify the differences between the two distribution channels (*equivalence principle*). In other words, the conditions should not aim to restrict online sales directly or indirectly.

For instance, in *Yatsan*,[633] the Board assessed that the prohibition of online sales imposed by Yatsan on its resellers could not be justified based on the preservation of brand image

---

[631]   Article 4(c) of Communiqué No. 2002/2.
[632]   Article 4(b)(1) of Communiqué No. 2002/2.
[633]   *Yatsan* (September 23, 2010; n. 166).

and potential concerns in terms of free riding. The Board found that Yatsan's products does not have special characteristics that may necessitate the prohibition of their sales to certain customers due to health and safety reasons, and thus, Yatsan's agreement with its resellers would not benefit from the block exemption. Furthermore, compared to the traditional sales methods, the internet is a significant tool that allows both resellers and suppliers to reach more and varied end-users, and online sales increase consumer welfare by decreasing search and comparison costs and easing the process of reaching a demanded product. The Board concluded that such restriction goes beyond what is necessary to attain the objective of preserving the brand image and prevent free riding.

On the other hand, in its *Antis*[634] decisions, the agreements set forth some restrictions for the authorised dealers. The authorised dealers cannot sell any product that they have purchased from Antis outside the area specified in the agreement. Moreover, Dermalogica branded professional products can only be sent to the dealers who have been trained for their application by Antis and, therefore, these products cannot be sold to any other undertaking by the authorised dealers, regardless of whether they are Antis' authorised dealers or not. Also, the authorised dealers cannot display or sell any products other than Antis' products in their stores and cannot sell Antis' products online without the prior consent of Antis. The Board found that Dermalogica's professional products require key personnel specifically trained for the application of those cosmetic products. In this respect, the Board stated that the rationale of Antis' selective distribution system is based on the nature of its professional cosmetic products and its need to preserve its brand image. To that end, the Board emphasised that in order for Antis to address the end-users' expectations for professional cosmetic products offered in the beauty centres, the presence of trained personnel could be objectively considered as necessary. Furthermore, given that (i) internet sales of Antis' resellers were not completely restricted, but require Antis' permission to conduct online sales and (ii) the restriction imposed by Antis only covers Dermalogica's professional cosmetic products, the Board indicated that requesting permission of Antis for online sales does not go beyond what is necessary and granted an individual exemption to the agreements in both decisions.[635]

In light of the foregoing, it can be said that in *Yatsan*, the Board did not consider the product's features and consumer behaviour, on the other hand, in *Antis* decisions, the grounds on which the selective distribution system is based have been accepted as justification for the restriction of online sales without discussing their transformative effects in purchase habits and accessibility, thus the Board did not evaluate the competitive benefit provided by the internet. All in all, the common approach adopted in both decisions is that if the inter-brand competition is sufficient, the decrease in intra-brand competition caused by the online ban will not create a significant competitive concern.[636]

On the other hand, the supplier may not restrict the members of the selective distribution system, either directly or indirectly, from selling products of a specific competing

---

[634]   *Antis* (n. 623); *Antis* (24 October 2013, 13-59/831-353).
[635]   For the sake of completeness, in *Antis* decision the Board granted an individual exemption for five years while in *Antis* decision it did not limit the time period of the individual exemption.
[636]   C. Yüksek, *Seçici Dağıtım Sisteminde İnternetten Satış Sınırlamaları* (Ankara: Rekabet Kurumu, 2017), p. 44.

supplier.[637] That being said, the supplier of a selective distribution system may impose non-compete obligations on the resellers to restrict them from selling all of the other suppliers' competing products instead of prohibiting the sale of a specific supplier's competing products.

Overall, the duration of the non-compete obligations imposed on the members of a selective distribution system may not be indefinite or even exceed five years. Moreover, post-term non-compete obligations may be imposed only if such obligations are (i) related to products or services that compete with the contracted products or services; (ii) indispensable to protect know-how transferred by the supplier to the reseller; (iii) limited to the point of sale or land from which the reseller has operated during the agreement; and (iv) limited to a maximum period of one year after the termination of the agreement. In *BBA Beymen*,[638] the Board concluded that a post-term non-compete obligation for six months would be within the scope of Communiqué No. 2002/2 as it is necessary to protect the information and experiences that can be considered as know-how of BBA Beymen. The relevant restriction has also been found to fulfil the other conditions set forth under the Communiqué No. 2002/2, which are related with the duration, subject, and geographic scope of such restriction.

5.1.4 Single Branding (Non-Compete Obligations)

Under Article 3(d) of Communiqué No. 2002/2, a non-compete obligation is defined as any kind of direct or indirect obligation preventing the buyer from producing, purchasing, selling or reselling products or services that compete with the products and services subject to the agreement. Furthermore, any contractual imposition that directly or indirectly obliges the buyer to purchase more than 80% of the products or services (or substitutes) in the relevant market (based on their previous calendar year purchases) from that particular supplier (or another undertaking designated by the same) is also considered as non-compete obligation.[639]

Non-compete obligations are beneficial for the suppliers as they prevent the buyers from selling other products by taking advantage of the suppliers' reputation and thus becoming competitors for the suppliers. As the main purpose of Law No. 4054 is to ensure competition in the market, it is clear that a non-compete obligation may constitute competition law violation as it may restrict the entry of different actors in the market and the commercial independence of the buyer. However, under certain circumstances, such provisions are permitted.

Non-compete obligations that do not exceed the scope of the agreement and are restricted to the undertakings party to the agreement can usually benefit from the block exemption

---

[637]   Article 5(c) of Communiqué No. 2002/2.
[638]   *BBA Beymen* (25 March 2004, 04-22/234-50).
[639]   *Hyundai* (n. 606).

under the assumption that the two pre-conditions have been fulfilled: (i) the duration of the non-compete obligation (lasting during the term of the agreement) does not exceed five years and (ii) the market share of the undertakings which are party to the vertical agreement is less than 40%.

A non-compete obligation that continues after the termination of the agreement may be more problematic. Article 5(b) of Communiqué No. 2002/2 sets forth the conditions for non-compete obligations that exceed the duration of the agreement. Overall, the evaluation of the scope of the non-compete obligation and its duration is important. According to Article 5 of Communiqué No. 2002/2, the non-compete obligations of the buyers cannot benefit from the exemption granted within the scope of the relevant communiqué if they exceed five years or are indefinite in duration. If the non-compete obligation could be tacitly renewed for a period that would exceed five years, this would be considered as an indefinite non-compete obligation.

Also, according to paragraph 38 of the Guidelines on Vertical Agreements, in case the provisions that include the non-compete obligation cannot be separated from the other provisions of the agreement, the agreement as a whole cannot benefit from the block exemption. On the contrary, if it is possible to separate the provisions referring to the non-compete obligation, the rest of the agreement may benefit from the block exemption. If the agreement in question cannot benefit from the block exemption due to the fact that the market shares of the undertakings party to the agreement exceed 40%, or the non-compete obligation lasts longer than the acceptable duration, the Board can still evaluate the conditions for individual exemption set forth under Article 5 of Law No. 4054.

In relation to the restrictions under non-compete terms brought to parties to the agreement, indeed, in *Mogaz*,[640] the Board confirmed that Communiqué No. 2002/2 does not contain any provision with regard to non-compete obligations that can be imposed on third parties which are not parties to the vertical agreement, yet also concluded that non-compete obligations set forth for third parties (i.e., rather than the dealer itself) cannot benefit from the block exemption and that the relevant clauses must be amended to restrict the reach of the term.

In relation to the five-year duration restriction of non-compete terms, in *Generali*,[641] *JTI*[642] and *IGA/THY*,[643] the Board decided that the agreements subject to the Board's evaluation could not benefit from the block exemption within the scope of Communiqué No. 2002/2 as the non-compete obligations exceeded five years. In this respect, in these decisions, the Board evaluated the conditions for individual exemption and decided that individual exemption could be granted to the agreements in question. For completeness, in *IGA/THY*, the Board granted an individual exemption for ten years. Having said that, in *Karbogaz*,[644] the Board evaluated that a non-compete obligation lasting for the term of the agreement, which is indefinite, may not benefit from an exemption.

---

[640]   *Mogaz* (31 July 2008, 08-49/702-277).
[641]   *Generali* (16 April 2020, 20-20/265-126).
[642]   *JTI Tobacco III* (13 February 2019, 19-07/81-33).
[643]   *IGA/THY* (n. 583).
[644]   *Karbogaz* (1 December 2005, 05-80/1106-317).

Moving on, in *BFIT*,[645] the Board evaluated the non-compete obligation, which continued after the termination of the franchise agreement, and decided that the scope of the obligation was more restrictive than necessary to protect the know-how within the scope of Article 5 of Communiqué No. 2002/2. The Board also decided that the non-compete provision had to be revised in order to be restricted to the operation or the franchise site, and that the duration of this provision should be limited to one year after the termination of the agreement, instead of two years.

In addition to the non-compete provisions, rights affecting the duration of the vertical relationship such as usufruct and lease obtained by the distributor on the property where the dealer operates are also considered within the scope of Article 5 of Communiqué No. 2002/2 as they may indirectly constitute non-compete obligations. According to paragraph 44 of the Guidelines on Vertical Agreements, the aforementioned rights exceeding five years cannot benefit from the block exemption. This matter is usually rendered to be problematic for the dealership agreements in the fuel oil sector. Despite this provision and the duration of the dealership agreement, which does not exceed five years, in practice the duration of the non-compete obligation may be de facto extended when the usufruct and lease rights established on behalf of the distributor through the vertical agreements (including non-compete provisions) entered between the entities exceed five years.[646]

Accordingly, in *Shell/Cabbaroğlu*,[647] while the Board admitted that lease and usufruct rights affected the duration of the non-compete obligation, it did not take this finding into consideration while evaluating the case in hand. As the non-complete obligations included in the agreements executed between Shell and its dealers were set forth for an indefinite period, the Board decided that the agreements in question may benefit from the block exemption under the condition that these obligations are limited to five years. Moreover, in *Güney Petrol/POAŞ*,[648] Güney Petrol claimed that the duration of the non-compete obligation must be taken into consideration with regard to the duration of the usufruct right but not the duration of the vertical agreement. The Board evaluated the dealership agreement with non-compete obligation and the usufruct right jointly and considered it within the scope of Article 4 of Law No. 4054, and concluded that they benefited from the exemption. In *Siyam Petrol*,[649] the Board stated that the agreement might benefit from the block exemption if only the provision included a limitation of five years for the usufruct right. Overall, according to paragraph 40 of the Guidelines on Vertical Agreements, the five-year period is calculated by taking into consideration both the date of termination of the vertical agreement and the termination of the lease and usufruct rights.[650]

In some product markets, the non-compete obligations may be rendered to lead to barriers to entry for competitors. For instance, the Board's decisions such as *JTI Tobacco I*,[651]

---

[645] *BFIT* (n. 515).
[646] A. K. Karauz, *Akaryakıt Bayilik Sözleşmesi* (doctoral thesis, Ankara: Yetkin Yayınevi, 2015), p. 168.
[647] *Shell/Cabbaroğlu* (2 October 2003, 03-64/770-356).
[648] *Güney Petrol/POAŞ* (7 February 2008, 08-12/123-40).
[649] *Siyam Petrol* (7 May 2020, 20-23/300-146).
[650] *Shell* (12 November 2019, 19-39/601-255).
[651] *JTI Tobacco I* (28 May 2002, 02-32/368-154).

JTI Tobacco II,[652] and *JTI Tobacco III*[653] concerning the non-compete obligations on the cigarette market are noteworthy as the Board took into consideration aspects such as the advertisement bans and the narrow oligopoly nature of this market during its evaluation, and concluded that the non-compete obligations in the stand agreements executed between cigarette producers and the dealers could lead to barriers to entry and market foreclosure for small undertakings. Accordingly, these kinds of provisions cannot benefit from the exemption and they should be eliminated from the agreements in the entire sector.

Similarly, the Board's decisions in the pharmaceutical sector are also noteworthy in terms of the evaluation of the conditions for individual exemption within the scope of Article 5 of Law No. 4054. In *Takeda*,[654] the Board concluded that the agreement could not benefit from the block exemption as the duration of the non-compete obligation was two years after the termination of the agreement by the distributor. However, this provision did not refer to a termination by the supplier. Thus, the Board decided that this provision did not restrict the competition more than necessary and the agreement could therefore benefit from an individual exemption. In *Sanofi-Aventis*,[655] as the market share of Sanofi-Aventis exceeded 40% in the relevant product market, the Board concluded that the agreement could not benefit from the block exemption. Therefore, as the conditions in Article 5 of Law No. 4054 were fulfilled, the Board granted an individual exemption.

5.1.5 Obligation to Supply to a Single Buyer

Pursuant to Article 3(h) of Communiqué No. 2002/2, obligation to supply to a single buyer can be defined as the supplier's direct or indirect obligation to sell the products or services subject to the agreement to solely one buyer in Turkey for the purpose of its own use or for resale. According to Article 2 of Communiqué No. 2002/2, exemption for the vertical agreements including the obligation to supply to a single buyer can be granted under the condition that the buyer's market share in the relevant market where it purchases the products and services subject to the vertical agreement does not exceed 40%, and that the other conditions set forth under Communiqué No. 2002/2 are fulfilled.

The Guidelines on Vertical Agreements set forth that the main competition concern arising from this obligation is market foreclosure for other buyers in the market. In the assessment of a provision setting forth that the buyer can restrict other buyers' access to the market that is their source of supply, the market share in the upstream market should be taken into consideration. However, the buyer's position in the downstream market is also important for the assessment of whether this may lead to any competition law concerns. In case the buyer does not have any market power in the downstream market, the negative effects of the arrangement on the consumers are considered to be less.

---

[652]   *JTI Tobacco II* (3 March 2004, 04-18/152-34).
[653]   *JTI Tobacco III* (n. 642).
[654]   *Takeda* (3 April 2014, 14-13/242-107).
[655]   *Sanofi-Aventis* (22 November 2012, 12-59/1570-571).

In this respect and in light of the Board's precedent,[656] the buyer's market share in the relevant product market should not exceed 40% in order to conclude that the obligation to supply to a single buyer does not lead to any competition concerns.

The duration and scope of the obligation to supply to a single buyer are important for the assessment of the relevant obligation. Generally speaking, the longer the duration of the obligation, the more likely it will lead to market foreclosure. An obligation to supply to a single buyer for a period exceeding five years is usually considered to be beyond the necessary extent to ensure efficiency for the investments.

In *Pankobirlik*,[657] *Marka Mağazacılık*,[658] *TEB/İDO*,[659] *Çaykur*[660] and *TTNET*,[661] while evaluating whether exemption can be granted to the vertical agreement, including the obligation to supply to a single buyer, the Board examined the total market size of the relevant product market as well as the undertakings' market shares. In this respect, the Board decided that the agreement may benefit from the block exemption as long as the market share of the buyer does not exceed 40%, and noted that if the market shares are exceeded, conditions for individual exemption within the scope of Article 5 of Law No. 4054 must be examined by the Board.

In *JTI Tobacco III*,[662] the Board stated that in order to not restrict competition in the significant part of the relevant market, it should be determined whether the competitor providers' access to the market is prevented, as well as the competitor buyers' access to the input(s).

In *Tuborg/Ecocaps*,[663] as the agreement contained a provision setting forth the obligation to supply solely to Ecocaps for Tuborg, the Board firstly examined the market shares. The market share of the supplier exceeded 40% in the relevant product market. However, the market share of the buyer was not certain. As there was a risk that the market share of the buyer may exceed 40%, the Board did not grant block exemption and decided to examine the conditions for individual exemption. Since the duration of the obligation was limited to the duration of the agreement, the Board decided that it did not restrict competition more than the necessary extent and concluded that the agreement might benefit from an individual exemption.

5.1.6 Most-Favoured Nation/Customer Clause

MFN arrangements, also referred to as selection or price parity arrangements, are essentially restrictions that prohibit a buyer from offering more favourable prices or conditions through its own means (i.e., directly to consumers) or through other means (i.e., to its customers).

---

[656] *Johnson & Johnson/Öz-sel* (8 November 2007, 07-85/1050-409).
[657] *Pankobirlik* (28 July 2020, 20-36/489-215).
[658] *Marka Mağazacılık* (4 November 2019, 19-15/208-93).
[659] *TEB/İDO* (6 January 2016, 16-01/7-2).
[660] *Çaykur* (19 December 2013, 13-71/972-418).
[661] *TTNET* (13 August 2014, 14-28/558-241).
[662] *JTI Tobacco III* (n. 642).
[663] *Tuborg/Ecocaps* (10 February 2016, 16-04/69-27).

Three types of MFN arrangements are recognised in the legal literature: (i) MFN-plus arrangements, (ii) narrow MFN arrangements and (iii) wide MFN arrangements.

MFN-plus arrangements guarantee the most favourable terms to a buyer. Narrow MFN arrangements compare terms with the direct channel of the supplier and require the application of the same terms adopted by the supplier. On the other hand, wide MFN arrangements extend to sales over other platforms or resellers (i.e., competing buyers) and require the application of the same terms offered by the supplier to other buyers.

Under Turkish competition law, there is no statutory provision explicitly allowing or prohibiting MFN arrangements. In other words, it could be said that price parity clauses are not considered illegal per se, and through the amendments in 2018, the Guidelines on Vertical Agreements recognise potential pro-competitive effects of MFN clauses alongside potential anti-competitive effects and adopt a rule of reason-based approach, without making a distinction between the three different types of MFN arrangements. Moreover, the potential pro-competitive and anti-competitive effects of MFN clauses especially in digital markets and more specifically across marketplace platform settings are evaluated under the Authority's Preliminary Report on the Sector Inquiry Concerning E-Marketplace Platforms.[664] In the relevant Preliminary Report,[665] the potential pro-competitive and anti-competitive effects of MFN clauses are explained with a focus on their adoption by gatekeeper marketplaces and their effects on inter-platform competition essentially driven by the commissions applied by the marketplaces. Taking into consideration the distinct features of narrow MFN arrangements and wide MFN arrangements, adopting a secondary legislation governing MFN arrangements in platform markets is advised.

Board's decisional practice to date and the relevant legislation show that MFN clauses are regarded as posing risks for competition if the market powers of the undertakings benefiting from such practices are high (i.e., above 40%). Indeed, in principle, an agreement containing MFN clauses may benefit from the block exemption provided that the market share of the party that is the beneficiary of the clause does not exceed 40% and that the other conditions stipulated in Communiqué No. 2002/2 are met.

As also recognised by the Authority's Preliminary Report on the Sector Inquiry Concerning E-Marketplace Platforms, the evaluation of MFN clauses in the traditional markets differs from those in the online platforms. For example, while the party that is the beneficiary of the clause is the buyer in the traditional markets, it may be either the supplier, the buyer or the intermediary in the online platform markets depending on the relevant product market. Therefore, Communiqué No. 2002/2 does not provide any indication as to which party's market share should be taken into account and provides that one should consider the market share of the beneficiary party of the agreement and the relevant MFN clauses. In case the market share thresholds are exceeded, individual exemption assessment must be carried out under Article 5 of Law No. 4054.

---

[664] E. İnce et al., "E-Pazaryeri Platformları Sektör İncelemesi Ön Raporu" (Sector Inquiry Preliminary Report), 2021, pp. 197–217.

[665] Ibid.

When analysing MFN clauses, factors to be taken into account include (i) the relevant undertakings' and their competitors' position in the relevant market; (ii) the object of the MFN clause in the relevant agreement; and (iii) the specific characteristics of the market. MFN clauses, especially when used by a strong player in the market, raise competition law concerns if and to the extent they have a resale price maintenance and collusion facilitating effect and they reduce "the motivation of undertakings that are not part of such practices to seek better prices and conditions", "artificially increase market transparency", "raise barriers to entry", or "raise competitors' costs", and lead to "price increase" or "price rigidity". For instance, retroactive MFN clauses which allow the beneficiary buyer to get more favourable offers in all cases, or which increase the supplier's costs for offering discounts to buyers that are not party to the clause such as by payment of the difference between (i) the low prices offered to buyers that are not party to the MFN clause and (ii) the price offered to the buyer party to the MFN clause, to the relevant buyer, are likely to harm competition. Besides, if parties to the MFN clause have a stronger market power compared to their competitors in the market, one may argue that such clauses are likely to further harm competition. In such cases, these clauses may lead to the exclusion of competitors that are not party to the relevant agreement and foreclosure of the market to the competitors. Moreover, the use of these clauses in concentrated markets is riskier compared to non-concentrated markets, as the likelihood of rival buyers that are not party to the clause to find an alternative supplier is relatively lower in concentrated markets. In addition to this, in cases where the use of MFN clauses has become widespread and thus a significant portion of the market has been subjected to these clauses, it is necessary to adopt a more sceptical approach in the evaluation of these clauses. This is because it is more likely that the restrictive effects arising from the clauses increase cumulatively where these clauses have become widespread in the market, and thus the likelihood of restriction of competition is higher. Similar concerns are raised in the Authority's Preliminary Report on the Sector Inquiry Concerning E-Marketplace Platforms.[666]

On the other hand, MFN clauses do not always have anti-competitive effects. They may have pro-competitive effects such as reducing costs arising from the repetition of transactions, encouraging investments specific to commercial relations, reducing delays in transactions and demand uncertainty, protecting the brand and preventing the free-rider problem, and preventing the interruption of product supply.[667]

For example, in the instances where neither of the parties to an agreement containing MFN clauses has market power, it is unlikely that the implementation of these clauses would create competition concerns. Moreover, when a small-scale buyer without any significant market power applies an MFN clause, this may allow buyers to benefit from favourable prices and sales conditions in the market. In the instances where the concentration level of the upstream market is low (i.e., upstream market is sufficiently competitive), competitive harm may not exist given that in such a situation current and potential competitors may choose the alternatives. In the case of a non-transparent

---

[666] Ibid., paras. 393–434.
[667] H. Adıyaman, Rekabet Hukukunda Fiyat Parite Anlaşmaları: En Çok Kayrılan Ülke/Müşteri Koşulu (Ankara: Rekabet Kurumu, 2017), p. 40.

market, the negative effects of MFN clauses would be relatively low given that in such situations, it is unlikely that parties will be able to effectively monitor the implementation of these clauses in the market. Again, the Authority has set forth similar points in the Preliminary Report on the Sector Inquiry Concerning E-Marketplace Platforms.[668]

Overall, the two landmark Board decisions on MFN clauses discussed below[669] refer to the exclusionary effects created and the extension of such exclusionary effects to competitors through the adoption of such clauses by undertakings that have more than 40% market share and/or are considered to be in a dominant position in the relevant market. In this regard, it should also be noted that assuming the beneficiary of the MFN clause is in the dominant position in the relevant market, the MFN clause could also result in abuse of dominant position within the meaning of Article 6 of Law No. 4054 and raise allegations on market foreclosure effects.

In *Booking*,[670] the Board indicated that the agreements executed by Booking and certain accommodation facilities (such as hotels, motels, etc.) that include MFN clauses might fall under Article 4 and Article 6. Considering that the evaluation of the actual effect of the MFN clause would be based on similar principles under both articles, instead of making a separate analysis of whether Booking was in dominant position, the Board decided to conduct its assessment based on Article 4 of Law No. 4054.

The Board alleged that clauses in the agreements (i) foreclosed the relevant market segment to competitors and reduced competition in the marketplace for "accommodation reservation services platforms"; (ii) reduced the incentives of Booking's competitors to offer lower commission rates to the accommodation providers that implement broad price parity clauses with Booking; (iii) prevented the application of downward competitive pressure on the commission rates charged by Booking; and (iv) protected Booking from competition by new entrants into the relevant market segment. The Board concluded that (i) broad price parity clauses could not benefit from the block exemption due to Booking's high market share, and (ii) such clauses did not satisfy the requirements for an individual exemption and therefore violated Article 4 of Law No. 4054. In other words, it can be said that the Board also makes a distinction between "wide" and "narrow" MFN clauses and decides to impose an administrative monetary fine on "wide" MFN clauses.

Similarly, in *Yemek Sepeti*,[671] which is the first case where MFN clauses were considered as an infringement of Law No. 4054, the Board assessed whether Yemek Sepeti violated Article 4 and Article 6 of Law No. 4054 through its MFN clauses. However, by concluding that Yemek Sepeti held a dominant position in the online meal order-delivery platform services market, it has focused its assessment on abuse of dominance. By examining Yemek Sepeti's price parity practices, the Board found that the restaurants that had been approached by Yemek Sepeti regarding the price parity clause had generally chosen to cease providing discounts on other platforms, and had, in some cases, even

---

[668] İnce et al., (n. 664), paras. 434–441.
[669] *Booking* (5 January 2017, 17-01/12-4) and *Yemek Sepeti* (n. 31).
[670] Ibid., *Booking* (n. 669).
[671] *Yemek Sepeti* (n. 31).

left competitors' platforms completely. As a result, the Board concluded that such price parity clauses had violated Article 6 of Law No. 4054 by leading to exclusionary effects.

The diversity of the MFN-like clauses used in practice is noteworthy. The platforms that only act as marketplaces for third parties and do not conduct their own sales generally use similar MFN clauses (as in *Yemek Sepeti* and *Booking*). However, platforms that also (or only) act as actual resellers (and therefore should be deemed as buyers in the traditional sense) may require different mechanisms to guarantee that they are getting the best deals from their suppliers.

In *Kitapyurdu*,[672] some of these mechanisms are brought before the attention of the Board. Kitapyurdu.com operated in the market for online retail book sales and held a market share below 40%. Unlike Yemek Sepeti and Booking, Kitapyurdu was not a marketplace for third-party sellers but a reseller that purchased books from different publishers and sold them online through its own website. As explained in the decision, in order to ensure that it remains competitive vis-à-vis other book resellers, Kitapyurdu regularly monitored the prices charged by its competitors at the retail level and contacted the suppliers when it detected any competitors offering more advantageous terms. In those contacts, Kitapyurdu generally requested the suppliers to give additional discounts over the wholesale price or asked them to grant Kitapyurdu additional discounts/campaigns that are available to the competitors. In certain exceptional cases, it was also seen that Kitapyurdu asked suppliers to interfere with the lower retail prices charged by some competitors.

The Board held that Kitapyurdu's requests for additional discounts and/or access to similar/ better discounts and campaigns than its competitors could be deemed as wholesale MFN clauses and considered that such practices would benefit from the protective cloak of Communiqué No. 2002/2, as Kitapyurdu's market share was below 40%.

Moreover, the Board examined the exceptional cases whereby Kitapyurdu asked suppliers to interfere with the lower retail prices charged by some competitors. Accordingly, the Board assessed that despite the wording of some of the communications between Kitapyurdu and its suppliers, which on their face appeared problematic, Kitapyurdu did not try to force the suppliers to interfere with the resale price of its competitors and sought to rather figure out whether these lower prices were stemming from better conditions offered at the wholesale level. The Board concluded that the aim of such communications was to make sure that Kitapyurdu was not put in a less advantageous position vis-à-vis its competitors. Hence, the Board decided that these could also be treated as wholesale MFN clauses that benefit from the block exemption.

Still, the Board noted that in case Kitapyurdu were to interfere with the resale prices of its competitors through the suppliers, this could no longer be regarded as an MFN clause and a further investigation as to whether such practices may amount to resale price maintenance would have to be conducted. On the other hand, in *Tourism Agencies*,[673] the Board evaluated the MFN clauses available in agreements signed between hotels and

---

[672]   *Kitapyurdu* (n. 27).
[673]   *Tourism Agencies* (25 October 2018, 18-40/645-315).

travel agencies and considering factors such as the presence of a high number of players in the relevant market with none exceeding a market share above 40%, it assessed that the price parity clauses applied by the travel agencies benefitted from the protective cloak of block exemption under Communiqué No. 2002.

The Board, in its decisions, often reviewed the scope of the MFN in order to analyse its effects on the market. For example, in *Hopi/Migros*,[674] the Board noted that MFN clauses would be applicable only within the specific periods of beneficiary's sale offer campaigns; at other times the supplier would be free to apply better conditions to other business partners. Similarly in *Arçelik/Sony*,[675] which concerns toll manufacturing agreement between competitors, the Board decided that the MFN clause would not raise restriction of competition in the LCD TV market for the competitors since (i) its scope was limited to toll manufacturing of the same quality product for a third party, and (ii) the market was competitive and the relevant product was diverse (many options available with different quality and features).

Moreover, in *Hopi/Migros*, the Board assessed the advantages of MFN clauses and indicated that Hopi (personalised online shopping offer platform) customers benefit from more "money points" as well as more opportunities due to the MFN conditions applied by Hopi to Migros (FMCG retail chain in Turkey). It has further indicated that the Hopi system aims the users to receive efficient service and benefit from special opportunities and concluded that with the applied MFN conditions, the consumers would benefit from the special offers under more favourable conditions and, therefore, the MFN clauses would actually be beneficial for the consumers. In addition to that, the scope of the MFN clause would be limited to (i) the general and mass special offer days of Hopi and (ii) direct competitors of Hopi. Thus, Migros was able to offer better conditions to other platforms or other business partners when Hopi was not conducting a campaign. As previously stipulated, MFN clauses are regarded as practices that may reinforce the effect of direct and indirect methods for resale price maintenance given that it is likely for them to decrease the supplier's incentives to sell its products to buyers other than the favoured customer for better prices and conditions. That being said, generally speaking, MFN clauses and similar practices that may reinforce the effects of resale price maintenance are not considered as practices that lead to resale price maintenance in and of themselves.[676] To date, there is no Board decision that assesses the resale price maintenance creating effects of MFN clauses.

5.1.7 Franchise Agreements

Under Turkish competition law, franchise agreements are considered as "atypical" agreements that combine the features/characteristics of various agreements (such as

---

[674] *Hopi/Migros* (3 May 2018, 18-13/238-111).
[675] *Arçelik/Sony* (8 December 2010, 10-76/1572-605).
[676] Guidelines on Vertical Agreements, para. 19.

sale/purchase agreements, agency agreements, service agreements, etc.). Franchise agreements are defined in the doctrine as well as by Turkish courts as follows:

> A franchise agreement is between two legally independent parties. It gives the franchisee (i) the right to market a product or service by using the franchisor's trademark or trade name, (ii) the right to market a product or service by using the franchisor's operation methods (know-how), (iii) the obligation to pay a royalty fee for such rights. It also obliges the franchisor to (i) provide know-how or license a trademark (or another IP right) and (ii) to support the franchisee.[677]

A similar definition is also provided in the Guidelines on Vertical Agreements. Accordingly, franchise agreements, which essentially provide a uniform distribution network for products, are defined as agreements containing licences of intellectual property rights and know-how relating in particular to trademarks, signs, etc., for the distribution of products or services and whereby the franchisor provides commercial or technical assistance to the franchisee in return for payment of royalty.[678] A franchise agreement brings about a vertical supply relationship between the franchisor and franchisee. Since franchise agreements usually contain vertical restraints such as non-compete, exclusivity or information exchange provisions, they are often considered under Article 4 of Law No. 4054. Depending on the market share of parties of the franchise agreement, the nature of the relationship between the parties and the content of the transferred know-how, franchise agreements may fall within the scope of application of Communiqué No. 2008/2,[679] or Communiqué No. 2002/2. These two communiqués introduce different and detailed conditions for block exemption. On the other hand, as per the Guidelines on Vertical Agreements, most of the obligations in the franchise agreements may be deemed necessary to protect intellectual property rights or maintain the common identity and product of the franchised network; therefore, they may be deemed to benefit from the protective cloak under Article 5 of Law No. 4054 and in such circumstances, fall outside the scope of Article 4 of Law No. 4054.

Overall, the Guidelines on Vertical Agreements[680] provide that the more important the transfer of know-how, the easier it is for the vertical restrictions to meet the exemption criteria.

Generally speaking, a franchisee may be obliged to sell products manufactured by the franchisor or third parties determined by the franchisor, provided they are necessary to protect the intellectual property rights of the franchisor and to maintain the identity and

---

[677] O. B. Gürzumar, *Franchise Sözleşmeleri ve Bu Sözleşmelerin Temelini Oluşturan Sistemlerin Hukuken Korunması* (Istanbul: Beta Yayımları, 1995), pp. 8–10; Court of Appeal, 19th Civil Chamber (25 June 2001, E. 2001/819, K. 2001/4917).

[678] Guidelines on Vertical Agreements, para. 188.

[679] The agreements where the licensor permits the licensee to use the licensed technology when producing the products specified in the agreement, and that are also technology transfer agreements under Article 4 of Law No. 4054, comprise the scope of this communiqué. This covers the agreements where the licence of the relevant intellectual property and know-how is granted separately or in combination. In case these agreements contain clauses about the sale, purchase of products or giving licence or transferring other intellectual property rights, it is accepted that they are in the scope of this definition, so long as they are the main purpose of the agreement and these are directly related to the production of the product.

[680] Guidelines on Vertical Agreements, para. 189.

Vertical Agreements

reputation of the franchise network. This is also confirmed in *Pınar*[681] and *LB Börekçilik*.[682] Moreover, certain prohibitions which are not generally permitted under other vertical relationships may be regarded as acceptable under franchise agreements. For example, in *Pizza*[683] and in *Dogati*,[684] the prohibition on sales and services in another franchisee's region and the penalty for non-compliance are not evaluated as restrictions on passive sales; instead, the Board concluded that the relevant provisions were determined in order to protect the product and service quality of the franchisor, to protect the brand name and prestige and to ensure customer satisfaction.

Furthermore, non-compete obligations may be subject to differing evaluations in franchise arrangements. The Guidelines on Vertical Agreements[685] provides that a non-competition obligation concerning the products or services purchased by the franchisee falls outside the scope of Article 4 of Law No. 4054 where such an obligation is necessary to maintain the common identity and prestige of the franchised network. In such cases, the duration of the non-competition obligation will not cause a problem under Article 4 either, as long as it does not exceed the duration of the franchise agreement itself.

In *Çelebi Gıda*[686] and in *Costa International*,[687] the Board indicated that although the duration of the non-compete clauses in the franchise agreements, which did not exceed the duration of the agreements, exceeded five years, they would not fall under Article 4 of Law No. 4054 as the non-compete obligation imposed by the franchisor to the franchisee was aimed to protect the identity and prestige of the franchise network. However, in *Starbucks*,[688] the non-compete obligation for fifteen years was not considered to be within the scope of Communiqué No. 2002/2; the Board indicated that the duration might be revised as five years but also the non-compete obligation for fifteen years would be granted with an individual exemption. In *Gap*,[689] the Board granted an individual exemption to non-compete obligation exceeding five years by referring that "a know-how transfer, such as a franchising agreement, may generally justify a non-competition obligation for the duration of the supply agreement".

Communiqué No. 2002/2 is applicable in case of imposition of a non-compete obligation that would be applicable post-expiration of the franchise arrangement. Accordingly, such a non-compete obligation may be imposed on the purchaser provided that it does not exceed one year as of the expiration of the agreement, with the conditions that the prohibition (i) relates to products or services in competition with the products or services which are the subject of the agreement; (ii) is limited to the facility or land where the purchaser operates during the agreement; and (iii) is compulsory for protecting the know-how

[681] *Pınar* (6 September 1999, 99-41/435-274). In the relevant decision, the franchise system has been considered within the scope of Block Exemption Communiqué No. 1998/7 on Franchise Agreements, which has been replaced by Communiqué No. 2002/2.
[682] *LB Börekçilik* (14 November 2019, 19-40/646-273).
[683] *Pizza Pizza* (8 May 2014, 14-17/322-140).
[684] *Dogati* (n. 546).
[685] Guidelines on Vertical Agreements, para. 189.
[686] *Çelebi Gıda* (12 October 2011, 11-54/1378-488).
[687] *Costa International* (16 December 2009, 09-59/1445-378).
[688] *Starbucks* (15 April 2004, 04-26/286-64).
[689] *GAP* (3 October 2013, 13-56/785-335).

transferred by the provider to the purchaser. If the non-compete obligation with regard to the period following the expiry of the franchise agreement exceeds one year[690] or if it is not limited to the facility or land where the purchaser operates during the agreement,[691] the non-compete clause would not benefit from a block exemption. However, an individual exemption assessment may be carried out under Article 5 of Law No. 4054.

5.1.8 Subcontracting Agreements

Subcontracting agreements generally refer to arrangements where one party (the contractor) entrusts the production of a product to another party (the subcontractor). Such agreements are deemed important for encouraging the use and creation of new technologies and increasing specialisation, lowering costs and enhancing efficiencies in production and distribution relationships. However, one needs to be cautious when such arrangements include certain restrictions. For instance, under subcontracting arrangements, the subcontractor may have to make use of the technology or equipment to be provided by the contractor in order to fulfil the requirements set out in the relevant agreement. Accordingly, the contractor may request such technologies or equipment to be used solely for the purposes of the agreement. In such cases, uncertainty may arise as to whether the subcontracting agreements are caught by Article 4 of Law No. 4054.[692] On this note, the Guidelines on Certain Subcontracting Agreements provide explanations on assessment of such arrangements.

Pursuant to paragraph 3 of the Guidelines on Certain Subcontracting Agreements, subcontracting agreements are defined as agreements under which an undertaking (subcontractor) commits to produce goods, provide services or perform work on behalf of or for another undertaking (the contractor) in line with such undertaking's instructions.[693] For instance, in *Henkel/Hobi*,[694] the subcontracting agreement sets forth the obligation for Hobi Kozmetik to produce and package Henkel's "Taft" branded hair gels in accordance with Henkel's specifications. In this respect, Henkel is under the obligation to buy the products from Hobi Kozmetik at the unit price determined in the agreement. The agreement also includes the transfer of Henkel's know-how to Hobi Kozmetik.

Subcontracting agreements are generally characterised as vertical agreements, as one of the parties produces a good and supplies it to the other party. However, in cases where the parties of a subcontracting agreement are also competitors to each other, these agreements are no longer accepted as vertical agreements.

Article 2(5) of Communiqué No. 2002/2 sets forth that vertical agreements concluded between competing undertakings may not benefit from the exemption granted by this communiqué. Competing undertakings are defined in Article 3(c) of Communiqué No. 2002/2

---

690   *LB Börekçilik* (n. 682).
691   *DiaSA* (25 November 2009, 09-57/1386-359).
692   Guidelines on Certain Subcontracting Agreements, paras. 1, 4.
693   Ibid., para. 3.
694   *Henkel/Hobi* (20 January 2009, 09-03/46-15).

as providers that operate or have the potential to operate in the same product market. Product market covers the products or services that are the subject of the agreement, and the products or services considered, in terms of the purchaser, to be interchangeable with or substitutable for them on the basis of their product characteristics, prices and intended uses.

On this note, if a subcontracting agreement is concluded between competing undertakings and it is considered as a horizontal subcontracting agreement, which constitutes a type of production agreement, they may be subject to the conditions of block exemption set out under Communiqué No. 2013/3 if they comprise unilateral and reciprocal specialisation agreements as well as subcontracting, signed with the aim of expanding production. Moreover, they may also benefit from the individual exemption mechanism, provided that they meet the relevant criteria.

For instance, in *Arçelik/Sony*,[695] the Board stated that the parties to the subcontracting agreement are competitors as they are both active in the production and distribution of LCD televisions. In this respect, the Board decided that the subcontracting agreement cannot benefit from the block exemption within the scope of Communiqué No. 2002/2 due to the fact that it may lead to competitive concerns arising from horizontal cooperation.

On this note, it must be highlighted that subcontracting agreements are executed commonly in the pharmaceutical sector as well. For instance, in *Novo Nordisk/Abdi İbrahim*,[696] the Board referred to paragraph 132 of the Guidelines on Horizontal Agreements, which states that the principles in these guidelines are valid for all forms of joint production agreements and horizontal subcontracting agreements. In this respect, the Board examined the market shares of the parties. As the market share of Novo Nordisk exceeded 25%, the Board did not grant block exemption to the subcontracting agreement, yet it did grant an individual exemption.

In *Bayer/Zentiva*,[697] the Board examined whether the supplier Bayer's transfer of information to the producer Zentiva constituted any competitive concerns. Bayer provided technical information to Zentiva, including raw material specifications, the characteristics of the raw materials and the packaging materials, the production and packaging process, quality standards, packaging and labelling specifications and know-how related to the product. Within the scope of the subcontracting agreement, Zentiva was under the obligation not to disclose this information to third parties. In this respect, the Board decided that the subcontracting agreement did not lead to any concerns within the scope of Article 4 of Law No. 4054.

Having said that, if the subcontracting relationship is formed at a vertical level, generally speaking, as long as the agreement provides that (i) the technology or equipment provided by the contractor may not be used except for the purposes of the subcontracting agreement; (ii) the technology or equipment provided by the contractor may not be made available to third parties; (iii) goods produced, services provided or work performed using such technology or equipment may be supplied only to the contractor or to a person to be

---

[695] *Arçelik/Sony* (n. 675).
[696] *Novo Nordisk* (28 July 2020, 20-36/493-218).
[697] *Bayer/Zentiva* (28 July 2015, 15-32/460-142).

indicated by the contractor, or may be carried out only on behalf of the contractor, provided that such technology or equipment is necessary for the subcontractor to produce the goods, provide the services or perform the work in accordance with the contractor's instructions and under reasonable conditions, then the subcontracting arrangements should not be considered restrictive under Article 4 of Law No. 4054. Accordingly, if the buyer transfers to the supplier only the detailed specifications describing the products and services to be provided, the subcontracting agreement may benefit from the block exemption within the scope of Communiqué No. 2002/2. The transfer of these specifications should be considered "necessary" within the scope of the execution of the subcontracting agreement in order not to be subject to the prohibition set forth under Article 4 of Law No. 4054. Pursuant to the Guidelines on Certain Subcontracting Agreements, "necessity of the technology or equipment provided by the contractor" means that in the absence of the subcontracting agreement, the subcontractor would be unable to produce the goods, provide the services or perform the work concerned by the contract, as an independent provider.[698] On this note, (i) industrial property rights owned by or at the disposal of the contractor in the form of patents, utility models, designs protected in a registered or an unregistered manner or other rights; (ii) secret knowledge or know-how owned by or at the disposal of the contractor; (iii) studies, plans or documents accompanying the information given which have been prepared by or for the contractor; (iv) dyes, patterns or equipment, tools and accessory equipment that distinctively belong to the contractor, which, even though not covered by industrial property rights nor containing any element of secrecy, allow for the production of goods that differ in form, function or composition from other goods produced or supplied on the market, are regarded as necessary specifications.[699] Generally speaking, provisions included in subcontracting agreements for the subcontractor to obtain inputs such as raw material to produce goods, or to purchase substances to be used in the provision of services or performance of work, in line with the instructions of the contractor, from the contractor itself or a person to be indicated by the contractor, are not restrictive of competition provided that they are necessary for the said goods, services or work to be carried out with a defined feature, standard or quality. Moreover, the contractor may also demand that subcontracting agreements include provisions about objectively reasonable safeguards to ensure that the goods to be produced, services to be provided or work to be performed have a defined standard or quality. On the other hand, it may be deemed justifiable to impose certain obligations such as (i) a non-disclosure obligation on the subcontractor to whom know-how is transferred; (ii) an obligation on the subcontractor not to make use of the manufacturing processes of secret nature, or of other elements that may be characterised as know-how both during the term and after the expiration of the agreement; (iii) an obligation on the subcontractor to pass on to the contractor the technical improvements or inventions it has made with respect to the agreement, during the term of the agreement on a non-exclusive basis; or (iv) restrictions on matters such as the use of a specific trademark, trade name, outlook, or package of the products subject to the agreement.[700] However, the restrictions under such agreements must be assessed very carefully.

---

[698] Guidelines on Certain Subcontracting Agreements, para. 5.

[699] Ibid., para. 6.

[700] Ibid., paras. 8, 9.

For instance, in *JTI/Sunel*,[701] as the parties did not operate in the same relevant product market, the Board examined the nature of the instructions transferred from JTI to Sunel in order to determine whether it constitutes the transfer of know-how or detailed instructions/specifications with regard to the products, and accordingly determine whether the subcontracting agreement may benefit from the block exemption under Communiqué No. 2002/2. Having considered the terms of the agreements, inter alia, in relation to the protection of know-how and technical information transferred JTI, the restriction of the use of standards and proprietary rights attached to such standards owned by JTI, the obligation to exclusively buy tobacco from a designated provider, restrictions on areas of production for the relevant products, pricing requirements at market and competitive levels, the Board conducted an individual exemption analysis and concluded that the relevant restrictions in the agreement which would have fallen within the scope of Article 4 of Law No. 4054 might benefit from an individual exemption.

5.1.9 Agency Relationship

Pursuant to Article 102 of Turkish Commercial Code No. 6102, in an agency relationship (i) the agent must negotiate and/or conclude contracts relating to a commercial enterprise; (ii) there must be an agreement that constitutes the basis of the agent's negotiations or contracting activities; (iii) such activities should be permanent; and (iv) the agent should pursue these activities as a profession.

Under the Turkish competition law practice, the relationship between an undertaking and its agency is in principle not considered as an anti-competitive agreement within the scope of Article 4 of Law No. 4054, due to the fact that the agency and the undertaking are considered to be within the same economic entity. In this respect, agency agreements are in principle not subject to Article 4 of Law No. 4054. The main factor which determines whether the agency agreements fall within the scope of Article 4 of Law No. 4054 is whether the agency takes a commercial or financial risk in relation to the activities assigned to it by its client.

According to the Guidelines on Vertical Agreements,[702] in case the agency does not assume any financial or commercial risks due to the agreement it concludes or mediates, the relationship between an undertaking and its agency is deemed to be beyond the scope of Article 4 of Law No. 4054. In such a case, the buying or selling activities of the agency are considered as a part of the relevant undertakings' activities. On the other hand, if the agency undertakes all of the risks, it would need to freely set its own marketing strategy in order to ensure a return on its investment. In this case, the agreement in question may fall under Article 4 of Law No. 4045 and may be assessed under Communiqué No. 2002/2.

While determining which party undertakes the risk, which is the crucial point for the application of Article 4 of Law No. 4054, the Board should take into consideration

---

[701] *JTI/Sunel* (14 September 2011, 11-47/1178-419).
[702] Guidelines on Vertical Agreements, para. 10.

the legal relationship between the parties as well as the economic characteristics of the market.

For instance, in *Western Union*[703] and *Aygaz*,[704] during its assessment of Article 4 of Law No. 4054, the Board examined which party undertook the financial and commercial risk and stated that in case the agency did not undertake any risk, its activities would be considered as a part of the undertaking. In *Eureko*,[705] the Board did not consider the relationship between Eureko and Garanti as an agency relationship due to the fact that the agency did not have the authority to apply rebates, refunds or waive its receivables. In this respect, the Board concluded that Eureko did not undertake any financial or commercial risk and that it cannot act independently within the scope of the executed agreements.

Agency agreements can generally include restrictions that prevent an undertaking from appointing another agency for the relevant transactions at the customer or regional level (exclusive agency clause) and/or prevent the agency from serving as an agency or distributor for competing undertakings (non-compete clause) (for instance, *HSBC/Euler*,[706] or *Yapı Kredi*[707]). Exclusive agency clause only concerns intra-brand competition and does not generally lead to anti-competitive effects. However non-compete obligations, including those related to the period following the termination of the agreement, concern inter-brand competition and may lead to anti-competitive effects if they create a foreclosure effect in the relevant market where the products or services in the agreement are being sold; as a result, this provision may fall under Article 4 of Law No. 4054.

Even when the agent does not undertake the aforementioned or similar financial and commercial risks, an agency agreement may still fall under the scope of Article 4 of Law No. 4054 if it facilitates anti-competitive cooperation, particularly if competing parties use the same agency and transfer important information to each other through the agency.

5.1.10 The Block Exemption Regulation for the Motor Vehicle Sector

The block exemption regulation for the motor vehicle sector was subject to changes in recent years. Communiqué No. 2017/3, published on 24 February 2017, revoked the previously applicable Communiqué No. 2005/4, and it currently stands as the relevant block exemption regulation for the motor vehicle sector.

Overall, Communiqué No. 2017/3 is applied to vertical agreements concerning the (i) purchase, sale or resale of new motor vehicles; (ii) purchase, sale or resale of spare parts of motor vehicles; and (iii) provision of maintenance and repair services for motor vehicles.

---

[703] *Western Union* (8 August 2018, 18-27/442-212).
[704] *Aygaz* (16 November 2016, 16-39/659-294).
[705] *Eureko* (10 March 2016, 16-09/152-67).
[706] *HSBC/Euler* (9 September 2015, 15-36/551-179).
[707] *Yapı Kredi* (26 June 2013, 13-40/521-230).

The communiqué does not apply (i) to vehicles that are not considered as motor vehicles, such as motorcycles with less than three tires and tractors; (ii) to motor vehicles that are not new; or (iii) to those accessories which are not deemed to be spare parts, like radios, luggage racks, navigation systems.[708] Additionally, as per the definition of spare parts in the communiqué, products such as motor oil and paint that may be used for different purposes may also fall outside the scope of the communiqué depending on their purpose of use or the field of operation of the buyer.

Vertical agreements concerning the distribution of this nature are only considered to fall under the scope of the communiqué where it is generally accepted that the products may be applied in or on to a motor vehicle, if the buyer is operating in the sector for maintaining and repairing motor vehicles or if it is providing goods for that sector. For vertical agreements covered by Communiqué No. 2017/3 to benefit from the exemption, the parties should not exceed certain market share thresholds in the relevant market depending on the nature of their distribution system and comply with the notice of termination periods specified in the communiqué.

The market share thresholds that are applied in order to determine whether an agreement would benefit from the block exemption have been harmonised under the communiqué for the quantitative distribution agreements and the exclusive distribution agreements. Communiqué No. 2005/4 had set market share thresholds for the application of the block exemption within the sales market at 30% for exclusive distribution and at 40% for quantitative selective distribution. However, with Communiqué No. 2017/3, the market share threshold provided for the quantitative selective distribution has been reduced from 40% to 30%. Communiqué No. 2017/3 does not provide a market share threshold for application of the block exemption to the qualitative selective distribution systems.

For the calculation of market share, initially, the parties must establish the market that they are operating in. In addition to the explanations provided in the Guidelines on the Relevant Market, the Guidelines on the Block Exemption in the Motor Vehicles Sector provide further guidance in defining the product market in the motor vehicle sector. As after-sales services such as maintenance and repair services are those that may be required following the purchase of a particular brand motor vehicle and must be procured specific to that vehicle, the relevant product markets for maintenance and repair services, as well as spare parts, are defined specific to the brand.

In principle, in the calculation of market share, the turnover generated by the players in the relevant market is taken into consideration. However, due to the difficulties in accessing the turnover data of all players in the motor vehicle sector, the market share of vehicle suppliers in the distribution of new motor vehicles is calculated based on sales quantity instead of sales value. Calculation of market share in the after-sales market is also considered to be challenging. In relation to the distribution of spare parts for motor vehicles, calculating market shares over sales quantity is not possible since a vertical agreement may concern spare parts of different types. Therefore, the rule of thumb in calculations for the spare parts market is the sales value. As the market value

---

[708] Self-propelled vehicles with three or more tires, used for transporting people, animals or cargo on roads.

is mostly unavailable in the after-sales market where independent services and chain service stations are operated in addition to authorised services, the market share of the vehicle supplier or the network founder in the relevant market where it provides maintenance and repair services will be calculated based on the proportion of the number of vehicles that procure maintenance and repair services from authorised service stations (the number of vehicles that are serviced) to the number of vehicles in the vehicle fleet of the relevant brand (vehicles with traffic registration).[709]

Communiqué No. 2017/3 indicates that in cases where a market share below 30% subsequently exceeds the threshold (without exceeding 35%), following two years after the year in which the 30% threshold is exceeded for the first time and if the market share exceeds 35% while it was below 30% initially, the year following the year in which the 35% market share threshold was first exceeded would still benefit from the block exemption.

It is seen that in the EU regulations on the automotive sector, the rules specifically pertaining to distribution network structures were removed and the issue was addressed under the guidelines. This may increase the possibility of granting individual exemptions in case of quantitative or exclusive distribution systems, with respect to distribution networks that exceed the relevant thresholds. However, it is seen that the Board does not grant individual exemptions for the brands exceeding the thresholds determined in Communiqué No. 2017/3.

In *Borusan Otomotiv*,[710] regarding the agreement based on quantitative selective distribution that will be executed between Borusan Otomotiv and the authorised dealers of Jaguar and Land Rover, the Board indicated that Borusan Otomotiv's market share in the after-sales maintenance and repair services and spare parts market for Jaguar and Land Rover branded vehicles, does not exceed 30% and meets the market share threshold in Communiqué No. 2017/3, and the agreements do not contain restrictions that would prevent them from benefitting from the Communiqué.

Whereas in *Mais*,[711] regarding the agreement based on quantitative selective distribution concerning the after-sales services for Renault and Dacia branded vehicles, the Board indicated that the market share threshold is met for Renault branded vehicles while Dacia's market share exceeds 30% and therefore a block exemption cannot be granted for Dacia branded vehicles. In terms of individual exemption analysis, the Board concluded that in case the quantitative selective distribution system is established for Dacia branded vehicles, competition will be restricted more than necessary and therefore the arrangement cannot be granted an individual exemption.

Similarly in *Tofaş*,[712] regarding the quantitative selective distribution systems that will be applied by Tofaş for after-sales services and spare parts of Fiat, Alfa Romeo, Jeep, and Lancia branded vehicles, the Board indicated that market shares of Tofaş do not

---

[709]   *Ford* (21 August 2013, 13-48/671-287); Ankara 6th Administrative Court's decision (31 December 2014, E. 2013/1839, K. 2014/1727).
[710]   *Borusan Otomotiv* (5 March 2020, 20-13/167-86).
[711]   *Mais* (21 June 2018, 18-20/353-174).
[712]   *Tofaş* (1 November 2018, 18-41/658-322).

exceed 30% for Fiat and Alfa Romeo branded vehicles; however, its market shares well exceed the relevant threshold for Jeep and Lancia branded vehicles. Therefore, it was concluded that the agreements concerning the markets for the services of the after-sales maintenance and repairs, and the distribution of spare parts market for Jeep and Lancia could not be granted block exemption under Communiqué No. 2017/3. Therefore the distribution network for Jeep and Lancia was assessed to be structured based on a qualitative distribution system.

As indicated above, within the scope of the qualitative selective distribution systems, the supplier authorises the resellers on the basis of objective criteria required by the nature of the product such as training of sales personnel, service provided at the point of sale, a certain range of products being sold. The quantitative selective distribution systems, on the other hand, set forth further criteria for selection that more directly limit the potential number of dealers by, for instance, requiring minimum or maximum sales, by fixing the number of dealers.

In *IVECO*,[713] regarding IVECO's quantitative selective distribution systems, the Board indicated that IVECO's market share did not exceed 30% in spare markets. However, the Board concluded that the clause obliging the dealer to notify IVECO regularly in terms of the market situation and competitors' activities should be removed from the agreement in order for the agreement to be granted block exemption, as the relevant clause may increase the transparency in the market. Furthermore, within the scope of the relevant case, the Board requested information from IVECO on its criteria for authorised services in different regions and levels. IVECO responded that it planned to make a categorisation of cities based on the gross national product and population density/distribution; and the criteria determined by IVECO for the transition to a higher class would be applied equally and transparently to all authorised services. Although Communiqué No. 2017/3 does not impose an obligation to implement the standards in a non-discriminatory, transparent manner where a quantitative selective distribution system is adopted, the Board concluded that certainty was achieved regarding the categorisation of criteria and application of principles and that the said criteria can be considered reasonable in the ordinary course of commerce.

With Communiqué No. 2017/3, the freedom to assign the agreements concluded between the distributors and the suppliers is no longer prerequisite to benefit from the block exemption. Likewise, a detailed, reasoned and written termination notice is no longer a requirement. Furthermore, granting the suppliers and the distributors the right to bring the conflicts arising from the agreement to an independent expert or to an arbitrator is also no longer a condition for benefiting from the block exemption.

On the other hand, the following provisions related to the time periods that apply to the termination notice are preserved in Communiqué No. 2017/3: (i) a six months' notice period is set for the agreements with terms of at least five years; (ii) a minimum two-year notice period, for agreements with an indefinite term; but the notice period is reduced to a minimum one-year period, where the supplier is contractually or legally

---

[713] *IVECO* (27 February 2020, 20-12/143-79).

required to pay appropriate compensation in case it terminates the agreement, or where the supplier terminates the agreement because it must reorganize a significant portion or the entirety of the distribution system.

Overall, Communiqué No. 2017/3 lists certain hard-core restrictions which, if included in a vertical agreement, result in the loss of entitlement to the block exemption for the agreement as a whole. The Communiqué also lists a number of specific conditions that cannot benefit from the exemption.

Similar to Communiqué No. 2002/2, vertical agreements that restrict the distributor's freedom to set its own sales price will not benefit from the block exemption granted by the relevant Communiqué. However, the supplier or the network founder may set maximum sales prices or make recommendations on sales prices, provided these do not transform into fixed or minimum sales prices as a result of pressure or encouragement from one of the parties. In *Maysan*,[714] the Board decided that Maysan Mando violated Article 4 of Law No. 4054 by determining the resale prices of dampers through the supply agreements with its dealers. The Board evaluated the relevant practice under Communiqué No. 2017/3 and held that further to Article 6 of Communiqué No. 2017/3, preventing the distributors' freedom to set their own selling prices is considered as a restriction, which aims to prevent competition both directly and indirectly, and any agreement that contains such restrictions cannot benefit from the block exemption provided within the scope of Communiqué No. 2017/3.

Whereas in *Mercedes-Benz*,[715] the individual exemption analysis for authorised dealership agreement included both recommended resale prices and maximum resale prices and the Board evaluated that both practices sought to reflect Mercedes' long-lasting experience in the relevant market and served as reference points for the authorised dealers, whilst also ensuring that the authorised dealers remain free to determine their resale prices.

Communiqué No. 2017/3 provides that territory or customer restrictions imposed on the distributors cannot benefit from the block exemption, apart from certain exceptions. Accordingly, in the exclusive distribution system, active sales made by the distributors into an exclusive territory, or an exclusive customer group, can be restricted. However, it is also provided that any restriction on passive sales would prevent the agreement from benefitting from the block exemption. Vertical agreements cannot benefit from the block exemption in cases where the above-mentioned restriction of active sales is imposed on the customers of the distributor. However, the sales to end-users by a buyer (distributor) operating at the wholesale level can be restricted. Moreover, in selective distribution systems, sales by selective distribution system members to unauthorised distributors within the region allocated by the supplier for the operation of the system concerned can be restricted. On this note, it must be highlighted that sales between the selective distribution system members cannot be restricted. In networks with selective distribution systems, no restriction can be imposed regarding active or passive sales by selective distribution system members operating at the retail level to final users. However, for agreements concerning the sales of new motor vehicles, the right to prohibit a system member from

---

[714]   *Maysan* (n. 570).
[715]   *Mercedes-Benz* (n. 541).

operating at a location where it is not authorised is reserved. On the other hand, if the supplier (manufacturer) restricts the buyer from selling the components provided for the purposes of assembling to the competitors of the supplier, this would prevent the agreement from the benefit of the block exemption. In *Arslanoğlu/Mercedes-Benz*,[716] the Board evaluated the allegations based on refusal to supply by Mercedes-Benz and upon its instructions its dealers. Arslanoğlu, an unauthorised reseller, alleged that Mercedes-Benz and its authorised dealers refused to supply motor vehicles to Arslanoğlu due to the fact that it exports such vehicles abroad. While evaluating these allegations, the Board stated that Mercedes-Benz adopted a quantitative selective distribution system, and therefore may restrict its dealers' sales to unauthorised resellers such as Arslanoğlu.

It was concluded in the Guidelines on the Block Exemption in the Motor Vehicles Sector that there were still problems with the potential to distort competition in the after-sales market, and therefore Communiqué No. 2017/3 preserved most of the provisions that make market penetration of alternative players such as independent service stations easier.

Communiqué No. 2017/3 provides that the obligations imposed on the authorised distributors by the supplier of motor vehicles to provide after-sales services with the sale, or the obligation imposed on the authorised services to distribute the new motor vehicle together with the after-sales services, cannot benefit from the block exemption. However, the vertical agreements which oblige the supply of maintenance and repair services together with the distribution of spare parts may benefit from the block exemption.

Communiqué No. 2017/3 also regulates the restrictions on the distribution of spare parts. Accordingly, restrictions on the ability of authorised distributors, authorised services and authorised spare parts distributors to sell the spare parts of motor vehicles to the independent services for use in the maintenance and repair of motor vehicles would preclude the relevant vertical agreement from the benefit of the block exemption. This regulation is deemed to be important, especially for captive parts (parts that can only be procured through the motor vehicle supplier) on which the private service stations depend. As a side note, a distributor that adopted the selective distribution system may restrict its authorised services or authorised spare parts dealers from selling the spare parts to unauthorised resellers for resale purposes.

Moreover, imposing a restriction on a supplier's ability to sell the relevant products to the authorised or independent distributors of spare parts, authorised services, independent services or end-users, by way of an agreement concluded between a supplier of the motor vehicle and its supplier of spare parts, or a supplier who provides equipment such as repair equipment or diagnostic devices, would also prevent the relevant vertical agreement from the block exemption benefit.

Although Communiqué No. 2017/3 preserved most of the previous provisions on access to spare parts and other devices, provisions regarding access to technical information, equipment and training have been removed based on the assumption that private service stations should have the same rights as authorised distributors and authorised service stations. The Guidelines on the Block Exemption in the Motor Vehicles Sector note

---

[716]   *Arslanoğlu/Mercedes-Benz* (11 November 2017, 17-38/613-268).

that private service stations' access to technical information is regulated in detail with the EU Regulations on vehicle emissions and access to maintenance and repair.[717] Since these regulations are considered sufficient for the purposes of private service stations' access to technical information, a separate regulation under the Communiqué has not been introduced. However, it should also be noted that disputes related to access to technical information may be evaluated under Article 6 of Law No. 4054.

In addition to that, apart from the free services under warranty, free maintenance and vehicle recall campaigns, the restriction of an authorised distributor's or authorised service's ability to use spare parts of matching quality or original spare parts sourced from a third-party undertaking and preventing the authorised distributor and authorised service from purchasing the original spare parts directly from the manufacturer of spare parts would prevent the relevant vertical agreement from benefiting from the block exemption. In this context, the main reason for such an obligation to use original parts in services such as work done under warranty terms is that the costs of these services are covered by the manufacturers or distributors.

The definition of "spare parts of matching quality" under Communiqué No. 2005/4 provided that compliance with the mandatory standards required by law was to be documented by the manufacturer, whereas, as a result of the amendment of the definition under Communiqué No. 2017/3, relevant parts should be certified by an accredited institution as being spare parts of matching quality, pursuant to the criteria such as mass, size, material, functionality.

As a separate note, in case spare parts of matching quality are used by authorised services, the obligation to inform customers that the relevant part used in the service work is a spare part of matching quality will not prevent the agreement to benefit from the block exemption. In *Doğuş Otomotiv*,[718] the Board examined the allegation that only contracted Castrol branded oils are used at Volkswagen authorised services and the relevant oils are not sold separately in the market. It was further alleged that Valvoline branded oil is not allowed to be used, despite being approved by Volkswagen and brought to the service by the customer himself. Firstly, the Board held that oils used for the operation and protection of motor vehicles will be considered as spare part. Thus, motor oils should have certain specifications in order to achieve the expected efficiencies regarding motor vehicles, and the relevant specifications may differ depending on the type of vehicle engine and they can be determined by the vehicle manufacturer. As for whether the motor oil maintenance of the vehicles is within the scope of the warranty, the use/change of the motor oil itself is not a repair within the scope of warranty, but a routine maintenance activity. Therefore, the use/change of motor oil was not found to be within the above-mentioned exception. Thus, motor oils of matching quality can be

---

[717] Regulation (EC) No. 715/2007 on type approval of motor vehicles with respect to emissions from light passenger and commercial vehicles (Euro 5 and Euro 6) and on access to vehicle maintenance and repair information, published in the Official Gazette dated 21 April 2009 and numbered 27207, and Regulation (EC) No. 595/2009 on type-approval of motor vehicles with respect to emissions from heavy duty vehicles (Euro 6) and on access to vehicle maintenance and repair information, published in the Official Gazette dated 3 August 2011 and numbered 28014.

[718] *Doğuş Otomotiv* (13 October 2016, 16-33/575-251).

used by the services. The Board concluded that the services were not required to use a certain brand; however, Doğuş Otomotiv has recommended certain brands or required certain standards; thus the practices complied with the block exemption. The Board further added that the clause indicating that the customer will be responsible in case any problem occurs due to the use of motor oil of matching quality would not be considered as an indirect obligation to use a certain brand.

Moving on, the restriction of the ability of a spare parts manufacturer to place its own trademark or logo on the components supplied to a supplier in an easily visible manner would preclude the relevant vertical agreement from the benefit of the block exemption.

Under the Communiqué, non-compete obligation and restrictions on opening additional facilities are regulated as provisions that are benefitting from the exemption. Communiqué No. 2005/4 regulated non-compete obligation regarding the sale, maintenance and repair of motor vehicles collectively. On the contrary, in line with Article 7 of Communiqué No. 2017/3, "distribution of motor vehicles", "distribution of spare parts" and "provision of maintenance and repair services" are explained separately within the Guidelines in terms of non-compete obligations. Communiqué No. 2017/3 (i) determines the threshold for non-compete obligations as 80% for the sales of motor vehicles and, therefore, allows abandoning the multi-branded distribution structure, and (ii) indicates that the non-compete obligations that do not exceed five years (or in cases where the extension after five years is only possible by both parties' mutual consent and there are no circumstances preventing the purchaser from terminating the non-compete obligation) will benefit from the block exemption.

Within the scope of Communiqué No. 2017/3, it is provided that, in terms of maintenance repair services and the distribution of spare parts, direct or indirect obligations that oblige the purchaser to make more than 30% of its purchases on a certain type of product cannot benefit from the block exemption. On the other hand, as an exception to the above-mentioned provision, non-compete obligations of up to five years imposed on (i) independent spare part distributors in terms of the spare part distribution networks established by independent spare part suppliers, and (ii) chain services in terms of maintenance and repair chains, may benefit from the block exemption.

Within this scope, an independent spare part distributor is defined as an undertaking distributing spare parts for motor vehicles without participating in a distribution system established by the vehicle supplier, while a chain service station is defined as an undertaking that provides maintenance and repair services under the framework of maintenance and repair chains. As backdrop to the exception of non-compete obligations on the distribution of spare parts, particularly in agreements that mineral oil, paint and tire suppliers conclude with the buyer undertakings, the said buyers are granted cash credits and/or equipment support in return for exclusive purchase requirements. However, the relevant spare parts also have some different characteristics than those procured from motor vehicle suppliers. Buyers are able to choose from among the options presented for the relevant products and then deal with whichever supplier they wish. Thus, the non-compete obligation will ensure a return on the investment made by the independent spare part distributor.[719] Similarly, in terms

---

[719]   *Shell&Turcas* (29 March 2007, 07-29/262-93); *BASF Coatings* (4 March 2010, 10-21/278-102).

of the grounds for the exception of non-compete obligations with respect to maintenance and repair chains, the establishment and popularisation of maintenance and repair chains may potentially lead to a general improvement in the sector by increasing the competition in the markets for distribution of spare parts and for maintenance and repair services. Therefore, the non-compete obligations introduced by the network founder with a period of up to five years will ensure a return on investment.[720]

Non-compete obligations (in terms of distribution of motor vehicles, distribution of spare parts and provision of maintenance and repair services) after the termination of the agreement are not included within the scope of the exemption.

In *Bosch*,[721] regarding the agreements concluded between Bosch and its qualitative selective distribution system members regarding the distribution of spare parts for motor vehicles and the provision of maintenance and repair services, the Board held that the agreements could not benefit from the block exemption, as the validity period of the agreement is one year and the termination notice period is limited to one month. Furthermore, the Board examined the provisions that the purchase of spare parts from brands other than Bosch may not exceed 70% of the purchases made in the last year and the obligation to make a minimum purchase commitment/notification, stating that these provisions may lead to indirect non-competition obligations when assessed with the premium systems and also the validity period and termination notice periods.

Similar to the non-compete obligation, as the level of competition is more restricted in after-sales market, rules concerning the distribution of motor vehicles, distribution of spare parts and the provision of maintenance and repair services are regulated separately. According to Article 7(1) of Communiqué No. 2017/3, in relation to the distribution of spare parts and/or maintenance and repair services, the exemption of the Communiqué will not be applied to direct or indirect obligations concerning the opening of additional facilities where a selective distribution system is implemented. While the supplier is allowed to restrict additional facilities to be opened by authorised distributors and authorised sellers under this Communiqué, restriction of opening additional facilities for the distribution of spare parts and/or maintenance and repair services will not benefit from the block exemption.

5.1.11 The Block Exemption Regulation on Technology Transfer Agreements

Communiqué No. 2008/2 provides a protective cloak for agreements involving the transfer of intellectual property rights and in particular technology licensing agreements. Technology transfer agreements are license agreements that set forth the transfer of the use of three main kinds of rights: (i) patents, (ii) know-how and (iii) software copyrights.[722] According

[720]   *Goodyear* (4 April 2011, 11-22/392-125).
[721]   *Bosch* (14 November 2019, 19-40/656-281).
[722]   F. Gözlükaya, *Teknoloji Transferi Sözleşmelerine İlişkin Rekabet Hukuku Uygulaması* (Ankara: Rekabet Kurumu, 2007), p. 8.

to Article 1 of Communiqué No. 2008/2, the main purpose of the relevant communiqué is to regulate the conditions for block exemption to be granted to technology transfer agreements, by means of which these agreements can be excluded within the scope of application of Article 4 of Law No. 4054. In Article 2 of Communiqué No. 2008/2, the scope of application for the Communiqué is defined as technology transfer agreements where the licensor authorises the licensee to use the licensed technology for the production of the products subject to the agreement and which fall under the scope of Article 4 of Law No. 4054.

Technology transfer agreements aim to protect the interest of the parties at the highest level and also contribute to the competition in the market by ensuring that new technology, new products and new services are effectively diffused and distributed in the market.[723] Technology transfer agreements which involve intellectual property rights–patents, utility models, industrial designs, integrated circuit topographies, plant breeders' rights or software rights– and know-how may bring about various economic efficiencies such as encouraging research and development activities, preventing waste of resources through duplication of research and development, facilitating the dissemination of knowledge and technology resulting from the aforementioned research and development activities, and increasing competition by the new and higher quality products brought to the market. In addition to the aforementioned economic efficiencies, as intellectual property rights bestow monopolistic powers to their holders, technology transfer agreements involving such rights, considering also certain other provisions they contain, may lead to the restriction of competition to a certain extent.[724]

Pursuant to Article 5 of Communiqué No. 2008/2, only agreements executed between two undertakings may benefit from the exemption and, therefore, the agreements concerning more than two undertakings cannot benefit from this Communiqué. In addition, the agreement in question must be related to the manufacture of the products subject to the agreement; more specifically, the licence granted to the licensee must ensure that the licensee can produce goods or provide services by using the transferred technology. The duration of the exemption equals the duration of the protection granted to the intellectual property right subject to the agreement. If the agreement includes know-how, the exemption is granted only if the know-how remains secret.

The exemption does not apply to all kinds of technology transfer agreements but only to agreements that do not exceed certain thresholds related to the market shares of the undertakings. Technology transfer agreements executed between competitors may benefit from the exemption if the total market share of the parties does not exceed 30% on the affected relevant technology and product market. On the other hand, in order to grant exemption to technology transfer agreements that are not executed between competitors, the total market share of the parties should not exceed 40% on the affected relevant technology and product market. The relevant market is defined by taking into consideration the technology subject to the licence, as well as the products to be manufactured by using this technology.

Article 6 of Communiqué No. 2008/2 regulates the restrictions that would preclude an agreement to benefit from the scope of application of this Communiqué. If the parties of a

---

[723] Ibid., p. 11.
[724] General Preamble of Communiqué No. 2008/2.

technology transfer agreement are competitors to each other, (i) the restriction of a party's right to determine its sales prices; (ii) the restriction of production and sales volumes of the products subject to the agreement; (iii) the allocation of markets and customers; and (iv) the restriction of a licensee's right to use its own technology, or the restriction of a party's right to carry out research and development activities unless such restriction is necessary in order to prevent the disclosure of the licensed know-how to third parties.

The restrictions that cause an agreement to fall out of scope in case the parties are not competitors are (i) the restriction of a party's right to determine its sales prices; (ii) the restriction of the territory or the customers that the licensee may passively sell the agreement products to; and (iii) the restriction of active or passive sales to end-users by a licensee carrying out activities at the retail level, without prejudice to the right to prohibit a member of a selective distribution system from carrying out activities at an unauthorised site.

It is noteworthy that Communiqué No. 2008/2 also sets forth some exceptions for the aforementioned restrictions. Accordingly, if a technology transfer agreement includes one of the restrictions listed above but falls under one of the exceptions, or if the provision that includes the restriction is severable, then the remaining part of the agreement can benefit from exemption, as per Article 7 of Communiqué No. 2008/2. If, however, the restrictive provision is not severable, then the agreement will be precluded as a whole from the block exemption benefits.

In *Molson Coors/Anadolu Efes*,[725] the Board granted an individual exemption to the distribution and licence agreement signed between Molson Coors and Anadolu Efes. The agreement regulates the production of Miller Genuine Draft by Anadolu Efes for Molson Coors, as well as its distribution and marketing by Anadolu Efes within the "Defined Territory". Under the agreement, Molson Coors has granted exclusive licence rights to Anadolu Efes, which include (i) the use of licensed know-how for the production and packaging of MGD-branded beers within the Defined Territory; (ii) the distribution and sale of MGD-branded beers in the Defined Territory (including the sub-licensing to the customers of Anadolu Efes) by way of using the trademarks; as well as (iii) the issuance of a non-exclusive marketing licence (due to the global characteristics of certain advertising or promotional materials).

The Board set forth that the agreement could not benefit from the protective cloak of Communiqué No. 2008/2, as the total market share of the parties in the market for beer in Turkey exceeded the 30% threshold set by the Communiqué. The Board also found that a vast majority of beer production in Turkey was conducted by Anadolu Efes and Türk Tuborg. Furthermore, the Board determined that the market shares of other manufacturers and importers that were active in Turkey in terms of beer were at significantly low levels. Although the Board categorised MGD-branded beers under the "premium beer" segment without providing any detailed analysis on this front, it proceeded to define the relevant product market as "the beer market" without distinguishing between plausible sub-segments, by way of referring to its well-established precedents for this market.

---

[725] *Molson Coors/Anadolu Efes* (18 April 2019, 19-16/218-97).

Given that the agreement could not benefit from the block exemption under Communiqué No. 2008/2 due to the relevant market share threshold, the Board continued its evaluation by assessing whether the agreement met the conditions for an individual exemption under Article 5 of Law No. 4054. The Board concluded that the agreement satisfied all the conditions set forth under Article 5 of Law No. 4054 and, therefore, granted an unconditional individual exemption to the agreement.

In *BKM/DFS*,[726] the Board evaluated whether the licence agreement executed between BKM and DFS fulfilled the conditions in order to benefit from the block exemption set forth under Communiqué No. 2008/2. In order to develop TROY, which is a card system brand of BKM, BKM intends to benefit from DFS's products and know-how within the scope of the executed agreement. The Board stated that these two undertakings are competitors. In this respect, the Board evaluated their market shares. Due to the fact that the market shares of the undertakings did not exceed 30% in the relevant product market, the Board stated that the agreement might be evaluated within the scope of Communiqué No. 2008/2.

It was further noted that Article 4.1. of the licence agreement prevents BKM from actively distributing the licensed products outside the determined area without the consent of the licensor. The Board referred to the fourth exception set forth under Article 6(c) of Communiqué No. 2008/2 and stated that this provision is not contrary to the Communiqué. The Board also evaluated Article 6 of the licence agreement, which regulates the obligation of the licensee or a third party acting on its behalf, to transfer the improvements made on the subject of the licence or the new application areas to the licensor free of charge and in a non-exclusive way. The Board referred to Article 7(2)(b) of Communiqué No. 2008/2, which sets forth that the communiqué does not apply to any direct or indirect obligation on the licensee to assign, partly or completely, to the licensor or a third party designated by the licensor the rights related to its own severable improvements on or new applications of the licensed technology. The Board decided that the provision in question cannot be evaluated within the scope of the relevant article of the Communiqué. Finally, the Board decided that the licence agreement may benefit from the Communiqué as long as the know-how remains secret.

---

[726]   *BKM* (n. 491).

Chapter 6
Concept of Dominance

GÖNENÇ GÜRKAYNAK, ESQ., BERFU AKGÜN[*] AND BEYZA TIMUR[**]

Under the Turkish competition law regime, for conduct to constitute an abuse of dominant position under Article 6 of Law No. 4054, the undertaking(s) in question must be in a dominant position.

Article 3 of Law No. 4054 sets forth the definition of dominance as "dominant position [is] the power of one or more undertakings in a particular market to determine economic parameters such as price, supply, the amount of production and distribution, by acting independently of their competitors and customers".

Accordingly, under paragraph 8 of the Guidelines on Abuse of Dominance, it is stated that "an undertaking with the power to behave to an appreciable extent independently from competitive pressure is considered to hold the dominant position". The dominant position could be enjoyed by one or multiple undertakings since Article 6 of Law No 4054 also makes reference to collective dominance as "the abuse, by *one or more undertakings*, of their dominant position in a market for goods or services within the whole or a part of the country on their own or through agreements with others or through concerted practices, is illegal and prohibited" (emphasis added). That said, in practice, the analyses conducted by the Competition Board in the great majority of the cases are concerned with the abusive conduct relating to the dominance that is held by one single undertaking. Hence, this chapter will mostly focus on dominance held by one single undertaking and subsequently provide brief explanations on collective dominance under the Turkish competition law regime.

Unilateral activities prohibited by Turkish competition law generally fall under the ambit of Article 6 of Law No. 4054, which prohibits abuse of dominance. Article 6 is closely modelled after Article 102 TFEU, andprovides that "The abuse, by one or more undertakings, of their dominant position in a market for goods or services within the whole or a part of the country on their own or through agreements with others or through concerted practices, is illegal and prohibited".[727] Article 6 of Law No. 4054 does not categorically define what would constitute an abuse; however, it does provide a non-exhaustive list of examples. It also does not prohibit dominance itself, but rather the abusive conduct exercised by the undertaking(s) in question through the utilisation of such power.

---

[*]   Associate, ELIG Gürkaynak Attorneys-at-Law, Istanbul <berfu.akgun@elig.com>.
[**]   Associate, ELIG Gürkaynak Attorneys-at-Law, Istanbul <beyza.timur@elig.com>.
[727] Article 102 of the TFEU reads as follows: "Any abuse by one or more undertakings of a dominant position within the internal market or in a substantial part of it shall be prohibited as incompatible with the internal market in so far as it may affect trade between Member States."

Moreover, dominance position is also a parameter taken into account for merger and acquisition transactions. Article 7 of Law No. 4054 deems it illegal to establish or strengthen the dominant position by merger and acquisition transactions in a way that restricts the effective competition in the relevant market. In line with EU competition law, the recent addition to the article replaces the current dominance test with the significant impediment of effective competition (SIEC) test. With this new test, the Competition Authority is now able to prohibit not only transactions that may create a dominant position or strengthen an existing dominant position, but also those that could significantly impede competition.

This chapter will mainly dwell upon the concept of dominance and the parameters that are taken into account in order to determine when an undertaking is deemed to be dominant in a given market and, therefore, potentially becomes subject to the prohibition under Article 6 of Law No. 4054. Accordingly, the relevant market is the first of the parameters to be assessed. After all, the concept of dominance refers to a position of economic strength in a properly defined relevant market.[728] Thereby, in order to determine whether a single undertaking has (or, as the case may be, a number of undertakings, collectively have) that economic strength, the analysis would firstly focus on setting the exact boundaries of that relevant market.

6.1 Definition of Relevant Markets

The prohibition set forth under Article 6 of Law No. 4054 would only be applicable in case the undertakings in question are deemed to be in a dominant position in a given market within the period when the alleged conduct is committed. However, it would only be possible to mention the existence of a violation under Article 6 in case the undertaking in question is in a dominant position. This will be analysed in detail under Chapters 7 and 8 on Abuse of Dominance and Theories of Harm.

The definition of the relevant market should be considered with utmost precision, as it constitutes one of the most significant factors in terms of any antitrust analysis when determining whether the undertakings in question enjoy market power that would confer them dominance.

In competition law practice, the purpose of the relevant market definition is to identify products, geographic areas, and market players that could exert competitive pressure on one another. In other words, the aim of the relevant market definition is to ascertain which competitors have the power to influence or restrict the behaviour of the undertaking(s) under examination. Thereby, for the purposes of the determination of a dominant position, the initial step would be the definition of the relevant market in order to be able to evaluate the market position of the undertaking(s) in question afterwards.

---

[728]   R. O'Donoghue and A. J. Padilla, *The Law and Economics of Article 102 TFEU*, p. 4.

Relevant market definition is a prerequisite in establishing dominant position under the Guidelines on Abuse of Dominance.[729] Additionally, pursuant to the Guidelines on the Relevant Market, the market definition is an instrument that "allows the Competition Board to set the framework for the application of the competition policy".[730] The Guidelines on the Relevant Market is issued for the purpose of minimising the uncertainties and of clarifying the methods adopted by the Competition Board in its decision-making practice in terms of the definition of the relevant product and geographic market. It is closely modelled on the Commission notice on the definition of relevant market for the purposes of Community competition law (97/C 372/03). The Guidelines consider the demand-side substitution as the primary standpoint of market definition, and the supply-side substitution and potential competition as secondary factors, as will be explained below.

6.1.1 Product Market Definition

The definition of product market is an initial step in terms of the analysis conducted under Article 6 of Law No. 4054. When a unilateral or a collective conduct is in question, dominance in a market is the primary condition for the application of the prohibition stipulated under Article 6. To establish the existence of a dominant position, one must first determine the relevant market and then the market position and all other elements used as tools to determine market power.

6.1.1.1 Demand-Side Substitution

"Demand-side substitutability", "demand substitution" or "cross demand elasticity" is the most important and primarily used concept in defining the relevant market.[731] Demand substitution measures the sensitivity of the demand for a product that is similar in terms of use and characteristics when the other product's price is altered. In case of a price increase, the fastest and most straightforward reaction against the increase would arise from the demand side. If the results show that the consumer's choices turn towards another product, then this would mean that there is substitutability between the products, and therefore they should be evaluated within the same relevant product market. That is the reason why demand substitution is the key element in terms of relevant market definition in Turkey.[732]

Although the characteristics and the purpose of use of a product are the primary factors in determining demand substitutability, they are not the only determinants. The Board also considers factors such as indications that the products were used as substitutes

---

[729] Guidelines on Abusive of Dominance, para. 9.

[730] Guidelines on the Relevant Market, para. 1.

[731] See C. Bellamy and G. Child *European Community Law of Competition* (5th edition, London: Sweet & Maxwell, 2001), p. 687.

[732] M. Çetinkaya, *İlgili Pazar Kavramı ve İlgili Pazar Tanımında Kullanılan Nicel Teknikler* (Ankara: Rekabet Kurumu, 2005), p. 80.

recently, quantitative tests specifically formulated for market definition, customers' and competitors' remarks, consumer preferences, costs and drawbacks on turning the demand to the substitutes, and different customer categories and price discrimination.[733]

6.1.1.2 Supply-Side Substitution

Within this context, the initial consideration would be the demand side in defining the relevant market. The supply substitution then could be considered in terms of whether it has an equivalent effect to demand substitution and is utilised as such.[734] Consequently, in consideration of supply substitution, the suppliers must be able to shift their production to other products when faced with small and permanent increases in relative prices and they must be able to market these products without having to tolerate additional costs and risks. When these conditions are met, the additional production introduced to the market would create competitive pressure on the undertakings under review. Such an effect is considered equivalent to demand substitution in terms of efficiency and quick results.[735]

6.1.2 Geographic Market Definition

Geographic market definition is the second step for defining the relevant market, since "a product market is meaningless without a corresponding definition of its scope".[736] Geographical markets are areas where undertakings operate in the supply and demand of their goods and services, in which the conditions of competition are sufficiently homogenous, and which can easily be distinguished from neighbouring areas, as the conditions of competition are appreciably different from these areas. According to the Guidelines on the Relevant Market,[737] when defining the geographical market, a preliminary opinion is prepared based on the indications concerning the distribution of the market shares of the parties and competitors, as well as on the price differentiation. Afterwards, the examination focuses on whether undertakings in different regions actually serve as an alternative source of supply for the customers. In this examination, demand structure is taken into consideration. Whether or not customers of the undertakings under examination can switch their orders to undertakings in other regions in a short period of time and at negligible costs would constitute the starting point in this examination.

The Guidelines on the Relevant Market indicate that:

> Based on the available information, the Board shall define a market the size of which may vary from local to international. Examples of local and international market definitions are available in the previous decisions of the Board.[738]

---

[733] H. Çeçen, *Avrupa Birliği ve Türk Rekabet Hukukunda Hakim Durumun Fiyat Uygulamaları ile Kötüye Kullanılması* (Istanbul: Legal, 2018), pp. 61, 62.

[734] *Mercedes-Benz* (27 August 2018, 18-29/498-239).

[735] Guidelines on the Relevant Market, paras. 8 and 13; *Torras/Sarrio* (Case No. IV/M.166) Commission Decision [1992] OJ C 58/5; Çetinkaya (n. 732), at 61; *Vetrerie Riunite S.p.A.* (21 November 2019, 19-42/707-305).

[736] O'Donoghue and Padilla (n. 728).

[737] Guidelines on the Relevant Market, para. 19.

[738] Ibid., para. 39.

Indeed, even though Article 2 of Law No. 4054 sets the scope of the Law as "within the borders of Republic of Turkey", the Board in its various past decisions defined the geographic scope of the relevant product market wider than Turkey for the purpose of evaluating the potential impact of a transaction/examination when the conduct in question has a wider scale.[739] For instance, in its *Ereğli Denizcilik* decision, given that the transport services conducted by capsize ships can be procured from undertakings operating worldwide without facing any obstacles, the Board considered that geographic market could be deemed as "global". Moreover, in *APMM/PONL*, it was stated that in cases where prices are determined by the international markets instead of players in Turkey, there is no barrier before imports, and competition takes place in the global markets, then the geographic market can be defined as "global".

In this sense, the relevant geographic market is defined on a case-by-case basis, and constitutes an imperative determinant in terms of the definition of the relevant market when determining whether any given undertaking holds a dominant position. The geographical borders of the relevant market vary on certain factors, including but not limited to the product's endurance, characteristics of the distribution system, demand conditions, price differences, entry barriers, quotas, taxes, and even local customs.[740]

6.2 Market Power and Dominant Position

Considering the definition of dominance in Article 3 of Law No. 4054, when evaluating a dominant position, the main factor to be investigated is to what extent the undertaking being examined can act independently from competitive pressures and while this is being conducted, the specific circumstances of each case should be taken into account in the relevant assessment. However, this should not be perceived as total independence. At this point, it is possible to say that a dominant undertaking acts independently, to some extent, from its competitors in determining its price (or, in some cases, the other inputs).[741] Therefore, market power in principle would refer to an undertaking's ability to manipulate the price of an item. For the sake of completeness, there are also markets in which price is not a relevant paradigm. As indicated under the Guidelines on Abuse of Dominance, an undertaking that is able to act independently from competitive pressures would also be able to manipulate and drag down the manufacture and distribution levels, the variety and/or quality of goods and services, and innovation below the competitive levels, in a way that would be to its own benefit but to the detriment of consumers.[742] Along the same lines, undertakings may sometimes choose to offer free goods and

---

[739] *Arçelik-Blomberg Werke – Brant Group* (28 May 2002, 02-32/367-153); *Eti Gümüş* (27 May 2003, 03-35/424-186); *Ereğli Denizcilik* (16 December 2004, 04-79/1147-287); *APMM/PONL* (21 July 2005, 05-48/689-182), *Metlac/ Akzo Nobel Coatings* (14 June 2012, 12-33/927-285); *International Paper Company/Weyerhaeuser Company* (23 September 2016, 16-31/519-233).

[740] A. Kaya, *Rekabet Hukukunda Ayrımcılık Suretiyle Hakim Durumun Kötüye Kullanılması* (Istanbul: On İki Levha Yayıncılık, 2018), p. 84.

[741] *Mey Alcoholic Beverage* (11 June 2020, 20-28/349-163).

[742] Guidelines on the Abuse of Dominance, para. 8

services for various economic reasons, which could, in turn, serve the purpose of providing them with significant commercial benefits–e.g., boosting the sales of their related products/services through several marketing tools such as bundling or tying strategies. These markets in which free goods and services are provided are referred to as "zero price markets". The economic compensation that the provider of a free product or service foregoes may be returned by generating other business profits or the accrual of other economic advantages to the service providers. These may include the collection of users' personal data for advertisement purposes, advertisements and marketing messages displayed on relevant free platforms for unrelated products, or the effects of the free product or service on increasing the popularity of interrelated products, among others.

Therefore, the common feature presented by zero-priced markets is that there is–almost always–an interrelated product or service that is offered in exchange for a non-zero price (i.e., sold for value, like regular goods and services), and which benefits from the popularity of the relevant zero-priced market.

In terms of the markets where the price is indeed determinant, the doctrine suggests that the ability to manipulate and raise prices and therefore being able to act independently in that regard could be facilitated via two different methods, which are referred to as the classical "Stiglerian power" and the exclusionary "Bainian power".[743] While the "Stiglerian power" is predominantly concerned with the restriction of the undertaking's own output, which could, in turn, provide it with the opportunity to control and raise prices and make profits; the "Bainian power" is concerned with limiting the competitors' output through ensuring that its costs are increased.

> Either way consumer welfare is reduced because output below the efficient competitive level denies consumers products that they value in excess of the marginal cost of production and transfers wealth from consumers to producers.[744]

It is argued that these two could be implemented together and the presence of one would ease the implementation of the other, when exercised by the undertaking in question. Therefore, a sound competition law analysis should check for the existence of both, and in cases where one is found, this should be considered sufficient to deem that market power is present.[745]

The Board describes market power as "the ability to profitably keep prices above competitive price levels for a period of time or to profitably keep indicators such as product quantity, quality and variety, or innovation below competitive levels for a period of time".[746] Therefore, the Board considers that a high amount of market power which enables an undertaking to act distinct from competitive pressures as bestowing the dominant position.

---

[743] T. G. Krattenmaker, R. H. Land, S. C. Salop, "Monopoly Power and Market Power in Antitrust Law", available at Justice.gov <https://www.justice.gov/atr/monopoly-power-and-market-power-antitrust-law> (last accessed 15 June 2021).

[744] Ibid.

[745] B. Ekdi, *Hakim Durumda Bulunan Teşebbüslerin Dikey Anlaşmalar Yoluyla Piyasayı Kapatması*, (Ankara: Rekabet Kurumu, 2009).

[746] *Göltaş/Batı Söke Çimento* (9 January 2014, 14-01/6-5).

As it is asserted in section 2.2 titled "Determination of the Dominant Position" of the Guidelines on Abuse of Dominance, the main principles considered in the determination of the dominant position are the relative market positions of the undertaking that is being examined and its competitors, entry and expansion barriers in the market, and the bargaining power of the buyers.

The factors outlined above, along with several other determinants that have been persistently taken into consideration in the Board's decisional practice in terms of the analysis on dominant position, are explained below.[747]

6.2.1 The Initial Step: Market Shares

Market share is the cornerstone of dominance assessment, and the indicator that is most referred to in terms of the analyses of dominance, since it is one of the data to be retrieved by the Authority with the least effort and definitive in measuring the market power in a particular product market. The high market share of an undertaking in a particular market constitutes a strong presumption for the existence of a dominant position. Market shares can be measured through different parameters such as turnover, number of sales, capacity, etc. In cases where the product is homogeneous/undifferentiated and the market operates at a point close to full capacity, these three data are expected to provide close results. In the Guidelines on the Relevant Market, it is asserted that, as a rule, sales figures in terms of both volume and value will provide useful information in the calculation of market shares.[748] In line with this, when it comes to differentiated products, it is articulated that, most of the time, the value of the sales figures and market shares linked to these numbers are considered to be better indicators for making a comparison between the market shares of suppliers.[749]

In terms of market share thresholds for dominance, it is accepted in the Board's precedents that undertakings with a market share below 40% are unlikely to be in a dominant position, and a more detailed examination is required for undertakings with a market share above this level.[750]

The Commission's precedents show that a market share over 70% constitutes a strong presumption for the existence of dominance.[751] In *Hoffmann-La Roche*[752] decision of the Commission, it was stated that a market share between 70% and 90% in various relevant product markets was at a sufficiently high level to prove the existence of a dominant

---

[747] Guidelines on Abuse of Dominance, paras. 10–21.
[748] Guidelines on the Relevant Market, para. 43.
[749] Ibid.
[750] Guidelines on Abuse of Dominance, para. 12; *Şafak Elektrik* (24 July 2019, 19-26/402-187); *Otomotive* (15 October 2020, 20-46/618-270); *Container Lineer* (24 September 2020, 20-43/591-264); *Mediamarkt* (12 May 2010, 10-36/575-205).
[751] R. O'Donoghue and A. J. Padilla, *The Law and Economics of Article 82 EC* (Oxford: Hart Publishing, 2006), s. 113.
[752] Case 85/76 *Hoffmann-La Roche & Co. AG v. Commission* [1979] ECR 461.

position. Similar explanations were provided in the *Hilti*[753] and *Tetra Pak*[754] decisions of the Commission, and it was stated in *Hoffmann-La Roche* judgment[755] of the European Court of Justice that having a high level of market share and maintaining this market share for a long time would point towards the existence of a dominant position in most cases, although it was also recognised that there may be exceptional cases where further analysis would be required. In *British Airways* decision of the Commission, a market share of 39.6%, which was seven times higher compared to the market share of the closest competitor, was utilised as one of the significant criteria in determining the dominant position.[756] Similarly, in the *AKZO* decision, it has been accepted that market shares above 50% indicate that the undertaking is in a dominant position in the relevant product market, unless otherwise proven.[757] The assessment of market shares was conducted more thoroughly in the *Hilti* decision and it was evaluated that a market share in the 70–80% band was a clear indication of a dominant position.[758] The decisional practice of the Commission has been significantly prominent in terms of providing guidance for the Board, since the Authority tends to follow the EU competition law precedents and regulations.

That said, it is also a widely accepted principle both in the literature[759] and the Board's practice[760] that market shares cannot be the sole indicator of market power. In its *Rockwood/Specialities Group*[761] decision (where the Board did not consider an aggregated market share of approximately 90% as resulting in a dominant position and cleared the relevant transaction), the Board explicitly set forth that even a 100% market share cannot be an indicator of a dominant position by itself and that market shares cannot be the only evidence for the existence of adequate competition. In this decision, the Board analysed the dynamics of the market by focusing on buyer power, potential competition and entry barriers. There are also numerous decisions in which the Board concludes that high market shares are not necessarily an indicator of a dominant position. In its *Arçelik*[762] decision, the Board decided a market share of 53%-54% is not sufficient on its own for establishing dominance. The Board relied on the presence of powerful potential competitors in the market as a basis for its conclusion. Likewise, in the *Kütahya Porselen* decision, the Board concluded that an undertaking with 72–85% market share was not in a dominant position.[763] That decision was justified based on broader economic parameters such as competition from duty-free imported products, the narrowing of demand, effects of the economic crisis, and changes to the interest rate.

---

[753]   Case T-30/89 *Hilti AG v. Commission* [1991] ECR II-1439, para. 92.

[754]   Case C-333/94 P *Tetra Pak International SA v. Commission* [1996] ECR I-5951.

[755]   *Hoffmann-La Roche & Co. AG v. Commission* (n. 752), paras. 38–40.

[756]   Case T-219/99 *British Airways v. Commission* [2003] ECR II-5917.

[757]   Case C-62/86 *AKZO Chemie BV v. Commission* [1991] ECR I-3359, para. 60.

[758]   Case T-30/89 *Hilti AG v. Commission* (n. 753), para. 92.

[759]   P. A. Posner and W. S. Landes, "Market Power in Antitrust Cases", *Harvard Law Review*, Vol. 94, No. 5, pp. 937–996.

[760]   *Coca-Cola* (23 January 2004, 04-07/75-18), p. 13: "When determining the dominant position, the structure of the relevant market is an indicator that is important as much as market share. In other words, the importance of market share becomes meaningful when it is assessed with the structure of the market together."

[761]   *Süd-Chemie* (29 December 2005, 05-88/1229-358).

[762]   *Arçelik* (17 October 2000, 00-39/436-242).

[763]   *Kütahya Porselen* (16 January 2001, 01-04/21-4).

In the Board's *Cisco/IBM* decision, it has been determined that Cisco's market share will increase to 70.5% and CR4[764] will increase to 89.7% post-transaction. However, the Board determined that the network market will expand around 30–40% every year, and will keep on growing in the upcoming years. Due to this reason, when the market entry conditions and the potential competition are evaluated, it has been determined that the transaction does not strengthen IBM's dominance.[765] Indeed, in its *Cisco/IBM* decision, the Board emphasised that even though the market demonstrates a firm oligopolistic structure, the fact that there are no barriers to entry or exit in the market may curb the behaviours of the undertakings in the market.

In line with the above, it is appropriate to claim that the market share of the undertaking and its competitors is one of the main criteria taken into account while evaluating the dominance in competition analysis. However, the sole examination of market shares is insufficient to determine that the undertaking is in a dominant position, and it is necessary to examine many other factors along with the market shares.[766] For example, the existence of barriers to entry and expansion forms the cornerstone of the assessment of whether the investigated undertaking would be able to maintain its market power derived from high market shares for a certain amount of time. Similarly, the presence of strong and effective buyers in the market could potentially prevent an undertaking to exert market power, and strong buyers would be able to play a significant role in terms of determining the economic parameters, thanks to the bargaining power they hold against the undertaking with a high market share.[767] The foregoing factors will be examined in the sections below.

6.2.2 Entry Barriers

Although market shares are deemed the most important criteria in the dominant position assessment, the existence and the extent of barriers to entry and expansion are among the factors that directly affect the market position of the undertaking under examination. It is unlikely that high market shares in the relevant market will transform into a dominant position if the entry into the market in question is rather easy. This is because the likelihood of expansion of undertakings operating in the market or of entry into the market by new undertakings can also exert competitive pressure on the behaviour of the undertaking examined.[768] Thus, the capability of existing competitors in the market to increase capacity or the threat stemming from the entry of potential competitors should also be considered when evaluating dominance. However, in order to create sufficient competitive pressure on the players in the market, market entry must be possible and capable of eliminating restrictive effects on competition in a timely manner.

---

[764]   Concentration level for the four undertakings with the highest market shares.
[765]   *Cisco/IBM* (2 May 2000, 00-16/160-82).
[766]   Guidelines on Abuse of Dominance para. 15.
[767]   *Varinak* (19 December 2019, 19-45/768-330); *Yonga Chipboard* (13 October 2016, 16-33/571-248).
[768]   Guidelines on Abuse of Dominance para. 15.

Entry barriers are broadly defined as "advantages of established sellers in an industry over potential entrant sellers, these advantages being reflected in the extent to which established sellers can persistently raise their prices above a competitive level without attracting new firms to enter the industry",[769] while George Stigler's definition is narrower: "a cost of producing... which must be borne by a firm seeking to enter an industry but it is not borne by firms already in the industry".[770] The Guidelines, on the other hand, accepts a broader concept, and provides examples of what could constitute entry barriers.[771]

In this context, first of all, it is examined whether market entry is possible and whether any potential entries could create competitive pressure on existing undertakings in the market. In order for market entry to be possible, entry should be profitable enough, considering the increase in the sales volume that would result from new entries along with the reactions of existing undertakings to such entries. In cases where it is necessary to establish large-scale facilities or bear sunk costs such as advertising/marketing expenses in order to enter the market in an economically profitable way, or in cases where the existing undertakings in the market offer long-term agreements to customers in order to maintain their market shares, the possibility of new entries to the market would be diminished to a great extent. If the risks and costs to be incurred in case the market entry efforts fail are high, this would also decrease the likelihood of market entries.[772] Potential new entrants face a number of entry barriers that determine the risk and cost of entry, and hence its profitability and likelihood. As outlined above, entry barriers are a set of advantages that existing undertakings in the market have over undertakings with the potential to enter the market, often arising from the characteristics of the market itself.[773] If the entry barriers are low, the market power of the existing undertakings may not be permanent, and on the contrary, if the entry barriers are high, the position of the existing undertakings in the market may be somehow guaranteed. While assessing entry barriers, it is important to consider whether the potential profitability of the undertaking to enter the market will create sufficient incentives, and examining any market in terms of past entries and exits can provide important information on the magnitude of entry barriers.[774]

The existence of entry barriers could also refer to specific competition law concerns depending on the type of abuse that is being examined in the scope of the case. For instance, the reason why the existence of entry barriers is considered as the main condition in the evaluation of excessive pricing is the assumption that in the absence of entry barriers in the market, high profits within the framework of the general functioning of the market economy will allow new undertakings to enter the market. The Board also emphasised this point with the following statement:

> In cases where it is possible for the market to remedy itself in the medium or
> long term, the duty of the competition authority should not be to intervene to

[769]   J. S. Bain, *Barriers to New Competition: Their Character and Consequences in Manufacturing Industries* (Cambridge, MA: Harvard University Press, (1956), p. 3.
[770]   G. J. Stigler, *The Organization of Industry* (Chicago: University of Chicago Press, 1968), p. 67.
[771]   The Guidelines on Abuse of Dominance, paras. 15–20.
[772]   *Varinak* (n. 767); *Mey Alcoholic Beverage* (n. 741).
[773]   *Mey Alcoholic Beverage* (n. 741).
[774]   Ibid. ; *Turkuvaz* (29 May 2018, 18-16/293-146).

interrupt the functioning of this process, but to take measures to accelerate this process. In other words, in markets where entry of new players is possible, competition authorities should avoid interfering with excessive pricing and focus on reducing barriers to entry.[775]

Barriers to entry or expansion may stem from the characteristics of the relevant market or from the characteristics or behaviour of the undertaking examined. Barriers stemming from the characteristics of the relevant market can take the form of legal and administrative barriers such as state monopolies, authorisation and licensing requirements and intellectual property rights, or they can be in the form of economic barriers such as sunk costs, economies of scale and scope, network effects, and switching costs faced by customers.[776] Entry barriers could also include, but are not limited to, high capital needs, excess capacity, customer loyalty, technology challenges, vertical integration and distribution channels.[777] There is no exhaustive list of entry barriers, and they are evaluated on a case-by-case basis.

A non-exhaustive list of categories that may be considered as entry barriers is provided below.

6.2.2.1 Legal Entry Barriers

The most common legal entry barriers are the market-specific regulations that require undertakings to obtain intellectual property or licensing before entering certain markets.[778] These entry barriers are sometimes considered as absolute. Licensing exists in many communication industries (radio and TV broadcasting), professions (doctors) and services (banking, off-licence or liquor stores). Although the terms of these licences vary, they often bring various restrictions to the firm, such as price, quality or extent of service. Therefore, licensing requirements represent important entry barriers in these industries.[779] In some cases, such as mobile communication services, licensing regulations might directly envisage restrictions over the number of undertakings which will operate in the market, which may again reveal itself as an entry barrier. In addition, one of the most prominent legal entry barriers would be legal monopoly, where the undertaking in question would enjoy absolute dominance in a given market. For instance, in *TTAŞ*,[780] when the Board examined Türk Telekomünikasyon A.Ş.'s position in the market in scope of the essential facilities doctrine, it stated that due to the existing voice transmission and telecommunications infrastructure, access to local users and leased lines from local telephone networks and cable TV networks are controlled by Türk Telekomünikasyon A.Ş. in the investigated relevant markets, where these services constitute the main input. Due to this characteristic of legal monopoly and well-established monopoly in terms of the leased

---

[775] *TMST* (10 June 2010, 10-42/756-243).
[776] Guidelines on Abuse of Dominance, para. 17.
[777] *Avrupa Topluluğu ve Türk Rekabet Hukukunda Hakim Durumun Kötüye Kullanilmasi*, Tez Serisi,
[778] B. Kesici, *Rekabet Hukukunun İhlalinden Kaynaklanan Haksız Fiil Sorumluluğu* (Istanbul: On İki Levha Yayıncılık, 2017), p. 73; H. Çeçen (n. 733) at 35.
[779] OECD, "Glossary of Industrial Organisation Economics and Competition Law", compiled by R. S. Khemani and D. M. Shapiro, commissioned by the Directorate for Financial, Fiscal and Enterprise Affairs, 1993, p. 26 <https://www.oecd.org/regreform/sectors/2376087.pdf> p. 52.
[780] *TTAŞ* (5 January 2006, 06-02/47-8).

lines, the Board deemed that it would be impossible for competitors to reasonably establish these infrastructures. Moreover, in *Belko*,[781] the Board emphasised that Belko, which is active in terms of coal sales and imports, was a legal monopoly so the barriers to entry in the particular market were absolute, and that Belko acted recklessly in its commercial affairs due to its reliance on its monopoly position, thereby abusing its dominant position.

An example in that regard would be related to the advertising and promotion bans that are amongst legal entry barriers. For instance, according to the provision in the first paragraph of Article 6 of Law No. 4250 on Alcohol and Alcoholic Beverages, – alcoholic beverages cannot be advertised in any way or promoted to consumers. In addition, those who produce, import and market alcoholic beverages cannot sponsor any activity by using the brands, emblems or signs of their products. In the *Mey Alcoholic Beverages* decision, the Board evaluated that the respective limitations in terms of the advertisement of the product constitute a significant obstacle for new market entries.[782]

Another example is related to the sales and marketing of natural gas. In its *BOTAŞ* decision, the Board established that when the qualification requirements from BOTAŞ and/or distribution companies and the tender specifications of station buyers are considered together, it was seen that the production and sales of natural gas pressure reduction and measurement stations are subject to certain legal entry barriers due to public safety and quality standards.[783] Moreover, in *Pietro/Gemsat*,[784] the Board determined the existence of legal entry barriers in the gas equipment market by stating that:

> Considering this article, the requirement to obtain a certificate of competence from BOTAŞ and/or distribution companies in order to obtain the 'Construction and Service Certificate' included in the Certificate Regulation and the tender specifications of the station buyers, it is seen that the market for natural gas pressure reduction and measurement stations appears to be subject to a number of legal entry barriers, in order to ensure the public safety and quality of the production and sales.

Another example is related to the refined sugar market. In the Board's *Türkiye Şeker Fabrikaları* decision,[785] the Board sets forth that the sale of surplus sugar production is subject to the permission of the Sugar Board, entrepreneurs that want to establish a factory for production are obliged to obtain permission from the Sugar Authority and sugar imports are subject to considerably high taxes. In line with the foregoing, the Board determined that the refined sugar market comprises legal entry barriers that render entries quite difficult.

6.2.2.2 Capital Requirement

If entry into a market requires the undertakings to make large investments, this would, in turn, lead them to be less inclined to enter that specific market. Capital requirement for market entry would be considered to be specifically important in areas where resources are scarce

---

[781]   *Belko* (6 April 2001, 01-17/150-39).
[782]   *Mey İçki* (12 June 2014, 14-21/410-178).
[783]   *Botaş* (7 May 2020, 20-23/301-147).
[784]   *Pietro/Gemsat* (18 April 2018, 18-11/197-93).
[785]   *Türkiye Şeker Fabrikaları* (18 July 2013, 13-46/589-259).

in the first place. This, in turn, gives rise to certain issues, since for instance, in Turkey, the banks are mostly holding banks and the use of capital is more expensive for small enterprises compared to holding companies, and in some cases the issue stems from the fact that it is not even possible for small enterprises to obtain the necessary loans they apply for.[786]

For instance, in the Board's *Trakya Cam/Düzcam Exemption* decision,[787] high level of capital requirement was considered as a prominent entry barrier. In this regard, in general, the basic production technology of flat glass products does not differ significantly among companies around the world. However, the glass industry is a production area that requires high capital and installation costs. Therefore in the flat glass market, it becomes more and more important to benefit from economies of scale in order to be able to operate nationally and/or internationally, due to the need for uninterrupted and energy-intensive production, which in turn causes growth in scale. In this context, companies that aspire to have a strong presence in the sector should ensure that they benefit from scale economies by establishing high-capacity facilities. The fact is that the foregoing increases the need for capital, and the necessity of continuous growth and modernisation of investments renders it difficult for producers who wish to enter the market. Furthermore, in several of its decisions,[788] the Board considered that high investment costs constitute significant entry barriers in the fertiliser industry. In this regard, it was determined that the chemical fertiliser market has high barriers to entry: due to the instability of the Turkish economy, the dependence of the sector on imports in terms of raw material resources, the uncertainties in the market due to its appeal to the agricultural sector, the cost of establishing a new production facility of USD 300 million, the validity of economies of scale in the transportation and production of fertilisers; in addition, the use of ports, which are of great importance for the sustainability of the activities, the establishment of a warehouse and packaging facility, and the difficulty and cost of establishing a dealer network.

As opposed to this, the contrary case–that is, capital requirements being below a certain level–has been evaluated by the Competition Board as a factor that renders it easy for undertaking to enter the market in certain instances. An example of such is related to data storage card market within the bank industry in Turkey, where there is no permission or licence regime, no regulatory entry barrier, or need for high capital strength or qualified personnel to carry out the respective activity. In this respect, the Board has in the past, for instance, in its *MIH Pavü* decision, deemed that market entries are easy for various organisations who wish to offer card data storage services, ranging from payment institutions to banks, e-commerce companies to software companies.[789]

6.2.2.3 Excess Capacity

Excess capacity, which occurs when an undertaking in a given market has supply capacity that is greater than the demand, discourages investments for entry. The incumbent undertaking is able to lower the prices when a new market player comes in, thus lowering

---

[786]   Ibid. at 30.
[787]   *Trakya Cam/Düzcam Exemption* (n. 210).
[788]   *Fertiliser* (24 April 2007, 07-34/339-121); *Fertiliser Producers* (24 January 2008, 08-08/82-24).
[789]   *MIH Pavü* (5 September 2019, 31/466-199).

the chances of the new market player to survive. The existence of excess capacity in the long term could represent a natural monopoly or monopoly power.[790]

The Board has, in many instances, determined that excess capacity poses a dissuading factor for undertakings who wish to enter the market since it is perceived that in case an additional need for demand arises, it could be easily and efficiently met by the undertakings running on low capacity that are already present in the market. For instance, in its *Bimpaş* decision[791] in relation to the beer market, the Board evaluated that Efpa, which has a 77% share in the beer market, has maintained this stable position for years. No significant changes were observed in the market share of Bimpaş, which ranks second after Efpa, with a market share around 22–23%. Despite the market's growth trend, the capacity utilisation of both undertakings in the market remained low. In 2003, Efpa used only 67% of its capacity, while Bimpaş used solely 61%. Based on the foregoing, the Board decided that entrance to the market, which is characterised by significant excess capacity, is discouraged from the investors' perspective. Another example is related to the cement sector, whereby the Board evaluated in its *Özgür Cement* decision[792] that excess supply in a sector constitutes a significant obstacle for entries. The Board set forth that even if there is an increase in demand, it seems unlikely that new undertakings will enter the market due to the excess capacity in the cement sector in Turkey and the fact that the undertakings already settled and active benefit from significant economies of scale. Again in line with this approach, in its Türk *Ytong Sanayi* decision[793] the Board considered that although there is no technical or legal barrier, excess capacity reaching 30–40% constitutes an entry barrier to new entrants to establish their own networks for authorised sellers.

6.2.2.4 Product Differentiation and Customer Loyalty

Product differentiation and customer loyalty could be categorised as potential entry barriers arising from strategic advantages of the undertaking that enjoys market power. As a result of the marketing activities (e.g., advertising) of a certain product, the product may become distinct from its substitutes, thereby establishing customer loyalty.[794] In addition, customer loyalty may be established when the customer has a commercial relationship with the supplier for a long time or there is no alternative to the product based on its qualities and technical features. Loyalty to the brand and inability to supply the product from another supplier may result in customer loyalty as well.[795] Product differentiation and advertisement may be deemed as an entry barrier through dissuading the strategic entrance or in certain situations utilised as a tool for market entry; therefore, its effects should be evaluated on a case-by-case basis.[796]

In simple terms, in markets where the customer/brand loyalty is significantly predominant and/or the degree of product differentiation is high, the market structure would be less

---

[790] Kaya (n. 740) at 74.

[791] *Bimpaş* (22 April 2005, 05-27/317-80).

[792] *Özgür Cement* (17 April 2008, 08-29/355-116).

[793] *Türk Ytong Sanayi* (16 December 2009, 09-59/1435-373).

[794] *Glaxo Wellcome/Smithkline Beecham* (Case No. IV/M.1846) Commission Decision [2000] O.J. C 170, paras. 107–123; *Nestlé/Perrier* (Case No. IV/M.190) Commission Decision 92/553/EEC [1992] OJ L 356/1.

[795] Kaya (n. 740) at 75.

[796] Ibid. at 33.

competitive and price competition would be less intense from the incumbent under-takings' perspective. This, in turn, would render entries less attractive, since any given undertaking that wishes to enter the market would have to show a greater amount of effort to render its product distinct and desirable from the consumers' perspective. One of the most prominent examples of this is related to the non-alcoholic beverages market in Turkey, where the incumbent undertakings have very well established and distinct products that the great majority of consumers are consistently inclined to purchase. In this regard, in its *Coca-Cola* decision,[797] the Board evaluated that Coca-Cola and Pepsi-Cola brands had a monetary value of billions of dollars in 2002–according to a survey of the world's top 100 brands regularly conducted by the economy magazine *Businessweek*–while Coca-Cola's brand value has reached approximately ten times when compared to Pepsi-Cola. The biggest impact of this indicator is that all products put on the market with the logo of "The Coca-Cola Company" have a certain priceless image in the eyes of consumers. High brand awareness and loyalty at the international level make Coca-Cola an indispensable product that must be kept stocked by resellers. This, in turn, provides Coca-Cola A.Ş. with bargaining power on significant aspects such as sales conditions, positioning on the shelves and promotion areas in the agreements it has with retailers. This extent of brand loyalty may even cause consumers who cannot find the Coca-Cola product at a sales point to go to another point instead of turning to competitor brands. The foregoing, evaluated together with the extensive advertisement expenditures that have been spent for marketing the brand, was found by the Board to grant significant advantage to undertakings such as Coca-Cola A.Ş. and Pepsi Group over their local competitors in creating brand image and loyalty, which have a decisive influence on the sales of carbonated-non-alcoholic drinks. Thereby entries to the market in question would be hindered to a great extent since it would certainly be very chal-lenging for a new entrant to capture market share from the incumbent firms, who have been conducting profitable activities for decades. Another example for distinct products towards which consumers demonstrate a significant amount of brand loyalty could be observed between a sports club and its customers (supporters), which are referred to as a power that is close to monopoly. This level of brand loyalty allows sports clubs to act independently from their competitors in terms of their economic activities, such as ticket and product sales, etc.[798]

On the other hand, it could be evaluated that when there is a multitude of players and brand loyalty for a single product is not observed, market entry is rather easy compared to the previous examples. For instance, in terms of ready-made clothing and footwear products, where demand and supply substitution are high, brand dependency is low for the majority of customers, as customer loyalty is low due to the presence of many different players in the sector and there are abundant alternative sales points, market entries could be considered facilitated.[799] Along the same line, in the yeast market, the low brand dependency due to the homogeneity of the product causes customers to easily switch between products, thereby rendering the market attractive for newcomers.[800]

---

[797]   *Coca-Cola* (n. 760), p. 11.
[798]   *Football Association* (12 September 2018, 18-31/532-262).
[799]   *Boyner* (16 April 2020, 20-20/271-130).
[800]   *Dosu Maya/Lessafre* (31 May 2018, 18-17/316-156).

6.2.2.5 Technology Challenges

Certain industries require undertakings to make large technological investments, which could, in turn, disincentivise investors from entering the market. Technological superiority of an undertaking may discourage other investors from entering the market that requires high-cost technologies, as it provides the undertaking having technological superiority with cost advantages and effective production.[801] For instance, in its *Ereğli Demir* decision, the Board evaluated that the iron-steel sector is open to global competition and thereby a competitive market; however, when it is considered that automotive and domestic appliance industrialists, who are customers of cold-rolled products, attribute importance to the quality of the products and that Erdemir's cold rolling facilities have the latest technology in the world, the Board deemed that Erdemir has a significant amount of market power.[802]

The effect of high technology challenges would be heightened in a market that requires ever-changing innovations and intellectual property.[803] In evaluating technology challenges as entry barriers, the cost and/or timeframe of the potential competitors acquiring or developing the technology are among the determinative factors.[804] For example, in its *Duygu Havacılık* decision, the Board evaluated that the DNA Barcode technology, which is a pre-requisite in order to comply with the conditions determined by the Ministry for entering the market, requires a great deal of know-how. The Board deemed that these can be considered as a barrier to market entry and thereby considered the requirement for the access to the respective technology and know-how as a significant determinant factor in its assessment of dominance.[805]

6.2.2.6 Vertical Integration and Distribution Channels

Vertical integration is referred to as the expansion of the company's activities into the supply of its inputs/commodities (backwards integration) or the inclusion of retail activities such as the distribution and sale of the products (forward integration) within its business framework. Gathering all activities from commodity procurement to retail sales under the same roof defines full vertical integration.[806] In more basic terms, vertical integration is the arrangement of consecutive production processes within a single firm, where a firm is defined as a business that produces goods and services.[807]

Vertical integration can provide a company with significant advantages over non-integrated companies such as lower transaction costs, security of inputs, and ability to remedy market failure.[808] Vertical integration can take several forms, ranging from a supply chain in which raw materials and other inputs are utilised to create an intermediate good, which

---

[801]   Kaya (n. 740) at 76.

[802]   *Ereğli Iron-Steel* (12 June 2001, 01-27/260-74).

[803]   Yanık (n. 777) at 36–37.

[804]   Çeçen (n. 733) at 40.

[805]   *Duygu Havacılık* (16 April 2020, 20-20/266-127), para. 40.

[806]   *Sias Alçı/ABS Alçı* (1 February 2007, 07-11/70-22).

[807]   M. H. Riordan, "What is Vertical Integration?" in *The Firm as a Nexus of Treaties*, M. Aoki, B. Gustafsson and O. E. Williamson, eds. (London: Sage Publications, 1990)

[808]   *Milyon Production* (15 October 2020, 20-46/621-273).

is then used as a component input in the creation of a final good, which is then supplied to customers via a retail channel. Forward vertical integration occurs when a company increases its scope of operations to include both the production and distribution of the final product.[809]

Internal expansion or mergers might result in vertical integration. Internally, a company might integrate backwards by constructing its own manufacturing facilities or forward by establishing its own distribution facilities. Vertical integration through the acquisition of new productive assets typically expands markets and hence does not pose a competitive threat. This is not to suggest that a vertically integrated market structure always outperforms a non-integrated one; in some industries, limits on vertically integrated firms' conduct may actually increase market performance.[810]

In terms of examples where the Board evaluated vertical integration as a determinant factor relating to entry barriers, in its *Luxottica* decision,[811] Luxottica Group was evaluated to be active in terms of the distribution of its own manufactured branded sunglasses and at the retail level through Sunglass Hut stores with an ever-increasing number. Hence, it was considered that Luxottica's position as a strong vertically integrated player at the global level constituted a significant barrier for entry. Along the same lines, in its *TTNET* decision,[812] the Board stated that Türk Telekom's vertically integrated structure might give rise to a strong and common distribution network, its wide product portfolio, high brand awareness and financial and economic strength were amongst the factors that create significant entry barriers within the sector.

6.2.2.7 Timespan for Entry

If entry into a market requires a long amount of time for certain industries, it may disincentive investors from entering the market. For instance, in the Board's *Novartis/Nestlé* decision,[813] the Board considered the entry of the equivalent medicine suppliers' entrance to the market as a factor that renders market entries difficult. Along the same lines, in the Board's *İzocam* decision,[814] the Board considered that the required duration for the establishment of the furnaces and the transition into the manufacturing period constitutes a considerable amount of time, which would be again deemed as an entry barrier for the new entrants to the market.

6.2.2.8 Switching Costs

In any given market, buyers make investments based on their relationships with suppliers. For instance, buyers may base their decision on (i) the time and effort necessary to change suppliers; (ii) the risk of disrupting normal operations of the business; (iii) their

---

[809]   M. H. Riordan, "Competitive Effects of Vertical Integration", Prepared for LEAR conference on "Advances in the Economics of Competition Law", Rome, 23–25 June 2005.

[810]   Ibid.

[811]   *Luxottica* (23 February 2017, 17-08/99-42).

[812]   *TTNET* (5 February 2015, 15-06/74-31).

[813]   *Novartis/Nestlé* (7 July 2010, 10-49/929-327).

[814]   *İzocam* (8 February 2010, 10-14/175-66).

knowledge regarding how to use a vendor's product; (iv) the ability to acquire complementary goods that only work with a specific vendor's products; and (v) the transaction costs (e.g., cancellation fees, opening and closing bank accounts) associated with finding and establishing a working relationship with a new supplier. These relationship-specific assets result in switching costs for a buyer who changes from one supplier to another.[815] Accordingly, switching costs may produce adverse effects on competition by making it difficult for new entries.

Switching costs are amongst the factors assessed by the Board when evaluating the existence of dominance. For example, in its *Enerjisa* decision, the Board held that the business model would result in providing other services, such as gas and telecommunication services, as well as electrical services to residential customers, and therefore make it easier for these customers who are faced with high switching costs to switch suppliers.[816] In line with these decisions, in *Doğan Yayın Holding* decision,[817] while assessing whether the undertaking is in a dominant position, the Board stated that:

> As a result, considering that each discount rate in the discount system implemented by Doğan Media Group and the cumulative effect of this discount system make Doğan Media Group an indispensable commercial partner for advertisers and as these discount rates can jump to dramatic levels, it can be said that it has the potential to greatly increase the customers' switching costs and create a loyalty-increasing effect.

In its *Siemens III* decision,[818] the Board examined six different parameters for assessing Siemens' market power in the after-sales markets, one of which was switching costs. In that regard, the Board evaluated that the switching costs were quite high due to the absence of a regulated active secondary product market, where in case of an increase in the prices of secondary products, manufacturers would have the ability to offer different prices to new consumers and locked-in consumers.

6.2.2.9 Sunk Costs and Network Effects

Sunk costs are defined as costs that a firm must bear to enter the market but cannot be recovered after exiting the market. For example, promotional expenditures to build brand loyalty, equipment that cannot be used for any other purpose, investments for network marketing, etc., are considered sunk costs. Sunk costs are seminal to the decision of new entrants to enter the market. The higher the investment cost requirement in terms of entering a market, the higher the sunk costs that the undertaking that wants to end its activities in the market will face. If it is necessary to bear significant sunk costs for entry to the market, this has a deterrent effect on the potential new entrant and the established firm can easily use this situation to its advantage. In this respect, sunk costs make it difficult to enter and exit the market.[819]

---

[815] J. Farrell and C. Shapiro, "Dynamic Competition With Switching Costs", *RAND Journal of Economics*, Vol. 19, No. 1, Spring 1988, p. 123.

[816] *Enerjisa* (8 August 2018, 18-27/461-224), para. 101.

[817] *Doğan Yayın* (30 March 2011, 11-18/341-103).

[818] *Siemens III* (19 November 2020, 20-50/695-306).

[819] *Milyon Production* (n. 808).

The network effect is when the value of a good is affected by the number of owners of the same good. For example, it is understood that online food ordering services are open to network effects, since the customers will be more willing to use the site as the number of restaurants on the site increases, and the restaurants will be willing to pay more for the service provided by the site as the number of registered customers and especially as chain restaurant brands increase on the site.[820] It is this network effect that differentiates the service in question for restaurants. In return for this service, the restaurant pays to the extent that it benefits from the network effect, in other words, a certain percentage of the sales generated by the site itself.

For instance, when evaluating the entry barriers in its *Sahibinden III* decision,[821] the Board dwelled upon the entry barriers that are specific to multisided platform economies, which prominently include network effects and sunk costs that arise from network effects. The Board stated that the network effect in this case–i.e., the value of the platform–is determined by decision units that want to benefit from the commercial interaction opportunities offered by the platform and are influenced by each other's preferences. The increase in the participation of one of the decision unit groups means that the value of the platform increases for the other groups.

In this respect, in practice, undertakings providing platform services increase the value of the platform by providing free or low-cost services to the end consumers, and the entrepreneur gains profit from the pricing of other decision unit groups within the platform. Therefore, the undertaking that increases the value of the platform (for all user groups through the network effect) by providing free or very low-cost services to end consumers who enter the market early and demand goods/services through the platform will gain a competitive advantage. This would create a significant entry barrier for late entrants.

Therefore, the Board concluded that in terms of entry barriers, the most challenging entry barriers in the relevant product market are network effects and sunk costs related to network effects.

6.2.2.10 Economies of Scale and Scope

Economies of scope mean that it costs less to produce two types of products together than to produce them separately. Economies of scope may have similar implications to economies of scale, as a potential entrant would prefer to enter the market with many as opposed to few products.[822]

In parallel, "economies of scale exist where average costs fall as output rises".[823] This, in turn, enables incumbent undertakings to conduct manufacturing activities at lower costs compared to their competitors and thereby enables them to sell their products at lower prices.[824]

---

[820] *Yemek Sepeti* (25 March 2004, 04-22/231-48).
[821] *Sahibinden III* (2 May 2019, 19-17/239-108).
[822] Office of Fair Trading, "Assessment of Market Power: Understanding Competition Law", 2004.
[823] Ibid.
[824] *Halk Ekmek* (15 November 2007, 07-86/1085-421).

For instance, in its *Vodafone/Türksat* decision,[825] when evaluating the entry barriers within the electronic communications sector, the Board determined that the respective sector significantly benefits from economies of scale and scope. It further evaluated that Türk Telekom is able to significantly benefit from economies of scale and scope due to its widespread network within Turkey and its vertically integrated structure. Türk Telekom is able to provide services such as leased circuits, phone and internet access via the same network, which enables the sharing the costs of employee expenditures, marketing and infrastructure, which significantly decreases its average costs in general. Thereby, the Board determined that alternative operators do not have the ability to exercise any competitive restraints on Türk Telekom in the short run due to the advantages it benefits from, including most prominently the economies of scale and scope.

6.2.3 Countervailing Buying Power

Another criterion used to determine whether an undertaking is in a dominant position within the scope of Law No. 4054 is the ability of the undertaking to act independently of its customers in the relevant market. In the Guidelines it is stated that if the customers in the market are relatively large, have knowledge with respect to the alternative sources of supply and have the opportunity to switch to another provider or create their own supply within a reasonable time, these customers have bargaining power–in other words, buyer power. In the *Mey Alcoholic Beverage* decision, the Board stated:

> In this context, in case there are customers who are effective and have significant bargaining power against the undertaking that is being examined, the relevant undertaking may not be able to determine all the parameters that may be a bargaining factor, especially the price, and will have to adjust its actions by taking into account the pressure from its customers. On the other hand, in cases where there is only a limited customer base, it can be evaluated that the buyer power does not create sufficient competitive pressure.

> In the Guidelines on Horizontal Mergers, balancing buyer power is defined as the bargaining power gained by buyers against their suppliers in commercial transactions based on the size of the customers, their importance vis-à-vis the supplier and their ability to switch to alternative suppliers.[826] It is accepted in the doctrine that even undertakings with a very high market share may not be deemed to be in a dominant position when customers have a significant purchasing power. In order to evaluate that the undertaking in question is not in a dominant position due to the structure of the market, certain buyers should be in a position to enable new entries to the market in the face of possible price increases or to protect the whole market from price increase by allowing existing competitors to increase their production. In this context, it can be said that the existence of buyer power can be accepted in cases where the buyer segment of the market is concentrated.[827]

---

[825]   *Vodafone/Türksat* (25 November 2018, 18-40/641-312).
[826]   Guidelines on Horizontal Mergers, para. 63.
[827]   *Mey İçki* (n. 741).

Thus, in case the customers of the undertaking examined are relatively large, sufficiently informed about alternative sources of supply and capable of switching to another supplier or creating their own supply within a reasonable period of time, then these customers may be said to have bargaining power or buyer power. In this case, the buyer power of the customers will present as a competitive factor restricting the conduct of the undertaking examined and may prevent the determination of a dominant position for the undertaking. However, buyer power may be considered not to form sufficient competitive pressure if it only ensures that a limited segment of customers is shielded from the market power of the dominant undertaking.[828]

For instance, in its *Varinak* decision,[829] the Board, in the scope of its examination, found that hospitals (or, in some cases, institutions that issue a tender bid process to procure services for the hospital) are customers in medical device maintenance and repair market. Radiotherapy devices are very expensive and it is understood that once purchased, the customers cannot easily switch to a different brand's device due to the high cost of transition. It has been observed that hospitals prefer to purchase from authorised distributors from time to time via direct procurement method, in which case the service is more costly. When it is considered that there are limited number and capacity of alternative undertakings that can provide maintenance and repair services to the Varian brand radiotherapy device, it is not possible to talk about the existence of a balancing buyer power in terms of the relevant market.

Similarly, in the Board's *Unmaş* decision,[830] it was articulated that the advantageous party in the contracts Unmaş has made with retail chains for the supply of packaged bread is the retailers that make the products accessible to consumers. As a matter of fact, it is seen that the provisions regarding termination, product returns and compensation in the contracts examined granted material rights to the retailers as purchasers of the products. Therefore, the claim that Unmaş is in a dominant position has no justifiable basis.

Moreover, in its *Luxottica* decision[831] the Board stated that the total market share of the eleven chain store opticians, despite increasing their share in the market, was spread among eleven chain enterprises and far from covering the market in general. Therefore, at this stage, the said eleven chain opticians cannot be considered to constitute a serious stabilising buyer power over Luxottica and its competitors. Moreover, a significant part of the market is still constituted by other large and small chains and opticians. Although it can be seen that the leading big chains at the retail level of the market can obtain better conditions thanks to their bargaining power, it does not seem possible to say that the remainder of the market, which shows a dispersed structure, constitutes the balancing buyer power.

On the other hand, there is a view in the literature that balancing buyer power should not only neutralise a power on the opposite side of the market, but should also offer benefits to the weaker buyers in the market. Thus, limited protection will be provided even though it will be limited to smaller buyers. The positive externality that the balancing

---

[828] Guidelines on Horizontal Mergers, para. 65.
[829] *Varinak (n. 767)*.
[830] *Unmaş* (2 March 2016, 16-07/136-61).
[831] *Luxottica (n. 811)*.

buyer power provides to small buyers in this way is known as the spillover effect, or the anti-waterbed effect. Within this framework, based on the determinations made in the *Firmenich International* decision[832] of the Board, the information and opinions obtained, it is evaluated that anti-competitive behaviours that may occur after the acquisition can be prevented by the existing buyer power in the market, the opportunity to change suppliers and the existence of strong and active competitors.

6.3 Collective Dominance

Article 6 of Law No. 4054 makes reference to collective dominance as "The abuse, by *one or more undertakings*, of their dominant position in a market for goods or services within the whole or a part of the country on their own or through agreements with others or through concerted practices, is illegal and prohibited" (emphasis added). The Guidelines on Horizontal Mergers provide that a merger could give rise to the creation or strengthening of dominance, and thereby significantly impede effective competition through two methods,[833] the first one being unilateral effects. The Guidelines make reference to unilateral effects as "creating or strengthening a dominant position as a result of the elimination of important competitive pressure on one or more undertakings (single dominant position)".[834] Besides this, the Guidelines also refer to collective dominance as "Changing the nature of competition in the relevant market, undertakings that previously were not coordinating their behaviour, significantly impede competition by rendering coordination (joint dominant position)".[835] It is also indicated that such merger may render existing coordination between undertakings in the relevant market easier, more stable or more effective compared to pre-merger conditions.[836]

As indicated under the EU Horizontal Guidelines, a merger in a concentrated market may significantly impede effective competition, through the creation or the strengthening of a collective dominant position, because it increases the likelihood that firms are able to coordinate their behaviour in this way and raise prices, even without entering into an agreement or resorting to a concerted practice within the meaning of Article 81 of the Treaty.[837] As provided under paragraph 41 of the EU Horizontal Guidelines, three conditions have been determined for cooperation/collective dominance to be sustainable within any given market:[838]

- The coordinating firms must be able to monitor to a sufficient degree whether the terms of coordination are being adhered to.

- Discipline requires that there is some form of credible deterrent mechanism that can be activated if deviation is detected.

---

[832] *Firmenich International* (25 June 2020, 20-31/388-174).
[833] Guidelines on Horizontal Mergers, para. 22.
[834] Ibid.
[835] Ibid.
[836] *Lesaffre/Dosu Maya* (15 December 2014, 14-52/903-411).
[837] EU Horizontal Guidelines, para. 39.
[838] Ibid. at para. 41.

–   The reactions of outsiders, such as current and future competitors not participating in the coordination, as well as customers, should not be able to jeopardise the results expected from the coordination.

Collective dominance constitutes a significant competition law matter in terms of the potential coordinative effects it may produce. Certain markets' structure renders it economically rational and therefore preferable for undertakings to adopt behavioural patterns that would allow them to conduct sales with high price levels, in a sustainable manner. In this sense, without resorting to an explicit agreement or concerted practice within the meaning of Article 4 of Law No. 4054, they would have the opportunity to coordinate and raise prices.[839]

In markets that render it easy for undertakings to reach a common understanding with regard to the form of cooperation, it is more probable for transactions to give rise to collective dominance or cooperation. In turn, undertakings being able to reach a common understanding would depend on the market structure itself. In this sense, cooperation would be easier in markets where a few players are active, one single homogenous product is being sold, the demand/supply structure is stationary, and the economic nature of the market is less complicated and placid . In addition to this, in case the operation of the market allows the allocation of customers and/or geographical regions, and in case the market players show similarities in terms of cost structures, market shares, vertical integration and capacities, the chances of cooperation would be even higher. On the other hand, in case of markets where there are differentiated products, the demand structure is volatile, market entries and exits are easier, it is convenient to obtain market share via technological advancements, it is less probable for undertakings to engage in any coordinative behaviour.[840]

In terms of the Board's decisional practice, precedents concerning collective dominance are not mature enough to allow for a clear inference of a set of minimum conditions under which collective dominance should be alleged. That said, the Board has considered it necessary to establish an economic link for a finding of abuse of collective dominance in certain decisions (see, for example, *National Roaming*, 9 June 2003, 03-40/432-186; *Biryay*, 17 July 2000, 00-26/292-162). In addition, in the scope of the *Gaziantep Çimento* decision,[841] where the Board evaluated the transaction relating to an acquisition is the cement sector, it was determined that there is no risk of collective dominance, since (i) there are no structural ties between the respective undertakings; (ii) no competitive coordination had been found in the past; and (iii) there is no risk of contact within multiple markets.

---

[839]   *Saudi Arabian Oil Company* (29 August 2019, 19-30/448-193); *BASF* (5 April 2018, 18-10/183-86); *Lesaffre/ Dosu Maya* (n. 836); *Asahi* (11 June 2020, 20-28/362-162).

[840]   *Ingenico SA* (24 January 2008, 08-08/89-29).

[841]   *Gaziantep Çimento* (28 April 2006, 06-31/379-96).

Chapter 7
Abuse of Dominance –
Exclusionary Practices

GÖNENÇ GÜRKAYNAK, ESQ., BETÜL BAŞ ÇÖMLEKÇI*
AND CEREN DURAK**

This chapter will mainly dwell upon (i) concept of abuse; (ii) concept of anti-competitive effect; (iii) objective justifications; and (iv) types of exclusionary practices–namely, price-based exclusionary practices and non-price based exclusionary practices. Under price-based exclusionary practices, this chapter will cover predatory pricing and margin squeeze; while under non-price based exclusionary practices, we will cover exclusive dealing, rebate systems, tying, and refusal to deal.

7.1 Concept of Abuse

Unilateral activities prohibited by Turkish competition law generally fall under the ambit of Article 6 of Law No. 4054, which is akin to Article 102 TFEU. Article 3 of Law No. 4054 defines dominance as "The power of one or more undertakings in a particular market to determine economic parameters such as price, supply, the amount of production and distribution, by acting independently of their competitors and customers ". Article 6 of Law No. 4054 is the primary legislation that applies specifically to dominant firm behaviour. It provides that "The abuse, by one or more undertakings, of their dominant position in a market for goods or services within the whole or a part of the country on their own or through agreements with others or through concerted practices, is illegal and prohibited".

Article 6 of Law No. 4054 only applies to dominant undertakings. As per paragraph 7 of the Guidelines on Dominant Position, for a behaviour that is investigated within the scope of Article 6 of Law No. 4054 to constitute a violation, both of the following conditions must be satisfied: (i) the investigated undertaking must be in a dominant position in the relevant market and (ii) the behaviour must constitute an abuse. As such, if the Board finds that the investigated undertaking is not in a dominant position, it may choose not to analyse the other factors and decide that the investigated undertaking is not violating Article 6.[842,843]

---

* Associate, ELIG Gürkaynak Attorneys-at-Law, Istanbul <betul.bas@elig.com>.
** Associate, ELIG Gürkaynak Attorneys-at-Law, Istanbul <ceren.durak@elig.com>.

[842] Guidelines on Abuse of Dominance, para. 7; Council of State, 13th Chamber, 3 April 2014, E. 2013/3006, K. 2014/1284 and 25 May 2015, E. 2009/5608, K. 2014/2054; and Ankara 14th Administrative Court, 2 October 2014, E. 2012/1803, K. 2014/1065.

[843] *Unilever* (28 August 2012, 12-42/1257-409); *Luxottica-Dünya Göz* (3 May 2007, 07-37/396-156); *Nuh Çimento* (18 February 2016, 16-05/118-53).

It should be underlined that being in a dominant position is not prohibited within the scope of Law No. 4054. However, abusive conduct of a dominant undertaking is restricted by Article 6 of Law No. 4054. Accordingly, although it does not expressly define "abuse", Article 6 of Law No. 4054 provides a non-exhaustive list of five abusive behaviours, which are forbidden within the scope of competition law:

–   directly or indirectly preventing entries into the market or hindering competitor activity in the market;

–   directly or indirectly engaging in discriminatory behaviour by applying dissimilar conditions to equivalent transactions with similar trading parties;

–   making the conclusion of contracts subject to acceptance by the other parties of restrictions concerning resale conditions such as the purchase of other goods and services; or acceptance by the intermediary purchasers of displaying other goods and services or maintenance of a minimum resale price;

–   distorting competition in other markets by taking advantage of financial, technological and commercial superiority in the dominated market;

–   limiting production, markets or technical development to the prejudice of consumers.

However, a definition of abuse can be found under the Guidelines on Abuse of Dominance, which were closely modelled after the EU Dominance Guidance to provide guidance for the assessment of dominance as a soft law instrument.

According to paragraph 22 of the Guidelines on Abuse of Dominance, "abuse" emerges when a dominant undertaking takes advantage of its market power to engage in activities that are likely, directly or indirectly, to reduce consumer welfare.

Moreover, Article 2 of Law No. 4054 adopts an effects-based approach to identifying anti-competitive conduct, with the result that the determining factor in assessing whether a practice amounts to an abuse is the effect on the market regardless of the type of conduct. In parallel, as per paragraph 24 of the Guidelines on Exclusionary Abuses:

> In the assessment of exclusionary conduct, in addition to the specific conditions of the conduct under examination, its actual or potential effects on the market should be taken into consideration as well.

The concept of abuse covers both exploitative and exclusionary practices, as well as discriminatory ones.

Along with the fact that Law No. 4054 does not set forth any definition of the concept of abuse, the Turkish competition law legislation and previous decisions of the Board (i) require dominant firms to exhibit a "special responsibility" in their conduct and (ii) prohibit them from reducing consumer welfare by exploiting the advantages of the market power they enjoy. Law No. 4054 and the relevant Guidelines ordain that dominant undertakings be considered to have a "special responsibility" not to allow their conduct to restrict competition.[844] A similar approach is observed in the precedents of the Commission, where it is set forth that "the undertaking concerned has a special responsibility not to allow its conduct to impair genuine undistorted competition on the common market".[845]

In its *Hoffmann-La Roche* decision,[846] the Commission has defined abuse as "an objective concept relating to the behaviour of an undertaking in a dominant position which is such as to influence the structure of a market where, as a result of the very presence of the undertaking in question, the degree of competition is weakened and which, through recourse to methods different from those which condition normal competition in products or services on the basis of the transactions of commercial operators, has the effect of hindering the maintenance of the degree of competition still existing in the market or the growth of that competition". According to the CJEU, "article 82 of the EC Treaty does not only apply to practices that can cause harm directly to consumers but also those that are harmful for them because of their influence on the structure of competition in the market. Abuse can also occur if an entrepreneur occupying the dominant position strengthens it in such a way that the degree of acquired dominance materially limits the competition".[847] The foregoing also influenced Turkish competition law as the Board and the administrative courts in Turkey adopted similar definitions.[848]

The list of specific abuses under Article 6 is not exhaustive, and it is very likely that other types of conduct may be deemed as abuse of dominance. For example, practices such as excessive pricing[849] and self-preferencing[850] were recognised as abusive practices by the Board despite the fact that they are not included within the non-exhaustive list under Article 6. Having said this, up until now, the Board did not render a decision concerning other forms of abuse such as strategic capacity construction, predatory product design or process innovation, failure to disclose new technology, predatory advertising or excessive product differentiation.

Article 6 of Law No. 4054 does not include a categorisation for types of abuse, and in practice it is not possible to completely separate such conduct from each other, in every one of the cases under examination. The Guidelines on Abuse of Dominance set out specific forms of abuse–namely, discriminatory, exploitative and exclusionary[851]–however, a particular conduct examined by the Board may constitute an example of more than one type of conduct listed under Article 6 of Law No. 4054.

---

[844] *Unilever* (18 March 2021, 21-15/190-80); *Tüpraş II* (17 January 2014, 14-03/60-24); *Radontek* (11 October 2018, 18-38/617-298); *UN Ro-Ro* (1 October 2012, 12-47/1413-474); *Bereket Enerji/Aydem/Gediz* (1 October 2018, 18-36/583-284); *Cine 5*, decision of the 10th Chamber of the Council of State (4 November 2003, E. 2001/355, K. 2003/4245); *Karbogaz* (1 December 2005, 05-80/1106-317); *Mey İçki* (12 June 2014, 14-21/410-178).

[845] Case 322/81 *Michelin v. Commission* [1983] ECR 3461, para. 57.

[846] Case 85/76 *Hoffmann-La Roche & Co. AG v. Commission* [1979] ECR 461, para. 91.

[847] Office for Competition and Consumers' Protection, "Abuse of a dominant position in the light of legal provisions and case law of the European Communities", Warsaw, 2003, p. 16.

[848] *Benkar/Fiba* (18 September 2001, 01-44/433-111).

[849] *Belko* (n. 781); *BOTAŞ-EGO-İDGAŞ* (8 March 2002, 02-13/127-54).

[850] *Google Shopping Unit* (7 November 2019, 19-38/575-243); *Google Local Search* (4 April 2021, 21-20/248-105).

[851] In recent decisions, the Board reiterates the classification of abuses under three groups, namely, discriminatory, exploitative and exclusionary: *Google Shopping Unit* (n. 850), p. 37; *Soda* (20 April 2016, 16-14/205-89), p. 1; *THY* (1 September 2015, 15-34/512-160), p. 11; *UN Ro-Ro* (n. 844), p. 34.

Similar to the EU Dominance Guidance, the Guidelines on Abuse of Dominance are limited to exclusionary abuses and do not include information on exploitative or discriminatory abuses. However, exploitative and discriminatory practices also fall under Article 6 of Law No. 4054. Exploitative prices or terms of supply may be deemed to be an infringement although the wording of Article 6 does not contain a specific reference to this concept. The main examples of exploitative abuses are excessive purchase or selling prices and imposing unfair and exploitative contract terms. As for discriminatory abuse, price and non-price discrimination may amount to an abusive conduct under Article 6.[852]

Further, Law No. 4054 does not recognise any industry-specific abuses or defences. Independent regulatory authorities have the jurisdiction to regulate the activities of dominant players in the specific regulated sectors. For instance, according to the secondary legislation issued by the Turkish Information and Communication Technologies Authority, firms with significant market power are prohibited from engaging in discriminatory behaviour among companies seeking access to their network and (unless justified) rejecting requests for access or interconnection. Similar restrictions and requirements are also applicable in the energy sector. Also, the secondary legislation issued by the Energy Market Regulatory Authority brings certain requirements for the retail electricity sales companies and distribution companies. The sector-specific rules and regulations provide structural market remedies for the effective functioning of the free market; however, these do not entail any dominance-control mechanisms. The Authority is the only regulatory body that investigates and condemns abuses of dominance. However, the Board takes into account the regulatory context to assess the nature of the market and whether the investigated undertaking's conduct is justified based on these regulations.[853]

One should note that, regarding the link between the various factors with respect to the prohibition of the abuse of a dominant position, usually it is not crucial for the abuse to take place in the market where the dominant position was established. Article 6 also prohibits abusive conduct in a market different from the market subject to dominant position. Accordingly, in its decisions concerning leveraging allegations, the Board also found incumbent undertakings to have infringed Article 6 by engaging in abusive conduct in markets neighbouring the dominated market.[854]

Finally, mergers and acquisitions are normally caught by the merger control rules under Article 7 of Law No. 4054. However, there have been some cases, albeit rare, where the

---

[852] Exploitative and discriminatory practices are examined in detail in Chapter 8.

[853] *Isttelkom* (11 April 2019, 19-15/214-94); *Bereket Enerji/Aydem/Gediz* (n. 844); *Enerjisa* (8 August 2018, 18-27/461-224).

[854] See, for example, *Google Shopping* (n. 28); *Google Android* (n. 29); *Volkan Metro* (2 December 2013, 13-67/928-390); *Türkiye Denizcilik İşletmeleri* (24 June 2010, 10-45/801-264); *Türk Telekom* (2 October 2002, 02-60/755-305) and *Turkcell* (20 July 2001, 01-35/347-95). In *Google Android*, which is one of the limited instances of the Board fining the incumbent firms based on tying or leveraging allegations, the Board found that Google used its dominant position in the market for licensable smart mobile operating systems and abused its dominance through its practices in the said market as well as other markets such as search and app store service market, by tying the search and app store services, engaging in exclusivity practices and preventing the use of alternative services by the manufacturers.

Board found structural abuses through which collectively dominant firms used joint venture arrangements as a backup tool to exclude competitors. This was condemned as a violation of Article 6 of Law No. 4054.[855]

7.2 Anti-Competitive Effect

Article 2 of Law No. 4054 adopts an effects-based approach for identifying anti-competitive conduct – "covers all agreements, decisions and practices which prevent, distort or restrict competition between any undertakings operating in or affecting markets for goods and services" – with the result that the determining factor in assessing whether a practice amounts to an abuse is the effect on the market, regardless of the type of conduct at issue. Paragraph 24 of the Guidelines on Abuse of Dominance states that:

> In the assessment of exclusionary conduct, in addition to the specific conditions of the conduct under examination, its actual or potential effects on the market should be taken into consideration as well.

Abuse of dominant position can have results which decrease consumer welfare such as price increase, decrease in product quality and innovation level, decrease in variability of products and deterioration of service quality.

There is no remedy for this lack of uniformity in definition even though the case law of the Board, as well as the doctrine, was used to achieve consistency in practice. Case law sheds light on the Board's approach and considerations in applying the prohibition of Article 6 of Law No. 4054. Within this scope, when sub-clause (a) and sub-clause (d) are observed respectively – "Preventing, directly or indirectly, another undertaking from entering into the area of commercial activity, or actions aimed at complicating the activities of competitors in the market" and "Conduct which aim to distort competitive conditions in another market for goods or services by means of exploiting financial, technological and commercial advantages created by dominance in a particular market " – it can be concluded that these examples show that the mere existence of a distortive or exploitative "aim" in such specific actions could be deemed as abusive behaviour.

The Guidelines on the Abuse of Dominance define anti-competitive foreclosure as "the obstruction or prevention of access to sources of supply or markets for actual or potential competitors as a result of the conduct of the dominant undertakings, to the detriment of consumers"[856] and follows that consumer harm occurs in cases of price increases, decrease in innovation and product quality and a lesser variety of goods and services.[857]

Because of the foregoing vagueness in the wording of the relevant legislation, in some of its precedents, the Board found it necessary to ground the finding of violation on the "aim

---

[855] *Biryay* (17 July 2000, 00-26/292-162). In this decision, the Board condemned Birleşik Basın Dağıtım A.Ş., YAYSAT Yayın Satış Pazarlama ve Dağıtım A.Ş. and BİRYAY Birleşik Yayın Dağıtım A.Ş. for abuse of collective dominance, whereas the Board assessed that the relevant joint venture did not constitute a concentration in terms of competition law.

[856] Guidelines on the Abuse of Dominance, para. 25.

[857] Ibid.

of exclusion", despite the fact that anti-competitive effect was proven.[858] On the other hand, interpretation of sub-clause (c) of the same article – "purchasing another good or service together with a good or service, or tying a good or service demanded by purchasers acting as intermediary undertakings to the condition of displaying another good or service by the purchaser, or imposing limitations with regard to the terms of purchase and sales in case of resale, such as not selling a purchased good below a particular price" – may lead to a conclusion that "the act itself" is prohibited, in certain examples such as tying practices. Thus, with regard to the relevant acts, the adoption of a per se unlawfulness approach may be deduced.[859] Lastly, from the interpretation of sub-clause (e) – "Restricting production, marketing or technical development to the [detriment] of consumers" – one might easily claim that the presence of "consumer harm" was put forward as a condition. Consequently, analysing the letter of the law reveals that sometimes the existence of a mere aim is deemed as an abuse, while sometimes the presence of consumer harm is a prerequisite to find an abuse; thus, incoherently, both a form-based approach and an impact-based approach are adopted.[860]

Article 6(a) of Law No. 4054 prohibits conduct that prevents, directly or indirectly, another undertaking from entering into the area of commercial activity, or actions aimed at complicating the activities of competitors in the market. The Board's assessments on exclusionary conduct concern whether the conduct of the dominant undertaking results/possibly will result in foreclosure of the market.[861] According to the Guidelines on the Abuse of Dominance, anti-competitive market foreclosure means that a dominant undertaking obstructs or prevents current or potential competitors to reach supply sources/market, which would result in diminishing consumer welfare.[862] Consumer harm may occur in the form of increased prices, decreased product quality and level of innovation, and reduced variety of goods and services.

The Guidelines on the Abuse of Dominance list the elements that are taken into account when examining whether there exists anti-competitive foreclosure.[863] The potential evidence concerning actual foreclosure is one of the elements to be considered in market foreclosure assessments. The importance of these elements stated under the Guidelines on the Abuse of Dominance may vary on a case-by-case basis, depending on the nature of the conduct under examination. Therefore, in order to establish market foreclosure, the Board evaluates these elements together since potential evidence concerning actual foreclosure is not sufficient on its own to find an anti-competitive market foreclosure.

Paragraph 26 of the Guidelines on Abuse of Dominance lists the following criteria, which must be taken into account when assessing whether the relevant practice leads to an anti-competitive foreclosure in the relevant market:

- The market position of the dominant undertaking: the stronger the dominant position, the higher the possibility of the conduct to cause anti-competitive foreclosure.

---

[858]   *Karbogaz* (n. 844); *Ulusal Basın* (2 August 2007, 07-63/777-283). It should be noted that the Board emphasised that "abuse" is an objective concept and stressed the significance of anti-competitive effect in *Karbogaz*, p. 58.

[859]   *Lineer Aktuatör* (8 March 2007, 07-19/188-60); *Doğan Yayın* (n. 817).

[860]   N. Sümer Özdemir, *Rekabete Aykırı Dışlayıcı Uygulamaların Tespitinde Etki Temelli Yaklaşım ve Etki Standartları* (Ankara:Rekabet Kurumu, 2015), pp. 56–57.

[861]   Guidelines on the Abuse of Dominance, para. 25.

[862]   Ibid.

[863]   Ibid., para. 26.

– The conditions in the relevant market: the higher the barriers to entry and growth in the market, the higher the possibility of the conduct in question to foreclose the market. Within this context, entry and growth conditions such as economies of scale and scope carry weight.

– The market positions of the dominant undertaking's competitors: a competitor who has a market share that is comparably lower may cause competitive pressure on a dominant undertaking.

– The position of the customers or suppliers: another aspect to consider in the anti-competitive foreclosure analysis is whether the conduct of a dominant undertaking has a selective nature or not.

– The scope and duration of the practice under examination: the higher the ratio of the sales in the relevant market over the total sales, the longer the conduct and the more regularly the behaviour is practiced, the higher the possibility of market foreclosure.

– Potential evidence related to actual foreclosure: if the conduct in question continues for a specific period of time, then the performance of both the dominant undertaking and its competitors in the market may be counted as direct evidence of anti-competitive market foreclosure.

– Direct or indirect evidence of exclusionary strategy: an analysis may be conducted in order to assess the intention of the dominant undertaking when performing the conduct in question.

The Board has repeatedly adopted the approach that in order to establish market foreclosure, it is not sufficient to solely examine one element. There are decisions in which the Board did not find anti-competitive market foreclosure by evaluating the elements mentioned in the Guidelines even if the examined undertaking has significant market power. For example, in assessing whether the alleged conduct leads to market foreclosure, the Board, in *İsttelkom*,[864] states that conditions in the relevant market are as important as the dominant position of the undertaking therein. In its *Trakya Cam* decision,[865] the Board found that Trakya Cam has high market power, portfolio power, financial power, and a strong position in the market. However, the Board did not find anti-competitive market foreclosure since Düzce Cam, which is a rival of Trakya Cam, did not experience a decrease in its sales and did not lose its consumers during the period of the alleged violation. In the *Türk Telekom* decision,[866] the Board evaluated the elements, including the possible evidence of actual foreclosure stated under the Guidelines. The Board assessed the market share trends of Türk Telekom and its rivals in the VPN service market and found that Türk Telekom did not experience a significant increase in its market share while its rivals' market share increased. The Board concluded that there was no need to launch an investigation against Türk Telekom since there was no evidence to show that the alleged conduct caused anti-competitive market foreclosure. Similarly, in the *Çiçek Sepeti* decision,[867] the Board decided that although

---

[864] *Isttelkom* (n. 853).
[865] *Trakya Cam* (9 February 2015, 15-08/110-46).
[866] *Türk Telekom* (19 September 2018, 18-33/545-269).
[867] *Çiçek Sepeti* (n. 30).

Çiçek Sepeti has significant market power in the online flower sales market, the duration of examined conduct and sales volume as a result of the conduct are not sufficient to establish an anti-competitive market foreclosure.

The Board indeed takes into consideration the above-mentioned factors when assessing whether the relevant practice leads to an anti-competitive foreclosure in the relevant market and provides explanations in its decisions on each factor. For example, in its *Bereket Enerji/Aydem/Gediz, Akdeniz/CK Akdeniz Elektrik* and *Enerjisa*[868] decisions, the Board assessed each factor in detail by referring to the relevant paragraphs of the Guidelines on Abuse of Dominance.

The importance of carrying out an effects-based analysis in dominance cases was underlined in the Board's landmark *Frito-Lay* decision of 2006,[869] in which it emphasised that: "It is not appropriate to forbid the undertakings' desire to pursue or strengthen their dominant position in a per se approach."[870] The Board had therefore made clear that a dominant undertaking's conduct cannot simply be presumed to be harmful. Among the considerations that the Board took into account in its assessment of the conduct were its duration and how much of the market was "covered" by the distribution channels in question. The Board endorsed this approach in its subsequent *Ceramic Adhesives* decision:

> In its precedents, the Competition Board held that, in assessing rebate/premium systems under Article 6 of Law No. 4054, effects on the market need to be taken into consideration and that these evaluations should centre around (i) analysis regarding the restriction of competition through the exclusion of competitors and (ii) whether the rebate systems indicate an exclusionary intent and have any such effect.[871]

In *Biletix*, and by reference to the actual economics at play in the relevant market (supply-side considerations, countervailing buyer power, barriers to entry, potential entrants, competitive constraints in the upstream market, coverage of the disputed agreements, and the existence of actual effects resulting from the conduct, among others), the Board concluded that "in order to determine whether an exclusive agreement forecloses the market, one should initially assess the ability of the agreement subject to examination to foreclose current and potential competitors".[872] The Board further validated this approach in its *Mey İçki Rakı* decision, in which it underlined the importance of conducting a thorough effect assessment in abuse of dominance cases.[873] Instead of proceeding on a presumption, the Board assessed all of the criteria set out in paragraph 26 of the Guidelines on Abuse of Dominance, including the

---

[868]   *Bereket Enerji/Aydem/Gediz* (n. 844); *Akdeniz Elektrik* (20 February 2018, 18-06/101-52); *Enerjisa* (n. 853).
[869]   *Frito-Lay* (6 April 2006, 06-24/304-71).
[870]   N. Sümer Özdemir, *Rekabete Aykırı Dışlayıcı Uygulamaların Tespitinde Etki Temelli Yaklaşım ve Etki Standartları*, (Ankara: Rekabet Kurumu, 2015) (Effects-Based Approach and Standard of Effect in Determining Anti-competitive Foreclosing Conducts, Thesis of Competition Experts, No. 146) available at <https://www.rekabet.gov.tr/Dosya/uzmanlik-tezleri/147-pdf>.
[871]   *Ceramic Adhesives Producers* (12 January 2011, 11-03/42-14).
[872]   *Biletix* (5 November 2013, 13-61/851-359).
[873]   *Mey İçki Rakı* (16 February 2017, 17-07/84-34).

nature of the product in question, the incumbent's position in the relevant market(s), and the margin between prices.

In its *Microsoft*[874] and *Mercedes-Benz*[875] decisions, the Board once again underlined the importance of assessment on the foreclosure effect by stating that "the fundamental part of the assessments of the Board on exclusionary conduct is to evaluate whether the conduct of the dominant undertaking results/possibly will result in foreclosure of the market".

7.3 Objective Justifications and Efficiency Claims

During the examination of an alleged abuse of dominance, the Board takes into consideration any claims that a dominant undertaking puts forward to justify its conduct. The chances of success of certain defences and what constitutes a defence depend heavily on the circumstances of each case. Thus, even if a conduct may restrict competition, it may not be regarded as abuse if there is an objective justification for the conduct.

As per paragraph 30 of the Guidelines on Abuse of Dominance, the Board considers the justifications put forward by a dominant undertaking through the perspective of "objective necessity"[876] or "efficiency", or both. Within this scope, if it can be appropriately demonstrated that the pro-competitive benefits balance out the anti-competitive impact, it is possible to invoke the efficiency defence. In order for the Board to consider such claims, an undertaking's justification claim needs to prove that the alleged conduct indeed provides a legitimate benefit and that such conduct is imperative in order to accomplish that benefit. Therefore. even when the exclusionary intent is demonstrated as a defence, objective justifications such as "objective necessity" and/or "efficiency" can be applied on that front.

As per paragraph 31 of the Guidelines on Abuse of Dominance, the burden of proof resides with the dominant undertaking. Accordingly, when the Board assesses the objective requirement justification, it considers (i) whether there is a legitimate interest protected by the conduct and (ii) whether such conduct is indispensable for the interest it tries to protect. Within this context, the dominant undertaking needs to prove that its conduct is indispensable to protect a legitimate interest.

Similar to its consideration of efficiency gains within the scope of Communique No 2010/4 in its various decisions,[877] the Board also assessed them within the scope of Article 6 of Law No. 4054.[878] When the Board's precedents are examined, it is observed that the

---

[874] *Microsoft* (24 April 2018, 18-12/227-102).
[875] *Mercedes-Benz* (27 August 2018, 18-29/498-239).
[876] *Congresium* (27 August 2020, 20-39/538-239).
[877] *Toros Gübre* (3 November 2000, 00-43/464-254); *Samsun Gübre* (5 May 2005, 05-30/373-92); *Antalya Airport* (16 May 2007, 07-41/452-174); *Schering/Merck* (21 October 2009, 09-48/1203-304).
[878] *OYAK* (18 November 2009, 09-56/1338-341); *Çamlıbel Electricity Distribution* (8 April 2010, 10-29/437-163); *Uludağ Electricity Distribution* (8 April 2010, 10-29/438-164); *Fırat Electricity Distribution* (8 April 2010, 10-29/439-165); *Van Gölü Electricity Distribution* (8 April 2010, 10-29/440-166); *Uludağ Electricity Distribution*

"refusal to deal" cases take the lead with regard to efficiency analysis. In most of the refusal to deal cases, the Authority stated that even if it is prima facie abusive, behaviours having objective justification, which by majority refers to efficiency gains, that outweigh the negative effects on competition do not infringe Article 6 of Law No. 4054.[879]

In its *Varinak* decision,[880] the Board has evaluated objective justification claims by referencing Article 31 of the Guidelines on Abuse of Dominance. In *UN Ro-Ro*,[881] the Board assessed that if the conduct of a dominant undertaking is based on an objective justification, then it is possible that such conduct may not be considered as abuse of dominance, even if it is anti-competitive. Moreover, in order for an objective justification to be accepted by the Board, the conduct should be proportionate and necessary, i.e., the effects that arise as a result of the conduct shall balance out the anti-competitive effects of the conduct and also be proportionate.[882]

In its *Sony* decision,[883] the Board assessed that no evidence could be obtained regarding whether or not Sony had a discriminatory strategy in its pricing campaigns. In certain documents obtained during the dawn raid, the Board assessed that one of the reasons for the fluctuations in the pricing strategy of Sony was because the game prices were indexed to foreign currency. In addition to this, the Board also considered the rapid fluctuation in the foreign currency as another reason for the constant changes in the game prices.

Similarly, in its *Dow* decision,[884] the Board assessed whether the aspects raised as justifications to the practice in question can be considered as objective justification.

Alongside the justification claims, as long as it can be appropriately demonstrated that the pro-competitive benefits outweigh the anti-competitive impact, it is possible to assert efficiency gains. In determining the efficiency justifications put forward by the dominant undertakings, the Board checks whether the following four cumulative conditions are all fulfilled:[885]

- Efficiencies must take place or be likely to take place as a result of the practice in question.

- The practice in question must be indispensable for the efficiencies to take place.

- Efficiencies that are likely to occur as a result of the practice in question must compensate for the possible adverse effects of such practice on the competitive landscape as well as consumer well-being within the relevant affected market.

- The practice in question should not eliminate effective competition by disabling all or majority of the sources of actual and potential competition.

(11 March 2010, 10-22/296-106); *Yeşilırmak Electricity Distribution* (11 March 2010, 10-22/297-107); *Çoruh Electricity Distribution* (11 March 2010, 10-22/298-108).

[879]   OECD, Policy Roundtables, "The Role of Efficiency Claims in Antitrust Proceedings", 2012, p. 170.

[880]   *Varinak* (n. 767).

[881]   *UN Ro-Ro* (n. 844).

[882]   Ibid., para. 142.

[883]   *Sony Eurasia* (7 February 2019, 19-06/47-16).

[884]   *Dow* (13 October 2016, 16-33/586-257).

[885]   The Guidelines on Abuse of Dominance, para. 32.

When evaluating an alleged abuse, the overall effect on consumer welfare is decisive. If efficiencies stemming from the conduct in question compensate for the anti-competitive harm, it should not constitute a violation.[886]

7.4 Exclusionary Practices

This section will address the concept of exclusionary practices under (i) price-based exclusionary practices (i.e., predatory pricing and margin squeeze) and (ii) non-price based exclusionary practices (i.e., exclusive dealing, rebate systems, tying, refusal to deal).

As stated earlier, there is no definition of exclusionary abuse under Law No. 4054. Although abuse can objectively be assessed in three categories, i.e., as exploitative, exclusionary and discriminatory practices, there is no rigid separation between them. In practice, as evidenced by many precedents of the Board, exclusionary pricing, exclusive dealing, leveraging, and refusing to deal may amount to exclusionary abuse.

7.4.1 Predatory Pricing

This section considers the extent to which predatory price amounts to an infringement of Article 6 of Law No. 4054.

7.4.1.1 Concept of Predatory Pricing in Turkish Competition Law

The concept of predatory pricing refers to a case where a dominant undertaking deliberately reduces its prices below cost, to loss-making levels, in order to discipline its existing competitors or to foreclose the market to a new entrant, and then increases the prices again, resulting in consumer harm. Predatory pricing involves the predator setting prices sufficiently low to reduce the competitors' ability or incentives to compete effectively or to exclude them from the market.[887] The Guidelines on Abuse of Dominance define predatory pricing as "an anti-competitive pricing strategy where a dominant undertaking deliberately incurs losses or foregoing profits in the short term ('sacrifices'), so as to exclude, discipline or otherwise restrict competitive conduct of one or more of its actual or potential competitors with a view to strengthening or maintaining its market power".[888]

It is difficult to determine or prevent predatory pricing for two main reasons: firstly, the predatory pricing strategy entails low prices and this is generally assumed to increase

---

[886]   Case C-62/86 *AKZO Chemie BV v. Commission* [1991] ECR I-3359, para. 655.
[887]   International Competition Network, "Unilateral Conduct Workbook Chapter 4: Predatory Pricing Analysis", 2012, p. 2.
[888]   Guidelines on Abuse of Dominance, para. 51.

consumer welfare, which is one of the principal aims of competition law, and thus deemed to be desirable for consumers; secondly, it is difficult to distinguish between pro- and anti-competitive low prices from a competition law point of view.

When a dominant undertaking engages in predatory pricing, even though consumers may initially enjoy lower prices, the implementation of this strategy may lead to undesirable consequences for consumers in the long term. Therefore, predatory pricing is prohibited, and undertakings that adopt predatory pricing strategies are subject to legal sanctions.

In the analysis of potential predatory pricing, the actual price of the relevant undertaking is compared with its costs in order to determine whether its pricing strategy could potentially foreclose the market to an as-efficient competitor.[889] In predatory pricing, even though consumers enjoy low prices in the short term, competition constraints can lead to undesired consequences in the mid and long term, such as high prices, low quality and a decrease in consumer choice. In such cases, the Board may impose an administrative fine on a dominant undertaking for predatory pricing.[890]

In general, the Board assesses the allegations of predatory pricing under six complementary stages:[891]

- dominant position
- whether prices are below a certain cost level
- intention to exclude competitors from the market
- possibility of recoupment following the exclusion of competitors
- (actual/potential) effects
- whether there is any objective justification.

In *Kale Kilit*[892] the Board enlisted the following factors in its assessment regarding predatory pricing: (i) financial superiority of the undertaking; (ii) unusually low prices; (iii) intention to impair competitors; and (iv) short-term losses in exchange for long-term profits. Although there are many precedents of the Board,[893] complaints on this basis are frequently dismissed by the Authority due to its reluctance to micromanage pricing behaviour. High standards are usually observed for bringing forward predatory pricing claims. For example, in *Sony Eurasia*, the Board concluded that prices that were set below costs for a limited amount of time were not enough to determine an Article 6 violation.[894]

In the predatory pricing analysis, which compares the price implemented by the dominant undertaking with the costs incurred with respect to the conduct under examination, the Board evaluates whether the conduct in question is likely to lead to market foreclosure

---

[889]   Ibid.
[890]   *UN Ro-Ro* (n. 844).
[891]   Guidelines on Abuse of Dominance, paras. 51–55; *Mey İçki*; Ankara 12th Administrative Court, *UN Ro-Ro* (9 October 2014, E. 2013/1754, K. 2014/1094).
[892]   *Kale Kilit* (6 December 2012, 12-62/1633-598).
[893]   *Trakya Cam* (17 November 2011, 11-57/1477-533); *Tüpraş II* (n. 844); *UN Ro-Ro* (n. 844).
[894]   *Sony Eurasia* (n. 883).

for an equally efficient competitor. The first phase of the predatory pricing analysis of the Board is the assessment of whether the dominant undertaking made a sacrifice in the short term with its pricing practice. If, by charging a lower price for all or a particular part of its output over the relevant time period, the dominant undertaking incurred or is incurring losses that could have been avoided, this will be considered a sacrifice. The Board also takes into account whether the undertaking suffered from particular costs whilst expanding its capacity and therefore applied predatory prices in order to exclude its competitors.

In assessing the existence of sacrifice in the dominant undertaking's conduct, it may be possible to rely upon direct evidence, such as a detailed plan by the said undertaking to sacrifice, aiming to exclude a competitor, to prevent entry or to pre-empt the emergence of a market. It is necessary for competitors to have actually exited the market for the Board to conclude that there has been an anti-competitive foreclosure through predatory pricing.[895]

As stated before, Article 6 of Law No. 4054 and the Guidelines on Abuse of Dominance are closely modelled after Article 102 TFEU and the Commission's Guidance on the Commission's enforcement priorities in applying Article 82 of the EC Treaty to abusive exclusionary conduct by dominant undertakings. The CJEU assessed predatory pricing for the first time in the *AKZO* case. According to the CJEU, prices below average variable cost[896] (AVC) by a dominant undertaking will be presumed abusive; while prices below average total cost[897] (ATC) but above AVC will be regarded as abusive if they are part of a plan to eliminate competitors. The CJEU's case law was later further developed in *Tetra Pak II*[898] and France *Télécom v. Commission*.[899] In *Tetra Pak II*, the CJEU indicated that "in the circumstances of the present case", whether the dominant undertaking had a "realistic chance of recouping its losses" is not needed to be shown. In *France Télécom v. Commission*, the CJEU held that the case law of the court did not require proving the possibility of recoupment of losses as a necessary precondition to establishing that such a pricing policy is abusive.[900] It further noted that the Commission could still consider the possibility of recoupment a relevant factor for predatory pricing analysis. In its very recent Qualcomm decision, the Commission concluded that the pricing strategy that Qualcomm adopted toward certain customers (i.e., Huawei and ZTE) between 1 July 2009 and 30 June 2011 were below cost, as they did not allow Qualcomm to cover its cost for developing and producing these chipsets.[901]

---

[895] Guidelines on Abuse of Dominance, para. 50 *et seq.*

[896] The costs of supply, which vary with changes in output (e.g., the costs of raw materials, distribution, etc.), averaged over the number of units produced.

[897] The combination of variable costs and fixed costs of production (e.g., monthly rental of premises), which remain constant irrespective of changes in output, averaged over the number of units produced.

[898] Case C-333/94P *Tetra Pak International SA v. Commission* [1996] ECR I-5951.

[899] C-202/07 P *France Télécom v. Commission* [2009] ECR 2369.

[900] In *France Telecom*, the Commission chose the adjusted costs method of calculation under which it spread the costs of acquiring customers over forty-eight months and made a separate assessment of adjusted variable costs and adjusted full costs.

[901] *Qualcomm (predation)* (Case COMP/39.711) Commission Decision [2019] C(2019) 5361 final; I. Lianos & V. Korah with P. Siliciani, *Competition Law: Analysis, Cases and Materials*, Oxford University Press, Oxford, 2019.

The Board's analyses in terms of predatory pricing are generally in line with the EU approach adopted in the *AKZO* decision.[902] According to the *AKZO* test,[903] there are two separate criteria for determining whether the prices in a particular case are predatory. If the price that the investigated undertaking imposes is under its AVC, then it is presumed that the undertaking is abusing its dominant position, since each item produced and sold entails a loss for the undertaking. In such a case, the CJEC does not need to establish any conceivable economic purpose for the pricing strategy other than the elimination of a competitor. As to the second criterion, the CJEU concluded that if the price that the undertaking imposed is above its AVC but below its ATC and an intention on the part of the undertaking to eliminate the competition through its pricing strategy is proved, the undertaking violates competition law rules.[904]

There are numerous cases where the Board applied the *AKZO* test.[905] In *UN Ro-Ro*,[906] the Board based its analysis upon three elements: (i) the proof of below-cost pricing, (ii) the existence of intention of elimination and (iii) anti-competitive foreclosure. Although UN Ro-Ro's prices were below its average avoidable cost (AAC), the Board nevertheless presented the existence of predatory intention in order to demonstrate that the only plausible explanation of the undertaking's strategy was to eliminate its competitor. Furthermore, the Board showed that UN Ro-Ro also had the possibility to recoup its losses while indicating that this was not a precondition for finding predatory pricing.

Turkish case law has established that apart from a dominant position, predatory pricing may amount to an infringement where the following are satisfied:[907] (i) unusually low price; (ii) intention to impair competitors; (iii) losses borne in the short term in exchange for long-term profits (possibility for recoupment); (iv) (actual/potential) anti-competitive effects; and (v) whether there is any objective justification.

In order to impose predatory prices, the undertaking in question must have a market power that gives it the ability to price its product low enough in the market to eliminate all competitors and thus deter any new entrants into the market. The undertaking's market power in other markets is also important as it enables the undertaking to compensate for the losses due to the lower prices from its activities in other markets.

In light of the foregoing, while predatory pricing may be regarded as a form of abuse as evidenced by many precedents,[908] complaints on this basis are frequently dismissed by the Authority, as it is reluctant to interfere in pricing behaviour unduly. This means that predatory pricing claims usually require high standards of proof.

---

[902]   Case C-62/86 *AKZO Chemie BV v. Commission* (n. 886).

[903]   Ibid., paras. 70–72.

[904]   G. Gürkaynak, A. Kağan Uçar and Z. Buharalı, "Data-Related Abuses in Competition Law", in *Frédéric Jenny Liber Amicorum: Standing Up for Convergence and Relevance in Antitrust*, Vol. I, N. Charbit and S. Ahmad, eds. (New York: Concurrences, 2019), pp. 293–310, p. 305, available at SSRN <https://ssrn.com/abstract=3318071>.

[905]   *Habaş* (19 September 2006, 06-66/887-256); *İşbak* (22 May 2006, 06-35/444-116); *Coca-Cola* (23 January 2004, 04-07/75-18).

[906]   *UN Ro-Ro* (n. 844).

[907]   Guidelines on Abuse of Dominance, paras. 51–55.

[908]   *Coca-Cola* (n. 905); *Feniks* (23 August 2007, 07-67/815-310); *Trakya Cam* (n. 893)

7.4.1.2 Pricing Strategy

One of the elements in establishing a prima facie case of predatory pricing is proof of sales below cost. The most important factor in predatory pricing analysis is whether the undertaking is sacrificing in the short term with its pricing strategy. In other words, whether the undertaking bears a loss that could have been avoided.[909]

The Guidelines on Abuse of Dominance provide that in order to decide whether the undertaking is sacrificing profits, the Board should conduct an average avoidable cost (AAC)[910] test.[911,912] Similar to the European practice, in its decisional practice, the Board generally applies the criterion of AAC in assessing whether a sale was below cost. Below cost pricing is usually a condition for establishing predation. In general, if the Board finds that an undertaking does not price below its costs, it will not proceed to investigate the practices.[913]

The starting point for the Board in identifying the products to include in the cost analysis is the relevant product market definition. For instance, if the market definition is "packaging", as a starting point, the Board is likely to include all packaging products in the cost analysis. The Board may then narrow the scope up to a point where the company is able to reasonably allocate the common costs to the relevant products.

In *UN Ro-Ro*,[914] the Board opted to use AAC as the relevant cost criterion, and while calculating it, it considered the undertaking's variable costs such as fuel, personnel, air transportation, Ro-La, port charges, technical management and insurance. Indeed, in the same vein, in its *THY* decision,[915] the Board examined the AAC, average prices and income and expenses for the period of five months to determine whether THY implemented predatory pricing strategies. The assessment looked at the relationship between average price and AAC, where the AAC was calculated by adding up variable direct expenses and fixed direct expenses. Furthermore, the Board considered "advertisement costs" avoidable costs as THY would have avoided these costs if it did not start flights from another airport.

Another cost criterion that can be used by the Board in predatory pricing assessment under certain exceptional circumstances in light of the conditions of the relevant market is the

---

[909] *Toypa* (14 November 2019, 19-40/664-285); *Huawei* (30 May 2019, 19-20/286-122); *Habaş* (7 March 2019, 19-11/125-53); *Techniques Surfaces* (3 January 2019, 19-02/2-1); *Çiçek Sepeti* (n. 30); *Hatay Ro-Ro* (January 6, 2016, 16-01/12-5); *UN Ro-Ro* (1 October 2012, 12-47/1413-474).

[910] AAC may be defined as the costs an undertaking would avoid or save if it had not produced a discrete amount of output. When calculating AAC, the sum of all variable and fixed costs directly related to production can be taken into account in order to calculate all costs incurred by the business for the production under examination. Since it is only possible to avoid variable costs in the short term, in most cases, AAC and average variable cost will be the same. However, in cases where the dominant undertaking must make additional investment in capacity in order to implement the conduct under examination, the fixed costs in question are also taken into account in cost calculation. In such cases, AAC is a more suitable criterion than average variable cost.

[911] Guidelines on Abuse of Dominance, para. 52.

[912] In certain circumstances, the Authority may alternatively consider the long-run average incremental cost (LRAIC). However, this measurement may not be readily applicable to all industries concerned.

[913] *Bilsing* (14 December 2017, 17-41/642-281).

[914] *UN Ro-Ro* (n. 844).

[915] *THY* (25 December 2014, 14-54/932-420).

long-run average incremental cost (LRAIC).[916] LRAIC might be more suitable for sectors like telecommunications where the undertakings are required to bear significantly lower variable costs than fixed costs or where the variable and/or avoidable cost criteria do not reflect the realities of the industry.[917] LRAIC is generally higher than AAC because, unlike AAC (which only includes fixed costs incurred within the examined period), LRAIC also includes fixed costs related to the product under examination, incurred in the period before the asserted abusive conduct. Where LRAIC is used as the relevant cost criterion, failing to meet LRAIC shows that the dominant undertaking did not recoup all costs concerning the production of the good or service in question, and an equally efficient competitor can be foreclosed. Where the price is above LRAIC, the conduct of the dominant undertaking will not be considered predatory pricing since equally efficient competitors will be able to continue their operations without incurring losses.[918]

However, in its *Knauf* decision, the Board acknowledged that the most comprehensive criterion is ATC, given that both AVC and AAC are basically calculated by removing some items from ATC, taking into account the stability, variability or avoidability of costs.[919] Based on this point, the assessment to be made within the framework of the file was limited to ATC in the first place. If it is determined that the prices are below ATC, an assessment regarding AAC or AVC will be included. Accordingly, the Board has taken into account both the average variable costs such as labour, energy and raw materials, as well as the fixed costs such as capacity creation and capacity increase not depending on the nature of the product. In this context, one may conclude that the Board determines the cost calculation method, as well as the relevant cost items, based on the dynamics of the case.

7.4.1.3 Intent

In general, the Board may take into account the dominant firm's "intent" in abuse of dominance cases (Guidelines on Abuse of Dominance, para. 26). Theoretically, in some instances, even a below-cost pricing strategy (if any) may have some objective and legitimate reasons.[920] The Board explicitly held in *Volkan/Öz Edirne* that if there is no proof of the relevant undertaking's intent to exclude its competitors through predatory pricing, a low price level cannot be considered as predatory pricing.[921] The administrative courts have also reiterated this point in their case law and emphasised that competitive pricing strategy and low prices resulting from the market pressure should be distinguished

---

[916]   LRAIC is the average of all (fixed and variable) costs a firm incurs to manufacture a product. ATC and LRAIC are good proxies for each other. In fact, these two types of costs are the same for single-product firms. On the other hand, for multi-product firms, LRAIC may be below ATC for each individual product where economies of scope are a factor. In the case of multiple products, any costs that could have been avoided by not producing a particular product cannot be considered common costs. However, in situations where common costs are significant, such costs may also be taken into account in the assessment concerning the exclusion of an equally efficient company. It may be said that LRAIC is a more suitable criterion for those markets with very low variable costs and very high fixed costs, such as network industries, technology markets and markets that require high R&D investments.

[917]   *Knauf* (16 December 2009, 09-59/1441-376).

[918]   Guidelines on Abuse of Dominance, para. 54.

[919]   Ibid.

[920]   Guidelines on Abuse of Dominance, para. 60.

[921]   *Volkan/Öz Edirne* (19 July 2017, 17-23/384-167).

from predatory pricing that will lead to abuse of dominance.[922] In assessing whether a dominant firm intended to exclude its competitors with predatory pricing, the Authority will take into account factors including:[923]

- – Written evidence that clearly demonstrates the intent;
- – Whether the predatory pricing has commercial rationale only within the framework of a destructive plan;
- – A competitor was or is likely to be pushed out of the market;
- – Pricing strategy targets only certain customer groups;
- – The relevant undertaking bears extra special costs for capacity increase;[924]
- – The scope, duration and continuity of predatory pricing;
- – Implementation of predatory pricing with other exclusionary actions;[925]
- – Possibility of the dominant undertaking to compensate its losses from other sales;
- – Possibility of the dominant undertaking to compensate its losses by applying higher prices in the future.[926]

In *UN Ro-Ro*,[927] however, the Board held that if the prices imposed by a dominant undertaking are below AAC, then there is no need to show predatory intent to establish a violation. The Board stated that unless there is a legitimate justification, the conduct that only causes damages for the dominant undertaking in the short term can solely be explained with the intention to exclude competitors and to turn the market conditions in favour of the dominant undertaking. On the other hand, the Board expressed that establishing the intent of the dominant undertaking that imposes below-cost prices with direct and indirect evidence is important to assess the defences and justifications in relation to the pricing, as well as the determination of the monetary fine.[928] In the Board's *Akdeniz Dağıtım* decision, the Board held that the abuse of a dominant position could only be mentioned provided that the intention and effect of the sales are proven.[929] In the same vein, in *Cevahir Alışveriş Merkezi*,[930] the Board assessed the potentially exclusionary behaviours and determined that no evidence of intent was available that shows that the undertakings developed a hostile attitude towards the complainant.

Theoretically, in some instances, even a below-cost pricing strategy (if any) may have some objective and legitimate reasons.[931] In *Coca-Cola*,[932] the Board stated that

---

[922] See, e.g., *UN Ro-Ro* (n. 844) at 21.
[923] *Knauf* (n. 917); *Avea* (4 November 2009, 09-52/1253-318); *Milangaz* (30 December 2009, 09-61/1498-394).
[924] *Knauf* (16 December 2009, 09-59/1441-376), para. 640.
[925] The Authority also analyses whether the predation was implemented together with any other exclusionary action to support its finding on intent. This is, however, not a condition alone, just an element used as further evidence of intent.
[926] *Avea* (n. 923).
[927] *UN Ro-Ro* (n. 844).
[928] Ibid., paras. 193–194.
[929] *Akdeniz Dağıtım* (4 July 2012, 12-36/1039-327).
[930] *Cevahir Alışveriş Merkezi* (15 June 2006, 06-44/540-142).
[931] Guidelines on Abuse of Dominance, para. 60.
[932] *Coca-Cola* (n. 905).

along with economic superiority and unusually low prices, the Board should take account of the intent of the undertaking. In *Coca Cola*, the Board found that there is no explicit evidence showing the intent; therefore, it evaluated whether a predatory intent is reasonable in terms of different scenarios. The Board concluded that there is no predatory intent and decided not to evaluate the effect of the relevant conduct. In the recent *Kamil Koç*[933] decision, it was also stated that when establishing predatory pricing, "economic superiority", "unusually lower prices", "intent", and "recoupment" elements become important.[934] Similarly, the Board explicitly held in *Volkan/Öz Edirne* that if there is no proof of the relevant undertaking's intent to exclude its competitors through predatory pricing, a low price level cannot be considered as predatory pricing.

7.4.1.4 Possibility for Recoupment

Recoupment is another important criterion for predatory pricing. Recoupment is intrinsic to any rational theory of predation; without such an expectation, predatory behaviour is not sensible economic behaviour.[935] However, neither the Guidelines on Abuse of Dominance nor the precedents of the Board deem actual recoupment a necessary element.[936] That said, in *UN Ro-Ro*, the Ankara 12th Administrative Court concluded that another criterion of predatory pricing is "recoupment", which is the ultimate purpose of predatory pricing.[937] Similarly, in *THY*,[938] the Board evaluated whether recoupment is possible when evaluating predatory pricing.[939]

When analysing whether pricing strategy targets only certain customer groups, the Authority analyses whether the dominant firm has the ability to recoup the losses that it incurred during the below-cost pricing period by increasing the price above competitive levels, after having excluded its competitors from the market through its predatory conduct in the previous period. If the dominant firm is expected to increase its market price after the predatory pricing strategy, the Board considers that recoupment is likely. As a requirement for establishing the allegation of "recoupment", the Board first should prove that the alleged below-cost pricing has an (actual or potential) exclusionary effect on the competitors.

7.4.1.5 Anti-Competitive Effect

In its effects analysis for predatory pricing, the Authority looks into actual or potential anti-competitive market foreclosure, i.e., whether access of actual/potential competitors

---

[933] *Kamil Koç* (14 November 2019, 19-40/658-283).
[934] Ibid. para. 20.
[935] M. de la Mano and B. Durand, "A Three-Step Structured Rule of Reason to Assess Predation under Article 82", *European Commission Office of the Chief Economist Discussion Paper*, December 2005, p. 26 <https://ec.europa.eu/dgs/competition/economist/pred_art82.pdf>.
[936] This is in line with the EU Commission's approach adopted in *France Télécom*(n. 899), where the Commission concluded that proof of recoupment of losses does not constitute a necessary precondition to a finding of predatory pricing.
[937] Ankara 12th Administrative Court, *UN Ro-Ro* (n. 891), p. 5.
[938] *THY* (n. 915).
[939] *Kamil Koç* (n. 933); *Metro Turizm* (14 July 2011, 11-43/915-284); *Milangaz* (n. 923); *Feniks* (n. 908).

222   *Gönenç Gürkaynak – Turkish Competition Law*

to supply sources or markets is prevented or obstructed. Factors the Authority takes into account in the foreclosure analysis include the following:[940]

- Market position of the dominant firm;

- Market conditions (e.g., entry/expansion barriers and economies of scale);[941]

- Competitors' position in the market (whether they are able to counter any potential strategy of a dominant firm to exclude competitors);[942]

- Customers'/suppliers' position (i.e., whether the predatory pricing strategy targets certain customers that are critical for competitors' entry/growth in the market);[943]

- The scope and duration of the conduct;[944]

- Evidence of market foreclosure (e.g., an increase in the dominant firm's market share due to reasons that could be linked to predatory pricing, a decrease in competitors' market share or exit of competitors for the same reason).[945]

The Authority usually uses the "as-efficient competitor test" (AECT) to analyse whether competitors could be excluded from the market due to a predatory pricing strategy. If the Board determines that an equally efficient competitor can effectively compete with the pricing strategies of an undertaking imposing predatory prices, in principle, it will not intervene based on the consideration that the pricing practice of the relevant undertaking does not have a negative effect on effective competition, and therefore the consumers. If, however, the pricing of the relevant undertaking has the potential to exclude equally efficient competitors, then the Authority will include that conclusion to its assessment of general anti-competitive foreclosure, taking into account other relevant quantitative and qualitative evidence. The Authority may also consider the impact on less efficient competitors.[946] However, this is exceptional, and the Board generally favours the "as efficient competitor test" to avoid false positives and deterring competition.[947] The analysis then boils down to whether or not competitors can apply effective counter-strategies for the contested portion of the customer's demand (without pricing below cost). If competitors are not able to apply such a counter-strategy, the pricing would then be considered exclusionary for as-efficient competitors.

In *Çiçek Sepeti*,[948] the Board examined whether Çiçek Sepeti abused its dominant position in the online flower sales market and hampered its competitors' activities through predatory pricing. The Board evaluated whether the conduct in question was likely to lead to market foreclosure for an equally efficient competitor when

---

[940] Guidelines on Abuse of Dominance, para. 26.
[941] *Çiçek Sepeti* (n. 30) ; *Huawei* (n. 909).
[942] *Mey İçki* (25 October 2017, 17-34/537-228); *Çiçek Sepeti* (n. 30).
[943] *Dow* (n. 884); *Çiçek Sepeti* (n. 30).
[944] *Sony Eurasia* (n. 883); *Çiçek Sepeti* (n. 30).
[945] *Çiçek Sepeti* (n. 30).
[946] *UN Ro-Ro* (n. 844).
[947] *Türk Telekom* (3 May 2016, 16-15/254-109).
[948] *Çiçek Sepeti* (n. 30).

assessing the allegations of predatory pricing. After conducting a price-cost analysis on products, the Board decided that an anti-competitive foreclosure could not be established.

From an effects-based perspective, in some cases, it is also possible that the Authority first makes a price-cost comparison before trying to determine whether the undertaking under investigation has a dominant position. In general, when it is understood that the second condition is not fulfilled, in other words, when the Authority finds that the undertaking under investigation does not price below its costs, the Authority does not proceed to investigate other conditions and closes the investigation.[949]

7.4.1.6 Objective Justification

The Board usually considers objective justification for predatory pricing to be unlikely. However, the Guidelines on Abuse of Dominance state that arguments on achieving economies of scale through low prices and efficiencies regarding market growth will be taken into account in this analysis.[950] More specifically, the Authority first considers whether there is a legitimate interest protected by the relevant conduct and whether this conduct is indispensable to achieve the benefit that the dominant firm aims for. For example, in *Knauf*, the Board accepted sudden cost increases as a "commercially reasonable" explanation.[951]

7.4.2 Margin Squeeze

This section includes an explanation of the concept of margin squeeze in Turkish competition laws and considers the extent to which margin squeeze amounts to an infringement of Article 6 of Law No. 4054.

7.4.2.1 Concept of Price/Margin Squeeze in Turkish Competition Law

Margin squeeze is a pricing strategy of a vertically integrated company that is (i) active both in the downstream and upstream market of a production/service chain, and (ii) in a dominant position in the upstream market. Margin squeeze is defined in the Guidelines on Abuse of Dominance as follows:

> Price squeeze is when an undertaking active in vertically related markets that is dominant in the upstream market sets the margin between the prices of the upstream and downstream products at a level that does not allow even an equally efficient competitor in the downstream market to trade profitably on a lasting basis. The undertaking dominant in the upstream may cause margin squeeze

---

949   *Bilsing* (n. 913).
950   Guidelines on Abuse of Dominance, para. 60.
951   *Knauf* (n. 917).

by increasing the price for the upstream product, by decreasing the price for the downstream product, or by doing both simultaneously. Thus, the dominant undertaking is able to transfer its market power over the upstream product to the downstream market and lead to the restriction of competition (para. 61).[952]

The company dominant in the upstream may cause margin squeeze (i) by increasing the price for the upstream product; (ii) by decreasing the price for the downstream product; or (iii) by doing both simultaneously. When such a company narrows the margin between the wholesale price of the input it controls in the upstream market and the price of the product in the downstream market, the profit margin for competitors in the downstream market is squeezed. Moreover, this anti-competitive conduct of the dominant company leads to abuse of dominance as the vertically integrated dominant company may exclude actual or potential competitors in the retail market, restrain their activities or market shares and prevent competition by transferring its market power on the input in the wholesale market to the retail market.

To summarise, the five key elements for a margin squeeze abuse are as follows:

- vertically integrated firm
- essential (indispensable) inputs for competition at another level of the supply chain
- market power at one level of the supply chain
- insufficient margin for downstream competitors
- harm to competition and consumers.

As for the structure of the undertaking, the undertaking must be vertically integrated. In other words, the undertaking must be active in upstream and downstream markets that are connected to each other in a production chain.

In evaluating whether the dominant undertakings pricing policy renders its downstream market competitors activities uneconomic or not, there are two alternative methods–namely, the as-efficient competitor test and the reasonably efficient competitor test. The Board, in *Turkcell*,[953] stated that the AECT evaluates the possibility that whether the dominant undertaking in the upstream market could operate profitably in the downstream market if it were obliged to pay the same amount of input cost and whether the as-efficient competitors would be excluded from the market by this way. Whereas for the reasonably efficient competitor test, the Board stated that it is used to evaluate whether a competitor could compete with a dominant undertaking by making a normal amount of profit in the downstream market and the data used is hypothetically based upon the theoretical costs of a reasonably efficient competitor. Lastly, between the two alternatives, the Board asserted that relevant authorities adopted the as-efficient competitor test.[954]

---

[952] Margin squeeze definition in the Guidelines is based on the Board's decision *Türk Telekom/TTNET* (19 November 2008, 08-65/1055-411).

[953] *Turkcell* (6 February 2020, 20-08/82-49), para. 47.

[954] *Turkcell* (8 November 2018, 18-42/670-329); *Türk Telekom/TTNET* (n. 952).

The approach in the Turkish legislation is in line with the margin squeeze definition adopted in the European Union.[955] Margin squeeze is explained in the EU Dominance Guidance as follows:

> A dominant undertaking may charge a price for the product on the upstream market which, compared to the price it charges on the downstream market, does not allow even an equally efficient competitor to trade profitably in the downstream market on a lasting basis (a so-called 'margin squeeze').[956]

When the decisional practice of the Board is observed, it can be asserted that it closely examines the allegations of margin squeeze and most of the cases examined within this scope belong to the telecommunications sector.

The Board did find a margin squeeze claim for the first time in the *Türk Telekom Student-Teacher Campaign* decision.[957] However, it rejected the claim on the grounds that the campaign of Türk Telekom was not within the scope of Law No. 4054 since it had been already approved by the Telecommunications Authority.[958]

In its decisional practice, one of the most important precedents of the Board is the *Türk Telekom* decision,[959] where an investigation was launched due to the allegations that Türk Telekom abused its dominant position in the internet access services market since (i) it determined network access tariffs so high that, in the relevant upstream market, its competitors could not compete, and (ii) it determined internet access tariffs very low in the downstream market. Consequently, the Board imposed an administrative monetary fine against *Türk Telekom*. The *Türk Telekom* decision was based on the theory of predatory pricing. However, the case could also have been concluded under the theory of margin squeeze.[960]

Another notable precedent of the Board is the *TTNET* decision.[961] The Board launched the investigation concerning the allegation that, in the wholesale broadband internet access services market, Türk Telekom abused its dominant position by way of its subsidiary TTNET's campaign in the retail broadband internet access services market. The Board decided to impose a monetary fine on Türk Telekom and TTNET. The *Türk Telekom TTNET* decision is important because it underlines the conditions of margin squeeze.

---

[955] See R. O'Donoghue and A. J. Padilla, *The Law and Economics of Article 82 EC* (Oxford: Hart Publishing, 2006), p. 303; A. Jones and B. Sufrin, *EU Competition Law: Text, Cases and Materials* (5th edition, Oxford University Press, 2014), p. 426; P. Roth QC and V. Rose (eds.), *Bellamy & Child: European Community Law of Competition* (6th edition, Oxford University Press, 2009), p. 993.

[956] "In margin squeeze cases the benchmark which the Commission will generally rely on to determine the costs of an equally efficient competitor are the LRAIC of the downstream division of the integrated dominant undertaking" (EU Dominance Guidance, para. 80).

[957] *Türk Telekom Student-Teacher Campaign* (8 September 2005, 05-55/833-226).

[958] Until the Council of State rendered decisions to the contrary (8 March 2012, E. 2008/14245-K. 2012/960; 20 November 2007, E. 2006/2052-K. 2007/7582), the Board persevered in its approach to reject claims regarding conduct or campaigns that the Telecommunications Authority previously approved.

[959] *Türk Telekom* (2 October 2002, 02-60/755-305). The Board evaluated this decision upon its annulment by the Council of State in its decision but did not change its position (5 January 2006, 06-02/47-8).

[960] Ş. D. Kaya, *Fiyat Sıkıştırması Ekonomik ve Hukuki Açıdan Bir Değerlendirme* (Ankara: Rekabet Kurumu Uzmanlık Tezleri Serisi No. 87, 2009), p. 24.

[961] *Türk Telekom/TTNET* (19 November 2008, 08-65/1055-411).

The main aspects of margin squeeze underlined in the *Türk Telekom TTNET* decision are as follows: (i) regarding the margin calculation, in order to detect whether the margin is negative, first a dominant undertaking's retail price and its wholesale price must be calculated; (ii) if such margin is not negative, then for the sales of the relevant product or service, whether or not this margin can compensate the equally efficient competitors' incremental costs must be decided; (iii) margin squeeze is different from predatory pricing, and it is not a necessity for the retail prices to be predatory to establish a margin squeeze; (iv) conducts' duration is important; and lastly (v) if the discounts are only applied for a short term, it could be asserted as an objective justification.

In determining abuse of dominance by price squeeze, along with dominance, the undertaking must hold a dominant position in the upstream market. The guidelines on Abuse of Dominance further state that even though the Board does not look for dominance in the downstream market, this may be taken into consideration as a factor that compounds the restrictive effects of the price squeezing behaviour on competition.

7.4.2.2 Indispensability

In determining the likelihood of conduct leading to anti-competitive foreclosure by margin squeeze, the upstream product must be indispensable for operating in the downstream market.[962]

For the indispensability condition, the Guidelines on Abuse of Dominance refer to the explanations under the Refusal to Deal section. For the indispensability condition, the Board evaluates whether a refusal to deal/margin squeeze by the dominant undertaking is likely to eliminate effective competition in the downstream market immediately or over time. The larger the share of the dominant undertaking in the downstream market, the greater the likelihood of elimination of effective competition in the downstream market will be.

7.4.2.3 Anti-Competitive Effect

In determining the likelihood of the conduct under examination leading to anti-competitive foreclosure by price squeeze, the Board, among others, takes the following factors into account: (i) structure of the undertaking; (ii) nature of the product; (iii) position of the undertaking in the relevant market(s); and (iv) margin between prices (see Guidelines on Exclusionary Abuses, para. 62).

The Guidelines on Abuse of Dominance state that the margin between the upstream and downstream products must be so low as to ensure that a competitor that is as efficient as the undertaking dominant in the upstream market would be unable to profit and operate in the downstream market on a lasting basis.[963] When establishing the costs of the equally efficient competitor, the Board will generally use LRAIC, calculated for the downstream product of an undertaking dominant in the upstream market.[964] For instance, in its *Knauf*

---

[962] Ibid.

[963] The Guidelines on Abuse of Dominance, para. 62.

[964] When calculating the aforementioned LRAIC, it is assumed that the undertaking dominant in the upstream market uses its upstream product at the same price it sells that product to its competitors downstream.

decision,[965] the Board stated that LRAIC is more suitable to be used in sectors such as the telecommunications industry where the undertakings are required to bear significantly lesser variable costs than fixed costs or where the variable and/or avoidable cost criteria cannot reflect the realities of the industry.

7.4.2.4 Objective Justification

The Board assesses the vertically integrated entity's objective justification allegations regarding margin squeeze.[966] Within this scope, the Board may consider the following aspects as objective justification: (i) that the market conditions caused the strategy subject of the claim; (ii) that the margin tightens due to the changes in the upstream market supply and downstream market demand; and/or (iii) that the product offered at a low price has just been launched to the market.

7.4.3 Exclusive Dealing

This section includes an explanation of the concept of exclusive dealing in Turkish competition laws and considers the extent to which exclusive dealing amounts to an infringement of Article 6 of Law No. 4054.

7.4.3.1 Concept of Exclusive Dealing in Turkish Competition Law

One of the most important areas of focus of the Turkish competition law enforcement is the practices that force the competitors out of the market and/or prevent the entry of new competitors. Exclusivity is one of these practices. The Guidelines on Exclusionary Abuses define exclusivity agreements as the agreements where a supplier obliges the buyer to purchase the entirety (or a significant portion) of its product requirements from a single supplier. This is similar to paragraph 32 of the EU Dominance Guidance, where exclusive dealing practices are defined as an action by a dominant undertaking to foreclose its competitors by hindering them from selling to customers through the use of exclusive purchasing obligations or rebates.

Although exclusive dealing normally falls under the scope of Article 4 of Law No. 4054, which governs restrictive agreements, concerted practices and decisions of trade associations, such practices could also be scrutinised within the scope of Article 6. Indeed, the Competition Board has already found in the past infringements of Article 6 on the basis of exclusive dealing arrangements.[967] Similarly, the Board imposed a fine on Mey İçki for its abusive conduct through which it prevented sales points from selling Mey İçki's competitors' products through exclusivity clauses and therefore foreclosed the market.[968]

---

[965]   *Knauf* (n. 917).
[966]   *Türknet/Türk Telekom* (20 June 2019, 19-22/325-144); *Türk Telekom/TTNET* (n. 952); *TTNET* (19 December 2013, 13-71/992-423); *TTNET* (9 February 2017, 17-06/53-20); *TTNET* (27 August 2018, 18-29/497-238); *TTNET* (17 October 2018, 18-39/621-301).
[967]   *Karbogaz* (n. 844).
[968]   *Mey İçki* (n. 844).

The Board investigated Trakya Cam for the purpose of determining whether Trakya Cam had violated Articles 4 and 6 of Law No. 4054 through the de facto implementation of its dealership system,[969] which was also subject to a Board decision where the Board did not grant an individual exemption to Trakya Cam's relevant conduct.[970] As a result of the investigation, the Board considered Trakya Cam's conduct as abusive.

On a separate note, Communiqué No. 2002/2 no longer exempts exclusive vertical supply agreements of an undertaking holding a market share above 40%. Thus, a dominant undertaking is an unlikely candidate to engage in non-compete provisions and single branding arrangements without any significant pro-competitive effects and efficiency.[971]

Article 6 of Law No. 4054 also applies to dominant purchasers. The Board found that TEB abused its dominance by entering into exclusive agreements with suppliers and imposing exclusive supply obligations upon them, thereby foreclosing the market to its competitors.[972]

7.4.3.2 Anti-Competitive Effect

It is necessary to show the foreclosure effects for the finding of an abuse under the unilateral conduct rules governing exclusive dealing. Market foreclosure means foreclosing an appreciable part of the market to competitors as a result of which competition in the market is weakened.[973]

By preventing the access of (actual and potential) competitors to necessary channels, exclusivity agreements foreclose relevant market(s) and thus may restrict the likelihood that other firms might emerge as an efficient competitor for the dominant undertaking.

The Board takes into account, along with the market positions of the undertaking and its competitors and the duration of the investigated conduct, the following factors in its assessment of exclusivity agreements signed by a dominant undertaking: (i) the scope of the conduct under examination; (ii) the level of trade; (iii) barriers to entry; (iv) the importance of the dominant undertaking for customers; and (v) the duration of exclusivity.[974]

When assessing the foreclosure effects, the Authority may take into consideration both direct and indirect evidence, i.e., market information, facts and data collected via various resources including market players, customers, the complainant, oral and written statements of employees of the dominant undertaking, competitors and customers, as well as qualitative/quantitative studies.[975]

---

[969]   *Trakya Cam* (n. 588).
[970]   *Trakya Cam/Düzcam Exemption* (n. 210).
[971]   The Board decided that *Mey İçki* was deemed as enjoying dominant position in the market for rakı and therefore it was determined that exclusive agreements concluded with the sales points and Mey İçki's well-established commercial practices aiming at creating de facto exclusivity cannot benefit from Communiqué No. 2002/2 (10 September 2007, 07-70/863-326).
[972]   *TEB* (6 December 2016, 16-42/699-3139).
[973]   International Competition Network, "Report on Single Branding/Exclusive Dealing", Presented at the 7th Annual Conference of the ICN, Kyoto, April 2008.
[974]   Guidelines on Exclusionary Abuses, para. 67.
[975]   *Isttelkom* (n. 853); *Trakya Cam* (n. 865); *Türk Telekom* (n. 866); *Çiçek Sepeti* (n. 30).

According to the Guidelines on Abuse of Dominance, exclusive dealing arrangements imposed on retailers may have more anti-competitive foreclosure effects than a similar arrangement imposed on a wholesale buyer.

7.4.3.3 Objective Justification

As in other abuse cases, the dominant company may establish an objective justification for its practices. However, the dominant undertaking will need to prove that its conduct achieves a legitimate objective. Within exclusivity, the following aspects may be considered as objective justification allegations: (i) the existence of investments that are specific to the commercial relationship; (ii) mitigating effects of exclusive regulations on cost; or (iii) its positive contribution to innovation.

Agreements with exclusive provisions of dominant undertakings may also promote efficiency. For instance, exclusive dealing may be used as a tool for the prevention of free riding.[976] Exclusive dealing may also allow suppliers to collect a return on their investments and increase output.[977] Another positive effect of exclusivity is that it ensures a regular product flow for the buying undertaking while providing a steady sales channel for the supplier. Exclusivity agreements increase the likelihood of the supplier making investments that are specific to the commercial relationship, as well. This is because exclusivity contributes to the return of investment process for the supplier as it does to the elimination of the hold-up problem,[978] especially when the duration is longer. In addition, exclusivity agreements may contribute to the competitive process and consumer welfare by focusing the buyer on a single product/brand and allowing it to make more effective promotions, by establishing a more robust inter-brand competition environment, and thus by ensuring an increase in product and service quality.

7.4.4 Rebate Systems

Rebate systems refer to discounts offered to customers in return for them engaging in a certain purchasing behaviour.[979] This section includes explanations on the concept of rebate systems in Turkish competition law and considers the extent to which rebate systems amount to an infringement of Article 6 of Law No. 4054.

7.4.4.1 Concept of Rebate Systems in Turkish Competition Law

Even though there is no explicit provision under the Turkish competition law regime that deems rebate systems illegal per se, rebate systems may give rise to competition law concerns under Article 4 (prohibiting restrictive agreements) and/or Article 6 (prohibiting abuse of dominance) of Law No. 4054.

---

[976] Guidelines of Abuse of Dominance, para. 65.

[977] A. F. Abbott and J. D. Wright, "Antitrust Analysis of Tying Arrangements and Exclusive Dealing", *George Mason University Law and Economics Research Paper Series* No. 8-37, 2008.

[978] The Guidelines of Abuse of Dominance refer to the Guidelines on Vertical Agreements, p. 32, for the detailed explanations on the hold-up problem.

[979] Guidelines on Abuse of Dominance, para 69.

Due to the nature of business life, rebate systems may occur in many different forms, and they may vary depending on their structure, function and effect. Some rebate systems have standardised purchase targets that are applied to all customers, whereas other systems have purchase targets specifically determined for each customer or certain groups of customers. As it is explicitly set forth in the Guidelines on Abuse of Dominance, the most fundamental distinction in the classification of rebate systems is between "single-product rebates" and "package rebates". Single-product rebates are discounts tied to the purchase of a single product, whereas package rebates represent discounts that are tied to the purchase of more than one product or market. In package rebates known as multi-product rebate or mixed packaging, the products may be offered for sale separately; however, when they are bought separately, the total price of the products adds up to more than the package price. Rebates that are offered depending on the customer purchasing at least two distinct products or purchasing a certain amount from the market in a certain time period are also considered package rebates.

Rebate systems that include standard purchase volume target(s) and accompanying standard discount rates, applicable without discrimination to all customers, can be characterised as "standardised rebates". However, where the relevant rebate systems include purchase targets that are adjusted depending on the demand of each customer or customer group, they are characterised as "individualised rebates". Individualised rebates may be formalised in various ways. For instance, such a purchase target may be a quantity target identified depending on the total demand of the customer in a certain period, or it may be identified as a portion of the purchases the customer will make in a certain period, or as a portion of the purchases the customer made in a reference period in the past.

The Board uses similar criteria in distinguishing between "quantity rebates" and "target rebates". Quantity rebates correspond to objective quantity-based conditions applying to all customers, whereas target rebates require that the customer satisfy a specific target in a given reference period. "Growth rebates", which are based on the buyer's increasing its sales from the relevant supplier in comparison to the previous reference period, can be regarded as a sub-specie of individualised rebates.

Rebate systems are also classified into retroactive rebates and top-slice rebates, depending on the scope of the discount. Rebate systems in which the customer can get discounts from the undertaking offering the rebate, for all of its purchases within the relevant period if it exceeds the threshold amount, are called "retroactive rebates" or "all-units rebates", while rebate systems in which the customer can only get discounts for its purchases over the rebate target are called "top-slice rebates". In this respect, retroactive rebates are considered to pose greater competition law concerns as (i) the sales price of the undertakings may become lower than their cost, which may give rise to predatory pricing, and (ii) undertakings already purchasing a certain amount from the given suppliers may be unwilling to switch a part of their demand to competitors where this causes them to lose their discount on all units. Lastly, rebate systems that only include a fixed discount rate are referred to as "fixed ratio rebates", whereas rebate systems that include progressively increasing discount rates based on increasing target purchase amounts are called "rebates with progressive rates".

7.4.4.2 Single-Product Rebates

If, in a rebate system, discounts are tied to the purchase of a single product, such rebates are considered to be "single-product rebates". The typical characteristic of single-product rebates is that the purchase condition included in the rebate system must be fulfilled within a certain period (reference period).

If each customer must meet a part of its demand in the reference period from the dominant undertaking every time, then the competitors will not be able to compete with the dominant undertaking under equal conditions for the entirety of the demand of the customer in question. By offering a retroactive rebate to such a customer, a dominant undertaking can prevent equally efficient competitors from selling to the said customer without dropping its prices below its costs. In assessing the risks posed by rebate systems, the Guidelines on Abuse of Dominance provide that "it is more likely for retroactive rebates to cause anti-competitive foreclosure where rebate targets are individualised, where the rebate percentage and rebate target constitute a significant part of the total demand of the consumer within the relevant reference period, and particularly where the competitors of the dominant undertaking are unable to compete with it under equal conditions for the entirety of each customer's demand".[980] The basis of the Board's assessment concerning retroactive rebates is the examination of whether, in response to the rebate, equally efficient competitors would be able to effectively compete with the dominant undertaking for the contestable portion of the customer's demand (that is to say, the amount for which the customer may prefer and be able to find substitutes). For instance, in its *Türkiye Petrol Rafinerileri I* decision, the Board stated that the following matters should be taken into account while assessing whether the rebate system applied by a dominant undertaking might lead to market foreclosure.[981] The Board firstly stated that the turnover premium system is not personalised and eliminates the risk of losing the rebate as a whole in case the buyers fail to meet the target sales. Therefore the market foreclosure effect of the turnover premium system is limited to a great extent. Still, the Board noted that the relevant rebate system had a retroactive character and therefore also assessed the potential of market foreclosure based on the equally efficient competitor test–i.e., whether the application of the rebate system in question could possibly lead to the exclusion of a hypothetical undertaking that is as effective as the dominant undertaking in the relevant market and whether the dominant undertaking's prices fall below cost. Similarly, in its *Doğan Yayın* decision, the Board has remarked that the assessment of whether a rebate system is individualised is of utmost importance in assessing its exclusionary effects.[982]

7.4.4.3 Package rebates

If the purchasing obligation of the rebate system covers more than one product or market, then the rebates in question are referred to as "bundled rebates".[983] The Board's assessments concerning the restrictive effects of bundled rebates on competition may vary

---

[980]   Guidelines on Abuse of Dominance, paras. 75–76.
[981]   *Türkiye Petrol Rafinerileri I* (20 October 2015, 15-41/675-237).
[982]   *Doğan Yayın* (n. 859)
[983]   *TTNET* (n. 812); *Doğan Yayın* (n. 859).

depending on whether competitors can (either alone or together with other competitors) compete by offering a reasonable alternative package.[984]

Pursuant to the Guidelines on Abuse of Dominance, equally efficient competitors are excluded from competition due to the rebate systems, where the package discount is attributed to any individual product within the package and if the effective price for the product in question[985] is lower than LRAIC for the same product.[986]

The products or services subject to the bundled rebates may be offered separately; however, the total price of the products bought separately is higher than the package price. Rebates that are offered to customers on the condition that they purchase at least two distinct products or a certain amount of the product in a given time period are also considered bundled rebates.

Justification claims, such as increasing output level and product variety, reducing trans-action costs stemming from buying the products separately, and preventing free riding by ensuring that resellers are focused on the products of the supplier may be considered by the Board when bundled rebates are evaluated.[987]

Moreover, the Board has evaluated whether the undertaking under review has abused its dominance through its rebate system in many different instances.[988] The Board has gener-ally analysed rebate schemes based on two main theories of harm: (i) the loyalty-inducing potential of the relevant rebate system, which may, in turn, create de facto or potential exclusionary effects (similar to the effects of non-compete obligations) on competitors; (ii) the discriminatory potential of the relevant rebate system amongst equally situated customers, which may, in turn, distort competition in the downstream market.[989]

In addition to the categories provided above, the Board's decisional practice also includes a variety of other factors that are relevant to the determination of whether a given rebate system is likely to result in exclusionary effects towards competitors. One of the most significant of these elements is the length of the reference period associated with the rebate. Particularly, for a retroactive rebate, the loyalty-inducing potential is considered to increase along with the reference period. This is because a longer reference period translates into more purchases on which the buyer stands to gain a discount if it meets the rebate target and, therefore, greater switching costs. The Board's past decisions have regarded a reference period of one year as a sufficiently long period for anti-competitive effects to emerge.[990] On the other hand, in *Doğan Yayın II*,[991] the Board used the fact

---

[984]   Guidelines on Abuse of Dominance, para. 69 *et seq.*
[985]   Effective price is calculated by subtracting the rebate offered for the whole package from the individual sale price of the product concerned.
[986]   Guidelines on Abuse of Dominance, para. 80.
[987]   Ibid., para. 81.
[988]   *Luxottica* (n. 811); *THY* (July 9, 2015, 15-29/427-123); *Kale Kilit* (n. 892); *Ceramic Adhesives Producers* (n. 871); *Doğan Yayın* (n. 859).
[989]   It is important to note that, where the resulting prices fall below cost, depending on the existence of certain other characteristics, rebates/discounting practices may also result in the abuse of dominance through predatory pricing.
[990]   *Doğan Yayın* (n. 859); *Unilever* (17 March 2011, 11-16/287-92).
[991]   *Doğan Yayın II* (23 February 2012, 12-08/250-81).

that the reference period had been reduced from one year to six months as a factor in concluding that Doğan Yayın's rebates no longer had a loyalty-inducing character.

Other factors taken into consideration include (i) the level of market power the dominant undertaking possesses (in other words, the extent of dominance); (ii) the extent of the market covered by the rebate system; (iii) the magnitude of the discounts; (iv) whether the dominant undertaking specifically targeted to harm its competitors; as well as (v) any specific characteristic of the relevant market that is pertinent to the analysis.[992] Additionally, the existence of exclusionary intent, if any, is a separate inquiry relevant to the rebate system's assessment but should be conducted based on evidence that demonstrates such intent. For instance, in *Ceramic Adhesives Producers*, when citing the Board's earlier case law, the Board stated that:

> In its past decisions, the Competition Board stated that, in the assessment of rebate/ discount systems, the analysis must focus on the effects in the market and concentrate on analyses regarding impediment of competition through the exclusion of competitors, and must assess whether the rebate systems point towards exclusionary intent and whether it has such effect.[993]

The Board found that "in the dawn raid on Kalekim, no internal documents have been found which point towards an exclusive intent vis-à-vis KUK-KUPS or in general".[994] Similarly, the Board stated that "as provided above, the dawn raid has not uncovered any documents which show that Unilever had an intent to cause exclusivity, to exclude its rivals or to foreclose the market".[995]

Moreover, rebate systems implemented by dominant undertakings may also give rise to predatory practice in certain circumstances. To be more specific, if the rebate systems result in the prices of the dominant undertakings to fall below a measure of cost, depending on the existence of certain other characteristics, rebate systems may also be deemed as an abuse of dominance. In other words, rebate systems that include a certain purchase condition, but do not limit the fulfilment of that condition to a certain reference period, could turn into predatory pricing and thus, foreclose or discipline one or more of the actual or potential competitors of the dominant undertakings, or otherwise prevent their competitive behaviour.

For instance, in *THY*, the Board evaluated whether the rebates and discounts applied under the incentive policy of the dominant airway company can be regarded as predatory pricing behaviour.[996] Since the final purchasing prices, including the rebate and discounts, were above the cost expenses, it was decided that the relevant rebate and discount systems did not lead to predatory pricing. The Board had also underlined that if there is a core demand linked to the dominant undertaking, the question of excluding competitors with equal effectiveness may arise even though the dominant undertaking does not engage

---

[992]   *Ceramic Adhesives Producers* (n. 871).
[993]   Ibid.
[994]   Ibid.
[995]   *Unilever* (n. 990).
[996]   *THY* (n. 988).

in predatory pricing practices, but only if the calculated effective price remains below the costs of the undertaking. However, in practice, the calculation of the core demand of the dominant undertakings is quite a difficult concept.

Lastly, by offering a retroactive rebate to a customer that must meet a part of its demand in the reference period from a dominant undertaking, the dominant undertaking can also prevent equally efficient competitors from selling to the relevant customer without dropping its prices below its costs. Nevertheless, it must be noted that such consequence clearly differentiates from predatory pricing as it does not necessarily require below-cost sales at all.

The Board conducted a preliminary investigation against Frito-Lay to examine whether Frito-Lay has abused its dominant position through, inter alia, rebate schemes. Before examining the specific allegations of the complainant, the Board provided some theoretical background on the subject matter and referred to its landmark decisions involving rebate systems. The Board first noted that, under the Guidelines on Abuse of Dominance, rebate systems are considered to be an important tool for increasing efficiency and consumer welfare, as well as fuelling competition among undertakings by lowering prices, increasing output and product diversity, reducing transaction costs resulting from the purchase of individual products, and preventing or reducing the "free-rider" problem. In this regard, the Board observed that, in case such discounts are granted by undertakings holding a dominant position in the relevant market, these might cause de facto or potential exclusionary effects in the market. Accordingly, the Board declared that a dominant undertaking might create de facto exclusivity and foreclose the market by preventing or hindering its competitors' access to the essential channels, thereby restricting its competitors' ability to appear as effective competitors against the dominant undertaking. The Board ultimately concluded that there were no grounds or factors leading the Board to initiate a fully-fledged investigation against Frito-Lay in connection with its rebate systems.[997]

The *Efe-Mey İçki* decision[998] was taken upon a complaint made by Efe Alkollü İçecekler Ticaret A.Ş. based on the allegations that Mey İçki continues its practices that lead to de facto exclusivity. This decision also provides very useful clues as to how the Board approaches the rebate systems. In this decision, the Board asserts that: (i) the rebates' effects on the market are important since the supplier in a dominant position may set the rebates in a way which may prevent the buyer from purchasing the contracted products from the competing undertakings; (ii) they may lead to de facto exclusivity by limiting the freedom of action as they are based on personalised targets regarding the amount of the purchases of the referenced period of time; (iii) "progressive" and "retroactive" rebate systems are considered as loyalty rebates if they lead a buyer to purchase the total amount of its needs from the seller.

In its Mercedes-Benz decision, even though the Board had found that "MBT applies the discount rates, which are defined in accordance with the annual purchase forecast, to the bodybuilders for each of their purchases within the year, within the scope of its discount system", and decided that MBT, in fact, does apply retrospective discounts, ultimately it did not impose an administrative monetary fine on the relevant undertaking on the grounds that, even if MBT's dominant position in the relevant market is established, it did not prevent its

---

[997]   *Frito-Lay* (n. 543).
[998]   *Efe-Mey İçki* (3 March 2011, 11-12/215-69).

competitors from entering the market by applying discount systems, directly or indirectly, or it did not obstruct its competitors' practices pursuant to Article 6 of Law No. 4054.[999]

Moreover, in 2017, the Board fined Luxottica for its activities in the wholesale of branded sunglasses by obstructing competitors' activities through its rebate systems.[1000] The Board also noted in this decision that, in order for a rebate system to produce exclusionary effects, the rebate targets must be personalised for a significant portion of customers in the market. Moreover, the Board evaluated that the effect of the rebate system on the basis of target turnovers implemented is deemed to be narrowing the room for competitors and incentivising Luxottica to attain a larger portion of the growing market than its market share. Although the Board explicitly indicates that no findings have been set forth to indicate that the competitors are actually excluded due to Luxottica's rebate system, still it was found sufficient that the characteristics and the foreclosure effects of the rebate system applied by Luxottica have the "exclusionary potential" and that the system produces exclusionary effects. Therefore it decided that Luxottica's target-based rebate system, which forces a wide product range, is creating exclusivity due to its loyalty-inducing features.

In its *Turkcell* decision, the Board condemned the defendant for abusing its dominance by, among other things, applying rebate schemes to encourage the use of the Turkcell logo and refusing to offer rebates to buyers that work with the competitors.[1001] In addition to that, the Board condemned the largest undertaking in the media sector (Dogan Yayın Holding) in Turkey for having abused its dominant position in the market for advertisement spaces in the daily newspapers by applying loyalty-inducing rebate schemes.[1002]

Furthermore, within its *ABBOTT* decision, the Board concluded that in order for any rebate scheme to be deemed a violation of Law No. 4054, it should be primarily analysed whether the relevant undertakings subject to allegations are dominant in the relevant product market or not.[1003] The Board has further decided that the relevant rebate scheme should be evaluated with respect to aspects such as increasing proportionality, retroactivity, etc., and it should be determined whether the applied rebate scheme actually has loyalty inducing and foreclosure effects.

7.4.5 Tying

This section includes explanations on the concept of tying and bundling in Turkish competition law and considers the extent to which tying and bundling amount to an infringement of Article 6 of Law No. 4054.

7.4.5.1 Concept of Tying in Turkish Competition Law

The Guidelines on Abuse of Dominance define tying as the practice of making the sale of one product (i.e., the "tying" product) a condition of the buyer's acceptance to

---

[999]   *Mercedes-Benz* (n. 875).

[1000]   *Luxottica* (n. 988).

[1001]   *Turkcell* (23 December 2009, 09-60/1490-379).

[1002]   *Doğan Yayın* (n. 859).

[1003]   *ABBOTT* (31 January 2013, 13-08/88-49).

simultaneously purchase another product (i.e., the "tied" product).[1004] Tying may also refer to the practice of conditioning the sale of the tying product on the buyer's acceptance not to purchase the tied product from any other seller.

Companies with or without market power may engage in tying. However, when conducted by a dominant undertaking in the tying market, these practices may lead to anti-competitive effects. The undertaking does not necessarily need to be dominant in the tied market, as well. However, because a dominant position in the tied market may render the abuse more likely, the competition authorities must properly define the relevant market(s) for both the tying and the tied product. When assessing tying, the Board generally first conducts a dominance analysis and then an effects analysis.

In general, the demand for the tying product is high, whereas there is a lower demand for the tied product, which would be more difficult to sell. In terms of Turkish competition law, tying may take various forms: (i) contractual tying; (ii) refusal to deal; (iii) withdrawal or withholding of guarantee; and (iv) technological tying. The Board generally reviews tying practices under contractual tying and technological tying. Contractual tying occurs when a customer is forced to buy the tied product along with the tying product–in other words, when the customer is forced to refrain from purchasing the tied product from a competitor. As to the technological tying, it occurs when the tied and tying products are sold together as the tying products cannot be separated, i.e., the tying product can only be utilised by the purchase of the tied product.[1005]

A dominant undertaking's tying practices may fall within the scope of Article 6 of Law No. 4054 when the necessary conditions for establishing abuse are met. Pursuant to the Guidelines on Abuse of Dominance, when assessing whether a dominant undertaking's practices in the tying product market violate Law No. 4054, the Board seeks to determine whether two elements are present, namely: (i) the tying product and the tied product should be two distinct products, and (ii) the tying practice should be likely to lead to anti-competitive foreclosure effects.[1006]

In *Microsoft*,[1007] the Commission took a five-step test and looked for the following conditions: (i) dominance in the tying market; (ii) distinct products; (iii) customers' inability to buy the tying product without the tied product; (iv) foreclosure effect; (v) no objective justifications. In general, the Commission considers tying or bundling to be abusive when the following conditions are met: (i) dominance in the tying market; (ii) the tying and tied goods are two distinct products; (iii) market distorting foreclosure effect; and (iv) lack of objective justifications or efficiencies.[1008,1009]

[1004] Guidelines on Abuse of Dominance, para. 82.

[1005] *TTNET* (n. 966).

[1006] Guidelines on Abuse of Dominance, para. 86.

[1007] *Microsoft* (Case COMP/C-3/37.792) Commission Decision No. C(2004)900 final.

[1008] DG Competition discussion paper on the application of Article 82 of the Treaty to exclusionary abuses, Brussels, December 2005, para. 183, available at <https://ec.europa.eu/competition/antitrust/art82/discpaper2005.pdf>.

[1009] Please also see *Google Android* (Case AT.40099) Commission Decision No. C(2018) 4761 final, for further reference to EU case law.

7.4.5.2 Two Distinct Products

The competition authorities apply different standards in order to assess whether two distinct products exist. In general, the authorities may consider whether the relevant products may be offered or priced separately and whether selling the products together improves the quality and efficiency of the combined product as well as the practices of other market players.

As for the definition of distinct products, in the absence of the tying practice, if a significant portion of the customers would purchase or would have purchased the tying product without purchasing the tied product, it is considered that these products are two distinct products. When assessing whether the tied and tying products are distinct, the Board may use direct evidence indicating that customers buy these products separately when they have a preference on this front, or it may also use indirect evidence such as the presence of undertakings in the market which are specialised in the production or sales of the tied product without the tying product.[1010]

In order to decide whether two tying and tied products are separate goods, the authorities should base their assessment on several factors, including "the nature and technical features of the products concerned, the facts observed on the market, the history of the development of the products concerned and also … commercial practice".[1011]

In several tying cases, the Board again examined the condition that customers cannot purchase the tied and tying products separately.[1012] In *Google Android*, the Board evaluated that "if a significant portion of the customers have purchased or would have purchased the tying product without purchasing the tied product in the absence of the tying practice, these products are considered to be two distinct products".[1013] In *Google Android*, which is one of the limited instances where the Board imposed an administrative monetary fine due to tying or leveraging allegations, it was found that Google abused its dominant position in the licensable smart mobile operating systems market and other markets such as the search and app store services market by tying the search and app store services, engaging in exclusivity practices and preventing use of alternative services by the device manufacturers.

In line with the EU precedents, the Board also evaluates whether customers can obtain the tying product without the tied product.[1014] In *Tetra Pak II*,[1015] the Court of First Instance stated that "where an undertaking in a dominant position directly or indirectly ties its customers by an exclusive supply obligation, that constitutes an abuse since it deprives the customer of the ability to choose his sources of supply and denies other producers access to the market".

[1010]   *Google Android* (n. 854).
[1011]   Case T-201/04 *Microsoft Corp. v. Commission* [2007] ECR II-3601, para. 925.
[1012]   *Google Android* (n. 29); *Petrol Ofisi* (11 January 2018, 18-02/20-10); *Microsoft* (n. 874); *Tüpraş II* (n. 844); *Superonline* (10 October 2012, 12-49/1431-484); *Microsoft* (3 May 2012, 12-24/661-183); *Logo Yazılım* (28 April 2011, 11-26/497-154); *Habaş* (12 November 2008, 08-63/1042-402).
[1013]   *Google Android* (n. 29), para. 207.
[1014]   *Digiturk I* (7 September 2006, 06-61/822-237).
[1015]   Case T-83/91 *Tetra Pak International SA v. Commission* [1994] ECR II-755, para. 137.

7.4.5.3 Anti-competitive Effect

In order to establish a tying case, the Board examines whether such practices lead to an anti-competitive foreclosure in either of the tied or tying product markets, or in both. The main direct anti-competitive effect of tying is possible foreclosure on the market of the tied product. In order to assess the foreclosure in the tied market, the authority should (i) first examine which customers are "tied" in the sense that competitors to the dominant company cannot compete for their business; (ii) second, should examine whether these customers "add up" to a sufficient part of the market being tied.[1016] Further, in *Microsoft*, the Board stated that in order to establish an anti-competitive effect, both of the following conditions should be met: (i) the tying product cannot be purchased without the tied product, and (ii) the tying conduct forecloses the market.[1017]

In addition to the criteria set forth under paragraph 26 of the Guidelines on Abuse of Dominance that must be taken into account for the assessment of anti-competitive foreclosure, the following circumstances must also be considered when assessing the likelihood of a tying practice conducted by a dominant undertaking to lead to anti-competitive foreclosure effects:[1018]

- The risk of anti-competitive foreclosure stemming from the conduct is higher when the dominant undertaking makes the relevant strategy permanent. Practices that are costly to reverse or undo, such as technological tying, are examples of this type of strategy.[1019]

- In certain tying cases, the relevant undertaking may be in a dominant position with respect to more than one product. As the number of such products involved in the tying practice increases, the likelihood of anti-competitive foreclosure increases as well.[1020]

- In instances where the production of the tied product benefits from economies of scale, it may become likely for competitors operating in the tied product market, who are deprived of potential customers due to their purchasing the tying product to fail to generate sufficient sales to achieve economies of scale. This, in turn, indicates that anti-competitive foreclosure is more likely.[1021]

- If the prices that the dominant undertaking can charge in the tying product market are regulated, the tying practice may allow the dominant undertaking to raise its prices in the tied product market in order to compensate for and recoup its revenue losses caused by the price regulation in the tying product market.[1022]

[1016] DG Competition discussion paper on the application of Article 82 of the Treaty to exclusionary abuses, (n. 1008), pp. 56–57.

[1017] *Microsoft* (n. 874), para. 78.

[1018] *Google Android* (n. 29), para. 209.

[1019] Guidelines on Abuse of Dominance, para. 89.

[1020] Ibid., para. 90.

[1021] Ibid., para. 91.

[1022] Ibid., para. 92.

- If the tied product is an important complementary product for customers of the tying product, a decline in the number of alternative suppliers of the tied product, and thus a reduction in the availability of that product, can make entry more difficult for an undertaking who wants to enter only the tying market.[1023]

7.4.5.4 Objective Justifications

Dominant undertakings may invoke an efficiency defence or show objective justifications, such as quality/reputation concerns, good usage of products, price efficiencies, savings in production, distribution and transaction. In principle, the competition authorities have the burden of proof to show the anti-competitive effects, whereas the undertakings must prove efficiencies and show that the conduct is justified.[1024]

When assessing the conduct, the Board considers efficiency defences of the investigated undertakings such as (i) creating production or distribution-related savings which ultimately benefit customers, or (ii) reducing transaction costs for customers who would otherwise have to buy the tied products separately.

It is established that tying may result in positive economic effects such as cost saving, standardisation, price efficiencies, savings in production, distribution and transaction. Companies may also engage in tying for reasons related to the quality, reputation and good usage of their products/services.[1025] As explained in the Guidelines on Abuse of Dominance, tying is a widespread commercial practice with no restrictive effects on competition in most circumstances.[1026]

For undertakings' tying conduct to be abusive, the Authority must prove that there is no objective justification and/or efficiency-enhancing conduct[1027] in addition to the first three conditions (i.e., distinct products, dominance, foreclosure). For instance, in *Digiturk*, the Board stated that in addition to the foreclosure effect, the Board should also evaluate whether the undertakings' sale strategy has a rational, objective justification.[1028] That said, the investigated undertaking's efficiency or objective justification defences are not always accepted.

7.4.6 Refusal to Deal

This section includes an explanation of the concept of refusal to deal in Turkish competition law and considers the extent to which refusal to deal amounts to an infringement of Article 6 of Law No. 4054.

[1023] Ibid., para. 93.
[1024] E. Aktekin, *Microsoft Davaları Işığında Yazılım Pazarında Bağlama Uygulamalarına Yaklaşım ve Öneriler* (Approaches and Suggestions Regarding Tying Practices in Software Markets in light of Microsoft Cases) (Ankara: Rekabet Kurumu, 2012), pp. 13–18.
[1025] Guidelines on Abuse of Dominance, para. 94.
[1026] Ibid., para. 83.
[1027] *TTNET* (9 October 2008, 08-57/912-363).
[1028] *Digiturk* (n. 1014), para. 32. Also see Aktekin (n. 1024), p. 127.

7.4.6.1 Concept of Refusal to Deal in Turkish Competition Law

In principle, any company, whether dominant or not, has the right to freely choose the counterparts with which it will do business. That said, in certain exceptional circumstances, refusal to deal by a dominant company may be considered abusive, in which case the dominant company may be required to deal and also face sanctions. Refusal-to-deal cases are analysed under Article 6 of Law No. 4054 as a form of abuse of a dominant position. Refusal to deal can take the form of halting an ongoing supply relationship concerning the goods, services or inputs,[1029] or it can be in the form of refusing the demands of potential customers for supply.[1030]

When assessing claims of refusal to deal, the Board looks for the presence of all of the following three conditions in order to find a violation:[1031] (i) the refusal should relate to a product or service that is indispensable to be able to compete in a downstream market; (ii) the refusal should be likely to eliminate effective competition in the downstream market; and (iii) the refusal should be likely to lead to consumer harm (see Guidelines on Abuse of Dominance, para. 43). In addition to these factors, the Board examines whether there is an indicator of anti-competitive intent.[1032] When evaluating anti-competitive intent, the Board also looks at whether the company refusing to deal with a certain party is active in the upstream or downstream market in which the relevant party is active. If this is not the case, the Board is less likely to find that the conduct was motivated by a desire to disrupt competition.

Refusal to license is also considered within the scope of refusal-to-deal cases.[1033],[1034] In parallel with the CJEU's Magill decision,[1035] the Board sets out the basis of the criteria required to establish an abuse of dominance for refusal to license: (i) the goods and services subject to the IP rights should be essential to supply a product–that consumers demand–in the downstream market; (ii) refusal to license should prevent the supply of that relevant product; (iii) there should be no objective justification for refusal; and (iv) the owner of the rights should eliminate the competition in the downstream market.[1036] Chapter 8 of this book provides detailed explanations on the abuse of dominance in relation to the use of IP Rights along with the refusal to license and standard essential patents.

Although obliging dominant undertakings to supply may increase the number of undertakings in the market and lead to short-term benefits, it also poses the risk of a reduction

---

[1029] *Maysan* (18 February 2016, 16-05/107-48); *Roche* (n. 612); *Volkan/Öz Edirne* (n. 921); *Novartis* (n. 614).

[1030] Guidelines on Abuse of Dominance, p. 9; *Tüyap* (25 October 2018, 18-40/644-314). For the EU case law, please see, e.g., Case C-7/97 *Oscar Bronner GmbH & Co KG v. Mediaprint* [1998] ECR I-7791; *Clearstream* (Case COMP/38.096) Commission Decision [2009] OJ C 165/5 (upheld Case T-301-04).

[1031] *Nuh* (7 November 2013, 10-63/1317-494); *POAS* (20 November 2001, 01-56/554-130); *Ak-Kim* (12 April 2003, 03-76/925-389); *Çukurova Elektrik* (10 November 2003, 03-72/874-373); *Congresium Ato* (27 October 2016, 16-35/604-269); *Sanofi* (29 March 2018, 18-09/156-76).

[1032] *Zeyport Zeytinburnu* (15 March 2018, 18-08/152-73); *Türkiye Petrol Rafinerileri II* (12 June 2018, 18-19/321-157); *Karabük Demir Çelik* (7 September 2017, 17-28/481-207); *TKİ* (19 October 2004, 04-66/949-227).

[1033] *Philips* (26 December 2019, 19-46/790-344); *Krea İçerik Hizmetleri* (8 September 2015, 15-36/544-176); *Surat Basım/Zambak* (19 March 2013, 13-15/230-114); *Digital Platform* (3 May 2012, 12-24/710-198).

[1034] For the EU case law please, see, e.g., Joined Cases C-241/91 P and C-242/91 P *Magill* [1995] ECR I-743; Case C-418/01 *IMS Health* [2004] ECR I-5039; Case 238/87 *AB Volvo* [1988] ECR 6211.

[1035] Joined Cases C-241/91 P and C-242/91 P *Magill* (n. 1034)

[1036] *Mesam* (22 August 2017, 17-27/451-193), para. 346.

in incentives for investment and innovation for both dominant undertakings and other undertakings and leads to a situation where a competitor can take a "free ride" on the investment of the dominant firm, which could be to the detriment of consumers in the long-run.[1037] Therefore, refusal-to-deal cases require the Board to conduct analysis both on short-term and long-term effects.

Refusals to supply and access to essential facilities are common forms of abuse with which the Authority is very familiar.[1038] According to the Guidelines on Abuse of Dominance, an undertaking's (i) refusal to supply the goods or services it produces as well as the tangible or intangible business inputs in its possession, or (ii) direct (outright) or indirect (constructive) refusal[1039] are considered instances of refusal to deal.[1040] Raw physical materials, infrastructure that is necessary for the provision of certain services, product distribution systems and intangible business inputs or information whether or not protected by intellectual property rights, as well as other assets demanded by undertakings, can be considered among the goods, services or inputs mentioned above.[1041]

The refusal to deal may also take the form of conditional and unconditional refusal. A dominant undertaking imposing certain conditions to supply the requested goods or services, such as non-compete clauses in the downstream market or exclusivity clauses, on the other hand, is considered conditional refusal to deal. If there are no such requirements, then it is deemed to be an unconditional refusal.[1042]

The practice of refusal to deal may be aimed at competitors of the dominant undertaking in the downstream market or at the customers that are not in competition with the dominant undertaking. The concept of "downstream market" refers to the market for which the input demanded is needed for manufacturing a product or providing a service. When the dominant undertaking and the undertaking it refused to supply in the downstream market are competitors (i.e., when the dominant undertaking is vertically integrated), the refusal to deal is more likely to lead to a restrictive effect on competition. In general, it is observed that the Board has rejected refusal-to-deal allegations relating to supplier and reseller relationships by concluding that there is no meaningful competition between a supplier and a reseller.[1043] In cases like *Unilever*[1044] and *Allergan*,[1045] the Board has rejected claims that a company has a duty to supply when the input is not indispensable,

---

[1037]   R. Whish and D. Bailey, *Competition Law* (8th edition, Oxford University Press, 2015), p. 698.

[1038]   *Eti Holding* (21 December 2000, 00-50/533-295); *POAS* (n. 1031); *Ak-Kim* (n. 1031); *Çukurova Elektrik* (n. 1031); *BOTAŞ* (17 April 2017, 17-14/207-85); *Sanofi* (n. 1031); *Lüleburgaz* (7 September 2017, 17-28/477-205); *Akdeniz Elektrik* (n. 868); *Enerjisa* (n. 853); *Isttelkom* (n. 853); *Medsantek* (28 March 2019, 19-13/182-80); *Varinak* (n. 767); *Google Shopping* (n. 28); *Congresium Ato* (n. 1031); O. Gürzümar, *Zorunlu Unsur Doktrinine Dayalı Sözleşme Yapma Yükümlülüğü*, Seçkin Yayınları, Ankara, 2006.

[1039]   *Türk Telekom* (27 February 2020, 20-12/153-83); *Radontek* (n. 844).

[1040]   Direct refusal occurs when a dominant undertaking refuses to deal, without providing any reason for such refusal, whereas constructive refusal occurs through conduct, including undue delays, restriction of product supply and imposition of unreasonable business conditions, etc.;

[1041]   Guidelines on Abuse of Dominance, para. 38.

[1042]   Guidelines on Abuse of Dominance, para. 41.

[1043]   *Novartis* (n. 614); *Johnson & Johnson* (14 November 2019, 19-40/642-270); *Baymak* (6 September 2018, 18-30/523-259).

[1044]   *Unilever* (n. 843).

[1045]   *Allergan* (3 January 2013, 13-01/3-3).

because alternative means for supply exist or will be available in the foreseeable future. However, in *Solmaz Mercan II*,[1046] the Board diverged from its consistent precedents and did not seek for the indispensability condition. In the relevant decision, the Board also did not evaluate whether the conduct led to an anti-competitive effect but stated that the "intent" in the present case is clearly to exclude competitors. The Board concluded that "even though Solmaz Mercan's activities have been restricted to some extent, there is no clear competition restricting effect on the pricing of the glass household goods" and therefore decided not to impose an administrative monetary fine on Anadolu Cam.[1047] The case was brought before the Council of State, which annulled the Board's decision. The Council of State stated that considering that (i) there was a significant decrease in supply levels and (ii) the Board already acknowledged that Anadolu Cam had abused its dominant position through its opinion letter to Anadolu Cam because the relevant conduct bore "the risk of turning into a violation", and the lack of effect in prices does not change the fact that Anadolu Cam abused its dominant position. Further to the Council of State's Decision, the Board decided to impose an administrative monetary fine on Anadolu Cam by concluding that the "intent" in the present case is clearly to exclude competitors.

The strict thresholds under Turkish law are reflections of international precedents. In *Oscar Bronner*, the leading EU case on this issue, the Advocate General explained that duties to supply and grant access to competitors interfere with "the right to choose one's trading partners and freely to dispose of one's property", and that "it is generally pro-competitive and in the interest of consumers to allow a company to retain for its own use facilities which it has developed for the purpose of its business".[1048] In *Bronner*, the CJEU set forth three cumulative conditions that must be met for a finding of abuse: (i) the refusal needs to eliminate all competition in the downstream market; (ii) the refusal must be incapable of objective justification; and (iii) the access to the service must be indispensable to carrying on that business.[1049]

7.4.6.2 Indispensability

When evaluating the indispensability condition, the Board tries to determine if the input in question is objectively necessary in order to compete effectively in the downstream market. This is the case where there is no actual or potential substitute for the relevant input on which competitors in the downstream market could rely so as to counter–at least in the long term–the negative effects of the refusal. When assessing whether there are actual or potential substitutes for the relevant input, the Board considers whether the competitors of the dominant undertaking could effectively duplicate the input in the foreseeable future.[1050] In general, if the relevant input is the result of a natural monopoly, if there are significant network effects, or if information can be acquired from a single source, it is generally concluded that it is impossible for the competitors

[1046] *Solmaz Mercan II* (26 August 2009, 09-39/949-236).
[1047] *Solmaz Mercan I* (5 June 2007, 07-47/506-181).
[1048] Case C-7/97 *Oscar Bronner GmbH & Co KG v. Mediaprint* [1998] ECR I-7791, Opinion AG Jacobs, paras. 56–57.
[1049] *Oscar Bronner GmbH & Co KG v. Mediaprint* (n. 1031).
[1050] *Superonline/Türk Telekom* (16 April 2020, 20-20/267-128); *Medical Gas* (1 September 2015, 15-34/502-155).

to duplicate the input.[1051] Nonetheless, the Board takes into account the dynamic structure of the market and the sustainability of the market power provided by the relevant input, separately, for each case.[1052]

The essential facilities doctrine applies to the indispensability condition, which is referred to as the "indispensability" of the product or service the dominant undertaking is alleged to deny access to. In *Daichii Sankyo*,[1053] the Board points out to such interrelation as:

> The essential facilities doctrine is immensely parallel with the aforementioned indispensability condition. That is because the essential facilities doctrine provides a useful framework that shall be applied to impose a supply obligation on the dominant undertaking under the EU law. The essential facilities doctrine uses the indispensability criterion to pose an exclusionary theory of harm.[1054]

In *Maysan*,[1055] the Board concluded that Maysan did not abuse its dominant position by refusing to supply as its products were not essential for reselling automotive spare parts. Therefore, the Board treats the indispensability criterion as the reflection of the essential facilities doctrine.

When the Board examines indispensability, it evaluates whether there is a potential or existing substitute for the relevant input.[1056] In assessing whether there exists a substitute, it is not relevant that some of these substitutes may be "less advantageous" for the competitor in question than using the service of the dominant undertaking.

When evaluating whether the indispensability condition is fulfilled, the Board takes into account the characteristics of the activities of the undertakings in downstream markets, which cannot obtain the input in question. The goods or services provided by the dominant undertaking are deemed to be indispensable to the extent they are used in production as "input" and adds value to a new and competitive end product. However, if the refusal only relates to the resale or distribution of a product supplied from the upstream market (when there is no added value), it is accepted that the first condition of refusal to deal is not fulfilled.[1057]

Refusal-to-deal cases may either stem from the disruption of the previous supply relationship or concern the supply of inputs that have not previously been provided. That said, a violation is more likely in case of the disruption of a current supply arrangement.

[1051] *Turkish Union of Chambers and Exchange Commodities* (14 November 2019; 19-40/650-276); *Doğan, Mozaik and Krea* (18 May 2016, 16-17/299-134).

[1052] Guidelines on Abuse of Dominance, para. 44.

[1053] *Daiichi Sankyo* (22 May 2018, 18-15/280-139), paras. 45–47.

[1054] Ibid, para 46. See also *Sanofi* (n. 1031) for similar explanations on essential facility doctrine and its relevance to the indispensability condition as provided under the Guidelines on Abuse of Dominance.

[1055] *Maysan* (n. 1038).

[1056] *Tema Fuarcılık* (2 July 2020, 20-32/396-178); *Maysan* (n. 1038); *Turkcell* (n. 954); *Dow* (n. 884); *Sasa* (3 November 2016, 16-36/608-271).

[1057] *Roche* (n. 1029), para. 202. Also see *Otis* (18 March 2010, 10-24/330-118); *Teknoform* (8 April 2010, 10-29/446-169); *Paşabahçe* (2 September 2010, 10-57/1155-439); *Samsung* (17 June 2010, 10-44/771-253); *White Goods* (14 July 2010, 11-43/942-306); *Allegan* (n. 1045); *Berko* (26 November 2014, 14-46/845-385); *Solgar* (18 February 2016, 16-05/116-51); *Sanofi* (n. 1031).

This would be taken into account as an important factor in identifying the relevant input as indispensable. Also, the fact that the dominant undertaking previously supplied the input in question may be considered an indication that supplying the product does not constitute a risk that the undertaking would be unable to receive sufficient compensation for its initial investment.[1058,1059]

7.4.6.3 Anti-Competitive Effect

Where it is established that the indispensability condition is met, the Board evaluates whether a refusal to deal by the dominant undertaking is likely to eliminate effective competition in the downstream market immediately or over time.[1060]

The likely exclusion of one individual competitor from the downstream market does not in itself constitute an abuse. An abuse may only arise when the exclusion of competitors is likely to have a negative effect on competition in the downstream market.[1061] This should, however, not be understood to mean the complete elimination of all competition, either. The extent to which the exclusion of one competitor has an impact on the level of competition depends on the pre-existing competition in the downstream market.[1062] The larger the share of the dominant undertaking in the downstream market, the greater the likelihood of eliminating effective competition in the downstream market. In addition, if the dominant undertaking has less capacity constraints relative to competitors in the downstream market and if the goods or services it produces are close substitutes for those of its competitors in the downstream market, the likelihood for the elimination of competition in the downstream market will increase.[1063] This is due to the fact that, in this case, the proportion of competitors affected by the refusal to deal will increase, as will the level of demand that will shift from the foreclosed competitors to the dominant undertaking.[1064]

In a no-go decision over alleged abusive conduct of *Aslan Tuğla*[1065] by means of a refusal to deal, the Board provides that "the cessation of commercial relation between the two undertakings did not lead to an exclusionary effect in the market" as it is established that the applicant could have and indeed did continue its operations in the downstream market by purchasing from alternative sources. Thereby, the Board establishes the significance of alternative sources in a possible foreclosure assessment. In *Lüleburgaz Terminal*, the Board assesses the anti-competitive effects when ODA (the company managing the Lüleburgaz terminal) refused to assign a place to Nişikli (a bus operator applicant) in the terminal. Similar to the above-mentioned case of Aslan Tuğla, the Board attributes great importance to alternative sources and concludes that the fact Nişikli was denied a place in the terminal does not amount to an anti-competitive foreclosure as (i) Nişikli could have used agents to lease out a place as some other bus operators did; (ii) in fact,

---

[1058] Guidelines on Abuse of Dominance, p. 10.
[1059] *Radontek* (n. 844); *Türk Telekom* (9 June 2016, 16-20/326-146).
[1060] Guidelines on Abuse of Dominance, p. 10.
[1061] *Congresium Ato* (n. 1031); *Radontek* (n. 844).
[1062] DG Competition discussion paper on the application of Article 82 of the Treaty to exclusionary abuses, p. 65.
[1063] The Guidelines on Abuse of Dominance, para. 46.
[1064] *Volkan/Öz Edirne* (n. 921); *Novartis* (n. 614).
[1065] *Aslan Tuğla* (31 May 2012, 12-29/839-242).

the number of undertakings operating as an agent has increased during the same period, and thus there are even more alternatives for bus operators to operate; and (iii) new rival bus operators have entered into the Lüleburgaz market during the same period. The Board notes no possible harm to consumers was demonstrated and affirms its position towards an effects-based approach by stating, "unless the competition is harmed in the market, non-interference is a more appropriate option".[1066]

7.4.6.4 Consumer Harm

The Board also assesses whether consumer harm is likely as a result of the dominant undertaking's refusal to deal.[1067] Consumer harm may be likely where, as a result of the dominant undertaking's refusal to deal, competitors are prevented from bringing innovative goods or services to market, are excluded from the market since they are unable to supply the product, which would lead to a decrease in the level of competition in the downstream market and consumer harm, or the consumers are unable to access the product subject to trade.[1068] The Board evaluates that if the dominant undertaking is not active in the downstream market (i.e., it is not vertically integrated), then one cannot conclude that the dominant undertaking forecloses the market for its own interest. In such cases, terminating a supply relation does not lead to direct consumer harm.[1069]

Consumer harm may occur through price increase, reduction in the quality of products, innovation or the variety of products and services.[1070,1071] When assessing consumer harm, the Board examines whether the negative consequences of the refusal to deal in the relevant market for customers outweigh the negative consequences that occur over time due to an obligation to supply. According to the Guidelines on Abuse of Dominance, if the dominant undertaking's refusal to deal prevents the competitor's innovation, then consumer harm may be likely.[1072] For instance, in *Radontek*,[1073] the Board expressed that if competitors are prevented from launching innovative products or services due to the refusal of the dominant undertaking, and/or refusal prevents innovation, there is consumer harm. The Board added that this is particularly the case if the undertaking that offered to deal has potential demand for new and improved products and services or aims to contribute technological development. If the purpose of the competitor in demanding this supply is to produce new or improved goods or services for which there is potential demand, or if the competitor is likely to contribute to technical development, without limiting itself to the goods or services already offered by the dominant undertaking, consumer harm is likely to occur.[1074] Furthermore, the Board also considers whether a refusal to deal would allow the dominant undertaking to gain more profits in the downstream market than it would normally do.[1075,1076]

[1066]   *Lüleburgaz Terminal* (n. 1038).
[1067]   *BP* (14 November 2019, 19-40/652-278); *Novartis* (n. 614); *Tüyap* (n. 1030); *Congresium Ato* (n. 1031).
[1068]   *Tüyap* (n. 1030); *Luxottica* (n. 988).
[1069]   *Novartis* (n. 614), para. 80.
[1070]   Guidelines on Abusive Conduct, para. 25.
[1071]   *Novartis* (n. 614), para. 81.
[1072]   Guidelines on Abuse of Dominance, para. 47.
[1073]   *Radontek* (n. 844).
[1074]   Ibid.
[1075]   Guidelines on Abuse of Dominance, para. 47.
[1076]   *Radontek* (n. 844), para. 112.

7.4.6.5 Objective Justification

In addition to the foregoing criterion, the investigated undertakings' claims of efficiencies or objective justification are also taken into account.[1077] If the undertaking asking for supply lacks commercial credibility, where the supply is temporarily or permanently halted due to capacity constraints, or lack of certain safety requirements, then the Board may decide that there is an objective necessity. However, for relying on such a justification, a dominant undertaking is obliged to show that its conduct is proportionate. May be considered as an efficiency defence claims that (i) the dominant undertaking would not realise adequate investment returns if it agreed to supply, or (ii) the dominant undertaking would need to exploit the input for a certain period of time in order to continue its investments or otherwise the incentives to invest would be negatively affected.[1078]

According to the precedents and doctrine, in refusal to deal cases, the investigated undertakings generally invoke the following justification or efficiency defences: (i) the lack of commercial credibility, technical inability, poor financial situation of the undertaking demanding the supply; (ii) inability to comply with safety/health conditions; (iii) technical inconsistency that would harm the dominant undertaking's infrastructure; (iv) capacity/input/stock constraints; (v) public restrictions on the supply of goods and services; (vi) dominant undertaking's plan to carry out activities in the downstream market; (vii) reduction in incentives for innovation.[1079,1080]

7.4.7 The Relationship Between IP Rights and Article 6

The abuse of dominance related to IP rights may be either exploitative, exclusionary or both. The Board states that IP rights are defined as rights that enable their owners to prevent others from using a certain intangible asset, categorised into three groups, namely, patents, copyrights and trademarks.[1081] The IP right provides its owner with an exclusive right, hence, the ability to obtain monopoly profit for a certain time.[1082]

The Guidelines on Horizontal Agreements provides that the main purpose of both intellectual property law and competition law is (i) to promote dynamic efficiency and efficiency in production and distribution and (ii) to increase innovation in the long run and thereby enhance consumer welfare.[1083] As the Board cites, the tension between the two disciplines of the law does not stem from the purpose but from the methods used when

---

[1077]   *Türk Telekom* (n. 1039); and *Maysan* (n. 570); *Tüyap* (n. 1030); *Radontek* (n. 844); *Congresium Ato* (n. 1031).
[1078]   Guidelines on Abuse of Dominance, paras. 48–49.
[1079]   Ibid., para.102.
[1080]   For EU case law, please see Case 27/76 *United Brands Company v. Commission* [1978] ECR 207; *Clearstream* (n. 1030).
[1081]   *Philips* (n. 1033), p. 10.
[1082]   A. Arıöz and Ö. C. Özbek, "Hakim Durumun Kötüye Kullanılmasının Sonucu Olarak Zorunlu Lisanslama: Değerlendirme Kriterleri ve Uygulanan Standartlar", *Rekabet Dergisi*, Vol. 11, No. 3, July 2010, pp. 11–49, p. 15.
[1083]   The Guidelines on the Horizontal Cooperation Agreements, para. 240.

pursuing their purposes.[1084] Competition law prohibits abuse of dominance in order to maximise efficiency, whereas intellectual property law promotes exclusivity in the market in order to encourage undertakings to innovate.[1085]

The Board argues that the current approach does not focus on the limits of IP rights and the sanctions to be imposed in the event of an infringement. Rather, the focus is to encourage R&D activities by removing the obstacles.[1086] It then notes that the competition authorities should consider the delicate balance between the exclusive rights of the IP rights holders and the benefit of the society.[1087]

Law No. 4054 does not contain a special provision on the applicability of competition law on IP rights; hence competition law applies to agreements and acts based on the use of IP rights as well.[1088] The Guidelines on the Technology Transfer Agreements also states that the IP right holders are subject to competition law even if the IP right provides them with exclusivity on the use of certain assets.[1089] Accordingly, the right holder cannot use its IP right as a defence for an act that has the effect or object of restricting competition.[1090]

There may be cases where vertical or horizontal agreements concerning IP rights are made in contravention of Article 4 of Law No. 4054. However, this section will only focus on how IP rights may be used in violation of Article 6 of Law No. 4054.

With regard to the relationship between dominance/market power and IP rights, the Guidelines on Horizontal Agreements state that the establishment of a standard may create or increase the market power for those undertakings holding the IP rights essential for that standard. However, the undertaking cannot be considered to have or be able to exercise market power solely because it holds the IP right essential for a standard. Hence, the market power assessment should be made on a case-by-case basis.[1091] Also, according to the Guidelines on the Technology Transfer Agreements, holding essential patents and having superior technologies are considered as competitive advantages when analysing the market power of an undertaking.[1092]

In *Philips*, the Board holds that holding a SEP does not necessarily follow that the right holder holds a dominant position in the market. Rather, a case-by-case analysis needs to be conducted. However, the Board found that Philips held a dominant position in the market for subtitling technology for digital video broadcasting because of the fact that, inter alia,

---

[1084] W. Cornish and D. Llewlyn, *Intellectual Property: Patents, Copyrights, Trademarks and Allied Rights*, cited with (5th edition, London: Sweet&Maxwell, 2003) cited in *Philips* (n. 1033), p. 10.
[1085] H. Hovenkamp, M. D. Janis, M. A. Lemley, *IP and Antitrust: An Analysis of Antitrust Principles Applied to Intellectual Property Law* (New York: Aspen Law & Business, 2005), pp. 1–13, cited in *Philips* (n. 1033), p. 10.
[1086] S. N. Bayramoğlu, *Rekabet Hukukunda Fikri Mülkiyet Haklarının Toplu Yönetimi: Patent Havuzları ve Standart Belirleme* (Ankara: Rekabet Kurumu, 2012), p. 1; also see *Philips* (n. 1033), p. 11.
[1087] *Philips* (n. 1033), p. 11.
[1088] Ibid., p. 11.
[1089] The Guidelines on the Application of Articles 4 and 5 of Law No. 4054 on the Protection of Competition to Technology Transfer Agreements, para. 5.
[1090] U. Petrovcic, *Competition Law and Standard Essential Patents: A Transatlantic Perspective* (Alphen aan den Rijn: Wolters Kluwer Law & Business, 2014), p. 44, cited in *Philips* (n. 1033), p. 12; also see *Mesam* (n. 1036), pp. 30–31.
[1091] Guidelines on Horizontal Agreements, para. 240.
[1092] Guidelines on the Application of Articles 4 and 5 of Law No. 4054 on the Protection of Competition, para. 112.

it was mandatory for television and set-top box producers to comply with the relevant standard and they had to use Philips' relevant patents for compliance with the standard.[1093]

In *Philips*, the Board provides the main examples of abuse of dominance related to IP rights as discriminating between the undertakings that obtained licences, excessive pricing and refusal to license.[1094] These examples, along with others, will be analysed below. For completeness, please note that there are also cases where the Board analysed tying and bundling[1095] and the application of rebate systems[1096] with respect to IP rights.

7.4.7.1 Refusal to License

Pursuant to the Guidelines on Abuse of Dominance, an undertaking's refusal to supply not only the goods or services it produces, but also the tangible or intangible business inputs in its possession to other undertakings, is considered as a refusal to supply. Accordingly, "intangible business inputs or information which are protected or unprotected by IP rights" are deemed among the inputs that may be subject to abuse of dominance.[1097] Also, according to the Board, refusal to license IP rights is a subcategory of refusal to supply.[1098]

The Board has dealt with the refusal to supply in relation to IP rights in many cases. In its landmark decision, *National Roaming*, the Board sets forth the conditions under which a refusal to supply may be deemed abusive.[1099] Accordingly, (i) the access to the essential facility must be essential for entry into the market; (ii) the undertaking requesting access must have sufficient capacity to supply the demand; (iii) the undertaking owning the essential facility must restrict competition in the market either for an existing or a potential product and/or service, or the demand must exceed the capacity of the undertaking owning the essential facility; (iv) the undertaking requesting access to the essential facility must be ready to pay a fee based on reasonable and non-discriminatory terms; and (v) there must be no objective justification for refusal to grant access. In more recent decisions concerning IP rights, the Board reiterates these conditions.[1100]

7.4.7.2 Refusal to License and Standard Essential Patents

The patented technologies declared to be necessary for complying with certain standards are named as SEPs.[1101] Standard setting means providing the common characteristics that must exist in a certain product or service.[1102]

[1093] *Philips* (n. 1033).
[1094] Ibid., p. 12.
[1095] See *Siemens Medical Devices* (20 August 2014, 14-29/613-266) (tying the sales of spare parts of its products to the sale of technical services for its products); also see *Logo Yazılım* (28 April 2011, 11-26/497-154) (tying the licensing of certain IP rights to the licensing of other IP rights).
[1096] See *Microsoft* (13 June 2013, 13-36/481-211).
[1097] Guidelines on Abuse of Dominance, para. 38.
[1098] *Lüleburgaz* (7 September 2017, 17-28/477-205), p. 20; *Karabük Demir Çelik* (7 September 2017, 17-28/481-207), p. 68; *Digital Platform* (3 May 2012, 12-24/710-198), p. 16.
[1099] *National Roaming* (n. 327), p. 43.
[1100] *Türk Telekom* (n. 1059); *Krea İçerik Hizmetleri* (n. 1033); *Surat Basım/Zambak* (n. 1033); *Digital Platform* (n. 1033); *Bilsa* (21 March 2007, 07-26/238-77) and *National Roaming* (n. 327).
[1101] *Philips* (n. 1033), p. 9.
[1102] OECD, Policy Roundtables, "Standard Setting", DAF/COMP(2010)33, 8 March 2011 <http://www.oecd.org/daf/competition/47381304.pdf> (last accessed on 25 May 2019), p. 10.

The Guidelines on Horizontal Agreements state that standardisation agreements, in principle, lead to positive economic outcomes by promoting competition and reducing the cost of production and sales. Standards may result in improved quality, ensuring interoperability and compatibility, thereby increasing benefits for consumers.[1103] Nevertheless, standardisation agreements may have anti-competitive effects as they may chill price competition and lead to the exclusion of or discrimination against competitors from the market by way of limiting technical development and preventing efficient access to the standard.[1104]

Accordingly, during the process of determining a standard, several technologies compete with each other for becoming the standard; however, once a technology is determined as a standard, the alternative undertakings and technologies might face a barrier to entry and might be excluded from the market. Hence, standards may limit technical development and innovation.[1105]

Moreover, some undertakings might be prevented from accessing a standard, or access to the standard might be made subject to prohibitive or discriminatory conditions. To eliminate this risk, the rules setting the standard should ensure effective access to the standard on fair, reasonable and non-discriminatory (FRAND) terms.[1106]

Last but not least, the Guidelines on Horizontal Agreements emphasise the risk that where one undertaking owns the IP right that is essential to comply with the standard, the relevant undertaking may indirectly control the standard and engage in anti-competitive behaviours, for example, by refusing to license the necessary IP right or through imposing excessive royalty fees for the access.[1107] For this reason, any participant wishing to have their IP right included in the standard must provide an irrevocable FRAND commitment, meaning that they would have to license their essential IP right to all third parties under fair, reasonable and non-discriminatory terms.[1108]

The decision where the Board explicitly refers to "FRAND" terms for the first time is *Digiturk II*. In its analysis on whether the agreement between the Turkish Football Federation and Digiturk may be granted an individual exemption pursuant to Article 5 of Law No. 4054, the Board notes that the licensing agreement must include FRAND terms.[1109] Nevertheless, the Board does not conduct an analysis on whether the agreement at hand complies with FRAND terms since it decides to grant an individual exemption to the agreement stating that it enables the licensees' platforms to access certain technical developments, thereby providing customer benefit.[1110]

Philips also is of utmost importance to show the application of competition law to standard setting and the use of SEPs. According to the Board, the possible forms of abuse of dominance related to SEPs are "refusal to license", "hold up", and "court injunction". The refusal to license by the SEP holder may lead to the exclusion of the producers using SEP in its products, particularly if these producers are currently "locked in" to the relevant standard and made their investments specific to the relevant standard. The SEP

[1103]   Guidelines on Horizontal Agreements, para. 235.
[1104]   Ibid., para. 236.
[1105]   Ibid, para. 238.
[1106]   Ibid., paras. 239, 252, 254.
[1107]   Ibid., para. 240.
[1108]   Ibid., para. 256.
[1109]   *Digiturk II* (10 February 2016, 16-04/82-36), p. 19.
[1110]   Ibid., pp. 20–21.

may use the power stemming from the lack of alternatives through applying excessive royalties or unreasonable licensing terms.[1111]

In *Philips*, the allegations against the undertaking were that Philips abused its dominant position since it (i) did not negotiate in good faith for the licensing of its SEPs on the subtitling technology; (ii) initiated lawsuits against Vestel to obtain an injunction for the destruction of its products;[1112] (iii) requested excessive royalties;[1113] (iv) imposed no-challenge and termination-upon-challenge clauses in the licensing agreement;[1114] (v) discriminated against Vestel through charging excessive royalty fees;[1115] and (vi) prevented Vestel from using its own technology by requiring Vestel to pay royalties for the modified products it produced unless Vestel proves that the modified products are manufactured based on its own technology.[1116]

In its analysis on the allegations of not negotiating in good faith for the licensing process and filing lawsuits, the Board notes that, in order not to be found to abuse its dominant position, the SEP owner should have taken certain steps before bringing a lawsuit in case of violation of the SEP. In this particular case, however, the Board decided that, even if Philips had offered to make a licence agreement before filing a lawsuit, it had abused its dominance, on the ground that when the parties could not agree on the royalty fees over two years, Philips should have referred to an independent third party for determination of the amount of the royalty before bringing a lawsuit.[1117]

Regarding the excessive royalty allegations, having noted the practical difficulties in analysing whether a royalty fee is excessive, the Board dismisses the allegation considering the ratio of the royalty imposed over the average TV selling price and Vestel's average unit cost.[1118]

On the discrimination allegation, the Board states that applying FRAND terms does not mean imposing the same price to every undertaking but it requires being transparent and able to explain any difference based on objective reasons. The Board then takes into account that Philips does not report some of its royalty fees on its website, which is not in compliance with the principle of transparency, and, for this reason, holds that Philips discriminated against Vestel.[1119]

The Board also analyses the termination-upon-challenge clause provided in the agreement between Philips and Vestel. The Board notes that if a termination-upon-challenge clause (providing that the agreement is terminated when the licensee challenges the concerned IP right) has the effect of a no-challenge clause by preventing the licensee from challenging the IP right due to the importance of using the licence, it may be regarded as a type of no-challenge clause. Furthermore, it states that if no-challenge clauses are applied by an undertaking holding SEP or an IP right granting its owner a significant market power,

---

[1111]   *Philips* (n. 1033), p. 14.
[1112]   Ibid., p. 27.
[1113]   Ibid., p. 31.
[1114]   Ibid., pp. 29–30.
[1115]   Ibid., p. 39
[1116]   Ibid., p. 41.
[1117]   Ibid., p. 29.
[1118]   Ibid., p. 39.
[1119]   Ibid., pp. 40–41.

they may lead to serious competitive risks. Accordingly, the Board finds that the termination-upon-challenge clause in the case at hand has the characteristics of a no-challenge clause, hence imposing such a clause constitutes an abuse of a dominant position.[1120]

Finally, about the allegation on preventing Vestel from using its own technology by requiring it to prove that its modified products are based on its own technology or otherwise pay a royalty fee for these products, the Board states that the burden of proof should be on the SEP holder if it claims that the licensee violated the SEP. Hence, reversing the burden of proof would violate the FRAND terms.[1121]

Therefore, the Board decides that Philips abused its dominant position as (i) it did not refer to an independent third party for the determination of the royalty amount before filing a lawsuit against the undertaking infringing its SEP; (ii) it did not publish the royalties in contrary to the principle of transparency; (iii) it prevented Vestel from using its own technology by reversing the burden of proof; and (iv) it included a no-challenge clause into the agreement, which was not in compliance with the FRAND terms.

7.4.7.3 Excessive Pricing

The Guidelines on Horizontal Agreements state that, when deciding whether the price charged for access to an IP right that is essential for complying with a standard is fair and reasonable, one should analyse whether there is a reasonable relationship between the fee charged and the economic value of the IP right. However, it is acknowledged that it is difficult to analyse the cost incurred for producing the asset subject to the IP right. According to the Guidelines on Horizontal Agreements, a comparison between the price imposed for the licence of the same IP right prior to and after the standard setting in the sector may be useful to decide whether the price is excessive. Also, the fee charged for IP rights that are essential for similar standards may be considered for the price comparison.[1122]

The main test applied by the Board to decide whether the price is excessive is the economic value test (EVT). The EVT is a two-stage test, the first stage being the price-cost analysis and the second stage, the price comparison. In *Philips*, the Board states that even if it is acknowledged that the Board may intervene if the price applied for licensing of the IP rights is excessive, it considers the difficulties in deciding whether the price charged for access to SEP is abusive. It states that, for the first stage of the EVT, using the marginal cost and AVC is not feasible given that undertakings incur high fixed costs for innovation, and the marginal cost and the AVC are equal to zero for each licensed patent. That said, the R&D costs may still be taken into account, since during such processes, most R&D activities result in no meaningful consequence; but it is hard to decide which R&D activities would need to be considered for calculation of the cost. Moreover, if the undertaking is active in the downstream market, the cost of R&D would need to be divided into both markets (i.e., the market for production

---

[1120]   Ibid., pp. 30–31.
[1121]   Ibid., pp. 150–151.
[1122]   Guidelines on Horizontal Agreements, para. 260.

and the market for licensing). For the second stage of the EVT, it is difficult to find a historical equivalent that could be compared to the IP right at hand because of the unique nature of IP rights. Also, it may not be meaningful to compare the prices applied by the undertaking at different times because undertakings charge lower prices in order to make customers accustomed to the relevant technology and then increase their prices.[1123]

Another decision that shows the difficulties of applying a price-cost analysis when the case concerns IP rights is the *Mesam* decision. In this decision, the Board holds that since the idea and creativity behind a musical product are non-quantifiable, it cannot conduct a price-cost analysis to determine whether the royalty fees imposed for the use of copyright of musical products are excessive.[1124]

7.4.7.4 Predatory Litigation

Predatory litigation is defined by the Board as cases in which mostly large companies expose small companies to long and wearisome litigation processes. The Board notes that under US antitrust law, these cases are considered to have been brought to court in order to hinder or obstruct the commercial activities of the rivals based on unsubstantiated grounds, and the lawsuits involving IP rights where the plaintiff abuses these rights are considered as predatory litigation.[1125]

In *Microsoft I*, when conducting an analysis on whether Microsoft Corporation abused its dominant position by seeking a court injunction to stop AMD Elektronik Bilgisayar Sanayi ve Ticaret A.Ş.'s sales, the Board notes that applying to the court to prevent or restrict the competitor's commercial activities, to force the competitor to settle and to save time without having a substantiated ground is contrary to competition law.[1126] Nevertheless, the Board found that Microsoft Corporation sought to protect its intellectual property before the court, so its act was justifiable.[1127]

7.4.7.5 Discrimination Against Licensees

The Board also condemns discrimination (i) among the licensees of IP rights and (ii) against the competitors by leveraging the market power derived from another market.

In *Siemens Medical Devices*, the Board reconsiders the allegations against Siemens San. ve Tic. A.Ş., among others, that the undertaking discriminates against the independent providers of maintenance and repair services for Siemens branded medical diagnosis and imaging devices. The Board finds that (i) the undertaking holds a dominant position in the market for the sale of spare parts to be used for maintenance and repair services for Siemens branded medical diagnosis and imaging devices; and (ii) it abused its dominant position in this market by charging prices for the spare parts that are purchased by the independent providers of maintenance and repair services for Siemens' products.

[1123]   *Philips* (n. 1033), pp. 32–33.
[1124]   *Mesam* (21 July 2005, 05-48/683-177), p. 3.
[1125]   *Microsoft I* (23 November 2000, 00-46/488-266), p. 4.
[1126]   Ibid., p. 4.
[1127]   Ibid., p. 5.

The spare parts were mostly under an IP right protection, and the undertaking was also active in the market for the provision of maintenance and repair services for its own branded products.[1128]

In another case, Siemens Product Lifecycle Management Software, Inc. and its distributors in Turkey were accused of violating Articles 4 and 6 of Law No. 4054 by refusing to supply Siemens NX CAD/CAM software to a certain customer, hence discriminating against it. However, in that case, the Board rejected the allegation of discrimination by stating that the relevant customer was not actually equal to other customers of Siemens because it had violated Siemens' IP right by using unlicensed software.[1129]

[1128]   *Siemens Medical Devices* (n. 1095), pp. 24–25.
[1129]   *Siemens II* (8 January 2015, 15-02/5-3), p. 17.

Chapter 8
Abuse of Dominance – Exploitative and Discriminatory Practices

GÖNENÇ GÜRKAYNAK, ESQ. AND ZEYNEP AYATA AYDOĞAN[*]

Both exclusionary and exploitative conducts are condemned as abuse of dominance under Turkish competition law. The main examples of exploitative practices are the imposition of excessive pricing and unfair and exploitative contract terms.

As indicated in the Board's decisions, intervention on the basis of the allegation of excessive pricing is controversial considering, among others, that (i) the market may self-correct without intervention since higher profits would attract new entries; (ii) there are practical difficulties in deciding whether the price is excessive; and (iii) it is difficult to impose the right remedy in case of the finding of infringement. The Board decides whether the price is excessive based on the EVT test by giving more weight to the findings derived from the second stage (i.e., the price comparison stage) compared to the first stage (i.e., the cost/price ratio analysis). In its assessment, the Board is likely to consider factors such as whether the relevant undertaking operates at or near monopolistic status and whether it is subject to regulation and, if this is the case, whether it complies with the relevant regulation. As for the more recent case law, the discussion about whether the EVT test is sufficient to determine the excessiveness of the prices becomes even more important given the Board analyses on the excessive pricing allegations brought forward in innovative sectors.

Regarding the case law on unfair and exploitative contract terms, the Board seems less willing to intervene if a specific law applies to the contract terms. Having said that, based on a recent investigation of the Board and the Preliminary Report on the Sector Inquiry Concerning E-Marketplace Platforms, it may be stated that the Board may take a more active stance against the use of exploitative contract terms in digital markets by associating, for example, "excessive data collection" with exploitative behaviour.

Finally, Law No. 4054 also provides that discriminating against equal customers may be considered an abuse of dominance. Whether competition authorities should intervene in discriminatory behaviour is also under debate considering that, among others, the overall effect of discriminatory practices may be beneficial for competition. The Board categorises discriminatory practices under two different groups. If an undertaking engages in discrimination which may have an impact only on its competitors (including potential

[*] Associate, ELIG Gürkaynak Attorneys-at-Law, Istanbul <zeynep.ayata@elig.com>.

rivals), it is considered as a primary line injury; whereas, if the discriminatory conduct of a dominant undertaking has an impact on competition among its customers, then its conduct is classified as a secondary line injury. Although "putting a customer at a competitive disadvantage" is not a prerequisite for condemning the behaviour pursuant to Law No. 4054, there are cases where the Board considered whether this condition is satisfied.

8.1 Exploitative Practices

Under Turkish competition law, in addition to the exclusionary practices aimed to exclude competitors, the exploitative practices aimed to exploit consumers are also condemned as a form of abuse of dominance, even if the latter does not lead to direct harm to competition. Excessive pricing and imposing unfair and exploitative contract terms are the main examples of exploitative practices. That said, the Board only rarely analyses the abuse of dominance instances through imposing unfair and exploitative contract terms; the debate on whether to intervene usually focuses on excessive pricing.

The concept of excessive pricing itself is controversial on the basis that (i) the market may self-correct in the absence of barriers to entry and (ii) the intervention may distort the competitive process in the market and have a chilling effect on the motivation to invest and innovate. Also, there are practical difficulties in deciding whether the price is excessive.

As briefly introduced above in Chapter 7, the Board employs the EVT to ascertain whether the price is excessive. However, unlike the approach of the CJEU, the Board gives more weight to the findings derived from the second stage (i.e., the price comparison stage) compared to the first stage (i.e., the cost/price ratio analysis).

8.2 Concept of Exploitation and Theory of Harm

With regard to the historical background of the classification of abuses, there has been a discussion under Turkish competition law on whether the intervention on the ground of excessive pricing as a sub-category of exploitative abuse has any basis in law.[1130] Unlike Article 102 TFEU, which states that "directly or indirectly imposing unfair purchase or selling prices or other unfair trading conditions" may be considered as abusive behaviour, Article 6 of Law No. 4054 provides examples of different types of abuses without making any classification for them. Some argue that the documents on the

---

[1130] K. C. Sanlı, "Rekabet Hukukunda Tekelci Fiyatlandırma", *Perşembe Konferansları* (Ankara: Rekabet Kurumu 2010), p. 108; Ç. Ünal, "Rekabet Hukukunda Tek Taraflı Sömürücü Davranışlar", *Rekabet Dergisi*, Vol. 11, No. 4, October 2010, p. 145.

drafting of Law No. 4054 do indicate that the aim of the legislator was not to include a prohibition on excessive pricing under Article 6.[1131] However, there is reason to believe that Article 6(1) provides sufficient legal basis for an intervention in terms of excessive pricing instances, as it prohibits all kinds of abuses of dominance.[1132]

In line with this opinion, in its landmark judgment *Belko*, the Board holds that monopoly pricing provides a case for intervention under competition law because of its exploitative effect on consumers, even though such pricing may not directly impact the competition in the market.[1133] In *BOTAŞ-EGO-İZGAZ-İGDAŞ*, the Board states that the types of abuses are not limited to the list of examples provided under Article 6 of Law No. 4054.[1134] Furthermore, by referring to Article 6(2)(e) of Law No. 4054, which provides that "restricting production, marketing or technical development to the prejudice of consumers" is abusive, the Council of State decides that excessive pricing is in violation of competition law because it exerts a direct negative impact on consumers.[1135] In *Garanti Bank*, the Board finds that the competition law concerns that may arise as a result of tying credit services with insurance policies offered by the same bank are both the "exploitation of consumers" and "foreclosure of the market". Accordingly, the Board defines exploitative conduct as "the pricing strategies and other practices that are directly detrimental to the consumer welfare. With such abuses, the dominant undertaking uses its advantage stemming from its market power to obtain undeserved profits from its sales to consumers, which those undertakings that do not hold a dominant position would not be able to obtain."[1136]

In *Türk Telekom/TTNET*, the Board holds that an abuse can be either exploitative or exclusionary, or both. Accordingly, the undertakings earn unjustified profits by way of exploitative conduct, and undertakings force their competitors to exit the market by way of exclusionary conduct with the aim to obtain the market power necessary to engage in exploitative behaviour.[1137] In *Tüpraş I*, the Board states that abuses are generally categorised under three classes, namely, exclusionary, exploitative and discriminatory abuses. Immediately afterwards, the Board published the Guidelines on Abuse of Dominance, which refer to the same three groups under which abuses may be classified. Along the same lines, the Guidelines on Abuse of Dominance emphasised two points. First, the same conduct may have the characteristics of more than one category of abuse (i.e., exclusionary, exploitative and discriminatory), and second, the conducts that are not listed in Article 6 of Law No. 4054 may be held to be abusive.[1138] In recent decisions, the Board reiterates the classification of abuses under the three groups[1139] and defines

[1131]   Sanlı (n. 1130), p. 109.
[1132]   G. Gürkaynak, "Hâkim Durumun Kötüye Kullanılmasının Özel Görünüm Şekli Olarak Aşırı Fiyatlama", *Çimento İşveren Dergisi*, Vol. 26, No. 6, 2012, p. 38.
[1133]   *Belko* (n. 781), p. 58.
[1134]   *BOTAŞ-EGO-İZGAZ-İGDAŞ* (8 March 2002, 02-13/127-54), p. 26.
[1135]   10th Chamber of Council of State (5 December 2003, E. 2001/4817, K. 2003/4770).
[1136]   *Garanti Bank* (5 August 2009, 09-34/787-192) pp. 4–5. In a similar vein, see also *Tüpraş* (4 November 2009, 09-52/1246-315).
[1137]   *Türk Telekom/TTNET* (19 November 2008, 08-65/1055-411), p. 119.
[1138]   Guidelines on Abusive Conduct, para 5. See also Preamble to Law No. 4054 (emphasising the same points).
[1139]   *Google Shopping Unit* (7 November 2019, 19-38/575-243), p. 37; *Soda* (20 April 2016, 16-14/205-89), p. 11; *THY* (1 September 2015, 15-34/512-160), p. 11; *UN Ro-Ro* (1 October 2012, 12-47/1413-474), p. 34.

exploitative behaviour as conduct such as excessive pricing, which the undertaking engages in to transfer value from customers.[1140]

The main examples of exploitative behaviour are excessive pricing and imposing unfair and exploitative contract terms. While the cases of unfair and exploitative contract terms are rare, the issue of whether to intervene in excessive pricing is considered by the Board in many cases. The Board explains two potential problems that may arise from excessive pricing.[1141] First, because monopolistic prices are higher than marginal costs, there would be an inefficient distribution of resources (i.e., deadweight loss).[1142] Second, since the prices are above the levels that would have existed in a perfectly competitive market, the surplus here would be gained by the monopoly, hence resulting in a value transfer from consumers to the monopoly.[1143] Thus, the ground for intervention seems to be straightforward. However, there are also strong arguments in favour of a hands-off approach.

In its decisions, the Board summarises the discussion for non-intervention by referring to the points raised in the US and EU jurisdictions. Accordingly, the main arguments against intervening in the markets, discussed in detail below, are as follows: (i) the concept is itself controversial; (ii) the market will self-correct in the absence of barrier to entries and intervention may distort the competitive process in the market by discouraging entries; (iii) intervention may reduce the motivation to invest and innovate; and (iv) there are practical difficulties in determining whether the price is excessive.[1144]

First of all, the concept itself is controversial since it is not easy to distinguish between the dominant undertaking's lawful strategy for profit maximisation and its exploitative abuse.[1145] Indeed, Article 3 of Law No. 4054 defines dominant position as "the power of one or more undertakings in a particular market to determine economic parameters such as price, supply, the amount of production and distribution, by acting

---

[1140] *Radontek* (n. 844), p. 24; *Bandırma* (11 October 2018, 18-38/618-299), pp. 34-35; *Sahibinden II* (1 October 2018, 18-36/584-285), p. 10; *Mesam* (n. 1036), p. 41.

[1141] *Sahibinden II* (n. 1140), p. 11; *Soda* (n. 1139), p. 13.

[1142] In a perfectly competitive market, there are many producers (sellers) and consumers (buyers). Since there are many alternative sellers from whom the consumers could buy the product, the sellers face a perfectly elastic demand curve, and therefore all sellers are price takers. That is, if a producer were to increase the price of the product to increase its profitability, the consumers would cease to buy from that producer and switch to another. And in case sellers can manage to increase the price, any profit would be swept away with new sellers' entry into the market since there are no entry barriers in the market. This functioning drives the product's market price to marginal cost level in perfectly competitive markets, where the price, the marginal revenue, is equal to the cost of producing this additional unit (marginal cost). At this market equilibrium, where the price is equal to marginal cost, all demand above the cost of production would be satisfied, and therefore there would be no deadweight loss, and resources would be allocated in the most efficient way. On the contrary, in monopolistic markets, the monopolistic firm may increase prices by reducing its output. In this case, not all demand above marginal cost will be satisfied, and the monopolist will gain larger profits which are higher than the marginal costs, but consumers will deprive the chance of purchasing products that could be produced otherwise. This will result in deadweight loss and an inefficient allocation of resources.

[1143] *Sahibinden II* (n. 1140), p. 10.

[1144] Ibid., pp. 11-12; *Soda* (n. 1139), pp. 14-15; *Fuel Oil* (13 March 2019, 19-12/137-61), p. 11.

[1145] *Sahibinden II* (n. 1140), pp. 11–12; *Soda* (n. 1139), p. 14; *Fuel Oil* (n. 1144). p. 11. Also see Ç. Ünal, *Aşırı Fiyat Kavramı ve Aşırı Fiyatlama Davranışının Rekabet Hukukundaki Yeri* (Ankara: Rekabet Kurumu, 2009), pp. 11–12.

independently of their competitors and customers". According to the Guidelines on Abuse of Dominance, dominant undertakings are those "which can behave independently from competitive pressure [and are] capable of profitably increasing [their] prices above the competitive level and maintain them at that level for a certain period of time".[1146] Thus, dominant undertakings are, by definition, able to earn high profits, and intervention may entail the risk of prohibiting undertakings that hold market power from pursuing profit maximisation.[1147]

The Board also underlines that the US authorities do not interfere with excessive pricing and EU authorities rarely bring cases, despite the existence of a legal ground in Article 102 of the TFEU, since the common view on both sides of the Atlantic is that the market will self-correct in short or middle term by attracting new entries.[1148] Accordingly, the assumption is that the possibility of earning supra-competitive prices, as the monopolist does, will attract new entries into markets, as a consequence of which the market will correct itself. Hence, in the absence of barriers to entry into the market, the intervention is undesirable since imposing an obligation to reduce the prices to the competitive level may prevent potential entries that are attracted by the opportunity of earning profit.[1149]

With regard to the self-correction of markets, some scholars argue that the market may not self-correct even in the absence of entry barriers. That is because the potential entrants may not foresee the price that the dominant undertaking would apply after their entry into the market. The possibility is that the dominant undertaking may change its strategy in a way to charge prices below the level that a newcomer would not be able to compete, since the latter's costs would probably be higher than those of the dominant undertaking. However, even those scholars do not claim that intervention is necessary in such cases because (i) it is still difficult to establish which price is excessive and (ii) the intervention still may have a chilling effect on the motivation for investment and innovation.[1150]

The possible long-run effect of intervention is a disincentive to invest and innovate.[1151] As the US Supreme Court emphasises in *Trinko*:

> The opportunity to charge monopoly prices–at least for a short period–is what attracts 'business acumen' in the first place; it induces risk taking that produces innovation and economic growth.[1152]

Nevertheless, in case that it is not plausibly foreseen that the market will correct itself due to, for example, legal barriers to entry into the market, the Board argues that both the US and EU legal systems acknowledge that the intervention in such circumstances might be

---

[1146] Guidelines on Abusive Conduct, para. 8.
[1147] *Sahibinden II* (n. 1140), pp. 11-12; *Soda* (n. 1139), p. 14; *Fuel Oil* (n. 1144), p. 11.
[1148] *Sahibinden II* (n. 1140), pp. 11-12; *Soda* (n. 1139); *Fuel Oil* (n. 1144), p. 11.
[1149] *Soda* (n. 1139), p. 14.
[1150] A. Ezrachi and D. Gilo, "Are Excessive Prices Really Self-Correcting?" *Journal of Competition Law & Economics*, Vol. 5, Issue 2, June 2009, pp. 249–268.
[1151] *Kırtur* (5 November 2020, 20-48/657-288), p. 14.
[1152] *Verizon Communications v. Law Offices of Curtis V. Trinko, LLP*, 540 US 398 (2004).

justified.[1153] This explains why in cases where the Board has acted, there existed almost always legal, natural or de facto monopolies.[1154] Even in this case, it is difficult to devise the right remedy to bring the infringement to an end.[1155] There is a range of options, from directly addressing the market failure or only alleviating its effects, to requiring the undertaking to reduce the price or imposing structural remedies.[1156] According to the Board, there are two opposite views on whether competition authorities should interfere with the price if the market is regulated under a sector-specific legislation.[1157] The Board explains that competition advocacy would be an option if the excessive prices are the result of the lack or insufficiency of the regulation.[1158] Indeed, to eliminate the risk of capping prices, which is an inefficient distribution of resources,[1159] competition authorities should focus on detecting the market failures (e.g., the inefficiency of legal monopoly) that distort the "auto-correction" function of the market.[1160]

Even if competition authorities agree on how to intervene, there are problems in deciding cases requiring intervention. The competition authorities are liable to err when deciding whether the price is supra-competitive.[1161] In light of the CJEC's holding in *United Brands v. Commission*,[1162] the Board applies the EVT to determine whether the price is so excessive as to be considered abusive.[1163]

As summarised by the Board,[1164] the main question set out in *United Brands v. Commission* is whether the profit earned by the dominant undertaking is greater than what it would have earned "if there had been normal and sufficiently effective competition".[1165] Accordingly, the abusive price is the one that bears no "reasonable relation to the economic value of the product supplied".[1166] To determine this, the EVT compares the price charged and the cost incurred in providing the product or service. One then analyses two other questions: (i) whether the price is excessive considering the difference between the cost and price and (ii) whether the price is unfair in itself or when compared to competing products.[1167] In any case, the price that is above the competitive level should be persistently maintained for a significant period of time for the relevant authority to consider it abusive.[1168]

[1153]   *Sahibinden II* (n. 1140), p. 11; *Soda* (n. 1139), p. 14; *Fuel Oil* (n. 1144), p. 11.

[1154]   See, e.g., *ASKİ I* (13 March 2001, 01-12/114-29); *ASKİ II* (20 December 2006, 06-92/1176-354); *Havaş* (3 January 2008, 08-01/5-4); *TEDAŞ* (30 April 2002, 02-26/262-102); *Bereket Jeotermal* (14 February 2008, 08-15/146-49); *İzmir Jeotermal* (15 July 2009, 09-33/739-176); *BOTAŞ-EGO-İZGAZ-İGDAŞ* (n. 1134); *MTS* (26 May 2006, 06-36/462-124) and *Tüpraş II* (17 January 2014, 14-03/60-24).

[1155]   *Sahibinden II* (n. 1140), pp. 14–15.

[1156]   OECD, Policy Roundtables, "Excessive Prices", DAF/COMP(2011)18, 7 February 2012 <https://www.oecd.org/competition/abuse/49604207.pdf> (last accessed on 26 March 2021), pp. 12–13.

[1157]   Also see Ç. Ünal, (n. 1145), p. 12 (on whether competition authorities are in the right position to intervene in excessive prices).

[1158]   See *Sahibinden II* (n. 1140), p. 15; *Soda* (n. 1139), p. 15; *Fuel Oil* (n. 1144), p. 12.

[1159]   *Kırtur* (n. 1151), p. 14.

[1160]   Whish and Bailey, (n. 1037), ch. 18, pp. 5–6.

[1161]   *Sahibinden II* (n. 1140); *Soda* (n. 1139), pp. 15-16; *Fuel Oil* (n. 1144), p. 13.

[1162]   Case 27/76 *United Brands Company v. Commission* [1978] ECR 207.

[1163]   *Sahibinden II* (n. 1140), p. 12; *Soda* (n. 1139), p. 15; *Fuel Oil* (n. 1144), p. 12.

[1164]   *Fuel Oil* (n. 1144), p. 12.

[1165]   *United Brands Company v. Commission* (n. 1162), para. 249.

[1166]   Ibid. para. 250.

[1167]   Ibid. para. 251.

[1168]   Case C-177/16 *AKKA/LAA*, EU:C:2017:689.

That said, it is fair to say that addressing these questions is not an easy task. First, as the Board sets forth, to determine the economic value of a product or service, it is necessary to take into account factors such as the consumer demand for the product or service. Hence, considering merely the cost or supply-related factors would not suffice.[1169] Also, reliable data about costs may not be available, and it is controversial whether the cost of the most efficient firm in the market or that of the undertaking should be considered.[1170] Moreover, it is difficult to establish which profit margin is large enough to be regarded as abusive. The value of investment, sunk costs, opportunity costs and characteristics of the sector are all determinative factors.[1171] Thus, the Board acknowledges that the EVT will not provide a meaningful result in all sectors and cases.[1172] In a recent decision, the Board also points out the difficulty of determining the cost when the undertaking provides multiple products/services or operates in more than one market.[1173] Although some methods have been developed to distribute the common costs among different products, a common view among scholars is that these methods are considerably flawed.[1174]

All in all, it would be proper to say that intervention may cause a negative systemic effect on markets due to the legal uncertainty associated with both the concept itself and the application of the law.[1175]

8.3 Examples

8.3.1 Excessive Pricing

Excessive pricing is the most common exploitative practice that the Board analyses. The Board defines excessive pricing as the price that is constantly applied significantly above the competitive level as a result of the exercise of market power.[1176] Following on from the theories of harm in the Board's decisions on excessive pricing, we now turn to (i) the criteria that should be met for a finding of excessive pricing; (ii) the test that the Board applies to decide whether the price is excessive; and (iii) remedies devised when abuse has been established.

According to the Board's decisional practice, the main factors that the Board considers for finding abusive pricing may be summarised as (i) operating at or near monopolistic status where there are barriers to entry and (ii) being subject to or complying with the regulation.

[1169] *Sahibinden II* (n. 1140), p. 12; *Soda* (n. 1139), p. 15; *Fuel Oil* (n. 1144), p. 12.
[1170] *Soda* (n. 1139), p. 15.
[1171] *Fuel Oil* (n. 1144), p. 12.
[1172] *Soda* (n. 1139), p. 15; *Fuel Oil* (n. 1144), p. 12.
[1173] *Sahibinden II* (n. 1140), p. 12.
[1174] R. O'Donoghue and A. J. Padilla, *The Law and Economics of Article 102 TFEU* (2nd edition, Oxford: Hart Publishing, 2013), pp. 750–751; Ünal (n. **Erreur ! Signet non défini.**), pp. 32–33.
[1175] OECD, Policy Roundtables, "Excessive Prices" (n. 1156), p. 26.
[1176] *Fuel Oil* (n. 1144), p. 10.

8.3.1.1 Operating at or near Monopolistic Status Where There Are Barriers to Entry

The 13th Chamber of Council of State holds that the Board may act in excessive pricing cases only if the undertaking applying the prices operates at or near monopolistic status.[1177] The Board also states that it refrains from intervening if the market is open to competition.[1178]

The Board's past decisional practice shows that it almost always applies this condition of operating at or near monopolistic status. By way of example, the relevant condition is found to be satisfied in (i) *ASKİ I*[1179] and *ASKİ II*,[1180] where the undertaking was a natural monopoly in the markets for collection of wastewater and distribution of mains water; (ii) *Havaş*,[1181] where the undertaking was a legal monopoly in providing passenger transportation by buses from the airports to the city centre in Ankara; (iii) *TEDAŞ*,[1182] where the undertaking was a legal monopoly in the distribution of electricity in certain regions; (iv) *İzmir Jeotermal*,[1183] where the undertaking was a natural monopoly in geothermic domestic heating; (v) *MTS*,[1184] where the undertaking was the only importer of spare parts of the boiler heater branded "Wolf" in Turkey; (vi) *Tüpraş II*,[1185] where the undertaking was the only refinery in Turkey which holds 91% market share; and (viii) *HP*,[1186] where the undertaking was the only producer of the spare parts and the only provider of the after-sale services for its own printers.

In *Cement*, the Board states that, although the undertakings charging excessive prices are dominant in the market, it will not consider their behaviour abusive because they do not constitute a natural or legal monopoly.[1187] In a similar vein, in *Bedir Nakliyat*[1188] and *Mars*,[1189] the Board states that it will intervene solely if the undertaking is either natural or legal monopoly. In *Ulusal Cad*, the Board emphasises that although the undertaking holds a dominant position, there are no high barriers to entry into the market.[1190]

Although there are decisions where the Board analyses the behaviour of undertakings that are not monopolies, it does not impose a fine after its analysis.[1191]

Indeed, the Board applied this condition even in investigations against multi-sided platforms until its *Sahibinden II* decision[1192], where it found that an online platform abused

---

[1177] 13th Chamber of the Council of State (1 February 2013, E. 2009/109, K. 2013/212).
[1178] *Tav* (29 June 2016, 16-22/395-183).
[1179] *ASKİ I* (n. 1154).
[1180] *ASKİ II* (n. 1154).
[1181] *Havaş* (n. 1154).
[1182] *TEDAŞ* (n. 1154).
[1183] *İzmir Jeotermal* (n. 1154).
[1184] *MTS* (n. 1154).
[1185] *Tüpraş II* (n. 1154).
[1186] *HP* (8 May 2001, 01-22/192-50).
[1187] *Cement* (1 February 2002, 02-06/51-24). Reviewed after the cancellation decision of the Council of State (24 March 2006, 06-29/354-86).
[1188] *Bedir Nakliyat* (12 March 2014, 14-10/191-81).
[1189] *Mars* (23 June 2016, 16-21/371-173).
[1190] *Ulusal Cad* (9 May 2012, 12-25/729-209).
[1191] *Biletix* (1 March 2007, 07-18/164-54); *Darfilm* (4 December 2008, 08-69/1123-439); *Tüpraş I* (n. 1136); *İzocam* (8 February 2010, 10-14/175-66).
[1192] *Sahibinden II* (n. 1140)

its dominant position by way of charging excessive prices. The Board stated that there is no natural or legal barrier to entry but decided that network effects may constitute significant barriers to entry into the market. Nevertheless, as one of the members of the Board's dissenting opinion emphasises, there were recent entries into the market. The decision was annulled by the 6th Administrative Court of Ankara on the ground that, among others, the possible effect of the entrance of the global players into the market was not analysed by the Board.[1193] The Court acknowledged that (i) in order to consider excessive pricing as an abuse of dominant position, there must exist high and permanent barriers to entry into the market, which lead to a monopoly or a near-monopolistic situation, or the existing monopoly or a near-monopolistic situation must have arisen from exclusive or special rights maintained in the current situation or the past; and (ii) even in this case, any intervention under competition law must be called for only if it is impossible for the competition authorities or other relevant authorities to eliminate the entry barriers.[1194] The Court decides that the Board's finding that the market would not correct itself in the short or midterm because competitive pressure is unlikely due to the entry barriers does not rely on concrete evidence and analysis; hence, it can be considered a mere observation or assumption.[1195]

8.3.1.2 Being Subject to or Complying With the Regulation

In *Belko*, the Board condemns the pricing strategy as abusive and emphasises that there is no legislation applicable in the market to the pricing strategy of undertakings.[1196] In some other decisions, the Board dismisses allegations solely on the ground that the sector is regulated.[1197] In *BOTAŞ-EGO-İZGAZ-İGDAŞ*, the Board states that it may only interfere with the prices of undertaking that are free to determine their prices and does not condemn the profit margin of 67–77%. In this case, it was the relevant Ministry that regulated the maximum and minimum price for natural gas as opposed to the undertakings.[1198] In *İzmir Jeotermal*, the Board notes that the domestic geothermal heating market where the undertaking is active is a natural monopoly and that the market is not subject to regulation, hence open to the risk of excessive pricing. It then decides to send an opinion to the relevant authorities advising a price regulation for the domestic geothermic heating market.[1199]

Nevertheless, there are decisions where the Board makes an excessive pricing analysis in regulated sectors, too.[1200] The question is whether the Board should intervene when there is already a regulation applying to the market, but it is not effective in curbing the anti-competitive behaviour.

[1193] 6th Administrative Court of Ankara (18 December 2019, E. 2019/246, K. 2019/2625). The annulment decision was upheld by the 8th Administrative Chamber of the Ankara Regional Administrative Court (20 January 2021, E. 2020/699, K. 2021/68).

[1194] 6th Administrative Court of Ankara (18 December 2019, E. 2019/246, K. 2019/2625), p. 4.

[1195] Ibid., p. 6.

[1196] *Belko* (n. 1133), p. 29. Reviewed after the cancellation decision of the Council of State (8 July 2009, 09-32/703-161).

[1197] *BOTAŞ-EGO-İZGAZ-İGDAŞ* (n. 1134), p. 33; *Amity Oil & Trakya Gazdas* (29 June 2006, 06-46/601-172) (stating that Energy Market Regulatory Authority regulates the prices); *Turk Telekom* (20 June 2007, 07-53/571-187); *Roche* (30 October 2008, 08-61/996-388).

[1198] *BOTAŞ-EGO-İZGAZ-İGDAŞ* (n. 1134), pp. 6, 26.

[1199] *İzmir Jeotermal* (n. 1154), p. 21.

[1200] *Ataköy Marina* (24 April 2008, 08-30/373-123); *ASKİ II* (n. 1154).

In *ASKİ II*, the Board argued that the price regulation in the market for the supply of mains water fell short of preventing excessive prices. However, it decided not to open an investigation and merely issued an opinion stating that ASKİ should reduce its prices and base its price calculations on its costs.[1201] It is argued that the Board's approach here was inconsistent with its approach in *Belko*, as the Board should have initiated an investigation as ASKİ had failed to comply with its obligations under the applicable regulation.[1202]

In *Bereket Jeotermal I*, the Board decided to monitor the pricing behaviour of the undertaking for five years.[1203] However, the Board ceased monitoring the pricing behaviour one year after the relevant decision, when the sector was brought under regulation.[1204] In *Haydarpaşa/Erenköy/Halkalı Gümrük Sahası Taşıyıcıları*, the Board decided that the price was not excessive since prices applied complied with the tariff imposed by the Istanbul Union of Chamber of Merchants and Craftsmen.[1205]

Therefore, it is fair to say that the Board refrains from making a direct intervention on the price in markets where there already exists a regulatory intervention, even if it determines that the pricing strategy may have an exploitative effect. Also, complying with the regulation seems to provide a shield from competition law intervention.

8.3.1.3 The Test Applied to Decide Whether the Price Is Excessive

According to the Board, the main test applied to decide whether the price is abusive is the EVT established by the CJEC in *United Brands v. Commission*, and other tests are drawn upon the framework provided under the EVT.[1206] The Board's interpretation of *United Brands v. Commission* is that the EVT is a two-stage test. The EVT first compares the price and the cost of the product or service. With this comparison, the EVT reveals the profit margin. Then, the question that needs to be answered is whether the profit exceeds a reasonable margin. In the second stage, the EVT compares the relevant price and costs with (i) the prices and costs of the rivals that are active in the same relevant product market and (ii) the prices that the dominant firm applied at different points of time, in different geographical markets and/or to different customer groups. This second stage of the analysis is conducted to eliminate the problems stemming from the difficulty of determining the cost or economic-value-related factors. Hence, if the findings from the first stage are not sufficient to analyse the case due to the problems related to the first stage of the EVT, these will be further assessed by taking into account the findings obtained in the second stage.[1207]

Having put forward the roles of these two stages in the analysis, the Board notes that although it applies a two-stage analysis, unlike the approach of the CJEU, it prefers the second stage–the comparison of the prices–over the first stage and that it conducts a cost-price analysis only if the costs can be easily detected.[1208] Accordingly, it finds a

---

[1201] *ASKİ II* (n. 1154)
[1202] Ünal (n. 1130), p. 149.
[1203] *Bereket Jeotermal* (n. 1154).
[1204] *Bereket Jeotermal II* (16 December 2009, 09-59/1452-383).
[1205] *Haydarpaşa/Erenköy/Halkalı Gümrük Sahası Taşıyıcıları* (26 April 2001, 01-21/191-49).
[1206] *Sahibinden II* (n. 1140), p. 12; *Soda* (n. 1139), p. 15; *Fuel Oil* (n. 1144), p. 12.
[1207] *Sahibinden II* (n. 1140), p. 13; *Soda* (n. 1139), pp.15–16; *Fuel Oil* (n. 1144), pp. 12–13.
[1208] *Kırtur* (n. 1151), p. 17; *Fuel Oil* (n. 1144), p. 14; *Congresium Ato* (27 October 2016, 16-35/604-269), p. 38.

mere price comparison sufficient for condemning excessive prices when the cost cannot be clearly understood or allocated.[1209]

In *United Brands v. Commission*, the CJEC sets out the cost-price comparison as one of the ways to decide whether the price is excessive.[1210] Nevertheless, the CJEU annuls the Commission's decision on the same case as the Commission did not make any analysis of the cost and price comparison of the bananas.[1211] It is true that the CJEU acknowledges that the data about the cost may not be available in some cases. This was the case, for example, in *Deutsche Post*, where the issue was whether the undertaking's fee charged for the transmission for cross-border mail,[1212] and in *AKKA/LAA*, where the Latvian Competition Council discussed whether a society for collecting copyright fees charged excessive prices for musical work performances.[1213] Nevertheless, AG Wahl in *AKKA/LAA* states that when the price-cost analysis is impossible or not feasible, the competition authorities should consider other factors such as whether (i) there are entry or expansion barriers into the market; (ii) the market is subject to sectoral regulation; or (iii) there is countervailing buyer power in the market to supplement their analysis.[1214] Further to AG Wahl's opinion in *AKKA/LAA*, the Board's approach is criticised. Some has argued that it should not be sufficient for the Board to conduct an analysis merely based on price comparisons and that, in cases where analysing the costs is not feasible, the Board should take into account other factors that may support the conclusion that prices are excessive as provided in AG Wahl's opinion.[1215]

The Board's landmark decision *Belko* is illustrative of the Board's approach on this front.[1216] In *Belko*, the Board analysed whether the legal monopolist on the sale of coal in Ankara (the capital of Turkey) applied excessive prices. In the decision, the Board stated that it would first compare the prices applied in other geographic markets that are open to competition because comparison between price and cost should only be made when the cost can easily be determined. The Board then made a comprehensive analysis of the costs and considered all accounting-based costs of the firm, including financing costs. As a result of its analysis, the Board found that Belko's costs were higher than those of its competitors. Nevertheless, because Belko's prices were higher than that of the undertakings providing equivalent products in other geographic markets, the Board imposed a fine.[1217]

Also, in *Tüpraş II*, the Board held that price-cost analysis of the refinery sale prices of unleaded fuel and diesel would not provide meaningful results. It then ran analyses based on the comparison between Tüpraş's refinery sale prices with that of Platts Italy CIF Med

---

[1209]   *Kırtur* (n. 1151), p. 17; *Sahibinden II* (n. 1140), p. 14.

[1210]   The ECJ used the phrase "inter alia" when introducing the price-cost comparison stage. See *United Brands v. Commission* (n. 1162), para. 251. For a similar interpretation of the case, see Whish and Bailey (n. 1160), ch. 18.

[1211]   *United Brands v. Commission* (n. 1162).

[1212]   *Deutsche Post AG – Interception of cross-border mail* (Case COMP/C-1/36.91) Commission Decision 2001/892/EC [2001] OJ L 331/40.

[1213]   *AKKA/LAA* (n. 1168).

[1214]   AG Wahl's Opinion in Case C-177/16, EU:C:2017:286, paras. 43–45.

[1215]   See E. Şahin, "Avrupa Birliği Adalet Divanı'nın AKKA/LAA Kararı Kapsamında Aşırı Fiyatlama Analizi ve Türk Hukuku Bakımından Çıkarımlar" (Within the scope of ECJ's AKKA/LAA decision, Lessons for the Analysis of Excessive Pricing and Turkish Competition Law), *Uygulamalı Rekabet Hukuku Seminerleri*, 2018.

[1216]   See *Congresium Ato* (n. 1208), p. 38 (analysing *Belko* (n. 1133)).

[1217]   *Belko* (n. 1133), pp. 53–54, 60.

and found that Tüpraş's prices were 14.5% higher for the sale of unleaded fuel and 15% higher for the sale of diesel. It also compared the domestic retail prices and export prices of Tüpraş and found around 20–30% price difference for unleaded fuel and approximately 20% for diesel. Based on this comparison, the Board decided that the prices were abusive.[1218]

Similar to its holding in *Belko*, in Congresium *Ato*[1219], the Board noted that it is hard to distribute different costs, and it compared the prices of the undertaking with those of competitors. Following this comparison, it decided that prices were not excessive, although the Board emphasised the fact that the undertaking was making loss from its activities of hiring out facilities and grounds for trade fairs would not have precluded a finding of excessive prices, in accordance with *Belko*.[1220]

Likewise, in *BOTAŞ-EGO-İZGAZ-İGDAŞ*,[1221] the Board compared the profit ratios of the legal monopoly providing natural gas with its peers in the EU and decided that even the 67–77% profit ratio cannot be regarded as abusive since it is below the profit ratios of the undertakings that are active in the same market in the EU. Also, in *Microsoft I*, the Board decided that the price is not excessive since the product sold for USD 90 in Turkey is sold above USD 150 in the US and EU.[1222]

The *Mesam*[1223] decision is illustrative of the difficulties in applying a price-cost analysis to decide whether the price is excessive. In *Mesam*, the Board held that it was not possible to analyse the costs in order to decide whether the royalties requested for the use of copyright of musical products is excessive since the idea and creativity behind the product are non-quantifiable. According to the Board, it could make a proper analysis solely based on comparing prices with those applied in other countries, but there was no suitable country with the same economic and social conditions as Turkey.[1224] This approach is also adopted in *MTS*, as well.[1225]

Nevertheless, there are decisions where the Board gave more weight to the price-cost analysis. In *TEDAŞ*, the Board analysed the price increase in the provision of electricity by conducting a price-cost analysis. The Board took into account all accounting-based costs and the inflation rate. It also compared the prices with the price of electricity in other OECD countries.[1226]

The *Havaş* decision is noteworthy because of the range of factors that the Board considers in finding an abuse. The Board analysed Havaş's prices for providing bus transportation to passengers from the airports to the city centre in Ankara. It first noted that Havaş is not facing any competitive pressure from potential competitors since the law prevents any entry into the market where Havaş is the only active player. It then analysed that

---

[1218]   *Tüpraş II* (n. 1154), p. 21.
[1219]   *Congresium Ato* (n. 1208).
[1220]   Ibid., p. 40.
[1221]   *BOTAŞ-EGO-İZGAZ-İGDAŞ* (n. 1134), p. 31.
[1222]   *Microsoft I* (n. 1125).
[1223]   *Mesam* (n. 1124).
[1224]   Ibid. For a similar approach see *MTS* (n. 1154).
[1225]   *MTS* (n. 1154).
[1226]   *TEDAŞ* (n. 1154).

Havaş's prices are higher than the prices charged for urban transportation. Also, it compared the profit margin of airline transportation that provides a service with higher economic value for passengers with that of Havaş and found that Havaş's profit margin is much higher. Based on this finding, the Board concluded that the price is excessive as it does not have any reasonable relation with the economic value of the product.[1227]

In light of the cases above, the Board's approach is that the comparison of prices prevails over the cost-price analysis and the Board condemns excessive pricing caused by cost inefficiency even if it does not result in excessive profits.[1228]

Hence, the Board gives more weight to the findings derived from the price comparison as opposed to analysis of the cost/price ratio. On this note, the Board is seen as deviating from the opinion of AG Wahl in *AKKA/LAA* by making an analysis solely based on the second stage of the EVT test, without supporting it with an analysis of other factors when it is not proper to make a price-cost assessment.[1229]

As to the excessiveness of the price, in *Biletix*, the Board held that 11–18% profit margin is not excessive.[1230] Also, in *MTS*, the Board does not deem that an undertaking's prices that are 25% higher than its competitors to be excessive.[1231] On the other hand, the difference of 14.5% and 15% when compared with competitors' prices is found excessive in *Tüpraş II*.[1232] In *Belko*, where the price is found abusive, Belko had 50%–60% higher prices compared to other undertakings.[1233]

One can argue that the most controversial decision of the Board about excessive pricing is *Sahibinden II*, where it finds that an online service platform for real estate and vehicle sales (Sahibinden.com) abused its dominant position by way of charging excessive prices.[1234]

Before moving to this controversial decision, one should first mention the Board's holding in *Sahibinden I*, which concerns a preliminary investigation on the same undertakings' pricing strategy related to fees charged for corporate subscriptions to the platform. In the relevant decision, the Board stated that it could not conduct an analysis on the price-cost ratio or the economic value of the service because Sahibinden.com is not able to provide its costs for each of its services separately due to the existence of common costs that it incurs for those services.[1235] It then noted that high prices in dynamic sectors are indeed competitive as they (i) provide a return for initial investment; (ii) may attract new entries into the market; and (iii) enable other undertakings active in the market to reach potential customers by competitive prices, thereby eliminating the consequence of network externalities that exist in the market.[1236]

[1227] *Havaş* (n. 1154).
[1228] *Kırtur* (n. 1151), p. 17; *Viessmann* (15 May 2017, 17-16/223-93).
[1229] Şahin (n. 1215).
[1230] *Biletix* (n. 1191).
[1231] *MTS* (n. 1154).
[1232] *Tüpraş II* (n. 1154), p. 21.
[1233] *Belko* (n. 1133), p. 60.
[1234] *Sahibinden II* (n. 1140).
[1235] *Sahibinden I* (19 February 2015, 15-08/109-45).
[1236] Ibid.

The holding of the Board in *Sahibinden I* may be seen as a reflection of understanding of the peculiarities of dynamic markets. Indeed, the EVT does not provide a meaningful result in all sectors, particularly in dynamic sectors. That is because, in short, "in dynamic industries (i) fixed costs are high and marginal costs are low, (ii) the products and services exhibit network effects, (iii) rates of return are high but prolonged, (iv) competition is dynamic,"[1237] (v) there are common costs incurred for different services and (vi) the products of competitors are not comparable.[1238]

Nevertheless, in *Sahibinden II*, it is fair to assert that the Board changed its approach towards this dynamic sector. It stated that it would not conduct a price-cost analysis by considering that Sahibinden.com's business model does not allow the calculation of individual costs for each of its services. However, the Board also noted that the return on equity and net profit on sales are considered to provide insight into the price-cost margin of undertakings. Accordingly, it conducted an analysis by comparing (i) the return on equity and net profit on sales of Sahibinden.com with the prices of the undertakings providing platform services and (ii) Sahibinden.com's prices with its previous prices.[1239] Based on these comparisons, the Board concluded that the prices are abusive as the return on equity and net profit on sales of Sahibinden.com are noticeably higher than those of its competitors and that the prices are higher than what would have been observed in competitive markets. It further noted that (i) the price increase does not result in a decrease in Sahibinden.com's market share; (ii) it is not foreseen that there would be competitive pressure in the future; and (iii) the market does not seem to correct itself in the short or midterm due to barriers to entry stemming from network effects. To that effect, the Board ordered Sahibinden.com to cease its breach by limiting its price increases to a reasonable extent that can be justified by the increase in costs. Nevertheless, one of the Board members' dissenting opinion provides that (i) it was only the strategic business decisions of the undertaking that contributed to its current position, which enables it to charge higher prices than those of its competitors; (ii) higher prices do not necessarily lead to a decrease in consumer welfare; (iii) there were indeed recent new entries into the market from strong local and global players such as Facebook Marketplace and Letgo, which had already started exerting more competitive pressure.

The justification of the Board, as well as the Board's remedies, is highly criticised because in innovative sectors, undertakings innovate to decrease their costs, and ordering them to increase prices only to a reasonable extent that can be justified by the increase in costs entails the risk of chilling innovation.[1240]

Sahibinden II was subsequently annulled by the 6th Administrative Court of Ankara.[1241] In the annulment decision, the court emphasised that the Board should intervene in excessive

---

[1237] See G. Gürkaynak, M. Bakırcı, S. Mutafoğlu, "Excessive Pricing Enforcement in Dynamic Sectors: Should You Stop Reading Now?" *The Academic Gift Book of ELIG, Attorneys-at-Law in Honor of the 20th Anniversary of Competition Law Practice in Turkey*", 2018, pp. 143–175.

[1238] *Sahibinden I* (n. 1235); *Sahibinden II* (n. 1140), p. 12.

[1239] *Sahibinden II* (n. 1140), pp. 25–33.

[1240] E. Köksal and B. Ikiler, "Dünyada ve Türkiye'de Platformlara Yönelik Güncel Rekabet Politikaları: *ABD'de Amex, Türkiye'de Sahibinden ve AB'de Google Shopping Kararları*", in *Uygulamalı Rekabet Hukuku Seminerleri*, K. C. Sanlı and D. Alma, eds. (Isanbul, On İki Levha, 2019), pp. 477–492.

[1241] 6th Administrative Court of Ankara (18 December 2019, E. 2019/246, K. 2019/2625).

pricing only in exceptional cases. In line with this, the Board must prove beyond any doubt that there exist exceptional circumstances requiring intervention in the case at hand, based on the data and facts provided. The Court also held that the Board must clearly prove that the intervention would have positive consequences. In more detail, first, the court found that the Board compared Sahibinden.com's prices with the prices of platforms that offer services in different markets while not comparing the prices with those applied in other countries, in particular the countries where global players are active. Second, the court analysed the Board's arguments that (i) even though the market shares of competitors are close to the market share of Sahibinden.com, the latter will hold a dominant position in the market in the long run due to network effects and the cost of being active in more than one category of services, and (ii) the market will not self-correct in the short or midterm. It found that these arguments do not rely on concrete findings or facts about similar sectors; the Board failed to analyse (i) how operating in different categories of services would affect the costs and (ii) how the global players' entrance would affect the market in the future. Moreover, it decided that the Board's argument that Sahibinden.com uses the first-mover advantage and the advantage of using the domain name "sahibinden", meaning "from the owner" in Turkish, is ill-founded. The Court also underlined that the Board could not find the exact margin between the price and the cost but ordered Sahibinden.com to make price increases to a reasonable extent that can be justified by the increase in costs. Accordingly, the court found that the Board's order and findings were inconsistent, as conducting a cost analysis is not feasible for the relevant undertaking.

Another decision of the Board on the allegation of excessive pricing by an online platform is *Google Shopping Unit*. In the relevant decision, the Board stated that the EVT test and the excessive pricing doctrine cannot be applied to the relevant case because, first, Google's advertising cost is correlated with the number of clicks that the product received, so it is impossible to find the profit ratio and decide on the reasonable profit margin, and second, in the online advertising market, the price of a product may change even in two subsequent searches made within one second, because the price is determined based on instant auctions, so it is impossible to compare the prices of the product at different times or the prices of the product seen on different platforms. Also, the Board noted that the auction price is determined by e-commerce firms rather than the relevant undertaking since the latter only provides the auction through algorithms.[1242] Hence, the Board dismissed the allegation that the undertaking abused its dominant position by way of imposing excessive prices because it was not the relevant undertaking but the e-commerce firms determining the auction prices and it was impossible to calculate the advertising cost of the undertaking or to make a price comparison.

8.3.1.4 Remedies Devised
When Abuse Has Been Established

The arguments against intervention in excessive pricing are, to some extent, based on the difficulty of applying the right remedy when abuse is established. That is because competition authorities should refrain from behaving as price regulators in order not to distort the efficient

---

[1242]   *Google Shopping Unit* (n. 1139), pp. 44–45.

distribution of resources. This is the reason why the Board holds back from determining the competitive price level itself and merely states that the price should be reduced to the competitive level. In *Belko*, the Board (i) ordered the undertaking to reduce its prices to the competitive level but refrained from stating which level of price is competitive; (ii) decided to inform relevant authorities on how to preserve competition in the market.

Such remedies necessarily require a monitoring procedure. In *Bereket Jeotermal*, the Board decided to monitor the pricing behaviour of the undertaking for five years. However, it ceased monitoring after one year, once the sector became regulated.[1243]

In *İzmir Jeotermal*, where the undertaking was a natural monopoly but there was no price regulation in the market, the Board did not decide on any remedy to bring the competition infringement to an end. The Board merely decided to inform the regulatory authority based on its role in competition advocacy.[1244]

In *Sahibinden II*, the Board ordered Sahibinden.com to cease its breach and to make price increases for the provision of the online service platform for real estate and vehicle sales only to a reasonable extent that can be justified by the increase in costs.[1245] Nevertheless, as discussed in detail earlier, the 6th Administrative Court of Ankara found the remedy to be unlawful on the ground that the Board cannot order the undertaking to link its prices with its costs when conducting an analysis of the cost is not feasible.[1246]

8.3.2 Unfair and Exploitative Contract Terms

Abuse of dominance through imposing unfair and exploitative contract terms have been analysed by the Board only very rarely. In its analysis on the contract terms imposed by *İzmirgaz*–as the only provider of natural gas in the region–pursuant to applicable legislation, the Board states that the regulator should order İzmirgaz to cease its conduct.[1247] Similar to the EU, there are only a few decisions in which abuse of a dominant position by imposing unfair and exploitative contract terms has been assessed. As was the case in *İzmirgaz* and in keeping with the rules pertaining to the hierarchy of norms, when there is a law that specifically applies to the contract terms under scrutiny, the Board states that the specific law will prevail over Law No. 4054 since the latter is regarded as the general law.

Having said that, the recent investigation of the Board against Facebook and WhatsApp is noteworthy on this front, as it may show the Board's willingness to take a more active stance against the use of exploitative contract terms in digital markets, as opposed to its approach in traditional markets. Following WhatsApp's notification to its users about the change in its privacy policy providing that if the users would like

---

[1243] *Bereket Jeotermal* (n. 1154).
[1244] *İzmir Jeotermal* (n. 1154).
[1245] *Sahibinden* (n. 1140), p. 33.
[1246] 6th Administrative Court of Ankara (18 December 2019, E. 2019/246, K. 2019/2625).
[1247] *İzmirgaz* (8 January 2009, 09-01/2-2). See also *Çalık* (1 November 2012; 12-53/1491-519); *Carrefour SA* (10 November 2020, 10-71/1487-570).

to continue using WhatsApp, they need to give consent that their data can be shared with other Facebook companies, the Board initiated an *ex officio* investigation against Facebook Inc., Facebook Ireland Ltd., WhatsApp Inc., and WhatsApp LLC in order to determine whether there is a violation of Article 6 of Law No. 4054.[1248] The Board stated in its announcement about the investigation that this update in the privacy policy would enable Facebook to collect, process, and use more data.[1249] In its decision, the Board also imposes an interim measure requiring Facebook to cease the execution of the new privacy policy and notify the same to all of its users regardless of whether they gave the relevant consent or not.[1250] WhatsApp then informed the Authority that the updated policy would not be executed with respect to any users in Turkey regardless of whether they gave consent to the application of the new terms.[1251]

As to the theory of harm with respect to collecting "excessive" data, in its Preliminary Report on the Sector Inquiry on E-Marketplace Platforms, the Board states that data becomes the currency used in digital markets. Consumers' demand elasticity is lower in cases where they pay for the services with their data as opposed to money. Because demand elasticity is low, companies are then able to collect even more data. As a result of this, "excessive data collection" replaces "excessive pricing" as a way to exploit consumers in digital markets.[1252] In addition, privacy that may be harmed through excessive data collection and processing is considered to be a parameter of quality competition,[1253] which is of great importance in markets where "free" services are offered.[1254] In this regard, "quality" increases if consumers are more sensitive in the amount and content of the data they share and if they have more control over the sharing of their data.[1255]

The investigation is in line with Bundeskartellamt's Facebook investigation, as a result of which the Bundeskartellamt decided that Facebook abused its market power by providing its social networking services conditional on the users' agreement that it can collect data through tracking their activities even outside its website on the internet or on smartphone apps, and merge the relevant data in its subscribers' Facebook account, and handed down an interim decision requiring Facebook to stop executing the relevant terms. Also, all data collected through the websites owned by Facebook, including WhatsApp and Instagram, can be merged with the users' Facebook account. Bundeskartellamt focuses on the extent that Facebook collects, uses and merges data in a user's account, the fact that users are not aware

---

[1248] *WhatsApp Investigation* (11 January 2021, 21-02/25-M).
[1249] The Announcement of the Authority (11 January 2021) available on the Authority's website <https://www.rekabet.gov.tr/tr/Guncel/rekabet-kurulu-facebook-ve-whatsapp-hakk-14728ae4f653eb11812700505694b4c6> (last accessed on 8 June 2021).
[1250] *WhatsApp* (n. 1248).
[1251] The Announcement of the Authority (5 May 2021) available at the Authority's website <https://www.rekabet.gov.tr/tr/Guncel/facebook-whatsapp-sorusturmasi-hakkinda--7f1270260cbaeb11812e00505694b4c6> (last accessed on 28 May 2021).
[1252] M. Botta and K. Wiedemann, "Exploitative Conducts in Digital Markets: Time for a Discussion after the Facebook Decision", *Journal of European Competition Law & Practice*, Vol. 10, Issue 8, 2019, p. 466 (cited in Preliminary Report on the Sector Inquiry on E-Marketplace Platforms p. 310).
[1253] M. C. Buiten, "Exploitative Abuses in Digital Markets: Between Competition Law and Data Protection Law", *Journal of Antitrust Enforcement*, Vol. 9, Issue 2, 2021, pp. 270–288, p. 284 (cited in Preliminary Report on the Sector Inquiry on E-Marketplace Platforms pp. 310–311).
[1254] Preliminary Report on the Sector Inquiry on E-Marketplace Platforms, p. 340.
[1255] Ibid., p. 312.

of this collection and that such a collection violates the data protection laws of Germany.[1256] The Düsseldorf Court of Appeal annulled the interim decision by stating that (i) the terms imposed by Facebook are also applied by other companies, hence their application cannot be attributed to Facebook's dominant position; (ii) the terms were not exploitative as users gave consent to them; and (iii) the violation of data protection laws is irrelevant to the case at hand.[1257] However, the Federal Supreme Court upheld the Bundeskartellamt's interim decision, finding that Facebook's conduct makes it more difficult for its rivals to compete for advertisements and decreases the choice of users given that they have to pay more (i.e., by allowing the collection of more of their data) for a service that they do not want in its entirety (i.e., since Facebook offers only a package service including these terms).[1258] Finally, on 24 March 2021, the Düsseldorf Court of Appeal decided to refer the case to the CJEU.[1259]

8.4 Discriminative Practices

Article 6(2)(b) of Law No. 4054 prohibits "making direct or indirect discrimination between purchasers with equal status by offering different terms for the same and equal rights, obligations and acts". Discriminatory practices are analysed as unilateral conducts under competition law, and may be considered abusive when certain conditions are met. Since undertakings, even if they hold a dominant position in the market, have the freedom to contract, their conducts may be prohibited under competition law only in exceptional circumstances.[1260]

Undertakings may engage in discrimination based not only on unilateral decisions but also by way of concerted practice or entering into agreements. If two or more undertakings agree on putting another player who has a commercial relationship with them at a competitive disadvantage, this conduct may be considered under the scope of Article 4 as opposed to Article 6 of Law No. 4054. By way of an example, in *Ecza Depoları*,[1261] the Board condemns the agreement of pharmaceutical warehouses on ceasing their forward sales to a pharmacy with the aim to make its operations more difficult, as an infringement of Article 4 of Law No. 4054.[1262]

The important point here is where to draw the line between discriminatory unilateral practices and agreements. For example, the following two cases are subject to different analyses. The first is the case that the supplier imposes different prices/trading conditions on its customers, and the second is the case that two or more undertakings (suppliers, or suppliers and their distributors) agree on putting a third-party undertaking, with whom the parties to

---

[1256] Bundeskartellamt's decision of 6 February 2019, No. B6-22/16; the Announcement of the Bundeskartellamt (7 February 2019) available on the Bundeskartellamt's website <https://www.bundeskartellamt.de/SharedDocs/Meldung/EN/Pressemitteilungen/2019/07_02_2019_Facebook.html> (last accessed on June 8, 2021).

[1257] The Düsseldorf Court of Appeal's (Oberlandesgericht Düsseldorf) decision of 26 August 2019, Case VI-Kart 1/19.

[1258] The German Federal Supreme Court's (Bundesgerichtshof) decision of 23 June 2020, Case KVR 69/19.

[1259] The Düsseldorf Court of Appeal's (Oberlandesgericht Düsseldorf) decision of 24 March 2021, Case Kart 9/2021.

[1260] C. Bellamy and G. Child *European Community Law of Competition* (5th edition, London: Sweet & Maxwell, 2001), pp. 716–720.

[1261] *Ecza Depoları* (9 March 2006, 06-18/212-53).

[1262] In this decision, the Board also analysed whether there were any objective justifications for such conduct in the specific case.

the agreement have a commercial relationship, at a competitive disadvantage. While the latter may be categorised as an agreement, the former should be analysed as a unilateral practice.[1263] As a result, the former may only be condemned if the supplier holds a dominant position and other conditions are met. That is because, otherwise, the freedom to contract may be unduly limited, and the customers who are not given a discount may bring frequent claims that the supplier engages in discriminatory practice under competition law.[1264] The Board's decisions are also in line with this view: the Board considers that applying different conditions to one's distributors cannot be analysed under Article 4 of Law No. 4054 since the relevant article only applies to those situations where there is an agreement between the supplier and its distributor(s) to apply different conditions to another distributor.[1265]

The Board categorised discriminatory practices under two different groups: discriminatory conduct leading to "primary line" injury and discriminatory conduct leading to "secondary line" injury.[1266] If an undertaking engages in discrimination that may have an impact only on its competitors (including potential rivals), it is considered as a primary line injury. On the other hand, if the discriminatory conduct of a dominant undertaking has an impact on competition among its customers, then its conduct is classified as a secondary line injury.

The discriminatory behaviour may be conducted through offering either different prices or transaction terms.[1267] Price discrimination is defined as the sale or purchase of different units of a good or service at prices that cannot be explained by the differences in the costs of providing them. This would be the case when, despite having reasons for differentiation of the prices due to different costs of supplying the products/services, the supplier refrains from making such differentiation. It may also be the case when there is no reason behind applying different prices to equal customers.[1268]

8.5 Concept of Discrimination and Theories of Harm

Just as the case for exploitative abuses, whether competition authorities should intervene in discriminatory behaviour is also under debate. The first argument against intervention focuses on the practical difficulty in determining whether the purchasers are indeed in equal status, or if they are not in an equal status, whether and to what extent differentiation of prices is justifiable to different purchasers.[1269]

[1263] G. Gürkaynak and K. Yıldırım, "Türk Rekabet Hukukunda Ayrımcı Uygulamaların Niteliğine ve Tabi Oldukları Hükümlere İlişkin Bir Değerlendirme", *Rekabet Forumu*, Issue 33, 2007, pp. 2–7, pp. 3–6.

[1264] Ibid., pp. 6–7.

[1265] *Brisa* (24 July 2020; 20-35/455-202), p. 12; *DSM* (20 February 2020, 20-11/127-73); *Baymak* (6 September 2018, 18-30/523-259); *Akbank* (12 February 2014, 14-06/116-55); *Timken* (10 October 2000, 00-38/419-235).

[1266] *DHMİ* (9 September 2015, 15-36/559-182); *Roche II* (n. 1197); *Ceramic Adhesives Producers* (12 January 2011, 11-03/42-14); *Doğan Yayın* (n. 817); *Kale Kilit* (6 December 2012, 12-62/1633-598).

[1267] *DHMİ* (n. 1266).

[1268] *Congresium* (27 August 2020, 20-39/538-239). Also see Ü. Görgülü, *Hakim Durumun Kötüye Kullanılması Kapsamında Fiyat Ayrımcılığı Uygulamaları* (Ankara: Rekabet Kurumu, 2003).

[1269] Whish and Bailey (n. 1160), ch. 18.

Second, in most cases, whether the overall effects of discriminatory practices are harmful or beneficial for competition is often controversial. It is true that discriminatory practices may cause anti-competitive effects by harming the operations of customers and competitors and hindering entry into the market. For example, if an undertaking operates in two product markets, it may charge higher prices in markets where the demand elasticity is low. Doing so may increase its profits to a level even above the monopoly price in the market where the demand elasticity is higher.[1270] This may strengthen its market power, may put its competitors in a disadvantaged position and may prevent new entries into the market.[1271]

Nevertheless, such behaviours may have positive effects on the quantity of supply, distribution of wealth, total welfare and small entities.[1272] The most important example of discriminatory practices is price discrimination, which is very often seen as a way to increase economic welfare.[1273] Public entities and regulated monopolies apply discriminatory prices as a method to provide redistribution of wealth among consumers.[1274] Also, price discrimination enables new consumers to purchase products that they could not afford in the absence of price differentiation. To provide its products to the new consumers, the undertaking increases its output, which enables it to reach economies of scale.[1275] As to the effect of the rule on discrimination on small entities, it is argued that the provision on discriminatory practices, along with other prohibitions provided under Article 6 of Law No. 4054, aims to protect small entities since their existence is necessary to provide effective competition in any market.[1276]

The pro-competitive effects of price discrimination are also acknowledged by the Board in *Roche II*.[1277] Accordingly, the Board notes the effect of discrimination on enhancing total welfare by increasing the total output. The Board further explains that, if the suppliers are prevented from discriminating against purchasers without providing any exception, this may lead to coordination among purchasers in the downstream market.[1278]

The Board emphasises that the undertaking holding a dominant position in the market would not have any incentive to put one or some of its purchasers in an advantaged position among others if it is not vertically integrated.[1279] The existence of effective competition in the downstream market is in favour of the dominant supplier. If some of the undertakings active in the downstream market exit the market due to discriminatory

---

[1270]   Görgülü (n. 1268), ch. 1.3.

[1271]   Ibid.

[1272]   A. Kaya, *Türk Rekabet Hukukunda Ayrımcılık Suretiyle Hakim Durumun Kötüye Kullanılması*, (Istanbul: On İki Levha, 2018).

[1273]   Görgülü (n. 1268), ch. 1.3.

[1274]   Ibid.

[1275]   E. Deliktaş, "Monopol Piyasası ve Fiyat Farklılaştırması-Erzurum Büyükşehir Belediyesi Su Fiyatlaması Üzerine Bir Uygulama", T.C. Yükseköğretim Kurulu Dökümantasyon Merkezi, Doktora Tezi, Erzurum, 1997, p. 28.

[1276]   K. C. Sanlı (n. 1), pp. 11–12.

[1277]   *Roche II* (n. 1197).

[1278]   D. Geradin and N. Petit, "Price Discrimination under EC Competition Law: The Need for a case-by-case Approach", *The Global Competition Law Centre Working Papers Series* No. 07/05, 2005 cited *Roche II* (n. 1197).

[1279]   *Congresium* (n. 1268); *Roche II* (n. 1197). Also see Ç. Tunçel, "Avrupa Rekabet Hukukunda İkincil Seviye Fiyat Ayrımcılığı – Etki Temelli Perspektiften Değerlendirme", *Rekabet Dergisi*, Vol. 15, No. 3, July 2014, pp. 50–51, p. 63.

behaviour, the downstream market will be more concentrated, decreasing the possibility of effective distribution and promotion of its products in the downstream market. This may indeed increase the counter-veiling buyer power, which would not be preferable. According to the Board, this explains why the EU authorities refrain from intervening in discriminatory practices leading to secondary line injury.[1280]

Undertakings mainly engage in practices leading to secondary line injury in two cases. First, state-owned undertakings discriminate against foreign companies in favour of domestic companies, and second, firms engage in these practices to complement another practice leading to primarily line injury.[1281] Hence, it is mostly the case that these practices are not solely related to a secondary line injury.[1282]

Indeed, in case the undertaking is vertically integrated, it may have the incentive to prevent effective competition in the downstream market through discriminatory practices as a way to leverage its power in the upstream market to the downstream market. Even in this case, the Board underlines that it is not necessary to apply a per se prohibition. Rather, the anti-competitive effects should be considered on a case-by-case basis.[1283]

Discriminatory prices may be exploitative, for example, when they are applied to lock in customers that are not able to switch to other suppliers.[1284] However, the theory of harm in discrimination cases does not need to be purely based on the exploitative effect. Rather, in light of the aforementioned explanations, the exclusionary effect of the conduct is frequently considered as a factor to decide whether the conduct was discriminatory, and so, abusive.[1285] Accordingly, in line with the decisional practice in the EU,[1286] the Board analyses whether the discriminatory practices result in exclusionary effects on the market in order to decide whether the conduct is abusive.[1287]

8.6 Examples

In its decisions where the allegation of discriminatory behaviour is analysed, the Board first considers whether the customers are in equal status.[1288] For this, the customers' purchase quantities, as well as their market power, are taken into account.[1289] In some

---

[1280] *Congresium* (n. 1268); *Roche II* (n. 1197). Also see ECJ, Case C-18/93 *Corsica Ferries Italia Srl v. Corpo dei Piloti del Porto di Genova* [1994] ECR I-1783; *Portuguese Airports* (Case No IV/35.703) Commission Decision 1999/199/EC [1999], OJ L 69/31.

[1281] R. O'Donoghue and A. J. Padilla, *The Law and Economics of Article 82 EC* (Oxford: Hart Publishing, 2006), pp. 573–574, cited in *Congresium* (n. 1268).

[1282] Tunçel (n. 1279), pp. 61–62.

[1283] *Roche II* (n. 1197).

[1284] Whish and Bailey (n. 1160), ch. 18.

[1285] Kaya (n. 1272).

[1286] R. Whish and B. E. Sufrin, *Competition Law* (3rd edition, London: Butterworths, 1993).

[1287] Kaya (n. 1272); also see *Roche II* (n. 1197).

[1288] *Alcon* (5 March 2015; 15-10/139-62); *Siemens II* (n. 1129); *Türk Telekomünikasyon* (24 September 2014; 14-35/697-309); *Draeger* (19 December 2013, 13-71/971-417); *Siemens I* (25 April 2012, 12-22/572-166).

[1289] *Siemens III* (19 November 2020, 20-50/695-306).

decisions, the Board states that the undertakings that are subject to discriminatory behaviour must be the competitors of the undertaking under scrutiny.[1290]

Since Article 6 of Law No. 4054 defines discriminatory behaviour as offering different terms for equal rights, obligations and acts, the Board takes into account promotional campaigns, payment conditions of the buyer, any extra cost that the buyer bears and commercial justifications for the behaviour, in addition to the price.[1291]

With regard to the price discrimination, the Board states that for finding of abuse, the undertaking must offer different terms to purchasers for equal rights, obligations and acts, and the purchasers must be equal. Hence, according to the Board, these are cumulative conditions.[1292]

8.6.1 Practices Leading to Primary Line Injury

According to the Board's definition, if an undertaking engages in discrimination (e.g., by applying different prices to its customers) that may have an impact only on its competitors (including potential rivals), such conduct is considered as a primary line injury.[1293] In other words, practices leading to primary line injury are those made in the markets where the dominant undertaking or its affiliated undertakings are active.[1294] In these cases, the dominant undertakings may increase the costs of its customers that compete with it in the downstream market, in order to force these customers to exit the market.[1295] Hence, the primary line injury refers to the exclusionary effect of the practice,[1296] and practices leading to primary line injury are usually found anti-competitive because of their exclusionary effect.[1297]

When the undertaking engaging in discriminatory practices is vertically integrated, the allegation may come up in relation to the refusal to supply. In *Eti Holding*, the Board analysed Eti Holding A.Ş.'s refusal to supply concentrated colemanite to Ceytaş Madencilik Tekstil San. ve Tic. A.Ş. for the latter's production of granular colemanite. Eti Holding A.Ş. holds a legal monopoly in the exploration, concentration and refinement of boron, as well as producing and marketing of end products made from it. First, the Board stated that there are two cases in which an undertaking must provide access to its input: (i) the purchaser must be a repeat customer or (ii) the input must be indispensable for the purchaser to conduct its activities. The Board stated that the market in which Eti Holding A.Ş. has a legal monopoly encompasses the production of granular colemanite, and Eti Holding A.Ş. does not have to provide its direct competitor with the input for its production even if there is no other undertaking from which Ceytaş Madencilik Tekstil San. ve Tic. A.Ş. can purchase the concentrated colemanite. Another issue the Board considered was that Eti Holding A.Ş. was

---

[1290]   *Google Shopping Unit* (n. 1139), p. 43; *Roche II* (n. 1197); *Cine 5* (11 October 1999, 99-46/500-316).

[1291]   *Siemens III* (n. 1289).

[1292]   Ibid.

[1293]   *Roche II* (n. 1197); *Ceramic Adhesives Producers* (n. 1266); *Doğan Holding* (n. 1266); *Kale Kilit* (n. 1266).

[1294]   *DHMİ* (n. 1266).

[1295]   *Congresium* (n. 1268).

[1296]   *Roche II* (n. 1197); *Ceramic Adhesives Producers* (n, 1266); *Doğan Holding* (n. 1266); *Kale Kilit* (n. 1266).

[1297]   *Congresium* (n. 1268).

supplying raw boron materials to its customers abroad so that they could produce granular boron. The Board decided that refusal to supply to Turkish customers is not discriminatory under Article 6 of Law No. 4054 since customers abroad and in Turkey were not equal. Interestingly, the Board stated that in order to decide whether the customers are equal, it should be analysed whether the customers are substitutable, not from the perspective of the supplier but from the customers' own perspective. The Board concluded that in this case, the customers abroad and in Turkey could not easily switch their roles.[1298]

The application of rebate systems may also sometimes be considered as discriminatory practice since rebates often might result in a situation where the customers are held to be exposed to different conditions. In its analysis of rebate systems, the Board refers to the CJEC's decisional practice.[1299] Accordingly, the Board notes that there is a separation between (i) the rebates applied to all customers and offered with equal and objective conditions and (ii) the rebates inducing loyalty.[1300] As the Board cites,[1301] the first decision that the CJEU made this separation is *Suiker Unie v. Commission*, where the condemned rebates were applied only if the customer made all of its purchase during the entire year from one undertaking. If the undertaking made any purchase from a competitor, it would not be eligible for a discount.[1302] The Board also cites the two main reasons that the CJEU put forward in *Hoffmann-La Roche v. Commission* regarding the different treatment of these two types of practices.[1303] The CJEU stated that, first, the loyalty inducing rebates may distort competition in favour of the dominant undertaking in the market for the sale of its products; second, they may also distort the competition among customers by putting some of them at a competitive disadvantage as a result of applying different conditions to equal transactions and customers.[1304]

8.6.2 Practices Leading to Secondary Line Injury

If the discriminatory conduct of a dominant undertaking (e.g., applying different prices to its customers) has an impact on the competition among its customers (i.e., undertakings having a vertical relationship with the dominant undertaking), then its conduct is classified as a secondary line injury.[1305] Hence, practices leading to secondary line injury occur in markets where the undertaking itself is not active,[1306] and they are imposed upon customers that do not compete with the dominant undertaking.[1307] According to the Board, Article 6 of Law No. 4054 refers to the secondary line injury.[1308]

[1298] *Eti Holding* (21 December 2000, 00-50/533-295).
[1299] *İzocam* (n. 1191).
[1300] Ibid.
[1301] Ibid.
[1302] Joined Cases 40 to 48, 50, 54 to 56, 111, 113 and 114-73 *Coöperatieve Vereniging "Suiker Unie" UA and others v. Commission of the European Communities* [1975] ECR 1663.
[1303] *İzocam* (n. 1191).
[1304] Case 85/76 *Hoffmann-La Roche & Co. AG v. Commission* [1979] ECR 461.
[1305] *Roche II* (n. 1197); *Ceramic Adhesives Producers* (n. 1266); *Doğan Holding* (n. 1266); *Kale Kilit* (n. 1266).
[1306] *DHMİ* (n. 1266).
[1307] *Congresium* (n. 1268).
[1308] *Roche II* (n. 1197).

Unlike Article 102(2)(c) TFEU, putting a customer at a competitive disadvantage is not a prerequisite for condemning the behaviour under Article 6 of Law No. 4054. However, there are cases where the Board requires this condition and not condemns offering different prices to equal customers, e.g., in *DHMI*. In this case, the Board pointed out that no customer had been put in a competitively disadvantaged position due to discrimination in rents charged, as the rent payments of the customers subject to heavier payment requirements constitute only a small portion of their overall cost, any differences in rent payment conditions would not have considerably disadvantaged the competitor .[1309]

Hence, in *Congresium*[1310], the Board summarised its case law by stating that in order to consider practices leading to secondary line injury as abuse of dominance, (i) the customers, transactions and obligations must be equal; (ii) the practice must cause a competitive disadvantage; and (iii) there must be no objective justification for the conduct.[1311]

Although annulled by the Council of State based on public interest grounds,[1312] the *Cine 5* decision of the Board is still of importance with respect to demonstrating the Board's approach to discrimination. In *Cine 5*, the analysis is purely based on the allegation of discrimination.[1313] In the decision, the Board assessed whether Cine 5, holding the exclusive right to broadcast football matches in Turkey's 1st Professional Football League, discriminates against some of its customers by imposing different commercial conditions in their agreements regarding the licence to broadcast these football matches in three minutes, for reporting purposes. The Board stated that in free-market economies, it is normal and sometimes inevitable that prices applied in the market differ based on supply and demand. The same product may be sold at different prices due to various factors. Hence, the Board noted that not all price differences are discriminatory. For example, perishable foods are sometimes sold at lower prices so that they would not expire before the sale. Also, excess stock and technological changes may lead to price differentiation.

The Board then set forth the criteria that need to be satisfied to consider price discrimination to be in breach of competition law: (i) the undertakings that are subject to discrimination must be competitors of each other; (ii) the practice must put one of the customers at a competitive disadvantage in favour of the other customer; and (iii) the commercial transactions must be equal.[1314]

In the assessment of whether the commercial transactions are equal, the following factors should be taken into account:[1315]

- The characteristics of the product subject to the commercial transaction: the type, quality, cost, etc., of the product;

[1309]   *DHMİ* (n. 1266).

[1310]   *Congresium* (n. 1268)

[1311]   Ibid. For a case where the Board finds that there was an objective justification see *MEDAŞ* (16 January 2020, 20-04/41-23).

[1312]   The 10th Chamber of the Council of State (4 November 2003, E. 2001/355, K. 2003/4245).

[1313]   *Cine 5* (n. 1290).

[1314]   Ibid.

[1315]   Ibid.

 – The circumstances under which the commercial transaction is made: only the conditions about how the customer approached the undertaking, for example, the delivery time and place, the type of payment (in advance or by instalments) and purchasing volume (amount).

In light of the foregoing and considering the relevant factors, the Board found that Cine 5's pricing strategy was not objectively determined.

Cine 5 argued that they divide their customers into different categories based on objective criteria–for example, whether the broadcasting channel is national or regional and if it is a national channel whether it generates more than USD 2,000,000 in a year from advertisements–and differentiate the prices based on these categories. Cine 5 also alleged that it provides the match video clips to the channels that have lower revenues by giving up their own profit in order to enable the viewers of this channel to watch the football matches. Hence, the practice is beneficial for TV viewers.

The Board, however, found that (i) the channels that are argued to be in the same category by Cine 5 generate, in fact, different revenues from advertisements, or (ii) the channels under the same category are made subject to different terms under their agreements. In addition, the Board noted that differentiation based on advertising revenues might not be in compliance with competition law since there may be other factors to be considered to decide whether the commercial transactions were equal. Accordingly, in order to apply objective criteria, Cine 5 should have considered the customers that demand the same product, in the same quantity, and under the same payment and delivery conditions, to be equal. Also, the Board analysed that the argument that Cine 5 gives up its own revenue in favour of the TV viewers does not seem to reflect the real situation as Cine 5 only made one free sale, which was to Star TV, and that was in fact based on a swap contract. Finally, the Board underlined that the delivery conditions in one of Cine 5's agreements are different; hence prices applied under this agreement may not be seen as discriminatory. Therefore, apart from the last one, the Board decided that the agreements violated Article 6 of Law No. 4054.

Nevertheless, the Council of State annulled the *Cine 5* decision by stating that the analysis must be made by considering the characteristics of the service, the end customers and also public interest. Since the purpose of Cine 5 is to provide the service to all TV viewers from different backgrounds, the conduct is seen to be for the benefit of the public. Cine 5 takes into account the different financial capabilities of the channels. Also, the price differences applied to channels are not excessive, and Cine 5 does not exceed the maximum price set out in its agreement with the Turkey Football Federation on the right of broadcasting football matches.[1316] The annulment decision was upheld by the Council of State, Plenary Session of the Chambers for Administrative Cases.[1317] Upon the annulment decision, the Board held that there is no merit for further analysis on the issue.[1318]

[1316]   10th Chamber of the Council of State (4 November 2003, E. 2001/355, K. 2003/4245).
[1317]   Council of State (3 May 2007, E. 2004/1188, K. 2007/864).
[1318]   *Cine 5* (1 November 2007, 07-83/1009-393).

In *Digiturk I*, the Board analysed two practices from the perspective of discrimination. First, Digiturk, having the exclusive right for broadcasting the matches played within the Turkey 1st Professional Football League, decided to license the right of broadcasting for reporting purposes on the condition that the video clips of all nine matches played in one week are purchased together; not just the popular games. Having found that Digiturk is the only broadcaster that owns the video clips of these football matches, hence holds a dominant position in the market for broadcasting matches within Turkey 1st Professional Football League, the Board focused on the two effects of tying the nine matches on the open TV broadcasting market: (i) putting the channels with inferior purchasing power in a disadvantaged position in favour of Show TV, the channel with which Digiturk has a close relationship, and (ii) making it complicated for these channels to have access to the right of broadcasting clips. The second practice that the Board analysed is Show TV's ability to broadcast the clips from the match for reporting purposes more quickly than other channels, which has led to the conclusion that Digiturk has provided Show TV with the videos in a quicker way, putting other channels in a competitive disadvantage. The decision is noteworthy not only because it demonstrates an analysis of tying practices from a discriminatory behaviour perspective but also because it shows how the Board approaches the discrimination by an undertaking in favour of a customer with which it has a close relationship.[1319]

As an example of the application of the condition of customers being equal in secondary line injury cases, in *Coca-Cola and Fruko-Tamek*, the Board considered that applying different prices and agreement terms to supermarkets and groceries are not discriminatory on the basis that (i) supermarkets have stronger buyer power due to their higher volume of purchases; (ii) transportation costs incurred for sales to groceries are higher as their purchases are less frequent and in lower amounts; (iii) supermarkets may order through the phone or e-mail while Coca Cola Group and Fruko-Tamek Group need to hire personnel for sales to groceries; (iv) supermarkets make their payments through banks while groceries make their payments to the personnel hired for receipt of payments. Hence, there is an economic justification for differentiation.[1320]

In *Roche II*, the Board noted that for discriminatory practices cases, it is not sufficient to merely show that different prices apply to equivalent consumers. Rather, the exclusionary effect of discrimination on the rival should also be established.[1321] In the decision, the Board rejected the allegation that Roche discriminates against hospitals by stating that the hospitals (state hospitals, university hospitals) that initiate tenders for Roche drugs are not competitors of Roche, nor are they competitors of each other. Hence, the Board found that the complainants do not explain the competition on which market is restricted and why.[1322]

In *Google Shopping Unit*, the Board rejected the discrimination allegation by stating, among others, that since the undertaking does not have any shareholding in any e-commerce com-

---

[1319]   *Digiturk I* (n. 1014).
[1320]   *Coca-Cola and Fruko-Tamek* (27 June 2000, 00-24/251-136).
[1321]   *Roche II* (n. 1197).
[1322]   Ibid.

panies, it has no incentive to discriminate against e-commerce companies when offering advertising services to them. Otherwise, the competition in the e-commerce market may be restricted, which may in the mid or long term decrease the profits generated from providing advertising services to e-commerce companies.[1323]

In *Turkcell-Vodafone*, the Board analysed the selective pricing of the undertaking with a focus on its discriminatory effect. The practice in question was Turkcell's conduct, where it identified its competitor Vodafone's customers by processing traffic data and offered them discounts or free mobile phones in exchange for subscribing to Turkcell. The allegation, thus, concerned whether Turkcell discriminates among its subscribers and applies selective pricing. The Board did not initiate a fully-fledged investigation, nor did it analyse the practice from the perspective of competition law, stating that the Telecommunication Authority had already notified Turkcell to cease its practice as it violates telecommunication regulations.[1324]

Finally, in *Sanofi-Aventis* the Board found that Sanofi-Aventis İlaçları Ltd. Şti. abuses its dominant position by changing its sales conditions and reducing the payment terms imposed on pharmaceutical warehouses for monthly purchases below a certain amount. The Board considered whether the reduction of the payment terms would put certain pharmaceutical warehouses, especially those of small or medium scale, at a competitive disadvantage. Accordingly, the Board found that, due to the characteristics of the sector, the warehouses would inevitably be in a position to reflect the cost of reduced payment terms to pharmacies, as otherwise they would incur significant costs. However, because the price elasticity of pharmacies is very high, it would cause the pharmacies to cease their purchases and start making purchases from large scale warehouses. The alternative methods that the small and medium warehouses could use would be making joint purchases with other warehouses, or make their purchases from other warehouses as opposed to Sanofi-Aventis İlaçları Ltd. Şti itself. However, the cost of these alternatives would be so high that small and medium warehouses would not be able to compete with the large warehouses. As a result of the above analysis, the Board imposed an administrative fine on Sanofi-Aventis İlaçları Ltd. Şti.[1325]

[1323]   *Google Shopping Unit* (n. 1139), p. 43.
[1324]   *Turkcell-Vodafone* (20 May 2008, 08-34/453-159). The Council of State ordered the stay of execution of the decision by its decision (25 June 2009, E. 2009/152). Nevertheless, the Board rendered its second decision on the issue in the same vein (8 October 2009, 09-45/1136-286).
[1325]   *Sanofi-Aventis* (20 April 2009, 09-16/374-88).

Chapter 9
Merger Control: Procedural Aspects

GÖNENÇ GÜRKAYNAK, ESQ. AND İ. BARAN CAN YILDIRIM[*]

Article 7 of Law No. 4054 prohibits the mergers and acquisitions that would result in a significant lessening of effective competition, particularly in the form of creating or strengthening a dominant position in any given market in Turkey.

The Board is authorised within the scope of Article 7 of Law No. 4054 to declare, via communiqués to be issued, the types of mergers and acquisitions which shall be notified to the Board in order for them to become legally valid. As such, the Board has published Communiqué No. 2010/4,[1326] which lays out which types of mergers and acquisitions are subject to a mandatory merger control filing in Turkey. Accordingly, any transaction that exceeds certain turnover thresholds set out under Article 7 of Communiqué No. 2010/4 is subject to a mandatory merger control filing, provided that such transaction also leads to a permanent change of control. Therefore, the notifiability analysis of a transaction is a two-fold test: (i) assessment of whether the transaction leads to change in control, and (ii) if so, assessment of whether the turnover thresholds stipulated under Article 7 of Communiqué No. 2010/4 are exceeded. This two-fold notifiability assessment of the Authority is explained below.

9.1 Jurisdictional Issues

9.1.1 Concept of Control

Under the Turkish merger control regime, "control" is understood to be the right to exercise decisive influence on strategic business decisions; and it can be exercised de jure or de facto. Control may take the form of sole or joint control over an undertaking.

Article 5(2) of Communiqué No. 2010/4 sets out various examples of instruments that are at the disposal of the transaction parties to grant them control, as follows:

> Control may be acquired through rights, contracts or other instruments which, separately or together, allow de facto or de jure exercise of decisive influence over an

[*] Associate, ELIG Gürkaynak Attorneys-at-Law, Istanbul <can.yildirim@elig.com>.
[1326] Communiqué No. 2010/4 on Mergers and Acquisitions Subject to the Approval of the Turkish Competition Board was published in the Official Gazette of 7 October 2010, No. 27722.

undertaking. In particular, these instruments consist of ownership right or operating right over all or part of the assets of an undertaking, and those rights or contracts granting decisive influence over the structure or decisions of the bodies of an undertaking. Control may be acquired by right holders, or by those persons or undertakings who have been empowered to exercise such rights in accordance with a contract, or who, while lacking such rights and powers, have de facto strength to exercise such rights.

As such, control may be acquired, among others, by way of acquisition of shares or assets and also through various types of contracts, including franchise agreements. The different means that may grant controlling rights to the undertakings are further elaborated below.

9.1.1.1 Acquisition of Shares or Assets

Acquisition of shares or assets is considered as one of the most common means for acquisition of control.[1327] As explained below under Section 9.1.3, agreements governing shareholders' rights and powers are also significant in terms of determinations as to the features of joint control.

9.1.1.2 Contracts

In order for a contract to lead to a change in control, the nature of control the provisions of the contract in question grant must be akin to the acquisition of shares or assets.[1328] For instance, in *AstraZeneca/Bristol/Amylin*,[1329] the Board underlined that within the subject transaction, parties would sign an "Agreement on Joint Offers", which would not entail any transfer of shares. However, the Board accepted said transaction as an acquisition leading to joint control by Bristol and AstraZeneca over Amylin. In making this assessment, the Board considered the terms that the parties would (i) equally share the obligations and (ii) jointly decide on all matters from product development to budget matters.[1330]

Paragraph 13 of the Guidelines on the Concept of Control provides that contracts that satisfy this condition would be long-term agreements. In assessing the "long-term" condition, the Board accepted that seven-year[1331] and five-year[1332] lease agreements would be sufficiently long term.

9.1.1.3 Other Means of Control

The Board may also take the nature of the economic relations into consideration while assessing whether there is a change in control on a lasting basis. For instance, if there is visible economic dependence, then this could lead to de facto control.[1333] Paragraph 14 of the Guidelines on the Concept of Control lists, in a non-exhaustive manner,

---

[1327] Guidelines on the Concept of Control, para. 12.
[1328] Guidelines on the Concept of Control, para. 13.
[1329] *AstraZeneca/Bristol/Amylin* (20 February 2013, 13-11/163-85)
[1330] Ibid., paras. 5–7.
[1331] *Migros/Hamoğlu* (14 August 2008, 08-50/721-281)
[1332] *Konya Cement/Erdoğanlar* (10 September 2012, 12-43/1323-436); *Cimpor/Babil* (30 October 2008, 08-61/998-390).
[1333] Guidelines on the Concept of Control, para. 14.

the following instances as possible economic dependence when coupled with structural links such as cross-shareholdings and/or cross-directorships: (i) long-term supply agreements concerning an essential component for undertaking's business[1334] and (ii) credits that suppliers or customers provide. For instance, in *Besler/Turyağ*, the Board determined that the transaction in question would not be considered a merger or acquisition as the structural links between the parties would diminish in time.[1335]

Further, paragraph 15 of the Guidelines on the Concept of Control sets forth that in certain cases, an action of a third party may trigger a transfer of control where the acquirer is in a passive position. For instance, the cases where the exit by certain shareholders would lead to a change of control could constitute an example of such third-party actions.[1336]

9.1.2 Sole Control

When one undertaking alone has a decisive influence on another undertaking, this would constitute sole control.[1337] Paragraph 40 of the Guidelines on the Concept of Control lists two general situations in which an undertaking is considered to have sole control:

– First, the undertaking that has sole control enjoys the right to determine the strategic commercial decisions of the other undertaking. This is generally the case where the relevant party acquires a majority of voting rights in a company.

– Second would be the "negative sole control", where only one shareholder is able to veto strategic decisions in an undertaking but does not have the power on its own to take such decisions. In this case, the shareholder holding negative sole control over the undertaking is not required to cooperate with other shareholders on strategic matters of the said undertaking. The shareholder with negative sole control would be able to create a deadlock situation by itself, thus having decisive influence over the strategic decisions.

For instance, in *Cinven Capital/Stichting/Barentz*, the Board, in order to determine whether a negative sole control issue existed in the case at hand, assessed whether Vakif and Cinven (the shareholders of Barentz) have to cooperate to appoint the senior management or whether Vakif is able to singlehandedly veto the appointment of the senior management. The Board found that Vakif is not able to veto such decision, and the parties have to cooperate. As such, it was concluded that Vakif does not enjoy a negative sole control.[1338]

Further, in *Akarlılar/Mavi Giyim*, the Board concluded that in a board structure, where three of six members are appointed by Akarlılar, Akarlılar has a negative sole control over the undertaking since it is able to veto all the decisions, even if it cannot take any decision without the participation of other members.[1339]

[1334] *Besler/Turyağ* (12 October 2010, 10-64/1355-498), p. 6.
[1335] Ibid., p. 9.
[1336] Guidelines on the Concept of Control, para. 15.
[1337] Ibid. 40.
[1338] *Cinven/Stichting/Barentz* (22 November 2019, 19-41/676-291), para. 9.
[1339] *Akarlılar/Mavi Giyim* (8 March 2018, 18-07/121-65), para. 9.

9.1.3 Joint Control

Pursuant to the Guidelines on the Concept of Control, joint control exists where two or more undertakings or persons have the possibility of exercising decisive influence over another undertaking[1340]. The main feature of joint control materialises when two or more parent companies have the right to reject strategic decisions and to create a deadlock situation in the decision process.[1341] The Guidelines on the Concept of Control provide the following definition with respect to the concept of decisive influence: "The power to block actions which determine the strategic commercial behaviour of an undertaking." Accordingly, if the minority shareholders retain veto rights for the "decisions which are essential for the strategic commercial behaviour", then the joint control would occur in terms of that joint venture.[1342]

While the veto rights that allow decisive influence over strategic decisions and business policies could effectively grant joint control, the veto rights of minority shareholders that protect the financial interests of the investors (i.e., changes in the master agreement of the joint venture, increase or decrease in the capital or liquidation) would not do so.[1343]

Paragraph 53 of the Guidelines on the Concept of Control exemplifies the veto rights that confer joint control as follows: decisions such as the budget, the business plan, major investments or the appointment of senior management. Importantly, it is not relevant whether or not the acquirer of joint control would, in fact, exercise its decisive influence.[1344] Accordingly, it is sufficient that such a right simply exists.

On another important note, the minority shareholders are not required to hold all or even a majority of the mentioned decisive influence veto rights.[1345] Paragraph 54 of the Guidelines on the Concept of Control sets forth that the points of consideration on this matter are (i) the content of the veto right and (ii) the significance that said right carries within the operations of the joint venture.

The Guidelines on the Concept of Control summarise some of the important veto rights as below.

9.1.3.1 Appointment of Senior Management and Determination of Budget

If the veto right in question grants the right to appoint or dismiss senior management officials such as board members, then this would be considered as having decisive influence over the commercial policy of the joint venture in question.[1346] Veto rights in terms of budget would also be considered as having decisive influence since it is determinative of the framework of the activities of the joint venture.[1347]

[1340] Guidelines on the Concept of Control, para. 48.
[1341] Ibid.
[1342] Ibid., para. 51.
[1343] Ibid., para. 52.
[1344] Ibid., para. 53.
[1345] Ibid., para. 54.
[1346] Ibid., para. 56.
[1347] Ibid.

9.1.3.2 Business Plan

The Guidelines on the Concept of Control provide that the business plan would consist of the objectives of the joints venture, as well as the plans to achieve these objectives[1348]. However, any and all veto rights relating to the business plan would not be considered as having decisive influence. For instance, if a veto right over the business plan simply comprises general statements on the business objectives, then this would not be sufficient to grant joint control.[1349]

9.1.3.3 Investments

The Guidelines on the Concept of Control emphasise that with respect to investments, the level of investment is a crucial point of consideration. If the veto rights concern a very high level of investment, then the Board may review these veto rights as more protecting the interests of minority shareholders rather than conferring joint control over the commercial policy of the joint venture.[1350] Moreover, the Board would also take into account whether or not the level of investment constitutes an essential feature in the relevant market.[1351]

Accordingly, paragraph 58 of the Guidelines on the Concept of Control emphasises that in certain markets, investments may not play as much of a significant role in the behaviour of the undertakings as in other markets where the level of investment is quite significant.[1352]

9.1.3.4 Market-Specific Rights

The Guidelines on the Concept of Control underline that while some veto rights are considered as having decisive influence irrespective of the market, certain veto rights are significant for specific markets[1353]. For instance, if the joint venture in question operates in a technology-related market, veto right over a decision on which technology the said joint venture is to use could constitute a determining influence.[1354] Moreover, in markets with a high level of product differentiation and innovation, veto rights over decisions on newly developing products may be considered as establishing joint control.[1355]

Paragraph 60 of the Guidelines on the Concept of Control sets forth that if there are multiple veto rights, these rights should not be reviewed separately while determining whether or not they confer joint control. Accordingly, the Board would review veto rights as a whole to assess whether or not they confer joint control.

Further, the Guidelines on the Concept of Control refer to the circumstance of "changing alliances" where (i) there is no stable majority in decision-making and (ii) the minority

---

[1348] Ibid., para. 57.
[1349] Ibid.
[1350] Ibid., para. 58.
[1351] Ibid.
[1352] Ibid.
[1353] Ibid., para. 59.
[1354] Ibid.
[1355] Ibid.

shareholders can attain a majority through various combinations.[1356] Under such circumstances, the Board would not be able to assume that the minority shareholders (or a certain group thereof) exercise joint control.[1357] For instance, in *Turkcell*,[1358] the Board assessed that the transaction could not be considered a joint control acquisition because both the general assembly and board of directors required different alliances for the decision-making process. In other words, the Board found that there was no joint control because the majority to obtain a decision could be reached with different combinations each time.

9.1.4 Turnover-Based Thresholds

As for the turnover-based thresholds, the Authority explains these thresholds under Article 7 of Communiqué No. 2010/4. Under Article 7(1) of Communiqué No. 2010/4, the transaction would be notifiable in case one of the following turnover thresholds is triggered:[1359]

- The aggregate Turkish turnover of the transaction parties exceeds TL 100 million, and the Turkish turnover of at least two of the parties to the transaction exceeds each TL 30 million (Article 7(1)(a)).

- The Turkish turnover of the transferred assets or businesses in *acquisitions* exceeds TL 30 million, and the worldwide turnover of at least one of the other parties to the transaction exceeds TL 500 million (Article 7(1)(b)),

- The Turkish turnover of any of the parties in *mergers* exceeds TL 30 million, and the worldwide turnover of at least one of the other parties to the transaction exceeds TL 500 million (Article 7(1)(b)).

As seen above, Article 7(1)(b) actually sets out two separate tests; Article 7(1)(b)(i) is applicable only in cases of acquisition transactions (as well as joint ventures), while Article 7(1)(b)(ii) is applicable only in cases of merger transactions.

The thresholds do not differ according to the sector. There are, however, certain other special merger control rules to be considered in respect of a number of specific sectors such as the banking sector. Further detailed explanations on such exceptions are presented below, under Section 9.1.6.

In case the jurisdictional thresholds are not exceeded, the transaction would not fall within the scope of Communiqué No. 2010/4, and thus the transaction would not be subject to the Board's approval. However, the fact that a transaction is not subject to the Board's approval does not mean that it is not contrary to the primary legislation of competition

---

[1356] Ibid., para. 66.
[1357] *CMLKK Liman* (31 May 2018, 18-17/303-152), paras. 10–14; *CMLKK Bilişim* (5 July 2018; 18-22/376-184), paras. 11–15; *CMLKK Parking/Exchange/Fuel* (2 August 2018, 18-24/426-200), paras. 24 and 26–30; *Camargo/ Cimpor* (n. 24), paras. 4–5.
[1358] *Automobile Project* (n. 431), paras. 17–18.
[1359] Pursuant to Article 8(6) of Communiqué No. 2010/4 and paragraph 24 of the Guidelines on Undertakings Concerned, Turnover and Ancillary Restraints, for the purpose of calculating the turnovers, the amounts in foreign currencies will be converted to TL in accordance with the applicable Turkish Central Bank average buying rate for the relevant year.

law, i.e., Law No. 4054. Indeed, while the question of whether the transaction is subject to the Board's approval should be taken into consideration within the scope of secondary legislation (i.e., Communiqué No. 2010/4), the question of whether the same transaction creates competition law sensitivities should be assessed within the scope of the primary legislation (i.e., Article 7 of Law No. 4054). In other words, in this particular case, as the primary legislation, the provisions of Law No. 4054 would be superior to the provisions of Communiqué No. 2010/4 and take precedence according to the hierarchy of norms.

As stated above, the assessment on whether a transaction creates competition law sensitivities is independent of the question of whether the transaction is subject to the Board's approval within the scope of Article 7 of Communiqué No. 2010/4. While Article 7 of Communiqué No. 2010/4 regulates the conditions of notification of transactions to the Board, the conformity of transactions with the competition law would be assessed considering Article 7 of Law No. 4054. As per the hierarchy of norms, the fact that a transaction is not subject to the Board's approval would not have an effect on the assessment of the same transaction in terms of its merits.

Under Article 7 of Law No. 4054 regulating the control of mergers and acquisitions, any merger by one or more undertakings, or acquisitions by any undertaking from another undertaking, which would result in a significant lessening of competition in a market for goods or services within the whole or a part of the country, are prohibited.

Therefore, Law No. 4054 deems mergers and acquisitions that would result in a significant lessening of competition as illegal, regardless of the question of whether the relevant turnover thresholds have been exceeded or not. The jurisdictional threshold provided under Communiqué No. 2010/4 acts as a filter by excluding some transactions from the notification obligation, as such transactions do not attain a certain economic size. One of the former members of the Board criticised this issue in the dissenting vote reasoned under the Board's *Swedish Match/Sağlam* decision.[1360]

Thus, even though some mergers or acquisitions between competitors are not notifiable, they could still be evaluated in accordance with the provisions of Law No. 4054. Parties may consider submitting a negative clearance application before the Board on the basis of Article 8 of Law No. 4054 in order to gain legal certainty for transactions that are suspected not to comply with the competition law rules but which are not subject to the Board's approval. Gaining legal certainty through this application may be imperative, especially when there are strong market players in a market with a low competitive environment.

9.1.4.1 Calculation Methods

Article 8 of Communiqué No. 2010/4 regulates the calculation of the turnover. Accordingly, to calculate the turnover of each transaction party, the Board takes the following into consideration:

– The turnover of the entire economic group, including the undertakings controlling the undertaking concerned, as well as all the undertakings controlled by the undertaking concerned, will be taken into account.

[1360]   *Swedish Match/Sağlam* (25 April 2012, 12-22/569-164).

- When calculating turnover in an acquisition transaction, only the turnover of the acquired part will be taken into account with respect to the seller.

- The turnover of jointly controlled undertakings (including joint ventures) will be divided equally by the number of controlling undertakings.

- Multiple transactions between the same undertakings realised over a period of three years are deemed to be a single transaction for turnover calculation purposes. They warrant separate notifications if their cumulative effect exceeds the thresholds, regardless of whether the transactions are in the same market or sector; and whether they were previously notified to the Authority or not.

For the purposes of the notifiability analysis, the turnover of the transaction parties generated as of the end of the financial year preceding the date of the notification should be taken into consideration. If this cannot be calculated, the turnover generated as of the end of the financial year closest to the date of notification should be taken into consideration.

The notifiability analysis of joint ventures in terms of turnover thresholds would take into consideration (i) the turnover figures of the parent companies which exercise joint control over the joint venture, as well as (ii) the Turkish turnover of the transferred assets/businesses to the joint venture (if applicable). When the transaction is a formation of a joint venture, the transaction would be evaluated under the turnover thresholds provided under Article 7(1)(a) or 7(1)(b)(i), as Article 7(1)(b)(ii) only applies to merger transactions.

It is important to note that, as per Article 8(2) of Communiqué No. 2010/4, the Board evaluates the transactions realised by the same undertaking concerned in the same relevant product market within three years as a single transaction, as well as two transactions carried out between the same persons or parties within a three-year period.

9.1.4.2 Instances of Where There are Two or More Transactions Between the Same Parties in the Same Relevant Product Market in the Last Three Years

The previous wording of Article 8(5) of Communiqué No. 2010/4 included the following provision:

> Two or more transactions falling under paragraph 2 of this Article, carried out between the same persons or parties within a period of two years, shall be considered as a single transaction for the purpose of calculating the turnovers listed in Article 7 of this Communiqué.

Whereas the current version of Article 8(5) of Communiqué No. 2010/4 (as amended by Communiqué No. 2017/2) reads as follows:

> Two or more transactions falling under paragraph 2 of this Article, carried out between the same persons or parties within a period of three years; or an undertaking realising two or more transactions in the same relevant product market within a period of three years, shall be considered as a single transaction for the purpose of calculating the turnovers listed in Article 7 of this Communiqué.

The rationale for this amendment is to ensure that the Authority is not deprived of the opportunity to take into consideration the cumulative effects of creeping acquisitions realised by the same buyer in the same relevant market within a relatively short period of time. By way of example, in the absence of this amendment, serial acquisitions by the market leader of its multiple smaller competitors (which have no connection whatsoever) would not have to be notified, regardless of what the combined effect of these transactions may be, merely because none of the targets in the said transactions generates turnovers in excess of the thresholds set forth in Communiqué No. 2010/4, although the combined turnovers of the targets may exceed the said thresholds.

For instance, the *MP Hotel/Magic Life/TUI/Bodrum Imperial/Alaçatı* decision[1361] lays down the principles concerning creeping acquisitions. In the relevant decision, the notified transaction concerned MP Hotel's acquisition of control over certain hotels in Turkey (namely, Magic Life, TUI, Bodrum Imperial, and Alaçatı Beach Resort) via long-term lease agreements. The Board first concluded that MP Hotel's lease and management of the target hotels would create a permanent change in control, and therefore, should be considered as an acquisition under Article 5 of Communiqué No. 2010/4. Afterwards, and by referring to Article 8(5) of Communiqué No. 2010/4, the Board examined other acquisitions realised by MP Hotel in the same relevant market. As an important point, the Board did not only consider the transactions realised after 24 February 2017, when the relevant amendment in Article 8(5) was made, and stipulated that all the transactions that were realised within the last three years should be assessed. In doing so, the Board rejected the parties' arguments regarding "non-retrospectivity". The Board determined that MP Hotel had acquired seven other targets operating in the same relevant market in the last three years and considered all these transactions as a single transaction for the purposes of turnover calculation. While the turnover generated by the targets to be acquired in the notified transaction (i.e., Magic Life, TUI, Bodrum Imperial, and Alaçatı Beach Resort) remained below the thresholds, the combined turnovers of all the targets that had been acquired in the last three years by MP Hotel did exceed the thresholds. Hence, the Board decided that the transaction was notifiable.

Moreover, it is understood from the final sentence of paragraph 35 of the Guidelines on Undertakings Concerned, Turnover and Ancillary Restraints that whether two or more acquisitions realised by a relevant undertaking in the same relevant market within the last three-year-period, which do not exceed the thresholds when examined individually, are subject to approval, shall be assessed considering the combined turnovers. As another important point, neither Article 8(5) of Communiqué No. 2010/4 nor the relevant guidelines set forth that the overlap must be in relevant markets in Turkey. Hence, a strictly literal interpretation of the said provision does not exclude the possibility of taking horizontal overlaps in different jurisdictions into consideration.

However, the Board does not define separate geographical markets for any jurisdictions other than Turkey, and the relevant markets in different jurisdictions do not fall within the scope of Law No. 4054. As a matter of fact, Article 2 of Law No. 4054 clarifies that the relevant law covers practices "affecting markets for goods and services within the borders of the Republic of Turkey".

[1361] *MP Hotel/Magic Life/TUI/Bodrum Imperial/Alaçatı* (22 November 2018, 18-44/699-343).

Accordingly, the Board confines its competitive assessments to affected markets in Turkey, and the fact that there may be horizontal overlaps between the activities of the target and other undertakings that had been acquired by the same buyer during the course of three years in jurisdictions other than Turkey would not have any material impact on the Board's assessments. Considering Article 8(5) was introduced to ensure that the cumulative effects of a series of individually non-notifiable transactions that were realised by the buyer in the same relevant market would not lead to a significant impediment of effective competition in Turkey, a teleological interpretation of Article 8(5) should exclude horizontal overlaps in jurisdictions other than Turkey.

Assessing the former precedents where the Board applied Article 8(5) (e.g., *UBM/UBM ICC/ UBM İstanbul/UBM NTSR*,[1362] *Gümüşdoğa/Baracuda*,[1363] *MP Hotel/Magic Life/TUI/Bodrum Imperial/Alaçatı*,[1364] *Mikro/Zirve*[1365]), it is seen that the Board has always taken into consideration the horizontal overlaps of the relevant markets in Turkey. Yet, there are no precedents where an assessment was conducted as to what the legal implications of horizontal overlaps in other jurisdictions would be from the perspective of the applicability of Article 8(5).

In addition to the foregoing, given that transactions with no Turkey nexus are also notifiable if the relevant turnover thresholds set forth in Communique No. 2010/4 are exceeded, taking horizontal overlaps in different jurisdictions into consideration for the purposes of conducting a notifiability assessment under Article 8(5) could unduly expand the scope of notifiable transactions and create legal uncertainty for undertakings.

9.1.4.3 Instances Where Two or More Transactions by the Same Undertaking Are Considered as a Single Transaction

Article 5(4) of Communiqué No. 2010/4 provides that closely related transactions that are tied to conditions or transactions, realised over a short period of time by way of expedited exchange of securities, are treated as a single transaction.

As detailed above, in terms of turnover calculation, the amended Article 8(5) of Communiqué No. 2010/4 provides that the Board would be in a position to evaluate the following transactions as a single transaction:

- Transactions realised by the same undertaking concerned in the same relevant product market within three years

- Two transactions carried out between the same persons or parties within a three-year period.

Accordingly, pursuant to paragraph 30 of the Guidelines on the Concept of Control, two or more transactions constitute a single concentration provided that the transactions are interdependent (i.e., one transaction would not have been carried out without the other)

[1362]   *UBM/UBM ICC/UBM İstanbul/UBM NTSR* (21 June 2018, 18-20/354-175).
[1363]   *Gümüşdoğa/Baracuda* (21 June 2018, 18-20/350-171).
[1364]   *MP Hotel/Magic Life/TUI/Bodrum Imperial/Alaçatı* (n. 1361).
[1365]   *Mikro/Zirve* (18 January 2018, 18-03/25-13).

and that the control is acquired by the same persons or undertaking(s). Paragraph 32 of the Guidelines on the Concept of Control sets forth that the conditionality of the transactions could be proven if the transactions are linked *de jure* (i.e., the agreements themselves are linked by mutual conditionality). Paragraph 32 of the Guidelines on the Concept of Control also provides that if parties are able to satisfactorily demonstrate the circumstances, then de facto conditionality may also suffice for treating the transactions as a single concentration.

For instance, in *APMC/GSEZ/TIPSP/Arise*,[1366] the Board considered that four different share transfer transactions constituted a single transaction pursuant to the information submitted by the parties. Such informationindicated that separate investments made to the different transaction parties were linked to one another; thus these transactions were interdependent.

9.1.5 Foreign-to-Foreign Transactions

Article 7 of Communiqué No. 2010/4 does not seek the existence of an "affected market" in assessing whether a transaction triggers a notification requirement. The concept of "affected market", however, still carries weight in terms of the substantive competitive assessment and the notification document. However, it should be emphasised that the Board decisions indicate that unless there is an extremely exceptional circumstance where the JV engages in an infrastructure-based business that has natural boundaries (e.g., railroad construction, electricity distribution, etc.) in transactions involving a JV where thresholds are triggered, a mandatory filing before the Board would be required.[1367]

The Board rendered multiple decisions on the matter, detailing several different aspects of foreign-to-foreign transactions. For example, in *Eksim/Rönesans/Acıbadem*, the Board decided that a greenfield healthcare JV in Kuwait would be notifiable.[1368] In this particular case, the Board stated that although the joint venture will be established and operated outside of Turkey (i.e., in Kuwait), the Turkish market could be indirectly affected. To explain the indirect effect, the Board reasoned that the parties forming the joint venture have companies that are active in Turkey and the increase of their market power through the turnover generated from the joint venture in Kuwait would indirectly increase their power in Turkey. As such, the Board concluded that the transaction would indirectly affect the Turkish market and thus should be subject to the approval of the Board. This approach of the Board indicates that it disregards "the ability to import products into Turkey" and still considers a JV transaction that will not have any effect in the near future in Turkey to be within the scope of Article 7 of Law No. 4054 (i.e., within the definition of mergers and acquisitions).

The Board's other precedents[1369] clearly indicate that even though the JV is not/will not be active in Turkey and will not have any effects in the near future on the Turkish markets,

[1366] *APMC/GSEZ/TIPSP/Arise* (19 December 2019, 19-45/757-326).
[1367] *Sorgenia/KKR* (14 July 2011, 11-43/919-288).
[1368] *Eksim/Rönesans/Acıbadem* (16 May 2012, 12-26/759-213).
[1369] *Sumitomo/Toyota* (13 February 2020, 20-10/101-59); *Galenica/Fresenius* (24 November 2011, 11-59/1515-540); *Blackstone/Lisa Germany* (17 November 2011, 11-57/1468-525); *Flabeg/Schott/SBPS/Ocean* (17 August 2011, 11-45/1106-382); *Sonangol/BP/Chevron/Eni/Total/ALNG* (25 April 2012, 12-22/564-162)

the transaction is still subject to notification. In *Galenica/Fresenius*,[1370] the JV was established abroad to undertake R&D and distribution activities for kidney treatment medicines. The JV did not have a nexus with Turkey, and the parties expected that the product would be distributed by as late as 2028. In its *Flabeg/Schott/SBPS/Ocean* decision,[1371] the Board ruled that even though there is no market for the power generation from solar energy plants based on parabolic trough technology in Turkey that may be affected by this acquisition, there is still a potential that with the advancement of technology, there may eventually be an effect on that market in Turkey. In its *Sonangol/BP/Chevron/Eni/Total/ALNG* decision[1372] in the market for the production and sale of liquefied natural gas (LNG), the Board ruled that, even though the JV does not consider Turkey as one of its target customers, in the future, with the increasing demand for LNG in Turkey, it would always be possible for the JV to consider Turkey as a customer. In *ADPM/Vinci Airports/Astaldi*,[1373] which concerns the formation of a greenfield airport management JV regarding the management of Santiago Airport in Chile, the Board decided that the transaction is still subject to notification even though the JV will not be operating in Turkey, and will execute all its economic activities on the management of Santiago Airport in Chile. In all these cases, the Board found the transactions to be notifiable and granted approval to them. In a recent case, *Sumitomo/Toyota*,[1374] while the Board acknowledged that the joint venture's activities would be limited to the USA, it still contemplated possible anti-competitive concerns under the assumption that the joint venture may still operate in Turkey.

Nucor/JFE[1375] concerned the formation of a joint venture which would be active in the sales and marketing of galvanised flat carbon steel products in Mexico. The joint venture's operations and activities would be limited to Mexico and, furthermore, would not have any assets outside of Mexico. The Board concluded that the relevant transaction would still require a mandatory notification even though the JV will not be operating in Turkey and will execute all its economic activities in Mexico.

Against this background, if the turnover thresholds are triggered, the joint venture transaction would be notifiable so long as the joint venture is a full-function joint venture. The fact that the JV's products/services will not be offered in Turkey would not change the analysis, and thus it would not be possible to avoid a notification in Turkey on that basis.

9.1.6 Exceptions

There are several exceptions to the notifiability analysis as explained above, regulated both within Communiqué No. 2010/4 and other non-antitrust regulations.

Article 6 of Communiqué No. 2010/4 provides the cases that are not considered as a merger or an acquisition as: (i) intra-group transactions and other transactions which do

---

[1370]   *Galenica/Fresenius* (n. 1369).

[1371]   *Flabeg/Schott/SBPS/Ocean* (n. 1369).

[1372]   *Sonangol/BP/Chevron/Eni/Total/ALNG* (n. 1369).

[1373]   *ADPM/Vinci Airports/Astaldi* (1 September 2015, 15-34/509-157).

[1374]   *Sumitomo/Toyota* (n. 1369).

[1375]   *Nucor/JFE* (23 June 2016, 16-21/383-177).

not lead to a change in control; (ii) operations of undertakings whose ordinary operations involve transactions with securities, temporarily holding on to securities purchased for resale purposes, provided that the voting rights from those securities are not used to affect the competitive policies of the undertaking; (iii) acquisition of control by a public institution or organisation by operation of law; and (iv) mergers or acquisitions occurring as a result of inheritance.

Moreover, the Banking Law No. 5411 provides that the provisions of Articles 7, 10 and 11 of Law No. 4054 shall not be applicable, as long as the sectorial share of the total assets of the banks subject to merger or acquisition does not exceed 20%. The Board distinguishes between transactions involving foreign acquiring banks with no operations in Turkey and those foreign acquiring banks already operating in Turkey while applying the exception rule in the Banking Law. Therefore, while the Board applies Law No. 4054 to mergers and acquisitions in cases where the foreign acquiring bank does not have any operations in Turkey, it does not apply Law No. 4054 if the foreign acquiring bank already has operations in Turkey under the exception rule in the Banking Law. The competition legislation provides no special regulation applicable to foreign investments. However, some special restrictions do exist on foreign investment in other legislations, such as media.

Another exception pertains to the Turkish Wealth Fund, which was incorporated as a company with Law No. 6741. Article 8(5) entitled "Exemptions and Exceptions" of Law No. 6741 sets out the legislation that is not applicable to the Turkish Wealth Fund itself and any companies established by the Turkish Wealth Fund, and Law No. 4054 is listed therein. Thus, any transactions performed by the Turkish Wealth Fund and/or companies established by the Turkish Wealth Fund would not be subject to the notifiability analysis detailed above.[1376]

9.1.7 Failure to Notify

As explained above, the Board declares which transactions need to be notified via communiqués, in accordance with Article 7 of Law No. 4054. Meanwhile, Article 11 of Law No. 4054 pertains to those cases where the parties fail to notify a transaction deemed notifiable via the legislation.

The relevant parties will face the consequences set out under Article 11 of Law No. 4054 if they do not notify a notifiable transaction in accordance with Communiqué No. 2010/4. This violation will be assessed by the Board when it becomes aware of the transaction, and the relevant parties will be imposed an administrative fine. It should also be noted that if the Board finds that the transaction in question violates Article 7 of Law No. 4054–i.e., significantly lessens effective competition–the parties will face further legal consequences as per Article 11.

It should be further noted that the Board is not required to determine and prove that the transaction would have any effect within the Turkish market when assessing if the

---

[1376] See, e.g., *Güneş Sigorta* (27 August 2020, 20-39/539-240).

relevant undertakings failed to notify a transaction, as seen in decisions such as *Cegedim/ Dendrite/Ultima*[1377] and *BMW/Daimler/Ford/Porsche/Ionity*.[1378] In the Cegedim decision, the Board made assessments regarding failure to notify in two different acquisitions made by Cegedim: (i) the acquisition of Dendrite Turkey Inc. and (ii) the acquisition of Ultima.

In the assessment of Cegedim's acquisition of Ultima, the Board found out that (i) Cegedim's vice-chairman was appointed to Ultima's board of directors; (ii) the announcement regarding the acquisition was made in Cegedim's financial report on half-year results; (iii) Cegedim had interfered in Ultima's invoicing practices during February 2008–May 2008 period; and (iv) the parties had exchanged information regarding Ultima's employment agreements, technical capacities, performance reviews and cash flow statements, as well as the printing of business cards for their employees. While said activities may or may not have an effect on competition in the relevant market, the Board imposed a fine on Cegedim and concluded that even though the share purchase agreement was approved on 20 November 2009, the de facto transaction was realised earlier than this date.

Furthermore, in the *BMW/Daimler/Ford/Porsche/Ionity* decision, the transaction concerned the establishment of a full-function joint venture in 2017, which actually had no presence nor any activity in Turkey, by four JV partners. The Authority became aware of that transaction within the scope of a notification made in 2020, with regard to another transaction that concerned the acquisition of joint control by a fifth JV partner alongside the existing JV partners. The Board assessed that the establishment of the joint venture is a notifiable transaction as the thresholds are met and found no overlap in the activities of the JV in Turkey. However, even though the Board unconditionally approved both transactions, it imposed administrative monetary fines on each of the four existing JV partners corresponding to 0.1% of their annual Turkish turnovers generated in their 2019 financial years for the violation of the suspension requirement.

The Board may become aware of such a transaction by way of complaints or through assessments of future transactions of the associated parties, or third parties in the same product market. Furthermore, the Board may also detect such a transaction via press coverage, such as the coverage of the Commission or other competition authorities' decisions on the transactions in question.

9.1.7.1 Monetary Fines

Article 11 of Law No. 4054 sets forth the consequences of failure to notify. The fines surrounding the failure to notify are provided under Article 16 of Law No. 4054.

Accordingly, if the Board becomes aware of a failure to notify, the undertakings concerned are imposed an automatic monetary fine of 0.1% of their turnover generated in Turkey within the financial year preceding the date of the decision. These undertakings are both merging parties in case of a merger and the acquiring parties in case of an acquisition. In joint ventures, as the acquiring parties will be ultimately controlling the newly formed joint venture, they will be liable for the fine. If the rate of 0.1% is found to be below

---

[1377]   *Cegedim/Dendrite/Ultima* (26 August 2010, 10-56/1089-411).
[1378]   *BMW/Daimler/Ford/Porsche/Ionity* (28 July 2020, 20-36/483-211).

the minimum administrative fine amount of the relevant year, then the minimum administrative fine amount is imposed.[1379]

While the frequency of such decisions has decreased, there are many instances where the Board fined the relevant undertakings due to (i) closing the transaction prior to notifying the transaction[1380] and (ii) not notifying the transaction at all.[1381] It should be noted that whereas such cases are considered as a violation of Article 4(1) and Article 7(1) of the EC Merger Regulation and two separate fines shall be imposed by the Commission,[1382] Law No. 4054 does not define two different violations and, therefore, the Board considers these two different acts as the same violation.

If the Board finds a violation of Article 7, then the undertakings concerned will be subject to further monetary fines and sanctions. In such case, as defined in Article 16(4) of Law No. 4054, the Board shall impose an additional monetary fine of up to 10% of the annual Turkish turnover of the undertakings concerned.

Furthermore, employees and executive Board members who had "decisive influence" in the infringement may also receive monetary fines of up to 5% of the fine imposed on the parties. However, it is a heavily disputed issue, and such a fine has not been imposed in a case of failure to notify, following the relevant amendments to Article 16 of Law No. 4054, which require a finding of formative effect.

If the transaction in question is found to be problematic, the Board may deem it necessary to take interim measures to protect the competition in the relevant market, which will be explained further in the following section. In the case of monetary fines, if the parties do not comply with the measures the Board has taken, as per Article 17 of Law No. 4054, the Board may further impose a daily administrative fine of 0.05% of annual gross revenues of the relevant undertakings, until the parties comply with the Board's decision.

However, there is no example that could be pointed out with regard to the imposition of daily fines in case of failure to notify, as there is no example where the parties closed

---

[1379]   The minimum administrative fine to be imposed as a result of the violation of Law No. 4054 is annually updated. The latest update indicates that the minimum fine is TL 34,809 (approx. USD 4,250 or EUR 3,500 as per the applicable currency rate as of 9 May 2021).

[1380]   E.g., *Brookfield/JCI* (30 April 2020, 20-21/278-132); *Labelon/A-Tex* (6 February 2016, 16-42/693-311); *DSG/ Electro World* (5 September 2013, 13-50/717-304); *Tekno İnşaat/Enerray/Tekno Ray* (23 February 2012, 12-08/224-55); *Zhejiang/Kiri* (2 June 2011, 11-33/723-226); *TOBB/Mesa Mesken* (26 August 2010, 10-56/1088-408); *CVRD Canada/Inco* (8 July 2010, 10-49/949-332); *Flir Systems Holding/Raymarine* (17 June 2010, 10-44/762-246); *Batıçim/Borares* (27 May 2010, 10-38/641-217); *Sarten/TKS* (15 April 2010, 10-31/471-175); *Simsmetal East/Fairless Iron & Metal* (16 September 2009, 09-42/1057-269); *Kiler/ Yimpaş* (15 July 2009, 09-33/728-168); *Verifone/Lipman* (13 April 2009, 09-14/300-73); *Fina/Turkon* (14 January 2009, 09-02/19-12); *Çallı/Turyağ* (12 November 2008, 08-63/1048-407); *Corio/ACT* (3 July 2008, 08-43/588-221); *Eastpharma/Deva* (24 April 2007, 07-34/355-133); *Total S.A./CEPSA* (20 December 2006, 06-92/1186-355); *Mauna/Tyco International* (29 June 2006, 06-46/586-159); *Dinter/Konfrut* (15 December 2005, 05-84/1149-329).

[1381]   E.g., *BMW/Daimler/Ford/Porsche/Ionity* (n. 1378); *Ersoy/Sesli* (25 June 2014, 14-22/422-186); *Cegedim/Dendrite/ Ultima* (n. 1377); *Kansai Paint/Akzo Nobel Coatings* (5 August 2009, 09-34/791-194); *Doğuş Otomotiv/ Katalonya* (22 August 2007, 07-66/813-308); *Doğan Yayın Holding/Turkish Daily News* (12 December 2000, 00-49/519-284).

[1382]   E.g., *Altice/PT Portugal* (Case M.7993) Commission Decision [2018] C(2018) 2418 final.

a transaction without notifying, which the Board prohibited. On the other hand, the Board has imposed a daily fine due to other violations such as (i) not allowing an on-the-spot inspection[1383] and (ii) not complying with the obligations imposed by the Board.[1384]

9.1.7.2 Other Possible Consequences of Failure to Notify

Besides the monetary fines, the main consequence of failure to notify shall be the invalidity of the transaction with all its legal implications, unless and until it is approved by the Board as stated in Article 10(4) of Communiqué No. 2010/4:

> A merger or an acquisition shall not become legally valid until a decision is taken, either explicitly under Article 10 paragraph 1 of the Law or tacitly under paragraph 2 of the same article, concerning the notification made on the merger or acquisition subject to authorisation.

Accordingly, as a notifiable merger or an acquisition cannot legally be valid until the approval of the Board, and such notifiable transaction cannot be closed in Turkey before the clearance of the Board, the parties shall be unable to enforce their rights under the transaction agreement(s) before Turkish courts, and build on this transaction in Turkey, prior to the clearance of the transaction by the Board.

If the parties were to engage in any official business with Turkish public authorities or administrations, this violation should be raised, and in any case, if the parties were to have a transaction in the future that has to be filed with the Authority, the Authority would halt the entire notification at that time, ask for a notification on the earlier transaction, review that, impose the administrative monetary fine and the decision for that particular case, and only then commence working on the actually notified transaction as seen in cases such as the above-mentioned *BMW/Daimler/Ford/Porsche/Ionity*,[1385] and *Ersoy/Sesli*.[1386]

In *Ersoy/Sesli*, the first transaction concerned the establishment of a joint venture–namely, Anayurt–between certain real persons, while the second transaction concerned the acquisition of a part of Anayurt's shares by another real person. The parties only notified the second transaction on 9 May 2014, and the notified transaction was unconditionally approved by the Board on 25 June 2014. However, within the scope of its review of the second transaction, the Board detected that the first transaction was not notified to the Board despite being subject to a mandatory merger control filing before the Authority. The Board also unconditionally approved the first transaction and despite the parties arguing that the purpose of establishing Anayurt was merely the acquisition of Gölbaşı (which was notified to the Board along with the second transaction–however, it was determined that this transaction was not subject to a mandatory merger control filing) decided that these two transactions were realised between the same undertakings within the last two years and they were interdependent in such a way that one transaction could not be realised without the other; therefore these two transactions, in fact, constituted a single transaction–which

---

[1383]   E.g., *Siemens* (7 November 2019, 19-38/581-247); *Mosaş* (21 June 2018, 18-20/356-176).
[1384]   E.g., *Google Android* (7 November 2019, 19-38/577-245).
[1385]   *BMW/Daimler/Ford/Porsche/Ionity* (n. 1378).
[1386]   *Ersoy/Sesli* (n. 1381).

was evident from the fact that Anayurt had not conducted any commercial activities since its establishment and its only expenditures were related to Gölbaşı. However, the Board did not accept these arguments and imposed administrative monetary fines against the incumbent parties for the violation of the suspension requirement regarding the first transaction.

Furthermore, pursuant to Article 9(1) of Law No. 4054, if the Board concludes that the transaction violates Article 7, "then it shall notify in its final decision the specific behaviors that the relevant undertaking or associations of undertakings must carry out or refrain from, in order to re-establish competition, and any structural remedies in the form of undertakings transferring certain businesses, partnership shares or assets". Hence, the Board may order certain remedies and direct the parties to take the necessary actions to restore the competitive environment before the closing of the transaction.

As referenced in the section above, the Board may also take interim measures if there is a possibility for serious and irreparable damages to occur. Article 11(b) of Law No. 4054 defines the Board's authority to take all necessary measures to (i) terminate the transaction; (ii) remove all de facto legal consequences of every action that has been taken unlawfully; (iii) return all shares and assets (if possible) to the places or persons they belonged to, before the transaction; or (iv) if this is not possible, assign them to third parties; and (v) forbid participation in the control of these undertakings until this assignment takes place, and to take any other necessary measures. In this context, the Board may take the measures stated above and any others it deems necessary to terminate the infringement of Article 7.

9.2 Types of Concentrations

9.2.1 Mergers

Article 7(1) of Law No. 4054, titled "Mergers and Acquisitions", prohibits mergers and acquisitions that lead to a significant lessening of effective competition in the relevant market, as follows:

> It is illegal and prohibited for one or more undertakings to merge, or for an undertaking or a person to acquire – except by inheritance – assets, or all or part of the partnership shares, or instruments conferring executive rights over another undertaking, where these would result in a significant lessening of effective competition within a market for goods or services in the entirety or a portion of the country, particularly in the form of creating or strengthening a dominant position.

Article 7(2) of Law No. 4054 imposes a duty upon the Board to regulate all matters pertaining to mergers and acquisitions through communiqués. Accordingly, the Board issued Communiqué No. 2010/4, which provides under Article 5(1)(a) that change of control on a lasting basis through the merger of two or more undertakings shall be a merger transaction within the meaning of Turkish competition law rules.[1387]

[1387]   Article 5(1)(a) of Communiqué No. 2010/4, which provides the definition of merger, is akin to Article 3(1)(a) of the EC Merger Regulation.

Paragraphs 5 and 6 of the Guidelines on the Concept of Control[1388] further set out the details of the types of mergers that can occur under the Turkish merger control regime:

- Two or more independent undertakings amalgamate into a new undertaking by terminating their legal entities,[1389]

- An undertaking is merged into another undertaking entirely, with one of the undertakings survive as an entity.[1390]

- The combining of the activities of previously independent undertakings results in the creation of a single economic unit, although the undertakings do not amalgamate into a single legal entity.[1391]

9.2.2 Acquisitions

The acquisition of direct or indirect control over all or part of one or more undertakings is considered a transaction of acquisition in the Turkish merger control regime. The acquisition could occur through the purchase of shares or assets, through a contract or through any other means.

Article 5(1)(b) of Communiqué No. 2010/4 concerns the acquisition transactions and indeed makes the definition below:

> The acquisition of direct or indirect control over all or part of one or more undertakings, by one or more undertakings or, by one or more persons who currently control at least one undertaking, through the purchase of shares or assets, through a contract or through any other means.[1392]

Under the Turkish merger control regime, full-function joint venture transactions are deemed as acquisitions pursuant to Article 5(3) of Communiqué No. 2010/4. Joint ventures are explained below under Section 9.2.3.

Acquisition of a minority shareholding may amount to a notifiable transaction if and to the extent it leads to a change in the control structure of the target entity. In other words, if minority interests acquired are granted certain veto rights that may influence the management of the company (e.g., privileged shares conferring management powers), then the nature of control could be deemed as changed (from sole to joint control) and the transaction could be subject to filing if the transaction clears the applicable turnover thresholds. These turnover thresholds are explained in detail above in Section 9.1.4.

As specified under paragraphs 52 and 53 of the Guidelines on the Concept of Control, such veto rights must be related to strategic decisions on the business policy, and

---

[1388] This regulation is closely modelled to paragraph 9 of the Commission Consolidated Jurisdictional Notice under Council Regulation (EC) No. 139/2004 on the control of concentrations between undertakings.
[1389] Guidelines on the Concept of Control, para. 5.
[1390] Ibid.
[1391] Ibid., para. 6.
[1392] Article 5(1)(b), which provides the definition of an acquisition, is akin to Article 3(1)(b) of the EC Merger Regulation.

they must go beyond normal "minority rights" protecting the financial interests of such shareholders. Veto rights that confer joint control typically include decisions pertaining to the budget, the business plan, major investments, or senior management appointment.

9.2.3 Joint Ventures

Article 5 of Communiqué No. 2010/4 defines joint ventures in a very similar manner to the EU law. There are essentially two criteria for a joint venture to qualify as a concentration subject to merger control:

- full functionality, i.e., the joint venture being established as an independent economic entity, on a lasting basis (having adequate capital, labour and an indefinite duration)

- the existence of joint control in the joint venture.

To that end, in order to be deemed "fully functional", a joint venture should:

- have sufficient resources to operate independently

- undertake activities beyond the one specific function for the parents

- be independent of the parent companies in its sale and purchase activities

- be operating on a lasting basis.

Overall, based on both the legislation and the Board's established jurisprudence, where a joint venture is not "full functional", it would not be subject to mandatory merger control filing.[1393]

However, such joint ventures could still fall under Article 4 of Law No. 4054, which prohibits restrictive agreements. In such cases, the parties could do a self-assessment individual exemption test on whether the joint venture meets the conditions of individual exemption as set out under Article 5 of Law No. 4054; or the conditions of a block exemption under Communiqué No. 2016/5 (for R&D agreements) or Communiqué No. 2013/3 (for specialisation agreements), among others, as discussed in detail under Chapter 4 of this book. This is not a positive duty of the parties but merely an option granted by the law.

[1393] *OMV Petrol Ofisi/Shell&Turcas* (5 June 2014, 14-20/382-166); *Omur Denizcilik/Ziraat/Güneş/Halk/Metropole/ Vitsan* (19 February 2014, 14-07/134-61); *Opet/Aygaz* (12 September 2013, 13-52/734-307); *Tamiran/SITA* (12 January 2012, 12-01/6-3); *Türkiye Petrol Rafinerileri/Akdeniz Akaryakıt* (4 July 2012, 12-36/1041-329); *Unmaş/Europastry* (27 December 2012, 12-60/1598-582); *Ravago/Barentz* (14 March 2012, 12-11/369-104); *Lur Berri/Alfesca* (14 December 2011, 11-61/1580-565); *Galenica/Fresenius* (n. 1369); *United Phosphorus/ Agromed* (14 July 2011; 11-43/938-302); *Ammann Group/Ammann Teknomak* (14 April 2011, 11-23/433-131); *Strategic Development/Yıldız Holding/Marsa* (9 February 2011, 11-08/151-49); *Netcell* (9 September 2002, 02-56/697-281).

9.2.3.1 Full Functionality

Section 5 of the Guidelines on the Concept of Control elaborates on the following conditions to establish the presence of full functionality:

9.2.3.1.1 Sufficient Resources to Operate Independently

A full-functional joint venture must operate as an undertaking that is normally carrying out certain tasks in a given market, independently of its parents with its own market presence. That is to say, even if the joint venture does not retain a strategic independence, it should be independent of the parent companies from an operational perspective. Paragraph 82 of the Guidelines on the Concept of Control provides the following criteria in assessing operational independence:

> The joint venture must have a management dedicated to its day-to-day operations and access to sufficient resources including finance, staff, and assets (tangible and intangible) in order to conduct its business activities on a lasting basis, within the area provided for in the joint-venture agreement.[1394]

Moreover, the joint venture's interactions with the parent companies should also occur within a normal commercial framework, and the joint venture should freely make its own employment decisions.[1395]

9.2.3.1.2 Conducting Activities Beyond the One Specific Function for the Parents

Joint ventures must separately access a given market or establish their own presence therein.[1396] For instance, in *Sumitomo/Toyota*,[1397] the Board considered that the proposed economic entity in question did not constitute a full-functional joint venture. The Board reached this conclusion due to the finding that (i) both parent companies maintained their activities in the same market and (ii) the distribution activities of the joint venture was limited to one group of products and exports.

Moreover, as specified within paragraph 83 of the Guidelines on the Concept of Control, joint ventures that are (i) solely focused on R&D and production, or (ii) principally acting as sales agencies for the products of their parent companies, would not fulfil this criterion of full functionality. Similarly, in terms of acquisition and/or holding real estate, while joint ventures may perform these tasks solely for their own behalf, the joint venture would not fulfil the full-functionality criteria if it performs these tasks for the parent companies by using their resources.[1398]

[1394]   See for example *Tamiran/SITA* (n. 1393), where the Board concluded that planned joint venture SITA fulfilled the criteria for independent operation as its financial and organisational structure and operational fields demonstrated that the joint venture would be operating as an independent financial entity.

[1395]   Guidelines on the Concept of Control, para. 82.

[1396]   Ibid., para. 83.

[1397]   *Sumitomo/Toyota* (n. 1369)

[1398]   Guidelines on the Concept of Control, para. 84.

9.2.3.1.3 Independence from the Parent Companies in Sale and Purchase Activities

Sales to Parent Companies

The Board would consider the ratio of the sales that the joint venture makes to the parent companies to its total production[1399] while assessing whether the joint venture (i) plays an active role in the relevant market and (ii) is economically autonomous from an operational perspective.[1400] Paragraph 86 of the Guidelines on the Concept of Control also emphasises that in any case, the relationship between the joint venture and the parent company should be purely commercial. Further, the Board would consider the general structure of the market as well.[1401]

In its decisional practice, the Board refrained from defining a specific ratio due to the unique circumstances that are at play in each case, suggesting a case-by-case analysis on this matter. However, as per paragraph 86 of the Guidelines on the Concept of Control, 50% is an important threshold in this consideration. Accordingly, if the joint venture makes more than 50% of its sales to third parties, then this would be a strong indicator of full functionality.[1402] However, if the ratio falls below 50%, then the Board would conduct a case-by-case analysis. In this case, the Board takes into account whether the parties sufficiently demonstrated that the joint venture (i) would supply its goods/services to the purchaser that pays the highest price and (ii) deal with its parent companies in a purely commercial environment.[1403]

Pursuant to an assessment in the above framework, if the Board concludes that the joint venture treats third parties and its parent companies equally, then allocating 20% of the planned sales to third parties could be deemed as sufficient.[1404,1405] In any case, paragraph 86 of the Guidelines on the Concept of Control sets forth that as the proportion of sales to parent companies increase, the parties would need to submit even more clear and concrete evidence as to the purely commercial relationship between the joint venture and the parent companies.

As an important example, in *TUSAŞ/Altınay*,[1406] the Board assessed a transaction where the operation of the parties would focus on prototype development for five years,

---

[1399] *See* for example: *Efes/Etap* (19 August 2009, 09-47/1161-295), where the Board reviewed the sales of Etap to the parent companies, as well as to third parties. Accordingly, the Board found that the portion of the sales that Etap makes to parent companies to its sales to third parties was not so high as to create an economic dependency on the parent companies. Accordingly, the Board concluded that Etap would operate as an independent economic entity.

[1400] Guidelines on the Concept of Control, para. 86.

[1401] *Efes/Etap* (n. 1399).

[1402] Guidelines on the Concept of Control, para. 86; *Celanese/Blackstone* (28 November 2017, 17-39/623-270).

[1403] Guidelines on the Concept of Control, para. 86.

[1404] Ibid., para. 86.

[1405] *Hitachi/Honda/Keihin/Showa/Nissin* (9 July 2020, 20-33/413-189).

[1406] *TUSAŞ/Altınay* (13 June 2019, 19-21/321-140); see also *TUSAŞ/Sarsılmaz* (15 March 2018, 18-08/137-67), where the Board found that even though the relevant joint venture would make most of its sales to the parent company TUSAŞ, this would not affect its full functionality due to the fact that (i) TUSAŞ is the sole producer of the products that would be produced with the products purchased from the joint venture and (ii) that TUSAŞ is planning to export its products globally.

following which they would move on to mass production, and subsequently to imports and sales to third parties. The Board recognised that initially, in this process, the joint venture would make most of its sales to one of the parties of the joint venture. However, it concluded that this would not hamper the full functionality of the relevant joint venture.

Purchases From Parent Companies

While assessing the purchases that the joint venture makes from parent companies, the Board would take into account whether and to what extent the joint venture provides any added value to the relevant product or service.[1407] Accordingly, paragraph 89 of the Guidelines on the Concept of Control provides that if the joint venture adds little value, then the Board would be critical of the joint venture's full-functional nature. For instance, in *SOCAR/BP*,[1408] the Board concluded that the joint venture would indeed add value to the products (i.e., raw material) purchased from parent companies as it would (i) produce the end product from the raw materials purchased from parent companies and (ii) would create an output of new products during the production process.[1409] Further, in *Celanese/Blackstone*,[1410] the Board conducted an analysis that went beyond the transformation of raw material to the final product. In *Celanese/Blackstone*, the Board emphasised that the joint venture would be able to purchase the product from other external resources, and also purchase the other production inputs from different suppliers. Accordingly, the Board concluded that the joint venture in question was indeed "full functional".

However, if the joint venture is active in a trade market and operates as a trading company, then the joint venture would still be considered "full functional".[1411] Accordingly, paragraph 90 of the Guidelines on the Concept of Control provides the following conditions for the joint ventures to be considered "full functional" under this assessment criteria:

> In order to constitute a full-function joint venture in a trade market, an undertaking must have the necessary facilities and be likely to procure a substantial part of its supplies not only from its parent companies but also from other competing sources.

Operation on a Lasting Basis

Generally, if the joint venture fulfils the above-mentioned full-functionality criteria, then this would demonstrate that the joint venture is operating on a lasting basis.[1412] Paragraph 91 of the Guidelines on the Concept of Control provides that if the agreement establishing the joint venture includes a provision for (i) dissolution of the joint venture or (ii) one of the parent companies to withdraw, this would not automatically mean that the joint venture is not operational on a lasting basis. However, if the joint venture is

1407 Guidelines on the Concept of Control, para. 89.
1408 *SOCAR/BP* (9 July 2020, 20-33/426-193).
1409 *See also Mitsui/Honshu* (7 January 2021, 21-01/4-3).
1410 *Celanese/Blackstone* (n. 1402).
1411 Guidelines on the Concept of Control, para. 90.
1412 Ibid., para. 91.

established for a specifically short period, then the joint venture would not be considered as operational on a lasting basis.[1413]

Moreover, the joint venture would also not be considered as operational on a lasting basis if essential decisions for the operation of the joint venture are being made by third parties.[1414]

Although the Guidelines on the Concept of Control do not indicate a particular duration or period, the Board indicated in *ADPM/Vinci Airports/Astaldi* that a joint venture that is established for a twenty-year period satisfies the condition of being operational on a lasting basis.[1415] Further in *Kalyon/Hanwha/YEKA*, the Board found a ten-year period is sufficient for the same purpose.[1416]

Joint ventures that do not fulfil the above criteria of full functionality are not subject to a mandatory merger control filing. However, such non-full-function joint ventures may fall under Article 4 of Law No. 4054, which prohibits restrictive agreements. Accordingly, a joint venture must not have the object or effect of restricting competition between the parties and itself.

9.2.3.2 Possible Review Under Articles 4 and 5 of Law No. 4054

As stated above, although joint ventures that do not fulfil the criteria for full functionality are not required to notify the merger, they may still be subject to review under Articles 4 and 5 of Law No. 4054. Article 13(3) of Communiqué No. 2010/4 specifically provides the following provision in this respect:

> The formation of a joint venture which has the goal or effect of limiting competition among undertakings and which would fulfil all of the functions of an independent economic entity on a lasting basis shall also be assessed within the framework of Articles 4 and 5 of the Act.

Further, the wording of the standard notification form also enables such analysis. Under Section 9 of the standard notification form provided by the Authority, Question 9.1 specifically requests parties' analysis as to a possible review of the transaction within the scope of Article 4 as well as Article 5 of Law No. 4054.

In its *DSM/Evonik*[1417] decision, the Board found that the proposed transaction did not fall under Article 7 of Law No. 4054. Accordingly, the Board evaluated that DSM and Evonik are competitors in the overall animal feed market and they have sales in vertical markets; therefore, the joint venture can be considered as a restrictive agreement under Article 4 of Law No. 4054. The Board also conducted an analysis pursuant to Article 5 of Law No. 4054 and, within the scope of its assessment, found that the transaction fulfilled the relevant criteria and therefore granted an individual exemption to the cooperation.

[1413]   Ibid., para. 92.
[1414]   Ibid., para. 93.
[1415]   *ADPM/Vinci Airports/Astaldi* (n. 1373).
[1416]   *Kalyon/Hanwha/YEKA* (21 December 2007, 17-42/658-290).
[1417]   *DSM/Evonik* (26 October 2017, 17-35/573-248).

9.3 Notification and Suspension Requirement

9.3.1 Phase I Review

The procedure surrounding a merger control filing is regulated under Article 10 of Law No. 4054. When all of the required information is provided with the filing made by the parties, phase I review begins where the Board is required to issue its decision on the application within a period of fifteen days. If the information provided in the notification form is deemed to be incomplete, the Authority may send requests for information and the relevant review period only begins on the date when all of the requested information is completed by the parties.

Moreover, the Board may send written requests to the parties, any other party relating to the transaction or third parties such as competitors, customers or suppliers during its reviews to scrutinise and possibly eliminate any competitive issue regarding the transaction.

The Board may also ask for another public authority's opinion in reviewing a transaction. As referenced in Article 11(2) of Communiqué No. 2010/4, "in case the opinion of a public institution or organisation is required in accordance with legislation, the time periods specified in Article 10 of the Act shall commence after the relevant opinion is received into the Board records". Therefore, the timing works similarly with an information request during phase I, so that the review period restarts on the date the relevant public authority submits its opinion. The phase I review pertains to the Board's preliminary review of the filing. The Board conducts the phase I review and renders its decision within the above-mentioned fifteen days. As a result, the Board either decides to approve the transaction or to investigate it further within the scope of a phase II Review. However, pursuant to Article 10 of Law No. 4054, if the Board takes no action or no decision during this period, this is understood as tacit approval, and the transaction becomes legally valid as of thirty days after the date of notification.

Similar to the duty of the parties to provide a complete filing, if the Board makes an information request to better assess the transaction during phase I, the period gets reset and starts anew after the responses to the information request are provided.

9.3.2 Phase II Review

Article 13 of Communiqué No. 2010/4 states that, in assessing whether a transaction would significantly impede effective competition in a given market, the structure of the relevant market, actual and potential competition among domestic- and foreign-based undertakings, the status of the undertakings within the market, their economic and financial power, their alternative sources for suppliers and customers, their ability to access sources of supply, barriers to entry into the market, supply and demand trends, consumer interests, activities benefiting consumers and other issues shall be taken into account. Although these elements do not present an exhaustive list, the Board gives them particular weight and takes the notified transaction to a phase II review should it find that the notified transaction has the potential to significantly impede effective competition in the market.

If the Board decides to take a transaction into phase II, it opens a fully-fledged investigation. Pursuant to Article 43 of Law No. 4054:

> Once the Board decides that an investigation shall be conducted, it designates the rapporteur or rapporteurs who shall conduct the investigation under the supervision of the head of department concerned. The investigation shall be concluded within 6 months at the latest. In cases where it is deemed necessary, an additional period of up to 6 months may be granted by the Board on a one-time-only basis.

Therefore, phase II shall be completed within six months from the date of the Board's decision, but it can be extended once, for up to six months if deemed necessary by the Board.

After the Board notifies the parties regarding the phase II review, along with sufficient information about the competitive issues raised, the parties are required to submit their first written defences within thirty days, similar to the procedure of a fully-fledged investigation.

The Board may decide to approve the transaction after the phase II review is completed. If not, the report shall be provided to the parties, and the procedure continues in parallel with the investigation procedure under Law No. 4054. As explained in further detail in Chapter 11, said procedure consists of the parties' second written defences, the additional written opinion, the parties' third written defence and the oral hearing. However, there are other aspects affecting the procedure and timing of merger control reviews in both of the phases.

9.3.3 Suspension Requirement

As explained above in Sections 9.1. and 9.2., any transaction triggering the thresholds defined under Article 7 of Communiqué No. 2010/4 is subject to a mandatory filing before the Authority. Even though no specific deadline is set with regard to the timing of the filing, an explicit suspension requirement is set out under Article 11(1)(a) of Law No. 4054 and Article 10(5) of Communiqué No. 2010/4. This suspension requirement dictates that the parties shall not close a notifiable transaction before obtaining the approval of the Board; therefore, the parties will be in violation if they do not notify such a transaction, or if they close said transaction while the assessment of the Board is yet pending.

Since the Board has the power to determine whether a transaction may significantly impede effective competition and accordingly decide to approve or reject said transaction, the suspension requirement performs a critical duty to prevent any notifiable transaction from being closed before the final decision of the Board. However, whether the Board approves the transaction or not, and whether an effect within the market occurs, do not affect the assessment on the violation of the suspension requirement. Once it is determined that the parties "jumped the gun" (i.e., violated the suspension requirement), a turnover-based fine is automatically imposed on the relevant parties and further legal consequences may arise in case the Board does not approve the transaction.

Pursuant to the suspension requirement, a notifiable merger or acquisition and all its legal consequences shall be deemed invalid unless and until it is approved by the Board. Therefore, no such transaction can be closed in Turkey before the Board grants its approval.

To understand whether a violation of the suspension requirement is in question, it is imperative to define what constitutes closing of a transaction according to Turkish competition law. As referenced in Article 5 of Communique No. 2010/4, completing or closing of the transaction may involve taking steps that could lead to the permanent change of control, such as exchanging commercially and competitively sensitive information, taking administrative actions and/or making recommendations, establishing joint marketing or working teams and initiating the integration process between the undertakings. Any activity showing that the transaction is implemented before the approval decision is indicative of a violation of the suspension requirement.

The Board is quite strict with regard to the assessment of gun jumping, and no effect or impediment on effective competition is needed to be determined for the Board to decide that the parties violated the suspension requirement. Furthermore, whilst determining whether the transaction was closed and the suspension requirement has been violated, the Board is not obliged to assess and prove any effect within the market in Turkey, either. This was demonstrated by the Board's decisions, such as *Ajans Press* and *Labelon/A-Tex*.

In *Ajans Press/PR Net*,[1418] the Board found that (i) the target PR Net's offices had been moved to the same building where the acquirer Ajans Press was located; (ii) that Ajans Press had been interfering with PR Net's daily business such as selection of phone numbers to publication subscriptions; (iii) the owner of Ajans Press had instructed PR Net's employees to conduct a meeting; and (iv) commercially sensitive information had been shared between the parties. Although these steps were all taken before any transfer of shares was made, the Board determined that these findings were sufficient to prove a violation of the suspension requirement.

Similarly, in *Labelon/A-Tex*,[1419] the Board determined that the transaction agreement was signed on 21 August 2015, and the change of control occurred on 27 August 2015, before any notification was made to the Board. Without any further assessment, the Board imposed an administrative monetary fine for violating the suspension requirement, as the transaction had been closed before the notification.

[1418]   *Ajans/Press/PR Net* (21 October 2010, 10-66/1402-523).
[1419]   Labelon/A-Tex (n. 1380).

9.3.4 Consequences of Violation of the Suspension Requirement

9.3.4.1 Monetary Fine

As indicated in the section above, pursuant to Article 16 of Law No. 4054, if the parties to a notifiable transaction violate the suspension requirement, a turnover-based monetary fine will be imposed on the undertakings concerned. The undertakings concerned are defined as both of the merging parties in case of a merger and the acquiring parties in case of an acquisition. In joint ventures, as the acquiring parties will be ultimately controlling the newly formed joint venture, similar to a case of acquisition, the acquiring parties will be liable for the fine.

In case of gun jumping, the undertakings concerned are imposed an automatic monetary fine of 0.1% of the turnover in Turkey generated in the financial year preceding the date of the decision. Even though recently the Board has fewer decisions where fines were imposed on undertakings for violations of the suspension requirement, which may be indicative of the undertakings' increasing awareness of competition law rules, it is not uncommon for the Board to impose an administrative monetary fine on the basis of violation of suspension requirement.[1420]

The above described monetary fine of 0.1% of the turnover is a fixed rate and levied automatically; the Board has no discretion regarding this fine once it finds a violation of the suspension requirement. If 0.1% of the turnover calculated is below the minimum administrative fine amount of the relevant year, then the minimum administrative fine amount is imposed.

As seen from the Board's precedents, the automatic monetary fine comes up only where the Board decides to approve the transaction. However, if the transaction does not pass the SIEC test (i.e., it is found to significantly impede effective competition), the Board shall decide against approving the transaction, and in such case, the violation of the suspension requirement may have further legal consequences.

9.3.4.2 Legal Consequences If the Transaction Is Not Approved

If the Board concludes that the transaction significantly restricts competition in any relevant product market, especially by way of creating or strengthening a dominant position, and thus the Board finds a violation of Article 7 of Law No. 4054, the concerned

---

[1420] E.g., *BMW/Daimler/Ford/Porsche/Ionity* (n. 1378); *Brookfield/JCI* (n. 1380); *Labelon/A-Tex* (n. 1380); *Ersoy/Sesli* (n. 1381); *DSG/Electro World* (n. 1380); *Tekno İnşaat/Enerray/Tekno Ray* (n. 1380); *Zhejiang/Kiri* (n. 1380); *Ajans Press* (n. 1418); *Cegedim/Dendrite/Ultima* (n. 1377); *TOBB/Mesa Mesken* (n. 1380); *CVRD Canada/Inco* (n. 1380); *Flir Systems Holding/Raymarine* (n. 1380); *Batıçim/Borares* (n. 1380); *Sarten/TKS* (n. 1380); *Simsmetal East/Fairless Iron & Metal* (n. 1380); *Kansai Paint/Akzo Nobel Coatings* (n. 1381); *Kiler/Yimpaş* (n. 1380); *Verifone/Lipman* (n. 1380), *Fina/Turkon* (n. 1380); *Çallı/Turyağ* (n. 1380); *Corio/ACT* (n. 1380); *Eastpharma/Deva* (n. 1380); *Doğuş Otomotiv/Katalonya* (n. 1381); *Total S.A./CEPSA* (n. 1380); *Mauna/Tyco International* (n. 1380); *Dinter/Konfrut* (n. 1380); *Doğan Yayın Holding/Turkish Daily News* (n. 1381).

undertakings will face further monetary fines and sanctions. Another fine which is heavily disputed and actually rarely seen in the Board's decisions is that which can be imposed upon the employees and members of the executive bodies of the parties if it is concluded that said individuals had a determining effect in the bringing about the violation. It should also be noted that such a fine has not been imposed in a case of violation of suspension requirement after the relevant amendments to Article 16 of Law No. 4054, which now require a finding of determining effect.

If a notifiable transaction is found problematic under the SIEC test applicable in Turkey, Article 11(b) of Law No. 4054 entitles the Board to *ex officio* launch an investigation in case the transaction was closed before approval. Based on this investigation, the Board may impose an additional monetary fine of up to 10% of the annual Turkish turnover of the undertakings concerned. Furthermore, as stated earlier, employees and executive members of the parties who are determined to have played a significant role in the infringement may also receive monetary fines up to 5% of the fine imposed on the parties, even though there is no recent case law where such a fine has been imposed.

Furthermore, pursuant to Article 9(1) of Law No. 4054, the Board is entitled to order remedies to take the necessary actions to restore the competitive environment that existed prior to the closing of the transaction (*restitutio in integrum*). Moreover, with the changes introduced by the Amendment Law, the Board shall order structural remedies only when behavioural remedies are found insufficient.

Similarly, the Board is authorised to take interim measures in cases where there is a risk of serious and irreparable damages until the final resolution is reached on the matter. As also stated in Article 11(b) of Law No. 4054, the Board is authorised to take all necessary measures to terminate the transaction, remove all de facto legal consequences of any unlawful action, return all shares and assets (if possible) to the places or persons they belonged to, before the transaction or, if such measure is not possible, assign these to third parties; and meanwhile forbid the parties' participation in the control of these undertakings until this assignment takes place, as well as any other necessary measures.

If the Board decides to take any or all of the above measures applicable, then the risk of additional daily fines (0.05%) cannot be discounted entirely. Indeed, as per Article 17 of Law No. 4054, if "obligations introduced or commitments made by a final decision or interim measure decision are not complied with", the Board may, for each day, impose on undertakings an additional administrative fine of 0.05% of their annual gross revenues, until the parties comply with the Board's decision.

As discussed above, there is no case law where the Board imposed a daily fine due to the fact that the parties closed a transaction that the Board prohibited. However, this may be due to the fact that there has not yet been an example where the parties closed a transaction that the Board had prohibited. That said, there are other examples of where the Board imposed a daily fine due to other violations such as (i) not allowing an on-the-spot inspection[1421] or (ii) not complying with the obligations imposed by the Board.[1422]

[1421]   E.g., *Siemens Healthcare* (n. 1383); *Mosaş* (n. 1383).
[1422]   E.g., *Google Android* (n. 1384).

9.3.4.3 Carve-Out and Hold-Separate Arrangements

While it may be possible to utilise carve-out and hold-separate arrangements to prevent an effect within the relevant market before obtaining the approval decision of the relevant authority, such practice is rarely seen in Turkey. It should be stated that there is no normative regulation allowing or disallowing carve-out arrangements; however, the decisional practice of the Board shows that there is a tendency to dismiss carve-out and hold-separate mechanisms under the Turkish merger control regime.

There are precedents of the Board in which it clearly dismissed carve-out arrangements.[1423] On the other hand, there are three cases that may serve as exceptions to the Board's outlook on carve-out and hold-separate arrangements. These cases–namely, *Prysmian S.p.A/Draka*,[1424] *Bekaert/Pirelli*[1425] and *APM Terminals B.V./Grup Maritim TCB, S.L.*[1426] – showed especially unique characteristics with regard to their market and business activities where the models envisaged allowed the prohibition of any effect in the relevant market in Turkey, or the foreign laws and regulations necessitated that the transaction was closed before obtaining the Board's decision.

9.3.4.3.1 Prysmian/Draka

In this case, the transaction consisted of Prysmian S.p.A ("Prysmian") acquiring all of Draka Holding N.V.'s ("Draka") shares with the agreement signed on 22 November 2010. After the discussions between the relevant parties, on 8 February 2011, Prysmian announced that their offer had become unconditional. As explained by the Board in the decision, per the laws of the Netherlands, Prysmian was under an obligation to make a payment to all shareholders of Draka, who requested Prysmian to purchase their shares in accordance with Prysmian's offer, within ten working days after Prysmian's offer became unconditional and the control of the shares were transferred to Prysmian subsequent to the payment. As the decision was rendered on 10 March 2011, it is clear that the transaction has been closed before obtaining the Board's decision.

As the parties recognised that this transaction would therefore violate the suspension requirement, Prysmian offered a commitment not to use its voting rights tied to Draka's shares to eliminate an effect before the Board's decision. While it may be derived from the decision that the Board accepted Prysmian's commitment as no fine was imposed due to a violation of the suspension requirement, it needs to be underlined as recognised by the Board that this case was unique since the parties had no choice to stall the transaction until they have obtained the final decision.

9.3.4.3.2 Bekaert/Pirelli

The transaction reviewed by the Board in this decision concerns NV Bekaert's ("Bekaert") acquisition of Pirelli Tyre's ("Pirelli") steel tire cord business. While the transaction was approved by the authorities of all of the relevant jurisdictions, the Turkish Board

[1423] *Total/CEPSA* (n. 1380), *CVR Inc/Inco Limited* (1 February 2007, 07-11/71-23).
[1424] *Prysmian/Draka* (10 March 2011, 11-15/259-87).
[1425] *Bekaert/Pirelli* (22 January 2015, 15-04/52-25).
[1426] *APMT/Grup Maritim* (11 May 2016, 16-16/267-118).

determined that the parties' market power had been increasing steadily within the market and that the transaction would increase their market power even more, which may, in turn, restrict competition in the market. Therefore, the Board decided to begin a phase II review of the transaction.

Çelikord A.Ş. is a separate company owned by Pirelli that operates in the market for manufacturing steel tire cords in Turkey. Since the Board had also determined that imports do not affect the market in Turkey in a major way, the parties arranged it so that they split the transaction into two parts based on these facts, taking into account that the Board may dismiss a so-called "carve-out" arrangement. The adopted arrangements pertained to two different sale and purchase agreements where the global parts of the business were transferred separately from the business in Turkey. As the global part of the transaction did not trigger the thresholds and raise any competitive issues, this was not found problematic by the Board.

The only notifiable part of the transaction was therefore concerning the transaction of the business in Turkey. In the assessment of the case and the decision, the Board determined that the acquisition of Pirelli's assets in Brazil, Italy, Romania and China is a separate transaction from the acquisition in Turkey, and Bekaert's behavioural commitments were adequate to eliminate the competitive issues raised by the phase II notification. Therefore, the transaction was approved conditionally.

As explained above, since the relevant parties and the market were able to completely distinguish between their business in Turkey and their operations in the rest of the world, they decided to form two different sale and purchase agreements rather than carving out the Turkish part of the deal from the transaction as a whole. Therefore, it would be hard to interpret this decision as a distinct instance of the Board's acceptance of a carve-out mechanism.

9.3.4.3.3 APMT/Grup Maritim

The most recent example to demonstrate the Board's outlook on carve-out and hold-separate arrangements concerned APM Terminals B.V.'s ("APMT") acquisition of Grup Maritim TCB S.L ("GMTCB"). As an international terminal operator, GMTCB had only one subsidiary active in Turkey, namely, TCE Ege Konteyner Terminal İşletmeleri A.Ş. ("TCE EGE").

While there is no detailed information on when the transaction was closed on a global level, the parties proposed an arrangement to the Board so that A. Perez y Cia S.L., GMTCB's largest shareholder, would take over TCE EGE as an interim buyer until the Board's final decision. Depending on the Board's approval of the transaction, A. Perez y Cia, S.L. would then transfer TCE EGE to APMT or transfer TCE EGE to another independent third party. Therefore, if the Board did not approve the decision, TCE EGE would not be part of the transaction, and no violation associated with TCE EGE would occur.

The Board defined the geographical market as "the city of İzmir", and no competitive issue was determined even with the narrow definition of a market about the transaction in question. Thus, the Board did not consider it a risk for a concentration of shipping terminals to have a significant impact on the market in Turkey.

In the final decision, the Board approved the transaction, which allowed APMT to obtain the shares of TCE EGE, and no administrative monetary fine was imposed. However, it is unclear whether the Board considered the proposed arrangement as a carve-out arrangement or a split of the transaction into two separate transactions similar to the *Pirelli/Bekaert* case, as no detailed assessment on this issue was given in the decision. Considering that the Board did not clearly set out which approach it took, this decision is not conducive to be a precedent to indicate that the Board may approve carve-out mechanisms.

9.4 Commitments

Another major aspect of the review process pursuant to Article 14 of Communiqué No. 2010/4 is the possible commitments to be proposed to the Authority during either phase of the review.

The relevant parties are allowed to propose commitments to eliminate the competition issues raised or that may arise with respect to Article 7 of Law No. 4054. There are many cases where the relevant parties have proposed commitments to limit the effect of the concentration in the market. In those cases, the Board has conditionally approved the transactions based on the commitments submitted.[1427] In certain other cases, the parties have not proposed the commitments directly to the Board, but the Board approved the concerned transactions conditional upon the commitments submitted to the Commission.[1428] There are also cases where the Board assessed the commitments submitted to the Commission but unconditionally approved the concerned transaction.[1429]

While commitments may be submitted during either phase of the review, it should be noted that as explained in paragraph 84 of the Guidelines on Remedies, for a commitment to be deemed sufficient during phase I, the competitive concern needs to be clearly and simply identifiable and the commitment in question needs to be equally clear.

[1427] *PSA/FCA* (30 December 2020, 20-57/794-354); *Harris/L3* (20 June 2019, 19-22/327-145); *Essilor/Luxottica* (1 October 2018, 18-36/585-286); *Arkas/Mardaş* (8 May 2018, 18-14/267-129); *Migros/Tesco* (9 February 2017, 17-06/56-22) ; *ABI/SABMiller* (1 June 2016, 16-19/311-140); *Anadolu/Migros* (9 July 2015, 15-29/420-117); *Novartis/GlaxoSmithKline* (29 January 2015, 15-05/59-26); *Bekaert/Pirelli* (n. 1425); *Lesaffre/Dosu Maya* (n. 836); *Sabiha Gökçen/THY Opet* (26 February 2014, 14-08/155-66); *Seagate/Samsung* (29 December 2011, 11-64/1656-586); *Mars/AFM* (17 November 2011, 11-57/1473-539); *Diageo/Mey İçki* (17 August 2011, 11-45/1043-356); *Besler/Turyağ* (n. 1334); *Türk Telekom/Invitel* (16 September 2010, 10-59/1195-451) ; *Mey İçki/Burgaz* (8 July 2010, 10-49/900-314) ; *OYAK* (18 November 2009, 09-56/1338-341); *ÇimSA/Bilecik* (2 June 2008, 08-36/481-169); *Doğan/Vatan* (10 March 2008, 08-23/237-75) ; *Toros Tarım/Mazıdağı* (21 February 2008, 08-16/189-62) ; *MGS/Gıdasa* (7 February 2008, 08-12/130-46); *Cadbury Schweppes/Intergum* (23 August 2007, 07-67/836-314).

[1428] *Synthomer/OMNOVA* (6 February 2020, 20-89/90-55); *Nidec/Whirlpool* (n. 39); *Bayer/Monsanto* (n. 39); *Valeo/FTE* (26 October 2017, 17-35/560-244); *Cookson/Foseco* (20 March 2008, 08-25/254-83); *P&G/Gillette* (8 September 2005, 05-55/836-228); *Syngenta/Advanta* (29 July 2004, 04-49/673-171); *DSM/Roche* (11 September 2003, 03-60/730-342).

[1429] *Maersk/HSDG* (4 May 2017, 17-15/210-89); *Agilent/Varian* (18 February 2010, 10-18/212-82); *Manitowoc/Enodis* (18 September 2008, 08-54/854-341); *TUI AG/CP Ships* (13 October 2005, 05-67/950-257); *Cytec/Surface* (6 January 2005, 05-01/3-3); *GlaxoSmithKline/Sanofi* (3 June 2004, 04-40/453-114).

With regard to the commitments to be submitted during phase II, paragraph 89 of the Guidelines on Remedies states that if the proposed commitments are found sufficient by the case handlers, the report and the commitments are submitted to the agenda of the Board without waiting for the statutory review period to be completed; however if the said commitments are found insufficient, the proposal shall be submitted to the Board's agenda together with the report completed in the legal time period.

If the Board finds the commitments insufficient, as per paragraph 90 of the Guidelines on Remedies, while the report is notified to the parties and their written pleas are requested, the relevant commitments may be developed further or new commitments may be proposed, together with the parties' second written pleas. In such case, these commitments are included in the Board's agenda together with the written additional opinion prepared by the case handlers. Any commitments submitted after the expiry of the period for the second written plea shall be ignored in order to ensure the proper functioning of the mechanism.

If the Board approves the transaction conditionally, the Board shall reference the proposed commitments in its decision and define them as "obligations" or "requirements". As explained in paragraph 92 of the Guidelines on Remedies, the distinction regarding obligations and requirements pertains to how the Board sets out the conditions on the application of the remedies in its decision, as obligations and requirements result in different legal consequences in a case of non-compliance.

In case of non-compliance with obligations, the parties may be subject to those administrative fines indicated under Article 17 of Law No. 4054, which is a turnover-based monetary fine at a rate of 0.05% based on the turnover generated in the financial year preceding the date of the fining decision.

Whereas in case of failure to comply with a requirement, the decision approving the transaction will automatically become invalid and the transaction unlawful, as the violation of Article 7 of Law No. 4054 is not resolved. Under those circumstances, the Board may apply the provisions of Article 16 of Law No. 4054, along with other legal consequences that would arise due to a violation of the suspension requirement.

Chapter 10
Merger Control: Substantive Aspects

GÖNENÇ GÜRKAYNAK, ESQ., İ. BARAN CAN YILDIRIM, LL.M.,[*]
BUĞRAHAN KÖROĞLU, LL.M.,[**] AND UZAY GÖRKEM YILDIZ[***]

Article 7 of Law No. 4054 sets down the rules on mergers and acquisitions prohibited under competition law, as explained in detail in Chapter 9. Accordingly, the Board is in charge of monitoring merger and/or acquisition transactions that may result in the significant lessening of effective competition in the relevant product markets for goods and services, in the entirety of the country or within certain regions.[1430]

To that end, during its assessment concerning the transactions, the Board (i) determines the relevant product and geographic markets affected by the transaction in question and then (ii) conducts its substantive assessment on whether the transaction will result in a significant lessening of effective competition.

Throughout this chapter, we will explain the rules governing the Board's substantive assessments and how the Board approaches the notified transactions. Generally, the Board starts by defining the markets that the transaction will affect and then assesses whether such transaction would result in a significant impediment in effective competition in those defined markets. In doing so, the Board looks into, among others, whether such transaction results in a dominant position, the competitive effects of such transaction and the possible efficiencies stemming from such transaction.

10.1 Market Definition for the Substantive Assessment of Concentrations

Market definitions are usually the starting point of the Board in every notified transaction. As such, the market definition identifies the markets in which the transaction presents its effects (i.e., where the competition takes place), by outlining the scope of the products and the geographical territory involved. In defining the markets, the Board identifies, among others, the products that are substitutable for each other (i.e., the relevant product

---

[*]   Associate, ELIG, Attorneys-at-Law, Istanbul <can.yildirim@elig.com>.
[**] Associate, ELIG, Attorneys-at-Law, Istanbul <bugrahan.koroglu@elig.com>.
[***] Associate, ELIG, Attorneys-at-Law, Istanbul <uzay.yıldız@elig.com>.
[1430] See Article 7 of Law No. 4054 on the Protection of Competition regarding the scope of the Board's competence with respect to the merger and acquisition transactions subject to mandatory merger control review in Turkey.

market) and the geographical territory where the supply and demand conditions are the same or similar (i.e., the relevant geographic market).

The Guidelines on the Relevant Market use the term "relevant market" to delineate the market concept used for competition law purposes. Thus, the starting point of the substantive analysis in Turkey is the "relevant market analysis". In order to find the answer to the question of whether a transaction will result in the significant lessening of the competition–particularly by the creation or strengthening of a dominant position–the possible relevant market definition with respect to such transaction should be properly analysed.

The reason behind such analysis is that with the relevant product and geographical markets outlined, the Authority could determine (i) whether there are horizontal or vertical overlaps between the parties of the transaction; (ii) the market power of the parties to the transaction within certain relevant product and geographic markets; and (iii) the level of competition in the relevant markets.

To that end, through a case-specific analysis depending on the parties' activities, the horizontal, vertical and/or conglomerate overlaps between the parties as well as the competitive structure of the markets, the Board determines different relevant product market definitions for each transaction as the initial step of its substantive analysis. Therefore, the approach of the Board on the definition of the potentially relevant market(s) becomes apparent in its decisional practice, as well as those of other competition authorities in different jurisdictions that inspire the Board's position on the matter.

As explained in detail under Chapter 6, "Concept of Dominance", there is a two-pronged analysis in defining the relevant market: (i) the relevant product (or services) market and (ii) the geographic market. While the analysis covers the time element as well, it is fused into the analyses of these two fundamental dimensions.

The "relevant product market" comprises the market that includes all of the goods and services deemed substitutable by the consumer in terms of price, purpose of use and quality, as well as other factors that might affect the definition of the relevant product market. Both the decisional practice of the Board and the scope of the Guidelines on the Relevant Market consider that demand substitution and supply substitution are the two main criteria employed for the relevant product market analysis. In this regard, while "demand-side substitutability" or "demand substitution" is the most important and widely used concept in defining the relevant market both at the Turkish[1431] and European levels,[1432] the "supply-side substitution" is also taken into account in the delimitation of the market in cases where it creates competitive pressure and prevents firms from engaging in monopoly activities.

[1431]   *ifm Electronic/Endress+Hauser* (24 December 2020, 20-55/771-343); *Cargill/Ekol Gıda* (29 March 2018, 18-09/159-79); *Munksjö/Ahlstrom* (1 November 2012, 12-53/1508-527); *Sümer Holding* (14 April 2011, 11-23/458-136); *Akzo Nobel/Dow Chemical* (18 March 2010, 10-24/339-123); *Medtronic/Kyphon* (1 October 2007, 07-83/1010-394); *Johnson & Johnson/Conor Medsystems* (29 January 2007, 07-10/64-13); *Shelby/Johnson & Johnson* (8 July 2005, 05-44/632-164); *Samsun Gübre* (22 April 2004, 04-27/317-72).

[1432]   See C. Bellamy and G. Child *European Community Law of Competition* (5th edition, London: Sweet & Maxwell, 2001), p. 687.

On the other hand, "relevant geographic market refers to those regions where undertakings operate for the supply and demand of their goods and services and that are readily distinguishable from the neighbouring regions because the competitive conditions are sufficiently homogenous, and especially, the competitive conditions are noticeably different from those in the neighbouring regions".[1433] The Board particularly takes certain aspects into account in the course of defining the relevant geographic market by considering the properties of the relevant goods and services, consumer preferences, entry barriers, and the existence of a noticeable difference between the relevant region and the neighbouring regions in terms of the market shares of the undertakings or prices of goods and services.

The determination of affected markets carries great importance in Turkey to assess whether the notified transaction will impede effective competition. On that front, it should be noted that before Communiqué No. 2010/4, which replaced Communiqué No. 1997/1 on the Mergers and Acquisitions Calling for the Authorization of the Competition Board, the transactions that do not affect the market in the geographical territory of Turkey were not subject to mandatory notification to the Authority, even if they exceeded the relevant turnover thresholds. Following the enactment of Communiqué No. 2010/4, which is still in force, the transactions that meet the relevant turnover thresholds have to be notified to the Authority, even if they do not lead to any effects on the relevant markets.

Although the mere wording of Communiqué No. 2010/4 does not indicate whether the affected markets outside the geographical territory of Turkey should be taken into consideration in assessing the transaction, in its decisional practice, the Board mostly assesses the affected markets in Turkey. As such, Article 2 of Law No. 4054 also provides that the scope of Law No. 4054 is limited to "the borders of the Republic of Turkey".

Within these lines, the second step following the delimitation of the relevant markets is the designation of the affected markets. Under the Turkish merger control regime, affected markets consist of relevant product markets that may potentially be affected by the notified transaction and where:

- two or more of the parties have commercial activities in the same product market (horizontal overlap) in Turkey

- at least one of the parties is engaged in commercial activities in markets that are upstream or downstream from the product market any of the other parties (vertical relationship) in Turkey.

In terms of the vertical overlaps, as a general rule under the Turkish merger control regime, a vertically affected market exists where at least one of the parties is engaged in commercial activities in Turkey in those markets which are upstream or downstream from the product market of any of the other parties' activities in Turkey. In other words, the presence of an actual commercial/supply relationship between the parties is not necessary, and it is sufficient that the parties are active (i.e., generate turnover) in vertically related product markets in Turkey.

[1433] Communiqué No. 2010/4 on Mergers and Acquisitions Subject to the Approval of the Turkish Competition Board was published in the Official Gazette of 7 October 2010, No. 27722.

10.2 Substantive Test

The substantive test is the main standard in examining whether a transaction should be allowed to proceed or not. For the competition authorities, determining a convenient substantial test is of great importance as it is the fundamental ground for prohibiting a notified transaction. Very recently, the Turkish competition legislation on this front, after years of trial and error, was amended and the go-to substantive test for merger control was changed to mirror the European legislative framework, the EC Merger Regulation.[1434] Through the Amendment Law, the previously used "dominance test" has been replaced with the SIEC test in Turkey. The details and application of both tests and how they differ are explained below.

10.2.1 Previously Applied "Dominance" Test

Before the Amendment Law, the substantive test used by the Authority for its merger review had been a typical dominance test, originating from Article 7 of Law No. 4054 (before being amended) and Article 13 of Communiqué No. 2010/4. Based on these articles, mergers and acquisitions that do not create or strengthen a dominant position and do not significantly lessen competition in a relevant product market within the whole or part of Turkey shall be approved by the Board. The substantive test is a two-prong test and the Board only blocks a merger or acquisition when the concentration not only creates or strengthens a dominant position but also significantly impedes competition. Simply put, before the amendment introduced the SIEC test, a contemplated transaction could be approved by the Board with very few exceptions unless it led to a new dominant position or reinforced an existing dominant position.[1435]

As elaborated under Chapter 6, "Concept of Dominance", dominant position is defined as "the power of one or more undertakings in a particular market to determine economic parameters such as price, supply, the amount of production and distribution, by acting independently of their competitors and customers"[1436] in Turkish competition law. Even though, in theory, a range of factors are taken into account when determining the existence of a dominant position, the Board's precedents show that a high level of market share is, most commonly, the primary indicator to consider whether an undertaking holds a dominant position.

According to the Guidelines on Abuse of Dominance, the threshold of 40% could only constitute a presumptive element for an undertaking having a dominant position. Therefore, the Board also considers various market characteristics as indicators of competitive pressures in the market, which can potentially set off or abate the effects of high market shares and concentration levels. Prominent examples of such factors are: (i) competitors' capacity to increase production in response to increases in price levels;

[1434] Council Regulation (EC) No. 139/2004 of 20 January 2004 [2004] OJ L 24/1.
[1435] See, e.g., *CMLLK Liman* (19 December 2019, 19-45/769-331).
[1436] Article 3 of Law No. 4054.

(ii) merged entity's capacity to impede the growth of competitors; (iii) countervailing buying power; and (iv) potential competition/lack of barriers to entry.

Against the foregoing, it is a generally accepted principle of antitrust law enforcement that the market share cannot be the sole indicator of market power. For instance, in *Rockwood/Specialties Group*,[1437] the Board explicitly set forth that even a 100% market share cannot be an indicator of a dominant position by itself and accurately pointed out that market share cannot be the only evidence of the company's ability to act independently from the competitors. Thereon, the Board assessed the dynamics of the market by focusing on buyer power, potential competition and entry barriers.

Furthermore, in *P&G/Aquarium/Gillette*,[1438] the Board indicated that even though P&G will become the market leader in the market for manual toothbrushes upon acquiring Gillette, which was the market leader prior to the transaction, the transaction would not result in the creation of a dominant position in this market as there exist global large-scale undertakings and two local producers. In the same decision, the Board did not raise any competitive concerns as regards the toothpaste market, where P&G has a significant market power through its Ipana brand, since there are two other global companies active in this market and Gillette's market share is very low.

Accordingly, as explained above and set forth under the Guidelines on Horizontal Mergers, market shares cannot by themselves establish the creation/strengthening of a dominant position and the significant lessening of competition in the market, and the Board also takes into account various characteristics of the specific relevant market (such as entry barriers, number of players active in the market, switching costs of the customers, countervailing buying power, import levels, etc.) as indicators of competitive pressures which can potentially set-off or abate the effects of high market shares.

10.2.2 Introduction of the SIEC Test

As explained above, the previously applied dominant test was replaced with the SIEC test, which is the substantive test that the Commission adopts to evaluate the competitive effects of mergers and acquisitions. The amended Article 7 of Law No. 4054 is as follows:

Mergers or Acquisitions

It is illegal and prohibited for one or more undertakings to merge, or for an undertaking or a person to acquire – except by inheritance – assets, or all or part of the partnership shares, or instruments conferring executive rights over another undertaking, where these would result in a significant lessening of effective competition within a market for goods or services in the entirety or a portion of the country, particularly in the form of creating or strengthening a dominant position.

[1437]   *Süd-Chemie* (n. 761).
[1438]   *P&G/Aquarium/Gillette* (8 October 2005, 05-55/836-228).

In the previous version of Article 7(1) of Law No. 4054,[1439] creating or strengthening of a dominant position was deemed as a precondition to prohibit a merger or acquisition. However, in line with the EC Merger Regulation No. 139/2004, the amended Article 7 of Law No. 4054 allows the Board to prohibit not only transactions that may result in creating a new dominant position or strengthening an existing dominant position, but also those that can significantly impede competition without changing the dominant position.

Nevertheless, the assessment on whether a dominant position would be created or strengthened as a result of a transaction would still be of great importance for the Board since, in most instances, effective competition would be significantly impeded via the creation or strengthening of dominance. On the other hand, the SIEC test may as well reduce over-enforcement, as it generally aims to examine whether and how much the competition is impeded post-transaction.[1440]

Post-amendment, the Board has started to include a brief wording regarding the SIEC test in its decisions.[1441] The most significant decision of this revised and upgraded merger control regime came with the *Marport/Terminal Investment* decision[1442] regarding the acquisition of sole control over Marport by Terminal Investment, which already enjoyed joint control over Marport. By specifically stating that it will apply the SIEC test, the Board analysed the markets in question in detail, examining Herfindahl-Hirschman Index (HHI) levels, capacities and market shares, and refused to grant approval to the relevant transaction based on the grounds that the notified transaction was likely to cause significant impediment of effective competition. Although there are not many instances where a no-go decision is rendered after a lengthy phase II review under the old dominance test, this is the first transaction that failed the SIEC test. Having checked this benchmark, the Board is expected to build further case law by making competitive analyses consider whether the envisaged transaction significantly impedes competition in the relevant market.

10.3 The Board's Review of Horizontal Concentrations

Horizontal concentrations refer to the mergers and acquisitions between companies operating in the same product markets.[1443] In other words, the parties to a horizontal transaction are actually firms competing in a given market, and following the

---

[1439] Article 7(1) of Law No. 4054 before the Amendment Law is as follows: "It is illegal and prohibited for one or more undertakings to merge, or for an undertaking or a person to acquire – except by inheritance – assets, or all or part of the partnership shares, or instruments conferring executive rights over another undertaking, where these would result in a significant lessening of effective competition within a market for goods or services in the entirety or a portion of the country, *with a view to create or strengthen a dominant position*" [emphasis added].

[1440] G. Gürkaynak and K. Yıldırım, "Digital Technology 2021", Law Business Research 2020, p. 73.

[1441] E.g. *Hegsakon/Unico* (25 June 2020, 20-31/393-176); *Baring/Travalex* (9 July 2020, 20-33/415-191); *Varian/Varinak* (28 July 2020, 20-36/491-216).

[1442] *Marport/TIL* (August 13, 2021, 20-37/523-231).

[1443] OECD, "Glossary of Industrial Organisation Economics and Competition Law", compiled by R. S. Khemani and D. M. Shapiro, commissioned by the Directorate for Financial, Fiscal and Enterprise Affairs, 1993, p. 58.

transaction, the number of competitors in the market inevitably decreases. As horizontal concentrations change the structure of the affected market in question, the competition authorities pay specific attention to transactions resulting in horizontal concentrations, and even more so if the envisaged transaction results in a high market share or concentration level.

The Board generally takes the following path in assessing whether a notified transaction significantly impedes effective competition in a market:

- Market Power: The Board first looks into whether the notified transaction may lead to the creation or strengthening of an existing dominant position in any of the affected markets. In doing so, the Board takes into consideration the market shares and concentration levels, among other things, as will be explained below.

- Anti-Competitive Effects: Following the assessment of dominance, the Board generally goes into the evaluation of possible anti-competitive effects of the notified transaction.

- Efficiencies: Lastly, the Board takes into consideration the efficiencies stemming from the notified transaction, which may include, among others, consumer welfare and decrease in costs of production.

10.3.1 Market Power

10.3.1.1 Market Share and Concentration Levels

The Board's assessment of horizontal concentrations is related to the change in competitive conditions in a given market before and after the envisaged transaction. This is based on the presumption of illegality, by showing that the merger would create an undertaking controlling an undue percentage of the relevant market, thereby resulting in a high concentration in the market.[1444] Per Article 7 of Law No. 4054, transactions resulting in a significant lessening of effective competition and creating a dominant position or strengthening an existing dominant position are not allowed. Therefore, when assessing a horizontal transaction, evaluating the market share and concentration level bears great importance.

The primary tools in the Authority's analysis are the parties' market shares, as well as the level of concentration in the market, for which the Authority usually uses the HHI. However, as explained above, the Authority considers these only as indicators and takes into account other parameters to reach a conclusion on potential competitive concerns, such as barriers to entry/expansion, switching costs of customers, buyer power and the ability of competitors to counter any potential anti-competitive strategy of the merged entity.

[1444] A. Chin, "Antitrust by Chance: A Unified Theory of Horizontal Merger Doctrine", *Yale Law Journal*, Vol. 106, 1997, p. 1167.

In calculating the market shares, the parties' sales revenue (e.g., turnover figures) or sales volume achieved in the market in question are taken into account. However, there is no "definitive" market share threshold that could be taken as a presumption that an undertaking holds a dominant position. Pursuant to the Guidelines on Horizontal Mergers, which is closely modelled after the EU Guidelines on Horizontal Mergers,[1445] a combined market share of 50% or more could be used as an indicator of dominance market.[1446] Moreover, the Guidelines on Abuse of Dominance[1447] and the Board's past precedents[1448] make it clear that an undertaking with a market share lower than 40% is unlikely to be in a dominant position. Accordingly, even though the Guidelines on Horizontal Mergers regard a combined 50% market share as an indicator of dominance, with certain decisions such as *Migros/Tesco*, the Board is seen to endorse the 40% market share indicated under the Guidelines on Abuse of Dominance. Thus, the Board conditionally approved the transaction in *Migros/Tesco* in light of efficient structural remedies[1449] within the districts in which the parties' activities horizontally overlapped and the aggregate post-transaction market share exceeded 40%.

That being said, the existence of a dominant position cannot be inferred from the market share alone. Market characteristics need to be analysed as a whole, based on the particulars of each case. In this regard, the Board has also been known to grant unconditional clearance to transactions where the combined market share had been higher than the thresholds mentioned above. This was the case for *Seagard/Samsung*, in which the aggregated market share was consistently around 70%.[1450] In such instances, the Board may grant clearance after a thorough examination of markets where the market shares were not deemed as indicators of permanent market power, for example, in innovative or technological markets or where the market shares are unstable, such as the case in the markets involving tender offers.

On the other hand, the competition law practice of the EU shows that dominance is more likely to be found in the market-share range of 40% to 50% than below 40%, although undertakings with market shares below 40% could also be considered to be in a dominant position. However, undertakings with market shares of no more than 25–35% are not likely to enjoy a (single) dominant position in the market concerned.[1451]

The concentration level provides insight into the competitiveness of a market hence the correlation to market shares. On the other hand, HHI is a measure of the size of companies in a market and an indicator of the amount of competition among the players in the relevant market.

[1445] European Commission's Guidelines on the assessment of horizontal mergers under the Council Regulation on the control of concentrations between undertakings, 2004/C 31/03, 5 February 2004 ("EU Guidelines on Horizontal Mergers").

[1446] Guidelines on Horizontal Mergers, para. 15; see also EU Guidelines on Horizontal Mergers, para. 17.

[1447] Guidelines on Abuse of Dominance, para 12.

[1448] *Mediamarkt* (12 May 2010, 10-36/575-205); *Pepsi Cola* (5 August 2010, 10-52/956-335) and *Egetek* (30 September 2010, 10-62/1286-487).

[1449] Behavioural remedies were offered as well, *Migros/Tesco* (9 February 2017, 17-06/56-22).

[1450] *Seagard/Samsung* (29 December 2011, 11-64/1656-586).

[1451] DG Competition discussion paper on the application of Article 82 of the Treaty to exclusionary abuses, Brussels, December 2005, available at <https://ec.europa.eu/competition/antitrust/art82/discpaper2005.pdf>.

HHI takes the market share levels into account and considers this as a pointer when assessing concentration levels. The Horizontal Merger Guidelines provide the following HHI thresholds:

- HHI < 1.000: The Board usually does not intervene as competitive concerns are highly unlikely at this level.

- 1.000 < HHI < 2.000: The market is considered of being mid-level concentrated. If the change in the index brought by the transaction is less than 250, the Board may consider disregarding competitive concerns.

- HHI > 2.000: If the HHI is above 2.000, but the increment is below 150, competitive concerns are unlikely except for the specific factors explained in the Guidelines.

HHI is calculated by taking the square of the market share of each participant in the market and then adding them together. To exemplify, the HHI for a market consisting of four undertakings with market shares of 40%, 30%, 15% and 15%, would be the sum of 1,600 + 900 + 225 + 225 = 2,950 HHI respectively. The final HHI value in this example is considered a highly concentrated industry since there are only four firms. However, the number of firms in a given market does not necessarily indicate anything about market concentration, which is why calculating the HHI is important.[1452]

While the Horizontal Merger Guidelines do not provide any other threshold for HHI levels above 2.000, the Board held in *Aygaz/Total Oil*[1453] decision that a HHI above 2.500 is a "highly concentrated" market by making reference to the Horizontal Merger Guidelines of the US Department of Justice and Federal Trade Commission.

Even though the Board adopts the HHI method to assess the concentration level in its merger control reviews, its precedents also indicate that HHI results are not the sole indicator for its assessment, and other characteristics of the market could be taken into account for a comprehensive analysis.[1454] The Guidelines on Horizontal Mergers provide a non-exhaustive list of factors that are likely to create competitive concerns, which the Board might consider for this purpose:[1455]

- One of the merging parties is a potential entrant or a recent entrant with a small market share

- Some of the merging parties are innovators in ways not reflected in market shares

- There are cross-shareholdings among the market participants

- One of the merging parties is competitive in a way that it may disrupt anti-competitive cooperation between market participants although it has small market share (the existence of a maverick firm)

[1452] S. Calkins, "The New Merger Guidelines and the Herfindahl-Hirschman Index", *California Law Review*, Vol. 71, 1983, pp. 402–429.

[1453] *Aygaz/Total Oil* (6 July 2011, 11-41/873-274).

[1454] *Ciner/Show* (26 June 2013, 13-40/526-233).

[1455] For example, see *Assan/Park Panel* (11 June 2009, 09-27/594-139); *Aşkale/Lafarge* (26 August 2009, 09-39/926-227); *HP/3Com* (18 February 2010, 10-18/213-83).

- Existence of past or ongoing anti-competitive cooperation between market participants or practices facilitating such cooperation
- One of the merging parties has a pre-merger market share of 50% or more[1456]

For example, in the above-mentioned case of *Aygaz/Total Oil*,[1457] the Board ultimately found no risk for dominance. This conclusion was reached after analysing various market conditions such as closeness of the parties as competitors, position of competitors and whether they have capacity limitations, whether or not the merged entity would have the ability to prevent competitors from entering/expanding in the market, switching costs and whether competitors could respond to a demand increase. In another decision,[1458] the Board held that while market share and concentration levels are important initial indicators of the market's structure and competitiveness, the analysis on whether the transaction significantly impedes competition in the relevant market should be based on a more thorough assessment of whether the transaction can indeed result in anti-competitive effects.

10.3.1.2 Countervailing Buyer Power

As an economic term, buyer power refers to the situation where the customer (buyer) has the ability to impact prices, supply and demand of a product. Therefore, the term "buyer power" might indicate an influence that potentially could lead to negative effects on competition. However, buyer power might have positive effect(s) on competition, especially when the customers could utilise the buyer power to impede the attempts of undertakings with a high degree of seller power to increase prices.[1459] Notwithstanding the positive effects, since buyer power can lead to competition law concerns in rare instances, it should be examined on a case-by-case basis to properly analyse the possible pro-competitive effects, most commonly as a balancing act in concentrations in the upstream level of the market.

The countervailing buyer power is the buyer's bargaining strength in its negotiations with the seller, due to the buyer's size, its commercial importance to the seller, and its ability to shift suppliers.[1460] In case the customers are relatively large and capable of switching to another supplier or creating their own supply within a reasonable period of time, then these customers would have bargaining power (i.e., buyer power). Thus, buyer power of customers will present a competitive factor, restricting the conduct of the undertaking examined and may prevent the finding of a dominant position.[1461]

Therefore, for the purpose of its review, the Authority analyses the transaction Parties' incentive and ability to foreclose the inputs in this market, based on factors such as countervailing buyer power or the existence of sufficient alternative suppliers. The

---

[1456] Guidelines on Horizontal Mergers, para.20.
[1457] *Aygaz/Total Oil* (n. 1453).
[1458] *Ajans Press/PR Net* (21 October 2010, 10-66/1402-523).
[1459] I. Kokkoris, "Buyer Power Assessment in Competition Law: A Boon or a Menace?" *World Competition* Vol. 29, No. 1, 2006, p. 140.
[1460] B. Yılmaz, *Rekabet Hukukunda Dengeleyici Alıcı Gücü* (Ankara: Rekabet Kurumu, 2020).
[1461] *Dosu Maya/Lessafre* (31 May 2018, 18-17/316-156); *Synthomer/OMNOVA* (6 February 2020, 20-89/90-55).

Horizontal Merger Guidelines explain that if customers have significant buyer power, even undertakings with very high market shares will not be able to attain a dominant position in the upstream market.[1462] In such cases, sellers are considered not to have the power to determine economic parameters independently, as there is significant pressure stemming from the customers. That means the Authority does not consider the presence of buyer power as an indication of a dominant position itself.

Based on the foregoing, countervailing buyer power could be defined as the power of a buyer to create or enhance competition on the other side of the market. Buyer market power is the market power in procurement arising from the lack of effective competition between buyers. The Horizontal Merger Guidelines explains that "countervailing buyer power should be understood as the bargaining strength that they gain vis-à-vis the seller in commercial transactions due to their size, significance for the seller and ability to switch to alternative suppliers".[1463]

In practice, the Board is likely to find countervailing buyer power where powerful buyers account for large percentages of the merged entity's sales and have the power to switch to alternative suppliers. Alternatively, the buyer may be in a position to sponsor the entry of potential competitors due to large purchase levels or even pose a credible threat of entering the market themselves as a response to the merged entity's conduct. Where such factors exist, the Board is likely to consider that this may prevent suppliers with large market shares from exerting dominance in the market.

In its *Henkel* decision, the Board stated that where the top five customers account for more than 40% of sales, this points to the likelihood of countervailing buyer power.[1464] Similarly, in its *Ceramics* decision, the Board stated that Kalekim is not dominant even if it has a market share between 42.6% and 47%, mainly considering the high degree of countervailing buyer power and other market characteristics.[1465] It should be emphasised, however, where select powerful customers are able to protect themselves and enjoy better conditions but the supplier can still increase prices and reduce supply for smaller customers, countervailing buyer power will not be considered to prevent the creation or strengthening of a dominant position, or the significant lessening of competition.[1466]

Similar to the *Henkel* decision, the Board might conduct a sectorial analysis when assessing whether the market has countervailing buyer power. For example, the Board has acknowledged in its precedent that the market for aircraft leasing is characterised by strong customers who enjoy countervailing buyer power to a significant extent. In its *Bohai/Orix-Avolon* decision,[1467] the Board remarked that considering that there were many players in the market and the customers in the aircraft financing market were usually corporate airline companies, they enjoyed countervailing buyer power. In particular,

---

[1462] The Horizontal Merger Guidelines, para. 62.
[1463] Ibid.
[1464] *Condat S.A./Henkel* (4 July 2007, 07-56/659-229).
[1465] *Ceramics Adhesive Producers* (12 January 2011, 11-03/42-14).
[1466] Guidelines on Horizontal Mergers, para. 63
[1467] *Bohai/Orix-Avolon* (26 September 2018, 18-34/567-280).

in its *Carmel/DAE* decision,[1468] the Board indicated that (i) a great number of buyers worked with multiple aircraft leasing companies; (ii) there was a wide range of alternative providers in the aircraft leasing market where more than fifty undertakings were active globally; (iii) the buyers could easily switch providers.Therefore, the buyers enjoyed significant buyer power.

10.3.1.3 Barriers to Entry

Barriers to entry could be defined as any kind of obstacles, legal, technical, economic or structural, which prevent or hinder companies from entering a specific market. Entry barriers may differ depending on the characteristic of a market structure.

As explained above, the Board takes into account many aspects (such as the number of players active in the market, switching costs of the customers, countervailing buying power, import levels, etc.) when assessing the potential anti-competitive impacts of an envisaged transaction. The assessment of whether the concerned market has entry barriers is also a very important aspect for the purpose of the Board's review. In this regard, Article 6 of Law No. 4054 indicates that "preventing, directly or indirectly, another undertaking from *entering into the area of commercial activity*, or actions aimed at complicating the activities of competitors in the market" and thereby preventing competitors from entering to a market, is considered as abusive behaviour in terms of dominant position.

Furthermore, the Guidelines on Horizontal Mergers indicate that where there are potential entrants whose ingress into the market is likely, timely and of a sufficient level, this can create significant competitive pressure on undertakings present in a market and prevent them from exercising market power.[1469] Therefore, where entry into a market is sufficiently easy, a merger/acquisition in that market is relatively unlikely to create a significantly anti-competitive outcome.

Even though many types of entry barriers could occur, the Guidelines on Horizontal Mergers set forth the following forms: (i) legal entry barriers; (ii) technical entry barriers; and (iii) consumer loyalty.[1470]

In cases where there are legal entry barriers, the relevant market requires the potential new entrants to have certain legal qualifications. For example, especially in regulated sectors such as telecommunication or pharmaceuticals, regulations might require the new market players to have the requisite licence to engage in the distribution channel. The technical entry barriers might cover the cases where entering a market requires proprietary technology, an extensive R&D, high-level experience specific to the market, know-how, favourable access to raw materials, favourable geographic locations, etc.

In cases where the market has customer loyalty, the incumbent players have existing customers loyal to established products. Brand loyalty is an important aspect for the Board to assess a transaction. The Board found in *OMV Petrol Ofisi* decision that a company with relatively low brand image/awareness could lose a significant number of

---

[1468]   *Carmel/DAE* (8 June 2017, 17-19/292-129).
[1469]   Guidelines on Horizontal Mergers, para. 66.
[1470]   Ibid., para. 69.

customers if it does not offer competitive prices.[1471] Similarly, in the *Luxottica/Essilor* decision, the Board analysed the market as a dynamic market where one of the parties to the transaction was the market leader with many other competitors in the market. The Board found that there were both horizontal and vertical effects from the transaction, after stating that there are many local and global competitors in the market, a high number of new entrances that grab a significant amount of share from the present undertakings in the market with high brand recognition.[1472]

As for the decisional practice of the Board, in its *Shell Turcas* decision, it was held that there are no significant legal barriers to obtain a fuel distribution licence to operate in the non-retail markets.[1473] That said, establishing a dealer network and the infrastructure required to operate as a wholesaler company could be considered as a sunk cost. Further, fuel stations are subject to certain licensing and zoning requirements. Acquiring the necessary licences and zoning permits to build a site could be costly, time-consuming and subject to geographic limitations.

In its *Greencastle/Amram* decision, the Board stated that the market has high sunk costs such as the advertisement costs since new entrance to the market requires high costs with brand recognition. Therefore, the Board has recognised the high costs required to enter the market as an entry barrier.[1474]

10.3.2 Anti-Competitive Effects

The Turkish merger control regime recently adopted the SIEC test in the evaluation of concentrations by amending Article 7 of Law No. 4054. Similarly, Article 13(II) of the Merger Communiqué indicates that mergers and acquisitions which do not create or strengthen a sole or joint dominant position and significantly lessen effective competition in a market shall be cleared by the Board. Accordingly, Turkish competition law provides the basis for the examination of both sole and joint dominant positions.

Sole dominant position is the creation of a dominant position or strengthening an existing dominant position by removing the substantial competitive pressure on one or more undertakings in the context of unilateral effects.[1475] On the other hand, joint dominant position is where the undertakings (whose behaviours indicate no previous coordination) impeding the competition substantially by coordinating and causing a change in the nature of competition in the relevant market.[1476] A merger transaction between such undertakings might cause the current coordination between undertakings in the relevant market to be easier, consistent and effective than the conditions before the merger.

[1471] *OMV Petrol Ofisi* (3 August 2011, 11-44/997-343).
[1472] *Essilor/Luxottica* (1 October 2018, 18-36/585-286).
[1473] *Shell Turcas Exemption* (24 June 2010, 10-45/806-267).
[1474] *Cadbury Schweppes/Intergum* (23 August 2007, 07-67/836-314).
[1475] Guidelines on Horizontal Mergers, para. 22.
[1476] Ibid.

10.3.2.1 Unilateral Effects

The unilateral effects of concentrations might be seen when the undertakings can increase the prices and reduce the quality, options or innovation by their own behaviour, without needing the collaborative response of their competitors.[1477] Therefore, the merged undertakings might have a mutual advantage by not losing their customers to their competitor in case a price increase occurs since they are already merged with their competitor.[1478]

In the non-collaborative oligopolies, a merger transaction might cause an increase in the prices and reduce the production by creating a market power without creating a sole dominant position or strengthening this dominant position or causing coordinated effects. This kind of effect is considered a unilateral effect in the non-collaborative oligopolies.

Many elements determine whether a horizontal merger transaction will cause unilateral effects which impede the competition substantially in the relevant market. As per the Guidelines on Horizontal Mergers, these elements are: (i) high market shares of the merging parties; (ii) merging parties being close competitors; (iii) customers having limited opportunity to change the suppliers; (iv) possibility for the competitors not increasing their productions in response to the price increase; (v) the merged undertaking having the power to prevent their competitors from expanding; and (vi) the merger transaction eliminating a substantial competitive force.[1479] Since these elements might not be considered decisive on an individual basis, it can be necessary to evaluate them all together.

10.3.2.2 Coordinated Effects

The coordinated effects of concentrations are related to the creation of an environment that facilitates the process of making explicit or confidential non-competitive arrangements between the undertakings in question. Coordination commonly occurs in the markets where it is more possible to reach a common understanding of the terms of coordination. A merging transaction might strengthen the current coordination between the undertakings that already conduct their activities in coordination before the merging transaction or might create an opportunity for the undertakings to coordinate on higher prices.

As per the Guidelines on Horizontal Mergers, three conditions are required for coordination to be sustainable: (i) the coordinating undertakings should be able to observe sufficiently whether the terms of coordination are being fulfilled; (ii) there should be some sort of credible deterrent mechanism that could be activated if a deviation is detected; and (iii) the reactions of the units outside the coordination, such as current and future competitors as well as customers, should not put the results expected from the coordination at risk.

While evaluating the coordinated effects, all kinds of available data should be considered, including the structural characteristics of the relevant market and the past behaviour of the undertakings in question.

[1477]   Guidelines on Horizontal Mergers, paras. 23–26.
[1478]   A. Hamza Şahin, "Türk Rekabet Hukukunda Birleşme ve Devralmalarda (Yoğunlaşmalarda) Yan Sınırlamalar", 2010, p. 13.
[1479]   Guidelines on Horizontal Mergers, paras. 27–37.

10.3.3 Efficiencies

Efficiencies are considered to be mitigating factors in mergers and acquisitions which may potentially impede effective competition. This is the case especially where the Board concludes that the efficiencies to be generated by the merger are likely to enhance the ability and incentive of the merged entity to act pro-competitively to the benefit of consumers. In order to consider the potential efficiencies to arise out of a merger, the Board conducts an overall assessment with respect to the merger, in which technical and economic improvements are taken into consideration.[1480]

An efficiency defence is expected to be transaction-specific and verifiable, while allowing consumers a fair share of the resulting benefit.[1481]

10.3.3.1 Benefit to Customers

In assessing efficiency gains, the Board requires that the efficiencies counteract the impacts of the merger on the effective competition. In other words, consumers should not be worse off as a result of the merger, as compared to pre-merger conditions. In this respect, efficiencies would be expected to substantially address the competition concerns in a timely manner.[1482]

Concentrations could bring about various types of efficiency gains that would be to the benefit of consumers, such as cost savings in production and distribution processes, reduction in variable and marginal costs. Likewise, efficiencies in the fields of R&D and innovation would allow consumers to reach higher-quality products and services as a result of the transaction. Increasing high-quality and low-cost production capabilities, efficiencies would also discourage coordination in the market, as the undertakings would prefer competing with other market players over coordinating with them.[1483]

In general, the Board favour efficiencies which yield timely results, compared to those taking effect in the long term. Further, potential efficiency gains should be in proportion to the competition concerns arising from the concentration. Therefore, if the transaction results in a high concentration level in the market, efficiencies to address such concerns should be equally effective.[1484]

10.3.3.2 Failing Firm Defence

In circumstances where one of the transaction parties is a failing firm, the Board may clear the transaction giving rise to anti-competitive effects if the lessening of competition

---

[1480]   *Shell&Turcas* (8 August 2007, 07-66/812-307), p. 6; *Coca-Cola Exemption* (10 September 2007, 07-70/864-327), p. 94; Guidelines on Horizontal Mergers, p. 21.
[1481]   *UN Ro-Ro/Ulusoy* (9 November 2017, 17-36/595-259), p. 57; *Kale Oto Exemption* (1 July 2010, 10-47/869-302), p. 4; Guidelines on Horizontal Mergers, p. 22.
[1482]   Guidelines on Horizontal Mergers, p. 22.
[1483]   *Yücel Boru/İlhanlar* (9 January 2014, 14-01/4-3), p. 5; *Antalya/Burgaz* (6 July 2011, 11-41/865-M), p. 14, *UN Ro-Ro/Ulusoy* (n. 1481) p. 53; Guidelines on Horizontal Mergers, p. 22.
[1484]   *UN Ro-Ro/Ulusoy* (n. 1481) p. 56; Guidelines on Horizontal Mergers, p. 23.

in the market is not caused by the transaction itself.[1485] In other words, if the competition level in the market were to deteriorate at least to the same extent in the absence of the merger, then this condition is met.[1486]

In assessing failing firm defence, the Board requires that the following criteria are met:[1487]

- If not acquired by another firm, the failing firm would be forced out of the market due to financial difficulties in the near future, resulting in the elimination of a market player.

- There must be no other, less anti-competitive alternative than the transaction.

- In the absence of the transaction, assets of the failing firm would inevitably exit the market.[1488]

Another point the Board puts emphasis on is whether there is collusion between the transaction parties to bypass the relevant legislation through the failing firm defence. In assessing this risk, the Board generally scrutinises the failing firm's debt structure to find out whether the concerned firm failed on purpose.[1489]

10.3.3.3 Other Issues to be Considered

10.3.3.3.1 Transaction specificity

For efficiencies to be considered a countervailing factor, the Board requires that they be a direct result of the transaction and not possible to be achieved through a less anti-competitive alternative way. In assessing transaction specificity of the efficiencies, the Board only considers alternative methods which are reasonably feasible, taking into account the established business practices in the market.[1490]

10.3.3.3.2 Verifiability

Efficiencies are required to be verifiable to the extent that the Board can be reasonably certain that they are likely to materialise, and be substantial enough to countervail the anti-competitive effects. In this respect, efficiency gains and potential share for consumers should be supported by the quantitative data to the extent possible.[1491]

Having first-hand information as to the structure of the transaction, transaction parties are expected to prove the feasibility and effectiveness of the efficiency arguments. The feasibility of efficiencies may be supported by internal corporate documents, market reports, pre-merger external experts' studies or market data obtained from previous transactions.[1492]

[1485]   *Mey İçki/Burgaz* (8 July 2010, 10-49/900-314), p. 47.
[1486]   *Doğan/Vatan* (10 March 2008, 08-23/237-75) p. 22; Guidelines on Horizontal Mergers, p. 24.
[1487]   *Yıldızlar/Yıldız* (13 August 2020, 20-37/525-233), p. 16; *Doğan/Vatan* (n. 1486), p. 23.
[1488]   Guidelines on Horizontal Mergers, p. 24.
[1489]   *Yıldızlar/Yıldız* (n. 1487), p.17; *Doğan/Vatan* (n. 1486), p. 23.
[1490]   *UN Ro-Ro/Ulusoy* (n. 1481), p. 80; Guidelines on Horizontal Mergers, p. 23.
[1491]   *UN Ro-Ro/Ulusoy* (n. 1481), p. 57; Guidelines on Horizontal Mergers, p. 23.
[1492]   Guidelines on Horizontal Mergers, p. 24.

10.4 Board's Review
of Non-Horizontal Concentrations

The Authority defines merger and acquisition transactions between undertakings operating in different relevant product markets as non-horizontal mergers and acquisitions.[1493] Non-horizontal mergers and acquisitions are segmented into two main categories: vertical mergers and conglomerate mergers. Vertical mergers and acquisitions relate to concentrations taking place between undertakings operating at different levels of the supply chain. Conglomerate mergers, on the other hand, concern concentrations between undertakings that are neither in a horizontal nor in a vertical relationship.

To set out the Authority's approach to vertical and conglomerate mergers and to give guidance to undertakings in the context of non-horizontal transactions, the Authority had issued the Guidelines Non-Horizontal Mergers in 2013. Compared to horizontal mergers, non-horizontal mergers are less likely to raise competition concerns, as they do not lead to the direct elimination or lessening of competition between undertakings operating in the same market.[1494] However, under certain circumstances, vertical integration of undertakings in the upstream and downstream markets may also give rise to serious competition problems.

Conversely, vertical mergers may generate significant efficiencies such as operational improvements, decreasing inventory costs, and new investments in production and marketing processes.[1495] It would eventually lead to lower prices for final products, contributing to product quality and innovation.

The section below first examines the assessment of market power in non-horizontal mergers, then explains the anti-competitive effects that may stem from non-horizontal mergers, and lastly, explains the vertical mergers and conglomerate mergers.

10.4.1 The Assessment of Market Power
in Non-Horizontal Mergers

The Guidelines on Non-Horizontal Mergers indicate that non-horizontal mergers would have no negative effect on competition unless the merged entity resulting from the non-horizontal merger transaction holds the dominant position in at least one of the relevant markets in question after the merger.[1496] Market shares and concentration levels are the main indicators concerning the market power of the merging undertakings and their competitors, as analysed in detail above under Horizontal Mergers.

[1493]   Guidelines on Non-Horizontal Mergers, para. 4.
[1494]   Ibid., para. 8; *Crown Holdings/Signode* (29 March 2018, 18-09/158-78), p. 3.
[1495]   Guidelines on Non-Horizontal Mergers, para. 14; *Deere/Wirtgen* (19 July 2017, 17-23/365-158), p. 2.
[1496]   Guidelines on Non-Horizontal Mergers, para. 25.

10.4.2 Anti-Competitive Effects

10.4.2.1 Vertical Concentrations

Vertical concentrations encompass mergers and acquisitions between undertakings operating at different levels of supply chains, including production, distribution and retail sales.[1497] In other words, undertakings that operate in the upstream markets generally provide the inputs to those operating in the downstream markets.[1498] However, in today's complex markets, this vertical structure might be a two-way relationship whereby the undertaking operating downstream provides a good or service to the undertaking in the upstream market, as well.[1499]

The vertical concentrations are generally assessed on the basis of two main theories of harm, namely unilateral and coordinated effects. Unilateral effects concern an individual incentive for the merged entity to raise prices, while post-merger tacit collusion is assessed within the scope of coordinated effects.[1500]

10.4.2.1.1 **Unilateral Effects**

Unilateral effects generally appear as the foreclosure of the market to actual or potential rivals through hampering their access to supplies or markets. The foreclosure may discourage market entries and expansion of competitors; it also may give rise to exclusionary effects. Market foreclosure effects are deemed to be anti-competitive where they allow merged undertakings and, possibly, some of their competitors to profitably increase their prices following the transaction.[1501]

Foreclosure effects might occur as "input foreclosure", which concerns restrictions on competitors' access to important inputs,[1502] and "customer foreclosure", which relates to restrictions on competitors' access to a customer base to operate effectively.[1503] Moreover, vertical integration may allow the merged entity to access its competitors' sensitive commercial information, thereby increasing transparency and facilitating anti-competitive conduct.[1504] For instance, a downstream player who has access to its competitors' cost structure through its upstream branch would be able to impose prices to exclude such competitors from the markets. Likewise, a vertically integrated structure may allow an undertaking to foreclose the downstream market to potential new entrants by denying them profitable access to inputs.[1505]

[1497] Guidelines on Non-Horizontal Mergers, para. 8

[1498] *Botaş* (7 May 2020, 20-23/301-147), p. 7; *CMLKK Liman* (n. 1435), pp. 13–14.

[1499] M. A. Salinger, "The Meaning of 'Upstream' and 'Downstream' and the Implications for Modeling Vertical Mergers", The Journal of Industrial Economics, Vol. 37, No. 4, 1989, p. 374.

[1500] *DIC/BASF* (28 July 2020, 20-36/497-222), p. 6, *Naturelgaz/Socar Turkey* (9 July 2020, 20-33/427-194), p. 14.

[1501] Guidelines on Non-Horizontal Mergers, para. 30.

[1502] *Calderys/Haznedar/Durer/Vender* (12 November 2020, 20-49/669-293), p. 12; Pietro/*Fio Gaz* (n. 1498), p. 8; Guidelines on Non-Horizontal Mergers, paras. 31 and 37.

[1503] *Migros/Dörtler* (16 January 2020, 20-04/38-20), p. 11; *Pigments* (17 September 2020, 20-42/579-259), pp. 14–15; *Demirören Medya* (3 May 2018, 18-13/248-113), p. 29; Guidelines on Non-Horizontal Mergers, para. 31.

[1504] *Anadolu/Migros* (9 July 2015, 15-29/420-117), p. 23.

[1505] Guidelines on Non-Horizontal Mergers, para. 32.

10.4.2.1.1.1 *Input Foreclosure*

Input foreclosure occurs when the merged entity limits or entirely ceases supplying input to downstream rivals or makes conditions of offer harder for downstream rivals, thereby raising their costs.[1506] For input foreclosure to lead to consumer harm, it is not strictly necessary for the rivals to be forced to exit the market after the merger. The benchmark in this assessment is whether increasing input costs would lead to higher prices charged to consumers.[1507] Foreclosure may also take different subtle forms, such as the incorporation of a new technology that is not compatible with that of the rivals or the degradation of the quality of input supplied.[1508] In its evaluation, the Board assesses whether the undertaking is an important supplier operating in the upstream market, which serves as a significant supply source for its customers operating in the downstream market. As such, the Board takes into consideration the merged entity's ability to foreclose, its incentive to do so and the potential effects of the foreclosure on competition altogether[1509] since they are closely intertwined.

The merged entity's ability to foreclose depends on whether the vertically integrated undertaking formed after the merger holds a certain level of market power in the upstream market.[1510]

The incentive for input foreclosure depends on the degree to which this restriction would be profitable for the merged undertaking. In other words, the merged entity that would conduct an input foreclosure should be able to increase its profit as a result of the trade-off between the profit lost due to input foreclosure in the upstream market and the profit gained from expanding its sales downstream or raising prices.[1511] In this respect, the incentive for the merged undertaking to engage in input foreclosure depends heavily on the extent to which downstream demand is likely to be diverted away from excluded competitors towards the merged undertaking. This diversion would be much higher if the concerned input is a determinant factor in pricing final products[1512] and the competitors' final products are highly substitutable with that of the merged entity. In this assessment, shareholding structure, previous strategies and business plans are also taken into consideration.[1513]

For input foreclosure to be a concern, the competitors who suffer cost increases must be important market players in the downstream market. While such players may generally be identified by their market shares, it is also possible for a small player with a relatively small market share to be an important market player and a determinant factor in other players' pricing and marketing strategies.[1514] Refusal to supply input to potential downstream competitors, or supplying input on less favourable terms than absent the

---

[1506]   *Calderys/Haznedar/Durer/Vender* (12 November 2020, 20-49/669-293), p. 12.
[1507]   Guidelines on Non-Horizontal Mergers, para. 33.
[1508]   Ibid., para. 36.
[1509]   *Boru Hatları* (8 May 2018, 18-14/254-120), p. 26.
[1510]   Guidelines on Non-Horizontal Mergers, para. 38.
[1511]   *Demirören Medya* (n. 1503), p. 29.
[1512]   *Turkuvaz* (n. 774).
[1513]   Guidelines on Non-Horizontal Mergers, para. 47.
[1514]   Guidelines on Non-Horizontal Mergers, para. 48.

merger, may also raise barriers to entry for potential competitors. If such input fore-closures would not allow potential competitors to enter the downstream market in an effective manner without entering the upstream market, then the effective competition may be deemed to be impeded.[1515]

On the other hand, certain factors such as alternative supply sources, buyer power, and potential entries to the upstream market may countervail the input foreclosures risks since these assert competitive pressure on the undertaking that has market power. In addition, those efficiencies arising out of vertical concentrations and which are substantiated by the parties can be taken into consideration, as long as they are merg-er-specific, verifiable and bring benefit to consumers. The most prominent efficiencies arising out of vertical concentrations are the elimination of double marginalisation, operational improvements, decrease in inventory costs, new investments in production and marketing processes.[1516]

10.4.2.1.1.2 Customer Foreclosure

Customer foreclosure concerns the restriction of actual or potential competitors' access to a significant customer base in the downstream market by making it harder for them to obtain the input under the pre-merger prices and conditions. Reducing the ability and incentive of its upstream rivals to compete, the merged undertaking, in turn, can profitably raise its prices in the downstream market. Therefore, the competitors' exiting the market is not a precondition for a finding of customer foreclosure, the rise in prices would be sufficient.[1517]

In assessing whether the merged undertaking would have the ability to foreclose the market by restricting customers, the Board examines whether there are sufficient alter-natives in the downstream market for the actual or potential upstream competitors to sell their products. In this regard, customer foreclosure takes effect in the downstream market where the undertaking party to the transaction is an important customer or a significant power. Therefore, customer foreclosure is unlikely where a sufficiently large customer base may switch to alternative suppliers.[1518]

In markets where significant economies of scale or scope exist, or demand structure is affected by network externalities, customer foreclosure can lead to higher input prices. In such circumstances, upstream competitors' ability to compete can be impaired.

As a result of the customer foreclosure, undertakings that have lost revenue streams would cut investments, R&D and product quality to save costs. This, in turn, would impair the undertakings' ability to compete and even lead to their exit from the market in the long run.[1519] On the other hand, the Board considers the counter-strategies which might be deployed by the downstream undertakings against the merged entity, in the foreclosure assessments. Therefore, the expectation is that those suffering the customer

---

[1515]   Boru Hatları (n. 1509), p. 27; Guidelines on Non-Horizontal Mergers, para. 49.
[1516]   CMLKK Liman (n. 1435).
[1517]   Saudi Arabian Oil Company (29 August 2019, 19-30/448-193), p. 13.
[1518]   Arkas/Mardaş (8 May 2018, 18-14/267-129), p. 51.
[1519]   Guidelines on Non-Horizontal Mergers, para. 66.

foreclosure use the concerned input in alternative markets, and implement counter-pricing or counter-marketing strategies in an efficient and timely manner, so as to mitigate or eliminate the effect of foreclosure.[1520]

Customer foreclosure may lead to price increases in the downstream and upstream markets, allowing the merged undertaking to generate additional revenue. However, this additional revenue comes with concessions because of the refusal to procure input from upstream competitors. Therefore, the net profit between the additional revenue and the cost of the customer foreclosure generally determines the undertakings' incentive to engage in customer foreclosure. Circumstances where the upstream division of the merged undertaking is less efficient than the foreclosed suppliers, offers less attractive products due to product differentiation, or operates under capacity constraints, would discourage the merged entity from conducting customer foreclosure.[1521] On the other hand, a high market share in the downstream market would suggest a higher profit margin as a result of customer foreclosure.

For a vertical merger to significantly reduce competition, a significant fraction of total upstream output should be affected by the merger in question.[1522] Therefore, if certain undertakings in the upstream market would still be in a position to compete effectively, then customer foreclosure would not yield results.

Customer foreclosure may affect not only the upstream market, but also undertakings operating in the downstream market in the long run. By impairing the upstream competitors' access to a significant customer base, the foreclosure puts them at a competitive disadvantage. In turn, downstream undertakings which source inputs from such upstream undertakings would also incur higher production costs. Consequently, the merged undertaking can profitably raise its prices or reduce the overall output in the downstream market.[1523]

10.4.2.1.2 Coordinated Effects

As elaborated under Section 10.3.2.2. above, the coordinated effects are relevant where companies which were operating without harmonising their behaviour before the merger are significantly more likely, post-merger, to raise prices or reduce competition through coordination. If undertakings in the market were already operating in coordination before the merger, a merger transaction realised in the market would help maintain the existing coordination in an easier, more stable and more effective manner. It will be assumed that, as a result of a merger with coordinated effects, a joint dominant position will be created or strengthened in the relevant markets, thereby significantly reducing competition.[1524] Having said that, in order for coordination to be deemed to take place, the Board's precedent requires three main conditions to be fulfilled in line with the Guidelines on Horizontal Mergers.[1525]

[1520] *Anadolu/Migros* (n. 1504), p. 25; *Demirören Medya* (n. 1503) p. 29; Guidelines on Non-Horizontal Mergers, para. 69.

[1521] Guidelines on Non-Horizontal Mergers, paras. 69–70.

[1522] *Gemsat* (18 April 2018, 18-11/197-93), p. 6.

[1523] Guidelines on Non-Horizontal Mergers, para. 73.

[1524] *Saudi Arabian Oil Company* (n. 1517), p. 14; Guidelines on Non-Horizontal Mergers, para. 79

[1525] *Dosu Maya/Lesaffre* (n. 1461), p. 26; *Asahi* (n. 839), p. 29; *Migros/Tesco* (n. 1449), p. 40; Guidelines on Non-Horizontal Mergers, para. 80.

Vertical concentrations may give rise to coordination in the market or strengthen the existing ones, on the grounds that:

- Elimination of certain market players as a result of the concentration would facilitate the coordination between the remaining undertakings.[1526]

- Increasing market transparency as a result of the concentration would allow the merged undertaking to access its competitors' sensitive information, thereby allowing the coordinating undertakings to monitor deviations from the coordination and take action against those who deviated.[1527]

- If a maverick player is a part of the vertical integration, the transaction would eliminate an important competitive force in the market, regardless of its market share.[1528]

- A vertically integrated undertaking would be able to effectively punish those deviating from the terms of coordination; therefore, it would strengthen undertakings' incentives to abide by the coordination.[1529]

- Vertical integration would raise the barriers to entry to the market and jeopardise the competitors' ability to compete as effective as before the transaction. Therefore, it would be much more difficult to undermine the existing coordination.[1530]

- An important downstream undertaking may tempt the coordinating upstream firms to deviate from the terms by concentrating a large part of its requirements on one supplier or by offering long-term contracts. The vertical integration of such a buyer would eliminate this chance.[1531]

10.4.2.2 Conglomerate Concentrations

Conglomerate mergers relate to concentrations between undertakings in a relationship that is neither horizontal (as competitors operating in the same market) nor vertical (as suppliers and customers). Although conglomerate mergers are considered unlikely to give rise to competition problems compared to vertical or horizontal mergers, in some cases, certain anti-competitive results may emerge out of conglomerate mergers.[1532]

10.4.2.2.1 **Unilateral Effects**

Supply of related products and services by a merged entity may allow it to use its strong position in one market into another through engaging in tying, bundling or other exclusionary conducts.[1533] By reducing the competitors' incentive and ability to compete,

---

[1526] *Viacom* (26 March 2020, 20-16/233-114).
[1527] *Boru Hatları* (n. 1509), p. 25; *EBS Automotive* (30 March 2016, 16-12/194-88), p. 4.
[1528] *Ajans Press/PR Net* (n. 1458), p. 26; *Mey İçki* (18 October 2009, 09-56/1325-331), p. 45.
[1529] Guidelines on Non-Horizontal Mergers, para. 87.
[1530] *Ülker/Şok* (17 August 2011, 11-45/1044-357), p. 34; *Şok/Onur* (13 August 2013, 13-47/635-274), p. 7; Guidelines on Non-Horizontal Mergers, para. 88.
[1531] *Ferrero* (8 January 2015, 15-02/8-6), p. 30.
[1532] Guidelines on Non-Horizontal Mergers, paras. 90–91.
[1533] *Essilor/Luxottica* (n. 1472), p. 35.

such conducts may eventually curtail the competitive pressure on the merged entity and thus raise prices in the market(s) in which it operates in the long run.[1534]

For a merged entity's tying and bundling practices to result in market foreclosure, the merged entity should be expected to hold a dominant position in at least one of the markets where it will operate.[1535] Moreover, tying and bundling practices would raise concerns, where:

- The products or services provided by at least one of the merging parties are deemed to be important and difficult to substitute by the customers.[1536]

- A large part of the customer portfolio is inclined to source the concerned products separately.[1537]

- There are economies of scale, or the current demand structure has dynamic implications affecting the conditions of supply in the future.[1538]

On the other hand, if the merged entity could not pursue bundling and tying practices as a long-running strategy, the impacts of their market foreclosure would be impaired. However, tying and bundling practices conducted for technical reasons are considered to be long-running strategies by the Board, as they would generate additional costs, when ceased.[1539]

In assessments of conglomerate mergers, the Board generally takes into consideration potential counter-strategies (e.g., counter-pricing or counter-marketing strategies) which might be deployed by the competitors against the merged entity, along with the fore-closure risks.

The incentive for market foreclosure through bundling or tying depends on the extent to which this restriction would be profitable for the merged undertaking. In order for a merged entity to engage in foreclosure, it should be able to make a profit as a result of the trade-off between the costs of anti-competitive practices and the gains.[1540] Therefore, the parties' incentives to carry out bundling or tying practices are assessed on a case-by-case basis from an economic point of view. For example, the pure bundling practices that do not allow sales of the tied products separately may lead to loss of customer base which generally prefers to purchase the products separately,[1541] despite certain gains. Likewise, a merged entity would be unlikely to engage in bundling practices in a relatively low-profitable market by risking its profit in a profitable market. In assessing the merged entity's incentive to engage in foreclosure, the Board also takes into consideration the shareholding structure, previous market strategies and business plans of the merging parties.[1542]

[1534] *Provus* (19 December 2013, 13-71/957-405) p. 3; *SOCAR* (2 May 2019, 19-17/235-106), p. 8; Guidelines on Non-Horizontal Mergers, paras. 92–93.
[1535] *Essilor/Luxottica* (n. 1472), p. 21; *Toyota* (6 April 2017, 17-12/143-63), p. 5; Guidelines on Non-Horizontal Mergers, para. 94.
[1536] *Provus* (n. 1534) p. 3; Guidelines on Non-Horizontal Mergers, para. 94.
[1537] Guidelines on Non-Horizontal Mergers, para. 95.
[1538] Ibid., para. 96.
[1539] Ibid., para. 97.
[1540] Ibid., para. 100.
[1541] Ibid., para. 101.
[1542] Ibid., para. 104.

In the long run, bundling and tying practices may impair sales of the incumbent firms which offer such products separately. Losses incurred by the incumbent firms may reduce such companies' ability and incentive to compete with the merged entity in the long term, thus creating a dominant position for the merged entity or strengthening an existing one.[1543] Slashing the newcomers' expectations for future sales and raising the market barriers, these practices also have the potential to discourage potential entries to the market. In cases where the tied products are complementary to each other, the tying and bundling practices would discourage new entries to other concerned markets, as well.[1544]

In assessing the impacts of bundling and tying practices, their possible outcomes are assessed together with the countervailing factors. In markets where (i) the competitors offering the products separately would be able to compete after the transaction,[1545] (ii) there is buyer power,[1546] (iii) or potential entries downstream or upstream are expected to maintain effective competition,[1547] the market dynamics may render all anti-competitive attempts futile.

On the other hand, conglomerate concentrations may generate efficiencies such as cost savings and operational improvements, despite the fact that they raise certain conglomerate effects.[1548] For example, the merged entities would tend to internalise small price changes in one of the tied products, while those offering the products separately would be unlikely inclined to do so (the Cournot effect). Further, tying the complementary products would bring certain advantages such as compatibility and quality guarantees for customers. The producers would also enjoy marketing advantages stemming from the sales of their products as a bundle.[1549] Likewise, offering more than one product may turn into an advantage in the markets where the customers generally prefer to source their needs from a single shop (one-stop-shopping).[1550]

10.4.2.2.2 Coordinated Effects

By eliminating certain market players, conglomerate mergers may increase the risk of coordination between the remaining competitors in the markets. Even though they are not prone to do so before the merger, the post-merger market structure may coerce the remaining competitors to engage in coordination, rather than challenging existing coordination or starting a price war with other market players colluding. These kinds of mergers may also facilitate monitoring compliance of firms operating in different markets in coordination and detecting any diversion therefrom.[1551] Therefore, all other coordination risks referred under the vertical mergers section are also present in conglomerate transactions.[1552]

[1543] Ibid., para. 107.
[1544] Ibid., para. 108.
[1545] Provus (n. 1534), p. 5; SOCAR (n. 1534), p. 9; Guidelines on Non-Horizontal Mergers, para. 109.
[1546] Guidelines on Non-Horizontal Mergers, para. 110.
[1547] Ibid.
[1548] Toyota (n. 1535), p. 4.
[1549] Guidelines on Non-Horizontal Mergers, para. 113.
[1550] Ibid., paras. 98–99.
[1551] Ibid., paras. 115–116.
[1552] Ibid., para. 114.

The Board's decisional practice with respect to conglomerate mergers is considerably limited as opposed to vertical and horizontal mergers. The Board's most remarkable decision in this field concerns the merger of Luxottica, an Italian eyewear company, with Essilor, a French ophthalmic lenses supplier. Since the merged entity was expected to become the market leader in the markets for wholesale of branded sunglasses, whole-sale of branded prescription frames and wholesale of ophthalmic lenses,[1553] the Board scrutinised the potential conglomerate effects that might arise out of the contemplated truncation. To address the Board's concerns, the parties offered certain behavioural remedies, committing (i) not to tie the sunglasses, optical frames and ophthalmic lenses and (ii) not to impose contractual or de facto exclusivity restricting the opticians to source competing products over a period of three years after the closing.[1554]

The transaction was ultimately approved by the Board, provided that certain amendments are made to the commitments.[1555] As for this decision, it is worth noting that the Board, rather than carrying out an assessment in line with the Guidelines on Non-Horizontal Mergers, has assessed the Luxottica merger within the scope of *portfolio* effects, which are not referred to under the Guidelines on Non-Horizontal Mergers.

10.5 Remedies and Their Application

10.5.1 General Principles for the Remedies

With a view to both ensuring the effective implementation of the merger control mechanism and enabling the economic efficiencies resulting from concentrations, Article 14 of Communiqué No. 2010/4 allows undertakings to propose remedies related to a concentration that raises competitive concerns under Article 7 of Law No. 4054.

Pursuant to the Guidelines on Remedies, if the Board has determined that there are serious concerns that a concentration might infringe Article 7 of Law No. 4054, it notifies this situation to the parties. To eliminate the competitive concerns and to obtain a clearance decision from the Board, the parties may choose to make suitable remedy proposals.[1556]

As per the Guidelines, parties may resort to remedies either (i) together with the merger control notification or (ii) upon the invitation of the Authority if it identifies serious competitive concerns in a concentration to take place. To allow parties to bring suitable and effective remedies, the Authority notifies parties of the competition concerns likely to arise out of the prospective concentration.

In this regard, under the Guidelines on Remedies, the remedies to be proposed by the undertakings must be structured on relevant legal and economic pillars–in other words,

---

[1553]   *Essilor/Luxottica* (n. 1472), p. 21.
[1554]   Ibid., p. 35.
[1555]   Ibid., p. 37.
[1556]   See Guidelines on Remedies, para. 6.

the proposal must be drawn up on the prevalent legal and economic principles. It is important to note that effective remedies aim to preserve both the efficiencies to arise out of the concentration to the extent possible and the competitive structure of the market, rather than competitors themselves.[1557]

In principle, the remedies must be clear, understandable and sustainable. As market conditions may change over time, they must be applicable in the short term. In responding to competitive concerns, they must leave no room for doubt. Parties must also address methods to be followed, relevant third-party rights, and difficulties in finding a buyer in divestiture processes, as well as any loss in value over the implementation period in the remedy proposal to be made. As set out in *Bekaert/Pirelli*,[1558] the Board also values transparency and predictability of the remedies to be proposed.

Remedies may be either behavioural or structural; the parties, however, may also resort to adopting behavioural and structural remedies together. A structural remedy relates to a structural change in the concentration, which generally requires the divestiture of a certain business, whereas a behavioural remedy concerns a promise by the parties as to how they will behave in the market post-transaction.

In assessing remedies, the Board carries out separate evaluations for both types, as the Guidelines on Remedies provide that if a concentration is likely to result in a significant lessening of competition in the market through creating or strengthening a dominant position, the most effective way of protecting competition in the market without resorting to the prohibition of the transaction concerned is to create the conditions that would give rise to a new competitor or to strengthen the existing competitors through the divestiture of a business.[1559]

Under the Turkish merger control regime, as reaffirmed by the Guidelines on Remedies and the precedents of the Board, structural remedies take precedence over behavioural remedies, as they constitute a long-lasting and immediate change in the competitive dynamics of the post-transaction market. To that end, the behavioural remedies can be considered in isolation only if (i) structural remedies are impossible to implement and (ii) behavioural remedies are beyond doubt as effective as structural remedies.[1560] A great majority of the conditional clearance decisions rely on structural remedies.[1561] In some of these cases,[1562] the parties had initially proposed purely behavioural remedies, which ultimately failed to pass muster.

In exceptional cases where the competitive problems arise from a market position based on the superiority of owning a certain technology or intellectual property right, the

---

[1557] Ibid., para. 12.
[1558] *Bekaert/Pirelli* (22 January 2015, 15-04/52-25).
[1559] Guidelines on Remedies, para. 20.
[1560] Ibid., para. 77.
[1561] Examples are *Migros/Tesco Kipa* (n. 1449); *AFM/Mars* (17 November 2011, 11-57/1473-539); *ÇimSA/Bilecik* (2 June 2008, 08-36/481-169); *Mey İçki/Diageo* (17 August 2011, 11-45/1043-356); *Mey İçki/Burgaz* (n. 1485); *Migros/Metro* (19 March 1998, 57/424-52); *Essilor/Luxottica* (n. 1472); *Harris/L3* (20 June 2019, 19-22/327-145).
[1562] *Cadbury Schweppes/Intergum* (23 August 2007, 07-67/836-314).

divestiture of the technology or intellectual property right may be considered as a suitable remedy. A divestiture package that includes only trademarks and relevant production and/or distribution assets may only be accepted as a suitable remedy if sufficient proof is adduced showing that at the hands of a suitable purchaser, the said package would turn into a competitive and viable asset immediately.[1563] By way of example, in *Novartis AG-GlaxoSmithKline*,[1564] the Board conditionally approved the transaction by way of accepting the divestiture of the relevant brands along with all of their elements. That said, there is no settled case law of the Board that would suggest that the brand divestment should be at least as large as the entire overlap, which would be parallel to the EU's recent tendency.

Once a proposal is made, the Board conducts an assessment on the type and the scope of remedies, parties' and competitors' market positions, the applicability of remedies in a timely and effective manner, along with other market conditions. Before rendering a decision, it also evaluates the proportionality of remedies with the competitive concerns at stake and makes sure that they meet the main conditions laid down for an acceptable solution. In its evaluation, the Board provides justification for each commitment made by the parties with regard to how a particular commitment addresses competitive concerns. During this evaluation process, being well aware of the feasibility and the efficiency of the proposed remedies, parties are expected to provide all information required by the Authority for a thorough assessment. In order to allow a concentration conditional approval at the end of an assessment process, the Authority should deem the remedies sufficient to eliminate competitive concerns without any doubt.

Another point to consider is the implementation process of remedies, which generally requires a continuous pursuit and audit. Except for divestiture measures, the implementation process of all remedies must be auditable at any time without leaving room for any efficiency loss by parties. To that end, effective audit mechanisms must be incorporated into remedy proposals. The Board may decline solutions failing to address feasibility questions and competitive concerns, especially on the grounds that they cannot be audited effectively and the failure to do so may give rise to efficiency losses in addressing competitive concerns.

10.5.2 Structural Remedies

As stressed above, the divestiture of a business is a largely accepted structural remedy that is believed to strengthen the existing competitors. In order to make sure that the divested business is able to compete effectively and on a long-term basis with the undertaking party to the transaction, it has to be viable on its own. In this respect, the divestment business must be independent of the parties such that it shall not require cooperation in the supply of inputs or similar matters, except during the transition period.

[1563] Guidelines on Remedies, paras. 34–35.
[1564] *Novartis/GlaxoSmithKline* (29 January 2015, 15-05/59-26).

Paragraph 22 of the Guidelines on Remedies indicates that divestiture of a viable and competitive business can be realised in two different ways:

- The divestiture of a whole business for which there is no doubt as to the viability and competitiveness in the market by itself,

- The formation of a new business that is viable and competitive by itself, through the combination of certain assets and/or divestiture of some of the existing ones. In order for a business to be viable and thus for an effective competitor to be created in the market, it may be necessary to include in the scope of the divestment business certain operations in markets where no competitive concerns exist.

According to paragraphs 34 and 35 of the Guidelines on Remedies, in exceptional cases where the competitive problems arise from a market position based on the superiority of owning a certain technology or intellectual property right, the divestiture of the technology or intellectual property right may be considered as a suitable remedy. A divestiture package that includes only trademarks and relevant production and/or distribution assets may be accepted as a suitable remedy only if sufficient proof is adduced showing that at the hands of a suitable purchaser, the said package would immediately turn into a competitive and viable asset.

As set out under paragraph 77 of the Guidelines on Remedies and in line with the precedents of the Board, under the Turkish merger control regime, the structural remedies take precedence over behavioural remedies. This is also seen in the decisional practice of the Board, where a great majority of the conditional clearance decisions rely on structural remedies.[1565] While the parties initially proposed purely behavioural remedies in some of these cases,[1566] these ultimately failed. Below are certain examples of recent conditional approval decisions rendered by the Board based on structural remedies.

In the above-explained *Luxottica/Essilor* decision,[1567] the parties have proposed structural and behavioural remedies to the Authority in order to address horizontal and conglomerate effects of the transaction. There were horizontal overlaps in the wholesale of branded sunglasses market and in the wholesale of branded prescription optical frame market. In order to resolve the competitive concerns anticipated by the Board, the parties proposed structural and behavioural remedies, which included the following:

- As a structural remedy, the parties proposed to divest Merve Optik in order to eliminate horizontal overlap in the markets concerned. The Board noted that the divestiture of Merve Optik would eliminate horizontal overlaps in the relevant markets, and therefore, the transaction would not lead to the creation or strengthening of a dominant position in the affected markets.

- In terms of behavioural remedies, it was proposed that (i) the parties and the combined entity would not implement tied sales of ophthalmic lenses, optical frames and sunglasses to opticians in Turkey, and (ii) the parties and the combined entity

---

[1565]   *Migros/Tesco* (n. 1449), AFM/Mars (n. 1561); *ÇimSA/Bilecik* (n. 1561); *Mey İçki/Diageo* (n. 1561); *Mey İçki/ Burgaz* (n. 1485); *Migros/Metro* (n. 1561).

[1566]   *Cadbury Schweppes/Intergum* (n. 1562).

[1567]   *Essilor/Luxottica* (n. 1472).

would not apply any contractual or de facto exclusivity provisions prohibiting or restricting the opticians from purchasing from their competitors. Although the Board noted that the combined entity guaranteed that it would not engage in any practices to restrict competition, it rejected the proposed remedy of the parties, which stated that upon a request of the optician(s), the parties would be permitted to engage in tied sales and conditionally approved the transaction.

In *Migros/Tesco*,[1568] the Board has conditionally approved the transaction pursuant to the commitments submitted by Migros, which included both (1) structural remedies with respect to efficient divestments within the districts in which the parties' activities horizontally overlapped and the post-transaction undertaking's market share exceeded 40%, and (2) behavioural remedies with respect to (i) maintenance of trade relationships with the competitors of Efes–significant beer producer in Turkey and sister company of Migros – (ii) maintenance of the shelf availability of the products of competitors of Efes, (iii) Anadolu Endüstri Holding, parent company of Migros, to refrain from sharing Tesco Kipa's confidential information with the competitors of Tesco Kipa (and vice versa), and (iv) launching a supervisory and reporting system for rendering the commitments, in order to eliminate the competition law concerns.

Turkish merger control rules applicable to remedies are akin to–if not the same as–the EU rules. Thus, in terms of the worldwide transactions that also have an effect within the Turkish market, the Board has a tendency to take into account the remedies submitted to the Commission so long as the relevant remedies also eliminate the competition law concerns that arise as a result of the transaction subject to review. In this regard, if the affected markets in Turkey are identical/similar to the affected markets in the EEA, there is a substantial likelihood for the Board to render its decision by considering the remedies submitted to the Commission and the Commission's approach to the relevant remedies.

There have been several decisions of the Board where concentrations were granted unconditional clearance in Turkey upon commitments submitted before the Commission.

For instance, in *Maersk Line/HSDG*,[1569] the Board took into consideration the commitments submitted before the Commission and their Turkey-specific effects in terms of its own review process. As a result, the Board granted its approval to the transaction unconditionally.

Moreover, in *Agilent/Varian*,[1570] the Board stated that the scope of the commitments submitted before the Commission, which include divestment of some businesses in the affected markets, is sufficient to resolve the competition law concerns in Turkey. To that end, the Board decided that the commitments would entirely eliminate the overlap between the parties' activities in Turkey. Therefore, the Board unconditionally cleared the proposed transaction.

The Board also conditionally cleared several concentrations that included commitments submitted before the Commission and had effects in Turkey. One of the most recent and significant examples of this is the *Bayer/Monsanto*[1571] transaction regarding

---

[1568] *Migros/Tesco* (n. 1449).
[1569] *Maersk/HSDG* (4 May 2017, 17-15/210-89).
[1570] *Agilent/Varian* (18 February 2010, 10-18/212-82).
[1571] *Bayer/Monsanto* (n. 39).

the acquisition of sole control over Monsanto Company by Bayer Aktiengesellschaft. The Board considered that the transaction might result in creating or strengthening Bayer's dominant position and thus significantly impede effective competition in the relevant market; therefore, it initiated a phase II review.

In terms of the potential competition law concerns regarding the horizontal overlaps, as well as the vertically related markets, the Board evaluated the Turkey-specific effects of the commitments submitted before the Commission. To that end, the Board indicated that the relevant structural remedies eliminated all of the Turkey-specific horizontal and vertical competition law concerns raised by the Authority during the phase II review. Accordingly, the Board granted approval to the transaction on the condition that the remedies submitted to the Commission will be implemented.

Moreover, in *Nidec/Embraco*,[1572] the transaction concerned the acquisition of sole control over the refrigeration compressor business of Whirlpool Corporation (namely, Embraco) by Nidec. Within the scope of its phase I review, the Board considered that the transaction would affect various markets in Turkey in which competition law concerns could realistically arise, and thus, decided to initiate a phase II review, likewise the Commission.

In terms of the potential competition law concerns regarding the horizontal and vertical overlaps, the Board evaluated the Turkey-specific effects of the commitments submitted before the Commission. Within the scope of the commitment, Nidec offered to divest its refrigeration compressor business for both household and light commercial applications.

The transaction was approved pursuant to the commitment package submitted to the Commission about the divestment of Nidec's own light commercial compressor and household compressor businesses as the Board concluded that the relevant commitments would eliminate the horizontal and vertical overlaps in Turkey.

In *Valeo-FTE*,[1573] the Board took into consideration the commitments submitted before the Commission in terms of the proposed transaction. In this respect, the Board concluded that the commitments would prevent the increase of the concentration in the market and preserve the market's competitive landscape. To that end, the Board conditionally approved the transaction, subject to the implementation of the commitments submitted before the Commission.

In *GlaxoSmithKline-Novartis*,[1574] the parties included Turkey in the geographical scope of the commitments submitted before the Commission and proposed some additional commitments for certain matters, rather than preparing a new remedy package for Turkey. The Board decided that the commitments would have Turkey-specific effects and came to the conclusion that conditional approval can be granted in view of the commitments submitted before the Commission. As a result, the Board conditionally approved the transaction subject to the implementation of the commitments.

[1572]   *Nidec/Whirlpool* (n. 39).
[1573]   *Valeo/FTE* (26 October 2017, 17-35/560-244).
[1574]   *Novartis/GlaxoSmithKline* (n. 1564).

10.5.3 Behavioural Remedies

As set out under the Guidelines on Remedies and in line with the precedents of the Turkish Competition Board, under the Turkish merger control regime, the structural remedies take precedence over behavioural remedies. However, there are certain limited and specific conditions where the behavioural remedies can be considered in isolation:

- When structural remedies are impossible to implement, and
- When it is beyond doubt that behavioural remedies are as effective as structural remedies.

Pursuant to Guidelines on Remedies, there are two types of behavioural remedies that can be defined as follows:

- Access remedies: The remedies that grant access to key infrastructure, networks, technologies such as patents, know-how or other intellectual property rights and essential inputs.

- Remedies involving change of long-term exclusive agreements: The remedies applicable when the change in the market resulting from the transaction causes the existing long-term exclusive agreements to be harmful to the competitive structure of the market. In such circumstances, termination or change of existing agreements may be applicable to eliminate such problems. Furthermore, in order for the remedy to be applicable, explanations and evidence available in the proposed remedy should be convincing that no de facto exclusivity will be created.

The requirements related to the structural remedies as set forth in the Guidelines on Remedies are applicable and should be taken into account for behavioural remedies as well.

One of the most recent decisions related to the behavioural remedies is the *Arkas/Mardaş*[1575] decision where the transaction concerned the acquisition of Mardaş Marmara Deniz İşletmeciliği A.Ş. that is conducting activities in Ambarlı Port, by Limar Liman ve Gemi İşletmeleri A.Ş. controlled by Arkas Holding.

Within the decision, in order to address the Board's concerns, the parties submitted a remedy package consisting of behavioural remedies targeting both horizontal and vertical concerns. The commitments submitted include (i) operational unbundling; (ii) legal unbundling; (iii) not changing the trade terms, operations and certain services offered to Mardaş's current feeder and/or deep-sea liner customers for thirty-six months from the date of the Share Purchase Agreement; (iv) not amending Mardaş's 2017 Standard Port Services Tariff for twelve months from the date of the Share Purchase Agreement; and (v) following this twelve-month period, determining new tariffs in light of competition in the market and avoid excessive pricing and upon request, informing the Authority of these prices every six months.

[1575]   Arkas/Mardaş (n. 1518).

The Board decided to grant approval to the notified transaction by a majority vote, within the framework of the behavioural remedies submitted to the Authority.

However, the 9th Administrative Court of Ankara has ordered a stay of execution on the Board's decision on *Arkas/Mardaş* on the grounds that (i) the proposed behavioural remedies would not eliminate competitive concerns; (ii) no effective implementation and monitoring mechanism were adopted with respect to the remedy package; and (iii) the Board failed to provide an adequate explanation on how these remedies would address concerns about the creation/strengthening of dominant position and coordination effects stemming from the transaction.[1576]

10.5.4 Board's Power to Apply Remedies

Article 7 of Law No. 4054 prohibits all concentrations and equivalent transactions that may result in a significant impediment of effective competition throughout the entire country or in a part of it. However, Law No. 4054 also vests the Authority with the authority to allow concentrations falling within the scope of Article 7 of Law No. 4054, on the basis of the communiqué to be issued.

In this regard, concentrations falling within the scope of Article 7 of Law No. 4054 shall be invalid under Turkish law unless the Authority grants an exemption either individually or through a block exemption communiqué to be issued in accordance with Article 5 of Law No. 4054. Parties failing to comply would not be able to enforce their rights under the transaction agreement(s) before Turkish courts nor before other public authorities if they fail to obtain an exemption for the transaction from the Board. In any case, parties would be precluded from building upon this transaction in Turkey in the future, too. This is to say, if they were to have a related transaction in the future which has to be filed with the Authority, the Authority would halt the new notification at that time and ask for a notification on the earlier transaction, in addition to imposing an administrative monetary fine for failing to notify the prior concentration.

Communiqué No. 2010/4, which was issued to guide parties in concentrations falling within the scope of Law No. 4054, leaves the remedies to parties' discretion; thus, the Authority is not entitled to impose any given remedy to parties, nor could it alter remedies brought to its attention in the filing. However, if it considers that proposed remedies fail to adequately address the competitive concerns, it may allow parties to alter the remedies that they have submitted.[1577] Failure to present adequate remedies at the end of the given period results in the prohibition of the prospective concentration by the Authority.[1578]

If the Authority deems the remedies adequate to eliminate competitive concerns, it then adopts these remedies proposed by parties and allows the transaction to take place along

---

[1576] The 9th Administrative Court of Ankara, 28 March 2019, E. 2018/2277.
[1577] *Dosu Maya/Lessafre* (n. 1461).
[1578] *UN Ro-Ro/Ulusoy* (n. 1481); *Setur* (30 April 2014, 15-29/421-118); *Mey İçki* (n. 1528).

with the commitments. After that point, as a matter of principle, no changes can be made. The Authority, however, may reconsider or alter its decision if (i) the decision is revealed to have been taken on the basis of incorrect or fallacious information or (ii) the parties fail to fulfil their commitments.

On the other hand, if a concentration falling into the scope of Article 7 of Law No. 4054 does not raise any competitive concern–in other words, is not deemed to result in a significant impediment of effective competition within the meaning of Article 7 –, the Authority authorises the transaction unconditionally without assessing the remedy proposals.

10.6 Sector-Based Assessment of Concentrations

Given the market-specific dynamics playing an important role in the conditions of the competition, the Board's approach towards concentrations varies according to the features of each concerned market. In this regard, the Board carries out a case-by-case analysis as to the market structure in each concentration, particularly in terms of economic and legal entry barriers, concentration level, supply and demand trends, alternative suppliers and customers, the buyer power and difficulties to access supply resources.[1579] To give insight into the factors taken into account in doing so, we provide below the dynamics of certain significant sectors that have been under the Board's scrutiny over a long time.

10.6.1 Cement and Ready-Mixed Concrete

The cement sector, deemed to be the driving force of infrastructure investments in Turkey, is characterised by high entry barriers due to sunk costs, as well as high investment costs, resulting in low supply elasticity in the market. According to the sector report issued by the Authority in 2016, one would need as much as USD 100 million to erect a cement production facility with an optimum capacity in Turkey.[1580]

The Board generally identifies cement as a product light in value but heavy in weight[1581] because of its high transportation cost compared to its low price. To set boundaries of the geographic market for this specific product, the Board employs several methods,

---

[1579]   Guidelines on Non-Horizontal Mergers, para. 26
[1580]   The Report on Cement Sector, Competition Authority, 5th Chamber, 2016, p. 19.
[1581]   *Medcem* (August 8, 2018, 18-27/451-220); *Adana Çimento* (4 January2018, 18-01/5-3); *Akçansa* (16 November 2016, 16-39/654-293), *Aegean Cement Producers* (n. 282), *Kars Çimento* (6 April 2012, 12-17/499-140), *Ünye Çimento* (14 September 2011, 11-47/1170-415, *Çimsa* (3 August 2011, 11-44/979-329), *Traçim* (16 June 2011, 11-37/779-245), *Göltaş* (n. 154), *OYAK* (18 November 2009, 09-56/1338-341)

including the Elzinga-Hogarty test,[1582] SSNIP test,[1583] 10% criterion,[1584] as well as the distance test.

– Elzinga-Hogarty test is based on two main transport data: LIFO (little in from outside) and LOFI (little out from inside). LIFO relates to the demand side of the market and measures the extent to which the demand is satisfied by the production made in the concerned area, whereas LOFI concerns the supply side and measures the flow of goods from the area in question to different areas. Employing the Elzinga-Hogarty test, the Board sets the boundaries of the geographic market until the LIFO and LOFI figures exceed the critical thresholds, which are generally considered as 0.8^{1585} or 0.85^{1586} by the Board in the market assessments. The developers of the test, Kenneth Elzinga and Thomas Hogarty, suggest a threshold of 0.75 in weak markets (i.e., where the flow of goods is not robust) or a threshold of 0.9 in strong markets (i.e., where there is a strong flow of goods).[1587]

– On the other hand, the SSNIP test assesses the consumers' possible reactions to a small but significant and non-transitory increase in relative prices of the product by a hypothetical monopolist. While the US Department of Justice applies an increase of 5%, the EU and the Authority implements a ratio of 10% in the cement sector.[1588]

– Ten per cent criterion, which has been developed by the Board itself, takes into account the percentage of the sales by a specific cement facility to a certain region in total consumption of such region. If the percentage is above %10, then the Board includes the concerned region in the geographic market definitions.[1589]

– The Board also carries out an analysis to determine the distance up to which the concerned cement supplier can economically sell its products, which generally suggests a geographic market within a 250–300 km distance from the production facilities, for the cement markets. This test is often employed by the Board since cement sales are not economically viable after a certain distance due to the high transportation cost compared to its price. That said, the Board has recently developed a new approach towards railways, considering them as an alternative low-budget transportation channel that allows the cement producers to make sales economically over long distances.[1590]

[1582] *Standart Çimento* (20 December 2005, 05-86/1187-339); *Ergani Çimento* (20 December 2005, 05-86/1194-346); *Van Çimento* (20 December 2005, 05-86/1192-344); *Trabzon Çimento* (20 December 2005, 05-86/1189-341); *Şanlıurfa Çimento* (20 December 2005, 05-86/1191-343); *Gaziantep Çimento* (28 April 2006, 06-31/379-96); *Şanlıurfa-Limak* (6 December 2007, 07-89/1130-441); *Göltaş* (10 November 2010, 10-71/1483-569); *Çimsa* (10 March 2011, 11-15/261-89); *Göltaş* (n. 1581); *Çimsa* (n. 1581); *Nuh Çimento* (18 February 2016, 16-05/118-53).

[1583] *OYAK* (n. 1581); *Biberci* (2 May 2019, 19-17/243-110); *Nuh Çimento* (n. 1582).

[1584] *Göltaş/Batı Söke Çimento* (January 9, 2014; 14-01/6-5); *Biberci* (n. 1583); *OYAK* (n. 1581); *Nuh Çimento* (n. 1582).

[1585] *Gaziantep Çimento* (20 December 2005, 05-86/1190-342); *Van Çimento* (n. 1582); *Gaziantep Çimento* (n. 1582).

[1586] *Çimsa* (n. 1582); *Çimsa* (n. 1581).

[1587] "The Handbook of Economic Analyses used in Turkish Competition Board Decisions" (English Version), Economic Analyses and Research Department, 2019, pp. 10–12.

[1588] Ibid., p. 14.

[1589] Ibid., p. 12.

[1590] *Biberci* (n. 1583), para. 97.

Based on outcomes of all or some of the methods above, the Board defines the relevant geographic market on a case-by-case basis by taking into account the data derived from the application of different tests.

With regard to the relevant product market, the Board generally divides the cement products into two, namely, grey and white cement, the latter being generally used for architectural and decorative purposes, while the former being the main input in the construction sector.[1591] The Board might further break down the grey cement market into bulk cement and bagged cement where necessary, two segments that generally target different customer groups.[1592] While the bulk cement is used by industrial customers and construction companies in large-scale projects, the bagged ones target small projects.

On the other hand, the ready-mixed concrete sector is generally in close vertical integration with the cement industry in Turkey since cement is an important input in the ready-mixed concrete production process. Nevertheless, there are a large number of independent ready-mixed concrete producers operating in Turkey due to the low entry barriers in the sector. In concentrations concerning the ready-mixed concrete market, the vertical integration between the cement and ready-mixed concrete markets generally raises foreclosure concerns through potential customer and input restrictions, especially where (i) the merged entity would have the ability to substantially foreclose; (ii) it would have the incentive to do so; and (iii) a fore-closure strategy would have a significant detrimental effect on competition in the downstream market.[1593]

The ready-mixed concrete producers enjoy a rather small geographic market as opposed to that of the cement producers because of the temporal restrictions in ready-mixed concrete transportation. Once produced, ready-mixed concrete is required to be consumed within a couple of hours, which limits its geographic market to a distance of 50–55 km from the production facilities.[1594] As for the product market, it is noteworthy that ready-mixed concrete categories are highly substitutable with each other despite different quality features, as opposed to the cement products.

10.6.2 Fast-Moving Consumer Goods

Having been under the Authority's scrutiny since the early 2000s, the FMCG sector has drastically changed over the last decade, as emphasised in the Authority's *Migros/Tesco* decision[1595] in 2017. Emerging vertical integration in the market, particularly *Ülker/Şok*[1596]

[1591] *Nuh Çimento* (n. 1582), p. 5.
[1592] *Akçansa* (16 October 2012, 12-50/1445-492), para. 16.
[1593] Guidelines on Non-Horizontal Mergers, paras. 34 and 60.
[1594] *Batıbeton* (24 July 2020, 20-35/453-200); *Elmalı* (August 9, 2017; 17-26/412-184); *Baştaş* (21 December 2017, 17-42/667-295); *Doğa Beton* (5 July 2018, 18-22/383-188).
[1595] *Migros/Tesco* (n. 1449), p. 8.
[1596] *Ülker/Şok* (n. 1530).

and *Anadolu/Migros*[1597] acquisitions, has allowed the vertically integrated undertakings to enjoy cost advantages and more competitive pricing in their operations.[1598] Given the fast developments in the market, the Authority had to initiate a second sector market inquiry, just seven years after the first sector report dated 2012.[1599]

As a multifaceted market, the FMCG sector has two significant axes, namely the traditional and the organised channels, which is an established distinction adopted by the Board.[1600] While the organised FMCG channel has significantly developed over the last decade, the grocery stores, kiosks/snack bars and similar traditional retailers continue their presence in the Turkish FMCG sector on a small scale.[1601]

The Board, in its precedents, generally assesses the organised channel under two or three subcategories, based on the sales are sizes. The categorisation mainly stems from the fact that discount stores with a limited space offer a limited range of products at low prices, as opposed to hypermarkets which cannot operate at such low costs. Sensitivity to price changes, free time costs, socioeconomic status of the customers also plays a vital role in this subdivision.[1602] For instance, the Board defined a twofold relevant market (the supermarkets with more than 1,000 m^2 net sales area and those with less than 1,000 m^2) in Carrefour/*Gima*[1603] and *Makromarket/Nazar*[1604] decisions, whereas it employed a threshold of 300 m^2 in *Migros-Tansaş*[1605] and *Canerler-Kiler*[1606] decisions.

On the other hand, the Board avoided breaking down the organised market segment in certain decisions on the grounds that it would not change the outcome or it would be extremely difficult to do so in an accurate manner.[1607] It is also worth noting that certain discount stores offering a range of products similar to that of hypermarkets, despite their limited space, renders any distinction based on market space futile.

The Board also identifies the supply market between the producers and the FMCG sector as a second market that would likely be affected by the concentrations taking place in the FMCG sector. Therefore, if deemed necessary, the Board also defines subcategories of the supply market on the basis of product types.[1608]

With regard to the geographic market, although the Board defined the geographic market on the basis of cities or towns in a large number of decisions,[1609] it has not yet developed a consistent approach. The last sector inquiry initiated in 2019 indicates that the

---

[1597]   *Anadolu/Migros* (n. 1504).
[1598]   Turkish Competition Authority, Preliminary Report on Turkish FMCG Sector, Economic Analysis and Research Chamber, February 2021, paras. 35–36.
[1599]   Turkish Competition Authority, Final Report on Turkish FMCG Sector, May 2012.
[1600]   *Migros/Dörtler* (n. 1503); *Anadolu/Migros* (n. 1504), para. 46; *Migros/Makro* (13 December 2018, 18-47/736-356) para. 18, *Migros/Tesco* (n. 1449).
[1601]   Preliminary Report on Turkish FMCG Sector (n. 1598), para. 21.
[1602]   *Migros/Tansaş* (31 October 2005, 05-76/1030-287), p. 6.
[1603]   *Carrefour/Gima* (17 June 2005, 05-40/557-136).
[1604]   *Makromarket/Nazar* (5 April 2007, 07-30/293-110).
[1605]   *Migros/Tansaş* (n. 1602).
[1606]   *Canerler/Kiler* (29 December 2010, 10-81/1693-644).
[1607]   *Migros/Kipa* (18 April 2018, 18-11/204-95); *Migros/Makro* (n. 1600).
[1608]   *Migros/Tansaş* (n. 1602); *Canerler/Kiler* (n. 1606); *Ülker/Şok* (n. 1530).
[1609]   *Makromarket/Nazar* (n. 1604); *Canerler/Kiler* (n. 1606); *Carrefour/Gima* (n. 1603).

market players do not have a uniform understanding regarding the geographic market, either. According to the preliminary report, while Kim, a Turkish discount market, takes into account other markets within a 1 km radius from a prospective location before opening up new shops, certain markets consider stores within 5–10 min and 10–15 min walking distances as competitors and adapt their marketing, sales and pricing strategies accordingly. Therefore, the preliminary report suggests that a case-by-case assessment for defining geographic markets in the FMCG sector would be much more accurate and effective than making a strict geographic market definition beforehand.[1610]

10.6.3 Pharmaceuticals

The pharmaceutical market widely diverges from the traditional health sector due to its unique structure where the intellectual property law and the product specifications play a vital role.[1611] The sector, which is the focal point of the governments' social policies, is highly regulated in Turkey as it is all over the world. Pharmaceutical companies, therefore, are subject to strict product safety regulations in every stage of the manufacturing process, from their production facilities to distribution.

In the Turkish pharmaceutical sector, no human medicinal product can be launched in the market without being licensed by the Turkish Ministry of Health, according to Article 5 of the Regulation on Licensing of Human Medicinal Products. Further, the pricing of human medicinal products is subject to a strict regulatory framework–namely, the Decree of the Council of Ministers No. 2017/9901 on Pricing of the Human Medicinal Products and the relevant communiqués issued by the Turkish Ministry of Health. This regulatory framework sets forth a strict pricing scheme, in which human medicinal products are set maximum prices according to reference country prices.[1612]

The Board generally defines the product markets in the pharma industry on the basis of the ATC classification introduced by the European Pharmaceutical Marketing Association, a well-established approach the Commission has adopted to date. The ATC scheme classifies the products hierarchically in 16 categories, based on their active pharmaceutical ingredients (API), target organs and systems in the body, as well as their therapeutic, pharmacological, and chemical characteristics. Each category is broken down into four scales from 1 to 4, 4 being the most detailed one. The Board mostly employs the ATC-3 scale, where medicines are categorised based on their therapeutic nature,[1613] although under exceptional circumstances, it also uses the ATC-4 scale, which categorises human medicines according to their API.[1614] For example,

---

[1610] Preliminary Report on Turkish FMCG Sector (n. 1598), paras. 127–129.

[1611] Turkish Competition Authority, Report on Pharmaceuticals Sector, 27 March 2013, para. 51.

[1612] The reference countries are France, Italy, Spain, Portugal and Greece according to Article 5 of the Communiqué on Pricing of Human Medicinal Products, 29 September 2017.

[1613] *Johnson & Johnson* (3 September 2020, 20-40/553-249); *Cheplapharm* (19 November 2020, 20-50/683-298); *Mylan* (20 February 2020, 20-11/125-72).

[1614] *Bayer/Medifar* (29 March 2018, 18-09/160-80); *Abdi İbrahim/Aksel Ecza Deposu* (19 July 2017, 17-23/372-163); *Roche/MTS Ecza Deposu* (16 November 2016, 16-39/642-288).

the Board has recently employed the ATC-4 classification in the *Astellas* decision, which concerned the purchases made by the public and private hospitals on the basis of APIs.[1615] Furthermore, in the *Astellas* decision, the Board indicates that the product market could be defined based on the pharmaceutical agent of the drug in terms of types of pharmaceutical purchases, in cases where the products with different pharmaceutical agents are not considered as competitors.

As for the geographical market, the distribution and the customer portfolio of medicinal products are somehow homogeneous all over the country; therefore, the Board generally defines the whole country as a single market.[1616] This is indeed a sound approach in the Turkish pharmaceutical sector, where the distribution network is not diversified on a regional basis.

10.6.4 Telecommunication

The growing population, rising digitalisation and urbanisation trends have made the telecommunication sector an indispensable part of our life. Over this period, the increasing competition in the telecommunication sector thanks to new technologies and innovative newcomers has incentivised the market players to be more innovative and competitive than a decade ago. Therefore, today's telecommunication companies are no longer mere communication companies; they are now technology companies aiming to meet the customers' needs even before they appear.[1617]

The telecommunication sector is characterised by high sunk costs, legal and administrative barriers, scale and scope economies and the resulting high entry barriers.[1618] To be able to compete with the incumbents, alternative service providers require the physical digital infrastructure or somehow access to it. Therefore, the incumbent firms hold an advantageous position in the sector. Likewise, given the characteristics of the sector, the Authority does not expect that Türk Telekom, which holds the largest telecommunication infrastructure in Turkey, will be replaced in the near future.[1619]

The telecommunication sector in Turkey involves a large number of sub-markets, especially in internet, television, mobile communication and landline areas. Although all sub-markets are somehow connected to each other, it is not possible to consider them substitutable to each other in the customers' eyes. On the other hand, evolving technology, changing customer preferences and different areas of use allow the Board to define new product markets or redefine the existing ones.[1620] Therefore, each case would require a specific market definition.

[1615]   *Astellas* (14 November 2019, 19-40/637-269).

[1616]   *Sanofi* (31 May 2018, 18-17/299-149); *Novo Nordisk/Aksel* (7 September 2017, 17-28/461-200); *Mylan* (n. 1613).

[1617]   KPMG, "Sektörel Bakış 2020 – Telekomünikasyon" (Sector Report 2020 – Telecommunications), p. 3.

[1618]   (Liberalization in the Telecommunication Sector), *Eskişehir Osmangazi Üniversitesi İİBF Dergisi*, Vol. 2, No. 2, 2007; and the *Superonline/Türk Telekom* (16 April 2020, 20-20/267-128), p. 11; *Türknet/Türk Telekom* (20 June 2019, 19-22/325-144), p. 15.

[1619]   *Superonline/Türk Telekom* (n. 1618), p. 11.

[1620]   For a different market definition, see *Türk Telekom* (27 February 2020, 20-12/153-83).

With regard to geographic markets, the Board has generally considered telecommunication services in Turkey as homogeneous all over the country in its precedents, although the infrastructure and the customer needs vary in rural and urban areas according to development levels. Therefore, the geographic market is generally considered as the whole country in the decisions rendered for the telecommunication sector.[1621]

10.6.5 Automotive

The automotive sector, which is an important industry in total consumer expenditures, is subject to different legal regimes than the traditional consumer markets in both the EU and Turkey.[1622] The multi-layered structure of the sector is generally reviewed under three separate markets, namely, the new motor vehicle distribution market, the replacement part market and the maintenance and repair market.[1623]

Distribution networks in the sector are generally organised through resale agreements, most of which involve certain market-specific competition restraints. The commonly used distribution systems in the automotive sector are the exclusive distribution system and the selective distribution system. Under the exclusive distribution system, a sole distributor is authorised to sell the products only in a given area, whereas the selective distribution systems (either quantitative or qualitative) prohibit the distributors from selling products to unauthorised resellers.[1624] To govern these sector-specific distribution networks, the Authority has issued a block exemption communiqué for the distribution agreements in the motor vehicle sector in 2005, which was replaced later on by Communiqué No. 2017/3.

The new motor vehicle market in Turkey involves a large number of players, allowing a competitive oligopolistic market with a low concentration level. Thus, consumers enjoy a wide range of products with different features and are able to choose the products that best fit their needs.[1625] In its precedents, the Board has reviewed the market under different sub-markets based on technical features, the intended use, the consumer portfolio, the taxation scheme, as well as the traffic regulations the vehicles are subject to.[1626] The prominent sub-markets are the passenger car market,[1627] the heavy[1628] and light commercial vehicle[1629] markets. However, new product markets such as hybrid and electric vehicles have recently emerged in the Board's decisions as a result of the fast-changing landscape in the sector.[1630]

[1621] *Turkcell* (6 February 2020, 20-08/82-49); *Türk Telekom* (n. 1620); *Vodafone* (13 February 2020, 20-10/110-66).

[1622] For this threefold market structure, see Block Exemption Communiqué No. 2017/3 on Vertical Agreements in the Motor Vehicles Sector.

[1623] Turkish Competition Authority, Motor Vehicles Sector Inquiry Report, 4th Chamber, p. 17.

[1624] Ibid, p.12.

[1625] Ibid., p. 11.

[1626] *Tofaş* (n. 215).

[1627] *Chrysler/DaimlerChrysler* (20 June 2007, 07-53/585-196).

[1628] *Volvo Exemption* (6 December 2016, 16-42/692-310).

[1629] *Tofaş Exemption* (24 December 2015, 15-45/755-277).

[1630] *Daimler/Geely* (24 July 2019, 19-26/396-183).

As opposed to the new motor vehicle market, the automotive aftermarkets have not reached the expected competition level, and the anti-competitive concerns remain in both the replacement market and the maintenance and repair market:[1631]

- The authorised technical services are still in an advantageous position over the private ones, and the profitability ratios are still high in the maintenance and repair market. The technical know-how required to deliver maintenance and repair services also gives rise to information asymmetries in the market. Long warranty periods granted by the resellers strengthen the market power of authorised technical services, limiting customers' choices in the after-sales market.[1632]

- With regard to replacement parts, the technical services remain dependent on the motor vehicle suppliers. The alternative producers have failed to get a foothold in the market with a 2% market share, indicating that the replacement part producers mainly supply to new motor vehicle producers.[1633]

Given the characteristics of the market, the Board defines the product markets on the basis of concerned brands and models in the automotive aftermarkets,[1634] as the consumers require model-specific parts and the specific technical know-how for maintenance and repair once they purchase a motor vehicle.[1635] Communiqué No. 2017/3 allows the parties to define a narrower product market limited to a particular model or type of a replacement part, where necessary.

Lastly, the Board generally defines the geographic market on a national level, as the distribution networks cover the whole country in most cases.[1636] However, it may narrow down the geographic market definition, where the competition problem relates to a specific region in an exclusive distribution system.[1637]

10.7 Ancillary Restraints

Ancillary restraints could be non-compete, non-solicit clauses imposed on the seller, and rarely on both parties. These are directly related to the concentration, necessary for the transaction's implementation, and to fully achieve the efficiencies expected from the concentration.

The Board's approval of the transaction will also cover the ancillary restraints (Article 13(5) of Communiqué No. 2010/4). Therefore, ancillary restraints will be covered to the extent that its nature, subject matter, geographic scope and duration are limited to what is necessary to fully achieve the efficiencies expected from the concentration.

[1631] Motor Vehicles Sector Inquiry Report (n. 1623), p. 9.
[1632] Ibid., p. 68.
[1633] Ibid., p. 124.
[1634] *Tofaş* (1 November 2018, 18-41/658-322); *Mais* (21 June 2018, 18-20/353-174).
[1635] Z. Şengören, Motorlu Taşıtlar Sektöründeki Dikey Anlaşmaların Düzenlenmesinde Yeni Dönem: AB Uygulamaları Işığında Türkiye İçin Yol Haritası (New Era in Regulating Vertical Agreements in the Motor Vehicles Sector: Roadmap for Turkey in Light of EU Practices), Competition Authority Dissertation, No. 126, (Ankara: Rekabet Kurumu, 2012), pp. 83-89.
[1636] *IVECO* (27 February 2020, 20-12/143-79); *Tofaş* (n. 1634); *Mais* (n. 1634).
[1637] *Mazda* (18 June 2009, 09-29/607-146).

General rules on ancillary restraints are defined in the Guidelines on Undertakings Concerned. The parties make a self-assessment as to whether a certain restriction could be deemed as ancillary.

A restriction such as a non-compete obligation should be (i) directly related and necessary to the concentration, (ii) restrictive only for the parties, and (iii) proportionate. As a result, for instance, it may be said that a restriction will be viewed as ancillary as long as its nature, geographic scope, subject matter and duration are limited to what is necessary to protect the legitimate interests of the parties entering the notified transaction.

As a rule, non-compete obligations must be limited to (i) those goods and services comprising the area of operations of the economic unit to be acquired before the transaction and (ii) the area of operations of the seller before the transaction.

The decisional practice of the Board and the Guideline on Undertakings Concerned recognise that non-compete obligations that do not exceed three years in terms of their duration are generally accepted as reasonable, and a non-compete provision that is binding on the JV parents during the life of the joint venture is deemed proportionate in terms of scope.

That being said, under the framework of ancillary restraints, it may be possible to accept non-compete obligations longer than three years, in case the customer tie-in lasts longer or it is required by the nature of the know-how transferred, provided that the scale required by the concrete case is not exceeded.

In its general decisional practice, the Board has deemed that post-term non-compete obligations of two years were proportionate; therefore, they constituted ancillary restraints. For instance, in *BBVA/Garanti Bankası*,[1638] concerning the acquisition of the shares of Doğuş Holding A.Ş. and Şahenk Family in the amount of 14.89% in Garanti Bankası by the existing shareholder, Banco Bilbao Vizcaya Argentaria S.A., the Board analysed the non-compete obligation in terms of the conditions of the ancillary restraints. The Board held that the non-compete obligation is proportionate considering that:

–   The non-compete obligation on both parties is directly related to the transaction since Doğuş Holding has significant know-how regarding the Turkish banking system, especially Garanti Bankası.

–   The non-compete obligation is restricted to former activities of Garanti Bankası and Turkey, and the parties.

Although the specific duration of the non-compete obligation has been redacted in the reasoned decision, the Board held that the duration is less than three years in any case. Therefore, the Board concluded that the non-compete obligation would be considered as an ancillary restraint.[1639]

[1638]   *BBVA/Garanti Bankası* (19 February 2015, 15-08/106-43).
[1639]   Ibid.; *Ajinomoto* (5 December 2013, 13-69/932-393); *Maspex-Tat* (26 December 2013, 13-72/1013-431); *LF Invest* (27 October 2010, 10-67/1423-539); *Alarm Systems* (23 December 2009, 09-60/1477-393); *Ekol* (9 December 2009, 09-58/1406-368); *Fayat* (February 2009, 09-06/119-36-36); *Enfes Gıda* (6 August 2009, 09-35/889-212); *Efes Etap* (19 August 2009, 09-47/1161-295).

Chapter 11
Public Enforcement and Procedures

GÖNENÇ GÜRKAYNAK, ESQ. AND NAZ ALTINSOY UÇAR[*]

Article 27 of Law No. 4054 regulates that the Board, as the competent body of the Authority, is entitled to (i) carry out, upon application or on its own initiative, examinations, inquiries and investigations about the activities and legal transactions prohibited in Law No. 4054; (ii) take the necessary measures for terminating infringements upon establishing that the provisions provided in Law No. 4054 are infringed, and to impose administrative fines on those responsible; (iii) evaluate the requests for exemption and negative clearance, and to grant exemption and negative clearance certificate to the appropriate agreements; and (iv) permit mergers and acquisitions.

This chapter will focus on the Authority's above duties and powers, and how the Board carries them out in accordance with the provisions of Law No. 4054 and related statutory instruments.

11.1 The Authority's Investigative Powers

11.1.1 *Ex officio* proceedings

The Board can decide to investigate a given conduct either following an application or through *ex officio* examination, similar to the Turkish criminal and administrative judicial procedures. Article 40 of Law No. 4054 states that "the Board decides to open a direct investigation, or to conduct a preliminary investigation to determine whether or not it is necessary to open an investigation, on its own initiative or upon the apllications filed with it".

Thus, the Board may autonomously decide whether to initiate an investigation, or to conduct a preliminary investigation to determine whether it is necessary to open an investigation, and assess whether further actions are necessary for the case at hand. During investigations, the Board's main purpose is to find the material facts, which can only be achieved by this method.

The Board may initiate a separate inquiry based on the documents and information obtained in another case that it handled. For instance, stating that the information provided within the scope of a previous preliminary investigation included indications of

---

[*]   Associate, ELIG, Attorneys-at-Law, Istanbul <naz.altinsoy@elig.com>.

a potential violation of Law No. 4054, the Board has initiated two separate preliminary investigations on the distributors of Toyota branded vehicles active in different regions. There are also examples where the Board has taken action based upon publicly available sources, such as news articles and opinion columns by journalists.[1640] In the *Turkish Banks Association* decision, the Board examined whether the Turkish Banks Association determined the interest rates for savings deposits and mortgage loans by relying upon a column published in the newspaper.[1641] The Board may also decide to carry out an investigation into current events. For instance, during the global COVID-19 pandemic, the Board has *ex officio* decided[1642] to launch an investigation against certain supermarket chains and their suppliers engaged in the trade of food and cleaning products in order to investigate their pricing behaviour and determine whether they have violated Article 4 of Law No. 4054. The Facebook investigation is another example of an *ex officio* proceeding where the Board decided to launch an investigation following an update announcement on WhatsApp's terms and privacy policy.[1643]

For those examinations initiated upon a complaint received by the Authority, the case handlers and the Board are not bound by the claims, arguments and evidence put forward by the complainants. Accordingly, the case handlers may investigate other related or unrelated issues during the process and propose different findings and/or remedies than those claimed by the complainant. Likewise, the Board may also establish a different finding and/or remedy than those suggested by the complainant, as well as the case handlers.[1644]

Finally, Turkey is one of the "effects theory" jurisdictions. There are many cases where the Board did not decline jurisdiction that involved undertakings based outside Turkey, to the extent their practices had an impact in Turkey.[1645] For instance, in *Şişecam/Yioula*, the Board decided to launch an investigation on territorial allocation allegations against Şişecam as well Yioula, an undertaking headquartered in Greece that was not active in Turkey, on the basis that the said practice could restrict imports into Turkey.[1646] Likewise, in *Russian Coal*, the Board reviewed and claimed jurisdiction over an anti-competitive agreement between undertakings that exported coal to Turkey.[1647] Two of the undertakings party to this agreement were based in Europe, with no representation in Turkey. One of these foreign undertakings, Krutrade AG, claimed that all of its sales agreements were made outside Turkey. However, the Board refused this argument and stated that these facts would not affect the Board's jurisdiction to the extent the said agreement had an effect in Turkey in the form of imports into the country.

[1640] *Toyota Distributors* (19 January 2012, 12-02/71-17 and 23 February 2012, 12-08/244-75).

[1641] *Turkish Banks Association* (20 July 2006, 06-53/689-196); *Marble-Cutters* (24 February 2005, 05-11/114-44), where the Board initiated a preliminary investigation pursuant to an article published in a newspaper titled "Marble-cutters raised their prices".

[1642] *Food & Cleaning Chain Stores and Suppliers* (7 May 2020, 20-23/298-M).

[1643] *WhatsApp* (11 January 2021, 21-02/25-M).

[1644] For instance, in *Koninklijke Philips*, the Board decided that Philips has violated Article 6 of Law No. 4054 and imposed an administrative monetary fine despite the case handlers' opinion that Philips' investigated conduct did not constitute a violation under Article 6 of Law No. 4054 (26 December 2019, 19-46/790-344).

[1645] *Syndicated Loans* (n. 44); *Rail Cargo Logistics* (n. 48); *Güneş Ekspres/Condor* (27 October 2011, 11-54/1431-507); *Imported Coal* (2 September 2010, 10-57/1141-430); Refrigerator Compressor (1 July 2009, 09-31/668-156); *Şişecam/Yioula* (n. 49) and *Gas Insulated Switchgears* (24 June 2004, 04-43/538-133).

[1646] *Şişecam/Yioula* (n. 49).

[1647] *Imported Coal* (n. 1645).

11.1.2 Information Requests

Article 14 of Law No. 4054 provides that the Board may request any information and documents that it deems necessary from all public institutions and organisations, undertakings and trade associations. The Board's power to request information and documents is not limited to the investigative stage and can be exercised at any time during the procedure, including after the Board's final decision. This power is also not limited to the investigated parties or the notifying parties in case of a merger control filing. The Board may request information from third parties, including customers, rivals and suppliers, as well as other persons related to the investigation or transaction notified to the Authority.[1648] The addressees are obliged to provide the requested information within the deadline set by the Authority. There have been cases where the Authority sends official information requests to undertakings based abroad within the scope of investigations conducted in Turkey, where the said undertaking has no appointed representatives or contacts in Turkey.

The Authority conveys its information and document requests by way of an official letter, informing the addressee of the scope of the proceeding, the legal basis of its request, the information and documents that are requested, the deadline for the addressee to convey their responses, as well as a warning on the applicable fines for failure to respond or the provision of incorrect or misleading information. The Authority may also conduct interviews with undertakings to obtain information.

The addressees are required to provide correct and complete information to the best of their abilities. Law No. 4054 does not include a provision allowing the addressees to refuse to provide certain information on the basis that it is not deemed necessary, or that it exceeds the scope of the inquiry or that it contains commercial secrets. In case of failure to provide the requested information or the provision of false, missing or misleading information, the Authority can impose a fine as per Article 16 of Law No. 4054. For instance, in the *Citibank* decision, a case involving four foreign financial institutions, the Authority requested the undertakings to provide information including the Bloomberg and Reuters chatroom conversations of foreign employees as part of a preliminary investigation.[1649] The Turkish branches of the relevant undertakings refused to provide the said information on the basis that the requested information and documents (i) concerned the parent undertaking; (ii) the data in question was not in their possession, and therefore; (iii) the relevant data were subject to laws and regulations of other countries and the service of the information request was not duly and legally made. The Board rejected these claims and decided to impose an administrative fine on the undertakings that did not submit the requested data.

A fining decision based on Article 16 of Law No. 4054 can be challenged before administrative courts.

[1648] In *Arçelik* (8 January 2009, 09-01/4-4), the Board reached the complainants via telephone to obtain further information on the allegations.

[1649] The Authority's preliminary investigation dated 17 January 2020 and numbered 20-05/48-M.

11.1.3 On-site Inspections

Article 15 of Law No. 4054 empowers the case handlers to carry out the following within the scope of an on-site inspection:

- Examine the books and all kinds of data and documents of undertakings and trade associations kept on physical or electronic media and in information systems, and take copies if deemed necessary.
- Request written or verbal statements on specific topics.
- Conduct on-site inspections with respect to any of the undertakings' assets.

The Authority may also collect information through on-site inspections conducted at the premises of the investigated undertaking (or a third-party undertaking that is not directly subject to investigation) without prior notice. The on-site inspection can be carried out during the preliminary investigation or investigation stage.

Article 15(2) of Law No. 4054 authorises the case handlers to raid the investigated undertakings' business premises without the need for a judicial decision. The Board's investigative powers under Law No. 4054 are, however, limited to the business premises. On the other hand, while the Authority does not need a judicial decision to raid business premises, case handlers cannot force themselves into the investigated undertakings' business premises if the undertaking refuses to allow the inspection. The Authority would need a judicial decision in that case, while the investigated undertaking would be imposed a monetary fine for obstructing the dawn raid.

In line with this, a refusal to grant the staff of the Authority access to business premises may lead to the imposition of a fixed fine of 0.5% of the turnover generated in the financial year preceding the date of the fining decision (or, if this is not calculable, the turnover generated in the financial year nearest to the date of the fining decision will be taken into account) pursuant to Article 16(1)(d) of Law No. 4054. It may also lead to the imposition of a daily monetary fine of 0.05% of the turnover for each day of the violation, in accordance with Article 17(1)(b) of Law No. 4054.[1650] For instance, in many cases where the investigated undertaking refused access, the Board has proceeded with the dawn raid by way of a judicial decision,[1651] and the undertaking subject to the dawn raid was imposed a monetary fine.

Before conducting a dawn raid, case handlers must be in possession of a deed of authorisation issued by the Board. The deed of authorisation must explicitly specify the subject matter and purpose of the investigation. But this document would not necessarily include detailed information on the scope of the investigation or the allegations subject to investigation. The scope of the case handlers' investigative power during the raid is

---

[1650]   Council of State's decision (4 February 2013, E. 2008/3425, K. 2013/347); *AntTur* (13 February 2019, 19-07/86-36); 13th Chamber of Council of State (22 March 2016, E. 2011/2660, K. 2016/775); 13th Chamber of Council of State (26 March 2013, E. 2009/5890, K. 2013/847).

[1651]   *Mars Sinema* (18 January 2018, 18-03/34-21); *Sodexo* (28 April 2006, 06-31/376-99); *Batıçim/Batısöke* (26 May 2006, 06-36/474-128).

limited to their authorisation. While the case handlers must not exercise their investigative powers for matters that would exceed the scope specified in the deed of authorisation, the Board may subsequently open a separate inquiry based on evidence obtained during a dawn raid.[1652]

The in-house counsels and external lawyers of the investigated undertakings are allowed to attend the on-site inspection. But the case law of the Board suggests that case handlers are not required to wait for the lawyers to start their inspection.[1653] The lawyers may interfere during the investigation if they suspect a potential violation of the investigated undertaking's rights during the on-site inspection, such as the collection of documents protected by attorney-client privilege, the request for documents and written or verbal information exceeding the scope of the inspection. As an example pertaining to the procedure of this interference, in *Çiçek Sepeti*,[1654] it is stated that during the on-site inspection, the attorneys have raised the objection that a three-page document extracted from the computer of a Çiçek Sepeti employee was protected by the attorney-client privilege. Pursuant to this objection, said documents were seized in a sealed envelope.

Upon completion of the inspection, the case handlers draw an on-site inspection affidavit to be co-signed by the case handlers and representatives of the inspected undertaking. The affidavit refers to the date and place of the on-site inspection, the scope of the documents collected by the case handlers together with hash values of the digital data where applicable, the verbal questions, as well as the responses conveyed during the on-site inspection.

11.1.3.1 Hard Copy Evidence

Article 15(1) of Law No. 4054 indicates that the case handlers are authorised to "examine the books, all types of data and documents of undertakings and associations of undertakings, kept on physical or electronic media and in information systems, take [digital and] physical samples thereof".

Thus, while the authority cannot seize the original documents, case handlers can make copies of the examined books, files and documents of undertakings and trade associations.

For instance, in *Lafarge Beton*,[1655] it is indicated that Lafarge had tried to prevent the case handlers from taking hard copies of certain documents that were relevant and could affect the course of the investigation. The Board imposed an administrative monetary fine in conclusion. Similarly, in *Ready-Mixed Concrete*,[1656] it is stated that the Board has taken the hard copy of the daily planner which belonged to the general coordinator of one of the investigated undertakings.

[1652] *General Motors* (18 July 2012, 12-38/1093-352).
[1653] *Çekok Gıda* (8 February 2018, 18-04/56-31).
[1654] *Çiçek Sepeti* (2 July 2020, 20-32/405-186).
[1655] *Lafarge Beton* (9 December 2009, 09-58/1396-364).
[1656] *Ready-Mixed Concrete* (5 August 2010, 10-52/1049-388).

11.1.3.2 Digital Evidence

The Guidelines on the Examination of Digital Data set out the process for the examination, processing and storage of digital data and documents held in the electronic media and information systems of the investigated undertakings during on-site inspections to be conducted pursuant to Article 15 of Law No. 4054.

The Guidelines provide that the Authority's case handlers are authorised to inspect digital environments containing all kinds of data belonging to the inspected undertaking, stored in the information systems such as servers, computers and portable devices as well as storage devices such as the undertakings' CDs, DVDs, USB flash drives, external hard disks, as well as back-up records and cloud storage.[1657] Case handlers are authorised to use keyword search tools installed on the undertaking's systems or other forensics IT software and hardware allowing them to conduct qualified searches for digital data. Case handlers can copy and retrieve previously deleted data from the undertaking's systems.[1658] All data carriers used during the review are deleted at the end of the inspection, except for the data found to have an evidentiary power. The case handlers make two copies of the digital data deemed relevant and necessary, with one copy to be delivered to the undertaking.[1659]

The undertaking is required to assist the case handlers during their inspection by providing full and active support in matters such as (i) providing information on software and hardware of the undertaking's internal systems; (ii) providing system administrator privileges; (iii) enabling remote access to the employees' email accounts; (iv) limiting the access of users to their corporate accounts; and (v) restoring backed-up corporate data.[1660] For instance, in *Groupe SEB*, the Board concluded that the on-site inspection was prevented and imposed an administrative monetary fine against Groupe SEB as the case handlers were not able to remotely access the emails of the former general director of Groupe SEB.[1661] In the said case, the case handlers' request has been transmitted to Groupe SEB's legal director in France as the relevant employee was working in France at the time of the inspection. The request was rejected by the company on the basis that granting access to the relevant email correspondence was not possible within the scope of the local laws and the EU General Data Protection Regulation. The case handlers responded that the correspondence would be examined to the extent they were of a professional nature and that the work-related correspondence exchanged during the term of duty cannot be deemed as personal data.

In *Siemens Healthcare*, although the case handlers were able to access the employees' e-mails, they were not granted access to the eDiscovery method.[1662] The case handlers indicated that the inspection would be limited to "Siemens Healthcare users", and the undertaking employees were welcome to be present during the inspection, to eliminate any legal concerns.

[1657] Guidelines on the Examination of Digital Data, p. 3.
[1658] Ibid.
[1659] Ibid., p. 8.
[1660] Ibid., p. 5.
[1661] *Groupe SEB* (9 January 2020, 20-03/31-14).
[1662] *Siemens* (7 November 2019, 19-38/581-247).

In response, the undertaking stated that granting access to the eDiscovery search would grant access to the information on all the Siemens Healthcare employees in the European Union and that this could raise risks in various jurisdictions. The Board concluded that the on-site inspection was prevented and imposed an administrative monetary fine to Siemens Healthcare Sağlık A.Ş. on the basis that the expected benefit from the on-site inspection was not achieved as the eDiscovery method was not available to the case handlers.

The Guidelines on the Examination of Digital Data also authorise the Authority to continue its inspection of digital evidence in the IT forensics laboratory of the Authority, if deemed necessary, except for mobile phones.[1663] This data is stored in three separate data carriers, with one left to the undertaking and the other two put in a sealed envelope to be transported to the Authority's headquarters. The Authority invites the undertaking to have a representative at the time of opening the sealed envelope and during the inspection to be conducted at the Authority's headquarters. The Guidelines on the Examination of Digital Data also provide that the Board may decide to return the sealed envelope containing the digital data to the relevant undertaking.[1664]

11.1.3.3 Personal Devices and Correspondences

The Board's case law and the Guidelines on the Examination of Digital Data establish that personal devices or e-mail accounts can also be examined within the scope of on-site inspections, provided that they contain information on the investigated undertaking.

The Board's *Orthodontics*[1665] and *Mosaş*[1666] decisions are two of the earlier cases where the Board examined mobile devices during the on-site inspection and seized correspondences on the mobiles as evidence. In *Mosaş*, the case handlers examined an employee's mobile phone because the employee was communicating through an online correspondence group on matters relating to the investigated undertaking. In *Orthodontics*, the relevant correspondences were realised through a mobile phone line that belonged to the undertaking but obtained from the computer of the employee.

Before the Guidelines on the Examination of Digital Data were issued, the Board sought to clarify the examination of mobile phones in its *Burdur Autogas* decision.[1667] In the decision, it is acknowledged that the investigation of correspondence via mobile devices give rise to concerns with regard to the privacy of personal life. But the Board then stated that any and all documents related to the commercial practices of the relevant undertaking, collected from any and all devices that were related to the commercial practices of the relevant undertaking, fall within the scope of Article 15 of Law No. 4054; referring to the aforementioned *Orthodontics* case; the Explanatory note on Commission inspections pursuant to Article 20(4) of Council Regulation No. 1/2003, as well as a judgment of a Spanish administrative court,[1668]

[1663]   Guidelines on the Examination of Digital Data, p. 6.
[1664]   Ibid., p. 10.
[1665]   *Orthodontics* (29 March 2018, 18-09/157-77).
[1666]   *Mosaş* (21 June 2018, 18-20/356-176).
[1667]   *Burdur Autogas* (9 January 2020, 20-03/28-12).
[1668]   CNMC (Comisión Nacional de los Mercados y la Competencia), 7 April 2016, Case S/DC/0503/14 *Fabricantes de Turrón*.

which acknowledged the Spanish Competition Authority's powers to examine an employee's mobile phone and obtain WhatsApp correspondences as evidence. The Board concluded that obtaining copies of correspondences related to business activities, which were sent/received through a mobile number belonging to the undertaking, satisfied the legality criteria and did not violate the right to privacy; therefore, the WhatsApp correspondences that were obtained by transferring them from the mobile phone belonging to the undertaking to a computer constituted legal/lawful evidence.

The Guidelines on the Examination of Digital Data enlist the principles governing the examination of mobile devices. Unlike the Explanatory note on European Commission inspections pursuant to Article 20(4) of Council Regulation No. 1/2003, the Guidelines on the Examination of Digital Data do not refer to the applicable data protection laws with respect to the collection of personal data.

The Guidelines on the Examination of Digital Data provide that mobile devices solely dedicated to personal usage are not subject to inspection. To understand whether employees' mobile devices contain professional data relating to the undertaking, the case handlers may "have a quick look" at the devices. If the devices contain data belonging to the inspected undertaking, case handlers will analyse the devices with forensic IT tools according to the Guidelines on the Examination of Digital Data. Case handlers may extract the files they deem to have evidentiary value, while all other data shall be permanently and irrevocably deleted. The inspection of the digital data contained in mobile devices shall, in any event, be completed at the undertaking's premises.

The Authority's case handlers also examine the personal email accounts of employees within the scope of on-site inspections. In *Ege Gübre*, the case handlers identified that the general manager of Ege Gübre used a personal email account for his business activities, and the emails sent to this account were also directed to his corporate email account. Ege Gübre refused to grant access to the general manager's personal email account.[1669] The Authority obtained a court order to continue its inspection, including the personal email account of the general manager. The Board decided that Ege Gübre has restricted the on-site inspection and imposed an administrative monetary fine. Similarly, in *Askaynak*, the case handlers found that Askaynak's general manager had a personal account where he communicated with competitors.[1670] In fact, in one of the correspondences, the relevant employee informed his recipients that he was purposely using his personal account, informed them that phone calls and face-to-face meetings were dangerous and requested them to respond through their personal accounts. When the case handlers informed Askaynak's general manager that they had findings indicating that personal accounts were being used for business purposes, relevant employees denied this pattern of usage. Furthermore, the general manager indicated that even if the case handlers wanted to continue their inspection in his personal email account, it would not be possible since he had forgotten the password. The case handlers retrieved the password and inspected the personal account that was being used for business purposes. Within the scope of the decision, the Board indicated that it was

---

[1669] *Ege Gübre* (7 February 2019, 19-06/51-18).
[1670] *Askaynak* (26 December 2019, 19-46/793-346).

ordinary to examine personal email accounts in case there was a suspicion that they were used for business purposes and in the present case, although the examination had started with the corporate emails, it was found in the corporate email account that the general manager of a competitor sent an email through his personal account which hinted the existence of anti-competitive cooperation. Therefore, it was understood that the relevant employees were using their personal email accounts for business purposes.

11.1.3.4 Employee Statements

Pursuant to Article 15 of Law No. 4054, case handlers can request verbal explanations during the on-site inspections. Accordingly, case handlers can interview the employees of the undertakings. Article 44 of Law No. 4054 provides that the case handlers can request "all kinds of information" during the interview. That said, in practice, if the requested information cannot be provided during the interview, the case handlers may grant additional time to respond to the said questions through a written submission. Further, as the case handlers have to respect the constitutional privilege against self-incrimination while exercising their investigative powers, interviewees are not compelled to make a statement that would incriminate them.

11.1.4 Privilege (Limitations)

Under Turkish Law, the attorney-client privilege is guaranteed under Article 36 of the Turkish Constitution on the basis of the fundamental "right to seek justice"[1671] as well as Article 6 and Article 8 of the European Convention on Human Rights,[1672] respectively on the "Right to respect for private and family life" and "Right to a fair trial" extended to the exchanges between lawyers and their clients by the European Court of Human Rights.[1673]

[1671] Article 36 of the Constitution: "Everyone has the right of litigation either as plaintiff or defendant and the right to a fair trial before the courts through legitimate means and procedures."

[1672] Article 8 of the European Convention on Human Rights (ECHR): "(1) Everyone has the right to respect for his private and family life, his home and his correspondence. (2) There shall be no interference by a public authority with the exercise of this right except such as is in accordance with the law and is necessary in a democratic society in the interests of national security, public safety or the economic well-being of the country, for the prevention of disorder or crime, for the protection of health or morals, or for the protection of the rights and freedoms of others."

[1673] See *Michaud v. France*, judgment of 6 December 2012, concerning an application on the obligation for French lawyers to report their suspicions on their clients' potential money laundering activities. The Court established that "while Article 8 protects the confidentiality of all 'correspondence' between individuals, it affords strengthened protection to exchanges between lawyers and their clients" as lawyers cannot carry out their duty if they are unable to guarantee that their exchanges with the clients will remain confidential (para. 118). The Court concluded that the protection provided by "Article 8 on the confidentiality of lawyer-client relations ... [led] the Court to find that ... legal professional privilege [while primarily imposing certain obligations on lawyers] is specifically protected by [Article 8]" (para. 119). See *Niemietz v. Germany*, judgment of 16 December 1992 concerning the search of a lawyer's office in the course of a criminal proceeding in Germany. The Court held that "where a lawyer is involved, an encroachment on professional secrecy may have repercussions on the proper administration of justice and hence on the rights guaranteed by Article 6 of the Convention" (para. 37).

Articles 46[1674] and 130[1675] of Law No. 5271 and Article 36(1)[1676] of Law No. 1136 explicitly refer to the attorney-client privilege. These provisions impose a duty on the lawyers not to disclose their clients' information and allow the members of the legal profession to be exempt from testifying against their clients and benefit from the protection of the attorney-client privilege for documents seized by public authorities to the extent they pertain to their clients.

Law No. 4054 and the related secondary legislation do not refer to the attorney-client privilege specific to competition law investigations. The extent of the attorney-client privilege during on-site inspections are therefore defined by the case law of the Board and the Ankara administrative courts.

The Board's early case law mostly referred to the EU law practices while setting the standard for the attorney-client privilege for investigations carried out under Law No. 4054. In its *Sanofi-Aventis*,[1677] the Board referred to the CJEU's *AM & S Europe v. Commission*[1678] to note that the attorney-client privilege could only apply to the inspected documents under two conditions: the relevant correspondence (i) should be made for the purposes and in the interests of the client's rights of defence and (ii) emanate from independent lawyers that do not have an employment relationship with the client.[1679] In *Sanofi-Aventis*, the Board also referred to the Court of First Instance's *Akzo Nobel* judgment[1680] to conclude that the correspondences held with the company's in-house lawyers would not fall within the scope of the attorney-client privilege.[1681]

This approach was later confirmed in the *CNR* decision,[1682] where the Board brought two additional clarifications concerning the collecting of documents that may benefit from the privilege. CNR, a Turkish trade fair organiser, objected to the collection of documents which consisted of the correspondences between the company attorney and two independent attorneys after the inspection was conducted, as part of their defences concerning the procedural aspect of the case. First, the Board referred to Article 130 of Law No. 5271 and stated that the attorney-client privilege and the sealed envelope procedure would only

---

[1674] Article 46(1) of Law No. 5271: "Those that are exempted from testifying because of their profession or permanent occupation as well as the subject and conditions of exemption are as follow: (a) lawyers and their trainees or paralegals, the information they acknowledge due to their roles or as part of their judicial duty".

[1675] Article 130(2) of Law No. 5271 indicates that "If the attorney whose office is searched, the president of Bar or the attorney representing the president of the Bar, objects to the search in respect to the items that are seized at the end of the search, on the basis that those items are related to the attorney-client relationship; the said items shall be put in a separate envelope or a package and be sealed. In the investigation phase, the judge of the court of peace; or in the prosecution phase the relevant judge or the Court, shall be asked to decide on this matter. In case the judge decides that the collected item falls within the scope of legal professional protection conferred by the attorney-client privilege, the said item shall immediately be returned to the attorney and the affidavits referring to the relevant act shall be destroyed. The decisions mentioned in this paragraph shall be taken within 24 hours."

[1676] Article 36(1) of Law No. 1136: "Lawyers are prohibited from divulging information conveyed to them or they have become aware of in the course of their duties as a lawyer or member of the Turkish Bar Association and bar associations."

[1677] *Sanofi-Aventis* (20 April 2009, 09-16/374-88), p. 2970.

[1678] Case 155/79 *AM & S Europe Limited v. Commission of the European Communities* [1982] ECR 1575.

[1679] Ibid., p. 2970.

[1680] Joined Cases T-125/03 and T-253/03 *Akzo Nobel Chemicals Ltd and Akcros Chemicals Ltd v. Commission of the European Communities* [2007] ECR 3523.

[1681] *Sanofi-Aventis* (n. 1677), p. 2990.

[1682] *CNR* (13 October 2009, 09-46/1154-290).

apply in case this is raised by the investigated undertakings.[1683] In other words, the case handlers do not have a duty to *ex officio* disregard documents that would benefit from the attorney-client privilege. Second, the Board stated that the relevant correspondence revealed an infringement under Law No. 4054 and could therefore not relate to the right of defence, i.e., the second condition laid down in *Sanofi-Aventis*.[1684]

Dow, a third important decision, involves an interesting procedure.[1685] Similar to the *CNR*, the employees of Dow did not raise any objection to the collection of correspondences between Dow and its external lawyers. Unlike CNR, Dow lodged a separate request asking the Authority to return the documents that would benefit from the legal professional privilege. Despite this request being made after the on-site inspection was concluded, the Board did review the contested documents and decided some of the documents should be returned to the undertaking as they fell within the scope of the attorney-client privilege. The Board noted that objections for attorney-client privilege should include information such as the sender and addressee of the relevant documents, the duties and responsibilities of both parties, and the purpose of the document.[1686]

Another major case is *Enerjisa*, which involves a judicial review stage. The Authority's case handlers collected a set of documents, including correspondence between Enerjisa and their external lawyer.[1687] Enerjisa raised an objection during the on-site inspection for a document regarding an internal audit report on the basis that this correspondence would fall within the scope of the attorney-client privilege. Those documents were collected in a sealed envelope for the Board to determine whether they would benefit from the privilege. The Board decided that the attorney-client privilege cannot be recognised for documents involving the correspondences aiming to assist a violation despite being related to an ongoing preliminary investigation, investigation or internal inspection to reject Enerjisa's application. Enerjisa appealed this decision before Ankara Administrative Courts. The local court annulled the Board's Enerjisa decision on the basis that the relevant correspondence relates to the exercise of the undertaking's right of defence and thereby falls within the scope of attorney-client privilege.[1688] Upon the Authority's request for appeal, the Ankara Regional Administrative Court removed the local court's decision on the basis that the audit report would not relate to the exercise of Enerjisa's right of defence as there was no competition law investigation launched or annulment lawsuit initiated at the time of the audit report.[1689]

Following this judgement of the Ankara Regional Court regarding *Enerjisa*, the Board rejected Warner Bros's objection against the seizure of correspondences between Warner Bros and its external lawyers during an on-site inspection.[1690] The Board referred to the *Enerjisa* court decision and stated that the documents subject to dispute were from a date prior to the launch of the preliminary investigation and cannot, therefore, be directly

---

[1683] Ibid., p. 27.
[1684] Ibid., p. 28.
[1685] *Dow* (2 August 2015, 15-42/690-259).
[1686] Ibid., p. 2.
[1687] *Enerjisa* (6 December 2016, 16-42/686-314), para. 4.
[1688] Ankara 15th Administrative Court's *Enerjisa* decision (16 November 2017, E. 2017/412, K. 2017/3045).
[1689] 8th Administrative Chamber of the Ankara Regional Court's *Enerjisa* decision (10 October 2018, E. 2018/658, K. 2018/1236).
[1690] *Warner Bros* (17 January 2019, 19-04/36-14).

related to Warner Bros's exercise of its right of defence. Accordingly, based on the Board's current practice, documents between an undertaking and external lawyers may not benefit from the legal professional privilege if the said undertaking is not investigated or party to an ongoing lawsuit concerning a Board decision at the time of the circulation of the document. That said, the judicial review phase of the above cases is not yet over; the Council of State, i.e., the highest plenary judicial body for administrative cases, has not ruled on the attorney-client privilege for documents seized during the Authority's on-site inspections.

In the *Huawei* decision, the Board also held that the correspondences (i) where the external counsel is only copied (carbon copied as a secondary email addressee) to the email message and there are no statements and/or assessments presented by him/her, and (ii) that do not carry the purpose to directly address the external counsel, would not benefit from the attorney-client privilege.[1691]

The Guidelines on the Examination of Digital Data also refer to the attorney-client privilege in line with the Board's case law. Accordingly, the Guidelines on the Examination of Digital Data enlist two cumulative conditions to benefit from the attorney-client privilege: (i) the relevant correspondence should be between the undertaking and their independent attorney (i.e., no employment relationship) and (ii) the correspondence should relate to the exercise of the undertaking's right of defence. The Guidelines on the Examination of Digital Data further provide that correspondences that are not directly related to the use of the undertaking's right of defence do not benefit from the privilege, especially if they consist in helping the undertaking to commit an infringement or concealing an ongoing or future violation.[1692]

11.2 Complaints

11.2.1 The Role of the Applicant

According to Article 9 of Law No. 4054, "natural and legal persons who have a legitimate interest are entitled to file a complaint" before the Authority. Communiqué No. 2012/2, deriving from Article 9 and Article 40 of Law No. 4054,[1693] regulates the application process before the Authority. According to Article 4 of Communiqué No. 2012/2, an application before the Authority can be submitted by way of a denunciation or complaint,[1694] or by request from the Ministry of Trade. Applications can be made by natural persons, public or private institutions, organisations, trade associations or other legal entities.

The formal and substantive requirements of applications are regulated under Article 5 of Communiqué No. 2012/2. While the applications are primarily made through written submission (via emails, letters delivered in person to the Authority, fax, e-Government

---

[1691]   *Huawei* (14 November 2019, 19-40/670-288).

[1692]   Guidelines on the Examination of Digital Data, p. 12.

[1693]   Article 40 of Law No. 4054 provides that the Board may decide to launch a preliminary investigation or an investigation *ex officio* or upon an application.

[1694]   Article 9(2) of Law No. 4054 specifies that "natural and legal persons [that] have a legitimate interest are entitled to file a complaint".

system or the Authority's official website), applications can also be made verbally. Verbal applications are considered denunciations under Communiqué No. 2012/2.

In case of a complaint or denunciation, the Board can either reject the application or decide to launch a preliminary investigation depending on whether the application is deemed to be serious. At this preliminary stage, undertakings subject to the application will not be notified unless the Authority decides to conduct an on-site inspection or address information requests.

Article 55 of the Regulation on the Turkish Competition Board's Operation Principles and Procedures provides that applications submitted to the Authority are conveyed to the relevant department. The case handlers of the relevant department would then conduct a preliminary assessment on the application and draft a first inspection report. Pursuant to this first inspection report, the department head would decide whether the subject falls within the scope of the Authority's remit. If the relevant department decides that the application does not fall within the scope, the relevant department notifies the rejection to the applicant. If the relevant department decides that the subject falls within Authority's remit, the Board would then discuss the matter to decide whether to initiate an investigation and/or preliminary investigation.

According to Article 5(4) of Communiqué No. 2012/2, the Authority shall not take any action for unsubstantiated requests that consist purely of abstract allegations, without including concrete information and/or evidence concerning the "form, place and time of the [alleged] infringement". The Authority shall also not take further action for applications where the Board finds the allegations not sufficiently serious or unsubstantiated despite meeting the formal conditions set under Article 5 of Communiqué No. 2012/2.

In any event, the Authority is not bound by the allegations within the application or the formal requirements set under Article 5 of Communiqué No. 2012/2. In addition to an outright rejection, the Authority may also choose to investigate part of the allegations within the application. The Authority may also launch an investigation despite the application not meeting the formal requirements set under Article 5(1) and 5(2) of Communiqué No. 2012/2 if the allegations are deemed serious enough.[1695]

Article 6 of Communiqué No. 2012/2 provides that the Authority's case handlers may contact the applicant through email or phone to request additional information on the allegation while determining whether to launch a preliminary investigation.

11.2.2 The Rights of the Applicant

11.2.2.1 The Rights of the Applicant During the Initiation of an Investigation

Pursuant to Article 42(1) of Law No. 4054, in case the Board deems that the claims put forward in a denouncement or complaint application are serious and sufficient, complainants

---

[1695] Article 5(3) of Communiqué No. 2012/2.

are notified in writing that the claims have been deemed serious and that an inquiry has been initiated. The Authority shall inform the applicant on the phases of their application within thirty days pursuant to Article 7 of Communiqué No. 2012/2 provided that the application meets the conditions set under Article 5 of Communiqué No. 2012/2.

On the other hand, in case the Board rejects a complaint, either through an explicit administrative act or implicitly by not responding to the application within the due period, Article 42(2) of Law No. 4054 grants the applicant the legal right to apply for a judicial review of the rejection. Although the "due period" for not notifying is not specified in Law No. 4054, the general view in competition law is that the due period should be deemed as sixty days in parallel to the procedures under administrative law pursuant to Law No. 2577.[1696]

On the other hand, the Authority has no duty to inform the applicant if the formal requirements set under Article 5(2) of Communiqué No. 2012/2 are not met.[1697] In fact, the Authority may take legal action against the "intentional supply of false or misleading information to the Authority".[1698] Indeed, in one of its decisions,[1699] the Board has explicitly decided to file a criminal complaint to the Public Prosecution Office against a natural person who has provided false/misleading information to the Board.

The applicant can ask for anonymity under Article 5(7) of Communiqué No. 2012/2. In this case, the name of the applicant is not disclosed during and after the investigation phase. Communiqué No. 2012/2 provides that any information that may reveal the identity of the applicant should not be included in any correspondences, including intra-Authority correspondences.[1700]

The applicant may also lodge a confidentiality request for the information it has submitted to the Authority pursuant to Communiqué No. 2010/3.

11.2.2.2 Rights of the Applicant During the Investigation

While Law No. 4054 and the secondary legislation do not provide an explicit mechanism allowing the applicant to make independent submissions during the investigation phase, in practice, the complainants do submit argumentative petitions, economic analyses, expert opinions and informative notes to the Authority. There are two main factors the Authority should take into account in deciding whether the Authority and the Board should consider the applicant's submissions. First, the Authority should assess whether

---

[1696] N. Inan, "Rekabet Kurulu Kararlarının Yargısal Denetimi" (Judicial Review of the Competition Board Decisions) (1999), Symposium of Competition Law and Jurisdiction, The Competition Authority Publications, Publication No. 30, Ankaraand Aslan (2001), p. 455, cited in G. Gürkaynak, H. Özgökçen, Z. Ortaç and S. Diniz, "Rekabet Hukuku Soruşturmalarında Şikayetçinin Konumu: Taraf Menfaatleri Ile Hakikatı Bulma Arasındaki Denge Üzerine Düşünceler" (The Position of the Complainant in Competition Law Investigations: Thoughts on the Balance Between the Interest of the Parties and Finding the Truth), *Rekabet Forumu*, March 2013, No. 72, p. 21.

[1697] There are, however, examples where the Authority informed the applicant on the deficiencies of the application with regard to formal and substantive requirements, which were completed later in due course (e.g., *Western Union* (8 August 2018, 18-27/442-212)).

[1698] Article 8 of Communiqué No. 2012/2.

[1699] *Turkcell* (18 May 2016, 16-17/285-128).

[1700] Article 5(7) of Communiqué No. 2012/2.

the applicant's submission is made in due time. The applicant should submit its petition before the finalisation of the Authority's Additional Opinion to allow the Authority time to review and provide its opinion on the submission. The applicant should, in any event, present its petition within a reasonable time before the submission of the third written defence. This is to allow sufficient time for the investigated undertaking to respond to the allegations and evidence set in the applicant's submission and ensure a final say is granted to the defending party in order to safeguard their rights of defence. Second, if the Authority decides to incorporate the submission in its case file, the Authority should immediately send a copy of the submission to the investigated undertaking if the said undertaking has already used its one and only right to access the Authority's file.

An additional element of the rights conferred to the applicants during the investigation relates to the right to attend the oral hearing. Article 4(2) and Article 6(3) of Communiqué No. 2010/2 specifies that the Board should notify the date and venue of the hearing to the complainant and to the Ministry of Trade in case the investigation was launched as per the Ministry of Trade request. According to Article 6(1) of Communiqué No. 2010/2, complainants need to submit a request for attendance to the oral hearing within the deadline to be set by the Board. Complainants are also entitled to have their representatives during the hearing under Article 7(1) of Communiqué No. 2010/2. The complainant can take the floor and make a presentation of their arguments at the beginning of the hearing. The chairperson of the Board may also allow the complainant to briefly respond to the investigated undertakings' arguments.

The complainant's right to access the file during the investigation stage has also been subject to discussion. Article 44(2) of Law No. 4054 on the access to files indicates that:

> Those parties which are notified of the initiation of an investigation against them may, until their request for enjoying the right to hearing, ask for a copy of any documents drawn up within the Authority concerning them, and if possible, a copy of any evidence obtained.

In an earlier decision, the Board accepted the complainant's request to review the investigation team's case file.[1701] But the Board's more recent case law consistently emphasises that the complainant cannot be deemed a party of the investigation and can therefore not access the case file for review.[1702]

11.2.3 Rights of the Complainant After the Final Decision

As also detailed under Chapter 13, according to Article 42 of Law No. 4054, only those persons/undertakings which have a direct or indirect interest in the matter may resort to

---

[1701] In *Renault Mais* (5 January 2006, 06-02/49-10), the Board accepted the complainant's request to actively participate to the investigation and submit evidence.

[1702] *Dow Turkey* (4 August 2016, 16-26/433-192); *Grup Maritim* (3 May 2016, 16-15/246-108); *Türk Telekomünikasyon* (11 May 2016, 16-16/263-115); *Roche* (19 September 2018, 18-33/557-275).

a judicial review against the rejection decision of the Board. The right of judicial review against decisions of the Board is addressed under Article 55 of Law No. 4054. Any real or legal person whose interests are harmed as a result of any final decision issued by the Board is entitled to apply for a judicial review. The complainant may also seek compensation before civil courts pursuant to Article 57[1703] of Law No. 4054.

11.3 Preliminary Investigation

Pursuant to Article 40 of Law No. 4054, the Board can either directly launch a fully-fledged investigation or launch a preliminary investigation in order to determine whether a fully-fledged investigation will be necessary.[1704] As evident from the wording of Article 40 of Law No. 4054, a preliminary investigation is not a compulsory step of the investigation. The Board is also entitled to directly initiate a fully-fledged investigation in cases where the Board deems that there is sufficient information at hand.

The Board may launch a preliminary investigation *ex officio*, upon complaint/denunciation or upon a leniency application. If the Board decides to launch a preliminary investigation, the Board should assign one or more of the Authority's case handlers as the rapporteurs to the case.[1705] These rapporteurs should submit all the information and evidence, as well as their opinion on the case, to the Board in a preliminary investigation report, within thirty days following their assignment.[1706] Accordingly, the preliminary investigation is a relatively fast procedure in order to see whether the allegations are serious enough to open an investigation. As noted in thegrounds of Law No. 4054, this is to make sure the Board treats each case rigorously, but without wasting considerable time and resources unnecessarily, in line with the principle of procedural efficiency.

Upon the submission of the preliminary investigation report, the Board should then decide within ten days whether to launch an investigation or not, based on the preliminary investigation report.[1707] The case handlers may conduct an on-site inspection as part of the preliminary investigation stage.

If the Board decides that there is no need to launch a fully-fledged investigation, it will issue a preliminary investigation decision, setting forth the reasons for not launching a fully-fledged investigation. This decision can be brought to judicial review.

In most cases, if the Board decides to launch a fully-fledged investigation pursuant to the documents and information collected during the preliminary investigation period, it notifies the relevant parties and usually announces it on its official website in due course.

[1703] Article 57 of Law No. 4054 states that "anyone who prevents, distorts or restricts competition via practices, decisions, contracts or agreements contrary to [Law No. 4054], or abuses his dominant position in a particular market for goods or services, is obliged to compensate the injured for any damage [incurred]".

[1704] Article 40 of Law No. 4054 provides that: "The Board decides to open a direct investigation, or to conduct a preliminary investigation to determine whether it is necessary to open an investigation, on its own initiative or upon an application received."

[1705] Article 40(1) of Law No. 4054.

[1706] Article 40(2) of Law No. 4054.

[1707] Article 41 of Law No. 4054.

11.4 Investigation

The Board may decide to initiate a fully-fledged investigation either directly or after conducting a preliminary investigation as per Article 40 of Law No. 4054. The Board may launch the investigation *ex officio* or in response to a complaint, denunciation or a leniency application under the same provision of the Law.

On the other hand, the Amendment Law that entered into force on 24 June 2020 has also introduced a set of new concepts that diverge from standard investigation rules and procedures. The new concepts that have direct effects on the investigation procedure include the application of the *de minimis* principle, as well as the settlement and commitment mechanisms.

11.4.1 Standard Investigation Procedure

The Board designates the department head, as well as the rapporteurs that will conduct the investigation–i.e., the investigation team.[1708] The investigation team needs to finalise their investigation within six months, but the Board may grant an additional period of six months if necessary.[1709] This additional period of six months can be granted either in one go or divided into two as three-month periods. For instance, in its *Turkcell* decision,[1710] the Board has granted an additional period of three months with its decision in December 2017, which was followed up by an additional period of three months granted in March 2018. The investigation process typically includes an exchange of the case team's written allegation reports and the investigated parties' written defences. The written phase of the investigation may be followed with a meeting for oral hearing, and the Board would issue its final decision at the end of the investigation process.

The Board notifies the parties concerned within fifteen days following the decision to initiate an investigation, i.e., the Investigation Notice.[1711] The Investigation Notice usually includes the preliminary allegations against the investigated undertakings. As per Article 43(3) of Law No. 4054, the Investigation Notice shall include sufficient information as to the type and nature of the allegations. After the Investigation Notice is formally served, the investigated parties have thirty calendar days to respond to the Investigation Notice by way of submitting their First Written Defences.[1712]

The Authority issues the Investigation Report within six months following the Board's investigation decision, which, if necessary, can be extended by an additional six months as explained above. The Investigation Report is the most comprehensive allegation report. It includes concrete allegations against the investigated parties and the evidence collected by the case handlers.

[1708] Article 43(1) of Law No. 4054.
[1709] Ibid.
[1710] *Turkcell* (8 November 2018, 18-42/670-329).
[1711] Article 43(2) of Law No. 4054.
[1712] Ibid.

Once the Investigation Report is served, the defendants will have thirty calendar days to respond by submitting their second written defence.[1713] These thirty calendar days set for the second written defence are extendable for a further thirty calendar days. Because the second written defence responds to the Investigation Report–i.e., the principal allegation document–this is also typically the instance where the investigated undertaking puts forward the backbone of its defences and arguments against the allegations. It is also important for the parties to present their defences before the Additional Opinion is issued, to allow the case team to assess their main arguments.

The investigation team will have fifteen calendar days to prepare their Additional Written Opinion after receipt of the Second written defence pursuant to Article 45(2) of Law No. 4054. This fifteen-calendar day period is extendable for an additional period of fifteen calendar days.[1714] The defending parties will have another thirty-day period, which is extendable for a further thirty calendar days, to reply to the additional opinion in a third written defence. This marks the last phase of the written pleas; the investigation team will not respond to the third written defence. That said, pursuant to Article 44(2) of Law No. 4054, the investigated parties are allowed to submit any information and evidence to the Board "at all times".

As discussed in detail above in "The Authority's Investigative Powers", the framework of the Authority's investigative powers is set under Articles 14 and 15 of Law No. 4054. In this scope, the Board is essentially entitled to conduct dawn raids, examine books, paperwork, documents, data and make written and verbal information requests to form its case. Article 44 of Law No. 4054 further stipulates that, during the investigation period, the Board may request the provision of any documents and information it deems necessary from the parties and other third parties concerned. If the conduct is prosecuted in a separate criminal investigation, the Board can also use the evidence obtained by the public prosecutor as part of the relevant criminal investigation (e.g., a recording of a telephone conversation).[1715]

Finally, the Authority is not entitled to establish its case based on illegally obtained evidence. For instance, in *Mey İçki*, the Board stressed that similar to criminal law cases, the principle of freedom of evidence governs the Authority's investigation procedure in terms of proving a violation but that this does not allow the Board to rely on illegally obtained evidence to support its case.[1716]

11.4.2 *De Minimis* Principle

The "*de minimis*" principle[1717] under Article 42(2) of Law No. 4054 provides that the Board may decide not to initiate an investigation on agreements, concerted practices and decisions and actions of associations of undertakings that "do not significantly

---

[1713]   Article 45(2) of Law No. 4054.
[1714]   Ibid.
[1715]   *Medical Devices* (n. 289).
[1716]   *Mey İçki* (17 November 2011, 11-57/1476-532), pp. 13–14.
[1717]   As further detailed under Chapter 2 "Article 4 and Article 5 of the Competition Law: Basic Principles".

restrict competition in the market" based on criteria such as the parties' market share and turnover. The same article notes that the *de minimis* principle does not apply to naked restrictions or hard-core restrictions such as price-fixing, territory or customer allocation and supply restrictions.

In order to clarify details on the process and procedure related to the application of the newly introduced *de minimis* principle, as well as the applicable market share and thresholds, the Authority published its Communiqué No. 2021/3 on 16 March 2021.

11.4.3 Commitment Procedure

Law No. 7246 introduced the commitment mechanism to the Turkish competition law regime by amending Article 43 of Law No. 4054. The recently issued Communiqué No. 2021/2 sets the relevant principles and procedures governing the commitment mechanism.

The amended Article 43(3) of Law No. 4054 provides that the investigated undertakings may offer commitments with respect to potential competition concerns under Articles 4 and 6 of Law No. 4054 during the preliminary investigation and the fully-fledged investigation processes. The same provision specifies that naked and hard-core restrictions such as price fixing between competitors, region and customer allocation, or supply restriction do not fall within the scope of the commitment mechanism.[1718] As for the nature of the commitments, Article 9 of Communiqué No. 2021/2 stipulates that the parties may submit behavioural and/or structural commitments to the Authority.

Article 5 of Communiqué No. 2021/2 provides that the investigated parties should first submit a request to offer commitments to the Authority in written form during the preliminary investigation or fully-fledged investigation phase, no later than three months following the service of the investigation notice.[1719] The Board would then review the request to determine whether it qualifies for the commitment mechanism. According to Article 6 of Communiqué No. 2021/2, the Board can either initiate the discussions with the parties or reject the proposed commitments and end the commitment procedure. If the Board finds that further examination is necessary in order to determine the competition law violation at the time of submission of the commitments, it can postpone the discussions with the parties.

The discussions may be made in oral or written form as per Article 6(4) of Communiqué No. 2021/2. The anti-competitive conduct subject to investigation will be clarified to the parties, and the documents and information that constitute a basis to the anti-competitive conduct will be presented to the parties during commitment discussions, except for confidential information and documents.[1720] However, it is possible for the Board not

---

[1718] Also, Article 2 of Communiqué No. 2021/2.

[1719] In *Arslan Nakliyat* (28 July 2020, 20-36/485-212) the Board rejected the commitments submitted by the investigated undertakings for failing to meet the deadline, as they had submitted their commitments after the investigation phase was completed.

[1720] Article 6(3) of Communiqué No. 2021/2.

to present the documents and information that serve as a basis for the competition law concern if the investigation notice has been provided to the parties as per Article 6(3) of Communiqué No. 2021/2.

The undertakings are then required to submit the commitment text within the deadline set by the Authority. For instance, pursuant to Article 7(1) of Communiqué No. 2021/2, "the parties shall send the commitment text, a copy of the commitment text free from trade secrets and confidential information, and a summary thereof, to the Authority within the period given". Article 7(2) of Communiqué No. 2021/2 further elaborates that "the period given for the submission of a commitment shall be determined by the Authority during the commitment discussions depending on the stage of the examination and the scope of the commitment".

Further, the content of the commitment text is specified under Article 8 of Communiqué No. 2021/2. Accordingly, the commitment text should be clear and include the following: (i) competition concerns to be solved by the commitment; (ii) implementation date and method as well as the duration of the commitment; (iii) the effect of the commitment on the market and how the commitment is expected to solve the competition concern; (iv) how the Authority will monitor compliance with the commitment and (v) other issues deemed necessary. In case a structural commitment is offered, the commitment text should include detailed explanations of the divestiture process. On the other hand, the commitment text should not include any alternative commitment proposal.

In case the Board does not find that the commitment is appropriate, the Board can either ask the parties to amend their commitment for one time only or decide to discontinue the commitment procedure.[1721] The Board may also ask for the complainant's and third parties' opinions regarding the commitment as part of its review under Article 11 of Communiqué No. 2021/2. In case the parties are required and willing to amend their commitments, the Board will continue the commitment discussions with the parties. In these discussions, the Board will explain its evaluations on the commitments and provide the parties with a copy of the confidential version of the third-party opinions, if any.

If the Board decides that the proposed commitments can solve the competition concerns, it may render these commitments binding for the relevant undertakings and decide not to initiate an investigation or to terminate an ongoing investigation as per Article 44(3) of Law No. 4054.[1722] The Board will then monitor the commitments through the periodic reports to be submitted by the parties regularly, appointing third parties for audit purposes, or cooperating with professional associations or relevant institutions and organisations, or by other means.[1723]

Finally, Article 44(4) provides that the Board can re-launch an investigation after rendering a commitment decision under Article 44(3) in the following cases: (i) there is a substantial change in any of the factors on which the decision was based, (ii) the relevant undertakings have violated the commitments, and/or (iii) the decision was based on missing, false or misleading information presented by the parties.

[1721] Article 10(3) of Communiqué No. 2021/2.
[1722] Article 10(2) of Communiqué No. 2021/2.
[1723] Article 15 of Communiqué No. 2021/2.

One of the Board's initial applications of the commitment mechanism is the *Havaş* decision.[1724] The Board has launched a fully-fledged investigation against Havaş and three other undertakings operating in the field of bonded temporary storage or warehouse services at airports in order to determine whether they violated Article 6 of Law No. 4054. Havaş submitted a commitment proposal within the scope of this investigation. The commitment procedure was concluded rapidly: The case handlers prepared their report within two weeks, and the Board rendered its decision in one month following the submission. The Board did not conduct a thorough competition law analysis but briefly identified the restrictions related to transfer fees for warehouse switching services. The Board decided that Havaş's commitment to terminate the fee practice was sufficient to eliminate competition law concerns.

As another example of the newly established commitment mechanism, the Board has also initiated the commitment mechanism in an investigation where the Board examined OSEM's standardisation and certification practices which were alleged to harm repair centres and equivalent part suppliers.[1725] As the commitments were found sufficient to eliminate the competition law concerns, the Board ended the ongoing investigation.

11.4.4 Settlement Procedure

The settlement procedure has also been introduced to the Turkish competition law regime with the Amendment Law. Article 43 of Law No. 4054 governs the settlement mechanism and the Regulation on the Settlement Procedure for Investigations on Anti-competitive Agreements, Concerted Practices, Decisions and Abuse of Dominant Position, which sets out the principles and procedure applicable to the settlement mechanism, was published on 15 July 2021. This procedure seeks to allow rapid resolution of the investigation process.

Article 43(5) of Law No. 405 provides that the Board can, *ex officio* or upon the investigated parties' request, initiate the settlement procedure with the investigated parties that acknowledge the existence and scope of an infringement until the official service of the investigation report. The Board may delay deciding on the applicant's request for settlement in case it deems more detailed research is necessary to establish the nature and scope of the violation.[1726] In case the Board initiates the settlement procedure on its own initiative, the parties should respond to the Board's invitation within fifteen days.[1727]

The Settlement Regulation foresees a list of provisions to allow the investigated undertaking to make a free and informed decision for settling. Accordingly, Article 6(2) of the Settlement Regulation includes an explicit provision highlighting that starting

---

[1724] *Havaş* (5 November 2020, 20-48/655-287).
[1725] *TSB/OSEM* (7 January 2021, 21-01/8-6).
[1726] Article 5(2) of the Settlement Regulation.
[1727] Article 5(3) of the Settlement Regulation.

settlement discussions with the Authority is not an acknowledgement of liability for the alleged violation(s). Likewise, during the discussion phase, the investigated undertaking is informed on (i) the content of the allegations; (ii) the nature and scope of the alleged violation; (iii) the reduction rate that may be applied to the administrative monetary in case of settlement; and (iv) an estimation of the range of likely fines.[1728] The investigated undertakings are also provided with non-confidential versions of the main evidence against them, limited to the scope and nature of the alleged violation.[1729]

The Board may decide to terminate the settlement procedure, for one or all of the parties, before reaching a final decision in case (i) it deems that the settlement will not bring the expected procedural efficiencies or it concludes that it will not be possible to find a common understanding with the parties to the settlement in terms of the existence and/or scope of the alleged violation; (ii) it considers there is a risk of evidence obfuscation; or (iii) the parties to the settlement do not respect the confidentiality requirements set under Article 12 of the Settlement Regulation.[1730]

Once the settlement discussions are finalised, the Board issues an interim decision. The interim decision includes, inter alia, the scope and nature of the alleged violation, the maximum amount of the fine and the reduction rate to be applied for settlement and leniency application (if any).[1731] In case the settlement request involves a leniency application, the reduction of fine granted for the settlement will be added to the reduction granted for the leniency application.[1732] The Board will also set a final deadline of fifteen days for the parties to submit their settlement text.[1733] The content of the interim decision cannot be made subject to discussion by the parties.[1734]

If the parties agree with the interim decision, they shall make a written submission (i.e., the settlement text) addressed to the Board within the deadline set by the Board as per Article 43(6) of Law No. 4054. Article 8(1) of the Settlement Regulation provides that the settlement text should include (i) an explicit declaration of admission concerning the existence and scope of the violation; (ii) the maximum rate and amount that the Board may have applied for a monetary fine and the settling undertaking's acceptance of such a fine; (iii) a recognition that the settling undertaking has been dully informed of the allegations and has been recognised the right to convey its own explanations and defences; and (iv) that the matter subject to settlement and the monetary fine cannot be litigated before the administrative courts. The fourth paragraph of the same article provides that the parties cannot retract settlement text submitted in due form.

Article 43(6) of Law No. 4054 provides that the Board will then issue its final decision establishing the infringement as well as the administrative monetary fine. As a result of

---

[1728]   Article 6(5) of the Settlement Regulation.
[1729]   Article 6(5)(c) of the Settlement Regulation.
[1730]   Article 4(6) of the Settlement Regulation.
[1731]   Article 7(1) of the Settlement Regulation.
[1732]   Article 7(3) of the Settlement Regulation.
[1733]   Article 7(1)(e) of the Settlement Regulation.
[1734]   Article 7(4) of the Settlement Regulation.

the settlement procedure, the Board can reduce the administrative monetary fine amount by 10% to 25% as per Article 43(7) of Law No. 4054 and Article 4(4) of the Settlement Procedure. In parallel with Article 8(1) of the Settlement Regulation, Article 43(8) of Law No. 4054 notes that the parties to a settlement cannot challenge the administrative fine and the provision of the settlement text before administrative courts if the process ends with a settlement.[1735]

Finally, the Settlement Regulation introduced a limitation concerning the resubmission of a settlement request. As per Article 11 of the said regulation, the parties cannot make another settlement request for the same case when (i) the process had not resulted in a settlement, or (ii) the parties did not accept, or respond in due time, to the Board's invitation for a settlement.

Unlike the EU competition law practice, the settlement procedure is not limited to cartel cases under Law No. 4054. Law No. 4054 does not foresee an exception to the settlement procedure in terms of the investigated conduct. Likewise, Article 1 of the Settlement Regulation explicitly provides that the settlement mechanism is applicable for violations prohibited under Articles 4 and 6 of Law No. 4054.

The first example of the settlement mechanism under Turkish competition law is the *Philips Home Appliances* case, concerning an investigation based on Article 4 of Law No. 4054.[1736] Following the parties' submission of their settlement text, the Board decided to conclude the settlement procedure for each of the parties.

11.5 Oral Hearings

Articles 46 and 47 of Law No. 4054, along with Communiqué No. 2010/2, govern the right and principles applicable to the oral hearing. The oral hearing is the fourth instance where the investigated party is allowed to present its defences. The hearing is held after the written phase of the investigation is closed. It gives the investigated undertaking an opportunity to orally address its defences directly to the Board. The preamble of Communiqué No. 2010/2 refers to the oral hearing meeting as a procedural safeguard for the investigated undertakings to effectively use their right of defence. The preamble notes that the oral hearing meeting seeks to allow the investigated undertaking to raise the essential points of their defences verbally and in person before the Board but also to allow the Board to ask questions to the investigated parties before reaching a final decision.

Oral hearings are not a mandatory step in the investigation process; they can be held upon the request of the investigated parties or *ex officio* by the Board if deemed necessary.[1737]

[1735]   Also, Article 4(4) of the Settlement Regulation.
[1736]   *Philips Home Appliances* (5 August 2021, 21-37/524-258).
[1737]   Article 46(1) of Law No. 4054.

11.5.1 Announcement of the Oral Hearing Meeting and Participants

Pursuant to Article 46 of Law No. 4054, oral hearings are held within at least thirty and at most sixty days following the completion of the written phase of the investigation. The oral hearing meeting invitation should be conveyed to the parties at least thirty days prior to the date of the hearing.[1738] The Board sets the date, venue and time of the meeting, and the notice duration for complainants and third parties that want to attend the meeting, which are also announced on the Authority' official website.[1739]

In addition to the parties to the investigation, Article 6(1) of Communiqué No. 2010/2 provides that the complainant(s) can attend the oral hearing if they make a written request within the notice period determined by the Board. Third parties can also request attendance, provided that they present information and documents showing their interest in the subject matter of the oral hearing, within the timings announced by the Authority. The Board would then decide on the requests and inform the relevant parties. The same article provides that the Board may also invite other third natural or legal persons deemed relevant or for the sake of obtaining information, either based on the investigation team's proposal or on its own initiative. For investigations launched upon request of the Ministry of Trade, the Ministry is also notified for attendance. All participants can attend the oral hearing meeting in person or via their representatives. Finally, the public can also attend the hearing pursuant to Article 8 of Communiqué No. 2010/2 as audience; provided that they are present at the premises of the Authority a reasonable time before the hearing; they can be admitted in order of arrival and depending on the capacity of physical facilities.

The Board may decide to postpone the hearing date if it is imperative to do so. In that case, parties, the complainant, third parties as well as the Ministry are individually informed while an announcement is also published on the Authority's official website.[1740]

11.5.2 Meeting Quorum

To reach the meeting quorum, the chairperson of the Board, or the deputy chairperson in the absence of the chairperson, as well as at least four Board members, should attend the hearing.[1741] In exceptional circumstances where the Board lost the necessary oral hearing meeting quorum due to the expiration of the term of office of more than two Board members, the Board decides to stay the hearing on its agenda until the necessary quorum is established.[1742]

[1738] Article 46(2) of Law No. 4054 and Article 5(1) of Communiqué No. 2010/2.
[1739] Article 4(2) of Communiqué No. 2010/2.
[1740] Article 19(1) of Communiqué No. 2010/2.
[1741] Article 47(2) of Law No. 4054.
[1742] See, e.g., *Philips* (n. 1644), *Chamber of Electrical Engineers* (26 December 2019, 19-46/791-345), *Chemotherapy Medicine Bids* (2 January 2020, 20-01/14-06).

11.5.3 Publicity of the Hearing

In principle, according to Article 47 of Law No. 4054 and Article 9 of Communiqué No. 2010/2, oral hearings are held publicly. However, the Board can decide to hear the meeting in private (on camera) for the protection of *"public decency"* and trade secrets according to the same provisions.

The request for confidentiality and its grounds should be notified to the Board latest by the end of the period for submissions of evidence, i.e., seven days before the hearing.[1743] In case the Board decides that the grounds presented for the confidentiality request are valid, the hearing would be held in a confidential session. The Board may also decide to hold a partially confidential oral hearing meeting.[1744] In a confidential session, all persons other than the party concerned, the investigation committee and the Authority personnel in charge of the case are taken outside the hearing room.[1745]

The Board is entrusted with a margin of appreciation for confidential session requests. The Board's publicly available case law does not provide substantial reasoning on this matter. In decisions where the Board accepted the parties' request for the oral hearing to be held in closed session, the Board only briefly refers to the said requests and notes that such request is accepted.[1746] The Board's rejection decisions contain more detailed reasoning, albeit still very limited. For instance, in the *8 Banks* decision, the Board states that the request does not fall under the definitions of public decency or confidentiality.[1747] The Board further notes that, in rejecting the request, it also considered the fact that other defendants did not request a confidential oral hearing. In *Dialyzer Machines*, the Board refused the confidentiality request of one of the defendants relating to cartel allegations and assessments of vertical relations.[1748] The Board's refusal of this request was based on the grounds that the requesting party did not include sufficient justification and the request was too broad.

11.5.4 The Oral Hearing Meeting

Pursuant to Article 15 of Communiqué No. 2010/2, the chairperson presides the hearing, and at least five Board members, including the chairperson, should attend the meeting. The meeting should be terminated in case none of the parties attends the meeting.[1749] The full hearing process is limited to five consecutive sessions, and multiple meetings held within the same day are deemed as one session.[1750]

[1743] Article 9(3) and Article 11(2) of Communiqué No. 2010/2.
[1744] *Automotive Industry* (20 November 2012, 12-58/1556-558).
[1745] Article 10 of Communiqué No. 2010/2.
[1746] For instance, see *Cargo Transportation* (16 January 2020, 20-04/47-25), *Enerjisa* (8 August 2018, 18-27/461-224) and *Akdeniz Elektrik* (20 February 2018, 18-06/101-52).
[1747] *8 Banks* (7 March 2011, 11-13/243-78).
[1748] *Dialyzer Machines* (23 December 2010, 10-80/1687-640).
[1749] Article 15(2) of Communiqué No. 2010/2.
[1750] Article 47(3) of Law No. 4054.

The process steps to be followed are also described under Article 15 of Communiqué No. 2010/2. Accordingly, the meeting starts with a public roll call. The investigation committee then briefly summarises the content of the case file and their claims or lack thereof. After the investigation committee's brief, the complainant(s), third parties and the Ministry are allowed to take the floor respectively to briefly summarise their claims. The complainant is not allowed to present new allegations during the hearing. The Board can also hear the parties, complainants and third persons, if any, separately or jointly in the hearing. The investigated parties then take the floor to present their defences before the Board. The chairperson has the right to change this order. During the meeting, the chairperson and the Board members can direct questions to the parties and complainants, third persons, witnesses and experts, if any, to explain themselves or complement their statements. The chairperson can also allow the complainant(s) or the investigation team to briefly respond to the arguments put forward by the investigated parties. The chairperson finally announces the verdict or the date of the verdict at the closing of the oral hearing meeting.[1751]

Pursuant to Article 18 of Communiqué 2010/2, the entire meeting shall be recorded by means of voice and/or visual recordings.

11.5.5 Submission of Evidence during the Oral Hearing

Article 47 of Law No. 4054 specifies the types of evidence and means of proof that can be used during the oral hearing. Article 47(5) of Law No. 4054 provides that parties are obliged to notify the Board of the evidence they will submit, at the latest by seven days prior to the hearing, and that the parties may not use the evidence if they fail to notify the Board in due time.

The parties are equipped with broad rights in terms of the type of evidence to be used as a means of proof during the hearing. Article 47(6) of Law No. 4054 refers to the Turkish Civil Procedure Code and states that the parties can use any evidence and means of proof enlisted in the said law. Similarly, Communiqué No. 2010/2 stipulates that the parties can have witnesses or experts heard during the hearing.

As per the matter of the witnesses, Article 12 of Communiqué No. 2010/2 stipulates that if the parties want to present witness evidence, they should submit to the Board a list of their witnesses together with an explanation as to their relevance to the case, and the issue about which they want the witness to be heard.[1752] The parties shall notify the Board within seven days before the hearing at the latest. In case the Board opines that it has obtained sufficient information at a given point during the hearing, it may decide not to listen to the rest of the listed witnesses. The Board hears the witnesses separately during the course of the hearing, but it may also decide to have the witnesses confront each other.[1753]

[1751]   Article 48(1) of Law No. 4054.
[1752]   Article 11(2) of Communiqué No. 2010/2.
[1753]   Article 12(3) of Communiqué No. 2010/2.

With regard to expert opinions, Article 13 of Communiqué No. 2010/2 stipulates that the parties can obtain a scientific expert's opinion with regard to the subject matter of the file. The Board may decide to hear the expert during the hearing, upon request or on its own initiative. The party which shall resort to an expert opinion in its oral defence shall notify the Board within seven days before the hearing at the latest. The party should submit the expert opinion together with all kinds of data analysis that form the opinion's basis.

11.6 Decisions

The Board's decisions constitute administrative acts. There are three types of decisions the Board may adopt at the end of the preliminary investigation or investigation process: the Board may issue an interim decision to open an investigation under Article 41 of Law No. 4054, an Opinion Letter under Article 9(3) of Law No. 4054, interim measures under Article 9(4) of Law No. 4054 or final decision under Article 9(1) of Law No. 4054.

As per the final decisions rendered upon an investigation, pursuant to Article 48 of Law No. 4054, the Board will render its final decision within fifteen calendar days following the hearing, if an oral hearing is held. If no oral hearing is held, then the Board will issue its final decision within thirty calendar days following the completion of the investigation process, as per the same provision. In case the parties to the investigation do not attend the scheduled oral hearing, the decision is made within one week following the date of the meeting determined, pursuant to the examination to be performed on the file.[1754]

11.6.1 Meeting and Quorum

Pursuant to Article 49 of Law No. 4054 and Article 21 of the Regulation on Procedure and Principles of the Turkish Competition Authority, the meetings during which the Board discusses and renders its decisions are confidential and not open to public access. According to Article 49 of Law No. 4054, the Board's members present at the hearing are obliged to participate in the meeting where the final decision is made.

With respect to the procedure, relevant meetings are chaired by the chairperson of the Board or, in his absence, the deputy chairperson. The chairperson of the Board or his/her deputy determines matters to be resolved. After such matters are discussed freely, the chairperson collects the votes and finally casts his/her own vote.[1755]

According to Article 51 of Law No. 4054 on the meeting and decision quorums, in its final decisions, the Board invites at least a total of five members, including the chairperson or the deputy chairperson, to the meeting. The decision quorum requires at least

---

[1754]   Article 48(3) of Law No. 4054.
[1755]   Article 50 of Law No. 4054.

four members casting the same vote. If the necessary decision quorum cannot be met in the first meeting, the chairperson shall ensure the participation of all members in the second meeting. In case it is not possible, the decision is taken by an absolute majority of the participants in the meeting. In case the voting in the second meeting results in a tie, the side which the chairperson's voted for shall be deemed to prevail.[1756]

Article 51(3) of Law No. 4054 provides that for all decisions (except the final decision) and particularly those decisions and transactions in the form of measures and recommendations, the meeting quorum requirement shall be the attendance of at least one third of the members of the Board; with the decision quorum set at an absolute majority of the attendees.

11.6.2 Constitutive Elements of Final Decisions

The short and non-confidential version of the Board's final decision will be published on the Authority's official website pursuant to Article 53(2) of Law No. 4054. It usually takes the Board around three to five months (from the announcement of the final decision) to serve a reasoned decision. That said, there is no mandatory provision regulating the date of service of the reasoned decision, but the constitutive elements of the decisions are enlisted under Article 52 of Law No. 4054.

Article 52 of Law No. 4054 and Article 23 of the Regulation on Procedure and Principles of the Turkish Competition Authority set out the constitutive elements of a decision as follows: (i) names of the decision Board members; (ii) names of the assigned case handlers; (iii) names and addresses of the parties; (iv) summary of the parties' claims; (v) summary of the examination and discussions of economics and legal matters; (vi) rapporteur's opinion; (vii) evaluation of all evidence and pleas submitted; (viii) reasoning and the legal basis of the decision; (ix) conclusion; and (x) dissenting opinions, if any.

Article 53 of Law No. 4054 and Article 24 of the Regulation on Procedure and Principles of the Turkish Competition Authority indicate that the chairperson or a member assigned by the chairperson writes the decision. If a member or multiple members do not agree on matters set forward in the final decision, they can issue their dissenting opinions individually or jointly. Once the decision is drafted, the Authority keeps the original; serves copies on the parties, and sends another copy to the Board's Publication Department to be published.

11.7 Leniency Applications

Leniency applications are regulated by the secondary legislation under Turkish competition law. These are the Regulation on Leniency and Guidelines on Active Cooperation, which derive from Article 16(6) of Law No. 4054.

[1756] Article 51(3) of Law No. 4054.

Leniency applications are specific to cartel cases, and they do not cover other types of violations under Law No. 4054 pursuant to Article 1 of the Regulation on Leniency. The Regulation defines cartels as "agreements restricting competition and/or concerted practices between competitors for fixing prices; allocation of customers, suppliers, territories or trade channels; restricting the amount of supply or imposing quotas, and bid rigging".[1757]

As noted in the general preamble of the Regulation on Leniency, because cartels are more difficult to detect compared to other violation types due to their secretive nature, the Turkish competition law regime provides a specific procedure to encourage cartel members' active cooperation with the Authority. Accordingly, the leniency procedure grants immunity or a reduction in administrative fines for those undertakings as well as managers and employees who are willing to actively cooperate with the Authority.[1758]

11.7.1 Application Process

Leniency applications can be made by undertakings but also by executives and employees. The application must be made independently from other undertakings allegedly part of the cartel and their managers and employees. The applicant may ask the Authority for leniency if there is no ongoing preliminary investigation or fully-fledged investigation. The applicant may also submit a leniency request once the preliminary or the fully-fledged investigation is launched, but the application should be submitted to the Authority before the service of the Investigation Report. Applications can be made in writing either by the concerned undertaking/person or by their representative. However, information and evidence in respect of the alleged cartel, including the products affected, the duration of the cartel, the names of the undertakings party to the cartel, specific dates, locations and participants of cartel meetings, may be submitted orally.[1759]

The Regulation on Leniency regulates the application procedure for undertakings under Article 6 and the application procedure for managers and employees under Article 9. These articles are structured almost identically. Accordingly, for a leniency application to be valid, the Authority requests the applicant to submit the following information: the products affected by the cartel, the duration of the cartel, the names of the cartelists, the date, location and participants of the cartel meeting(s), and other information or documents on the cartel. The Authority may grant additional time to the applicant to complete its submission, provided that information on the affected products, duration of the cartel and the name of the cartelists are submitted in the first instance.

The documents to be submitted to the Authority may consist of any means of proof such as invoices, notes, appointment books, meeting minutes, internal and external correspondences, travel records, digital records, credit card statements, etc.[1760] The Leniency

---

[1757]   Article 3(1)(c) of the Regulation on Leniency.
[1758]   Leniency Guidelines, para. 6.
[1759]   Article 6 of the Regulation on Leniency.
[1760]   Leniency Guidelines, para. 33.

Guidelines provide that the applicant must also submit any new evidence and documents that it comes across after the application until the Board adopts its final decision.[1761]

The Board's *Yeast Producers* decision is a landmark case in terms of leniency applications.[1762] The Board examined the allegations that four yeast producers colluded in order to fix the sales prices of fresh bread yeast. After the initiation of the investigation process, Mauri Maya made a leniency application and stated that the investigated undertakings did indeed have meetings to fix prices, also submitting its evidence. The evidence included Mauri Maya's lengthy internal correspondences referring to meetings held with the investigated undertakings, as well as multiple supporting documents such as ferry and parking tickets, hotel and restaurant bills. While the investigated undertakings argued that the relevant documents constituted secondary evidence and can only be considered in the presence of primary evidence, the Board decided that the evidence submitted by the applicant, as well as those collected during the on-site inspection, clearly confirmed the information submitted in the leniency application. The matter was later brought before judicial review. The Council of State made a detailed analysis of the primary and secondary evidence to decide that the submission of internal correspondences within the scope of a leniency application would not in and of itself jeopardise the evidentiary value of the said documents.[1763] On the other hand, the Council of State's decision indirectly sets forward the "adding value" criterion that is sought for the evidence presented within the scope of a leniency programme in the EU but not required in the Turkish leniency legislation.

Leniency applicants can request anonymity until the investigation report is officially served.

11.7.2 Review Process

Article 6 and Article 9 of the Regulation on Leniency set forth a number of rules the applicants should abide by during the leniency period. Accordingly, the leniency applicant (i) should end its involvement in the alleged cartel, except when the Authority request otherwise on the basis that it would make it more difficult to detect the cartel; (ii) should not conceal or destroy any information or evidence related to the alleged cartel; (iii) keep the application confidential until the investigation report is served, unless the Authority requests otherwise; and (iv) maintain active cooperation with the Authority until the Board adopts its final decision.

As for the confidentiality of the application, the Leniency Guidelines provides that the investigating unit may grant some exceptions, which, for instance, may include providing information to other competition authorities and/or institutions.[1764] But this

---

[1761]   Ibid., para. 34.
[1762]   *Yeast Producers* (n. 299).
[1763]   13th Chamber of the Council of State (11 December 2019, E. 2015/3353, K. 2019/4244).
[1764]   Leniency Guidelines, para. 43.

should not, in any event, jeopardise the security of the investigation. If, on the other hand, the employees of the applicant undertaking disclose the leniency application to other undertakings allegedly party to the cartel and breach the confidentiality principle, the Board will evaluate whether this is an isolated incident or whether the breach can be attributed to the applicant undertaking.[1765] If the Board finds that the incident stems from a high-level manager or if the undertaking failed to take the necessary precautions or if the undertaking failed to urgently notify the Authority after becoming aware of the breach, the Board may then decide that the confidentiality principle has been violated.[1766]

The Regulation on Leniency and the Leniency Guidelines do not include a definite timing for the Board to decide on the leniency application. The Leniency Guidelines only refer to a "prompt notification of the application result".[1767] The Board should, in any event, decide on the leniency application before the investigation is completed. In case of a rejection decision, if it is requested that the application should not be assessed under Article 5 or Article 8 of the Regulation on Leniency, and if the Board decides that no immunity can be granted, the applicant may request that the information and documents submitted to the Authority be returned, pursuant to the Leniency Guidelines paragraph 71. The Board should no longer be in a position to take these documents into consideration in its final decision.

The acceptance of a leniency application does not suggest finding a violation; rather, it is similar to a decision to launch an investigation.[1768] For instance, in the *Arçelik/Vestel* decision, concerning an investigation launched following a leniency application, the Board did not identify any competition law violation in its final decision.[1769] In line with this, a leniency application would not de facto lead to a cartel case, either, even in case the Board identifies a competition law violation. For instance, in the *Syndicated Loans* decision, despite the preliminary investigation being launched upon a leniency application, the Board classified the violation finding under the type "other" instead of a cartel violation.[1770]

11.8 Exercise of Defence Rights in the Authority's Proceedings

11.8.1 Burden of Proof

Article 38(1) of the Turkish Constitution sets forth the presumption of innocence by indicating that "no one shall be considered guilty until proven guilty in a court of law". Additionally, Article 36 of the Turkish Constitution also guarantees the right to a fair trial: "Everyone

---

[1765] Ibid., para. 44.
[1766] Ibid.
[1767] Ibid., Section 4.4.
[1768] Ibid., para. 69.
[1769] *Arçelik/Vestel* (2 January 2020, 20-01/13-5).
[1770] *Syndicated Loans* (n. 1645).

has the right of litigation either as plaintiff or defendant and the right to a fair trial before the courts through legitimate means and procedures." Thus, the presumption of innocence and the right to a fair trial requires the Authority to prove its case against the respondent. Furthermore, Article 6(2) titled "Right to a fair trial" of the European Convention on Human Rights (ECHR), stating that "everyone charged with a criminal offence shall be presumed innocent until proved guilty according to law", is also applicable in Turkey.

Accordingly, under competition law, the burden of proof rests with the Authority except for concerted practice allegations. Article 4(3) and 4(4) of Law No. 4054 indicate that:

> In cases where the existence of an agreement cannot be proved, a similarity of price changes in the market, or the balance of demand and supply, or the operational regions of undertakings to those markets where competition is prevented, distorted or restricted, constitutes a presumption that the undertakings are engaged in concerted practice.Each of the parties may relieve itself of the responsibility by proving, on the basis of economic and rational facts that it has not engaged in concerted practices.

Likewise, Article 59(1) of the No 4054 on civil damage claims provides that "should the injured party submit to judicial bodies proofs such as… which give the impression of the existence of an agreement, or the distortion of competition in the market, then the burden of proof is on the defendants to show that the undertakings are not engaged in concerted practice". Therefore, the plaintiff must provide evidence pointing to the existence of an agreement or the distortion of competition in the market, to shift the burden of proof to the defendant.

Apart from Articles 59(1), Law No. 4054 does not include any other provisions that shift the burden of proof from the Authority to the investigated undertakings. In this regard, aside from the instances where concerted practice is presumable, the Authority is fully responsible for proving its case through meeting the requisite standard of proof established in the legislation and case law.

On the other hand, the Board considers that the investigated undertakings bear the burden to prove their efficiency claims.[1771]

11.8.2 Right to be Heard

In administrative law proceedings, it is crucial to note that the investigated individual/ legal entity is facing the claims of an administrative entity. Therefore, it is only natural that the investigated individual/legal entity should be granted a reasonable amount of time and all the relevant information and evidence in the case against it, enabling the investigated party to prepare and present its defences.

During the investigation phase, the Authority must inform the undertakings of the charges they face without omitting or hiding any element of its case, to allow a full right of defence. In line with this, Article 44(3) of Law No. 4054 establishes that "the Board

---

[1771]   *Microsoft* (3 May 2012, 12-24/661-183) and *Samsung* (23 June 2011, 11-39/838-262)

may not base its decisions on issues about which the parties have not been informed and granted the right to defence".

The investigated undertaking must be given the opportunity to submit their defences. Accordingly, the administrative procedure set forth under Law No. 4054 guarantees the right to present three written[1772] and one oral defence submissions to the undertakings that are subjected to an investigation. In addition to this, Article 44(1) provides that the investigated undertakings may submit any information or evidence to the Board at all times during the investigation period.

11.8.3 Self-Incrimination

Article 38 of the Turkish Constitution sets out that "no one shall be compelled to make a statement that would incriminate themselves or their legal next of kin, or to present such incriminating evidence". Accordingly, no one can be forced to make statements or provide evidence incriminating themselves under Turkish law.

In line with this, given the comprehensive scope of the investigative powers granted to the Board, coupled with the fact that the Board's power to request information is not subject to any restriction under Law No. 4054 or secondary legislation, the Board has to respect the constitutional privilege against self-incrimination while exercising its investigative powers. This is also recognised by the Board. For instance, the Board's *Custom Consultants Association decision*[1773] explicitly recognises that forcing a person and/or a legal entity to make statements or provide evidence incriminating themselves would contradict the fair trial principle. But the Board also noted that the scope of this privilege is not unlimited and that the provision of false or misleading information under Article 16(c) of Law No. 4054 does not fall within the scope of this privilege. In *Luxottica*, the Board assessed whether Luxottica provided wrong or misleading information to the Board within the scope of an investigation conducted against Luxottica concerning its sales policies and other practices.[1774] The Board held that the investigated undertaking's response letters collected under Article 14 of Law No. 4054 should be considered within the scope of the privilege against self-incrimination. The Board also held that response letters constitute statements that the investigated undertaking did not violate Law No. 4054 and can therefore not be considered as false or misleading information under Article 16(c) of Law No. 4054.

11.8.4 Protection of Trade Secrets

The protection of trade secrets is regulated under Communiqué No. 2010/3. Communiqué No. 2010/3 lists the conditions for information and documents to qualify as trade secrets

---

[1772] The written phase of the investigation may be followed with an oral hearing meeting and the Board would issue its final decision at the end of the investigation process.
[1773] *Custom Consultants Association* (6 February 2020, 20-08/77-44), pp. 3–4.
[1774] *Luxottica* (23 February 2017, 17-08/88-38), p. 5.

under Law No. 4054, and sets the procedures and principles concerning the exercise of the right to confidentiality.

As per Article 2 of Communiqué No. 2010/3, the protection of trade secrets is applicable to all kinds of information and documents obtained by the Authority within the scope of Law No. 4054. Accordingly, confidentiality can be claimed for documents obtained during an on-site inspection as well as for all defences and response petitions submitted to the Authority within the scope of Law No. 4054. Unless the undertakings expressly claim confidentiality, the presumption is that the information and documents are not confidential; nevertheless, the Authority can also ask the undertakings for an evaluation on the confidentiality of the information and/or documents, or make an *ex officio* evaluation.[1775]

Article 12 of Communiqué No. 2010/3 defines a trade secret as any information and document relating to the field of activity of undertakings that undertakings wish to keep confidential, that is only known to and can be accessed by a certain and restricted group of persons, and that is likely to result in serious damage to the undertaking concerned when disclosed to third parties, especially competitors, and to the public. The same provision further stipulates:

> Depending on the characteristics of the case and the undertaking, information and documents such as the internal structure and organisation of undertakings, their financial, economic, credit and liquidity status, research and development activities, operational strategy, raw material resources, technical information related to production and manufacturing, pricing policies, marketing tactics and costs, market shares, wholesale and retail customer potential and networks, contractual connections that are subject to or not subject to authorisation, can be considered as trade secrets.

On the other hand, Article 12(3) of Communiqué No. 2010/3 provides that information and documents relating to contracts, agreements, settlements and practices that are in violation of Law No. 4054 will not be considered as trade secrets, even if their disclosure is likely to result in damages to the undertaking concerned, or its competitors. Article 12(4) also notes that information that has already been made publicly available or information that has lost its commercial significance (e.g., due to reasons such as by publication in official records, or the fact that it is five years old or more) may not be deemed a trade secret.

According to Article 13 of Communiqué No. 2010/3, the burden of identifying whether the document submitted contains trade secrets and justifying such claim rests with the undertakings. The documents for which the undertakings do not make a confidentiality claim are deemed non-confidential. But the Authority may still ask the undertakings to review the said documents if the Authority considers that they may include confidential information. The Authority may also proceed with the redaction of the said documents. The undertakings that do not make a confidentiality assessment despite the Authority's request cannot claim confidentiality at a later stage.[1776]

[1775]   Article 14 of Communiqué No. 2010/3.
[1776]   Article 14(3) of Communiqué No. 2010/3.

The confidentiality claim should include the following in writing: (i) list of the information and documents that contain trade secrets; (ii) the grounds explaining the nature of the trade secrets within the identified information and documents; and (iii) redacted versions of the said documents.[1777] The undertakings are also required to identify each and every document deemed confidential–the Authority would not accept a confidentiality claim for the entirety of the documents.[1778]

In case the Authority accepts the confidentiality claims regarding the trade secrets, it shall refrain from disclosing them as per Article 15 of Communiqué No. 2010/3. The Authority is not authorised to disclose the confidential information to third parties, and any request from third parties to access the file is evaluated within the framework of general provisions. The Authority is also required to redact the confidential information in its reasoned decisions that are published on its website. For instance, trade secrets that are not imperative to proving the infringement should not be disclosed in Board decisions, as it is possible to adopt other methods such as providing approximate values or ranges, depending on the nature of the information.[1779] On the other hand, the Authority is able to reject confidentiality requests for information and documents that are indispensable as evidence of infringement as per Article 15(2) of Communiqué 2010/3. In these cases, the Authority may disclose such information and documents that could be considered as trade secrets by taking into account the balance between public and private interest, in accordance with the principle of proportionality.

Finally, the officials of the Authority and Board members themselves also have a duty of confidentiality. For instance, Article 25(4) of Law No. 4054 stipulates:

> The members and staff of the Board may not disclose and use in their own or others' interests, the confidential information pertaining to the Authority, and trade secrets of undertakings and associations of undertakings that they learn during the implementation of this Act, even if they have left their office.

11.8.5 Access to the File

The right to access the file allows applicants to access the documents within the Authority's case file pertaining to the investigation. It has two legal grounds under the Turkish competition law regime: (i) Communiqué No. 2010/3 applicable to procedures governed by Law No. 4054 and (ii) the broader Law No. 4982 on the Right to Information applicable to public institutions and professional organisations which qualify as public institutions.

Access to the file can be requested any time until the end of the period for submitting the last written defence as per Article 8(3) of Communiqué No. 2010/3. That said,

---

[1777]   Article 13(2) of Communiqué No. 2010/3.
[1778]   Article 13(5) of Communiqué No. 2010/3.
[1779]   Article 15(3) of Communiqué No. 2010/3.

the Authority may delay the timing of the access to the file until after the Investigation Report is served to the relevant parties, it is deemed necessary to preserve the confidentiality of the investigation and prevent the destruction of evidence.[1780] Unless there has been new evidence obtained during the investigation, the right to access to the file can only be used once, according to Article 5(1) of the Communiqué 2010/3.

With regard to the scope of the information and documents that fall under the right of access to file, Article 6 of Communiqué No. 2010/3 indicates that the parties can have access to any document that has been prepared and any evidence that has been obtained by the Authority which concerns them. Exceptions to this provision are the internal correspondence of the Authority[1781] and information and/or documents that include trade secrets and other confidential information about other undertakings, associations of undertakings and persons.

In case their request is accepted, the parties can exercise their right to access the file by receiving the photocopies or electronic copies of the documents in the file and have been rendered accessible. However, Article 10(2) of Communiqué 2010/3 points out that certain pieces of information that have been obtained within the framework of Article 6(3) and Article 9(3) of the Regulation on Active Cooperation for Detecting Cartels, as well as other intra-Authority correspondences that have the nature of exculpatory or accusatory evidence, can only be examined at the headquarters of the Authority.

The access to file applications made under Communiqué No. 2010/3 are reviewed by the investigation committee. If the application is accepted, the method, time and other matters regarding access to the file are notified to the applicant in writing. However, if the request is denied, the Board issues a reasoned decision as a separate administrative act.

On the other hand, Law No. 4982, which forms the basis of the right to information and the relevant procedure before public authorities, is also applicable to the process before the Authority. According to Article 3 and Article 4 of this law, all natural and legal persons are entitled to exercise their right to information before public authorities. Applicants are required to make a written submission. While the applications under Law No. 4982 on the Right to Information are first lodged before the Authority, if the information access application is refused, such decision can be brought before the Information Request Evaluation Committee for review.[1782]

[1780] Article 8(2) of Communiqué No. 2010/3
[1781] Article 7 of Communiqué No. 2010/3 states that, "(1) Intra-Authority correspondences are correspondences between departmental units, which have the nature of preparatory acts for the final decisions taken by the Board. (2) Information and documents that have been obtained within the framework of Article 6 paragraph three and Article 9 paragraph three of the Regulation on Active Cooperation for Detecting Cartels, as well as correspondences between the Authority and those from whom information was obtained such as other public institutions, professional organisations that have the nature of public institution or natural and legal persons in the private sector, are accepted as internal correspondence."
[1782] The Information Request Evaluation Committee is established under Law No. 4982. The Committee reviews and decides on the public authorities' exercise concerning the right to information under Law No. 4054.

11.9 International cooperation

The Authority takes part in the projects led by the Organisation for Economic Cooperation and Development (OECD), the United Nations Conference on Trade and Development (UNCTAD), the World Trade Organization (WTO) and the World Bank (WB).[1783]

The Authority is also party to bilateral cooperation agreements signed with the competition agencies in other jurisdictions. As of 2021, the Authority has signed bilateral cooperation agreements with 23 competition agencies in jurisdictions such as South Korea, Romania, Bulgaria, Portugal, Bosnia-Herzegovina, Russia, Croatia, Austria, Mongolia and many others.[1784] The scope of these cooperation agreements typically covers compliance to competition policies and exchange of information in this regard, including cartel enforcement.

Article 43 of Decision No. 1/95 of the EC-Turkey Association Council (Decision No. 1/95) authorises the Authority to notify and request the European Commission's Directorate-General for Competition to apply relevant measures if the Board believes that cartels organised in the territory of the EU adversely affect competition in Turkey. The provision grants reciprocal rights and obligations to the parties (the EU and Turkey), and thus the European Commission has the authority to request the Board to apply relevant measures to restore competition in relevant markets.

There have been many cases of the Authority requiring the cooperation of competition authorities in other jurisdictions concerning information exchange, service of notifications, and the collection of monetary fines. These requests are made via the Ministry of Foreign Affairs and the Ministry of Justice.[1785]

For instance, within the scope of the investigation[1786] initiated following the leniency application made by Deutsche Bahn against certain suppliers of rail freight forwarding services for block trains and cargo train service, concerning allegations on customer allocation, the Board has notified certain investigated parties through the embassies located in foreign countries. According to the publicly available version of the Board's decision, the petition submitted by the Turkish General Consulate of Budapest stated that the notification to a certain investigated party had been duly made, while the Turkish General Consulate of Zurich stated that the notification in Switzerland was not successful as the Authority was required to contact Switzerland's judicial authorities. On the other hand, in *Glencore/Minerkrom*[1787] decision, it is observed that the Board's efforts to notify the investigated parties in Austria and Switzerland,

---

[1783]   <https://www.rekabet.gov.tr/tr/Sayfa/Kurumsal/uluslararasi-iliskiler/genel-cerceve> (last accessed on 1 April 2021).
[1784]   <https://www.rekabet.gov.tr/tr/Sayfa/Kurumsal/uluslararasi-iliskiler/iki-tarafli-iliskiler/diger-rekabet-kurumlari-yla-yapilan-i> (last accessed on 1 April 2021).
[1785]   *Rail Cargo Logistics* (n. 48); *Imported Coal* (n. 1645); *Glencore decision* (11 September 2006, 06-62/848-241). See also G. Dere, "Jurisdictional Problems for Competition Authorities and Solution Suggestions for Turkey", Turkish Competition Authority, Dissertation No. 127, 2012.
[1786]   *Rail Cargo Logistics* (n. 48).
[1787]   *Imported Coal* (n. 1645).

by virtue of the Ministry of Foreign Affairs, remained inconclusive. In the case of Austria, the notification pertaining to the investigation conducted by the Authority could not be duly made since the content of the notification was deemed to concern administrative (i.e., not criminal or judicial) processes, and there are no bilateral or multilateral agreements executed between Turkey and Austria regarding the notification of such matters.

Chapter 12
Sanctions and the Termination
of Infringements

GÖNENÇ GÜRKAYNAK, ESQ., HAKAN DEMIRKAN,*
ESMA AKTAŞ** AND UZAY GÖRKEM YILDIZ***

Under the Turkish legal regime, competition law violations are classified as misdemeanours and accordingly, sanctions imposed by the Board are subject to Law No. 5326.[1788]
As the general law applied to misdemeanours, Law No. 5326 defines misdemeanour under
Article 2 as "a tort for which the law requires imposition of administrative sanctions".
Therefore, sanctions that the Board may impose in accordance with Law No. 4054 are
of administrative nature. In this regard, breach of Law No. 4054 leads to administrative
fines (and civil liability) but does not lead to criminal sanctions.

On the other hand, there have been cases where the matter also involved a breach of
criminal law and thus had to be referred to a public prosecutor after the competition law
investigation was completed: For example, bid-rigging activities may be criminally prosecuted in accordance with Section 235 *et seq.* of the Turkish Criminal Code. Illegal price
manipulation (i.e., manipulation through disinformation or other fraudulent means) may
also be punished by up to two years' imprisonment and a judicial monetary fine under
Article 237 of the Turkish Criminal Code, as explained below in detail under Section 12.3.

All in all, sanctions that the Board may impose are administrative in nature and subject to the
judicial review of administrative courts as regulated under Article 55 of Law No. 4054.[1789]

To that end, the Authority has been structured as an independent administrative authority.
Its autonomy and regulatory functions are supported by its power to impose administrative sanctions on undertakings violating competition law rules. These characteristics of
the Authority are reflected under Article 20 of Law No. 4054, which reads as follows:

> The Competition Authority having a public legal personality, and an administra-
> tive and financial autonomy is established in order to ensure the formation and
> development of markets for goods and services in a free and sound competitive
> environment, to observe the implementation of this Act, and to fulfil the duties
> assigned to it by the Act.

---

*   Associate, ELIG Gürkaynak Attorneys-at-Law, Istanbul <hakan.demirkan@elig.com>.
**   Associate, ELIG Gürkaynak Attorneys-at-Law, Istanbul <esma.aktas@elig.com>.
***   Associate, ELIG Gürkaynak Attorneys-at-Law, Istanbul <uzay.yildiz@elig.com>.
[1788] G. Karabel, *Rekabet Hukukunda Ne Bis In Idem İlkesi* (Ankara: Rekabet Kurumu), 2015, p. 15.
[1789] For further information, please see Chapter 13.

Accordingly, the Authority fulfils its duty to protect competition and, as an autonomous authority, is authorised to impose sanctions for those violating the rules of competition law.

On the other hand, the Board is the decision-making body of the Authority with extensive regulatory, supervisory and executive powers. The Board is vested with the power to enforce administrative sanctions in performing its duties. More specifically, the Board is authorised to impose administrative fines in cases of violation of Law No. 4054. In addition to the administrative monetary fines, the Board is also authorised to take all necessary measures to terminate the violation, to remove all de facto and legal consequences of every conduct that has been performed unlawfully, and to take all other necessary measures in order to restore the level of competition and the status quo which existed before the violation.[1790]

With its power to impose sanctions under administrative law enforcement, the Board undertakes the Authority's duty to ensure an environment of free and robust competition in the Turkish markets.

12.1 Principles Regarding Administrative Monetary Fines

12.1.1 Purpose and Scope

The principles and the framework surrounding administrative monetary fines to be imposed by the Board are set forth under Law No. 4054, as well as the Regulation on Fines published by the Authority.

Even though there are different views in literature focusing on the purpose of administrative sanctions, such discussions are fundamentally grouped into two categories, namely, retribution and deterrence. On the other hand, in terms of competition law sanctions, it is widely accepted that the purpose of administrative monetary fines is to provide clear deterrence for undertakings and prevent them from violating the rules of competition law.[1791] Indeed, "ensuring that fines are both specifically and generally deterrent" is listed among the purposes of the Regulation on Fines. The general preamble of the Regulation on Fines provides:

> Specific deterrence is preventing those undertakings, which are the addressee of fines, from violating the Act. General deterrence is dissuading those undertakings which are likely to violate the Act or which continue a violation that has not been detected yet. In this context, fines should be determined in such a way that they ensure both types of deterrence.

[1790] See Article 9 and Article 27 of Law No. 4054.
[1791] E. Aygün, *Rekabet Hukukunda Para Cezaları: Teori ve Uygulama* (Ankara: Rekabet Kurumu, 2008), pp. 3–4.

Article 16 of Law No. 4054 constitutes the legal basis of the administrative monetary fines to be imposed for violations of competition law. The said article regulates the principles of the imposition of administrative monetary fines.

In relation to competition law violations, Article 16(3) of Law No. 4054 provides that:

> To those who commit behavior prohibited in Articles 4, 6 and 7 of this Act, an administrative fine shall be imposed up to ten percent of annual gross revenues of undertakings and associations of undertakings or members of such associations to be imposed a penalty, generated by the end of the financial year preceding the decision, or generated by the end of the financial year closest to the date of the decision if it would not be possible to calculate it and which would be determined by the Board.

Accordingly, Law No. 4054 sets an upper limit to the administrative monetary fines that may be imposed by the Board, at 10% of annual gross revenues of undertakings, associations of undertakings or members of such associations.

Moreover, the Board shall take into account the annual gross revenues generated by the end of the financial year preceding the Board's decision; and if it would not be possible to calculate this, then the revenue generated by the end of the financial year closest to the date of the decision will be applicable.

Apart from undertakings, associations of undertakings or members of such associations themselves, the Board may also impose administrative fines on their employees or managers who have a decisive influence over the infringement of competition law. Pursuant to Article 16(4) of Law No. 4054, the administrative fine to be imposed on such employees or members of the executive bodies can reach up to 5% of the fine imposed on the undertaking or association of undertaking itself, as explained in detail under Section 12.2.2 below.

12.1.2 Principles Relating to the Determination of Fines

Article 16 of Law No. 4054 provides that the principles to consider in determining the administrative fines shall be set out under the secondary legislation to be published by the Board. Accordingly, the Authority has issued its Regulation on Fines, which lists the following goals in its preamble:

- Ensuring transparency, objectivity and consistency in the fining procedure.
- Taking into account the conduct of the undertakings, such as assistance during proceedings and active cooperation, while determining administrative fines and promoting them.
- Ensuring that administrative fines are specifically and generally deterrent.

The principles of determining the administrative monetary fines are set out under Article 4 of the Regulation on Fines, which provides a two-step process. Accordingly, the Board shall (i) first determine the base fine–details of which are explained in the next section–(ii) then take into account aggravating and mitigating factors. The maximum fine that the Board can impose is 10% of annual gross revenues, and the Board determines administrative fines within the boundaries of competition law legislation in Turkey as well as the general principles of administrative law.

The Regulation on Fines provides that the Board shall calculate the base fine separately for each conduct in case more than one individual conduct/behaviour is found to be in violation of competition law. In this regard, it is necessary to first evaluate the concept of single continuous infringement.

12.1.2.1 Single Continuous Infringement

Single continuous infringement is a concept enabling competition authorities to consider a series of agreements or conducts having the same objective to distort competition in the market as one single continuous infringement. Similar to the approach followed in the EU, the Authority also takes this concept into account while assessing a case under Article 4 of Law No. 4054. Although not expressly recognised in the relevant legislation, the concept is evaluated and acknowledged in the case law.

In its decisions, the Board sets forth the conditions for single continuous infringement by referring to the Commission's decisions on the matter.

In *Hyundai Dealers*,[1792] the Board stated that the use of the concept essentially depends on the existence of three main conditions. First, there must be a framework agreement or a common objective. Second, the agreement or concerted practices that emerge in time must be complementary in nature. In this context, the agreement or concerted practices must be executed through a common economic plan (the framework agreement), and such behaviour should constitute an integral whole. The third condition for single continuous infringement is the undertakings' participation in the agreement or concerted practices.

In *Nevsehir Driving Schools*,[1793] the Board investigated the driving schools for allegedly determining the sales prices and conditions, and creating pools for revenue sharing through different agreements between 2006 and 2012. The Board concluded that these separate agreements formed a single continuing infringement. The Board stated that the investigated undertakings had reached agreements on several matters within the scope of meetings that started in 2004 and continued until June 2012. The agreements were related to offsetting the driving school fees and private driving lessons, determination of the payment methods, creating pools for revenue sharing between the driving schools and sharing university students equally between the driving schools. Against this background, the Board decided that the agreements have distorted competition within the meaning of Article 4 of Law No. 4054. Moreover, the Board added that although the parties had reached different agreements at different times, the meetings were a part of the same process, and therefore the said agreements were considered as a single violation.

[1792] *Hyundai Dealers* (16 December 2013, 13-70/952-403).
[1793] *Nevsehir Driving Schools* (13 June 2013, 13-36/482-212).

In *12 Banks*,[1794] the Board has imposed administrative monetary fines on the investigated undertakings on the ground that they violated Article 4 of Law No. 4054 by engaging in concerted practices in the current accounts, credits and credit card services market. The Board further stated that each of the agreements and/or concerted practices between the undertakings suggests a single continuous infringement to fix the interest rates in terms of the current accounts, credits and credit card services. Although the undertakings' appeal to the Council of State was first rejected, certain banks' request for re-appeal was later accepted. The Council of State set forth that in order for a series of actions to be considered as a single continuous infringement, there must be a framework agreement or a common plan, whose scope and limits should be determined carefully. However, these framework agreements can be applied in various products and/or markets. The Council of State stated that in order for a single continuous infringement, it is not necessary for undertakings to be involved in all of the stages of the violation. It further added that an undertaking should be liable for violations conducted in different products and/or markets if it is proven that the relevant undertaking was either aware of or was in a position to know the framework agreement or common plan. On the other hand, the Council of State said that in cases where the relevant undertaking cannot be expected to know about the framework agreement or common plan, it could only be liable for violations that it actively committed. In its assessment on the merits of the case, it concluded that the Board's decision did not satisfy the necessary standard of proof. More specifically, it concluded that the decision failed to prove (beyond a reasonable doubt) that the investigated banks acted in accordance with a framework agreement and common practice in terms of the conducts in the current accounts, credit and credit card services market. Consequently, the Council of State revised its previous decision and directed the court of first instance to reconsider its decision.[1795] Although the court of first instance has not complied with the Council of State's decision, the case is expected to be brought before the highest decision-making body of the Council of State in the following stages.

12.1.2.2 *Ne bis in idem*

Ne bis in idem is one of the general legal principles acknowledged and discussed in the Board's decisions within the context of imposition of monetary fines. Basically, the principle sets forth that there should not be multiple judgments and punishments imposed upon the same conduct or matter. In other words, as per this principle, a conduct that is subject to a sanction cannot be fined twice. In terms of determination of monetary fines, this principle is of utmost importance for the implementation of competition law as it aims to avoid double penalisation.

The relevant principle is acknowledged and reflected as a fundamental right in international conventions and national legislation. For instance, Article 50 of the Charter of Fundamental Rights of the European Union sets forth that "no one shall be liable to be tried or punished again in criminal proceedings for an offence for which he

---

[1794]   *12 Banks* (8 March 2013, 13-13/198-100).
[1795]   13th Chamber of the Council of State (21 May 2019, E. 2016/4069, K. 2019/1783).

or she has already been finally acquitted or convicted within the Union in accordance with the law. *"Ne bis in idem* is also reflected in the Turkish statutory regime. To that end, Article 15(1) of Law No. 5326 sets forth that "if more than one misdemeanour is committed through an act, and the imposition of an administrative monetary fine is the only sanction provided for these misdemeanours, then the heaviest administrative monetary fine will be imposed". The relevant provision evidently indicates that Law No. 5326 adopts *ne bis in idem* by necessitating the imposition of (only) the heaviest fine if multiple misdemeanours are committed through an act.

Similarly, Article 4(1) of the Regulation on Fines provides:

> The base fine shall be calculated within the framework of Article 5 of this Regulation. In case more than one independent conduct–in terms of the market, nature, and chronological period–prohibited under Articles 4 and 6 of the Act is detected, the base fine shall be calculated separately for each conduct.

Therefore, the Regulation on Fines also adopts *ne bis in idem* by requiring the existence of separate individual conducts for separate fines. The Regulation on Fines, therefore, recognises that separate base fines should only be applied in respect of independent conduct, and independent conduct should be deemed to exist where three cumulative conditions are satisfied: namely, the examined behaviours take place in different markets, have different natures (i.e., constitute different types of violations) and take place in different chronological periods. The Board's decisions show that it conducts detailed assessments on the evaluation of the principle of *ne bis in idem* and takes into account this principle in determining the sanctions to be imposed on undertakings infringing competition law.[1796] In its landmark *Mey İçki* decision,[1797] the Board evaluated the allegations that Mey İçki abused its dominant position in the markets for vodka and gin in Turkey. In its substantive assessment, even though the Board found that Mey İçki enjoys a dominant position in the vodka and gin markets and has violated Article 6 of Law No. 4054, it decided not to impose an administrative fine on the undertaking, on the ground that Mey İçki had already been fined due to the same commercial strategy in another investigation conducted in the rakı (traditional Turkish spirit) market.[1798] The Board also factored in the fact that the previous fine has been calculated based on Mey İçki's total turnover rather than its turnover in the concerned market. Even though the Board's decision was appealed by Mey İçki's competitors, later on, the Council of State eventually upheld the Board's decision.[1799]

[1796] *Bereket Enerji/Aydem/Gediz* (1 October 2018, 18-36/583-284), para. 552; *Enerjisa* (8 August 2018, 18-27/461-224), para. 663; *Pınar Milk Products and Dimes Food Industry* (22 April 2004, 04-27/339-81); *SEK Milk Industry Institution* (22 April 2004, 04-27/340-82); *İzocam* (8 February 2010, 10-14/175-66); *Frito-Lay* (29 August 2013, 13-49/711-300); *Turkcell* (6 June 2011, 11-34/742-230); *Samsun Driving Schools* (15 May 2013, 13-28/387-175); *Cargo* (3 September 2010, 10-58/1193-449); *Booking* (5 January 2017, 17-01/12-4), para. 271; *Mars* (18 January 2018, 18-03/35-22), para. 39.

[1797] *Mey İçki* (25 October 2017, 17-34/537-228).

[1798] *Mey İçki Rakı* (16 February 2017, 17-07/84-34).

[1799] 13th Chamber of the Council of State (2 December 2020, E. 2020/1941, K. 2020/3508); 13th Chamber of the Council of State (2 December 2020, E. 2020/1939, K. 2020/3507).

The Board's *Mey İçki* decision and the Council of State's judgment are the latest reflection of *ne bis in idem* principle in Turkish competition law and are expected to set a precedent on the matter for the future.

12.1.3 Base Fine

As the first step of the imposition of administrative fines, the Board shall determine the base fine to be taken into account, at rates varying between 0.5% and 4% of total turnover under Turkish competition law.[1800]

The Regulation on Fines provides that the Board shall calculate the base fine separately for each conduct in case it is found that there is more than one individual conduct/ behaviour that was in violation of the competition law. In assessing whether there exists more than one behaviour/conduct, the Board considers factors such as the relevant market and the nature and chronological order of behaviours (Article 4 of the Regulation on Fines).

The Regulation on Fines sets forth the base fines for different types of conduct. Accordingly, the base fine is calculated at a rate between (i) 2% and 4% for cartels, and (ii) 0.5% and 3% for other violations, on the basis of the annual gross revenues of undertakings and association of undertakings or members of such associations that engaged in conducts listed under Articles 4, 6 and 7 of Law No. 4054, generated at the end of the fiscal year preceding the final decision (or if that cannot be calculated, at the end of the fiscal year closest to the date of the final decision).

As per the Regulation on Fines, annual gross revenue is defined as "net sales in the uniform chart of accounts, or if this cannot be calculated, the revenue closest to the net sales, which is to be determined by the Board". In this regard, it is important to note that the Turkish competition law regime does not make a distinction between domestic vs overseas revenues, or the part of revenues generated in the only relevant markets; it refers to the total turnover. On the other hand, as explained above, in some of its decisions, the Board imposed administrative monetary fines on undertakings by taking into account only the turnovers generated in the relevant markets,[1801] which led to discussions in the literature within the context of consistency and legal certainty.[1802]

In determining the level of the monetary fine, Article 16 of Law No. 4054 refers to Article 17 of Law No. 5326, directing the Board to consider factors such as recidivism, duration of the infringement, market power of relevant undertakings, the level of role

---

[1800] The turnover referred to herein corresponds to the concerned undertaking's annual gross revenue over the year preceding the decision, as per Article 3 of the Regulation on Fines.

[1801] *Türk Telekom/TTNET* (19 November 2008, 08-65/1055-411); *Sarten TKS* (15 April 2010, 10-31/471-175); *Medical Gas* (11 November 2010, 10-72/1503-572); *8 Banks* (7 March 2011, 11-13/243-78); *Güneş Express/ Condor* (27 October 2011, 11-54/1431-507).

[1802] K. C. Sanlı, "Rekabet Kurumunun Ceza Yönetmeliği Taslağı: Hukuk ve Ekonomi Perspektifinden Bir Değerlendirme", *Rekabet Dergisi*, Vol. 15, No. 1, January 2014.

in the realisation of infringement, compliance with commitments and the severity of the damage occurred or possible damages, etc. Similarly, for the determination of base fine, the Regulation on Fines provides that "factors such as the market power of the undertakings or associations of undertakings concerned, and the gravity of the damage which occurred or is likely to occur as a result of the violation shall be considered".

In this regard, "market power of undertakings" and "gravity of the damage" are also the subject of discussions in the literature due to their ambiguity since the Regulation on Fines does not explain how these concepts should be construed. In fact, this provision is in line with Article 17 of Law No. 5326, which lays down certain criteria for the assessment of the administrative fines, such as the degree of wrongdoing and the fault of the offender. To that end, the Board's interpretation of "market power of undertakings" and "gravity of the damage" becomes much more important. Reviewing the Board's decisions, it is seen that the Board generally does not provide detailed explanations on how it construes these concepts and confines itself to merely referring to the provisions of the Regulation on Fines.

That said, there are some rare decisions showing how and to what extent the Board took these factors into account in imposing the particular fines on undertakings. For instance, in *Sodaş Sodyum*,[1803] the Board stated that the damage arising as a result of the sodium sulphate cartel is limited due to the low share of sodium sulphate in textile costs, and this factor should be taken into account in the determination of the base level of the fine.

Moreover, Regulation on Fines provides that base fine shall be increased (i) by half for violations that had lasted between one and five years, and (ii) by one fold for violations that lasted longer than five years. As regards to the duration, the Council of State does not require evidence that clearly demonstrates the continuity of the conduct when assessing the period when the infringement takes place. It rather assumes that the infringement continued during the period for which no clear evidence exists if there is objective and consistent evidence indicating the continuity.[1804] The Board has subsequently adopted the Council of State's approach, as well.[1805]

12.1.4 Duration of the Violation

The duration of the violation plays an important role for the determination of the monetary fines and directly affects the amount of the fine to be imposed on the undertakings violating competition law rules. In determining the duration of the violation, the Board (i) evaluates the information and documents collected in the scope of the relevant case file and (ii) determines how long the violation has lasted, accordingly.

As explained above, competition law violations are considered misdemeanours. To that end, Article 5 of Law No. 5326 sets forth that a misdemeanour is deemed to be committed

---

[1803] *Sodaş Sodyum* (n. 299).
[1804] 13th Chamber of the Council of State (11 December 2019, E. 2015/3353, K. 2019/4244).
[1805] *Gaziantep Auto Experts* (9 July 2020, 20-33/439-196); *Syndicated Loans* (n. 44).

on the date when the perpetrator engaged in the conduct in question. Accordingly, a competition law violation is deemed to have occurred when the relevant undertaking engaged in conduct infringing competition law rules. On the other hand, competition law violations may end in various ways, e.g., they may be terminated by the undertaking itself or through the Board's powers such as opinion letters and interim measures, as explained under Section 12.3. Undertakings may also violate competition law rules for a certain limited period of time, which is particularly the case when a violation is committed through an agreement or conduct that has been implemented for a specific period of time. In practice, determination of the duration of the competition law violations generally requires the Board to conduct in-depth analyses on the nature/sequence of conducts and the information and documents obtained during the investigation stages. In this regard, the Board's decisions may shed some light on how the Board evaluates the duration of competition law violations, as there is yet no legislative framework governing the calculation of the duration with respect to fines.

To that end, the Board generally takes into account the earliest correspondence or document proving the existence of the violation. For instance, in its *Syndicated Loans* decision,[1806] the Board decided that three banks (i.e., Bank of Tokyo-Mitsubishi UFJ Turkey A.Ş. (BTMU), The Royal Bank of Scotland Plc. Istanbul Branch (RBS) and ING Bank A.Ş. (ING)) violated Law No. 4054 by way of exchanging competitively sensitive information on loans. In terms of the exchange of information between BTMU and RBS, the Board concluded that the violation started on the date of the first contact between the parties (28 January 2014) and ended on the date of the closing date of the relevant loan transaction (30 May 2014); and that thus the violation between BTMU and RBS lasted less than one year. Similarly, with regard to the violation between BTMU and ING, the Board assessed the date of the correspondences, including exchange of information and the closing date of the relevant loans and decided that ING had violated Article 4 of Law No. 4054 for a period of approximately two years.[1807]

In its *Unilever II* decision,[1808] the Board decided that Unilever Turkey violated Articles 4 and 6 of Law No. 4054 and imposed administrative fines separately for (i) abuse of dominant position through implementing anti-competitive discount systems in the ice cream market, and (ii) implementing a non-compete clause in its agreements with Getir, a mobile application for grocery delivery services. In terms of the violation under Article 6 of Law No. 4054, the Board stated that it evaluated the discount systems in 2016, 2017, 2018 and 2019. It also added that the investigated undertaking did not submit any information that the discount systems have been amended. Accordingly, the Board stated that the discounts have been implemented for a period longer than five years as of the date of the oral hearing on the investigation, and increased the base fine by one fold. As to the violation of non-compete obligation, the Board has taken into account the period between the (i) signing date of the contract with Getir and (ii) the date of the Additional Protocol terminating the non-compete condition, when assessing the duration.

[1806] *Syndicated Loans* (n. 1805).
[1807] BTMU was not imposed with an administrative monetary fine by the Board due to its leniency application.
[1808] *Unilever* (18 March 2021, 21-15/190-80).

On the other hand, there are Board decisions where, despite the existence of earlier evidence indicating violation of competition law, the Board took into account the period when the anti-competitive conduct has been committed on a frequent and continuous basis. In *Yemeksepeti*,[1809] the Board found that Yemeksepeti, an online food delivery platform, violated Law No. 4054 by way of imposing most favoured customer clauses in its agreements. In terms of the duration of the violation, the Board stated that apart from a document dated 2011, the conducts in question have occurred during the period between May 2014 and February 2015 on a frequent and continuous basis. The Board also stated that it imposed an interim measure on Yemeksepeti on the termination of the relevant clauses. Accordingly, the Board concluded that the violation has lasted less than one year and did not increase the monetary fine on the basis of the duration of the violation.

In its *Maysan*[1810] decision, the Board concluded that Maysan Mando, a manufacturer of shock absorbers for the automotive sector, violated competition law by way of fixing resale prices of its dealers in terms of shock absorbers and imposed an administrative fine on the undertaking. As to the determination of the duration of the violation, the Board noted that a document dated 2015 indicates that the violation had existed in 2014, although the precise date it commenced is unknown. The Board stated that the latest document pointing to the violation is dated 4 January 2018. Accordingly, the Board concluded that in any event, the duration of the infringement would be between one and five years and increased the base fine by half.

After its evaluations on the duration of the violation, the Board takes the aggravating and mitigating factors into account for determining the monetary fines.

12.1.5 Aggravating Factors

In setting the administrative monetary fine, the Board takes into account the following aggravating factors set out under Article 6 of the Regulation on Fines:

(1) The base fine shall be increased by half, up to one fold;

  – For each instance of repetition, in case the violation is repeated,
  – In case the cartel is maintained after the notification of the investigation decision.

(2) The base fine may be increased;

  – by half up to one fold, where the commitments made for the elimination of the competition problems raised within the scope of Article 4 or 6 of Law No. 4054 are not met,
  – by up to half, where no assistance is provided during the examination,
  – by up to one fourth in cases such as coercing other undertakings into the infringement.

[1809] *Yemek Sepeti* (n. 31).
[1810] *Maysan* (n. 570).

These aggravating factors are listed on the basis of the *numerus clausus* principle under the Regulation on Fines, i.e., only these particular factors cited can be taken into consideration by the Board, on a case-by-case basis. The following sections examine the aggravating factors in more detail.

12.1.5.1 Recidivism

Recidivism of an infringement, which is considered as an aggravating factor under Regulation on Fines, may be defined as the repetition of the same infringement by the same undertaking after being fined for the first one. Article 6(1)(a) of the Regulation on Fines indicates that the base fine shall be increased by half to one fold for each repetition of the infringement.

On the other hand, the Regulation on Fines and Law No. 4054 does not provide a clear definition and conditions for recidivism. Therefore, exactly which conducts would be considered recidivism and from which moment remain unanswered and are still a controversial topic under Turkish competition law. In this regard, the Board's decisions bring some clarity on the enforcement of recidivism clauses.

The Board's decisions involving recidivism show that the Board does not require finalisation of the judicial proceedings for applying recidivism clauses, and deems a previous Board decision concerning infringement by the same undertaking, to be sufficient to invoke recidivism.[1811] Therefore, to apply recidivism, there should be a determination of infringement committed previously by the same undertaking. A final decision imposing a monetary fine as a result of an investigation would be an example on that front.

On the other hand, it should be noted that not all of the Board's decisions may constitute a basis for recidivism. For example, the Board's decisions rendered under Article 9(3) of Law No. 4054 (opinion letters) are considered interim decisions[1812] and therefore cannot form a basis for recidivism.

Moreover, it is also important to determine the specific point in time when the violation was detected. While it is accepted that the violation is deemed to be detected with the issuance of the Board's reasoned decision, there are views advocating that pronouncing the Board's judgment should be sufficient for the determination of violation in the context of recidivism.[1813]

The lack of a legislative framework in defining the concept has led to certain discussions in terms of the application of recidivism in determining administrative monetary fines. While it is not clear which conducts may be taken into consideration in applying recidivism, some of the Board's decisions suggest that there must be two conducts infringing the same provision of Law No. 4054 (specific recidivism).[1814] There are also views arguing

---

[1811] In the lawsuit initiated with the request for the annulment of Article 6 of Regulation on Fines (Case No. 2018/1706, 13th Chamber of the Council of State), the Authority argued that finalisation of the judicial process is not required for an assessment of recidivism. The Court having accepted this argument, rejected the annulment request of the applicant.

[1812] 13th Chamber of the Council of State (12 September 2011, E. 2011/2383, K. 2011/3671).

[1813] N. Sağlam, *Rekabet Hukuku Uygulamasında Tekerrür* (Ankara: Rekabet Kurumu, 2015), p. 52.

[1814] *Doğan Yayın* (n. 817) and *UN Ro-Ro* (1 October 2012, 12-47/1413-474).

that there should not be a differentiation between the types of violations in order not to hinder the deterrence of this concept.[1815] On the other hand, the Board's decisional practice shows that the Board tends to apply recidivism where more than one violation exists, regardless of whether the conducts in question are similar or pertain to the same relevant product market.[1816] Moreover, it should be noted that the Board did not apply recidivism in some of its decisions despite the existence of the conditions sought for recidivism.[1817]

Consequently, while recidivism is considered as an aggravating factor in the determination of administrative monetary fines under Turkish competition law, the lack of a legislative framework on the concept has made it difficult to be applied consistently when determining monetary fines.

As for the statute of limitations with respect to the recidivism, the Board applies an eight-year period (as determined under Law No. 5326) with a view to relieving undertakings from the risk of being imposed aggravated fines for an infringement committed many years ago. The Board and the Council of State calculate the eight-year period from the date on which the first infringement decision is rendered rather than the date of the infringement itself.[1818] For instance, the Board, in *Aegean Cement Producers*, has taken into consideration a previous fine imposed three years ago as a legal ground to increase the monetary fine by half, after referring to the eight-year statute of limitations provided under Law No. 5326.[1819] This approach has been followed in the Board's other decisions, as well. Three years after *Aegean Cement Producers* decision, certain white meat producers were fined higher than what was supposed to be imposed in the first place due to recidivism arising from the first infringement approximately four years prior. The Board, once again, emphasised the eight-year statute of limitations in the *White Meat* decision.[1820]

12.1.5.2 Maintaining the Cartel After the Notification of the Investigation Decision

This aggravating factor is determined specifically for cartel cases in the Regulation on Fines. On the other hand, a review of the Board's decisions shows this factor has rarely been taken into account by the Board, possibly due to the potential discussions that may arise as a result of its application.[1821]

In this regard, in its *Bodrum Express* decision,[1822] when calculating the administrative monetary fine to be imposed on the relevant undertaking, the Board stated that the cartel has not been considered as a violation by the parties and that they have maintained the cartel even after the notification of the investigation decision. Accordingly, this factor

---

[1815]   See the dissenting opinion of Board members Mustafa Ateş and İsmail Hakkı Karakelle in *Un-Ro Ro* (n. 1814). See also B. Arı,(n. 43), p. 62.

[1816]   *Turkcell* (10 January 2019, 19-03/23-10).

[1817]   *Medical Gas* (n. 1801).

[1818]   13th Chamber of the Council of State (11 December 2019, E. 2015/3353, K. 2019/4244); *Turkcell* (n. 1816).

[1819]   *Aegean Cement Producers* (n. 282).

[1820]   *White Meat* (n. 400).

[1821]   Arı (n. 1815), p. 65.

[1822]   *Bodrum Express* (3 November 2009, 09-51/1245-314).

has been taken into account as an aggravating factor by the Board and resulted in an increase in the administrative monetary fine imposed on the relevant undertaking.

12.1.5.3 Failure to Comply With Commitments

The two factors explained above directly apply in cases where the nature of the violation fulfils the required conditions. In the application of other factors listed in the Regulation on Fines, the Board has been given discretion on whether to apply the aggravating factors in the determination of the monetary fines.

As per Article 6(2)(a) of the Regulation on Fines, the Board may increase the fine for failure to comply with the commitments given in order to eliminate the competition concerns raised within the scope of Article 4 and Article 6 of Law No. 4054.

It should be noted that the conditions sought for this aggravating factor are not defined explicitly in the Turkish competition law legislation, and the question of what should be understood from the term "commitment" has remained unclear. That said, given that the commitment procedure has been introduced with the Amendment Law, it may be argued that this factor is likely to be recognised and discussed more frequently in the Board's future decisions. On the other hand, the Board decisions suggest that this aggravating factor does not encompass a failure to comply with the Board's opinion letters sent under Article 9(3) of Law No. 4054.[1823]

12.1.5.4 Other Aggravating Factors

The Regulation on Fines also lists "not assisting examinations" and "coercing other undertakings to infringe [the law]" as aggravating factors that may be taken into account by the Board in determining monetary fines. Therefore, the Board may increase monetary fines for those undertakings that do not cooperate during the Board's proceedings and have played a more significant role in the violation.

12.1.6 Mitigating Factors

Article 7 of the Regulation on Fines provides the mitigating factors that may be taken into account by the Board in determining monetary fines. The relevant article provides:

> The base fine may be reduced at a rate of one fourth to three fifths in case the undertakings or association of undertakings concerned prove certain facts such as provision of assistance to the examination beyond the fulfilment of legal obligations, existence of encouragement by public authorities or coercion by other undertakings in the violation, voluntary payment of damages to those harmed, termination of other violations, and occupation of a very small share by practices subject to the violation within annual gross revenues.

[1823]   See, e.g., *TABGIS* (27 November 2008, 08-67/1091-424).

That said, the factors listed in Article 7 are not an exhaustive list, and other factors that are not included in the Regulation on Fines may also be taken into account by the Board in calculating the fines to be imposed.

12.1.6.1 Assisting Examination

The Board may consider this mitigating factor in case of collaboration or assistance beyond the fulfilment of legal obligations, such as responding to information requests from the Authority.

In other words, the Board does not consider undertakings' inputs/efforts provided in the scope of a request by the Board and seeks for further assistance performed by undertakings under examination. For instance, in its *Cargo* decision[1824] where three major undertakings in the Turkish cargo market have been fined for engaging in a collusive scheme, the Board did not accept undertakings' defences that they have fulfilled the Authority's information requests in a timely and complete manner. To that end, theBoard held that providing information and documents requested by the Authority is a legal duty for undertakings and did not consider this as a mitigating factor in the context of assisting examination.

In its *Bakers* decision,[1825] the Board has taken into consideration the bakeries' collaboration with the Authority, stressing their contribution to the investigation through applying leniency procedures. Accordingly, certain bakeries who have fixed the bread prices in Aydın's Didim district, a seaside town and holiday resort, have benefited from significant reductions in the administrative monetary fines due to their collaboration with the Authority.[1826] In the same vein, in the *Sivas Driving Schools* decision, the Board has granted significant reductions in the monetary fines imposed on the driving schools, which have facilitated the Authority's investigation with certain documents, although they have been fined for indulging in a price-fixing scheme.[1827]

Therefore, to apply this criterion as a mitigating factor, the Board does not deem that the undertakings' efforts made in accordance with their legal obligations (such as providing information in response to an information request); rather, it takes into account the undertakings' proactive efforts in facilitating the Board's investigative proceedings.

12.1.6.2 Encouragement by Public Authorities or Coercion by Other Undertakings

Encouragement by public authorities or coercion by other undertakings in the infringement of Law No. 4054 may be taken into account as a mitigating factor by the Board.

A review of the Board's decisions shows that this factor may be taken into consideration in cases where public authorities may have an impact on the undertakings' conduct

---

[1824] *Cargo* (n. 1796).
[1825] *Bakers* (22 January 2014, 14-04/80-33).
[1826] See also *Gaziantep Auto Experts* (n. 1805).
[1827] *Sivas Driving Schools (22 March 2010, 10-25/350-124).*

found to be infringing, particularly in the regulated markets. Apart from encouragement by public authorities, coercion by other undertakings may also be considered as a mitigating factor. For instance, in its *Medical Gas* decision, the Board decreased the monetary fines to be imposed on undertakings that have been forced to the infringement by another undertaking.[1828] Moreover, in its *Isttelkom* decision,[1829] the Board evaluated the allegations that Isttelkom hindered the activities of its competitors through its facility sharing arrangements. As a result of its assessment of the allegations, the Board found Isttelkom to be in a dominant position in the electronic communication infrastructure and that it had abused its dominant position through its facility sharing arrangements. On the other hand, in determining the monetary fine to impose on Isttelkom, the Board decreased the monetary fine by 60% since it found that Istanbul Metropolitan Municipality, which is the public authority ultimately controlling Isttelkom, had an encouraging role in the violation of competition law. In the same decision, the Board also decided to send an opinion letter to the Istanbul Metropolitan Municipality requesting it to act on a non-discriminatory and equal basis towards Isttelkom's rivals in terms of access requests.

Moreover, in the *TSSF* decision, the Board examined the allegation that the Turkish Federation of Underwater Sports abused its dominant position through various practices in swimming training systems and decided to impose an administrative monetary fine. In its defence, the investigated federation alleged that other public authorities, particularly the Department of Sports Services in Turkey, played a significant role in the infringement. However, the Board rejected the relevant defence and did not decrease the monetary fine, deeming that in this case, the facts did not constitute a mitigating factor. To that end, the Board set forth that in order for the existence of encouragement by public authorities, undertakings must be forced by public authorities to engage in conduct infringing the competition law rules and that their free will must be eliminated on that front.[1830] The Board also stated that it is not possible for an undertaking to be relieved of liability when it chooses to violate competition law of its own will.

Therefore, to apply this mitigating factor, the Board requires genuine encouragement by public authorities or coercion by other undertakings in a way that would eliminate the undertakings' free will as to the infringement of competition law.

12.1.6.3 Other Mitigating Factors

The Regulation on Fines lists (i) voluntary payment of damages to those harmed; (ii) termination of other violations; and (iii) cases where the practices in violation constitute a small share within the overall turnover as mitigating factors in the determination of monetary fines.

The most commonly applied mitigating factor in the Board's decisions is where the investigated conduct only constitutes a small part of the relevant undertaking's total turnover.

[1828]   *Medical Gas* (n. 1801).
[1829]   *Isttelkom* (11 April 2019, 19-15/214-94).
[1830]   *TSSF* (7 August 2014, 14-26/530-235).

In this regard, in several cases, the Board has reduced the monetary fines imposed on the relevant undertakings on the ground that the effect of the infringing conduct has remained limited since the conduct in question constitutes a small share within their total turnover. In its *Consumer Electronics*[1831] decision, the Board decreased the fine imposed on the investigated undertakings on the ground that the conduct constitutes a very small share within relevant undertakings' annual gross revenues.[1832]

In parallel, the Board wrote off 50% of the fine imposed on Sony for engaging in resale price maintenance, on the ground that Sony's activities subject to the investigation amounted to a relatively small share in the total of its turnover.[1833]

Given that the Regulation on Fines does not set forth an exhaustive list for mitigating factors, the Board may also take into account other case-specific factors as a mitigating factor. For instance, in its *Tekhnelogos* decision,[1834] the Board stated that the relevant market is an emerging market where there have been recent entries. The Board considered these features as sufficient grounds to reduce the base fine imposed on Tekhnelogos. The duration of the infringement was another feature factored in the reduction of the fines by the Board in the *Tekhnelogos* case.

On the other hand, the Board generally rules out the competition law compliance programmes and similar training programmes adopted by the undertaking in its assessment of mitigating factors and merely appreciates these efforts.[1835]

12.1.7 Draft Regulation on Fines

After the first five-year period that the Regulation on Fines has come into force, the Authority published a Draft Regulation on Fines for public consultation on 17 January 2014 to clarify certain issues that the Regulation on Fines did not specifically address, such as the turnover generated in the relevant market and the calculation of turnovers of association of undertakings. The Draft Regulation on Fines was set to replace the Regulation on Fines; however, it has not been enacted yet.

As stated above, even though there is no precise provision referring to the turnover obtained in the *relevant* product market to be used as the basis for the calculation of the administrative monetary fines under the current Regulation on Fines, the Draft Regulation provides that the turnover generated in the relevant markets should be taken into account, which has been adopted in some of the Board's previous decisions.[1836]

[1831]   *Consumer Electronics* (7 November 2016, 16-37/628-279).
[1832]   See also *3M* (9 June 2016, 16-20/340-155); *Bakers* (n. 1825); *TSSF* (n. 1830); *UN Ro-Ro* (n. 1814); *Sodaş Sodyum* (n. 299).
[1833]   *Sony Eurasia* (n. 182).
[1834]   *Tekhnelogos* (16 September 2014, 14-33/666-292).
[1835]   *Industrial Gas* (n. 596); *Insurance Market* (23 January 2020, 20-06/61-33).
[1836]   See *Türk Telekom/TTNET* (n. 1801), *Sarten/TKS* (n. 1801), *Medical Gas* (n. 1801), *8 Banks* (n. 1801), and *Güneş Express* (n. 1801).

Moreover, the Draft Regulation on Fines provides a more detailed framework on recidivism in order to eliminate the gaps in the application of this concept. In this regard, the Draft Regulation on Fines made it clear that recidivism shall be applied if Law No. 4054 is violated by an undertaking again within eight years after the notification of the Board's reasoned decision finding infringement of the same undertaking. It also states that for the application of recidivism, it is not required to violate the same provision of Law No. 4054. Therefore, the Draft Regulation on Fines adopts general recidivism and does not require the infringement of the same provision of Law No. 4054. Moreover, it also provides an explicit period for the application of recidivism starting from the notification of the Board's decision finding infringement on the same undertaking, which is, in fact, re-articulation of the established case law explained in detail under Section 12.1.5.1 above.

With respect to the aggravating factors, the Authority's Draft Regulation on Fines does not include "not assisting examinations" as an aggravating factor. That said, it lists "coercing other undertakings and playing an active role in the infringement" as an aggravating factor, similar to the current Regulation on Fines.

In light of the foregoing, although it has not been enacted yet, the Draft Regulation on Fines provides clearer guidance in terms of the administrative monetary fines applicable to competition law violations. Moreover, it should be noted that the Draft Regulation on Fines is an attempt to bring the Turkish competition law legislation more in line with the EU legislation. For instance, similar to the Commission's guidelines on setting monetary fines, the Draft Regulation on Fines sets a monetary fine of up to 30% of undertakings' turnover in the relevant market multiplied by the number of years of participation in the infringement as a maximum limit for the administrative monetary fines. Moreover, the reference to the turnover generated in the markets affected by the infringement is another similarity with the EU legislation. Although it has not yet entered into force, the Draft Regulation on Fines is expected to lead to future legislative efforts concerning monetary fines.

12.2 Types of Administrative Fines

12.2.1 Fines Imposed on Procedural Violations

Article 16(1) of Law No. 4054 provides that the Board shall impose an administrative monetary fine for the following cases:

- Providing false or misleading information or documents in applications for exemption and negative clearance, as well as merger control filings

- Completing those mergers and acquisitions that are subject to the Board's approval, without the Board's decision

- Providing incomplete, false or misleading information in response to the Authority's requests for information and during on-site inspections

- Refusing or hindering on-site inspections.

12.2.1.1 Providing False or Misleading Information in Exemption and Negative Clearance Notifications as well as Approval Notifications for Mergers and Acquisitions

In the Turkish competition law regime, merger control or exemption notifications are prepared and submitted by undertakings, which are then evaluated by the Board based on the information and explanations contained in these submissions. On the other hand, in case these notifications contain false or misleading information, the Board shall impose an administrative monetary fine calculated at 0.1% of the annual gross revenues of relevant parties generated by the end of the financial year preceding the Board's decision.

In its *Anadolu Efes/Tekel* decision, the Board stated that merger notifications are evaluated on the basis of the information provided by parties within submitted filings, and it renders its decision based on the information provided by undertakings. It further added that the Turkish competition law regime adopts a system where relevant parties are obliged to provide accurate information within such applications to the Authority, by way of sanctioning submission of false or misleading information to the Authority.[1837]

Likewise, the Board, in its *Brookfield/JCI* decision, stressed that even if the false or misleading information would not change the Board's appraisal for a case, the mere fact that the parties provide false or misleading information gives rise to an administrative fine in accordance with Article 16(1) of Law No. 4054.[1838]

In this regard, it is worth noting that undertakings' duty to provide accurate information in applications for mergers and acquisitions, and exemption/negative clearance notifications, is an objective obligation and the Board does not consider how important or how crucial the false or misleading information is. Likewise, the Council of State does not take into consideration whether the false or misleading information plays a substantive role in the assessment or whether such information was provided on purpose or by mistake. In other words, it does not seek a subjective element in assessing the nature of false or misleading information.[1839]

12.2.1.2 Completing Merger and Acquisitions that are Subject to the Board's Approval without the Board's Decision

As explained under Chapter 9, there is an explicit suspension requirement under the Turkish merger control regime, and thus a notifiable transaction cannot be closed before obtaining the approval of the Board.

If the parties to a notifiable transaction violate the suspension requirement (i.e., they (i) close a notifiable transaction without the approval of the Board or (ii) do not notify

---

[1837] *Anadolu Efes/Tekel* (7 February 2019, 19-06/54-20).
[1838] *Brookfield/JCI* (30 April 2020, 20-21/278-132).
[1839] 13th Chamber of the Council of State (13 December 2012, E. 2009/1523, K. 2012/3795).

the notifiable transaction at all) once such violation of the suspension requirement is detected, the Authority is obliged to enforce the sanctions and legal consequences set forth under Turkish merger control regime. In other words, the relevant legislation does not give the Authority any discretion other than following the procedural steps specified within the legislation. To that end, as also evident from its decisional practice, the Board imposed administrative monetary fines on undertakings in numerous cases so far, for either (i) closing the transaction prior to Board's approval or (ii) not notifying the transaction at all. As such, imposition of a fine for violating the suspension requirement is a usual occurrence in the Turkish merger control regime, and there are a number of examples in the Board's decisional practice.[1840]

Pursuant to Article 16 of Law No. 4054, if the parties to a notifiable transaction violate the suspension requirement, a turnover-based administrative monetary fine (based on the Turkish turnover generated in the financial year preceding the date of the fining decision at a rate of 0.1%) will be imposed on each of the responsible firms under Law No. 4054. In case of an acquisition, these would be the acquirer(s) or the joint venture partners; or both of the merging parties in the case of a merger).

Accordingly, in case of the violation of the suspension requirement, assuming a transaction which would not be deemed problematic under the applicable SIEC test, each of the parties ultimately acquiring control will be subject to administrative monetary fine at a rate of 0.1% based on the Turkish turnover they generated in their financial year preceding the date of the fining decision.

For the cases where the turnover-based monetary fine remains below the minimum administrative fine amount at that time, the administrative fine is set at the minimum amount applicable at the time of the fining decision. The relevant minimum amount of the administrative monetary fine is determined annually through the secondary legislation based on the re-evaluation rate specified within the scope of the General Communiqué on Tax Procedure Law and published on the official gazette every year. To that end, an administrative monetary fine imposed as a result of a violation of suspension requirement shall, in any event, not be less than TL 34,809 (approx. USD 5,000) until 31 December 2021.[1841]

12.2.1.3 Providing Incomplete, False or Misleading Information or Documents, Failure to Provide on Time or not Providing at all

Article 14 of Law No. 4054 entitles the Board to request any information and documents it deems necessary from all public institutions and organisations, undertakings and trade associations.

[1840]   See, e.g., *BMW/Daimler/Ford/Porsche/Ionity* (28 July 2020, 20-36/483-211); *Brookfield/JCI* (n. 1838); *Labelon/A-Tex* (6 February 2016, 16-42/693-311); *Ersoy/Sesli* (25 June 2014, 14-22/422-186); *DSG/Electro World* (n. 1380); *Tekno İnşaat* (23 February 2012, 12-08/224-55); *Zhejiang/Kiri* (2 June 2011, 11-33/723-226); *Ajans Press/PR Net* (21 October 2010, 10-66/1402-523); *TOBB/Mesa Mesken* (26 August 2010, 10-56/1088-408).

[1841]   See Article 1 of Communiqué No. 2021/1 Concerning the Increase of the Minimum Administrative Fines Specified in Paragraph 1 of Article 16 of Law No. 4054 (published on 18 December 2020).

Officials of these bodies, undertakings and trade associations are obliged to provide the requested information within the period determined by the Board. In this regard, there is no legal ground that would allow the undertakings to refuse the Authority's request for information; accordingly, these undertakings are obliged to provide accurate and complete information to the extent possible within their capabilities. Otherwise, they would be faced with an administrative monetary fine of 0.1% of the turnover generated in the financial year preceding the Board's decision (if this is not calculable, the turnover generated in the financial year nearest to the date of the fining decision will be taken into account).

On the other hand, in case the requested information or document is not provided within the duration determined by the Board within Articles 14 and 15 of Law No. 4054, the Board shall, for each day, impose an administrative fine of 0.05% of the annual gross revenues generated by the undertakings by the end of the financial year preceding the Board's decision (or by the end of the financial year closest to the date of the decision, similar to the above).

In its *Foreign Exchange* decision, the Board decided to impose an administrative monetary fine on Citibank, ING Bank, JPMorgan, and Garanti Bankası pursuant to Article 16(1)(c) of Law No. 4054, on the ground that the investigated banks did not submit the requested information and documents to the Authority within the scope of the preliminary investigation initiated as per the Board's decision of 17 January 2020.[1842]

Similarly, the Board also imposed an administrative fine on Apex, a producer of face masks and non-woven fabric,[1843] for failing to provide the information requested within the scope of an investigation that was launched into antiviral face mask producers through the Board's decision of 7 May 2020. There are also a number of other examples where fines were levied on undertakings for providing false and/or misleading information.[1844]

That said, there have been exceptional cases where the Board diverged from its established practice and adopted a more lenient approach with respect to information requests. For instance, in its *A101* decision, A101 failed to submit within the determined duration the information and documents requested by the Authority for its sector inquiry on fast-moving consumer goods. That said, the Board did not fine A101 on the ground that it subsequently submitted the requested information and documents before the Board had rendered a decision on the matter.[1845] The *A101* decision may be interpreted in a way that the Board may adopt a more lenient approach in cases where the requested information and documents do not relate to an investigative proceeding initiated directly against the relevant undertakings.

[1842] *Foreign Exchange* (2 July 2020, 20-32/397-179).
[1843] *Apex* (20 August 2020, 20-38/528-236).
[1844] *Brookfield/JCI* (n. 1838); *Çerkezköy* (23 January 2020, 20-06/49-26); *Garanti Oto* (22 November 2019, 19-41/681-294); *DVS Doğalgaz Mühendislik* (7 November 2019, 19-38/588-254); *TEB* (7 November 2019, 19-38/582-248), *Güven Beton* (13 March 2019, 19-12/147-68) and *Türk Telekom* (3 May 2016, 16-15/255-110).
[1845] *A101* (22 October 2020, 20-47/638-280).

12.2.1.4 Refusing or Hindering On-site Inspections

Article 15 of Law No. 4054 authorises the Board to conduct on-site investigations. Accordingly, the Board may:

- Examine the books, all types of data and documents of undertakings and associations of undertakings kept on physical or electronic media and in information systems, and take copies and physical samples thereof,
- Request written or oral statement on particular issues,
- Perform on-site examination of any assets of undertakings.

As per Article 16 of Law No. 4054, in cases where an on-site inspection is refused or obstructed, the Board shall impose an administrative monetary fine of 0.5% of the turnover the undertaking generated in the financial year preceding the date of the fining decision (or, if this is not calculable, the turnover generated in the financial year nearest to the date of the fining decision will be taken into account).

Hindering on-site inspections may also be subject to a proportional administrative monetary fine which would be levied for each day the obstructive conduct continues. Accordingly, Article 17 of Law No. 4054 lists hindering or complicating on-site inspection among cases for which "the Board shall, for each day, impose on undertakings and associations of undertakings an administrative fine by five in ten thousand of annual gross revenues of the relevant undertakings and associations of undertakings and/or members of such associations generated by the end of the financial year preceding the decision, or generated by the end of the financial year closest to the date of the decision if it would not be possible to calculate it…"

A review of the Board's decisions shows that it is not uncommon for the Board to impose an administrative monetary fine for the obstruction of on-site inspections. To that end, in *Mosaş*, the Board imposed an administrative monetary fine on the undertaking since Mosaş hindered the Authority's on-site inspection at its premises.[1846] It is stated in the decision that the Authority's case handlers duly informed Mosaş's employees of the Authority's preliminary investigation before conducting the inspection, and presented their authorisation documents along with their identity cards. During the case handlers' inspection of the computers at Mosaş's premises, the internet connection was interrupted twice. The case handlers also noticed that the e-mails on one of the computers were being deleted during their inspection. Additionally, the case handlers discovered that there were certain communications among Mosaş employees in an online chat group, where some employees instructed others to "disconnect the internet so that they [case handlers] cannot access", "break down the modem", and "delete the e-mails". The case handlers took screenshots of these conversations as evidence of obstruction of their inspection by Mosaş's employees. Consequently, the Board imposed administrative monetary fines on Mosaş under both Articles 16 and 17 of Law No. 4054.

In another investigation carried out against TTNET, an internet service provider, the competition experts experienced a similar incident. Certain files which had been

---

[1846] *Mosaş* (21 June 2018, 18-20/356-176).

accessed at the beginning were deleted by the TTNET employees during the course of the on-site inspection. Although the same files have been provided to the Authority by TTNET later on, the Board, irrespective of the content of such documents, has imposed an administrative monetary fine on TTNET.[1847] In an annulment lawsuit initiated for the administrative monetary fine, the Ankara 13th Administrative Court upheld the Board's approach with respect to on-site inspections, emphasising that the objective of Article 15 of Law No. 4054 is to access the document as is at the time of the on-site inspection.[1848]

In 2020, the Board fined a number of undertakings for hindering on-site inspections. In this respect, in its *Groupe SEB İstanbul* decision,[1849] the Board imposed a monetary fine of 0.5% of its turnover generated in 2018 on Groupe SEB İstanbul for hindering an on-site inspection. Similarly, the Board imposed a fine of 0.5% upon Unilever for failing to grant access to Unilever's electronic systems in a timely manner due to privacy concerns with respect to Unilever's global users. The competition experts were able to access Unilever's electronic systems only after completion of the inter-company approval procedure, which took about eight hours.[1850]

The Board has taken a similar approach vis-à-vis Siemens Healthcare, which had not granted access to its electronic systems on the raid date due to the potential legal risks that may arise in other jurisdictions.[1851] Although the IT team of Siemens Healthcare technically demonstrated that no record had been distorted, in a second visit paid by the competition experts upon Siemens Healthcare's official invitation, it did not relieve Siemens Healthcare of an administrative fine for obstructing the on-site inspection. The Board, in *Siemens Healthcare*, stressed that the on-site inspections are required to be conducted whenever the Authority deems necessary and any intervention by undertakings are deemed to be a hindrance of on-site inspections.

12.2.1.5 Failure to Comply With Commitments

The last procedural violation set forth in Law No. 4054 relates to non-compliance with obligations introduced or commitments made under a final or interim measure decision. In such a case, Article 17 of Law No. 4054 sets forth that the Board shall, for each day, impose an administrative monetary fine of 0.05% of annual gross revenues of undertakings generated by the end of the financial year preceding the decision (or, if it is not possible to calculate it, by the end of the year closest to the date of the decision).

Article 17 provides that the daily administrative monetary fine may be imposed as of the lapse of the period granted for compliance. If no specific time period was granted for compliance, then the administrative monetary fine may be imposed from the day following the date the decision was notified to the undertaking.

[1847] *TTNET* (18 July 2013, 13-46/601-M).
[1848] Ankara 13th Administrative Court (24 October 2014, E. 2013/1598, K. 2014/1495).
[1849] *Groupe SEB İstanbul* (9 January 2020, 20-03/31-14).
[1850] *Unilever I* (7 January 2019, 19-38/584-250). *See* also *Anıtur* (n. 1650); *Mosaş* (n. 1846).
[1851] *Siemens* (7 November 2019, 19-38/581-247).

A review of the Board's decisions shows that the Board generally determines a specific period for compliance with obligations or commitments, and tends to impose the daily monetary fine to accrue starting from the expiry of the duration determined by the Board until the date of compliance. For instance, in *Isttelkom II*, the Board evaluated whether Isttelkom complied with the obligations set forth in the Board's *Isttelkom* decision.[1852] The Board stated that Isttelkom had failed to comply with the obligation within the period granted, i.e., until 18 January 2020. In this regard, the Board deemed that the date for Isttelkom's compliance with the Board's decision was the date when it submitted the necessary changes made on its facility sharing arrangements (7 February 2020) and therefore decided to impose a daily monetary fine on Isttelkom for the period starting from the lapse of the period determined for compliance in the Board decision, until the date of the compliance (for twenty days).

12.2.2 Fines on Managers and Employees

Apart from the administrative monetary fines to be levied on undertakings infringing competition law, Article 16 of Law No. 4054 may also hold employees and managers personally liable in cases where managers or employees of undertakings play a significant role in the infringement of competition law. Accordingly, the relevant article provides that the Board shall impose an administrative fine, for up to 5% of the fine that was imposed on the undertaking or association of undertaking itself, on the managers or employees of the undertaking or association of undertaking that had a decisive influence in the infringement.[1853]

For instance, in the *White Meat Cartel* decision, the Board fined an executive of the relevant association of undertakings in the white meat market for playing a decisive role in the continuity and functionality of the cartel.[1854]

Before being amended in 2008, Law No. 4054 had also set forth a fine on managers for failure to notify mergers and acquisition to the Authority, for up to 10% of that imposed on the concerned undertaking or the concerned association of undertakings.

Article 8 of Regulation on Fines regulates the details of fines on individuals. The relevant article provides that:

> Each of the managers and employees of the undertaking who were detected to have had a decisive influence on the cartel shall be separately fined between 3% and 5%t of the fine imposed on the undertaking, taking into account points such as active cooperation.

[1852]   *Isttelkom* (n. 1829).

[1853]   The Board's decisional practice is quite limited where an administrative monetary fine was imposed on individuals (see, e.g., *Fresenius* (24 January 2008, 08-08/92-32); *White Meat* (25 November 2019, 09-57/1393-362), *Sodaş Sodyum* (n. 299).

[1854]   *White Meat* (n. 1853).

The relevant managers or employees who actively cooperate with the Authority for the uncovering of the violation may benefit from reduced fines, depending on the extent, effectiveness and timing of cooperation. In such a case, either no fine will be imposed on them or reductions will be applied. For instance, in the *Sodaş Sodyum* decision,[1855] relevant managers who were found to have brought the parties around the table for the price-fixing and customer allocation purposes enjoyed reductions in their monetary fines for their cooperation with the Authority.

Sanctions that could be imposed under Law No. 4054 are administrative in nature and limited to monetary fines; Law No. 4054 does not impose criminal sanctions. Accordingly, competition law infringements will not result in imprisonment against implicated individuals, unless the anti-competitive conduct also constitutes bid rigging in a public tender, or involves price manipulation, which are listed as offences under the Turkish Criminal Code.

12.3 Termination of an Infringement

In addition to the monetary sanctions, the Board is authorised to take all necessary measures to terminate restrictive agreements, to remove all de facto and *de jure* consequences of each unlawful action taken by the undertakings, and to take all other necessary measures in order to restore the level of competition and status quo to what it was before the infringement. Furthermore, such restrictive agreements will be deemed to be legally invalid and unenforceable, with all the legal consequences this entails. Similarly, the Turkish competition law regime authorises the Board to take interim measures that would restore the status before the infringement, and not to exceed the scope of the final resolution until the final resolution on the matter in case there is a possibility of serious and irreparable damages. Therefore, in brief, the Board is authorised to take all necessary measures to: (i) terminate the restrictive conduct or agreement; (ii) remove all factual and legal consequences of every action that has been taken unlawfully; and (iii) take all other necessary measures to restore the level of competition and status to what it was before the infringement.

Article 9 of Law No. 4054 was amended on 16 June 2020. The new provision titled "Termination of Infringement" provides that:

> If, in response to a denouncement, a complaint or the request of the Ministry or on its own initiative, the Board determines that there is an infringement of Article 4, 6 or 7 of this Act, then it shall notify in its final decision the behaviours that the relevant undertaking or associations of undertakings must carry out or refrain from in order to re-establish competition, and any structural remedies in the form of undertakings transferring certain businesses, partnership shares or assets. Behavioural and structural remedies must be proportionate to the infringement and necessary to bring the infringement effectively to an end. Structural

---

[1855] *Sodaş Sodyum* (n. 299).

remedies shall only apply where previous behavioural remedies imposed have been ineffective. In case the final decision finds that behavioural remedies have been unsuccessful, relevant undertaking or associations of undertakings shall be given at least 6 months to comply with the structural remedy.

To that end, while the previous version of the article did not refer to structural remedies, the amended provision explicitly includes structural remedies requiring the divestment of businesses, shares or assets as a tool that may be introduced by the Board to eliminate infringement. Moreover, Article 9 sets forth that the Board may impose such structural remedies if it is found that behavioural remedies would not yield the expected results.

Therefore, in case an infringement is detected, Article 9 urges the Board to assess whether the relevant violation may be eliminated through behavioural remedies. The Board will include its assessment on the sufficiency of behavioural remedies in its final decision. In cases where structural remedies are deemed necessary and accordingly introduced, the Board should give at least six months to the relevant undertakings to comply with the structural remedy brought by the Board.

Article 9 of Law No. 4054 requires behavioural or structural remedies introduced by the Board to be proportionate and also necessary for eliminating the relevant infringement in an effective manner. Even though the relevant provision may be found vague and unclear, it is an important element that delineates the Board's extensive powers to impose remedies for violations. Therefore, the Board should take into account "proportionality" and "necessity" elements when deciding on the behavioural or structural remedies to be imposed on undertakings infringing competition law rules.

Apart from introducing structural or behavioural remedies, the Board also has other extensive powers such as sending an opinion letter to the investigated party and taking interim measures for the termination of violations that may be exercised prior to a final decision, as discussed below.

It should also be noted that the commitment and conciliation mechanisms introduced in 2020 allow undertakings and association of undertakings to end ongoing investigations, as well as wholly or partly avoid significant administrative fines and negative publicity as a result of possible violation decisions.[1856]

12.3.1 Opinion Letter under Article 9(3)

Article 9(3) of Law No. 4054 concerns the opinion letters that may be sent to undertakings by the Board, which set forth the Board's opinions/view on the termination of an infringement. Accordingly, prior to taking a final decision on the infringement, the Board may "inform in writing the undertaking or associations of undertakings concerned of its opinions concerning how to terminate the infringement.". In practice, opinion letters

---

[1856] For further information, please see Chapter 11.

are used in cases where the preliminary assessment would be sufficient to handle the violation, and there is no need to initiate a fully-fledged investigation. The Board also uses this mechanism in cases where the effect of the investigated conduct/practice on competition would be limited.

For instance, in its *Hayal Seramik*,[1857] the Board examined the allegations that Qua Granit violated Article 4 of Law No. 4054 by imposing territorial restrictions and hindering its dealers' sales to other regions. In its evaluation of Qua Granit's dealership agreements, the Board found that these agreements included clauses such as (i) territory allocation and exclusivity; (ii) the restriction of dealers' sales outside their designated territory; (iii) a penalty clause for breach of the restriction on the dealers' sales; and (iv) the permission requirement for marketing activities of the dealers for Qua Granit products. To that end, the Board concluded that the relevant provisions of the dealership agreements could be considered to restrict not only the dealers' active sales but also their passive sales as well. The Board also found that clauses contained in Qua Granit's dealership agreements would not benefit from block exemption and individual exemption due to the nature of the clauses.

The Board then conducted an extensive analysis of the relevant market structure, market shares of the undertakings operating in the market, Qua Granit's market position compared to its competitors, and the effect of passive sales restriction on total sales. As a result of this assessment, the Board concluded that the competitive effect of relevant clauses on passive sales in the market would be very limited. Qua Granit also provided the Board with its proposed amendments to be made to its agreements. After reviewing the proposed amendments submitted by Qua Granit, the Board found them sufficient to eliminate the violation and issued an opinion letter instead of initiating a fully-fledged investigation against Qua Granit under Article 43 of Law No. 4054.

Similarly, in its *Raw Meatball Producers* decision,[1858] the Board evaluated the allegations that certain raw meatball producers in Gaziantep (a city located in the South-eastern Anatolia region of Turkey) violated Article 4 of Law No. 4054 by way of determining the sale prices of raw meatballs sold in the market, during a meeting of the Gaziantep Chamber of Commerce. It was also alleged that the relevant raw meatball producers had also determined a penalty for those who did not comply with the determined prices.

In its assessment of the allegations, the Board found a document indicating a fixed price was determined by relevant undertakings for raw meatballs, certain arrangements agreed for the sale of the product, and a penalty mechanism for those who failed to comply.

To that end, even though the Board established that the relevant arrangements constituted an infringement of competition law, it decided to issue an opinion letter to the relevant undertakings in order to terminate the violation, despite the opinion of the investigation team indicating that a fully-fledged investigation should be initiated. In its assessment, the Board also referred to the judgment of the Council of State in *Burdur Consumer Protection Association*,[1859] which states that the Board must initiate a fully-fledged investigation

---

[1857]   *Hayal Seramik* (n. 598).
[1858]   *Raw Meatball Producers* (10 January 2019, 19-03/13-5).
[1859]   13th Chamber of the Council of State (30 May 2014, E. 2010/4818, K. 2014/2197).

if the information and findings necessary to clarify the case subject to the preliminary investigation could not be obtained during the preliminary investigation phase; however it might also decide not to initiate a fully-fledged investigation and apply the different measures provided within Law No. 4054, in cases where (i) no finding of violation could be established; (ii) it is possible to fully shed light on the case during the preliminary investigation phase; (iii) the violation is so minor that initiating an investigation is not needed; (iv) it is also possible to eliminate entirely the effects of the violation and compensate the anti-competitive effects of the violation; or (v) the violation is made in markets which are not completely open to competition due to structural and legal barriers.

Consequently, in the above cases, the Board may use the opinion letter as a tool to terminate the infringement instead of inspecting relevant conducts under a fully-fledged investigation.

That said, the introduction of the "*de minimis*" principle into Turkish competition law in 2020 is expected to turn the tides in the use of opinion letters. It would be a more appropriate (and legally less controversial) measure for the Authority to handle low-profile cases and save red-tape costs that the Authority incurs in the investigation processes, especially when the infringement concerns only a small market. However, it still remains to be seen whether the introduction of the *de minimis* exception will put an end to the excessive use of Article 9(3) altogether, given that hard-core restrictions in small markets would still not benefit from the *de minimis* provision.

12.3.2 Interim Measures

In cases where there is a genuine urgency due to risks of serious and irreparable damage, as per Article 9(4) of Law No. 4054, the Board is entitled to take interim measures before rendering a final decision on the conduct investigated in order to maintain the situation prior to the infringement.

In order to apply interim measures, there must be strong indications necessitating the imposition of a measure on relevant undertakings before the final decision is rendered. A review of the Board's decisions shows that the Board applies interim measures in exceptional cases which require such a measure due to their particular dynamics.

For instance, in its *Türk Telekom/TTNET* decision,[1860] before rendering its decision on the allegations that Türk Telekom violated Law No. 4054 in the broadband internet access services market, the Board has imposed an interim measure on Türk Telekom requesting Türk Telekom to terminate its relevant campaigns for internet services.

Similarly, in its *WhatsApp* case in 2021, the Board announced its decision to launch a fully-fledged investigation against Facebook in relation to its updated privacy policy, which also included an interim measure against WhatsApp.[1861] WhatsApp's announcement

---

[1860]   *Türk Telekom/TTNET* (n. 1801).
[1861]   *WhatsApp* (11 January 2021, 21-02/25-10).

of its update notice regarding privacy policy in January 2021 had resulted in a public outrage in Turkey, which urged the Board to assess the data-sharing policy of WhatsApp in terms of competition law rules.

After analysing the details of the amended policies, the Board stated that other Facebook companies would be able to access and use WhatsApp users' data if the amended terms of use and privacy policy issued by Facebook were accepted by users. To that end, the Board concluded that if it were to cancel Facebook's newly issued terms of use and privacy policy at the end of a fully-fledged investigation, it would be difficult to eliminate the advantages that other Facebook companies would have already benefited through the use of the data obtained with the new policy. Accordingly, the Board indicated that implementation of the new privacy policy would create a situation that could not be rectified unless an interim measure were implemented. Moreover, by taking into account Facebook's market power in the relevant markets, the Board stated that it was likely that the newly adopted privacy policy, which required WhatsApp users to share their data with other Facebook companies, could cause serious and irreparable damages before a final decision could be rendered following a fully-fledged investigation. Consequently, the Board proceeded to impose an interim measure against WhatsApp before its final decision.

Consequently, interim measures are another tool that may be implemented by the Board in order to terminate violations, in case it is found that waiting for a final decision would create serious and irreparable harm that cannot be rectified.

Chapter 13
Judicial Review

GÖNENÇ GÜRKAYNAK, ESQ. AND ALI KAĞAN UÇAR[*]

The Board is a part of the administrative structure of the Authority as its decision-making body and is formed in accordance with Law No. 4054. Although the Board's procedures have quasi-judicial characteristics,[1862] the Board is ultimately an administrative authority, which unilaterally declares its intentions through implementing administrative acts.

As per Article 125 of the Constitution, "recourse to judicial review shall be available against all actions and acts of administration". In a democratic society, it is a compulsory element and a natural consequence of the "rule of law" that the administration considers itself to be bound by the laws of the land and that it faces a "sanction" in case of a violation of these rules.[1863] In Turkish competition law, in line with the provision of the Constitution, Article 55 of Law No. 4054 authorises the administrative courts for judicial review of the decisions of the Board, with the extent explained below.

13.1 Nature of the Board's Decisions

Decisions of the Authority and the Board are administrative acts.[1864] Since the Constitution explicitly states that all administrative acts and actions are subject to judicial review, the regulatory,[1865]

---

[*] Associate, ELIG Gürkaynak Attorneys-at-Law, Istanbul <kagan.ucar@elig.com>.

[1862] E. Koç, "4054 Sayılı Rekabetin Korunması Hakkında Kanun'da Düzenlenen İdari Para Cezaları İçin Öngörülen İdari Usul", *TBB Dergisi*, No. 98, 2012, p. 234 <http://tbbdergisi.barobirlik.org.tr/m2012-98-1127> (last accessed on 28 May 2021).

[1863] A. Ş. Gözübüyük, *Yönetsel Yargı*, Gözden Geçirilmiş (9th edition, Ankara: Turhan Kitabevi, 1993).

[1864] ECCHR defines the administrative action as "a legal action concerning the conduct of a public administrative body. This kind of action can for example lead to the reversal of certain decisions by public bodies or compel an authority to take a certain action" <https://www.ecchr.eu/en/glossary/administrative-action/#:~:text=An%20administrative%20action%20is%20a,to%20take%20a%20certain%20action> (last accessed on 12 May 2021).

[1865] Regulatory decisions are unilateral administrative actions of a general and impersonal nature. (K. Gözler and G. Kaplan, *İdare Hukukuna Giriş*, Bursa: Ekin Yayıncılık, 2017, p.185.) The Presidency of the Authority is authorised to prepare and publish communiqués and regulations. Such regulatory actions of the Authority are subject to judicial review as per Article 24/1(c) of Law No. 2575 on the Council of State. Regulation on Fines to Apply in Cases of Agreements, Concerted Practices and Decisions Limiting Competition, and Abuse of Dominant Position, published in the Official Gazette on 15 February 2009, numbered 27142; Communiqué No. 2010/4 Concerning the Mergers and Acquisitions Calling for the Authorisation of the Competition Board, published in the Official Gazette on 7 October 2009, numbered 27722; Guidelines on Vertical Agreements dated 29 March 2018, numbered 18-09/179-RM (1) are examples of the regulatory decisions of the Board.

organisational[1866] and substantive[1867] decisions of the Authority and the Board may, in principle, be judicially reviewed. This chapter of the book mainly concentrates on the Board's decisions concerning substantive issues related to its main duties in order to keep the focus on the aspects of judicial review regarding competition law, as other types of decisions are more in the purview of administrative law.

Law No. 4054 provides that legal actions against *administrative sanctions* may be pursued before the administrative courts.[1868] Law No. 4054, therefore, clarifies that the Board's decisions that impose sanctions may be challenged. However, not all of the Board's decisions concerning substantive issues involve an administrative sanction. For instance, the Board, in carrying out its duties, may request information from undertakings[1869] or perform on-site examinations at undertakings' premises.[1870] Similarly, the Board's decisions to launch a preliminary investigation[1871] do not in and of themselves involve any administrative sanction.

At this point, it should also be noted that Law No. 4054 divides the Board's decisions into two main categories, namely, final decisions and interim decisions.[1872] Final decisions of the Board are subject to judicial review, which means that interim decisions cannot, in principle, be directly challenged before the Board renders its final decision on the substance of the matter. There is, however, a specific type of interim decision, i.e., interim measure decision, which Law No. 4054 allows to be brought to judicial review without having to wait for the Board's final decision as the relevant interim decision involves an administrative sanction. Indeed, a Board decision that imposes an interim measure may be directly subject to an action for annulment.

13.1.1 Final Decisions

Article 48 of Law No. 4054 entitled "Final Decision" provides that the final decision shall be rendered after the oral hearing or at the end of the investigation phase. In other words, the relevant provision only addresses the final decisions rendered as part of the fully-fledged investigations. Accordingly, it remains unclear whether decisions other than those that are given as a result of an investigation (such as negative clearance, individual exemption decisions, etc.) also constitute a final decision under Law No. 4054.

That said, Article 48 does not seem to intend to cover all final decisions that the Board may adopt under Law No. 4054. Indeed, looking at the order of provisions and structure of Law

---

[1866] The Board may render decisions on organisational matters within the Authority. Such decisions can be brought to judicial review as per general provisions of Law No. 2577.

[1867] The term "substantive decisions" refers to the Board's decisions concerning the Board's substantive duties such as no-go decisions, decisions rendered at the end of the investigation phases, clearance decisions, etc.

[1868] Article 55 of Law No. 4054 reads as follows: "Lawsuits against administrative sanctions shall be brought before the competent administrative courts."

[1869] Article 14 of Law No. 4054.

[1870] Article 15 of Law No. 4054.

[1871] Article 40 of Law No. 4054.

[1872] Article 51 of Law No. 4054 differentiates between the "final decisions" and "decisions except the final decision" when setting the meeting and decision quorums.

No. 4054, Article 48 is situated after the articles concerning the hearing, as the last part of the section on the stages of the investigation phase (Articles 43–48). Furthermore, the wording of Article 48 also indicates that the term "final decision" in the relevant article refers to the decisions rendered after the oral hearing or at the end of the investigation phase only.

From an administrative law perspective, there is no doubt that the final decisions the Board may render are not limited to the decisions at the end of the investigation phase. General principles in administrative law apply in determining whether an administrative act of the Board constitutes a final decision.[1873] Accordingly, yet explains the term "final act" as follows:

> The notion of final act in the Administrative Law includes acts that arise as a result of a sequence of acts consisting of many ensuing stages and that conceive a new legal status.[1874]

As Articles 14(3)(d) and 15(1)(b) of Law No. 2577 initially require the existence of "a final administrative act that must be executed" for the administrative courts to start evaluating the request for annulment,[1875] the Board's decisions that may be subject to judicial review must, in principle, constitute a final and executive act.[1876] Accordingly, the Board's decisions concerning individual exemption, negative clearance, mergers and acquisitions, administrative fines and a no-go decision after the preliminary investigation phase may be subject to judicial review as they are final and executive acts.[1877]

13.1.2 Interim Decisions

Administrative bodies may adopt ensuing and interconnected acts in the decision-making process in order to provide a final and executive act. In the doctrine, interconnected (*chain*) acts are defined as "a sequence of acts that pursue each other and complement each other in order to assemble a definite and final result".[1878]

[1873]   H. Bolatoğlu, *Rekabet Kurumu Kararlarının Yargısal Denetimi* (Ankara: Rekabet Kurumu, Ankara, 2004), p. 9.

[1874]   O. Yet, *Rekabet Kurulu Kararlarının Yargısal Denetimi*, Panel II. Oturum, Rekabet Hukuku ve Yargı Sempozyumu (Ankara: Rekabet Kurumu, Bilgi İşlem, İstatistik ve Enformasyon Dairesi Başkanlığı, 1999), p. 72.

[1875]   Similarly, the judgment of the 8th Chamber of the Council of State (23 January 2004, E. 2003/3030, K. 2004/309) states that as the application of annulment/judicial review does not refer to a final administrative act that must be executed, the application should have been rejected in the preliminary examination and that it was unlawful [for the first instance court] to have reviewed the case on merits.

[1876]   M. Günday, *İdare Hukuku* (Ankara: İmaj Yayıncılık, 1998), p. 98, "The administrative acts which establish, change or terminate a legal status are deemed executive acts. On the other hand, expressions of intent and opinion, regulations that guide the practices of administration or preparatory processes before an administrative decision are considered as non-executive acts of administration."

[1877]   The decision of the 13th Chamber of the Council of State (9 July 2018, E. 2018/1837, K. 2018/232) is highly exceptional as the Court annulled the decision of the 7th Administrative Chamber of the Ankara Regional Administrative Court which upheld the decision of the 14th Administrative Chamber of the Ankara Administrative Court reversing the request of annulment of the Multinet decision of the Board (15 May 2017, 17-16/224-M) concerning the initiation of an investigation against Multinet Kurumsal Hizmetler A.Ş. The 13th Chamber of the Council of State stated that the Administrative Court should have examined the case by merits, implying that even the Board decisions concerning the initiation of an investigation may satisfy the prerequisites of being a final decision.

[1878]   C. Erkut, *İptal Davasının Konusunu Oluşturma Bakımından İdari İşlemin Kimliği*, Ankara: Danıştay Yayınları No. 51, 1990, p. 121.

As a consequence of the rule underlying in Article 14 of Law No. 2577, interim decisions at the stage of actualising a final decision are not subject to judicial review.[1879] Such that, the preliminary investigation decisions, investigation decisions, decisions to hold a hearing, the decisions on requesting information and on-site examinations are interim decisions intended to create a final decision, and since they are not considered as separate decisions, they cannot be subject to an annulment action.[1880]

13.2 Action for Annulment

Action for annulment is a type of lawsuit aiming at the annulment of an administrative act, i.e., retroactive removal of an administrative act's provisions and consequences, by the administrative courts.[1881] It also aims to disprove the presumption of legality of the administrative act.[1882] Article 2 of Law No. 2577 defines the annulment actions as "lawsuits that are brought by persons whose interests were violated by an administrative act which is claimed to be illegal or erroneous in terms of competence, form, reason, subject and purpose".

Although the main request in an action for annulment is evidently the annulment of the administrative act, it is also possible to request a stay of execution,[1883] inspection, expert examination and hearing.[1884]

13.2.1 Competent Courts and Court Hierarchy

The administrative judiciary system is organised in three levels as per the amendment brought by Law No. 6545 to Law No. 2576. Within the administrative justice organisation, the courts of first instance are the administrative courts, tax courts and the Council of State while dealing with the cases listed in Article 24 of Law No. 2575. As per Article 5 of Law No. 2576, administrative courts are the courts of first instance with general jurisdiction under the administrative branch of the judiciary.[1885] In other words, administrative courts have jurisdiction over the actions for annulment and damages if the administrative court that has jurisdiction over the case is not prescribed in other specific codes.

[1879] C. Karavelioğlu, İdari Yargılama Usulü Kanunu (Trabzon: Top-Kar Matbaacılık,1997), p. 19.

[1880] Yet (n. 1874), p. 77.

[1881] Gözler and Kaplan (n. 1865), p. 353.

[1882] Ibid., pp. 120, 353.

[1883] Article 27 of Law No. 2577.

[1884] Article 17 of Law No. 2577 reads as follows: "Hearing shall be held upon the request of one of the parties, in cases of annulment actions; damages claims against exceeding 57,000 Turkish liras; and tax cases concerning taxes, fees, duties and other similar financial obligations or increases and penalties concerning these obligations exceeding 57,000 Turkish liras in total." (Relevant monetary thresholds are revised annually in accordance with the revaluation figures published by the state.)

[1885] Gözler and Kaplan (n. 1865), p. 340: "There are four branches of judiciary in [the] Turkish legal system, which are the constitutional, civil [and] administrative courts and the court of jurisdictional disputes." P. 351: "As per the Article 158 of the Turkish Constitution, the Court of Jurisdictional Disputes is empowered to deliver final judgments in disputes between civil and administrative courts concerning their jurisdiction and judgments."

The actions for annulment against the Board's decisions are examined by the administrative courts. However, the annulment actions initiated against the Board's regulatory decisions fall within the jurisdiction of the Council of State as a court of first instance.[1886]

After the administrative courts render their decision as the court of first instance, regional administrative courts have appellate jurisdiction as the intermediate courts of appeal and they are authorised to carry out the second step of the judicial review process.

Finally, the Council of State is the last instance of the judicial reviewing process. The 2nd, 5th, 6th, 8th, 10th, 11th, 12th and 13th Chambers of the Council of State are authorised to review the administrative actions, where the remaining chambers resolve the disputes concerning tax, fees, duties and other similar fiscal obligations.[1887]

The Council of State also comprises two assemblies: (i) Plenary Session of Administrative/Tax Law Chambers and (ii) Assembly on the Unification of Conflicting Judgments. The main functions of the Plenary Session of Administrative Law Chambers are to review the following cases on appeal: (i) decisions of administrative courts insisting on their previous judgments, despite its reversal by a decision of a chamber of the Council of State, (ii) judgments of the administrative chambers of the Council of State sitting as the first instance court.[1888] In this regard, the Plenary Session of Administrative Law Chambers would have jurisdiction in appeals regarding the decisions given by the Council of State as the first instance court on requests for annulment of the Board's regulatory decisions.

Jurisdiction as to venue refers to the location of the court that the petition shall be filed with. That said, if the administrative court that has jurisdiction over the case is not prescribed in the other provisions of Law No. 2577 or in other specific statutory acts, the administrative court presiding in the region where the public authority whose act is being challenged is located shall have jurisdiction over the case.[1889] Accordingly, actions for the annulment of the Board's decisions concerning substantial issues must be commenced before the Ankara administrative courts, as the Authority is located in Ankara.

As a prerequisite for an action for annulment, the case should be brought before the court that has jurisdiction as to the subject matter and venue; accordingly, these issues are assessed under a preliminary examination.[1890] The determination of jurisdiction both as to subject and venue[1891] is regarded as requirements of public order. Thus, these prerequisites are examined *ex officio* by the court, and a decision of dismissal due to lack of jurisdiction can be given at every stage of the lawsuit. The decisions rendered by courts without jurisdiction are deemed unlawful.

[1886]   Article 24 of Law No. 2575.
[1887]   <https://www.danistay.gov.tr/icerik/26> (last accessed on 24 March 2021).
[1888]   Article 38 of Law No. 2575.
[1889]   Article 32 of Law No. 2577.
[1890]   Article 14(3)(a) of Law No. 2577.
[1891]   Article 32(2) of Law No. 2577.

13.2.2 Parties

A plaintiff is a person who brings a lawsuit with or without being represented by legal counsel.[1892] In addition to legal standing, i.e., the "legal capacity to be a party to a lawsuit" and the "legal capacity to sue", which are the objective criteria,[1893] there is also a need to show (sufficient) interest in the matter according to Article 2(1)(a) of Law No. 2577, which states, "an interest of the plaintiff must have been violated by an administrative act". This requirement is considered a prerequisite for the plaintiff.

As the "violation of interest" is a broader concept than the "violation of personal rights" required in actions for damages against the public authorities (full remedy actions,[1894] which is another type of administrative suit), it is accepted that there is a violation of interest if there is a current, serious, legitimate interest or relationship between the act/matter under action and the plaintiff.[1895]

On the other hand, the defendant is the public legal entity that implemented the administrative act that is subject to the action for annulment. In cases concerning the judicial review of the Board's decisions, the defendant public legal entity is the Authority.

13.2.3 Time Limits
for Judicial Review Proceedings

As per Articles 7 and 8 of Law No. 2577, administrative acts can be brought to judicial review by filing an appeal within sixty calendar days from the date on which the reasoned decision is received by the plaintiff unless other time limits are provided under specific codes.[1896] Having said this, Law No. 4054 does not contain any specific provision regarding the time limits for litigation and follows the general procedure set out under Law No. 2577. As this sixty calendar day period is expressed as a peremptory term, applications received after this time shall be dismissed as provided by Articles 13(3)(e) and 14(1)(b) of Law No. 2577. Appeals against Board's decisions should be filed before the Ankara administrative courts, and the proceedings involve two separate rounds of petition exchanges and an oral hearing in Ankara, if requested.[1897]

The time limit to bring an annulment action against the Board's regulatory decisions before the Council of State is also sixty days. The plaintiff may either initiate an action against

---

[1892] Gözler and Kaplan (n. 1865), p. 358.

[1893] Articles 50 and 51 of Law No. 6100.

[1894] Article 2(1)(b) of Law No. 2577.

[1895] Ş. Gözübüyük, *Amerika Ve Türkiye'de İdarenin Kaza Denetlenmesi* (Ankara: Üniversitesi Siyasal Bilgiler Fakültesi Yayınları, 1961), p. 175; Decision of Plenary Session of Administrative Law Chambers dated 10 December 2009 with docket number 2008/860 and decision numbered 2009/2836.

[1896] The Council of State has precedents stating that "it is not possible to examine the merits of the case since it is filed with request of annulment of an act that is not final or executable" where the plaintiffs filed upon the service of the Board's short-form decision (10th Chamber of Council of State (2 April 2002, E. 1999/3957, K. 2002/894); 10th Chamber of Council of State (7 October 2002, E. 2002/4182, K. 2002/3508)).

[1897] Gözler and Kaplan (n. 1865), p. 353.

(i) the regulatory decision from the day following the promulgation date (if promulgation is required); (ii) the act itself, upon the implementation of the regulatory decision on the plaintiff; or (iii) both of them.[1898] Thus, the interested parties may request the annulment of the regulatory decision, which is the basis of the specific act applied to them, even though sixty days after the promulgation date has already passed.

The parties may appeal the first instance court's decision before the Regional Administrative Court within thirty days as of its service.[1899] Similarly, the time limit to file an appeal against the Regional Administrative Court's decision before the Council of State is thirty days as of the service of the Regional Administrative Court's decision.[1900]

13.2.4 Applicable Procedural Rules

13.2.4.1 Applying to Superior Authorities

As per Article 11(1) of Law No. 2577, before initiating an action for annulment, the person concerned may request the abolishment, withdrawal, alteration of the administrative act or the implementation of a new act from the superior authority, i.e., the administrative body at a higher level of the administration; or, if there is no superior authority, from the authority that implemented the act. This application is not mandatory, i.e., it is not a prerequisite for applying to the judicial review. However, as per Article 11(1) of Law No. 2577, application to the superior authority stops the time limit for bringing an action before the court, as it starts to run on the date the reasoned decision was served on the plaintiff. As per Article 11(2) of Law No. 2577, if the authority does not respond within sixty days, the request is deemed to be dismissed. Following that, the time limit for filing for an annulment action resumes when the application is dismissed or deemed to be dismissed. According to Article 11(3) of Law No. 2577, the period passed until the date of application to the superior authority shall also be taken into account.

13.2.4.2 Jurisdiction in Connected Cases

As mentioned, while explaining the time limit to bring an annulment action against Board's regulatory decisions, the person concerned may bring an action (i) against the regulatory decision or (ii) against the specific act, which is applied to the person as a result of this regulatory decision or (iii) against both of them. Therefore, if the plaintiff is applying for the judicial review of both, these are deemed to be connected cases[1901], and the Council of State would have jurisdiction over both since one of the connected

---

[1898] Article 7(4) of Law No. 2577.

[1899] Article 45(2) of Law No. 2577.

[1900] Article 46 of Law No. 2577.

[1901] According to Article 38(1) of Law No. 2577, connected cases are defined as those cases "arising from the same facts or legal reasons or those where a decision given in one affects the other".

cases (judicial review of the regulatory decision) falls under its jurisdiction.[1902] It is an exceptional rule, as ordinarily, the Ankara administrative courts have jurisdiction over the Board's decisions regarding substantive issues, in the absence of a connected case under the general jurisdiction rule.

13.2.4.3 Stay of Execution

The application for the judicial review of Board decisions to the Ankara Administrative Courts does not automatically stay the execution of the decision. However, this could be requested any time before the final verdict is given as a separate injunctive relief from the court. As per Article 27(2) of Law No. 2577, the court may decide to stay the execution as an interim decision only if (i) the execution of the decision is likely to cause irreparable damages; and (ii) there is a prima facie case in favour of the plaintiff.

In certain exceptional cases, the decisions to stay the execution of administrative acts can be granted before waiting for the administration's defence, e.g., where there is some urgency due to a risk of irreparable harm. As per Article 27(6) of Law No. 2577, the stay of execution order can be given after a security payment is deposited with the court; however, depending on the specifics of the case, it may be waived.

As to the decisions concerning the stay of execution order; as per Article 27(7) of Law No. 2577, objections can be lodged against the decisions of a chamber of the Council of State before the Plenary Session of the Administrative Law Chambers; against the decisions of the regional administrative court, before the nearest regional administrative court; against the decisions of administrative courts or against a decision rendered by a single judge, before the regional administrative courts.

Parties can bring objections against the specific stay of execution order only once and have a time limit of seven days from the notification of the decision. The relevant judicial bodies must also decide on the objection within seven days. Decisions rendered upon objections are final.

As per Article 28 of Law No. 2577, the time limit for the administration to implement the stay of execution orders, under no circumstances, can exceed thirty days from the date the decision is notified to the administration.

13.2.5 Grounds for Annulment

Upon the application of the plaintiff, the Ankara Administrative Court goes through the case file to see whether the Board's decision complies with the law in terms of (i) subject, (ii) form, (iii) purpose, (iv) jurisdiction, and (v) reason. According to Article 2 of Law No. 2577, an administrative act, which is illegal due to a mistake made in one of the aforementioned elements, may be annulled by the court.

[1902]   Article 38(3) of Law No. 2577.

13.2.5.1 The "Subject" Element

The subject of a final decision is the legal consequence that is targeted by and arises as a result of the decision.[1903] If the administrative authority misapplies the substantive law, this results in illegality in terms of subject.[1904]

Regarding the subject element of administrative acts, the 4th Chamber of the Council of State's *Sirküler* decision[1905] sets forth the following:

> Considering the legal characteristics determined in the doctrine as well as the case law, 'the legal consequence of an administrative act' is deemed to be the subject of that act. The consequences of administrative acts whose subject must be legitimate and possible, have been pre-determined by laws and other regulatory acts. Accordingly the relevant [administration] is not authorised to change the legal consequences of an act or describe it as they wish.

In parallel to the Council of State's precedent, in the academic literature, Akyılmaz states that "the subject of the act must be possible and legitimate", in order for an administrative act to be considered lawful.[1906] In the same vein, Gözler argues that if the subject of an administrative act is impossible, the act would be established unlawful.[1907]

13.2.5.2 The "Form" Element

Academic literature has defined the element of form in administrative acts in various ways, but it is agreed that non-compliance with formalities will require the annulment of the relevant administrative acts.[1908] This is supported by the Council of State's decision[1909] where the 5th Chamber of the Council of State emphasised that form constitutes one of the essential elements of the legal validity of an administrative act. Indeed, the Council of State stated that "the failure to comply with the formal (procedural) requirements stipulated by the Law in the establishment of an administrative transaction may render it invalid or lead to annulment". As clearly stated in the Council of State's decision and the literature, when executing an administrative act, the administration is bound by the rules of form and procedure, which are determined by legal norms such as the Constitution, laws, regulations as well as international law. The failure by the Board to follow these rules leads to the annulment of the decision.

Accordingly, the Board must issue its final decision in accordance with the procedural (formal) rules set out under Articles 48 to 54 of Law No. 4054. In particular, the quorums indicated under Article 51, and subparagraphs under Article 52 listing the elements that must be included in a decision, are considered as material procedural

---

1903   Bolatoğlu (n. 1873), p. 64.
1904   Ş. Gözübüyük and T. Tan, *İdare Hukuku Cilt: 1 Genel Esaslar* (Ankara: Turhan Kitabevi, 2001), p. 492.
1905   4th Chamber of the Council of State (23 May 2011, E. 2009/248, K. 2011/4403).
1906   B. Akyılmaz, *İdari Usul İlkeleri Işığında İdari İşlemin Yapılış Usulü* (Ankara:Yetkin Yayınları, 2000), p. 429.
1907   K. Gözler, *İdare Hukuku (Administrative Law)* (Bursa: Ekin Kitap Evi, 2019), p. 932.
1908   A. Kadıoğlu, "İdari İşlemin Şekil Unsuru", T. C. Selçuk Üniversitesi Sosyal Bilimler Enstitüsü Kamu Hukuku Anabilim Dalı Yüksek Lisans Tezi, 2010, p. 109.
1909   5th Chamber of the Council of State (22 November 1988, E. 1988/2749, K. 1988/2845).

(formal) rules.[1910] On the other hand, although non-compliance with the procedure and form constitutes a violation of law, it is accepted that such violation does not always result in the annulment of the contested decision; in such a case, the legal consequences of such illegality on the contested decision must be observed.[1911]

According to Article 52(1)(k) of Law No. 4054, the dissenting opinions, if any, must be included in the decision and failure to include it is considered as an infringement of the law in terms of form. In the *Akçansa* judgment,[1912] the 10th Chamber of Council of State annulled the Board's *Ege Bölgesi Çimento* decision[1913] stating that excluding the dissenting opinions from the decision constituted a material infringement of law. Upon the annulment of the decision, when serving the decision to Batıçim (another undertaking investigated under the *Ege Bölgesi Çimento*), the Board delivered its former decision again, but this time annexed to a letter of dissenting opinions.[1914] Upon appeal by Batıçim, the 10th Chamber of the Council of State found the Board's service of the *Ege Bölgesi Çimento* decision once again, unlawful, stating that:[1915]

> Annulment decisions are those judicial decisions which may constitute a definitive judgment and result in the revocation of the administrative act retrospectively from the date such administration act was implemented, if the administrative court reviewing the lawfulness of an administrative act finds a defect that affects its validity.
>
> In cases requiring the implementation of a new act, the administration cannot act in a way that would eliminate the definitive judgment character of the annulment decision. In some cases, it is possible to re-implement the annulled action. It may not be considered unlawful, if the Board re-implements an administrative action, which was annulled for illegality due to defects in jurisdiction, form, reason or a lack of sufficient research.
>
> However, since the annulled act is removed from the body of rules retrospectively from the date of its implementation, it is obligatory to establish a new administrative act complying with the procedural rules for it to take effect as and on the date of re-establishment....
>
> Accordingly, the Board should have issued a new decision which would have become valid on the date it was taken. It is unlawful to instead impose, an administrative act by serving the [same] annulled decision with a cover letter signed by the Chairperson of the Board and annexing the dissenting opinions of the annulled decision, which disregards the reasoning of the annulment decision and the fact the former act has been revoked, taking into account the 'collective nature' of the decision even though the dissenting opinions were subsequently notified.

Accordingly, the Board's decisions that do not comply with the law in form may be annulled.

[1910] Bolatoğlu (n. 1873), p. 59.
[1911] 10th Chamber of the Council of State (27 February 2001, E. 1998/5517, K. 2001/738).
[1912] 10th Chamber of the Council of State *Akçansa* judgment (15 January 2001, E. 2000/1432, K. 2001/54) rendered upon Akçansa's appeal of the *Ege Bölgesi Çimento* (17 June 1999, 99-30/276-166).
[1913] *Ege Bölgesi Çimento* (n. 1912), pp. 59–64.
[1914] *Ege Bölgesi Çimento* (n. 1912) served on Batıçim, annexing the Board's letter dated 4 April 2002 and numbered 000385.
[1915] 10th Chamber of the Council of State (23 December 2003, E., 2002/3686, K. 2003/5292).

13.2.5.3 The "Purpose" Element

The aim of any administrative act is to serve the underlying reason that compelled the administration to adopt the act in the first place. The factual event or the legal context instigating the administrative action must be appropriate and the ultimate aim must be the public's welfare.

Within the context of competition law, the enforcement regime's contribution to the public interest is manifested as an increase in public welfare. An investigation conducted by the Authority should serve the public interest, and its goal should be to increase public welfare. Similarly, the decisions of the Board should aim to prevent the distortion of the marketplace through anti-competitive conduct, and it should further benefit the public by ensuring the facilitation and protection of competition in the marketplace.

More specifically, the purpose of competition law is to ensure (i) free and healthy competition and, where necessary, (ii) to restore the competition in a market following a violation.[1916] The competition laws seek to enhance consumer welfare by preserving and encouraging vigorous rivalry between independently competing firms. Competition law does not seek to protect the interests of individual competitors. It seeks to protect the competitive process.

As the Board has frequently emphasised,[1917] and as also set out in the preamble to Law No. 4054, "it is necessary for the proper functioning of a market economy that there should be a dynamic competitive process between competitors and successful undertakings".

The wording shows that the preamble to Law No. 4054 puts the emphasis on the competitive process, not on particular competitors. Hence, in its *illerarasımesafe.com* decision, the Board stated as follows: "the protection of consumer welfare does not mean protection of competitors operating in the market".[1918]

Accordingly, as the Board established in its *Türk Hava Yolları* decision,[1919] it is in no way the purpose of competition law "to ensure that competitors less efficient than the undertaking with the dominant position should remain on the market". On the contrary, "competition on the merits may, by definition, lead to the departure from the market or the marginalisation of competitors that are less efficient, and so, less attractive to consumers in terms of price, choice, quality or innovation, among other things".

Accordingly, the Board's decisions that do not comply with the purpose of the competition laws can be annulled by the administrative courts.

Furthermore, decisions violating the principle of proportionality can also be annulled on the grounds of illegality in terms of the purpose element. Administrative authorities,

---

[1916] K. E. Gönen, *Rekabet Hukukunda İdari Para Cezaları*, (Ankara: Seçkin Yayıncılık, 2003), p. 66.
[1917] *Malatya Belediyesi* (19 August 2009, 09-36/918-225), p. 4; *İzmir Municipality* (11 February 2010, 10-16/183-70), p. 4; *Yeşil Körfez Su Birliği* (11 July 2013, 13-44/553-247) para. 12.
[1918] *illerarasımesafe.com* (16 November 2016, 16-39/638-284), para. 82.
[1919] *THY* (25 December 2014, 14-54/932-420) paras. 167, 168, which endorses the *Intel* Judgment of the General Court (Seventh Chamber, Extended Composition) of the ECJ (Case T- 286/09 [2014]).

including the Board, should strike a fair balance between (i) the protection of a natural or legal person's rights and (ii) the protection of the rights and interests of the administration or the public.

Article 13 of the Constitution requires that any limitation of a fundamental right must respect the principle of proportionality. The principle of proportionality, in turn, requires that the means, tools, and measures used by the administration to make a decision should be proportionate to the objectives it pursues. To comply with this principle, an administrative authority should consider all circumstances of the specific case at hand. The decision adopted by the administration should also be reasonable and fair, meaning that it must not cause disadvantages that are disproportionate to the aim pursued.[1920] In other words, natural or legal persons' rights should not be restricted in a disproportionate way.[1921] Indeed, the Turkish Constitution Court has also underlined that it is obligatory to comply with the principle of proportionality in the acts by public authorities by stating the following:

> In judicial jurisprudence and doctrine, in such cases it is accepted that the discretionary power has not been used objectively, by referring to concepts such as clear error, disproportionality, balance, reasonable measure in the control of the legality of the discretionary power. After the constitutional court judgment, it has emerged that the principle of proportionality, which includes the sub-principles of commensurability, necessity and convenience, should be applied as a means of lawfulness, in administrative law.[1922]

Accordingly, the Board's decisions that do not comply with the law in terms of the element of purpose may be annulled.

13.2.5.4 The "Jurisdiction" Element

The administrative acts must be enacted by the authorised competent public bodies and administrations, to be legally valid in terms of jurisdiction.[1923] Also, failure to use the authority is considered as a ground for annulment as well, since the public administration is mandated to exercise its authority, unlike in private law.[1924] To that end, the Board must render its decisions within the boundaries of its jurisdiction. Lack of jurisdiction is a clear ground of annulment in terms of the Board's decisions.[1925]

[1920] Y. Oğurlu, "A Comparative Study on The Principle of Proportionality in Turkish Administrative Law", *Kamu Hukuku Arşivi (KHukA)*, İlhan Akın'a Armağan, March 2003 (1), also available at: <http://www.idare.gen.tr/ogurlu-proportionality.htm>.

[1921] J. G. Erdem, "Ölçülülük İlkesinin Kullanımının İdarenin Takdir Yetkisinin Kullanımındaki Yeri", *Ankara University School of Law Magazine*, Vol. 62, No. 4, 2013, pp. 984–992.

[1922] 1st Chamber of Turkish Constitution Court (19 October 1992, E. 1991/1619, K. 1992/1423).

[1923] H. Kalabalık, "İdarenin Takdir Yetkisinin Sınırları ve Yargısal Denetimi", *Gazi Üniversitesi Hukuk Fakültesi Dergisi*, Vol.1, Issue 1, 1997, pp. 172–211.

[1924] Gözübüyük and Tan (n. 1904), p. 414.

[1925] For instance, according to the decision of the 1st Chamber of the Council of State (5 July 1984, E. 1984/72, K. 1984/155), "The rules of authority are among the provisions regarding public order in a narrow and special sense, they are among the most important elements of administrative proceedings, the defects in the element of authority cannot be remedied with subsequent approval or permission, therefore the administration has to strictly comply with the rules of authority, and the rules of authority are subject to narrow interpretation. It is one of the known principles of administrative law that it should be adhered to the application methods.

13.2.5.5 The "Reason" Element

A legal consequence of an administrative act cannot be in conflict with (or contrary to) what the law dictates as the legal reason for that action (i.e., the element of reason).[1926]

For instance, the reasons for granting an individual exemption are explained under four subparagraphs of Article 5 of Law No. 4054. That is to say, there are two affirmative conditions: (i) to ensure new developments and improvements, or economic or technical development in the production or distribution of goods and in the provision of services, and (ii) to allow consumers a fair share of the resulting benefit; and two negative conditions: (i) not to eliminate competition in a significant part of the relevant market and (ii) not to limit competition more than what is required for achieving the goals set, which constitute the element of reason in the individual exemption decisions.[1927]

Furthermore, the element of reason for a negative clearance decision is that the application or the collusive behaviour subjected to the notification does not violate Articles 4, 6 or 7 of Law No. 4054.[1928]

One of the most significant examples showing that the Board must always observe the element of reason in its decisions is the *Sahibinden* judgment of the Ankara 6th Administrative Court.[1929] In its *Sahibinden* judgment, the Ankara 6th Administrative Court annulled the Board's *Sahibinden* decision[1930] concerning an abuse of dominance case in the (i) "online platform services market for the sale/renting of real estate" and in the (ii) "online platform services market for vehicle sales". The *Sahibinden* judgment constitutes a highly valuable and relevant precedent about legal standards to be applied to abuse of dominance cases. The main findings in the *Sahibinden* judgment are that, in abuse of dominance cases, the applicable legal standard requires the Board to conduct "clear and precise assessments beyond any doubt". The court criticised the Board's *Sahibinden* decision for relying on "*mere observations and assumptions*". In particular, the court underlined that "reaching a conclusion based on doubt is legally insufficient". Rather, "the requisite legal standard requires the allegation to be proven with concrete evidence and justifications establishing that the doubt is valid".

The *Sahibinden* judgment follows a well-established line of precedents in Turkish law[1931] as pointed out by the court. In its judgment, the court has emphasised that the obligation for the Authority is to set "concrete criteria on the factors to be taken into consideration to assess

---

Decision-making ability, which is called the element of authority in the narrow sense, is a power granted to certain organs, authorities and public officials by the Constitution and laws in terms of subject, place and time." (*Danıştay Dergisi*, Y. 1985, pp. 58–59, p. 76.)

[1926] H. Kalabalık, *Introduction to Administrative Procedural Law*, 2014, p. 184.

[1927] Bolatoğlu (n. 1873), p. 31.

[1928] Ibid., p. 36.

[1929] Ankara 6th Administrative Court's *Sahibinden* judgment (18 December 2019, E. 2019/946, K. 2019/2625).

[1930] *Sahibinden* (n. 1140).

[1931] The requirement for the establishment of an infringement with "clear and precise evidence beyond any doubt" is recognised by the Council of State (see, e.g., 15th Chamber, 13 November 2015, E. 2015/4441, K. 2015/7545 and 11 November 2015, E. 2015/2514, K. 2015/7361), and the High Court of Appeals (see, e.g., 15th Criminal Chamber, 20 January 2016, E. 2015/14529, K. 2016/634).

whether evidence in the Board decision" sufficiently meets the standard of proof. Specific to excessive pricing allegations, the court ruled that difficulties related to the calculation of different parameters "makes it impossible to establish price cost comparison objectively and perfectly" and held that the Authority failed to base its assessment on precise criteria.[1932]

In the *Servet Ünsal* decision,[1933] the Plenary Session of the Council of State reversed the decision of the Board on the grounds that the Board did not consider the new legal circumstances brought by the regulation in fines and did not apply the more favourable rule.

In its *Promesis* judgment,[1934] the 13th Chamber of the Council of State annulled the Board's *Promesis* decision[1935] on the basis that the Board imposed a fine based on the documents signed by the third parties whose relationship with the case could not be determined. Although the court's *Promesis* judgment was then reversed,[1936] the Plenary Session of the Administrative Law Chambers stated that "it is clear that aforementioned determinations cannot be accepted as evidence against the plaintiff".

13.3 Substantive Issues

As mentioned under Section 13.2 above, this chapter of the book mainly focuses on the Board's decisions on substantive issues related to its main duties under competition law. Below are certain significant examples of the Board's different types of decisions that have been subject to judicial review.

13.3.1 Individual Exemption

The Council of State annulled the *Akpet/Lukoil* decision[1937] on the grounds that the start date of the individual exemption granted by the Board had been determined in error.[1938] Although the Council of State did not object to the individual exemption itself, it emphasised that the Board should have considered the date of the dealership agreement as the beginning of the individual exemption instead of the date of the rental agreement concerning the relevant gas station.

[1932] The *Sahibinden* judgment reads as follows: "The said Decision provides that 'In the second phase concerning price comparison, the price of the product/services should be compared both with the price of the relevant undertaking and the prices of the rival undertakings'. However, examining the decision as a whole, one would observe that the decision (i) makes a comparison with the undertakings operating in different markets, that are inadequate for such a comparison, and (ii) does not make a price comparison with different jurisdictions and particularly with countries involving major global players."

[1933] Plenary Session of the Administrative Law Divisions (26 September 2012, E. 2012/1266, K. 2007/307).

[1934] 13th Chamber of Council of State *Promesis* judgment (2 February 2010, E. 2007/9330, K. 2010/1325)

[1935] *Promesis* (16 March 2007, 07-24/236-76).

[1936] Plenary Session of the Administrative Law Chambers' *Promesis* Verdict (20 February 2014, E. 2010/3333, K. 2014/437).

[1937] 13th Chamber of Council of State (14 April 2011, E. 2011/688, K. 2015/1456).

[1938] Plenary Session of the Administrative Law Divisions (9 April 2018, E. 2015/3253, K. 2017/3542).

In a very similar case, the Council of State annulled the Board's *Opet/Emka* individual exemption decision[1939] which started the individual exemption as of the date of the rental agreement between Opet and Emka. The Council of State emphasised that the non-compete obligation has entered into force through the execution of the dealership agreement, and therefore the individual exemption period should have commenced as of the date of the dealership agreement instead of the rental agreement.[1940]

13.3.2 Negative Clearance

The Board may, after issuing a negative clearance certificate, revoke its opinion at any time in case of a change in any circumstance that constituted the basis of the relevant decision to issuance the negative clearance certificate, as per Article 13 of Law No. 4054. In a dispute concerning the revocation of the Board's negative clearance decision,[1941] the Council of State explicitly ordered that the Board can and should revoke its previous negative clearance decision if the relevant circumstances have changed in the meantime, by stating that "the revocation decision of the Board is in compliance with the laws as the market conditions and the mutual exclusivity system approved by the Board's negative clearance decision have been then turned into a unilateral practice of the plaintiff, which hindered the market entries".[1942]

Furthermore, the 13th Chamber of the Council of State annulled the Board's *Ulusoy* decision[1943] which dismissed the request for a negative clearance certificate for the agreement concluded between Ulusoy Deniz Yolları İşletmeciliği A.Ş. and UN Ro-Ro İşletmeleri A.Ş., for entirely procedural reasons, stating that "it is against the law to take the decision by forming a quorum which consists of more than seven members, after the Law No. 5388 came into force on July 13, 2005", which had reduced the total number of Board members to seven.[1944]

13.3.3 Mergers and Acquisitions

In *DSG/Electro World* decision, the Board cleared the transaction where 40% of Electro World's shares were acquired by DSG but imposed an administrative monetary fine on DSG on the ground that the transaction was realised before obtaining the Board's approval, thus violating the suspension requirement.[1945] DSG filed an annulment lawsuit claiming that Electro World is planned to be sold to a potential buyer and the acquisition at hand is only a temporary transaction that would not ultimately lead to a lasting change in the control structure. Ankara 4th Administrative Court accepted these claims

---

[1939]   *Opet/Emka* (2 December 2010, 10-75/1544-597).
[1940]   13th Chamber of Council of State (14 April 2015, E. 2011/710, K. 2015/1459).
[1941]   *Benkar/Fiba* (18 September 2001, 01-44/433-111).
[1942]   10th Chamber of the Council of State (23 December 2003, E. 2002/693, K. 2003/5295).
[1943]   *Ulusoy* (27 October 2005, 05-74/998-279).
[1944]   13th Chamber of the Council of State (12 December 2006, E. 2006/313, K. 2006/4716).
[1945]   *DSG/Electro World* (n. 1380).

and annulled the Board's decision on the grounds that (i) the relevant share transfer was made in order for DSG to ultimately cease its shareholding in Electro World and exit the Turkish market entirely; (ii) the relevant sales process was already notified to the Authority; and (iii) the acquisition at hand was only a temporary transaction which would not have led to a lasting change in the control structure of the undertaking concerned.[1946] The Council of State upheld the Ankara 4th Administrative Court's decision.[1947]

Furthermore, in the *Van Et* decision,[1948] the Board had imposed an administrative monetary fine on Mr Galip Öztürk, stating that "he should have applied for approval from the Board, when he started to buy the shares from İstanbul Stock Exchange in order to take over the management of Van Et". Upon Mr Galip Öztürk's application for the annulment of the Board's decision, the Council of State has dismissed the case, stating:

> In terms of the nature of stock market transactions; publicly traded/quoted shares are exchanged during the session periods determined by the stock exchange officers. Although it is understood that it is not possible for such acquisitions and mergers to take place by getting an approval from the Board beforehand, notification to the Board within a reasonable time from the execution of the transaction, and permission from the Board is required.[1949]

13.3.4 No-Go Decision at the End of the Preliminary Investigation Phase

In the *Ford* judgment,[1950] the 10th Chamber of the Council of State annulled the Board's *Ford* decision[1951] concerning a no-go decision rendered upon the preliminary investigation phase, stating that "it is concluded that sufficient examination and research has not been done on the allegations submitted in the complaint petition". The Plenary Session of the Administrative Law Chambers also upheld the *Ford* judgment.[1952]

Similarly, in the *Allergan* judgment,[1953] the 13th Chamber of Council of State annulled the decision of the first instance court, which had approved the Board's *Allergan* decision[1954] concerning the no-go as a result of a preliminary investigation on the allegations that Allergan A.Ş. violated Article 6 of Law No. 4054 by not supplying Botox branded products. In its decision, the Council of State stated that "because the action subject to complaint was the unilateral conduct of Allergan, it should have been examined within the scope of Article 6

[1946] The 4th Administrative Court Ankara (26 November 2014, E. 2013/1811, K. 2014/1609).

[1947] 13th Chamber of the Council of State (5 June 2015, E. 2015/698, K. 2015/2125).

[1948] *Van Et* (26 May 2006, 06-36/459-121).

[1949] The decision of the 13th Chamber of the Council of State (29 January 2008, E. 2006/4192, K. 2008/1666) was subsequently approved by the decision of the Plenary Session of the Council of State (14 February 2013, E. 2008/2191, K. 2013/506).

[1950] 10th Chamber of the Council of State (7 October 2003, E. 2002/4519, K. 2003/3811).

[1951] *Ford* (21 December 1999, 99-58/624-398), p. 5.

[1952] The Plenary Session of the Administrative Law Chambers (22 December 2005, E. 2004/106, K. 2005/3262).

[1953] 13th Chamber of the Council of State (28 July 2020, E. 2014/462, K. 2020/1774).

[1954] *Allergan* (3 January 2013, 13-01/3-3), p. 6.

of the Law No. 4054 and evaluated in light of the information, documents and evidence to be obtained by the defendant administration by expanding the inquiry, and a fully-fledged investigation should have been launched to clarify the conduct without any doubts", and evaluated that not to initiate an investigation and to reject the complaint at the preliminary investigation stage was based on incomplete examination and overruled the decision of the first instance court.

13.3.5 Termination of Infringement

13.3.5.1 Behavioural and Structural Remedies

With its *Kumport* judgment,[1955] the 9th Administrative Court of Ankara annulled the Board's *ARKAS/Mardaş* decision[1956] concerning the acquisition of all shares of Mardaş Marmara Deniz İşletmeciliği by Limar Liman ve Gemi İşletmeleri (through its wholly-owned subsidiary Arter Terminal İşletmeleri), which is ultimately controlled by Arkas Group. Considering the competitive concerns arising from the transaction, the parties submitted a remedy package comprising behavioural remedies targeting both horizontal and vertical concerns.[1957] Subsequent to the Board's decision, Kumport (another port operating in Northwest Marmara) filed an administrative lawsuit against the Board's decision and also requested the stay of execution of the Board's decision.

In its reasoned decision, the court stated:

> When these commitments are examined, it is understood that all of the commitments are behavioural commitments ... in the decision of the Board, it is not sufficiently explained how the remedies submitted within the scope of the acquisition subject to the lawsuit will have a positive effect regarding the dominant position, the cooperative effects that will arise as a result of the transaction and regarding the concerns about the vertical restriction of competition; the submitted remedies are not qualified to solve the competitive concerns, there is no efficient implementation and control system for these remedies.

As a result, the court annulled the Board's *ARKAS/Mardaş* decision.

In the *Doğan/Vatan* decision,[1958] the Board approved the acquisition of Bağımsız Gazeteciler Yayıncılık A.Ş. and Kemer Yayıncılık ve Gazetecilik A.Ş. by Doğan Gazetecilik A.Ş., on the condition that certain obligations/remedies stated in the decision are complied with. Upon the application for partial annulment of the Board's decision concerning these conditions, the 13th Chamber of the Council of State ruled in *Doğan/Vatan* judgment[1959] that the conditions set forth in the decision have no legal basis and are based on hypothetical

---

[1955]   The 9th Administrative Court Ankara (21 October 2019, E. 2018/2277, K. 2019/2087).
[1956]   *Arkas/Mardaş* (8 May 2018, 18-14/267-129).
[1957]   G. Gürkaynak and Ö. İnanılır, "Recent competition law developments in Turkey: the administrative court's stay of execution decision regarding behavioural remedies", *The In-House Lawyer*, Summer 2019.
[1958]   *Doğan/Vatan* (10 March 2008, 08-23/237-75).
[1959]   13th Chamber of Council of State (15 March 2010, E. 2008/13171, K. 2010/2225)

and unforeseeable situations. The court further emphasised that it is even debatable that the Board has the power to bring forward such conditions for approval. Accordingly, the court accepted the partial annulment request and annulled the part of the Board's decision pertaining to these conditions.

13.3.5.2 Opinion Letter (Article 9(3) Letter)

In *TURÇEF*,[1960] the Ankara 12th Administrative Court annulled the Board's *TURÇEF* decision[1961] on sending an opinion letter as per Article 9/3 of Law No. 4054, stating that the association should terminate any decisions and practices involving the publishment of a price list that might be considered to fall under Article 4 of Law No. 4054 and should repeal those provisions in their by-laws in the preparation of a price list. In its decision, the court stated:

> It was found that the Board did not assess all of these factors together to establish that the plaintiff violated Article 4 of Law No. 4054 by publishing a price list, and that an action under Article 9(3) of the Law No. 4054 could only be taken following an establishment of violation under the legislation. In the lawsuit at hand, the Board's decision, which asked that the decisions and practices aimed at the publishing of price lists based on the risk of infringement be terminated and any provisions in the by-law concerning the preparation of price lists be repealed, was found to be noncompliant with the law.

However, the *TURÇEF* judgment is reversed by the 8th Regional Administrative Court on the grounds that the Board's *TURÇEF* decision is not a final and an executive decision, making it impossible to assess the case on the merits.

On the other hand, in the *EMDR* judgment,[1962] the Administrative Court accepted that the Board's decisions on sending an opinion letter under Article 9(3) of Law No. 4054 might be subject to judicial review. The merits of the relevant judgment concerned (i) the request of the annulment of the Board's *EMDR* decision[1963] on sending an opinion letter under Article 9(3) of Law No. 4054, which provided that the EMDR European Association should consider objective elements based on training for assessments during the approval process regarding foreign instructors, and that the seminars, workshops and similar kinds of activities not within the scope of EMDR European Association's rules on foreign instructors can be organised without any restriction; and (ii) the request of the annulment of the Board's decision[1964] concerning the rejection of the application to the superior authority under Article 11(2) of Law No. 2577 for the re-examination of the *EMDR* decision on the grounds that the application was not made within the statutory period. While the court annulled the Board's decision rejecting the application made under Article 11(2) of Law No. 2577, stating that the application was made within the statutory period, the court has not handed down a decision for the *EMDR* decision as it

---

[1960] Ankara 12th Administrative Court (15 June 2020, E. 2018/2099, K. 2019/2342).
[1961] *TURÇEF* (3 May 2018, 18-13/230-105), para. 37.
[1962] Ankara 3th Administrative Court (27 October 2020, E. 2020/1059, K. 2020/2043).
[1963] *EMDR* (18 May 2016, 16-17/284-127); Opinion Letter was dated 10 May 2017, numbered 5694.
[1964] *EMDR 2* (10 August 2017, 17-26/396-175).

shall be re-examined by the Board. The court, in the *EDMR* judgment, emphasised that the Board's decision on sending an opinion letter under Article 9(3) of Law No. 4054 not only delivers an opinion but also affects the plaintiff's interests; thus may be subject to judicial review. Upon the annulment of the decision concerning the rejection of the application to the superior authority under Article 11(2), the Board has reassessed the request and decided to uphold its decision on sending an opinion letter under Article 9(3).[1965]

13.3.5.3 Interim Measure

In the *Cine 5* judgment,[1966] the 10th Chamber of the Council of State annulled the Board's interim measure decision[1967] rendered during the investigation phase regarding the Board's *Cine 5* decision[1968] since the interim measure decision did not include the dissenting opinion, which constitutes a violation of the element of form, and a violation of the principle of service of a reasoned decision.

Moreover, during the investigation process of the *Türk Telekom* decision,[1969] the Board has decided to implement interim measures on Türk Telekomünikasyon A.Ş. and urged the company to cease cross-subsidy and complicating the activities of its competitors. However, *Türk Telekom* has been annulled by the 13th Chamber of the Council of State on the grounds that the Board member who conducted the investigation has also voted during the implementation of the final decision at the Board, which results in the violation of the principle of impartiality.[1970]

13.3.6 Periodic Monetary Fine

The 13th Chamber of Council of State annulled Board's *Sodexo* decision[1971] with its *Sodexo* judgment[1972] on the ground that the Board had imposed a fixed monetary fine stipulated under Article 16(1)(b) of Law No. 4054 instead of imposing a periodic (daily) monetary fine under Article 17(1)(d) of the same, as it was clear that the on-site inspection was prevented.

In the *Mosaş* decision,[1973] the Board imposed an administrative monetary fine of TL 8,150.09 (corresponding to 0.05% of the undertaking's gross revenues for 2017), pursuant to Article 17 of Law No. 4054, for each day that Mosaş Akıllı Ulaşım Sistemleri A.Ş. ("*Mosaş*") refrained from inviting the Authority to conduct the on-site inspection and thus ending the violation. Ankara 2nd Administrative Court has agreed with the Board's decision, stating:

> The authority to carry out on-site inspections is given to the Board in accordance with Article 15 of Law No. 4054. On-site inspections, by their nature, need to be

[1965] *EMDR 3* (28 January 2021, 21-05/56-23).
[1966] 10th Chamber of the Council of State (27 February 2001, E. 1998/5517, K. 2001/738).
[1967] *Cine 5 interim measure* (13 August 1998, 78/601-111).
[1968] *Cine 5* (11 October 1999, 99-46/500-316).
[1969] *Türk Telekom* (2 October 2002, 02-60/755-305).
[1970] 13th Chamber of the Council of State (1 July 2005, E. 2005/1700, K. 2004/3392).
[1971] *Sodexo* (28 April 2006, 06-31/376-99).
[1972] 13th Chamber of the Council of State (25 September 2007, E. 2006/3356, K. 2007/5248).
[1973] *Mosaş* (21 June 2018, 18-20/356-176).

carried out suddenly, without notice to undertakings, and with no interruptions. From the moment that the case-handlers initiate the on-site inspection and until the necessary information is given, the managers of the undertakings should in no way engage in acts of obfuscation of evidence.[1974]

13.3.7 Final Decision at the end of the Investigation Phase

In its *Mey İçki Non-Fining* decision,[1975] the Board found that (i) Mey İçki holds the dominant position in vodka and gin markets, (ii) Mey İçki has violated Article 6 of Law No. 4054 in the vodka and gin markets, and (iii) as Mey İçki has already received an administrative monetary fine for the consequences of the same strategy in the rakı market,[1976] Mey İçki should not be subject to another administrative monetary fine.

Mey İçki's competitors initiated an action for annulment against the Board's *Mey İçki Non-Fining* decision. These lawsuits were dismissed as the courts found that the no-fining part of the decision was lawful.[1977] However, the 8th Administrative Chamber of the Ankara Regional Administrative Court accepted the appeals of the plaintiff competitors, reversed the judgments of the first instance courts and annulled the Board's Non-Fining Decision,[1978] noting that the vodka and gin markets are distinct from the rakı market and that a violation in the vodka and gin markets should also be sanctioned.

Upon Mey İçki's appeal of the Regional Administrative Court's decision, the Council of State accepted that the principle of *ne bis in idem* should apply and dismissed the Regional Administrative Court's decision. Accordingly, the non-fining part of the Board's *Mey İçki Non-Fining* Decision became valid again.[1979]

13.4 Consequences of an Annulment Decision

The administrative act or decision annulled becomes invalid as of the date it was rendered.[1980] Although the rule is to annul the act in full, if the unlawful part of the decision is severable

---

[1974] Ankara 2nd Administrative Court (17 March 2020, E. 2018/2415, K. 2019/2649).

[1975] *Mey İçki* (25 October 2017, 17-34/537-228), para. 660.

[1976] *Mey İçki Rakı* (16 February 2017, 17-07/84-34).

[1977] Ankara 12th Administrative Court (7 March 2019, E. 2018/1145, K. 2019/475) and Ankara 2nd Administrative Court (27 June 2019, E. 2018/1292, K. 2019/1292).

[1978] Ankara Regional Administrative Court (8th Administrative Chamber) (4 March 2020, E. 2019/2944, K. 2020/424 and 20 February 2020, E. 2019/3384, K. 2020/320).

[1979] 13th Chamber of the Council of State (2 December 2020, E. 2020/1941, K. 2020/3508) and 13th Chamber of the Council of State (2 December 2020, E. 2020/1939, K. 2020/3507).

[1980] Günday (n. 1873), p. 353.

Judicial Review

from the rest of the decision, the administrative act can be partially annulled.[1981] In case of the annulment of the regulatory decision of the Board, the substantive decision rendered based on this regulatory decision will sustain its validity by virtue of the doctrine of acquired rights.

The annulment decision may have different consequences regarding the re-implementation of the act, depending on the reason why the act was annulled. The 10th Chamber of the Council of State stated in its judgment:

> In cases requiring the establishment of a new act by the administration upon annulment decisions, no decision can be taken to eliminate the effect of the definitive judgment. The re-implementation of the administrative act is possible in some cases; in cases of the annulment of the administrative act, which does not comply with the law in terms of jurisdiction, form, reason or which lacks sufficient research, the re-implementation of the administrative act by complying with the law may not be considered unlawful.[1982]

In the *Armatörler Liman İşletmeciliği* decision,[1983] the judgment of the 10th Chamber of the Council of State was reversed on the basis that the administrative act subject to the judicial review should have been made by the Board, instead of the Presidency of the Authority. Administrative acts annulled due to the lack of jurisdiction, unless there is lack of jurisdiction in terms of time, can be reimplemented by the person or body vested with the competent jurisdiction.[1984] Furthermore, the doctrine suggests that if the administrative act is annulled on the grounds of insufficient examination and research, which constitutes an illegality in the form, it may be reimplemented by re-initiating the examination and the research.[1985]

For instance, in *SIEMENS No-Go* decision[1986] Siemed Tıbbi Sistemleri Elektrik Elektronik İletişim Sağlık Hizmetleri Danışmanlık Bilgisayar ve San. Tic. Ltd. Şti. (*"Siemed"*) filed a complaint claiming that Siemens Healthcare Sağlık A.Ş. (*"Siemens"*) abused its dominant position by excluding competitor undertakings, discriminating and acting contrary to the obligations stipulated under *Medical Device Obligations*[1987]. Upon Siemed's complaint, the Board dismissed the claims and did not initiate a fully-fledged investigation.

However, as a result of the appeal of Siemed requesting the annulment of *Siemens* decision, the Ankara 7th Administrative Court decided that the Board's decision on not taking action in relation to Siemed's complaint was based on insufficient examination and research, and therefore the Court annulled the decision.[1988] Upon the annulment, the Board initiated a preliminary investigation which then turned into a fully-fledged investigation to determine whether Siemens violated Article 6 of Law No. 4054. (*Siemens* decision)[1989]

[1981]   R. Çağlayan, "İdari Yargı Kararlarının Değerlendirilmesi ve Uygulanması", İstanbul Üniversitesi Sosyal Bilimler Enstitüsü, İstanbul, 1999, p. 115.
[1982]   10th Chamber of the Council of State (26 April 2004, E. 2001/2004, K. 2004/4070).
[1983]   Plenary Session of the Administrative Law Chambers (28 September 2001, E. 2001/480, K. 2001/637).
[1984]   Bolatoğlu (n. 1873), p. 77.
[1985]   Ibid.
[1986]   *Siemens* (13 November 2016, 16-36/620-M).
[1987]   *Medical Device Obligations* (18 February 2009, 09-07/128-39).
[1988]   Decision of the Ankara 7th Administrative Court (26 December 2018, M. 2017/203, K. 2018/2471).
[1989]   *Siemens III* (19 November 2020, 20-50/695-306).

If the act is annulled for not complying with the law in terms of the purpose, the decision may not be taken based on the same grounds. Indeed, in its precedent, the 12th Chamber of the Council of State has stated that "the administrative act may not be reimplemented on the same grounds, which have been argued during the first action which has been overruled".[1990] Lastly, a decision annulled in terms of the subject can be renewed if it is annulled on the ground that an error was made in determining the subject; however, a decision annulled due to an illegality in the element of purpose may not be renewed.[1991]

[1990]   12th Chamber of the Council of State (13 May 1968, E. 1682, K. 1099).
[1991]   Bolatoğlu (n. 1873), p. 78.

Chapter 14
Private Enforcement

GÖNENÇ GÜRKAYNAK, ESQ., TUĞBA ULUAY,[*]
GÖRKEM YARDIM[**] AND BÜŞRA KIRIŞÇIOĞLU[***]

While breaches of Articles 4, 6 and 7 of Law No. 4054 would result in administrative monetary fines, they could also result in possible compensation claims in the scope of private enforcement in the Turkish law regime. Before delving into the details of compensation based on the violation of Law No. 4054, this section will focus on the legal nature of liability under competition law, types of breaches and their conditions of compensation, including Article 4, 6 and 7 of Law No. 4054, scope of the damage, determination and termination of the damage, including set-off of the damage, treble damages as well as further explanations on the procedural issues including parties to the claim, competent court, time bars and issues on evidence.

14.1 Private Enforcement in General

One of the most distinctive features of the Turkish competition law regime is that, unlike most jurisdictions, it allows private parties to bring lawsuits for treble damages.[1992] Hence, administrative enforcement is also supplemented with private enforcement, which is regulated by Article 57 *et seq.* of Law No. 4054, which entitles damaged parties to request compensation from the undertakings[1993] which have caused the harm, as further discussed below.

14.1.1 Legal Nature of Liability Under Competition Law

Aside from the general provisions stipulated under the Code of Obligations, Law No. 4054 also includes specific articles regarding the compensation of damages arising

---

[*]   Associate, ELIG Gürkaynak Attorneys-at-Law, Istanbul <tugba.uluay@elig.com>.
[**]   Associate, ELIG Gürkaynak Attorneys-at-Law, Istanbul <gorkem.yardim@elig.com>.
[***]   Associate, ELIG Gürkaynak Attorneys-at-Law, Istanbul <busra.kiriscioglu@elig.com>.
[1992] G. Gürkaynak and Ö. İnanılır, in *Global Legal Insights – Cartels: Enforcement, Appeals & Damages Actions* (8th edition, London: Global Legal Group, 2020).
[1993] Gürkaynak (n. 1992).

from Law No. 4054,[1994] going into detail regarding the breaches that require compensation, determination of compensation amounts and the standard of proof sought. As will be further detailed below, the primary reason for lawmakers to include private enforcement within Law No. 4054 in addition to the administrative sanctions is to compensate for the damages of the suffering parties, including competitors, consumers, and other affected entities.[1995] However, this is not the sole reason; private enforcement also aims to create a compensation risk to deter any entities that attempt to breach Law No. 4054. The aim to create a compensation risk is also supported by the regulation of compensation up to three times the damage[1996] (treble damages) discussed under section 14.2.2.3 below.

Accordingly, while the competitive structure of a market can be reconstructed through administrative sanctions, it is necessary to also include private enforcement to compensate the damages of consumers or entities to provide effective competition[1997] and erase any traces of an unlawful act. Articles 56–59 of Law No. 4054 stipulate the consequences (i.e., compensation for or invalidity of) of any agreement, decision or practice contrary to the rules set under Articles 4, 6, and 7 of Law No. 4054. In the scope of these articles, agreements and decisions of undertakings will be deemed invalid, and the parties who suffer from damages will have the right to claim compensation.[1998] The relevant sections of Articles 56 and 57 are provided below, respectively:[1999]

> Article 56 – Any agreements, and decisions of associations of undertakings, contrary to Article 4 of this Act are invalid.[2000]

> Article 57 – Anyone who prevents, distorts or restricts competition via practices, decisions, contracts or agreements contrary to this Act, or abuses his dominant position in a particular market for goods or services, is obliged to compensate for any damages of the injured.[2001]

Thus, breaches of Law No. 4054 will not only result in an administrative monetary fine but also in invalidity and possible compensation claims. In this context, while administrative fines are mandatory for the proper application and deterrence of breach of Law No. 4054, it is accepted that private enforcement in forms of invalidity and compensation is not mandatory for the application of Law No. 4054 and at the discretion of the

---

[1994] K.C. Sanlı, "Rekabetin Korunması Hakkında Kanun'un Özel Hukuk Alanındaki Sonuçları" Sorunlar ve Çözüm Önerileri Sempozyumu, 17.06.2011,İstanbul Bilgi Üniversitesi, p. 16.

[1995] M. Eroğlu, *Rekabet Hukukunda Uygulanan Yaptırımlara İlişkin Tartışmalar* (Istanbul: On İki Levha Yayıncılık, 2019), pp. 137–139.

[1996] C. Akcan, "Rekabeti Kısıtlayıcı Anlaşmalardan Doğan Tazminat Sorumluluğu", Rekabet Kurumu, 2019, p. 8.

[1997] M. Demirci, "Rekabet Hukukunun İhlalinden Doğan Tazminat Sorumluluğunun Hukuki Niteliği" (Master Thesis), Hacettepe Üniversitesi, 2019, p. 1.

[1998] Kesici (n. 778), p. 13.

[1999] The official English version of Law No. 4054 can be accessed through the following link: <https://www.rekabet. gov.tr/en/Sayfa/Legislation/act-no-4054> (last accessed on December 29, 2020).

[2000] For the sake of completeness, because Article 56 does not explicitly refer to Articles 6 and 7 of Law No. 4054, the invalidity only covers any agreements and decisions of associations of undertakings which are contrary to Article 4 of Law No. 4054.

[2001] Although Article 57 of Law No. 4054 does not specifically point out to certain articles, the statements "prevents, distorts or restricts competition via practices, decisions, contracts or agreements contrary to this Act" refers to Article 4 of Law No. 4054 and the statements "or abuses his dominant position in a particular market for goods or services" refers to Article 6 of Law No. 4054.

injured parties.[2002] Thus, while administrative fines are primary sanctions, the invalidity and compensation consequences are considered supplementary sanctions under Law No. 4054, meaning that Law No. 4054 carries a two-fold sanction scheme[2003] to protect both the competitive structure of the market and the individuals. This dualist approach indicates that providing compensation to the damaged party and proper execution of Law No. 4054, through administrative sanctions, are of utmost importance to the lawmaker.[2004]

However, although Article 57 of Law No. 4054 stipulates compensation, it specifies neither the legal nature of the compensation nor the legal basis for the compensation claim. Thus, while certain exceptions regarding compensation for the loss of profit will be further detailed below, the legal nature of this compensation can be defined as tort liability and therefore, the general provisions of the Code of Obligations regarding tort law, which requires an unlawful act, fault, damage, and causal connection, will be applicable.[2005] While this is the case, it is also crucial not to consider the legal nature of the compensation claim strictly under tort liability solely from a theoretical perspective but also consider whether Article 60[2006] of the Code of Obligations should be taken into consideration in cases where there are several sources that may result in compensation claims.[2007]

As elements of tort will be different for each breach under Law No. 4054, it should be explained whether the compensation under Article 57 can be applied for Articles 4, 6, and 7.

14.1.2 Types of Breaches and Conditions under the Law No. 4054 for Compensation

By using the phrase "unlawful act", Article 49 of the Code of Obligations stipulates that compensation under tort law only arises in case of an act in breach of the law. Although the Code of Obligations provides a general explanation as to what comprises an "unlawful act" for the acts that can be subject to compensation claims, Article 57 of Law No. 4054 specifically cites the acts that can raise compensation claims as:[2008]

> Anyone who prevents, distorts or restricts competition via practices, decisions, contracts or agreements contrary to this Act, or abuses his dominant position in a particular market for goods or services, is obliged to compensate for any damages of the injured.

[2002] Sanlı (n. 1994), p. 13.
[2003] Kesici (n. 778), p. 5.
[2004] Ibid., p. 16; T. Yeşil, "Rekabet İhlallerinin Özel Hukuk Sonuçları" (Master Thesis), Ankara Üniversitesi, 2020, p. 48.
[2005] İ. Yiğit, *Rekabet İhlallerinden Doğan Tazminat Sorumluluğu* (Istanbul: Vedat Kitapçılık, 2013), p. 5; Sanlı (n. 1994), p. 17; A. Kaya, *Rekabet Hukukunda Ayrımcılık Suretiyle Hakim Durumun Kötüye Kullanılması* (Istanbul: On İki Levha Yayıncılık, 2018), pp. 339–341.
[2006] Article 60 of the Code of Obligations provides that the judge should choose the basis of liability that provides the best remedy for the damage in cases where liability can be attributed to more than one action/reason.
[2007] Demirci (n. 1997), p. 3; Akcan (n. 1996), pp. 12–13.
[2008] Yiğit (n. 2005), p. 6.

In light of the wording of this article, it is accepted that only Articles 4 and 6 of Law No. 4054 are included within the breaches that can be subject to compensation claims. Thus, in order for a breach to be compensated, it is accepted that the breach should fall within the scope of either Article 4 or Article 6 of Law. No 4054. However, since the wording of Article 57 of Law No. 4054 does not include mergers and acquisitions, the doctrine has conflicting views regarding whether breaches arising from Article 7 can be compensated,[2009] and will be analysed separately below.

14.1.2.1 Compensation for Breaches under Article 4 of the Law. No 4054

As discussed under Chapter 2, Article 4 prohibits all agreements, decisions by associations of undertakings and concerted practices, object or effect of which is prevention, restriction or distortion of competition.[2010] This serves to allow each undertaking in the market to create its own commercial policies and conduct its activities in the market on its own.

Thus, unlawful acts within the meaning of Article 4 should satisfy the following three criteria: (i) there should be two or more entities involved; (ii) there should be concerted practices or agreements between these entities; and finally (iii) these practices or agreements should limit competition, aim to or risk limiting competition.[2011] Only then will such concerted practices of agreements be prohibited by Law No. 4054. However, if such practices stipulated under Article 4 also carry the conditions of the exemption set out under Article 5, such practices will be exempted from the prohibition of Article 4.[2012] Thus, causing damage due to the breach of Article 4 can be considered to be an unlawful act and compensated within the scope of Article 57 of Law No. 4054 provided that they do not fall within the exemptions under Article 5[2013], and they fulfil the criteria of a fault, loss, and causal connection which will be explained below.

14.1.2.2 Compensation of Breaches Under Article 6 of Law No. 4054

As explained under Chapter 6, Article 6 prohibits abusive unilateral conducts of a dominant undertaking, without providing a specific definition for "abuse" but through providing examples of prohibited abusive behaviours.[2014] While Article 6 stipulates the abuse of dominance of one undertaking in principle, in certain cases, this may also include collective dominance. Since the specific wording of the article states "the abuse, by one or more undertakings, of their dominant position",[2015] collective dominance is also included within compensation of breaches under Article 6 of Law No. 4054.

[2009]   Ibid.

[2010]   G. Gürkaynak, E. Uçtu, and O. Özgümüş, "Turkish Antitrust: An overview of Turkish competition law", *e-Competitions* Turkish Antitrust, art. No. 96461. p. 2.

[2011]   Kesici (n. 778), p. 57.

[2012]   Ibid., p. 118.

[2013]   Ibid., p. 57.

[2014]   Gürkaynak et al. (n. 2010), p. 4.

[2015]   Kesici (n. 778), p. 74.

Contrary to Article 4, Article 6 prohibits the actions of entities themselves instead of the relations between different entities. The importance of the breach in this article relies on the basis that the undertaking engaging in such act should be in a dominant position and an action that can be considered as "abuse of dominance" should be present; which can, in some cases, occur even without any action by the relevant undertaking.[2016] However, the crucial point in these types of breaches is that the behaviour should have a detrimental impact on the competition and welfare of the consumer. Thus, in light of the above explanations, two criteria should be met for the application of Article 6: (i) the undertaking should be in a dominant position in the market (defined as an undertaking's power to determine the economic parameters such as price, demand, production and distribution amounts of its competitors independent from the customers in a certain market as per by Article 3), and (ii) the existence of an action that can be considered as abuse of dominant position. Unlike Article 4, there is no exemption stipulated for Article 6. Thus, the Board analyses each defence specific to the particular case individually.

14.1.2.3 Compensation of Breaches Under Article 7 of Law No. 4054

As discussed within Chapter 9, Article 7 regulates the mergers and acquisitions and the requirements for them to be deemed legally valid. Under Article 57, an unlawful act is required for compensation liability. Considering that any merger or acquisition that has not been implemented cannot be considered as an unlawful act and cannot result in any losses, an un-implemented merger or acquisition will not be subject to any compensation request.[2017] Additionally, an implemented merger or acquisition that has also been cleared by the Board will be lawful, and thus compensation claims cannot be directed to these mergers or acquisitions.[2018] Thus, in order for a merger or acquisition to result in losses and be subject to compensation claims, such merger or acquisition should be implemented without any clearance decision related to it,

On the other hand, the doctrine is divided on whether a breach of Article 7 can be considered as an unlawful act and whether compensation can be requested for losses arising from mergers and acquisitions that exceed the turnover threshold and lead to the creation of dominant position have not been filed with the Board. The dominating view is that the possibility for awarding compensation pursuant to Article 7 is very low, and even if it is deemed applicable for some reason, the same compensation can, in any event, be requested through Article 6.[2019] Thus administrative fines should be sufficient for mergers and acquisitions, and no additional compensation

---

[2016] Ibid., pp. 68–69.

[2017] Yeşil (n. 2004), p. 62.

[2018] Yiğit (n. 2005), p. 7.

[2019] A. Kaya (n. 2005), pp. 344–346. While this is the case, certain scholars assert that the purpose of the norm shall be taken into consideration if the Board reevaluates the transaction at a later stage and finds that it is unlawful due to the creation of a dominant position. In this scope, it is believed that the norm does not mean to protect the benefit of private persons but rather focuses on public interest. Thus, it can be stated that the protection of the market with an aim to lower the public costs that would be incurred by a merger and acquisition would be considered as public benefit and is included within the purpose of the norm. Kesici (n. 778), pp. 212–219.

sanction should be awarded since Article 7 does not aim to protect individuals.[2020] Contrary to this view, certain scholars suggest that a breach of Article 7 can raise compensation claims mainly for the reason that the wording of Article 57 includes all types of breaches within Law No. 4054 without naming any particular provisions.[2021] Thus, while there are different views within the doctrine, it is generally accepted that the unlawful acts under tort would be the actions that breach Articles 4 and 6 of Law No. 4054, and so a breach of Article 7 would not result in compensation claims.[2022]

Hence, this section will first delve into explanations on substantive conditions for the claim of damages, including elements of compensations on tort, direct and joint liability, the legal concept of acting without authority within subsection 14.2.1. We will then explain the concept of harm or loss, paying special attention to the classification of losses under Section 14.2.2. Within the same section, we will also provide explanations on the determination of harm, the existence of a fault, and causal connection. Section 14.3 will mainly focus on the procedural issues in the claim of damages, including parties to the claim, competent court, statute of limitations, and issues of evidence. This will be followed by the last section on the contradictions between civil procedure and the Board decisions under the administrative procedure.

14.2 Substantive Conditions for the Claim of Damages

14.2.1 Elements of Compensation

As explained under Chapter 11, the legal nature of the compensation under Law No. 4054 can be defined as tort liability[2023], and the general provisions of the Code of Obligations regarding tort law (which require an unlawful act, fault, loss, and causal connection) will be applicable.[2024]

[2020] Additionally, with the new amendments, which passed through parliament on 16 June 2020 and entered into force on 24 June 2020, the dominance test within Law No. 4054 was replaced with the significant impediment of effective competition (SIEC) test. With this new test, the Authority will be able to prohibit not only transactions that may create a dominant position or strengthen an existing dominant position, but also those that could significantly impede competition. Thus, with the introduction of the SIEC test, it is considered that compensation through Article 7 may have a higher probability, since the SIEC test now introduces "significantly impediment of competition" in addition to dominance; thus, not all infringements of Article 7 will be able to be fit into Article 6.

[2021] Yiğit (n. 2005), p. 8.

[2022] Sanlı (n. 1994), p. 79.

[2023] Ibid., p. 37.

[2024] Yiğit (n. 2005), p. 5; Sanlı (n. 1994), p. 17; Kaya (n. 2005), pp. 339–341.

Similar to the legal systems in Europe, any person or undertaking that seeks compensation for the losses it has incurred due to an infringement of competition law should prove all of the following four elements:[2025]

- Existence of an unlawful act: in antitrust cases, the unlawful act is a breach of competition law in accordance with Article 57, i.e., an action, decision or agreement which is contrary to Law No. 4054;

- Occurrence of a loss caused by a breach of competition law;

- Appropriate causal link between the breach of competition law and the loss suffered as a result of that breach; and

- Fault (intention or negligence) of the infringers in committing the unlawful act.

14.2.2 Occurrence and Scope of the Loss

14.2.2.1 Concept of Loss

The concept of loss constitutes the most crucial parameter of liability, and thus compensation.[2026] An infringement that does not have any harmful effect on third parties may not be subject to a claim for compensation since tort liability requires the existence of loss.[2027] Accordingly, although Article 49 of the Code of Obligations stipulates the occurrence of harm, it does not provide a specific definition for the scope of the losses.[2028] However, the doctrine generally defines loss as the diminishment of a person's assets contrary to their will.[2029]

Accordingly, Article 57(1) of Law No. 4054 stipulates that for compensation claims to arise, competitors and/or third parties should have suffered losses, in addition to the anti-competitive effects of agreements, decisions by associations of undertakings and concerted practices.[2030] Under Article 58(1) of Law No. 4054, the relevant loss is the difference between the price that the injured parties paid and the price that they would have paid if the competition had not been limited, indicating that the actual losses suffered by the plaintiff will be compensated.[2031] The same article sets out that the competitors of the infringing undertaking(s) who were not themselves involved in the competition law violation and who suffered harm due to the competition law violation can claim compensation for "all of their losses" stemming from the violation, that is, actual losses and loss of profit. For instance, decreases in sales volumes and market share, or products that could not be sold because of the competition law infringement can be claimed as "loss

---

[2025] P. Güven, "Rekabet Hukukuna Dayalı Tazminat Davalarının Mahkeme Kararları Işığında Değerlendirilmesi", Rekabet Hukukunda Güncel Gelişmeler Sempozyumu V, Kayseri 2007, p. 213.

[2026] Demirci (n. 1997), p. 36.

[2027] M. Şahin, "Rekabet Hukukunda Tazminat Talepleri, ABD, AB ve Türk Rekabet Hukuklarında", İzmir, 2013, p. 136.

[2028] Kesici (n. 778), p. 155.

[2029] Demirci (n. 1997), p. 36.

[2030] Sanlı (n. 1994), p. 38; Kesici (n. 778), p. 157.

[2031] Kesici (n. 778), p. 167.

of profit", which qualifies as "harm" that is subject to compensation. Thus any harm to the injured party may be subject to a claim for compensation according to Articles 57 and 58 of Law No. 4054.[2032]

Accordingly, types of loss under Turkish legislation can be categorised under (i) actual losses and loss of profit; (ii) direct and indirect losses; (iii) reflective losses; and (iv) pecuniary and non-pecuniary losses. In this scope, according to Article 58(1) of Law No. 4054, pecuniary losses can be compensated, and actual losses and loss of profit are also included in the scope of compensation.[2033] On the other hand, while direct losses can be compensated, indirect losses[2034] can only be compensated if there is a causal link with the unlawful act that caused the direct harm in the first place. Furthermore, it is accepted within the doctrine that Law No. 4054 also includes[2035] reflective losses.[2036] However, although Article 57 of Law No. 4054 states "all losses" and thus includes material/pecuniary losses, it is not clear whether non-pecuniary damages are included as well. There are contradicting views in the doctrine on whether non-pecuniary losses can also be compensated in the scope of Law No. 4054[2037] or whether they should be compensated under general provisions of the Code of Obligations.[2038]

14.2.2.2 Determination of the Damages

For the court to decide on compensation, first, the amount of loss amount should be determined, which is a complex and crucial step due to the diversity of injured parties, the effect of the damage, and the requirement of economic analysis.[2039] In the scope of general provisions under the Code of Obligations, the upper limit for compensation should be equal to the loss amount. While this is the case, the court may also decide to set off losses in cases where the unlawful act also provided certain benefits to the injured party, which is also accepted under Turkish competition law.[2040]

14.2.2.2.1 Calculation of the Loss

Regarding the scope of damage, the first thing that should be established is the occurrence of harm; then, the relevant losses can be calculated.[2041] The method for calculating the losses is set out under Article 58 of Law No. 4054. Accordingly, the damage is the

---

[2032]   Ibid., p. 161.

[2033]   Şahin (n. 2027), pp. 136–140; 170–177.

[2034]   Indirect losses are those losses that are linked to another direct loss.

[2035]   Şahin (n. 2027), p. 174.

[2036]   The term "reflective losses" is defined as losses suffered by parties other than the person directly affected by the damage. It is also important to note that the doctrine includes different views on reflective losses: one group supports the idea that the reflective losses should not be compensated since they do not have an independent nature, they fail to establish a connection with illegality and the lack of causal connection; whereas the second group within the doctrine is of the view that the reflective losses can be compensated if they meet the conditions of compensation. See Kaya (n. 2005), p. 354.

[2037]   Demirci (n. 1997), p. 41; Şahin (n. 2027), pp. 175–176.

[2038]   Kesici (n. 778), p. 188.

[2039]   Ibid., p. 230.

[2040]   Yiğit (n. 2005), p. 247.

[2041]   C. Doğan et al., "Güncel Yargı Tatbikatı Işığında Rekabet Kurulu'nun 12 Banka Kararı Üzerine Açılan Tazminat Davaları Bağlamında Ampirik Bir İnceleme", *Banka ve Ticaret Hukuku Dergisi*, 2018, p. 195.

difference between the cost the injured parties incurred and the cost they would have incurred if the competition had not been limited. The article clarifies that in determining the extent of the damage, all profits expected to be gained by the injured undertakings should be calculated by taking into account the balance sheets of the previous years, as well.[2042] This type of damage suffered by the injured undertakings would be the "loss of profits".

Thus, the court should first determine the price of a product before the competition was restricted to calculate the difference between the cost the injured parties incurred and the cost they would have incurred if the competition had not been limited. This can be conducted through different methods, including (i) comparison of the prices before the limitation of competition to obtain an understanding of the price of the product, had the competition not been limited; (ii) comparison of the prices of the product to similar products in the same sector, or to the ones in similar sectors without competition restrictions; and (iii) comparison of the potential profit of an undertaking in a market where the competition has not been limited, with the potential profit in a market with limited competition.[2043] The judge may follow any one of these calculation methods in line with the case at hand.

Another crucial point within the calculation of losses is that the loss may differ from one breach under Law No. 4054 to another. So to say, in breaches of horizontal price-fixing, the loss consists of the extra payments made by the purchaser undertakings involved to the cartels.[2044] In such a case, first, the prices before the limitation of competition should be estimated and then compared to the price after the limitation of competition.[2045] This would calculate the loss suffered by a purchaser that had overpaid due to a breach. In order to correctly calculate this, the time period between the beginning and end of the breach should be ascertained.[2046] On the other hand, in cases of predatory pricing breaches, first, the price should be estimated if the competition had not been limited, and then the fall in sales revenue of the injured party (i.e., the infringing parties' gains) should be calculated based on this price.[2047] Additionally, in cases of exclusionary breaches, the damage can be calculated by (i) the before and after method, which is the calculation of the plaintiff's business status prior to, during and after the breach, and thus calculation of plaintiff's loss of profit due to the breach; (ii) comparison method which is the comparison made between the plaintiff and another undertaking active in a market with similar market conditions that is not affected by the breach; and (iii) loss of market share method which calculates the loss in the sales of the plaintiff.[2048] Finally, although losses related to the breaches in blocking entry to market cannot be clearly calculated, the views within the doctrine support that if an undertaking can prove that it tried its best to enter the market but could not due to the breach of Law No. 4054, then its losses arising from sunk costs may be subject to compensation claims.[2049]

[2042] Sanlı (n. 1994), p. 125.
[2043] Kesici (n. 778), pp. 230–232.
[2044] Yiğit (n. 2005), pp. 228–241.
[2045] Ibid., p. 177.
[2046] Demirci (n. 1997), p. 230.
[2047] Yiğit (n. 2005), p. 177.
[2048] Akcan (n. 1996), pp. 242, 244.
[2049] Yiğit (n. 2005), p. 178.

14.2.2.2.2 **Establishing the Date of the Damage**

Under Article 117(2) of the Code of Obligations, the losses should be calculated as of the day on which the unlawful act has occurred. In line with this approach, in terms of Law No. 4054, the dominant view within the doctrine is also that the damage should be determined on the day on which the unlawful act has occurred.[2050] However, the doctrine provides exceptions due to the ongoing nature of competition law breaches and deems that in ongoing breaches, the date on which the unlawful act ends should be taken into consideration.[2051] It should also be added that in case the harm incurred comes to an end before the unlawful act is ceased, then the end date of the damage should be considered.[2052] Thus (i) continuity of the competition law breach and (ii) whether the damage of the third party increases or not during the breach affect the date to be used in the calculation of the damage.[2053]

14.2.2.2.3 **Set-off**

The court may decide to set off damages in cases where the unlawful act also provided certain benefits to the damaged party, by subtracting the benefits of an unlawful act from the losses calculated.[2054] The existence of a causal link between benefits and unlawful act is a crucial point for set-off. As explained under Chapter 12, the date of the benefit should be calculated based on the same as the date of damage.

For instance, in competition law breaches concerning vertical restrictions, the quality of the product in terms of supply and presentation may be increased, which leads the consumer to purchase the product at a higher price while obtaining a product with better quality.[2055] Further, in cartels, although the non-party undertakings will face losses in their turnover, they will also gain more profit through the sale of products at higher prices.[2056]

14.2.2.2.4 **Discretion of the Court on the Amount of Losses**

As will be further detailed under Section 14.3.4, pursuant to Article 50(1) of the Code of Obligations, the injured party carries the burden of proof in compensation claims. However, Article 50(2) of the Code of Obligations states that the judge has the discretionary power to determine the amount of loss, if the existence of harm is certain but the amount cannot be exactly quantified. Article 50 of the Code of Obligations is also applied within the discretion on the damage amount under Law No. 4054. Additionally, the judge may also request the guidance of an expert in determining the loss.[2057]

[2050] Kesici (n. 778), p. 251.
[2051] Ibid.
[2052] Ibid.
[2053] Yiğit (n. 2005), p. 245.
[2054] Yeşil (n. 2004), p. 93.
[2055] Ibid., p. 94.
[2056] Ibid.
[2057] Kesici (n. 778), p. 225.

14.2.2.3 Determining the Compensation

14.2.2.3.1 The Amount of Compensation

Under the general provision of the Code of Obligations, the award of damages aims to compensate for the losses of a party, and thus, compensation cannot exceed the amount of loss; however, it is possible for the compensation to be lower than the actual loss.[2058] On the other hand, the compensation stipulated under Law No. 4054 also aims to deter undertakings from any competition law breach, in addition to compensating the damages of a party. Thus, as will be further detailed in the following section, the judge may also rule for treble damages.

Accordingly, pursuant to Article 51 of the Code of Obligations, the judge holds the power for determining both the amount and the method of compensation. The compensation can be paid in two methods: (i) pecuniary compensation and (ii) compensation in kind.[2059] While pecuniary compensation does not carry a specific importance within Law No. 4054, it is considered to be important in case of treble damages since it allows for payment in instalments.[2060] Since treble damages create a significant amount of burden on an undertaking, it is believed within the doctrine that pecuniary compensation provides a certain amount of relief to the injured person/undertaking and, thus, is crucial.[2061] On the other hand, while Article 58 of Law No. 4054 accepts pecuniary compensation, it does not stipulate any restriction on compensation in kind.

14.2.2.3.2 Compensation by Treble Damages

Article 58(2) of Law No. 4054 reads as follows:

> If the damage arises from an agreement or decision or gross negligence of the parties, the judge may, upon the request of the injured, award compensation by three fold of the material damage incurred or of the profits gained or likely to be gained by those who caused the damage.

According to Article 58 of Law No. 4054, the "injured parties" that are entitled to bring claims under Article 57 of Law No. 4054 are also eligible to claim damages of up to threefold of their losses. However, according to the doctrine, while all the injured parties (i.e., purchasers, competitors, or final customers) may claim damages for their pecuniary losses, only competitors should be eligible to claim treble damages based on the profits gained or likely to be gained by the infringers.[2062] However, there are other views that persons and undertakings that are "directly" harmed by the violation may claim treble damages, even if they were not the direct targets of the infringing conduct.[2063] On that note, one cannot rule out the possibility that any person or under-

---

[2058] M. N. Aksoy, *Rekabetin Korunması Hakkındaki Kanuna Aykırılığın Özel Hukuk Alanındaki Sonuçları* (Ankara: Rekabet Kurumu, 2004), p. 247.
[2059] Yiğit (n. 2005), pp. 249-259.
[2060] Ibid., p. 249.
[2061] Ibid.
[2062] O. Sekmen, *Rekabet Hukukunda Tazminat Sorumluluğu* (Ankara: Bilge Yayınevi, 2013), p. 90.
[2063] M. Topçuoğlu, "Rekabet Hukukunda Üç Kat Tazminat", Sorumluk ve Tazminat Hukuku Sempozyumu, 2009, pp. 41-42.

taking who can prove "direct" losses may be eligible for treble damages if they meet the conditions set forth below:

- the damage should be the result of an agreement or decision of the parties, or their act of gross negligence,[2064]

- the damage should be pecuniary (and not moral/non-pecuniary)[2065] since the wording of Article 58(2) only refers to actual pecuniary losses,[2066]

- the injured party should specifically and expressly request treble damages since the judge may not apply under its own discretionary without an explicit request by the injured party.[2067]

In addition to the above, there are certain discussions within the doctrine stating that if the undertakings actively cooperate with the Authority and make leniency application, treble damages should not be ruled for these cooperating undertakings. The doctrine further states that in the compensation lawsuits filed against these cooperating under-takings, there is a need for a regulation that allows the judge (on its own or upon request) to limit the damages to the material losses caused, or the amount of profit obtained or likely to be obtained by those who caused the damage, instead of treble compensation.

In practice, due to treble damages being available to litigants, private antirust compensa-tion cases are increasingly making their presence felt in the cartel enforcement arena.[2068] In the *12 Banks* decision,[2069] the Board had launched an investigation to determine as to whether twelve banks violated Article 4 of Law No. 4054. The Board imposed administrative fines ranging between 0.3% and 1.5% to the investigated undertakings involved. Moreover, the Board ruled that courts shall have absolute discretion to award treble damages in competition law based damage claims.[2070]

In addition to the above, certain objections within the doctrine generally focus on three main points, stating that treble damages (i) do not increase productivity; (ii) may be misused, and (iii) are unfair and lead to extreme deterrence.[2071] One of the views within the doctrine also criticises the lack of adequate discretionary power of the judge in the Turkish competition law in comparison to other jurisdictions (e.g., Germany, Denmark, and Italy). In this scope, while other jurisdictions provide a broader sense of discretionary power to the judges who allow them to hypothetically calculate the damages in cases where it is not possible to specifically calculate the exact amount of damages,[2072] the view criticises that the discretionary power within Turkish

---

[2064] Z. Arı, "Rekabet Hukukunda Üç kat Tazminat", *Rekabet Forumu Dergisi*, Rekabet Derneği, Vol. 26, No. 10, 2006; Yiğit (n. 2005), p. 273.
[2065] Yiğit (n. 2005); S. Sert, "4054 sayılı RKHK Madde 58/2: Üç Kat Tazminat, Doç. Dr. Mehmet Somer'in Anısına Armağan", *Marmara Üniversitesi Hukuk Araştırmaları Dergisi*, Armağan Özel Sayısı, p. 713.
[2066] Yiğit (n. 2005); *supra* n. 2068, p. 713.
[2067] Yeşil (n. 2004), p. 23; Yiğit (n. 2005), p. 274.
[2068] Gürkaynak (n. 1992).
[2069] *12 Banks* (8 March 2013, 13-13/198-100).
[2070] Gürkaynak (n. 1992); Ö. Ş, Kırkbeşoğlu and H. Tokbaş, *Sorularla 12 Bankaya Karşı Üç Kat Tazminat (Kartel Tazminatı) Davası Rehberi* (Istanbul: Aristo Yayınevi, 2017).
[2071] *Supra* n. 2005.
[2072] As in Fondalio Igleelo decision within G. Gürkaynak's opinion stated within Gürkaynak *supra* n. 1992.

competition law is not as broad and tries to stick by the rule of hybrid nature of the compensation, by trying to bring the "compensation up to three times rule, while protecting the profit loss and the potential harm, but determining the loss based on material damage only".[2073] The view concludes that this practice should be abandoned and it should be accepted that one cannot calculate losses exactly to the penny, and there should be a broader room for discretionary power in Turkish competition law to attain realism in law.

14.2.2.4 Existence of an Unlawful Act, Causal Connection and Fault

14.2.2.4.1 Existence of an Unlawful Act

In order for a competition law infringement to be considered in the scope of tort liability, the unlawful act should infringe the norms within Law No. 4054 as also stipulated under Article 57 of Law No. 4054; thus, unlike the frame scope provided within Article 49(1) of Code of Obligations, Law No. 4054 explicitly lists the unlawful acts. Additionally, as also explained below under Section 14.3, the court does not have to wait for the decision of the Board regarding the existence of an infringement, and it is sufficient for the court to conduct its analysis based on Article 49 of the Code of Obligations and Article 57 of Law No. 4054.

On the other hand, in practice, there are precedents of the High Court of Appeals where it is held that in cases of private enforcement, the courts must wait for the finalisation of the Board's decision before rendering a decision on the merits of the case, i.e., competition law violations and related losses.[2074] The High Court of Appeals states that the Board's decision must be handled as a preliminary matter, and so delay the rendering a decision on the merits of the case, rather than a necessary cause of action. However, the decision of the Board will not be sufficient for the existence of unlawful act on its own; thus, in any case, the existence of such unlawful act shall have to be proven through the rules of evidence.

14.2.2.4.2 Existence of Causal Connection

After having established the existence of an infringement of competition law and the existence of damage, the plaintiffs should also prove the causal link between the infringement of competition law and the damage they have suffered.

Under Turkish legislation, a causal connection can be established in two separate ways; first, the "logical link", i.e., the factual causation requiring that the damage should exist and be directly linked to the unlawful act, and second "appropriate link", requiring that the unlawful act should be reasonably foreseeable to cause the said damage within the ordinary course of life.[2075] The appropriate causal link is accepted within Turkish competition law since only accepting logical causal link and keeping the radius of causal

---

[2073]   Sanlı, G. Gürkaynak's opinion stated within *supra* n. 1994.

[2074]   11th Civil Chamber of the High Court of Appeals (5 October 2009, E. 2008/5575, K. 2009/10045); 11th Civil Chamber of the High Court of Appeals (23 June 2006, E. 2005/3755, K. 2006/7408).

[2075]   Sanlı (n. 1994), p. 45.

connection too wide could bring a burden on the infringing parties.[2076] In this manner, the causal connection in Turkish competition law has been defined as "the appropriate link of a damage that can occur within the ordinary course of life".[2077]

14.2.2.4.3 Existence of Fault

Finally, the injured party is required to demonstrate the last condition, i.e., the fault of the undertakings that have committed the unlawful act. Law No. 4054 does not specify whether a fault is necessary for compensation claims under Law No. 4054.[2078] In claims for damages caused by antitrust conducts, except in certain specific cases, when the existence of an infringement of competition law is established, there is no need to demonstrate the existence of the fault separately since the fault is generally included within the definition of this infringement.[2079]

Determining the existence and the degree of the fault is significant for determining the extent of the damages rather than determining the liability.[2080] For instance, to claim treble damages as per Article 58, the plaintiffs should prove that the loss suffered arises from an agreement or decision of the parties, or their gross negligence, i.e., the existence of a high degree of fault. In other words, treble damages require that a high degree of fault exists, in addition to a breach due to the defendants' aim to restrict competition.

As explained under Chapter 3, in 2009, the Board introduced the Leniency Regulation, which provides immunity from or reduction of fines to those undertakings which actively cooperate with the Authority. While the Leniency Regulation is an important tool for the determination of cartels, as discussed below, there are no regulations that address whether compensation can be claimed from the undertakings that cooperative with the Authority within the scope of Leniency Regulation.[2081]

14.3 Procedural Issues in the Claim of Damages

14.3.1 Parties to the Claim

14.3.1.1 Defendants

The action for compensation claims can be brought against undertakings, association of undertakings or members who implement the decision of the association of undertakings that are parties to the alleged agreement and/or concerted action acting contrary

---

[2076]   Yiğit (n. 2005), p. 285.
[2077]   Ibid., p. 286.
[2078]   Yeşil (n. 2004), p. 85; Eroğlu (n. 1995), p. 43.
[2079]   Sanlı (n. 1994), pp. 43–44.
[2080]   Ibid., p. 43.
[2081]   Gürkaynak (n. 1992), p. 57.

to Article 4 of Law No. 4054. Furthermore, it is also possible to address damages claims to undertaking(s) abusing their (sole or joint) dominant positions contrary to Article 6 of Law No. 4054. Finally, it is also possible to initiate an action against the parties that consummate the economic concentration prohibited under Article 7 of Law No. 4054.[2082]

One issue with respect to identifying potential defendants is whether a lawsuit can be filed against undertakings or associations of undertakings that indirectly benefit from the violation, although they are not directly involved in it.[2083] If the undertakings are not parties to the act or agreement that violates the competition law rules, it is not possible to file a lawsuit against those who have indirect benefits from the violation.[2084] Regarding this issue, the example generally cited is the price increase by undertakings that are not a party to the cartel, which consequently results in customers paying higher fees to their products and/or services. To that end, it does not seem possible for such customers to file compensation claims against undertakings that are not parties to the cartel.

14.3.1.2 Plaintiffs

According to Article 57 of Law No. 4054, anyone who prevents, distorts or restricts competition via practices, decisions, contracts or agreements contrary to this Act, or abuses his dominant position in a particular market for goods or services, is obliged to compensate the injured for any losses. In this context, the plaintiff can be expressed as the person or persons who claim to have suffered damage due to the violation of competition law rules. Based on Article 57 of Law No. 4054, it can be interpreted that Law No. 4054 does not impose any restriction on the scope of being a plaintiff; thus, it would be prudent to state that it is possible for consumers, existing or potential competitors and other undertakings (distributors, wholesalers and retailers) to file a compensation lawsuit.

In the doctrine, one of the most important questions concerning the issue of plaintiff is whether the undertakings that are party to the collusive relationship can file a lawsuit against each other due to the violation, where they can be evaluated as plaintiffs.[2085] In this context, it is possible for two competing undertakings to violate competition horizontally or to create a violation through vertical agreements.

Considering horizontal violations, the provisions of Law No. 6098 can be applicable since there is no regulation provided under Law No. 4054.[2086] In this context, from the perspective of the code of obligations, it should not be assumed that an undertaking that knows the terms of the agreement in advance and is a party to the agreement can, in principle, file a claim for compensation with the claim to benefit from its own unlawful

---

[2082]   For the sake of completeness and clarity, as elaborated under Section 14.1.2.3 above, it is accepted that the breach of Article 7 will not result in compensation claims.

[2083]   Kesici (n. 778), p. 487.

[2084]   K.C. Sanlı, "Türk Rekabet Hukukunda Haksız Fiil Sorumluluğu", Rekabet Hukukunda Güncel Gelişmeler Sempozyumu I, 2003, Kayseri: Erciyes Üniversitesi, pp. 211-277.

[2085]   Kesici (n. 778), p. 457.

[2086]   Doğan (n. 2041).

behaviour.[2087] It is also evaluated that cartel members cannot file a lawsuit against each other since they are outside the scope of the protection of Law No. 4054.[2088]

With respect to vertical agreements, it can be stated that an undertaking that is seen as the weaker side of the contract might be coerced to accept the terms due to fear of being alienated from the market.[2089] Thus, it would be prudent to state that a strict argument against such undertakings filing an action for damages would be inherently unfair. As a matter of fact, with respect to vertical agreements, there are High Court of Appeals decisions stating that the contracting party who suffered losses could file claims for compensation.[2090] For this reason, if one party imposes the terms of the contract on the other party, which becomes a party to the contract in order to maintain its economic existence, it can be argued that the injured person has no consent and may file a lawsuit for compensation.

Furthermore, it is considered that consumers (meaning, the end-users) are included in the group directly harmed by the restriction of competition.[2091] Indeed, it is argued that limiting the protective goal of the provisions giving rise to the liability under Law No. 4054 only to competitor undertakings may lead to a too narrow interpretation of Law No. 4054.[2092] In this context, although Law No. 4054 does not clearly describe who can be a plaintiff, the doctrine view accepts that consumers and other customers can be plaintiffs.

Generally, the effects of restricting competition are felt by competing undertakings and potential competitors. There is no doubt that there is a right of action to compensate for the damages of competing undertakings that have been harmed by the restriction of competition. This is because restriction of competition makes it difficult for competing undertakings to continue their activities and may potentially result in diminishing their market sales/services.[2093] As a matter of fact, Article 58 of Law No. 4054 provides that "competing undertakings affected by the limitation of competition may request that all of their damages are compensated by the undertaking or undertakings which limited competition. In determining the damage, all profits expected to be gained by the injured undertakings are calculated by taking into account the balance sheets of the previous years as well".

Lastly, it is one of the most controversial issues in compensation liability as to which party will have legal standing as plaintiff in the compensation case in the event that competitors and customers transfer damages ultimately to consumers.[2094] For instance,

---

2087 Kesici (n. 778), p. 459.
2088 Ibid. at 459.
2089 Kesici (n. 778), p. 460.
2090 19th Civil Chamber of the High Court of Appeals (21 April 2005, E. 2004/9634, K. 2005/4463); 13th Civil Chamber of the High Court of Appeals (25 December 2002, E. 2002/12626, K. 2002/14028).
2091 O. B. Gürzumar, "Özel Hukuk Açısından 4054 Sayılı Rekabetin Korunması Hakkında Kanun, 4054 Sayılı Rekabetin Korunması Hakkında Kanun ve Bu Kanun'da Değişiklik Yapılmasına İlişkin Taslak", Sempozsum, Bildiriler-Tartışmalar-Panel, 7-8 Ekim 2005, Banka ve Ticaret Hukuku Araştırma Enstitüsü (Editör: Cavid Abdullahzade).
2092 Kesici (n. 778), p. 462.
2093 Ibid. at 464.
2094 Ibid.

certain scholars contend that the competitors' right to file a lawsuit is clearly stated in the relevant article that there is a possibility of harm to persons other than undertakings and the role of plaintiff is open to everyone under Article 57 of Law No. 4054.[2095] In the same vein, it is also argued that although consumers are not explicitly mentioned in the first sentence of Article 58 of Law No. 4054, the prudent approach would be that consumers are implicitly intended to be included in the relevant provision.[2096]

However, in the doctrine, it is also contended that the consumer's damage is never borne by the buyer.[2097] To that end, it could not be considered as reflected damage, and it cannot be stated that these damages are in a proper causal link with the infringing act. However, even if subsequent buyers suffer, it is impossible to determine the extent of this damage because a product reaches the consumer through multiple stages in the supply chain. In this context, it is impossible to determine how much of the loss is borne by the (initial/direct) buyer and how much by the other subsequent buyers. In addition, in the event that the consumers, who are essentially ndirect buyers, have the right to file a lawsuit, a large number of lawsuits is likely to be initiated.

On the other hand, in the EU practice, Article 13 of Directive 2014/104 stipulates that the right to compensation is recognised for any natural or legal person–consumers, undertakings and public authorities alike–irrespective of the existence of a direct contractual relationship with the infringing undertaking, and regardless of whether or not there has been a prior finding of an infringement by a competition authority.

14.3.2 Competent Court

In the light of Articles 20 and 27 of Law No. 4054, the Authority is exclusively authorised to enforce administrative sanctions in case of violation of competition law.[2098] On the other hand, the competent court empowered to deal with claims for compensation arising from the violation of the material prohibitive provisions of Law No. 4054, as well as other claims such as prevention, suspension and requests for invalid transactions, are the civil courts.[2099]

Looking at the relevant provisions of Law No. 4054 with respect to consequences of compensation claims (i.e., Articles 57–59), it is observed that Law No. 4054 does not specifically determine a competent court.

Under Law No. 6100, the civil procedure has divided the duties between the civil courts of first instance and the civil courts of peace in the lawsuits, regardless of the claim amount or the value of the case.[2100] Accordingly, under Article 2(2) of Law No. 6100,

---

[2095] *12 Banks* (n. 2069).
[2096] Z. Arı, *Rekabet Hukukunda Danışıklık Kavramı ve Hukuki Sonuçlar* (Ankara: Seçkin, 2004).
[2097] Sanlı (n. 2084).
[2098] Kesici (n. 778), p. 420.
[2099] Güven (n. 2025), p. 232.
[2100] Kesici (n. 778), p. 422.

the court with general duty is the civil courts of first instance in the cases regarding property rights and personal assets.[2101] In this context, in line with Article 2(2) of Law No. 6100, considering the fact that the compensation arising from the violation of competition law is related to the property rights of the owner, the relevant court will be the civil court of first instance.

On the other hand, according to the subject matter of the case and the legal status of the plaintiff, the dispute subject to compensation can also fall under the jurisdiction of civil courts (e.g., commercial).[2102] Commercial cases are divided into absolute (objective) commercial cases and subjective commercial cases. In absolute commercial cases, it does not matter whether the parties are merchants or whether the entity in question is a commercial business; they fall under the jurisdiction of commercial courts.[2103] The compensation lawsuits to be filed due to violation of competition have not been listed among the absolute commercial cases under the Commercial Code, and there is no explicit regulation under Law No. 4054 on commercial lawsuits.[2104]

Furthermore, it is of utmost importance to underline that in the tort that arises as a result of the violation of competition, it may be the competitors or consumers who suffer damage. Since the concept of undertaking under Law No. 4054 includes commercial enterprises and real persons, it may not always be possible to consider who suffered loss as a commercial enterprise. In such a case, if, for example, a loss has been incurred due to the violation of competition, although the parties may refer to a damage caused to their commercial businesses through agreements, there may exist a tort that is not related to the commercial business of consumers.[2105] In such a scenario, compensation lawsuits arising from competition law will not be considered as commercial cases; however, if the tort affected the commercial business of each of the parties, it will be considered to be a commercial case.[2106] Thus, the competent court in case of non-commercial disputes will be the civil court of first instance under Law No. 6100; and if it is accepted as commercial, then the commercial court of first instance will have jurisdiction.

Lastly, if there are specialised courts, the choice of court to file for damages can change depending on the subject matter, considering that the High Court of Appeals rendered that the specialised Istanbul Maritime Court had jurisdiction in a case where it was alleged that a cartel was formed in relation to maritime transport and thus suffered from an infringement of competition.[2107]

In cases of compensation arising from a violation of competition, the jurisdiction is determined according to the relevant provisions of Law No. 6100. Accordingly, under Article 16 of Law No. 6100, for actions arising from tort, the court in the jurisdiction where the tortious act was committed or where the act occurred or will likely to show

---

[2101]   Kesici (n. 778)
[2102]   T. Koyuncu, *Rekabet Hukukunda Tazminat Davalarının Etkinliği Perspektifinden Toplu Dava Modelleri* (Ankara: Rekabet Kurumu, 2012).
[2103]   Güven (n. 2025), p. 233.
[2104]   Ibid.
[2105]   Doğan (n. 2041).
[2106]   Kesici (n. 778), p. 423.
[2107]   11th Civil Chamber of the Court of Appeals (10 October 2007, E. 2006/9834, K. 2007/12673).

its effect, or the court at the domicile of the aggrieved person shall have jurisdiction. In this context, it would be prudent to state that if the violation of competition affected entire Turkey, lawsuits could be filed wherever the harmful effect was experienced.

Furthermore, according to Article 17 of Law No. 6100, merchants or public legal entities may also mutually determine which court(s) shall have jurisdiction in case of an existing or future dispute under a contract. Unless the parties provide otherwise, these courts specified in their agreement shall have exclusive jurisdiction.

According to Article 57 of Law No. 4054, if the damage occurred due to the acts of more than one person, they shall be jointly responsible for the damage. Therefore, if the violation is committed by more than one undertaking, the competent court must be determined accordingly.[2108] As a rule of procedural law under Article 7(1) of Law No. 6100, if there are multiple defendants, it is possible to initiate the case in any of the courts where they reside. However, the exception is when the law specifies a court with joint authority for all the defendants, according to the subject matter of the case. In cases where there is more than one plaintiff, the case should be filed at the court where the tort was committed, which is the joint jurisdiction.[2109,2110]

Last, if there is a foreign element, the competent court will be determined according to the provisions of Law No. 5718. Accordingly, Article 40 of Law No. 5718 indicates that the international jurisdiction of the Turkish courts is determined by the rules of domestic law.[2111] Unlike insurance, consumer and employment contracts, no special jurisdiction rule has been adopted for violations of competition law. Therefore, as indicated above, where the plaintiff or the defendant is a foreign entity or person, the competent court would be determined in accordance with the provisions of Law No. 6100.

14.3.3 Statute of Limitations (Time Bars)

The statute of limitations can be defined as follows:[2112] "The debtor or the creditor loses the opportunity to recover their receivable by way of court litigation and execution proceeding because the debtor or the creditor fails to fulfil the actions stipulated by the law within the time period prescribed." That said, there are no specific periods of limitations under the scope of Law No. 4054 with respect to compensation cases to be filed.

To that end, it would be prudent to apply Article 72 of the Code of Obligations which refers to limitation periods for claims under tort. The relevant provision is as follows:

> A claim for compensation becomes time-barred two years from the date on which the injured person becomes aware of the damage and of the identity of the person

---

[2108] Güven (n. 2025), p. 235.
[2109] Yeşil (n. 2004).
[2110] An exception to this rule is that the application of the joint jurisdiction rule is subject to all defendants being sued for the same claim in the case.
[2111] Güven (n. 2025), p. 236.
[2112] M. Erdem, *Özel Hukukta Zamanaşımı* (Istanbul: On İki Levha Yayıncılık, 2010).

liable for it, but in any event ten years after the date on which the act was committed. However, if the action for damages is derived from an offence for which a longer limitation period is envisaged under criminal law, the longer period applies. Where the tort has given rise to a claim against the injured person, he may always refuse to satisfy the claim even if his own claim in tort is time-barred.

As seen above, Article 72 of the Code of Obligations sets out three different limitation periods for torts, two cumulative and one alternative, namely: (i) two years from the date the injured party becomes aware of the damage and of the identity of the infringers/tortfeasors (i.e., subjective limitation period); and (ii) ten years starting from the date of the infringement (i.e., objective limitation period); or (iii) if the violating act in question constitutes a crime in the context criminal law and the laws provide a longer limitation period for that crime, then that longer period. For the sake of completeness, prosecution of offences of a criminal nature (such as bid-rigging and price manipulation) is subject to criminal statutes of limitations, which may vary depending on the severity of the sentence to be imposed.

The limitation periods of two years and ten years provided under Article 72 are cumulative. This means that if the two-year time period has expired after the injured party became aware of the damage and the identity of the infringer, the objective limitation period of ten years can no longer be relied upon, and an injured party can no longer file a compensation suit. Furthermore, the two-year period is deemed to start from the date when the injured party becomes aware of both the damage and of the identity of the tortfeasors.[2113]

As regards the question of which specific moment should be considered as the moment when "the injured party becomes aware of the damage and of the identity of the infringers", certain decisions note that becoming aware of the damage refers to becoming aware of the full extent and amount of the damage, and therefore the date when the plaintiff could be aware of such information is the date when the expert witness report on the subject is received.

Furthermore, there are certain decisions wherein courts of first instance rejected the argument that the date when the decision of the Board is published on the official website of the Authority, should be deemed as the date when the injured party becomes aware of the damage. In the said decisions, the courts relied on the statements of the plaintiffs concerning the date when they had become aware of the damages and deemed these dates declared by the plaintiffs as the dates they had become aware of the damage.[2114]

Based on the wording of Article 72 of the Code of Obligations, the ten-year limitation period starts from the date on which the act that is subject to the claim takes place. The moment at which the damage occurs is not decisive, according to the majority of scholars who are assertive on the principle that the ten-year limitation period should start from the moment the infringement occurs and not at the moment of the occurrence of harm.

[2113] Marmaris 1st Civil Court of First Instance (14 November 2017, E. 2017/17, K. 2017/494).
[2114] Istanbul 12th Consumer Court, decision dated 23 May 2017, File No. 2016/23, Judgement No. 2017/184, and decision dated 23 May 2017, File No. 2016/979, Judgement No. 2017/191.

This is also in line with the case law of the High Court of Appeals, which considers the objective limitation period as starting from the date of infringement in question.[2115]

However, according to Article 20/4 of Law No. 5326, the statute of limitations is considered as "eight" years, contrary to Article 72 of the Code of Obligations. Article 20/4 of Law No. 5326 sets forth that the eight-year limitation period should start from the date on which the unlawful act (misdemeanour) has been committed, or its consequences have occurred.

There are precedents where the courts decided that the eight-year limitation period stipulated under Law No. 5326 must be applied for claims based on infringement of competition law.[2116] In these precedents, the court concluded that because competition law violations are sanctions as per Law No. 5326, which makes the violation a misdemeanour, the period of limitations (i.e., eight years) stipulated under Law No. 5326 should apply; and these must also be considered as offences in the context of criminal law. Accordingly, the court asserted that further to the Code of Obligations, the longer period of limitation provided under Law No. 5326 (i.e., eight years) shall apply for competition law violations as well, not the two-year period provided under Article 72 of the Code of Obligations.

14.3.4 Issues on Evidence

In competition law, there is generally a significant asymmetry of information regarding the violation, between the plaintiffs and defendants in compensation cases.[2117]

One of the important problems in compensating the losses incurred as a result of competition law infringements is the issue of proof of connection/association. In this respect, similar to the presumption of concerted action under Article 4, Law No. 4054 has provided under Article 59 certain rules regarding the evidencing of concerted actions in a way that helps the plaintiffs to overcome the difficulty of the burden of proof, as follows:[2118]

> Should the injured submit to judicial bodies proofs such as, particularly, the actual allocation of markets, stability observed in the market price for quite a long time, price increases within close intervals by undertakings operating in the market, which give the impression of the existence of an agreement, or the distortion of

---

[2115] 10th Civil Chamber of Court of Appeals, File No. 2003/835, Judgment No. 2003/1628, dated 6 March 2003; 3rd Civil Chamber of Court of Appeals, File No. 2009/17737, Judgment No. 2009/18986, dated 23 November 2009; 4th Civil Chamber of Court of Appeals, File No. 2016/3818, Judgment No. 2016/6946, dated 25 May 2016.

[2116] İstanbul 16th Commercial Court of First Instance, File No. 2017/976, decision No. 2019/211, dated 15 March 2019; Istanbul 16th Commercial Court of First Instance, File No. 2017/91, decision No. 2019/845, dated 4 October 2019; Batman Civil Court of First Instance (acting as the Consumer Court), File No. 2016/463, Judgment No. 2017/147, dated: 21 February 2017; 11th Civil Chamber of Court of Appeals, File No. 2014/13296, Judgment No. 2015/4424, dated 30 March 2015; File No. 2015/15, Judgement No. 2015/5128, dated 13 April 2015.

[2117] Güven (n. 2025), p. 250.

[2118] Ibid.

Private Enforcement

competition in the market, then the burden of proof is on the defendants that the undertakings are not engaged in concerted practice.

The existence of agreements, decisions and practices limiting competition may be proven by any kind of evidence.

In addition, the violation decision of the Board and the evidence within such decision are not the only legal instruments for establishing the proof, considering that Article 192 of Law No. 6100 indicates the following: "In cases where the law does not require proof with specific evidence, other pieces of evidence not regulated in the law may be used."

In light of the above, the evidence that can be used in the compensation claims can be both conclusive and discretionary evidence.[2119] Conclusive evidence refers to evidence where the terms, conditions and consequences are defined by law, and which (if submitted) the judge is bound to take into account without exercising judicial discretion. Conclusive evidence consists of definitive judgments (*res judicata*), deed (i.e., documentary proof) and oath.[2120]

To that end, the issue that needs to be addressed within the scope of conclusive evidence is *res judicata*. Res judicata is regulated under Article 303 of Law No. 6100 and states that in order for a court verdict to constitute direct evidence in another case, the parties, the subject and the grounds of the case must be the same.

We will also explain the rules surrounding evidence and the matter of the burden of proof under the Code of Civil Procedure for the lawsuits filed for compensation of damages arising from anti-competitive acts, by discussing the evidentiary value of the Board decisions if a plaintiff relies on this decision in its claim. As will be explained in more detail in Section 14.4, the verdicts rendered by the administrative courts and the Council of State in judicial reviews of the Board decisions do not constitute definitive judgments in the context of the compensation cases.[2121]

The category of evidence that the judge has the discretion to assess freely and does not bind the judge as in conclusive evidence is considered discretionary evidence. To that end, the important point to be mentioned with respect to discretionary evidence is that according to Article 293(1) of Law No. 6100, an expert opinion can constitute discretionary evidence.

The duty of the parties to submit the materials their case relies on is a basic principle in Turkish procedural law. In this context, it is up to the parties to put forward the facts that will justify their claim and to gather and present the relevant evidence to the court. The principle is also applicable in compensation claims arising from infringement of competition law.

Furthermore, Article 219 of Law No. 6100 reads as follows:

The parties are obliged to submit to the court all the documents that they or the other party rely on as evidence and are in their possession. Electronic documents,

[2119] Kesici (n. 778), p. 496.
[2120] Ibid., p. 497
[2121] Ibid., p. 499.

on the other hand, are printed and recorded in an electronic environment suitable for examination when requested and submitted to the court.

In this framework, the relevant article stipulates that both parties have to submit the documents they have in their control to the court file. On the other hand, failure of the parties to submit documents is stipulated in Article 220 of Law No. 6100. Accordingly, if the document summoned for submission is essential to prove the alleged matter, and the court has concluded this request to be lawful; if the other party admits that this document is in its possession, or it is concluded with an official record that the document exists or it has been confirmed in another document, the court grants a definite time for the submission of this document. In such a scenario, if the relevant party denies that the document summoned is in its possession, the court offers an oath to him, declaring that such a document is not in its possession, that it cannot find it despite diligent its search, and that it does not know where it is.

Furthermore, Article 220(3) of Law No. 6100 stipulates that if the party that was decided to submit the document failed to do it in the given time and does not give an acceptable excuse and evidence why it failed to do so, or denies that the document is in its possession and does not accept or execute the proposed oath, the court shall, in that case, accept the statements of the other party unilaterally.

14.4 Conflicts between Civil and Administrative Procedures regarding Competition Law Matters

With regard to the implementation of civil law sanctions and examining the decision of the Board, the Council of State is the authorised appellant court in Turkey. On the other hand, the High Court of Appeals is the appellant court in compensation cases arising from competition law. In this case, if a compensation lawsuit is filed for the same infringement and an investigation is carried out by the Board at the same time, the issue may be simultaneously brought before the courts and evaluated by the Board, and decisions can be rendered separately.[2122] Therefore, it is possible to have two different decisions as a result of applying to both the Board and the civil courts.

For instance, if those who are harmed by the abuse of a dominant position file a lawsuit in the civil courts demanding compensation for the damage, the court will first have to determine whether there is a dominant position, then whether the dominant position has been abused, and ultimately to decide whether it has resulted in any loss. When the same claim is brought before the Board, the Board will be able to apply the administrative sanctions specified in Law No. 4054 by determining whether a dominant position exists and whether it has been abused. To that end, for instance, when the Board decides that there is no abuse of the dominant position and therefore there is no need to impose an

---

[2122] Ibid., p. 215

administrative monetary fine, but the courts decide on compensation, then two different decisions will emerge.[2123]

When the doctrine is assessed with respect to such issue, İnan indicates that since the Board is an administrative body and not a judicial one, the courts will not be bound by the decision of the Board, and even after the Board's decision has been examined and finalised by the Council of State, the courts are not bound by this decision.[2124] As a matter of fact, İnan argues that if there is a finalised decision of the High Court of Appeals and the Council of State at the same time, a judgement conflict will not arise because the subject matter, parties and the purpose of the lawsuit are different.[2125]

In the same vein, there are others that defend that since the Board's decision does not refer to the existence or the extent of any alleged damage, it cannot be stated that the injured party will become aware of its damage via the Board's decision.[2126] Undertakings that have suffered losses resulting from an unlawful act may discover the identity of the infringers, regardless of the existence of the Board's decision.[2127] Therefore, it would be disproportionate to declare that a decision from the Board is necessary in each instance to establish the existence of the damage and the identity of the infringers.

On the other hand, some argue that the existence of a violation of competition law is a prerequisite for compensation claims. On that basis, determining whether agreements between undertakings or practices are violating the competition law rules is a complicated analysis, which is very difficult, even impossible, to be carried on by private persons. Therefore, such an analysis should be done by specialised authorities such as the Board, which has the competence to verify and define the conformity of the arrangements with competition law. As a consequence, according to this approach, if a court of first instance were to accept a claim for compensation without awaiting the decision of the Board related to the infringements that have caused the alleged damage, it is very likely that the High Court of Appeals will reverse the decision of the court of first instance.

Despite the lack of a legal requirement for the existence of the Board's decision, the High Court of Appeals has well-established case law according to which the civil judges should stay their analysis on compensation claims arising from competition infringements until the Board has rendered its decision on the contested infringements. To illustrate, the 11th Civil Chamber of the High Court of Appeals upheld the decision of the court of first instance[2128] and stated that the plaintiff should apply before the Competition Board before filing for a compensation claim. The court recognised that such an application before the Board is a necessary cause of action for compensation claims, as follows:[2129]

> The Court dismissed the ... actions on the grounds that the cause of action has not been satisfied and the period for initiating a lawsuit before the court has not

---

[2123]   Ibid, p. 216
[2124]   N. İnan, "4054 Sayılı Rekabetin Korunması Hakkında Kanun'un Özel Hukuka İlişkin Hükümlerine Eleştirisel Bir Bakış", Rekabet Hukukunda Güncel Gelişmeler Sempozyumu II, 2004, Kayseri, Rekabet Kurumu Yayını.
[2125]   Ibid at p. 63
[2126]   İ. Yiğit, Rekabet İhlallerinden Doğan Tazminat Sorumluluğu (İstanbul: Vedat Kitapçılık, 2013), p. 330.
[2127]   Ibid. at 331
[2128]   İzmir 2nd Commercial Court of First Instance, decision No. 2007/112, dated 16 March 2007, File No. 2006/726.
[2129]   11th Civil Chamber of the High Court of Appeals (5 October 2009, E. 2008/5575, K. 2009/10045).

started since the plaintiff applied before the Competition Board as regards the subject matter of this file on January 19, 2007, and had not applied to the relevant authority prior to initiating the lawsuit.

Previously, the 11th Civil Chamber of the High Court of Appeals recalled in its decision[2130] that the Authority is the competent authority for determining whether a behaviour constitutes a breach of competition law and stated that:

> Articles 57 and 58 of Law No. 4054 regulate requests for compensation following the finding of a restriction of competition; and the courts are deemed competent for such compensation requests. In order to decide on a compensation claim, it should be determined whether the relevant action or agreement is contrary to Law No. 4054. The Authority is the body primarily competent for such an examination and the Council of State is the competent court for reviewing the Board's decisions. On that basis, the sitting court should investigate whether the plaintiff has first introduced an application before the Authority and if it is the case, pronounce its judgment after the outcome of this application alleging that the defendant's actions are violating the provisions of Law No. 4054. If the plaintiff has not introduced an action before the Authority, the claim at hand cannot be heard without having first applied to the Authority and thus ... it rendered its judgment while the time to bring an action has not yet started. Therefore, the decision of the Court of first instance is reversed in favour of the defendant.

There are other precedents of the High Court of Appeals where it is held that the courts must wait for the finalisation of the Board's decision before rendering a decision on the merits of the case, i.e., competition law violations and damages connected to these violations. The High Court of Appeals states that the Board's decision must be handled as a preliminary matter that must be waited before rendering a decision on the merits of the case rather than a necessary cause of action.

For instance, the 11th Civil Circuit of the High Court of Appeals has annulled the decision of the Court of First Instance, which had dismissed the case on the grounds that the Board's decision was not final.[2131] The High Court of Appeals stated that the court should have heard the case on the merits and considered and evaluated the Board's decision as a preliminary issue. Accordingly, the Court of First Instance should have waited for the outcome of the appeal of the Board's decision and that it should have rendered its decision pursuant to the outcome of the appeal process.

In the same vein, the 19th Civil Chamber of the High Court of Appeals had annulled the decision of the Court of First Instance[2132] given that the action on damages, which was based on the abuse of dominant position allegation, had been rendered without considering whether there was an application filed before the Authority, and concluded that the application before the Authority should have been considered as a preliminary issue.

[2130] 11th Civil Chamber of the High Court of Appeals (23 June 2006, E. 2005/3755, K. 2006/7408).
[2131] 11th Civil Chamber of the High Court of Appeals (8 March 2016, E. 2015/5134, K. 2016/2543).
[2132] 19th Civil Chamber of the High Court of Appeals (1 November 1999, E. 99/3350, K. 99/6364).

There are many other similar cases where the High Court of Appeals emphasised the principles stated above.[2133] However, it is worth noting that there are some isolated instances where a different approach has been followed:

For instance, in one of the decisions of the 19th Civil Chamber of the High Court of Appeals,[2134] the Court considered a dispute regarding the execution of a vertical sales agreement between two undertakings. Izmir Court of First Instance accepted the claim of the plaintiff, who argued that the defendant behaved in violation of the sales agreement by selling competitors' products.[2135] Upon the appeal of this decision by the defendant and its annulment by the High Court of Appeals, the file was sent again before the Court of First Instance. Consequently, in its second decision, the Court of First Instance stated that although the Board's decision had not been finalised yet, it would not have any effect on this lawsuit which could be judged without awaiting the end of the appeal process against the Board's decision.[2136] This finding has been confirmed by the decision of the High Court of Appeals[2137] and again by the re-appeal chamber of the High Court of Appeals following an application of re-appeal on the 9 October 2007, decision.[2138]

Furthermore, in another decision,[2139] a compensation claim has been lodged by the plaintiff on the grounds that the defendant had terminated the authorised dealer and authorised service agreements. The Court of First Instance accepted the plaintiff's claim and decided that certain provisions of the aforementioned agreements were contrary to Article 4 of Law No. 4054. However, as to the compensation claim resulting from the damage related to the infringements at stake, the Court of First Instance rejected the claim on the ground that the plaintiff failed to show concrete evidence for the losses it claimed to have incurred due to the violation of competition law principles—namely, the prohibition of price-fixing, discrimination and preventing the sales of competitors' products.[2140]

High Court of Appeals reversed the Court of First Instance's decision on the ground that it failed to order an expert report in order to examine the plaintiff's claim on the basis of its balance sheets for the previous years, its commercial books and records, as well as the defendant's arguments on these allegations.

[2133] Please see 19th Civil Chamber of the High Court of Appeals decision No. 1999/6364, dated 1 November 1999, File No. 3350, where the High Court of Appeals decided that the Board should render a decision on the abusive conduct in order for a court to decide on compensation and the court should wait for the decision of the Board as a preliminary matter. Please see for the same approach, 19th Civil Chamber of the High Court of Appeals, decision No. 2006/10346, dated 6 November 2006, File No. 2006/2809, and 19th Civil Chamber of the High Court of Appeals, decision No. 2007/10677, dated 29 November 2007, File No. 2008/3229.

[2134] 19th Civil Chamber of the High Court of Appeals decision No. 2007/8775, dated 9 October 2007, File No. 2007/5290.

[2135] İzmir 4th Commercial Court of First Instance decision No. 2004/905 dated 2 December 2004, File No. 2004/466.

[2136] İzmir 4th Commercial Court of First Instance decision No. 2007/155 dated 12 April 2007, File No. 2006/507.

[2137] 19th Civil Chamber of the High Court of Appeals decision No. 2007/8775 dated 9 October 2008, File No. 2007/5290.

[2138] 19th Civil Chamber of the High Court of Appeals decision No. 2008/2858 dated 24 March 2008, File No. 2008/27.

[2139] 19th Civil Chamber of the High Court of Appeals decision No. 2008/731 dated 4 February 2008, File No. 2007/7136

[2140] Kadıköy 3. Commercial Court of First Instance, decision No. 2006/266, dated 4 April 2006, File No. 2002/793.

In light of these isolated decisions,[2141] it could be argued that a decision from the Authority is not always a precondition for bringing a claim for compensation. Then again, it is possible to conclude that the current practice adopted by the High Court of Appeals is to wait for the finalisation of the Board's decisions before deciding on the merits of the cases brought for compensation claims.

[2141] Please also see 19th Civil Chamber of the High Court of Appeals, decision No. 2002/7580, dated 29 November 2001, File No. 2002/2827. In this decision, the High Court of Appeals annulled the decision of the Court of First Instance and stated that it is not required to await the administrative action filed due to the violation of Law No. 4054 before deciding on the court file. However, the dissenting opinion in this decision argues that the Board should decide that there is a violation of Law No. 4054 in order for the civil court to decide on compensation pursuant to Article 58 of Law No. 4054. According to the dissenting opinion, in order to eliminate contradictory decisions, the civil courts await until the Board finalise its decision on the alleged violation.

BIBLIOGRAPHY

Books and Theses

Adıyaman, H., *Rekabet Hukukunda Fiyat Parite Anlaşmaları: En Çok Kayrılan Ülke/Müşteri Koşulu*, Ankara: Rekabet Kurumu Uzmanlık Tezleri Serisi No.150, 2017.

Akcan, C., "Rekabeti Kısıtlayıcı Anlaşmalardan Doğan Tazminat Sorumluluğu", Ankara: Rekabet Kurumu, 2019.

Aksoy, M. N., *Rekabetin Korunması Hakkındaki Kanuna Aykırılığın Özel Hukuk Alanındaki Sonuçları*, Ankara: Rekabet Kurumu Uzmanlık Tezleri Serisi No.144, 2004.

Akyılmaz, B., *İdari Usul İlkeleri Işığında İdari İşlemin Yapılış Usulü*, Ankara: Yetkin Yayınları, 2000.

Arı, B., *Karşılaştırmalı Hukukta Rekabet İhlallerine Verilen Cezalar*, Ankara: Rekabet Kurumu Uzmanlık Tezleri Serisi No.344, 2020.

Arı, Z., *Rekabet Hukukunda Danışıklık Kavramı ve Hukuki Sonuçlar*, Ankara: Seçkin, 2004.

Aşçıoğlu Öz, G., *Avrupa Topluluğu ve Türk Rekabet Hukukunda Hakim Durumun Kötüye Kullanılması*, (Abuse of Dominance in Turkish Competition Law and European Community), Ankara: Rekabet Kurumu Tez Serisi, No. 880, 2000.

Ayber, M., *Markaiçi ve Markalararası Rekabetin Dengelenmesi Gereken Hallerde Rekabet Otoritelerinin Yaklaşımı*, Ankara: Rekabet Kurumu Uzmanlık Tezleri Serisi No.128, 2003.

Aygün, E., *Rekabet Hukukunda Para Cezaları: Teori ve Uygulama*, Ankara: Rekabet Kurumu Uzmanlık Tezleri Serisi No. 220, 2008.

Kocabaş, B., *İndirim Sistemleri ve Rekabet: Tek taraflı Davranışlar Açısından Bir Değerlendirme*, Ankara: Rekabet Kurumu Uzmanlık Tezleri Serisi No. 224, 2009.

Bain, J. S., *Barriers to New Competition: Their Character and Consequences in Manufacturing Industries*, Cambridge, MA: Harvard University Press, 1956.

Bayramoğlu, S. N., *Rekabet Hukukunda Fikri Mülkiyet Haklarının Toplu Yönetimi: Patent Havuzları ve Standart Belirleme*, Ankara: Rekabet Kurumu Uzmanlık Tezleri Serisi No. 287, 2012.

Bellamy, C., and G. D. Child, *European Community Law of Competition*, Peter Roth QC, ed., 5th edition, London: Sweet & Maxwell, 2001.

Bolatoğlu, H., *Rekabet Kurumu Kararlarının Yargısal Denetimi*, Ankara: Rekabet Kurumu Uzmanlık Tezleri Serisi No.163, 2004.

Çağlayan, R., "İdari Yargı Kararlarının Değerlendirilmesi ve Uygulanması", İstanbul Üniversitesi Sosyal Bilimler Enstitüsü, 1999.

Can, O., "4054 Sayılı Rekabet Kanunu'na Göre Rekabeti Sınırlandıran Anlaşmalar Ve Uygulamada Sıkça Rastlanan Anlaşma Örnekleri", Kırıkkale Üniversitesi, 2004.

Çatalcalı, O. T., *Kartel Teorisi İhracat Kartelleri ve Kriz Kartelleri*, Ankara: Rekabet Kurumu Uzmanlık Tezleri Serisi, 2007.

Çeçen, H., *Avrupa Birliği ve Türk Rekabet Hukukunda Hakim Durumun Fiyat Uygulamaları ile Kötüye Kullanılması*, Istanbul: Legal, 2018.

Bibliography

Çetinkaya, M., *İlgili Pazar Kavramı ve İlgili Pazar Tanımında Kullanılan Nicel Teknikler*, Ankara: Rekabet Kurumu Uzmanlık Tezleri Serisi No. 86, 2005.

Charbit, N., and S. Ahmad (eds.), *Frédéric Jenny Liber Amicorum: Standing Up for Convergence and Relevance in Antitrust*, Vol. I, New York: Concurrences, 2019.

Cornish W. and D. Llewlyn, *Intellectual Property: Patents, Copyrights, Trademarks and Allied Rights*, cited with (5th edition, London: Sweet&Maxwell, 2003).

Deliktaş, E., "Monopol Piyasası ve Fiyat Farklılaştırması-Erzurum Büyükşehir Belediyesi Su Fiyatlaması Üzerine Bir Uygulama", T.C. Yükseköğretim Kurulu Dökümantasyon Merkezi, Doktora Tezi, Erzurum, 1997.

Demirci, M., "Rekabet Hukukunun İhlalinden Doğan Tazminat Sorumluluğunun Hukuki Niteliği", (Master Thesis) Hacettepe Üniversitesi, 2019.

Eğerci, A., *Rekabet Kurulu Kararlarının Hukuki Niteliği ve Yargısal Denetimi*, Ankara: Rekabet Kurumu, 2005.

Ekdi, B., *Gümrük Birliği Çerçevesinde Damping ve Yıkıcı Fiyat Uygulamaları*, Ankara: Rekabet Kurumu Uzmanlık Tezleri Serisi No. 89, 2003.

Ekdi, B., *Hakim Durumda Bulunan Teşebbüslerin Dikey Anlaşmalar Yoluyla Piyasayı Kapatması*, Ankara, 2003.

Erdem, M., *Özel Hukukta Zamanaşımı*, Istanbul: On İki Levha Yayıncılık, 2010.

Erkut, C., *İptal Davasının Konusunu Oluşturma Bakımından İdari İşlemin Kimliği*, Ankara: Danıştay Yayınları No. 51, 1990.

Eroğlu, M., *Rekabet Hukukunda Uygulanan Yaptırımlara İlişkin Tartışmalar*, Istanbul: On İki Levha Yayıncılık, 2019.

Fisher, F. M., J. J. McGowan and J. E. Greenwood, *Folded, Spindled, and Mutilated: Economic Analysis and U.S. v. I.B.M.*, Cambridge: MIT Press, 1983.

Gönen, K. E., *Rekabet Hukukunda İdari Para Cezaları,* Ankara : Seçkin Yayıncılık, 2003

Görgülü, Ü., *Hakim Durumun Kötüye Kullanılması Kapsamında Fiyat Ayrımcılığı Uygulamaları*, Ankara: Rekabet Kurumu Uzmanlık Tezleri Serisi No. 118, 2003.

Gözler, K. and G. Kaplan, *İdare Hukukuna Giriş*, Bursa: Ekin Yayıncılık, 2017.

Gözler, K., *İdare Hukuku (Administrative Law)*, Bursa: Ekin Kitap Evi, 2019.

Gözlükaya, F., *Teknoloji Transferi Sözleşmelerine İlişkin Rekabet Hukuku Uygulaması*, Ankara: Rekabet Kurumu Uzmanlık Tezleri Serisi, 2007.

Gözübüyük, A. Ş., *Yönetsel Yargı*, Gözden Geçirilmiş, 9th edition, Ankara: Turhan Kitabevi, 1993.

Gözübüyük, Ş., and T. Tan, *İdare Hukuku Cilt: 1 Genel Esaslar*, Ankara: Turhan Kitabevi, 2001.

Günday, M., *İdare Hukuku*, Ankara: İmaj Yayıncılık, 1998.

Gürkaynak, G., *Türk Rekabet Hukuku Uygulaması için "Hukuk Ve İktisat" Perspektifinden "Amaç" Tartışması,* Ankara: Rekabet Kurumu, 2003

Gürkaynak, G., in *The Cartels and Leniency Review*, C. A. Varney, ed., 2d edition, London: Law Business Research, 2014, Chapter 30 (Turkey).

Gürkaynak, G., *The Academic Gift Book of ELIG Attorneys-at-Law in Honor of the 20th Anniversary of Competition Law Practice in Turkey*, Istanbul: Legal Yayıncılık A.Ş., 2018.

Gürkaynak, G., B. Aktüre and D. Benli, "What Standard of Competition Law Review to Ensure Healthy Competition for Talent?" *The Academic Gift Book of ELIG Attorneys-at-Law in Honor of the 20th Anniversary of Competition Law Practice in Turkey*, Istanbul: Legal Yayıncılık A.Ş., 2018.

Bibliography

Gürkaynak, G., M. Bakırcı and S. Mutafoğlu, "Excessive Pricing Enforcement in Dynamic Sectors: Should You Stop Reading Now?" *The Academic Gift Book of ELIG Attorneys-at-Law in Honor of the 20th Anniversary of Competition Law Practice in Turkey*, Istanbul: Legal Yayıncılık A.Ş., 2018.

Gürkaynak, G., E. Ergul and S. Buğrahan Köroğlu, "Gun-Jumping through Pre-Closing Information Exchanges in M&A Transactions and Alternative Safeguard Mechanisms", *The Second Academic Gift Book of ELIG Gürkaynak Attorneys-at-Law on Selected Contemporary Competition Law Matters*, Istanbul: Legal Publishing Inc., 2019 pp. 141-184.

Gürkaynak, G., A. Kağan Uçar and Z. Buharalı, "Data-Related Abuses in Competition Law", in *Frédéric Jenny Liber Amicorum: Standing Up for Convergence and Relevance in Antitrust*, Vol. I, N. Charbit and S. Ahmad, eds., New York: Concurrences, 2019.

Gürkaynak, G., and K. Yıldırım, in *Cartel Regulation 2021*, Lexology Getting the Deal Through in association with Dechert LLP, London: Law Business Research Ltd, 2020.

Gürkaynak, G., and Ö. İnanılır, in *Global Legal Insights – Cartels: Enforcement, Appeals & Damages Actions*, 8th edition, London: Global Legal Group, 2020.

Gürkaynak, G., and Ö. İnanılır, in *Global Legal Insights – Cartels: Enforcement, Appeals & Damages Actions*, 9th edition, London: Global Legal Group, 2021.

Gürzumar, O. B., *Franchise Sözleşmeleri ve Bu Sözleşmelerin Temelini Oluşturan Sistemlerin Hukuken Korunması*, Istanbul: Beta Yayımları, 1995.

Gürzumar, O. B., *Zorunlu Unsur Doktrinine Dayalı Sözleşme Yapma Yükümlülüğü*, Ankara: Seçkin Yayıncılık, 2006

Güzel, O., *Rekabet Hukukunda Teşebbüs ve Teşebbüs Birlikleri*, Ankara: Rekabet Kurumu, 2003.

Hovenkamp, H., M. D. Janis and M. A. Lemley, *IP and Antitrust: An Analysis of Antitrust Principles Applied to Intellectual Property Law*, New York: Aspen Law & Business, 2005.

Hovenkamp, H., *The Antitrust Enterprise: Principle and Execution*, Cambridge: Harvard University Press, 2005.

Ivaldi, M., B. Jullien, P. Rey, P. Seabright, and J. Tirole, "The Economics of Tacit Collusion: Implications for Merger Control", in *The Political Economy of Antitrust*, V. Ghosal and J. Stennek, (eds.), Bingley: Emerald Group Publishing Limited, 2007.

Jones A. and B. Sufrin, EU Competition Law: Text, Cases and Materials, 5th edition, Oxford University Press, 2014; P. Roth QC and V. Rose (eds.), Bellamy & Child: European Community Law of Competition, 6th edition, Oxford University Press, 2009.

Kadıoğlu, A., "İdari İşlemin Şekil Unsuru", T. C. Selçuk Üniversitesi Sosyal Bilimler Enstitüsü Kamu Hukuku Anabilim Dalı Yüksek Lisans Tezi, 2010.

Kalabalık, H., *Introduction to Administrative Procedure Law*, 2014.

Karabel, G., *Rekabet Hukukunda Ne Bis In Idem İlkesi*, Ankara: Rekabet Kurumu Uzmanlık Tezleri Serisi No. 316, 2015.

Karauz, A. K., *Akaryakıt Bayilik Sözleşmesi*, Doctoral Thesis, Ankara: Yetkin Yayınevi, 2015.

Karavelioğlu, C., *İdari Yargılama Usulü Kanunu*, Trabzon:Top-Kar Matbaacılık, 1997.

Kaya, A., *Rekabet Hukukunda Ayrımcılık Suretiyle Hakim Durumun Kötüye Kullanılması*, Istanbul: On İki Levha Yayıncılık, 2018.

Kaya, Ş. D., *Fiyat Sıkıştırması Ekonomik ve Hukuki Açıdan Bir Değerlendirme*, Ankara: Rekabet Kurumu Uzmanlık Tezleri Serisi No. 221, 2009.

Kesici, B., *Rekabet Hukukunun İhlalinden Kaynaklanan Haksız Fiil Sorumluluğu*, Istanbul: On İki Levha Yayıncılık, 2017.

Bibliography

Khemani, R. S. (ed.), *A Framework for the Design and Implementation of Competition Law and Policy*, Washington, DC, World Bank Publications, 1999 <http://www.oecd.org/daf/competition/prosecutionandlawenforcement/27123114.pdf>

Kırkbeşoğlu, Ö. Ş., and H. Tokbaş, *Sorularla 12 Bankaya Karşı Üç Kat Tazminat (Kartel Tazminatı) Davası Rehberi*, Istanbul: Aristo Yayınevi, 2017.

Kocadağ, N., *Rekabet Hukuku Kapsamında Ana Şirketin Yavru Şirket İhlallerinden Doğan Sorumluluğu*, Ankara: Rekabet Kurumu Uzmanlık Tezleri Serisi No. 312, 2015.

Köksal, E., and B. Ikiler, "Dünyada ve Türkiye'de Platformlara Yönelik Güncel Rekabet Politikaları: *ABD'de Amex, Türkiye'de Sahibinden ve AB'de Google Shopping Kararları*, in *Uygulamalı Rekabet Hukuku Seminerleri*", K. C. Sanlı and D. Alma (eds.), Istanbul, On İki Levha, 2019.

Koyuncu, T., *Rekabet Hukukunda Tazminat Davalarının Etkinliği Perspektifinden Toplu Dava Modelleri*, Ankara: Rekabet Kurumu Uzmanlık Tezleri Serisi No. 293, 2012.

Lianos I., V. Korah, and P. Siciliani, *Competition Law Analysis, Cases, & Materials*, Oxford: Oxford University Press, 2019

O'Donoghue, R., and A. J. Padilla, *The Law and Economics of Article 82 EC*, Oxford: Hart Publishing, 2006.

O'Donoghue, R., and A. J. Padilla, *The Law and Economics of Article 102 TFEU*, 2nd edition Oxford: Hart Publishing, 2013.

O'Donoghue, R., and A. J. Padilla, *The Law and Economics of Article 102 TFEU*, 3rd edition, Oxford: Hart Publishing, 2020.

Öztürk, E., *Türk İdare Sisteminde Rekabet Kurumunun Yeri ve Diğer Bağımsız İdari Otoritelerle Karşılaştırılması*, Ankara: Rekabet Kurumu Uzmanlık Tezleri Serisi No. 124, 2003.

Petrovcic, U., *Competition Law and Standard Essential Patents: A Transatlantic Perspective*, Alphen aan den Rijn: Wolters Kluwer Law & Business, 2014.

Porter, M., *Competitive Strategy*, New York: Free Press, 1980.

Sağlam, N., *Rekabet Hukuku Uygulamasında Tekerrür*, Ankara: Rekabet Kurumu Uzmanlık Tezleri Serisi No. 320, 2015.

Şahin, A. H., "Türk Rekabet Hukukunda Birleşme ve Devralmalarda (Yoğunlaşmalarda) Yan Sınırlamalar", Yüksek Lisans Tezi, 2010.

Şahin, E., "Avrupa Birliği Adalet Divanı'nın AKKA/LAA Kararı Kapsamında Aşırı Fiyatlama Analizi ve Türk Hukuku Bakımından Çıkarımlar", in *Uygulamalı Rekabet Hukuku Seminerleri*, K. C. Sanlı and D. Alma, eds., Istanbul: On İki Levha, 2019.

Sanlı, K. C., *Rekabetin Korunması Hakkındaki Kanun'da Öngörülen Yasaklayıcı Hükümler ve Bu Hükümlere Aykırı Sözleşme ve Teşebbüs Birliği Kararlarının Geçersizliği*, Ankara: Rekabet Kurumu, 2000.

Sanlı, K. C., and S. Ardiyok, "The Legal Structure of Competition Policy in Turkey", in *The Political Economy of Regulation in Turkey*, T. Çetin and F. Oğuz, eds., New York: Springer, 2011, Chapter 5 <http://repository.bilkent.edu.tr/bitstream/handle/11693/38351/The_Legal_Structure_of_Competition_Policy.pdf,%20jsessionid=F92DB772727FE4D7FE30B367D1799D09?sequence=1>

Sekmen, O., *Rekabet Hukukunda Tazminat Sorumluluğu*, Ankara: Bilge Yayınevi, 2013.

Şengören, Z., *Motorlu Taşıtlar Sektöründeki Dikey Anlaşmaların Düzenlenmesinde Yeni Dönem: AB Uygulamaları Işığında Türkiye İçin Yol Haritası*, Ankara: Rekabet Kurumu Uzmanlık Tezleri Serisi No. 291, 2012.

Stigler, G. J., *The Organization of Industry*, Chicago: University of Chicago Press, 1968.

Sümer Özdemir, N., *Rekabete Aykırı Dışlayıcı Uygulamaların Tespitinde Etki Temelli Yaklaşım ve Etki Standartları*, Ankara: Rekabet Kurumu Uzmanlık Tezleri Serisi No. 321, 2015.

Bibliography

Tokgöz, M., *Münhasır Dikey Anlaşmaların 4054 sayılı Kanun'un 4. veya 6. Maddesi Kapsamında Değerlendirilmesi Sorunu*, Ankara: Rekabet Kurumu Uzmanlık Tezleri Serisi No. 326, 2017.

Topçuoğlu, M., *Rekabeti Kısıtlayan Teşebbüsler Arası İşbirliği Davranışları ve Hukuki Sonuçları*, Ankara: Rekabet Kurumu, 2001

Toprak, D., *Avrupa Birliği Uygulamaları Işığında Türk Rekabet Hukukunda Pişmanlık Programının Değerlendirilmesi*, Ankara: Rekabet Kurumu Uzmanlık Tezleri Serisi No. 359, 2020.

Ünal, Ç., *Aşırı Fiyat Kavramı ve Aşırı Fiyatlama Davranışının Rekabet Hukukundaki Yeri*, Ankara: Rekabet Kurumu Uzmanlık Tezleri Serisi No. 254, 2009.

Uzun, A. Ö., *Stratejik İşbirliklerine Genel Bakış*, Ankara: Rekabet Kurumu Uzmanlık Tezleri Serisi, 2007.

Whish, R., and B. E. Sufrin, *Competition Law*, 3rd edition, London: Butterworths, 1993.

Whish, R., and D. Bailey, *Competition Law*, 7th edition, Oxford University Press, 2012.

Whish, R., and D. Bailey, *Competition Law*, 8th edition, Oxford University Press, 2015.

Yanık, M., *Rekabet Hukukunun Hakim Durum ve Hakim Durumun Kötüye Kullanılması Uygulamalarında Piyasa Giriş Engelleri*, Ankara: Rekabet Kurumu Uzmanlık Tezleri Serisi No. 101, 2003.

Yeşil, T., "Rekabet İhlallerinin Özel Hukuk Sonuçları" (Master Thesis), Ankara Üniversitesi, 2020.

Yiğit, İ., *Rekabet İhlallerinden Doğan Tazminat Sorumluluğu*, Istanbul: Vedat Kitapçılık, 2013.

Yılmaz, B., *Rekabet Hukukunda Dengeleyici Alıcı Gücü*, Ankara: Rekabet Kurumu Uzmanlık Tezleri Serisi No. 355, 2020.

Yüksek, C., *Seçici Dağıtım Sisteminde İnternetten Satış Sınırlamaları*, Ankara: Rekabet Kurumu Uzmanlık Tezleri Serisi No. 330, 2017.

Articles and Research Papers

Abbott, A. F., and J. D. Wright, "Antitrust Analysis of Tying Arrangements and Exclusive Dealing", *George Mason University Law and Economics Research Paper Series* No. 8-37, 2008.

Arı, Z. "Rekabet Hukukunda Üç Kat Tazminat", *Rekabet Forumu Dergisi*, Rekabet Derneği, Vol. 26, No. 10, 2006.

Arıöz, A., and Ö. C. Özbek, "Hakim Durumun Kötüye Kullanılmasının Sonucu Olarak Zorunlu Lisanslama: Değerlendirme Kriterleri ve Uygulanan Standartlar", *Rekabet Dergisi*, Vol. 11, No. 3, July 2010, pp. 11–49.

Beggs, A., and P. Klemperer, "Multi-Period Competition With Switching Costs", *Econometrica*, Vol. 60, No. 3, 1992, pp. 651–666.

Botta, M., and K. Wiedemann, "Exploitative Conducts in Digital Markets: Time for a Discussion after the Facebook Decision", *Journal of European Competition Law & Practice*, Vol. 10, Issue 8, 2019, pp. 465–478.

Buiten, M. C., "Exploitative Abuses in Digital Markets: Between Competition Law and Data Protection Law", *Journal of Antitrust Enforcement*, 2020.

Calkins, S., "The New Merger Guidelines and the Herfindahl-Hirschman Index", *California Law Review*, Vol. 71, 1983, pp. 402–429.

Caves R. E., and M. E. Porter, "From Entry Barriers to Mobility Barriers: Conjectural Decisions and Contrived Deterrence to New Competition", *The Quarterly Journal of Economics*, Vol. 91, No. 2, 1977, pp. 241–261.

Bibliography

Cengiz, D., "Assessment of the Presumption of Concerted Practices and the Applications of the Competition Board Regarding Such Presumption", *Rekabet Dergisi*, Vol. 35, 2008.

Chin, A., "Antitrust by Chance: A Unified Theory of Horizontal Merger Doctrine", *Yale Law Journal*, Vol. 106, 1997, pp. 1165–1195.

Dennis, A. Y., and S. S. Desanti, Game Theory of Industrial Organization, 247, 1988 (as cited in N. Petit, "The Oligopoly Problem in EU Competition Law" (2012).

Doğan, C. et al., "Güncel Yargı Tatbikatı Işığında Rekabet Kurulu'nun 12 Banka Kararı Üzerine Açılan Tazminat Davaları Bağlamında Ampirik Bir İnceleme," *Banka ve Ticaret Hukuku Dergisi*, 2018.

Erdem, J. G., "Ölçülülük İlkesinin Kullanımının İdarenin Takdir Yetkisinin Kullanımındaki Yeri", *Ankara University School of Law Magazine*, Vol. 62, No. 4, 2013, pp. 984–992.

Ezrachi, A., and D. Gilo, "Are Excessive Prices Really Self-Correcting?" *Journal of Competition Law & Economics*, Vol. 5, Issue 2, June 2009, pp. 249–268.

Farrell, J., and C. Shapiro, "Dynamic Competition With Switching Costs", *RAND Journal of Economics*, Vol. 19, No. 1, Spring 1988, pp. 123–137.

Gal, M. S., and N. Elkin-Koren, "Algorithmic Consumers", *Harvard Journal of Law & Technology*, Vol. 30, No. 2, 2017, pp. 309–353.

Garrod, L., and M. Olczak, "Explicit vs tacit collusion: The effects of firm numbers and symmetries", *International Journal of Industrial Organization*, Vol. 56, Issue C, 2018, pp. 1–25.

Geradin, D., and N. Petit, "Price Discrimination under EC Competition Law: The Need for a case-by-case Approach", *The Global Competition Law Centre Working Papers Series* No. 07/05, 2005.

Gözübüyük, Ş., "Amerika ve Türkiye'de İdarenin Kaza Denetlenmesi", Ankara: Üniversitesi Siyasal Bilgiler Fakültesi Yayınları, 1961.

Gürkaynak, G., et al., "A Discussion on Proof Matters in Turkish Competition Law Focusing on Proof of Concerted Practices", *Rekabet Dergisi*, Vol. 12, No. 4, October 2011, pp. 75–125.

Gürkaynak, G., "Hâkim Durumun Kötüye Kullanılmasının Özel Görünüm Şekli Olarak Aşırı Fiyatlama", *Çimento İşveren Dergisi*, Vol. 26, No. 6, 2012, pp. 37–42.

Gürkaynak, G., and K. Yıldırım, "Türk Rekabet Hukukunda Ayrımcı Uygulamaların Niteliğine ve Tabi Oldukları Hükümlere İlişkin Bir Değerlendirme", *Rekabet Forumu*, Issue 33, 2007, pp. 2–7.

Gürkaynak, G. et al., "Naked Application of the Presumption of Concerted Practices in Turkish Law: *Baker's Yeast* Decision", Symposium on Board and Judiciary Decisions Regarding Competition Law, 15–16 October 2010.

Gürkaynak, G., and A. G. Yaşar, "Re-assessing Object Restrictions: A New Day in Light of the "Groupement des cartes bancaires v Commission' Decision", *Rekabet Dergisi*, Vol. 16, No. 1, January 2015, pp. 41–103.

Gürkaynak G., and Ö. İnanılır, "Recent competition law developments in Turkey: the administrative court's stay of execution decision regarding behavioural remedies", The In-House Lawyer, Summer 2019.

Gürkaynak, G., "The Turkish Competition Authority publishes a decision regarding an agreement granting access to infrastructure and support services between two telecom companies (*Vodafone / Superonline*)", *e-Competitions* August 2018, art. No. 88979 <https://www.concurrences.com/en/bulletin/news-issues/august-2018/the-turkish-competition-board-publishes-a-decision-regarding-an-agreement> (last accessed 30 June 2021).

Gürkaynak, G., and B. Can, "GCR Know-How: Information Exchange 2020", *Global Competition Review*, 2020.

Gürkaynak, G., E. Uçtu, and O. Özgümüş, "Turkish Antitrust: An overview of Turkish competition law", October 2020, *e-Competitions* Turkish Antitrust, art. No. 96461.

Bibliography

Gürkaynak, G., and K. Yıldırım, "Digital Technology 2021", Law Business Research 2020.

Gürkaynak, G., and B. Yüksel, Practical Law Cartel Leniency Global Guide, "Cartel Leniency in Turkey", Thomson Reuters, 2020.

Gürkaynak, G., B. Yüksel, C. Yıldırım, and Z. Ayata Aydoğan, "The Factors Affecting the Use of Essential Facilities Doctrine in Light of the Lithuanian Railway v Commission Decision: A Comparison with the Turkish Practice and Potential Implications", available at <https://www.gurkaynak.av.tr/docs/baf8f-the-factors-affecting-the-use-of-essential-facilities-doctrine-in-light-....pdf>.

Harrington, J. E., "A Theory of Tacit Collusion", *Working Paper* No. 588, The Johns Hopkins University, Department of Economics, 2012, pp. 2–3.

Ince, E., "Gizli Anlaşma: İktisadi Temelleri ve Rekabeti Kısıtlayıcı Anlaşmalar Rejimi İçin Çıkarımlar", *Rekabet Dergisi*, Vol. 20, Issue 2, December 2019, pp. 4–70.

Kadar, K., "Article 102 TFEU and Efficiency Pleas: A 'Fact-Check'" (26 August 2020), SSRN <https://ssrn.com/abstract=3681299> (The original version of this article was published in *Richard Whish QC (Hon) Liber Amicorum: Taking Competition Law Outside the Box*, N. Charbit and S. Ahmad, eds., New York, Concurrences, 2020).

Kalabalık, H., "İdarenin Takdir Yetkisinin Sınırları ve Yargısal Denetimi", *Gazi Üniversitesi Hukuk Fakültesi Dergisi*, Vol. 1, Issue 1, 1997, pp. 172–211.

Karakılıç, H., "Avrupa Birliği Rekabet Hukukunda Hakim Durumda Olmayan Teşebbüslerin Tek Yanlı Uygulamaları", *Rekabet Dergisi*, Vol. 14, No. 4, October 2013, pp. 3–48.

Koç, E., "4054 Sayılı Rekabetin Korunması Hakkında Kanun'da Düzenlenen İdari Para Cezaları İçin Öngörülen İdari Usul", *TBB Dergisi*, No. 98, 2012, pp. 231–282 <http://tbbdergisi.barobirlik.org.tr/m2012-98-1127>.

Kokkoris, I., "Buyer Power Assessment in Competition Law: A Boon or a Menace?" *World Competition* Vol. 29, No. 1, 2006.

Kovacic, W. E., R. C. Marshal, L. M. Marx and H. L. White, "Plus Factors and Agreements in Antitrust Law", *Michigan Law Review*, Vol. 110, Issue 3, 2011, pp. 393–439.

Krattenmaker, T. G., R. H. Land, and S. C. Salop, "Monopoly Power and Market Power in Antitrust Law", available at Justice.gov <https://www.justice.gov/atr/monopoly-power-and-market-power-antitrust-law> (last accessed 15 June 2021).

Kyprianides, G. P., "Should Resale Price Maintenance Be Per Se İllegal?" *European Competition Law Review*. Vol. 33, No. 8, 2012, pp. 376–385.

Mano, M. (de la), and B. Durand, "A Three-Step Structured Rule of Reason to Assess Predation under Article 82", *European Commission Office of the Chief Economist Discussion Paper*, December 2005 <https://ec.europa.eu/dgs/competition/economist/pred_art82.pdf>.

Müftüoğlu, M. T., "Rekabet Kanunu ve İki Yıllık Uygulaması," *Rekabet Kurumu, Rekabet Dergisi*, No. 1, 2000.

Oğurlu, Y., "A Comparative Study on The Principle of Proportionality in Turkish Administrative Law", *Kamu Hukuku Arşivi (KHukA)*, İlhan Akın'a Armağan, 2003.

Osborne, D. K., "Cartel Problems", *American Economic Review*, Vol. 66, No. 5, 1976, pp. 835–838.

Panzar, J., and R. D. Willig, "Sustainability Analysis: Economies of Scope", *The American Economic Review*, Vol. 71, No. 2, 1981, pp. 268–272.

Posner, R. A., and W. S. Landes, "Market Power in Antitrust Cases", *Harvard Law Review*, Vol. 94, No. 5, 1981, pp. 937–996.

Salinger, M. A., "The Meaning of 'Upstream' and 'Downstream' and the Implications for Modeling Vertical Mergers", *The Journal of Industrial Economics*, Vol. 37, No. 4, 1989, pp. 373–387.

Sanlı, K. C., "Rekabetin Korunması Hakkında Kanun'da Değişiklik Yapılmasına Dair Kanun Tasarısı Taslağı'nın Özel Hukuk Alanında Getirdiği Değişikliklerinin Değerlendirilmesi," *Rekabet Kurumu, Rekabet Dergisi*, No. 30, 2008.

Sanlı, K. C., "Rekabet Kurumunun Ceza Yönetmeliği Taslağı: Hukuk ve Ekonomi Perspektifinden Bir Değerlendirme", *Rekabet Dergisi*, Vol. 15, No. 1, January 2014, pp. 65–109.

Sert, S., "4054 sayılı RKHK Madde 58/2: Üç Kat Tazminat, Doç. Dr. Mehmet Somer'in Anısına Armağan", *Marmara Üniversitesi Hukuk Araştırmaları Dergisi*, Armağan Özel Sayısı

Stigler, G. J., "The Economies of Scale", *The Journal of Law & Economics*, Vol. 1, 1958, pp. 54–71.

Stigler, G. J., "A Theory of Oligopoly", *The Journal of Political Economy*, Vol. 72, Issue 1, 1964, pp. 44–61.

Şahin, A.H., "Türk Rekabet Hukukunda Birleşme ve Devralmalarda (Yoğunlaşmalarda) Yan Sınırlamalar", 2010

Tamer, H., "Rekabet Hukukunda Ekonomik Bütünlük Kavramı ve Hukuki Sonuçları", Marmara University, 2017 < https://tez.yok.gov.tr/UlusalTezMerkezi/tezDetay.jsp?id=vgS15QTODAu9XUQE-0MeR8w&no=qFD_aZESAypExtKr1gg8wQ> (last accessed on 11 June 2021).

Tunçel, Ç., "Avrupa Rekabet Hukukunda İkincil Seviye Fiyat Ayrımcılığı – Etki Temelli Perspektiften Değerlendirme", *Rekabet Dergisi*, Vol. 15, No. 3, July 2014, pp. 37–73.

Ünal, Ç., "Rekabet Hukukunda Tek Taraflı Sömürücü Davranışlar", *Rekabet Dergisi*, Vol. 11, No. 4, October 2010, pp. 111–164.

Van Doorn, F., "Resale Price Maintenance in EC Competition Law: The Need for a Standardised Approach", SSRN, 2009 <https://papers.ssrn.com/sol3/papers.cfm?abstract_id=1501070> (last accessed: 28 June 2021).

Wright, J. D. and M. C. Mungan, "The Easterbrook Theorem: An Application to Digital Markets", *The Yale Law Journal*, Vol. 130, 2021, pp. 622–646.

Conferences, Reports, Others

"Competition Law Handbook for small and medium-sized enterprises (SMEs)", External Affairs, Department of Education Competition Advocacy, Ankara, February 2016 ("KOBİ'ler için Rekabet Hukuku El Kitabı", Dış ilişkiler, Eğitim ve Rekabet Savunuculuğu Dairesi Ankara, Şubat 2016).

"The Handbook of Economic Analyses used in Turkish Competition Board Decisions" (English Version), Economic Analyses and Research Department, 2019.

8. Five Year Development Plan, Competition Law and Politics Specialisation Commission Report, 2000

Atiyas I., and G. Gürkaynak, "'Uyumlu Eylem Karinesi' Üzerine Hukuki ve Ekonomik Çözümle-meler" (Legal and Economic Analyses on the 'Presumption of Concerted Practice') 4th Symposium on Recent Developments in Competition Law, Erciyes University, 7 April 2006 , p.4, p.11.

Atiyas, İ., and G. Gürkaynak, "'Presumption of Concerted Practice': A Legal and

Bundeskartellamt, Press Release (7 February 2019) <https://www.bundeskartellamt.de/SharedDocs/Meldung/EN/Pressemitteilungen/2019/07_02_2019_Facebook.html> (last accessed on 8 June 2021).

DG Competition discussion paper on the application of Article 82 of the Treaty to exclusionary abuses, Brussels, December 2005, available at <https://ec.europa.eu/competition/antitrust/art82/discpaper2005.pdf>.

Europe Economics, "Study on Assessment Criteria for Distinguishing between Competitive and Dominant Oligopolies in Merger Control", 2001.

Bibliography

European Commission, "Glossary of Terms Used in EU Competition Policy: Antitrust and Control of Concentrations, Archived, 2012 <https://ec.europa.eu/translation/spanish/documents/glossary_competition_archived_en.pdf> (last accessed on 31 January 2021).

European Commission, Commission Staff Working Document, "Guidance on restrictions of competition 'by object' for the purpose of defining which agreements may benefit from the *De Minimis* Notice", SWD(2014) 198 final, 25 June 2014.

European Commission, Commission Staff Working Document, "Turkey 2020 Report," SWD(2020) 355 final, 6 October 2020.

European Commission, Guidelines on Vertical Restraints (2010/C 130/01)

Grounds for Articles for Law No. 4054 on the Protection of Competition <https://www.rekabet.gov.tr/en/Sayfa/Legislation/act-no-4054/grounds-for-the-articles> (last accessed on 19 April 2021).

Gürkaynak, G. et al., Chambers Global Practice Guides: "Cartels 2020", 2020.

Gürkaynak, G. et al., "Rekabet Hukuku Soruşturmalarında Şikayetçinin Konumu: Taraf Menfaatleri Ile Hakikatı Bulma Arasındaki Denge Üzerine Düşünceler" (The Position of the Complainant in Competition Law Investigations: Thoughts on the Balance Between the Interest of the Parties and Finding the Truth), Rekabet Forumu, March 2013, No. 72,

Gürzumar, O. B., "Özel Hukuk Açısından 4054 Sayılı Rekabetin Korunması Hakkında Kanun, 4054 Sayılı Rekabetin Korunması Hakkında Kanun ve Bu Kanun'da Değişiklik Yapılmasına İlişkin Taslak", Sempozsum, Bildiriler-Tartışmalar-Panel, 7-8 Ekim 2005, Banka ve Ticaret Hukuku Araştırma Enstitüsü (Editör: Cavid Abdullahzade).

Güven, P., "Rekabet Hukukuna Dayalı Tazminat Davalarının Mahkeme Kararları Işığında Değerlendirilmesi", Rekabet Hukukunda Güncel Gelişmeler Sempozyumu V, Kayseri 2007.

In re: Railway Industry Employee No-Poach Antitrust Litigation, Civil No. 2:18-MC-00798-JFC, MDL No. 2850 <https://www.justice.gov/atr/case-document/file/1131056/download>.

İnan, N., "Judicial Review of the Competition Board Decisions", Symposium of Competition Law and Jurisdiction, Rekabet Kurumu, 2001.

İnan, N., "4054 Sayılı Rekabetin Korunması Hakkında Kanun'un Özel Hukuka İlişkin Hükümlerine Eleştirisel Bir Bakış", Rekabet Hukukunda Güncel Gelişmeler Sempozyumu II, 2004, Kayseri, Rekabet Kurumu Yayını.

İnan, N., "Rekabet Kurulu Kararlarının Yargısal Denetimi" (Judicial Review of the Competition Board Decisions) (1999), Symposium of Competition Law and Jurisdiction, The Competition Authority Publications, Publication No. 30

İnce, E. et al., "E-Pazaryeri Platformları Sektör İncelemesi Ön Raporu" (Sector Inquiry Preliminary Report), 2021.

International Competition Network, "Report on Single Branding/Exclusive Dealing", Presented at the 7th Annual Conference of the ICN, Kyoto, April 2008.

International Competition Network, "Unilateral Conduct Workbook Chapter 4: Predatory Pricing Analysis", 2012.

Ivaldi, M., B. Jullien, P. Rey, P. Seabright, and J. Tirole, "The Economics of Tacit Collusion", IDEI Toulouse, Final Report for DG Competition, European Commission, 2003.

KPMG, Telecommunications Sector Report, 2020. <https://assets.kpmg/content/dam/kpmg/tr/pdf/2020/05/sektorel-bakis-2020-telekomunikasyon.pdf > (last accessed on 24 June 2021).

Mondaq, Turkey: Competition and Antitrust, "Turkey: Market Sharing Practice Guide", ELIG Gürkaynak Attorneys-at-Law.

OECD, "Glossary of Industrial Organisation Economics and Competition Law", compiled by R. S. Khemani and D. M. Shapiro, commissioned by the Directorate for Financial, Fiscal and

Enterprise Affairs, 1993 <https://www.oecd.org/regreform/sectors/2376087.pdf> (last accessed on 24 June 2021).

OECD, "Recommendation of the OECD Council Concerning Effective Action Against Hard Core Cartels", 1998.

OECD, Policy Roundtables, "The Role of Efficiency Claims in Antitrust Proceedings", DAF/COMP(2012)23, 2 May 2013

OECD, Policy Roundtables, "Standard Setting", DAF/COMP(2010)33, 8 March 2011 <http://www.oecd.org/daf/competition/47381304.pdf> (last accessed on 25 May 2019).

OECD, Policy Roundtables, "Information Exchanges Between Competitors under Competition Law", DAF/COMP(2010)37, 11 July 2011 <http://www.oecd.org/competition/cartels/48379006.pdf> (last accessed on 29 March 2021).

OECD, Policy Roundtables, "Excessive Prices", DAF/COMP(2011)18, 7 February 2012 <https://www.oecd.org/competition/abuse/49604207.pdf> (last accessed on 26 March 2021).

OECD, Policy Roundtables, "Unilateral Disclosure of Information with Anticompetitive Effects", DAF/COMP(2012)17, 11 October 2012.

OECD, "Algorithms and Collusion – Note by the European Union", DAF/COMP/WD (2017)12, 14 June 2017.

OECD, "Algorithms and Collusion: Competition Policy in the Digital Age" (2017) <https://www.oecd.org/daf/competition/Algorithms-and-colllusion-competition-policy-in-the-digital-age.pdf> (last accessed on 24 June 2021).

OECD, "It's a Feature, not a Bug: On Learning Algorithms and What They Teach Us – Note by Avigdor Gal", Roundtable on Algorithms and Collusion, 21–23 June 2017, DAF/COMP/WD(2017)50, 7 June 2017.

OECD, "Competition Concerns in Labour Markets – Background Note", DAF/COMP(2019)2, 13 May 2019.

OECD, "Competition Policy for Labour Markets – Note by Herbert Hovenkamp", DAF/COMP/WD(2019)67, 17 September 2020.

Office of Fair Trading, "Assessment of Market Power: Understanding Competition Law", 2004.

Riordan, M. H., "Competitive Effects of Vertical Integration", Prepared for LEAR conference on "Advances in the Economics of Competition Law", Rome, 23-25 June 2005.

Riordan, M. H., "What is Vertical Integration?" in The Firm as a Nexus of Treaties, M. Aoki, B. Gustafsson and O. E. Williamson, eds. (London: Sage Publications, 1990)

Şahin, M., "Rekabet Hukukunda Tazminat Talepleri, ABD, AB ve Türk Rekabet Hukuklarında", İzmir, 2013.

Sanlı, K. C., "Türk Rekabet Hukukunda Haksız Fiil Sorumluluğu", Rekabet Hukukunda Güncel Gelişmeler Sempozyumu I, 2003, Kayseri: Erciyes Üniversitesi.

Sanlı, K. C., "Rekabet Hukukunda Tekelci Fiyatlandırma", Perşembe Konferansları, Ankara: Rekabet Kurumu, 2010.

Sanlı, K. C., "Rekabetin Korunması Hakkında Kanun'un Özel Hukuk Alanındaki Sonuçları", Sorunlar ve Çözüm Önerileri Sempozyumu, 17 June 2011, İstanbul Bilgi Üniversitesi.

Topçuoğlu, M., "Rekabet Hukukunda Üç Kat Tazminat", Sorumluk ve Tazminat Hukuku Sempozyumu, 2009.

Turkish Competition Authority, Final Report on Turkish FMCG Sector, May 2012.

Turkish Competition Authority's Statement concerning the Transfer of Şok Stores to Ülker Group (27 December 2012) <https://www.rekabet.gov.tr/en/Guncel/statement-concerning-the-transfer-of-sok-01afdd1d66654b2f9af1249ce49213e0> (last accessed on 29 June 2021).

Turkish Competition Authority, "Glossary of Competition Definitions", 5th edition, April 2014.

Turkish Competition Authority, Strategic Plan for 2014–2018, Rekabet Kurumu, 2014.

Turkish Competition Authority, Strategic Plan 2019–2023, Rekabet Kurumu, 2019.

Turkish Competition Authority, Pharmaceuticals Sector Report, 27 March 2013

Turkish Competition Authority, Preliminary Report on the Sector Inquiry on E-Marketplace Platforms, 2021.

Turkish Competition Authority, Preliminary Report on Turkish FMCG Sector, Economic Analysis and Research Chamber, February 2021.

Turkish Competition Authority, The Report on Cement Sector, 5th Chamber, 2016

Turkish Competition Authority, Motor Vehicles Sector Inquiry Report, 4th Chamber, 2014

Turkish Competition Authority, Announcement (11 January 2021) <https://www.rekabet.gov.tr/tr/Guncel/rekabet-kurulu-facebook-ve-whatsapp-hakk-14728ae4f653eb11812700505694b4c6> (last accessed on 8 June 2021).

Turkish Competition Authority, Announcement (5 May 2021) <https://www.rekabet.gov.tr/tr/Guncel/facebook-whatsapp-sorusturmasi-hakkinda--7f1270260cbaeb11812e00505694b4c6> (last accessed on 28 May 2021).

US Department of Justice, Federal Trade Commission, Antitrust Guidance for Human Resource Professionals (October 2016) <https://www.justice.gov/atr/file/903511/download> (last accessed on 29 March 2021).

Yet, O., *Rekabet Kurulu Kararlarının Yargısal Denetimi*, Panel II.Oturum, Rekabet Hukuku ve Yargı Sempozyumu, Ankara: Rekabet Kurumu, Bilgi İşlem, İstatistik ve Enformasyon Dairesi Başkanlığı, 1999.

Case Law: Turkey

Agreements and Concerted Practices Between Undertakings, and Decisions and Practices of Associations of Undertakings

LPG *(26 November 1998, 93/750-159)*

Ege Bölgesi Çimento *(17 June 1999, 99-30/276-166)*

Pınar *(6 September 1999, 99-41/435-274)*

Cine 5 *(11 October 1999, 99-46/500-316)*

Istanbul Bread *(27 October 1999, 99-49/536-337)*

Besler Gıda *(22 November 1999, 99-53/575-364)*

Isdemir/Odak *(15 December 1999, 99-59/639-406)*

Ford *(21 December 1999, 99-58/624-398)*

Advertising Space *(1 February 2000, 00-4/41-19)*

Milk *(23 March 2000, 00-11/109-54)*

Coca-Cola and Fruko-Tamek *(27 June 2000, 00-24/251-136)*

Yeast *(27 June 2000, 00-24/255-138)*

Biryay *(17 July 2000, 00-26/292-162)*

Timken *(10 October 2000, 00-38/419-235)*

Bibliography

Sesa (6 November 2000, 00-44/472-257)

Microsoft I (23 November 2000, 00-46/488-266)

Motor Renewal Firms (27 February 2001, 01-10/100-24)

Haydarpaşa/Erenköy/Halkalı Gümrük Sahası Taşıyıcıları (26 April 2001, 01-21/191-49)

Turkcell (20 July 2001, 01-35/347-95)

Water Distributors (22 January 2002, 02-04/39-20)

TMMOB (22 January 2002, 02-04/40-21)

Cement (1 February 2002, 02-06/51-24)

JTI Tobacco (28 May 2002, 02-32/368-154)

Glaxo Wellcome-PNG (26 September 2002, 02-57/727-289)

Philip Morris/JTI (24 December 2002, 02-80/937-385)

SSK-I (27 May 2003, 03-35/416-182)

State Retirement Fund (19 June 2003, 03-44/501-221)

Yonga Levha (14 August 2003, 03-56/650-298)

Shell/Cabbaroğlu (2 October 2003, 03-64/770-356)

Ak-Kim (4 December 2003, 03-76/925-389)

JTI Tobacco (3 March 2004, 04-18/152-34)

BBA Beymen (25 March 2004, 04-22/234-50)

Starbucks (15 April 2004, 04-26/286-64)

Sodima (8 June 2004, 04-46/597-145)

Gas Insulated Switchgears (24 June 2004, 04-43/538-133)

Marble-Cutters (24 February 2005, 05-11/114-44)

Philip Morris (11 March 2005, 05-14/170-62)

Tofaş – Fiat – Peugeot (8 July 2005, 05-44/628-161)

Television Series Producers (28 July 2005, 05-49/710-195)

Çimento (13 September 2005, 05-57/850-230)

Yeast (23 September 2005, 05-60/896-241)

Ulusoy (27 October 2005, 05-74/998-279)

Karbogaz (1 December 2005, 05-80/1106-317)

Konya Mechanical Engineers (15 December 2005, 05-84/1150-330)

Renault Mais (5 January 2006, 06-02/49-10)

Ceramic (2 February 2006, 06-08/121-30)

Sodexo (28 April 2006, 06-31/376-99)

İşbak (22 May 2006, 06-35/444-116)

Batıçim/Batısöke (26 May 2006, 06-36/474-128)

Turkish Banks Association (20 July 2006, 06-53/689-196)

Sakarya Bus Firms (25 July 2006, 06-55/713-203)

Kütaş Teekanne (24 August 2006, 06-59/773-226)

Digiturk (7 September 2006, 06-61/822-237)

Glencore (11 September 2006, 06-62/848-241)

Sodexho (28 September 2006, 06-67/905-262)

Bibliography

Aegean Cement (19 October 2006, 06-77/992-287)

Fuel Oil (15 November 2006, 06-84/1059-306)

Frito-Lay (11 January 2007, 07-01/12-7)

Alarko (21 February 2007, 07-15/142-45)

Şişecam/Yioula (28 February 2007, 07-17/155-50)

Promesis (16 March 2007, 07-24/236-76)

Shell&Turcas (29 March 2007, 07-29/262-93)

Fertiliser (24 April 2007, 07-34/339-121)

Hyundai (11 July 2007, 07-59/684-240)

Goodyear (25 July 2007, 07-61/716-248)

Çimento (26 July 2007, 07-62/740-268)

Newspapers Publishers (26 July 2007, 07-62/742-269)

Vira Kozmetik (2 August 2007, 07-63/767-275)

Göltaş Çimento (20 September 2007, 07-76/908-346)

Cine 5 (1 November 2007, 07-83/1009-393)

Johnson & Johnson/Öz-sel (8 November 2007, 07-85/1050-409)

Gas Stations (13 December 2007, 07-90/1162-454)

Fertiliser Producers Decision (24 January 2008, 08-08/82-24)

Güney Petrol/POAŞ (7 February 2008, 08-12/123-40)

Gillette (20 March 2008, 08-25/261-88)

Antis (8 May 2008, 08-32/401-136)

Kuralkan (27 May 2008, 08-35/462-162)

Levi's (27 June 2008, 08-41/565-213)

Ginnery (27 June 2008, 08-41/567-215)

Benckiser (3 July 2008, 08-43/591-223)

Astur (17 July 2008, 08-45/626-238)

Mogaz (31 July 2008, 08-49/702-277)

Oligopoly (11 September 2008, 08-52/783-312)

Armada Bilgisayar (18 September 2008, 08-54/852-340)

Habaş (12 November 2008, 08-63/1042-402)

Yeast (12 November 2008, 08-63/1050-409)

TABGIS (27 November 2008, 08-67/1091-424)

Xerox (4 December 2008, 08-69/1121-437)

Henkel/Hobi (20 January 2009, 09-03/46-15)

Unilever (18 February 2009, 09-07/129-40)

Ter-Tuz/Alkan (24 April 2009, 09-20/404-99)

Akmaya (20 May 2009, 09-23/491-117)

Automotive (24 June 2009, 09-30/637-150)

Mazda (18 June 2009, 09-29/607-146)

Refrigerator Compressor (1 July 2009, 09-31/668-156)

Dagi (15 July 2009, 09-33/725-165)

Bibliography

Garanti Bank (5 August 2009, 09-34/787-192)

Arcon Cosmetics (9 September 2009, 09-41/987-249)

ODD (9 September 2009, 09-41/998-255)

Parrafin and Vaselin (28 October 2009, 09-49/1220-308)

Bodrum Express (3 November 2009, 09-51/1245-314)

KWS (25 November 2009, 09-57/1365-357)

DiaSA (25 November 2009, 09-57/1386-359)

White Meat (25 November 2009, 09-57/1393-362)

Lafarge Beton (9 December 2009, 09-58/1396-364)

Knauf (16 December 2009, 09-59/1441-376)

Costa International (16 December 2009, 09-59/1445-378)

Doğuş Otomotiv (28 January 2010, 10-10/90-40)

International Transporter's Association (28 January 2010, 10-10/94-42)

İzocam (8 February 2010, 10-14/175-66)

İzmir Municipality (11 February 2010, 10-16/183-70)

Sivas Driving Schools (22 March 2010, 10-25/350-124)

Roche-Corena I (17 June 2010, 10-44/785-262)

Doğan Yayın (1 July 2010, 10-47/858-296)

TEB (8 July 2010, 10-49/912-321)

White Goods (14 July 2010, 11-43/942-306)

Pepsi Cola (5 August 2010, 10-52/956-335)

Ready-Mixed Concrete (5 August 2010, 10-52/1049-388)

Peugeot (6 August 2010, 10-53/1057-391)

Imported Coal (2 September 2010, 10-57/1141-430)

Cargo (3 September 2010, 10-58/1193-449)

Yatsan (23 September 2010, 10-60/1251-469)

Medical Consumables (7 October 2010, 10-63/1325-497)

Anamur-Ankara Bus Companies (4 November 2010, 10-69/1466-564)

Göltaş (10 November 2010, 10-71/1483-569)

Medical Gas (11 November 2010, 10-72/1503-572)

Meat and Fish Authority (25 November 2010, 10-73/1509-577)

Arçelik/Sony (8 December 2010, 10-76/1572-605)

İstikbal (16 December 2010, 10-78/1624-624)

Dialyzer Machines (23 December 2010, 10-80/1687-640)

Ceramics Adhesive Producers (12 January 2011, 11-03/42-14)

Fertilizers (19 January 2011, 11-04/64-26)

Private Schools (3 March 2011, 11-12/226-76)

8 Banks (7 March 2011, 11-13/243-78)

Göltaş (31 March 2011, 11-20/378-117)

Automotive Market (18 April 2011, 11-24/464-139)

Henkel (26 May 2011, 11-32/650-201)

Bibliography

Turkcell (6 June 2011, 11-34/742-230)

Koçaklar (9 June 2011, 11-36/757-234)

Traçim (16 June 2011, 11-37/779-245)

Samsung (23 June 2011, 11-39/838-262)

BSH (14 July 2011, 11-43/941-305)

Karadeniz Tüpgaz (14 July 2011, 11-43/953-307)

Çimsa (3 August 2011, 11-44/979-329)

OMV Petrol Ofisi (3 August 2011, 11-44/997-343)

Ünye Çimento (14 September 2011, 11-47/1170-415)

JTI/Sunel (14 September 2011, 11-47/1178-419)

Çelebi Gıda (12 October 2011, 11-54/1378-488)

Arçelik (18 October 2011, 11-53/1353-479)

Boyner (27 October 2011, 11-54/1379-489)

UFO (27 October 2011, 11-54/1380-490)

TFF (27 October 2011, 11-54/1385-495)

Güneş Ekspres/Condor (27 October 2011, 11-54/1431-507)

Konya-Akşehir Bus Companies (17 November 2011, 11-57/1461-519)

Izmir-Konya Bus Companies (24 November 2011, 11-59/1521-546)

Şırnak Bus Companies (29 December 2011, 11-64/1666-596)

Toyota Distributors (19 January 2012, 12-02/71-17)

Setre (9 February 2012, 12-06/191-53)

Toyota Distributors (23 February 2012, 12-08/244-75)

Kars Çimento (6 April 2012, 12-17/499-140)

Peugeot (12 April 2012, 12-20/557-141)

Sodaş Sodyum (3 May 2012, 12-24/711-199)

Bayburt İnşaat (31 May 2012, 12-24/666-188)

BSH (12 June 2012, 12-32/916-275)

Fuel Sector Preliminary Investigation (4 July 2012, 12-36/1040-328)

General Motors (18 July 2012, 12-38/1093-352)

Biletix (9 August 2012, 12-41/1159-376)

BASF Coatings-Riwax (27 September 2012, 12-46/1396-469)

UN Ro-Ro (1 October 2012, 12-47/1413-474)

SMC/Entek (10 October 2012, 12-49/1439-490)

Steel Ring Manufacturers (30 October 2012, 12-52/1479-508)

Altınbaş Petrol (6 November 2012, 12-54/1517-535)

Automotive Industry (20 November 2012, 12-58/1556-558)

Sanofi-Aventis (22 November 2012, 12-59/1570-571)

Konya Exchangers and Goldsmiths Association (14 February 2013, 13-10/152-75)

Ankara-Adana Highway (20 February 2013, 13-11/165-87)

12 Banks (8 March 2013, 13-13/198-100)

Aygaz (13March 2013, 13-14/204-105)

Bibliography

Samsun Driving Schools (15 May 2013, 13-28/387-175)

Reckitt Benckiser (13 June 2013, 13-36/468-204)

Nevsehir Driving Schools (13 June 2013, 13-36/482-212)

Yapı Kredi (26 June 2013, 13-40/521-230)

Cement (26 June 2013, 13-40/528-235)

Yeşil Körfez Su Birliği (11 July 2013, 13-44/553-247)

Mercedes-Benz (13 August 2013, 13-47/644-282)

Ford (21 August 2013, 13-48/671-287)

Linde (29 August 2013, 13-49/710-297)

Industrial Gas (29 August 2013, 13-49/710-297)

Frito-Lay (29 August 2013, 13-49/711-300)

GAP (3 October 2013, 13-56/785-335)

Çağdaş (24 October 2013, 13-59/825-350)

Antis (24 October 2013, 13-59/831-353)

Biletix (5 November 2013, 13-61/851-359)

Hyundai Dealers (16 December 2013, 13-70/952-403)

Çaykur (19 December 2013, 13-71/972-418)

Şölen (16 January 2014, 14-02/35-14)

Gürsel Turizm (16 January 2014, 14-02/40-18)

Tüpraş II (17 January 2014, 14-03/60-24)

Bakers (22 January 2014, 14-04/80-33)

Akbank (12 February 2014, 14-06/116-55)

Takeda (3 April 2014, 14-13/242-107)

Pizza Pizza (8 May 2014, 14-17/322-140)

Mey İçki (12 June 2014, 14-21/410-178)

Ready-Mixed Concrete (25 June 2014, 14-22/441-199)

White Cement (25 June 2014, 14-22/460-202)

TTNET (13 August 2014, 14-28/558-241)

Çilek (20 August 2014, 14-29/597-263)

Pamukkale Taşımacılık (1 October 2014, 14-37/713-318)

Dogati (22 October 2014, 14-42/764-340)

Yeast Producers (22 October 2014, 14-42/783-346)

Turkish Football Federation (26 November 2014, 14-46/834-375)

Beylikdüzü Municipality (26 November 2014, 14-46/847-386)

Diye Danışmanlık (12 December 2014, 14-51/900-410)

Siemens II (8 January 2015, 15-02/5-3)

Alcon (5 March 2015, 15-10/139-62)

Bayer/Zentiva (28 July 2015, 15-32/460-142)

THY (1 September 2015, 15-34/512-160)

Medical Devices (1 September 2015, 15-34/514-162)

HSBC/Euler (9 September 2015, 15-36/551-179)

Bibliography

Mars Cinema (20 November 2015, 15-41/682-243)

Trakya Cam/Düzcam Exemption (2 December 2015, 15-42/704-258)

Rail Cargo Logistics (16 December 2015, 15-44/740-267)

TEB/İDO (6 January 2016, 16-01/7-2)

Aegean Cement Producers (14 January 2016, 16-02/44-14)

ArcelorMittal (21 January 2016, 16-03/54-19)

Tuborg/Ecocaps (10 February 2016, 16-04/69-27)

Digiturk (10 February 2016, 16-04/82-36)

BKM (18 February 2016, 16-05/106-47)

Maysan (18 February 2016, 16-05/107-48)

Solgar (18 February 2016, 16-05/116-51)

Sinop Ready-Mixed Concerete (18 February 2016, 16-05/117-52)

Eureko (10 March 2016, 16-09/152-67)

Soda (20 April 2016, 16-14/205-89)

Mastervolt/Artı Marin (11 May 2016, 16-16/278-122)

Doğan, Mozaik and Krea (18 May 2016, 16-17/299-134)

LMC Gıda (1 June 2016, 16-19/313-142)

3M (9 June 2016, 16-20/340-155)

Yemek Sepeti (9 June 2016, 16-20/347-156)

Doğuş Otomotiv II (13 October 2016, 16-33/575-251)

Mixed Feed (27 October 2016, 16-35/596-264)

Consumer Electronics (7 November 2016, 16-37/628-279)

Aygaz (16 November 2016, 16-39/659-294)

Antalya Tour Operators (21 November 2016, 16-40/662-296)

Forex (24 November 2016, 16-41/667-300)

Booking (5 January 2017, 17-01/12-4)

Suction Glass Tubes (2 February 2017, 17-08/100-43)

Social Security Institution (13 July 2017, 17-22/362-158)

Traffic Insurance (19 July 2017, 17-23/383-166)

Mesam (22 August 2017, 17-27/451-193)

Ready-Mixed Concrete (22 August 2017, 17-27/452-194)

BSH (22 August 2017, 17-27/454-195)

Karabük Demir Çelik (7 September 2017, 17-28/481-207)

Yataş (27 September 2017, 17-30/487-211)

Traffic Insurance (27 September 2017, 17-30/500-219)

Teknosa (9 November 2017, 17-36/578-252)

Arslanoğlu/Mercedes-Benz (11 November 2017, 17-38/613-268)

Syndicated Loans (28 November 2017, 17-39/636-276)

Mechanical Engineering (14 December 2017, 17-41/640-279)

Trakya Cam (14 December 2017, 17-41/641-280)

Mates-Atek (4 January 2018, 18-01/1-1)

Bibliography

Petrol Ofisi (11 January 2018, 18-02/20-10)

Mars (18 January 2018, 18-03/35-22)

Jotun (15 February 2018, 18-05/74-40)

Duru Bulgur (8 March 2018, 18-07/112-59)

Zeyport Zeytinburnu (15 March 2018, 18-08/152-73)

Orthodontics (29 March 2018, 18-09/157-77)

Adıyaman Autogas (29 March 2018, 18-09/180-85)

TURÇEF (3 May 2018, 18-13/230-105)

Hopi/Migros (3 May 2018, 18-13/238-111)

Frito-Lay (12 June 2018, 18-19/329-163)

IQVIA Health (12 June 2018, 18-19/330-164)

Mais (21 June 2018, 18-20/353-174)

Mosaş (21 June 2018, 18-20/356-176)

Doğa Beton (5 July 2018, 18-22/383-188)

Western Union (8 August 2018, 18-27/442-212)

Mutlu Akü (8 August 2018, 18-27/446-216)

Medcem (8 August 2018, 18-27/451-220)

Baymak (6 September 2018, 18-30/523-259)

Mey İçki (19 September 2018, 18-33/547-270)

Google Android (19 September 2018, 18-33/555-273)

Henkel (19 September 2018, 18-33/556-274)

Roche (19 September 2018, 18-33/557-275)

Tourism Agencies (25 October 2018, 18-40/645-315)

Tofaş (1 November 2018, 18-41/658-322)

Meal Coupons/Cards (15 November 2018, 18-43/694-339)

Association of Steel Guard Rails and Road Safety Systems (22 November 2018, 18-44/702-344)

Sony Eurasia (22 November 2018, 18-44/703-345)

Unilever (7 January 2019, 19-38/584-250)

Raw Meatball Producers (10 January 2019, 19-03/13-5)

Turkcell (10 January 2019, 19-03/23-10)

Ege Gübre (7 February 2019, 19-06/51-18)BFIT

(7 February 2019, 19-06/64-27)

JTI Tobacco III (13 February 2019, 19-07/81-33)

Anıtur (13 February 2019, 19-07/86-36)

Bereket (21 February 2019, 19-08/100-40)

Automotive Dsitributors Association (28 February 2019, 19-10/115-46)

Okan Okandan (7 March 2019, 19-11/129-56)

Güven Beton (13 March 2019, 19-12/147-68)

White Meat (13 March 2019, 19-12/155-70)

Abalıoğlu (13 March 2019, 19-12/156-71)

Molson Coors/Anadolu Efes (18 April 2019, 19-16/218-97)

Bibliography

Ambarlı Ro-Ro (18 April 2019, 19-16/229-101)

Customs Brokers Association (20 June 2019, 19-22/352-158)

Maysan (20 June 2019, 19-22/353-159)

Marka Mağazacılık (4 November 2019, 19-15/208-93)

TEB (7 November 2019, 19-38/582-248)

DVS Doğalgaz Mühendislik (7 November 2019, 19-38/588-254)

Shell (12 November 2019, 19-39/601-255)

Johnson & Johnson (14 November 2019, 19-40/642-270)

Turkish Pharmacists' Association II (14 November 2019, 19-40/643-271)

Çaykur II (14 November 2019, 19-40/645-272)

LB Börekçilik (14 November 2019, 19-40/646-273)

BP (14 November 2019, 19-40/652-278)

Bosch (14 November 2019, 19-40/656-281)

Garanti Oto (22 November 2019, 19-41/681-294)

Paşabahçe (12 December 2019, 19-44/737-314)

Keşan Cement (19 December 2019, 19-45/758-327)

Red Bull (19 December 2019, 19-45/767-329)

Hayal Seramik (26 December 2019, 19-46/772-333)

IGA/THY (26 December 2019, 19-46/786-343)

Chamber of Electric Engineers (26 December 2019, 19-46/791-345)

Askaynak (26 December 2019, 19-46/793-346)

İzmir Container Transporters (2 January 2020, 20-01/3-2)

Arçelik/Vestel (2 January 2020, 20-01/13-5)

Chemotherapy Medicine Bids (2 January 2020, 20-01/14-06)

Kubota (9 January 2020, 20-03/21-11)

Burdur Autogas (9 January 2020, 20-03/28-12)

Groupe SEB (9 January 2020, 20-03/31-14)

Cargo (16 January 2020, 20-04/47-25)

Çerkezköy (23 January 2020, 20-06/49-26)

Insurance Sector (23 January 2020, 20-06/61-33)

Yataş (6 February 2020, 20-08/83-50)

Philips/Group SEB (13 February 2020, 20-10/109-65)

DSM (20 February 2020, 20-11/127-73)

IVECO (27 February 2020, 20-12/143-79)

TÜKEBİR (27 February 2020, 20-12/145-80)

Borusan Otomotiv (5 March 2020, 20-13/167-86)

Mosaş (12 March 2020, 20-14/191-97)

Fuel Companies (12 March 2020, 20-14/192-98)

Yozgat Ready-Mixed Concrete Manufacturers (19 March 2020, 20-15/215-107)

Baymak (26 March 2020, 20-16/232-113)

Generali (16 April 2020, 20-20/265-126)

Food & Cleaning Chain Stores and Suppliers (7 May 2020, 20-23/298-M)

Siyam Petrol (7 May 2020, 20-23/300-146)

Foreign Exchange (2 July 2020, 20-32/397-179)

Gaziantep Auto Experts (9 July 2020, 20-33/439-196)

Brisa (24 July 2020, 20-35/455-202)

Pankobirlik (28 July 2020, 20-36/489-215)

Novo Nordisk (28 July 2020, 20-36/493-218)

Şanlıurfa Autogas (28 July 2020, 20-36/505-223)

Apex (20 August 2020, 20-38/528-236)

Johnson & Johnson (3 September 2020, 20-40/553-249)

Automative (15 October 2020, 20-46/618-270)

Kitapyurdu (5 November 2020, 20-48/658-289)

Reckitt Benckiser II (19 November 2020, 20-50/684-299)

İSDER (19 November 2020, 20-50/687-301)

Van Natural Gas Association (19 November 2020, 20-50/694-305)

Turkcell (3 December 2020, 20-52/723-320)

Unilever (18 March 2021, 21-15/190-80)

Individual Exemption

Advertising Space (1 February 2000, 00-4/41-19)

Biryay (17 July 2000, 00-26/292-162)

JTI Tobacco (28 May 2002, 02-32/368-154)

Netcell (9 September 2002, 02-56/697-281)

Glaxo Wellcome-PNG (26 September 2002, 02-57/727-289)

Shell/Cabbaroğlu (2 October 2003, 03-64/770-356)

BBA Beymen (25 March 2004, 04-22/234-50)

Starbucks (15 April 2004, 04-26/286-64)

Automotive Distributors Association (15 April 2004, 04-26/287-65)

Pınar Milk Products and Dimes Food Industry (22 April 2004, 04-27/339-81)

SEK Milk Industry Institution (22 April 2004, 04-27/340-82)

Sodima (8 June 2004, 04-46/597-145)

Yemek Sepeti (20 September 2004, 04-60/869-206)

Philip Morris (11 March 2005, 05-14/170-62)

Bimpaş (22 April 2005, 05-27/317-80)

Ulusoy I (27 October 2005, 05-74/998-279)

Karbogaz (1 December 2005, 05-80/1106-317)

Alarko (21 February 2007, 07-15/142-45)

Shell&Turcas (29 March 2007, 07-29/262-93)

Hyundai (July 11, 2007, 07-59/684-240)

Goodyear (July 25, 2007, 07-61/716-248)

Vira Kozmetik (2 August 2007, 07-63/767-275)

Bibliography

Pfizer-Dilek (2 August 2007, 07-63/774-281)

Shell&Turcas (8 August 2007, 07-66/812-307)

Coca-Cola Exemption (10 September 2007, 07-70/864-327)

Johnson & Johnson/Öz-sel (8 November 2007, 07-85/1050-409)

Antis (8 May 2008, 08-32/401-136)

Kuralkan (27 May 2008, 08-35/462-162)

GlaxoSmithKline/Pfizer (20 June 2008, 08-40/535-201)

Mogaz (31 July 2008, 08-49/702-277)

Xerox (4 December 2008, 08-69/1121-437)

Henkel/Hobi (20 January 2009, 09-03/46-15)

Akmaya (20 May 2009, 09-23/491-117)

Arcon Cosmetics (9 September 2009, 09-41/987-249)

Fayda Mağazacılık (11 November 2009, 09-54/1291-325)

KWS (25 November 2009, 09-57/1365-357)

DiaSA (25 November 2009, 09-57/1386-359)

Türk Ytong Sanayi (16 December 2009, 09-59/1435-373)

Costa International (16 December 2009, 09-59/1445-378)

Government of Singapore Investment/Citigroup (6 January 2010, 10-01/17-10)

Doğuş Otomotiv (28 January 2010, 10-10/90-40)

Arçelik-Sony Eurasia (4 February 2010, 10-13/145-61)

İzocam (8 February 2010, 10-14/175-66)

BASF Coatings (4 March 2010, 10-21/278-102)

Tuborg (18 March 2010, 10-24/331-119)

Shell Turcas Exemption (24 June 2010, 10-45/806-267)

Kale Oto Exemption (1 July 2010, 10-47/869-302)

Cargo (3 September 2010, 10-58/1193-449)

Yatsan (23 September 2010, 10-60/1251-469)

Opet/Emka (2 December 2010, 10-75/1544-597)

Arçelik/Sony (8 December 2010, 10-76/1572-605)

Dialyzer Machines (23 December 2010, 10-80/1687-640)

Goodyear (4 April 2011, 11-22/392-125)

Logo Yazilim (28 April 2011, 11-26/497-154)

Karadeniz Tüpgaz (14 July 2011, 11-43/953-307)

JTI/Sunel (14 September 2011, 11-47/1178-419)

Petder (22 September 2011, 11-48/1215-428)

Tofaş (5 October 2011, 11-51/1288-453)

Çelebi Gıda (12 October 2011, 11-54/1378-488)

Arçelik (18 October 2011, 11-53/1353-479)

Boyner (27 October 2011, 11-54/1379-489)

Sanofi-Aventis (22 November 2012, 12-59/1570-571)

Doğan Yayın II (23 February 2012, 12-08/250-81)

Bibliography

Swedish Match/Sağlam (25 April 2012, 12-22/569-164)

MSD (18 July 2012, 12-38/1086-345)

OSD (20 September 2012, 12-44/1350-455)

BASF Coatings-Riwax (27 September 2012, 12-46/1396-469)

SMC/Entek (10 October 2012, 12-49/1439-490)

Altınbaş Petrol (6 November 2012, 12-54/1517-535)

Biovesta (27 November 2012, 12-60/1597-581)

Trakya Cam/Isıcam Exemption (24 January 2013, 13-07/73-42)

ABBOTT (31 January 2013, 13-08/88-49)

Tofaş – Fiat – Peugeot (31 January 2013, 13-08/93-54)

Ceramic (13 March 2013, 13-14/201-103)

Samsun Driving Schools (15 May 2013, 13-28/387-175)

Yapı Kredi (26 June 2013, 13-40/521-230)

Mercedes-Benz (13 August 2013, 13-47/644-282)

Ford (21 August 2013, 13-48/671-287)

Industrial Gas (29 August 2013, 13-49/710-297)

Frito Lay (29 August 2013, 13-49/711-300)

GAP (3 October 2013, 13-56/785-335)

Antis (24 October 2013, 13-59/831-353)

Petroleum Industry Association (21 November 2013, 13-64/904-384)

Çaykur (19 December 2013, 13-71/972-418)

Göltaş/Batı Söke Çimento (9 January 2014, 14-01/6-5)

Takeda (3 April 2014, 14-13/242-107)

Pizza Pizza (8 May 2014, 14-17/322-140)

TTNET (13 August 2014, 14-28/558-241)

Dogati (22 October 2014, 14-42/764-340)

Say Reklamcılık (15 January 2015, 15-03/25-11)

TTNET (5 February 2015, 15-06/74-31)

Novo Nordisk (5 February 2015, 15-06/71-29)

Reckitt Benckiser (7 July 2015, 15-28/344-114)

Bayer/Zentiva (28 July 2015, 15-32/460-142)

HSBC/Euler (9 September 2015, 15-36/551-179)

Türkiye Petrol Rafinerileri I (20 October 2015, 15-41/675-237)

Mars Cinema (20 November 2015, 15-41/682-243)

Trakya Cam/Düzcam Exemption (2 December 2015, 15-42/704-258)

Tofaş Exemption (24 December 2015, 15-45/755-277)

TEB/İDO (6 January 2016, 16-01/7-2)

ArcelorMittal (21 January 2016, 16-03/54-19)

Tuborg/Ecocaps (10 February 2016, 16-04/69-27

Digiturk (10 February 2016, 16-04/82-36)

BKM (18 February 2016, 16-05/106-47)

Bibliography

Eureko (10 March 2016, 16-09/152-67)

EBS Automotive (30 March 2016, 16-12/194-88)

Kamrusepa (1 June 2016, 16-19/312-141)

Server-Zirve (23 June 2016, 16-21/363-169)

Yonga Chipboard (13 October 2016, 16-33/571-248)

Doğuş Otomotiv II (13 October 2016, 16-33/575-251)

Roche/MTS Ecza Deposu (16 November 2016, 16-39/642-288)

Aygaz (16 November 2016, 16-39/659-294)

Volvo Exemption (6 December2016, 16-42/692-310)

Elmalı (9 August 2017, 17-26/412-184)

Mesam (22 August 2017, 17-27/451-193)

BSH (22 August 2017, 17-27/454-195)

Novo Nordisk/Aksel (7 September 2017, 17-28/461-200)

Garanti/THY (7 September 2017, 17-28/465-204)

Traffic Insurance (27 September 2017, 17-30/500-219)

Devlet Malzeme Ofisi (10 October 2017, 17-31/522-226)

Teknosa (9 November 2017, 17-36/578-252)

Arslanoğlu/Mercedes-Benz (11 November 2017, 17-38/613-268)

Trakya Cam (14 December 2017, 17-41/641-280)

Trakya Cam/Düzcam Exemption (21 December 2017, 17-42/670-298)

Mates-Atek (4 January 2018, 18-01/1-1)

Turkey Construction Industrialists Employers Union (18 January 2018, 18-03/31-18)

Leasing, Factoring and Financing Companies Union (15 February 2018, 18-05/79-43)

Hopi/Migros (3 May 2018, 18-13/238-111)

Sanofi/Abdi İbrahim (31 May 2018, 18-17/299-149)

Mais (21 June 2018, 18-20/353-174)

Başkent Gaz (5 July 2018, 18-22/374-182)

Vodafone/Superonline (8 August 2018, 18-27/438-208)

Western Union (8 August 2018, 18-27/442-212)

Mutlu Akü (8 August 2018, 18-27/446-216)

Football Association (12 September 2018, 18-31/532-262)

Mey İçki (19 September 2018, 18-33/547-270)

Automobile Project (26 September 2018, 18-34/566-279)

Roche (26 September 2018, 18-34/577-283)

Tourism Agencies (25 October 2018, 18-40/645-315)

Tofaş (1 November 2018, 18-41/658-322)

Vodafone/Türksat (25 November 2018, 18-40/641-312)

*Turkish Insurance, Reinsurance and Retirement Companies Associations
(20 December 2018, 18-48/751-364)*

BFIT (7 February 2019, 19-06/64-27)

JTI Tobacco III (13 February 2019, 19-07/81-33)

Bibliography

Anıtur (13 February 2019, 19-07/86-36)

Bereket (21 February 2019, 19-08/100-40)

Okan Okandan (7 March 2019, 19-11/129-56)

Vodafone (11 April 2019, 19-15/203-90)

Molson Coors/Anadolu Efes (18 April 2019, 19-16/218-97)

Neova (30 May 2019, 19-20/290-125)

BKM (30 May 2019, 19-20/291-126)

Tuborg (20 June 2019 19-22/335-152)

Maysan (20 June 2019, 19-22/353-159)

*Chinese National Nuclear Corporation/Tsinghua Tongfang
(31 October 2019, 19-37/550-226)*

Marka Mağazacılık (4 November 2019, 19-15/208-93)

Shell (12 November 2019, 19-39/601-255)

Johnson & Johnson (14 November 2019, 19-40/642-270)

Çaykur II (14 November 2019, 19-40/645-272)

LB Börekçilik (14 November 2019, 19-40/646-273)

THY (14 November 2019, 19-40/653-279)

Turkey Port Managers Association (14 November 2019, 19-40/655-280)

Bosch (14 November 2019, 19-40/656-281)

Roche Exemption (12 December 2019, 19-44/732-312)

Paşabahçe (12 December 2019, 19-44/737-314)

Keşan Cement (19 December 2019, 19-45/758-327)

Red Bull (19 December 2019, 19-45/767-329)

Hayal Seramik (26 December 2019, 19-46/772-333)

IGA/THY (26 December 2019, 19-46/786-343)

Philips (26 December 2019, 19-46/790-344)

Kubota (9 January 2020, 20-03/21-11)

Cargo (16 January 2020, 20-04/47-25)

Yataş (6 February 2020, 20-08/83-50)

Vodafone (13 February 2020, 20-10/110-66)

IVECO (27 February 2020, 20-12/143-79)

Borusan Otomotiv (5 March 2020, 20-13/167-86)

Baymak (26 March 2020, 20-16/232-113)

Generali (16 April 2020, 20-20/265-126)

Boyner (16 April 2020, 20-20/271-130)

Turkish Bankers' Union (30 April 2020, 20-21/280-134)

Construction Equipment (7 May 2020, 20-23/293-141)

Financial Institutions Union (7 May 2020, 20-23/296-143)

Siyam Petrol (7 May 2020, 20-23/300-146)

Air France (4 June 2020, 20-27/329-154)

Trakya Cam/Düzcam Exemption (25 June 2020, 20-31/382-171)

Bayer (28 July 2020, 20-36/488-214)

Pankobirlik (28 July 2020, 20-36/489-215)

Novo Nordisk (28 July 2020, 20-36/493-218)

Turkish Ceramic Federation (20 August 2020, 20-38/526-234)

Güneş Sigorta (27 August 2020, 20-39/539-240)

Johnson & Johnson (3 September 2020, 20-40/553-249)

Casting Agencies (24 September 2020, 20-43/588-262)

Kitapyurdu (5 November 2020, 20-48/658-289)

Insurance Information and Supervision Center (12 November 2020, 20-49/672-294)

Reckitt Benckiser II (19 November 2020, 20-50/684-299)

İSDER (19 November 2020, 20-50/687-301)

İSDER II (19 November 2020, 20-50/688-302)

2020 Efes (26 November 2020, 20-51/701-310)

Turkcell (3 December 2020, 20-52/723-320

Zurich Sigorta/TEB (3 December 2020, 20-52/735-326)

Insurance (24 December 2020, 20-55/769-341)

BNP Paribas (4 February 2021, 21-06/73-33)

Unilever (18 March 2021, 21-15/190-80)

Unilateral Conduct (Abuse of Dominance)

Pınar (6 September 1999, 99-41/435-274)

Cine 5 (11 October 1999, 99-46/500-316)

Advertising Space (1 February 2000, 00-4/41-19)

Coca-Cola and Fruko-Tamek (27 June 2000, 00-24/251-136)

Biryay (17 July 2000, 00-26/292-162)

Timken (10 October 2000, 00-38/419-235)

Arçelik (17 October 2000, 00-39/436-242)

Eti Holding (21 December 2000, 00-50/533-295)

Kütahya Porselen (16 January 2001, 01-04/21-4)

ASKİ I (13 March 2001, 01-12/114-29)

Belko (6 April 2001, 01-17/150-39)

*Haydarpaşa/Erenköy/Halkalı Gümrük Sahası Taşıyıcıları
(April 26, 2001, 01-21/191-49)*

HP (8 May 2001, 01-22/192-50)

Ereğli Iron-Steel (12 June 2001, 01-27/260-74)

Turkcell (20 July 2001, 01-35/347-95)

POAS (20 November 2001, 01-56/554-130)

Cement (1 February 2002, 02-06/51-24)

BOTAŞ-EGO-İZGAZ-İGDAŞ (8 March 2002, 02-13/127-54)

TEDAŞ (30 April 2002, 02-26/262-102)

ASKİ (8 August 2002, 02-47/587-240)

Bibliography

Türk Telekom (2 October 2002, 02-60/755-305)

SSK-I (27 May 2003, 03-35/416-182)

National Roaming (9 June 2003, 03-40/432-186)

Çukurova Elektrik (10 November 2003, 03-72/874-373)

Ak-Kim (4 December 2003, 03-76/925-389)

Coca-Cola (23 January 2004, 04-07/75-18)

Yemek Sepeti (25 March 2004, 04-22/231-48)

TKİ (19 October 2004, 04-66/949-227)

Mesam (21 July 2005, 05-48/683-177)

Karbogaz (1 December 2005, 05-80/1106-317)

Turk Telekom Student-Teacher Campaign (8 September 2005, 05-55/833-226)

TTAŞ (5 January 2006, 06-02/47-8)

Frito-Lay (6 April 2006, 06-24/304-71)

İşbak (22 May 2006, 06-35/444-116)

MTS (26 May 2006, 06-36/462-124)

Cevahir Alışveriş Merkezi (15 June 2006, 06-44/540-142)

Digiturk (7 September 2006, 06-61/822-237)

Habaş (19 September 2006, 06-66/887-256)

ASKİ II (20 December 2006, 06-92/1176-354)

Frito-Lay (11 January 2007, 07-01/12-7)

Biletix (1 March 2007, 07-18/164-54)

Turk Telecom (1 March 2007, 07-18/165-55)

Lineer Aktuatör (8 March 2007, 07-19/188-60)

Bilsa (21 March 2007, 07-26/238-77)

Luxottica-Dünya Göz (3 May 2007, 07-37/396-156)

Solmaz Mercan I (5 June 2007, 07-47/506-181)

Turk Telekom (20 June 2007, 07-53/571-187

Ulusal Basın (2 August 2007, 07-63/777-283)

Feniks (23 August 2007, 07-67/815-310)

Cine 5 (1 November 2007, 07-83/1009-393)

Halk Ekmek (15 November 2007, 07-86/1085-421)

Havaş (3 January 2008, 08-01/5-4)

Bereket Jeotermal (14 February 2008, 08-15/146-49)

Gillette (20 March 2008, 08-25/261-88)

Ataköy Marina (24 April 2008, 08-30/373-123)

Turkcell-Vodafone (20 May 2008, 08-34/453-159)

Armada Bilgisayar (18 September 2008, 08-54/852-340)

Habaş (12 November 2008, 08-63/1042-402)

Türk Telekom/TTNET (19 November 2008, 08-65/1055-411)

İzmirgaz (8 January 2009, 09-01/2-2)

Arçelik (8 January 2009, 09-01/4-4)

Bibliography

Sanofi-Aventis (20 April, 2009, 09-16/374-88)

İzmir Jeotermal (15 July 2009, 09-33/739-176)

Malatya Belediyesi (19 August 2009, 09-36/918-225)

Solmaz Mercan II (26 August 2009, 09-39/949-236)

Turkcell-Vodafone (8 October 2009, 09-45/1136-286)

CNR (13 October 2009, 09-46/1154-290)

Parrafin and Vaselin (28 October 2009, 09-49/1220-308)

Tupras (4 November 2009, 09-52/1246-315)

Avea (4 November 2009, 09-52/1253-318)

Knauf (16 December 2009, 09-59/1441-376)

Bereket Jeotermal (16 December 2009, 09-59/1452-383)

Turkcell (23 December 2009, 09-60/1490-379)

Milangaz (30 December 2009, 09-61/1498-394)

İzocam (8 February 2010, 10-14/175-66)

Turkcell (4 March 2010, 10-21/271-100)

Otis (18 March 2010, 10-24/330-118)

Teknoform (8 April 2010, 10-29/446-169)

Mediamarkt (12 May 2010, 10-36/575-205)

TMST (10 June 2010, 10-42/756-243)

Samsung (17 June 2010, 10-44/771-253)

Türkiye Denizcilik İşletmeleri (24 June 2010, 10-45/801-264)

Doğan Yayın (1 July 2010, 10-47/858-296)

White Goods (14 July 2010, 11-43/942-306))

Pepsi Cola (August 5, 2010, 10-52/956-335)

Paşabahçe (2 September 2010, 10-57/1155-439)

Meat and Fish Authority (25 November 2010, 10-73/1509-577)

Ceramics Adhesive Producers (12 January 2011, 11-03/42-14)

Efe-Mey İçki (3 March 2011, 11-12/215-69)

Çimsa (10 March 2011, 11-15/261-89)

Unilever (17 March 2011, 11-16/287-92)

Doğan Medya (30 March 2011, 11-18/341-103)

Turkcell (6 June 2011, 11-34/742-230)

Metro Turizm (14 July 2011, 11-43/915-284)

Çimsa (3 August 2011, 11-44/979-329)

OMV Petrol Ofisi (3 August 2011, 11-44/997-343)

Mey İçki (17 November 2011, 11-57/1476-532)

Trakya Cam (17 November 2011, 11-57/1477-533)

Siemens I (25 April 2012, 12-22/572-166)

Microsoft (3 May 2012, 12-24/661-183)

Digital Platform (3 May 2012, 12-24/710-198)

Aslan Tuğla (31 May 2012, 12-29/839-242)

Bibliography

Biletix (6 June 2012, 12-30/896-274)

Akdeniz Dağıtım (4 July 2012, 12-36/1039-327)

Esgaz (9 August 2012, 12-41/1171-384)

Unilever (28 August 2012, 12-42/1257-409)

UN Ro-Ro (1 October 2012, 12-47/1413-474)

Superonline (10 October 2012, 12-49/1431-484)

Çalık (1 November 2012, 12-53/1491-519)

Kale Kilit (6 December 2012, 12-62/1633-598)

Allergan (3 January 2013, 13-01/3-3)

Hepsiburada (3 January 2013, 13-01/7-7)

Surat Basim/Zambak (19 March 2013, 13-15/230-114)

Microsoft (13 June 2013, 13-36/481-211)

Türkiye Şeker Fabrikaları (18 July 2013, 13-46/589-259)

TTNET (18 July 2013, 13-46/601-M)

Biletix (5 November 2013, 13-61/851-359

Nuh (7 November 2013, 10-63/1317-494)

Volkan Metro (2 December 2013, 13-67/928-390)

TTNET (19 December 2013, 13-71/992-423)

Tüpraş (17 January 2014, 14-03/60-24)

Akbank (12 February 2014, 14-06/116-55)

Bedir Nakliyat (12 March 2014, 14-10/191-81)

Mey İçki (12 June 2014, 14-21/410-178)

TSSF (7 August 2014, 14-26/530-235)

Siemens Medical Devices (20 August 2014, 14-29/613-266)

Tekhnelogos (16 September 2014, 14-33/666-292)

Türk Telekomünikasyon (24 September, 2014, 14-35/697-309)

Turkish Football Federation (26 November 2014, 14-46/834-375)

Berko (26 November 2014, 14-46/845-385)

THY (25 December 2014, 14-54/932-420)

Siemens II (8 January 2015, 15-02/5-3)

Trakya Cam (19 February 2015, 15-08/110-46)

Sahibinden (19 February 2015, 15-08/109-45)

Alcon (5 March 2015, 15-10/139-62)

THY (9 July 2015, 15-29/427-123)

Medical Gas (1 September 2015, 15-34/502-155)

THY (1 September 2015, 15-34/512-160)

Krea İçerik Hizmetleri (9 September 2015, 15-36/544-176)

Mars Cinema (20 November 2015, 15-41/682-243)

Hatay Ro-Ro (6 January 2016, 16-01/12-5)

Tuborg/Ecocaps (10 February 2016, 16-04/69-27)

Digiturk (10 February 2016, 16-04/82-36)

Bibliography

Maysan (18 February 2016, 16-05/107-48)

Solgar (18 February 2016, 16-05/116-51)

Nuh Çimento (18 February 2016, 16-05/118-53)

Unmaş (2 March 2016, 16-07/136-61)

Soda (20 April 2016, 16-14/205-89)

Türk Telekom (3 May 2016, 16-15/254-109)

Türk Telekom (3 May 2016, 16-15/255-110)

Türk Telekomünikasyon (11 May 2016, 16-16/263-115)

Doğan, Mozaik and Krea (18 May 2016, 16-17/299-134)

EMDR (18 May 2016, 16-17/284-127)

Turkcell (18 May 2016, 16-17/285-128)

LMC Gıda (1 June 2016, 16-19/313-142)

Türk Telekom (9 June 2016, 16-20/326-146)

Yemek Sepeti (9 June 2016, 16-20/347-156)

Mars (23 June 2016, 16-21/371-173)

Tav (29 June 2016, 16-22/395-183)

Dow Turkey (4 August 2016, 16-26/433-192)

Dow (13 September 2016, 16-33/586-257)

Yonga Chipboard (13 October 2016, 16-33/571-248)

Congresium Ato (27 October 2016, 16-35/604-269)

Sasa (3 November 2016, 16-36/608-271)

illerarasımesafe.com (16 November 2016, 16-39/638-284)

Congresium Ato (27 October 2016, 16-35/604-269)

TEB (6 December 2016, 16-42/699-3139)

TTNET (9 February 2017, 17-06/53-20)

Mey İçki Rakı (16 February 2017, 17-07/84-34)

Luxottica (23 February 2017, 17-08/99-42)

BOTAŞ (27 April 2017, 17-14/207-85)

Viessmann (15 May 2017, 17-16/223-93)

Social Security Institution (13 July 2017, 17-22/362-158)

Volkan/Öz Edirne, (19 July 2017, 17-23/384-167)

Mesam (22 August 2017, 17-27/451-193)

Lüleburgaz (7 September 2017, 17-28/477-205)

Karabük Demir Çelik (7 September 2017, 17-28/481-207))

Mey İçki (25 October 2017, 17-34/537-228)

Arslanoğlu/Mercedes-Benz (11 November 2017, 17-38/613-268)

Trakya Cam (14 December 2017, 17-41/641-280)

Bilsing (14 December 2017, 17-41/642-281)

Petrol Ofisi (11 January 2018, 18-02/20-10)

Mars (18 January 2018, 18-03/35-22)

Akdeniz Elektrik (20 February 2018, 18-06/101-52)

Bibliography

Çiçek Sepeti (8 March 2018, 18-07/111-58)

Zeyport Zeytinburnu (15 March 2018, 18-08/152-73)

Sanofi (29 March 2018, 18-09/156-76)

Microsoft (24 April 2018, 18-12/227-102)

Daiichi Sankyo (22 May 2018, 18-15/280-139)

Frito-Lay (12 June 2018, 18-19/329-163)

IQVIA Health (12 June 2018, 18-19/330-164))

Türkiye Petrol Rafinerileri (12 June 2018, 18-19/321-157)

Enerjisa (8 August 2018, 18-27/461-224)

TTNET (27 August 2018, 18-29/497-238)

Mercedes-Benz (27 August 2018, 18-29/498-239

Baymak (6 September 2018, 18-30/523-259)

Türk Telekom (19 September 2018, 18-33/545-269)

Google Android (19 September 2018, 18-33/555-273)

Roche (26 September 2018, 18-34/577-283)

Bereket Enerji/Aydem/Gediz (1 October 2018, 18-36/583-284)

Sahibinden (1 October 2018, 18-36/584-285)

Radontek (11 October 2018, 18-38/617-298)

Bandırma (11 October 2018, 18-38/618-299)

TTNET (17 October 2018, 18-39/621-301)

Tüyap (25 October 2018, 18-40/644-314)

Turkcell (8 November 2018, 18-42/670-329)

Techniques Surfaces (3 January 2019, 19-02/2-1)

Unilever I (7 January 2019, 19-38/584-250)

Sony Eurasia (7 February 2019, 19-06/47-16)

Habaş (7 March 2019, 19-11/125-53)

Maysan (28 March 2019, 19-13/182-80)

Isttelkom (11 April 2019, 19-15/214-94)

Novartis (11 April 2019, 19-15/215-95)

Sahibinden (2 May 2019, 19-17/239-108)

Huawei (30 May 2019, 19-20/286-122)

Türknet/Türk Telekom (20 June 2019, 19-22/325-144)

Maysan (20 June 2019, 19-22/353-159)

Google Shopping Unit (7 November 2019, 19-38/575-243)

Google Android (7 November 2019, 19-38/577-245)

Siemens (7 November 2019, 19-38/581-247)

Johnson & Johnson (14 November 2019, 19-40/642-270)

Çaykur II (14 November 2019, 19-40/645-272)

LB Börekçilik (14 November 2019, 19-40/646-273)

Turkish Union of Chambers and Exchange Commodities (14 November 2019, 19-40/650-276)

BP (14 November 2019, 19-40/652-278)

Kamil Koç (14 November 2019, 19-40/658-283)

Toypa (14 November 2019, 19-40/664-285)

Keşan Cement (19 December 2019, 19-45/758-327)

Varinak (19 December 2019, 19-45/768-330)

Philips (26 December 2019, 19-46/790-344)

MEDAŞ (16 January 2020, 20-04/41-23)

Turkcell (6 February 2020, 20-08/82-49)

Google Shopping (13 February 2020, 20-10/119-69)

DSM (20 February 2020, 20-11/127-73)

Türk Telekom (27 February 2020, 20-12/153-83)

Duygu Havacılık (16 April 2020, 20-20/266-127)

Superonline/Turk Telekom (16 April 2020, 20-20/267-128)

Mey Alcoholic Beverage (11 June 2020, 20-28/349-163)

Tema Fuarcılık (2 July 2020, 20-32/396-178)

Brisa (24 July 2020, 20-35/455-202)

Pankobirlik (28 July 2020, 20-36/489-215)

Congresium (27 August 2020, 20-39/538-239)

Container Lineer (24 September 2020, 20-43/591-264)

Outomative (15 October 2020, 20-46/618-270)

Milyon Production (15 October 2020, 20-46/621-273)

Kırtur (5 November 2020, 20-48/657-288)

Carrefour SA (10 November 2020, 10-71/1487-570)

Siemens III (19 November 2020, 20-50/695-306)

WhatsApp Investigation (11 January 2021, 21-02/25-M)

WhatsApp (11 January 2021, 21-02/25-10)

EMDR (28 January 2021, 21-05/56-23)

Unilever (18 March 2021, 21-15/190-80)

Google Local Search (4 April 2021, 21-20/248-105)

Garanti Bank (5 August 2009, 09-34/787-192)

Darfilm (4 December 2008, 08-69/1123-439)

Draeger (19 December 2013, 13-71/971-417)

Amity Oil & Trakya Gazdas (29 June 2006, 06-46/601-172)

Fuel Oil (13 March 2019, 19-12/137-61)

DHMİ (9 September 2015, 15-36/559-182)

Merger Control

Migros/Metro (19 March 1998, 57/424-52)

Cisco/IBM (2 May 2000, 00-16/160-82)

Arçelik (17 October 2000, 00-39/436-242)

Toros Gübre (3 November 2000, 00-43/464-254)

Microsoft I (23 November 2000, 00-46/488-266)

Bibliography

Doğan Yayın Holding/Turkish Daily News (12 December 2000, 00-49/519-284)

Bilkom (9 January 2001, 01-03/10-3)

Çimentas (7 August 2001, 01-39/391-100)

Benkar/Fiba (18 September 2001, 01-44/433-111)

Arçelik-Blomberg Werke – Brant Group (28 May 2002, 02-32/367-153)

ParıltıSofra (4 October 2002, 02-61/759-307)

Eti Gümüş (27 May 2003, 03-35/424-186)

DSM/Roche (11 September 2003, 03-60/730-342)

GlaxoSmithKline/Sanofi (3 June 2004, 04-40/453-114)

Syngenta/Advanta (29 July 2004, 04-49/673-171)

Ereğli Denizcilik (16 December 2004, 04-79/1147-287)

Cytec/Surface (6 January 2005, 05-01/3-3)

TCDD (3 March 2005, 05-12/145-52)

Alstom Power (4 March 2010, 10-21/264-97)

Samsun Gübre (5 May 2005, 05-30/373-92)

Carrefour/Gima (17 June 2005, 05-40/557-136)

APMM/PONL (21 July 2005, 05-48/689-182)

P&G/Gillette (8 September 2005, 05-55/836-228)

TUI AG/CP Ships (13 October 2005, 05-67/950-257)

Migros/Tansaş (31 October 2005, 05-76/1030-287)

Dinter/Konfrut (15 December 2005, 05-84/1149-329)

Standart Çimento (20 December 2005, 05-86/1187-339)

Trabzon Çimento (20 December 2005, 05-86/1189-341)

Gaziantep Çimento (20 December 2005, 05-86/1190-342)

Şanlıurfa Çimento (20 December 2005, 05-86/1191-343)

Van Çimento (20 December 2005, 05-86/1192-344)

Ergani Çimento (20 December 2005, 05-86/1194-346)

Süd-Chemie (29 December 2005, 05-88/1229-358)

Gaziantep Çimento (28 April 2006, 06-31/379-96)

Van Et (26 May 2006, 06-36/459-121)

Mauna/Tyco International (29 June 2006, 06-46/586-159)

Total S.A./CEPSA (20 December 2006, 06-92/1186-355)

Sias Alçı/ABS Alçı (1 February 2007, 07-11/70-22)

CVR Inc/Inco Limited (1 February 2007, 07-11/71-23)

Makromarket/Nazar (5 April 2007, 07-30/293-110)

Eastpharma/Deva (24 April 2007, 07-34/355-133)

Antalya Airport (16 May 2007, 07-41/452-174)

Turk Telekom (20 June 2007, 07-53/571-187)

Chrysler/DaimlerChrysler (20 June 2007, 07-53/585-196)

Condat S.A/Henkel (4 July 2007, 07-56/659-229)

Doğuş Otomotiv/Katalonya (22 August 2007, 07-66/813-308)

Bibliography

Cadbury Schweppes/Intergum (23 August 2007, 07-67/836-314)

Misbis (8 November 2007, 07-85/1039-401)

Şanlurfa-Limak (6 December 2007, 07-89/1130-441)

Kalyon/Hanwha/YEKA (21 December 2007, 17-42/658-290)

Ingenico SA (24 January 2008, 08-08/89-29)

Fresenius (24 January 2008, 08-08/92-32)

MGS/Gıdasa (7 February 2008, 08-12/130-46)

Toros Tarım/Mazıdağı (21 February 2008, 08-16/189-62)

Doğan/Bağımsız Gazeticiler/Kemer (10 March 2008, 08-23/237-75)

Cookson/Foseco (20 March 2008, 08-25/254-83)

Özgür Cement (17 April 2008, 08-29/355-116)

ÇimSA/Bilecik (2 June 2008, 08-36/481-169)

Corio/ACT (3 July 2008, 08-43/588-221)

Migros/Hamoğlu (14 August 2008, 08-50/721-281)

Manitowoc/Enodis (18 September 2008, 08-54/854-341)

Cimpor/Babil (30 October 2008, 08-61/998-390)

Çallı/Turyağ (12 November 2008, 08-63/1048-407)

Fina/Turkon (14 January 2009, 09-02/19-12)

Fayat (11 February 2009, 09-06/119-36)

Verifone/Lipman (13 April 2009, 09-14/300-73)

Assan/Park Panel (11 June 2009, 09-27/594-139)

Kiler/Yimpaş (15 July 2009, 09-33/728-168)

ČEZ Bohunice (15 July 2009, 09-33/763-183)

Kansai Paint/Akzo Nobel Coatings (5 August 2009, 09-34/791-194)

Enfes Gıda (6 August 2009, 09-35/889-212)

Efes Etap (19 August 2009, 09-47/1161-295)

Aşkale/Lafarge (26 August 2009, 09-39/926-227)

Simsmetal East/Fairless Iron & Metal (16 September 2009, 09-42/1057-269)

Schering/Merck (21 October 2009, 09-48/1203-304)

Mey İçki (18 November 2009, 09-56/1325-331)

OYAK (18 November 2009, 09-56/1338-341)

Ekol (9 December 2009, 09-58/1406-368)

Alarm Systems (23 December 2009, 09-60/1477-393)

Citigroup/US Treasure (6 January 2010, 10-01/18-11)

Novartis/Nestlé (8 February 2010, 10-49/929-327)

Agilent/Varian (18 February 2010, 10-18/212-82)

HP/3Com (18 February 2010, 10-18/213-83)

Uludağ Electricity Distribution (11 March 2010, 10-22/296-106)

Yeşilırmak Electricity Distribution (11 March 2010, 10-22/297-107)

Çoruh Electricity Distribution (11 March 2010, 10-22/298-108)

Altıparmak Gıda (31 March 2010, 10-27/393-146)

Bibliography

Çamlıbel Electricity Distribution (8 April 2010, 10-29/437-163)

Uludağ Electricity Distribution (8 April 2010, 10-29/438-164)

Fırat Electricity Distribution (8 April 2010, 10-29/439-165)

Van Gölü Electricity Distribution (8 April 2010, 10-29/440-166)

Sarten/TKS (15 April 2010, 10-31/471-175)

Mediamarkt (12 May 2010, 10-36/575-205)

Batıçim/Borares (27 May 2010, 10-38/641-217)

Flir Systems Holding/Raymarine (17 June 2010, 10-44/762-246)

Mey İçki/Burgaz (8 July 2010, 10-49/900-314)

CVRD Canada/Inco (8 July 2010, 10-49/949-332)

TOBB/Mesa Mesken (26 August 2010, 10-56/1088-408)

Cegedim/Dendrite/Ultima (26 August 2010, 10-56/1089-411)

Türk Telekom/Invitel (16 September 2010, 10-59/1195-451)

Egetek (30 September 2010, 10-62/1286-487)

Besler/Turyağ (12 October 2010, 10-64/1355-498)

Ajans Press/PR Net (21 October 2010, 10-66/1402-523)

LF Invest (27 October 2010, 10-67/1423-539)

Canerler/Kiler (29 December 2010, 10-81/1693-644)

Strategic Development/Yıldız Holding/Marsa (9 February 2011, 11-08/151-49)

Prysmian/Draka (10 March 2011, 11-15/259-87)

Ammann Group/Ammann Teknomak (14 April 2011, 11-23/433-131)

Zhejiang/Kiri (2 June 2011, 11-33/723-226)

Antalya/Burgaz (6 July 2011, 11-41/865-M)

Aygaz/Total Oil (6 July 2011, 11-41/873-274)

Sorgenia/KKR (14 July 2011, 11-43/919-288)

Diageo/Mey İçki (17 August 2011, 11-45/1043-356)

Ülker/Şok (17 August 2011, 11-45/1044-357)

Flabeg/Schott/SBPS/Ocean (17 August 2011, 11-45/1106-382)

Blackstone/Lisa Germany (17 November 2011, 11-57/1468-525)

Mars/AFM (17 November 2011, 11-57/1473-539)

Galenica/Fresenius (24 November 2011, 11-59/1515-540)

Lur Berri/Alfesca (14 December 2011, 11-61/1580-565)

Seagard/Samsung (29 December 2011, 11-64/1656-586)

Tamiran/SITA (12 January 2012, 12-01/6-3)

Tekno İnşaat/Enerray/Tekno Ray (23 February 2012, 12-08/224-55)

Ravago/Barentz (14 March 2012, 12-11/369-104)

Sonangol/BP/Chevron/Eni/Total/ALNG (25 April 2012, 12-22/564-162)

Camargo/Cimpor (3 May 2012, 12-24/665-187)

Ulusal Cad (9 May 2012, 12-25/729-209)

Eksim/Rönesans/Acıbadem (16 May 2012, 12-26/759-213)

Metlac/Akzo Nobel Coatings (14 June 2012, 12-33/927-285)

Bibliography

Türkiye Petrol Rafinerileri/Akdeniz Akaryakıt (4 July 2012, 12-36/1041-329)

Konya Cement/Erdoğanlar (10 September 2012, 12-43/1323-436)

Akçansa (16 October 2012, 12-50/1445-492)

Unmaş/Europastry (27 December 2012, 12-60/1598-582)

AstraZeneca/Bristol/Amylin (20 February 2013, 13-11/163-85)

Ciner/Show (26 June 2013, 13-40/526-233)

Şok/Onur (13 August 2013, 13-47/635-274)

DSG/Electro World (5 September 2013, 13-50/717-304)

Opet/Aygaz (12 September 2013, 13-52/734-307)

Ajinomoto (5 December 2013, 13-69/932-393)

Provus (19 December 2013, 13-71/957-405)

Maspex-Tat (26 December 2013, 13-72/1013-431)

Yücel Boru/İlhanlar (9 January 2014, 14-01/4-3)

Omur Denizcilik/Ziraat/Güneş/Halk/Metropole/Vitsan (19 February 2014, 14-07/134-61)

Sabiha Gökçen/THY Opet (26 February 2014, 14-08/155-66)

Setur (30 April 2014, 15-29/421-118)

OMV Petrol Ofisi/Shell&Turcas (5 June 2014, 14-20/382-166)

Ersoy/Sesli (25 June 2014, 14-22/422-186)

Lesaffre/Dosu Maya (15 December 2014, 14-52/903-411)

Ferrero (8 January 2015, 15-02/8-6)

Bekaert/Pirelli (22 January 2015, 15-04/52-25)

Novartis/GlaxoSmithKline (29 January 2015, 15-05/59-26)

BBVA/Garanti Bankası (19 February 2015, 15-08/106-43)

Anadolu Endüstri/Moonlight (9 July 2015, 15-29/420-117)

ADPM/Vinci Airports/Astaldi (1 September 2015, 15-34/509-157)

Labelon/A-Tex (6 February 2016, 16-42/693-311)

Grup Maritim (3 May 2016, 16-15/246-108)

APMT/Grup Maritim (11 May 2016, 16-16/267-118)

ABI/SABMiller (1 June 2016, 16-19/311-140)

Nucor/JFE (23 June 2016, 16-21/383-177)

International Paper Company/Weyerhaeuser Company (23 September 2016, 16-31/519-233)

Akçansa (16 November 2016, 16-39/654-293)

Migros/Tesco (9 February 2017, 17-06/56-22)

Toyota (6 April 2017, 17-12/143-63)

Maersk/HSDG (4 May 2017, 17-15/210-89)

Carmel/DAE (8 June 2017, 17-19/292-129)

Deere/Wirtgen (19 July 2017, 17-23/365-158)

Abdi İbrahim/Aksel Ecza Deposu (19 July 2017, 17-23/372-163)

Karabük Demir Çelik (7 September 2017, 17-28/481-207)

Bibliography

Valeo/FTE (26 October 2017, 17-35/560-244)

DSM/Evonik (26 October 2017, 17-35/573-248)

UN Ro-Ro/Ulusoy (9 November 2017, 17-36/595-259)

Celanese/Blackstone (28 November 2017, 17-39/623-270)

Baştaş (21 December 2017, 17-42/667-295)

Trakya Cam/Düzcam Exemption (21 December 2017, 17-42/670-298)

Adana Çimento (4 January2018, 18-01/5-3)

Mikro/Zirve (18 January 2018, 18-03/25-13)

Akarlılar/Mavi Giyim (8 March 2018, 18-07/121-65)

TUSAŞ/Sarsılmaz (15 March 2018, 18-08/137-67)

Crown Holdings/Signode (29 March 2018, 18-09/158-78)

Bayer/Medifar (29 March 2018, 18-09/160-80)

BASF (5 April 2018, 18-10/183-86)

Gemsat (18 April 2018, 18-11/197-93)

Migros/Kipa (18 April 2018, 18-11/204-95)

Demirören Medya (3 May 2018, 18-13/248-113)

Boru Hatları (8 May 2018, 18-14/254-120)

Bayer/Monsanto (8 May 2018, 18-14/261-126)

Arkas/Mardaş (8 May 2018, 18-14/267-129)

Turkuvaz (29 May 2018, 18-16/293-146)

CMLKK Liman (31 May 2018, 18-17/303-152)

Dosu Maya/Lessafre (31 May 2018, 18-17/316-156)

Gümüşdoğa/Baracuda (21 June 2018, 18-20/350-171)

UBM/UBM ICC/UBM İstanbul/UBM NTSR (21 June 2018, 18-20/354-175)

Mosaş (21 June 2018, 18-20/356-176)

CMLKK Bilişim (5 July 2018, 18-22/376-184)

CMLKK Parking/Exchange/Fuel (2 August 2018, 18-24/426-200)

Bohai/Orix-Avolon (26 September 2018, 18-34/567-280)

Automobile Project (26 September 2018, 18-34/566-279)

Essilor/Luxottica (1 October 2018, 18-36/585-286)

MP Hotel/Magic Life/TUI/Bodrum Imperial/Alaçatı (22 November 2018, 18-44/699-343)

Migros/Makro (13 December 2018, 18-47/736-356)

DENSO/Aisin Seiki (17 January 2019, 19-04/32-13)

Anadolu Efes/Tekel (7 February 2019, 19-06/54-20)

Daimler/Volkswagen-MT Holding (7 February 2019, 19-06/61-25)

Leoni/Hengtong (21 February 2019, 19-08/93-38)

Nidec/Whirlpool (18 April 2019, 19-16/231-103)

SOCAR (2 May 2019, 19-17/235-106)

Biberci (2 May 2019, 19-17/243-110)

TUSAŞ/Altınay (13 June 2019, 19-21/321-140)

Harris/L3 (20 June 2019, 19-22/327-145)

Bibliography

Daimler/Geely (24 July 2019, 19-26/396-183)

Şafak Elektrik (24 July 2019, 19-26/402-187)

Saudi Arabian Oil Company (29 August 2019, 19-30/448-193)

MIH Pavü (5 September 2019, 31/466-199)

Faurecia/Michelin-SymbioFCell (26 September 2019, 19-33/491-211)

Siemens (7 November 2019, 19-38/581-247)

Astellas (14 November 2019, 19-40/637-269)

Vetrerie Riunite S.p.A. (21 November 2019, 19-42/707-305)

Cinven/Stichting/Barentz (22 November 2019, 19-41/676-291)

CDC/Total (29 November 2019, 19-42/700-299)

Astorg/eResearch Technology (12 December 2019, 19-44/730-310)

Bamesa/Steel Center (12 December 2019, 19-44/739-316)

Engie/EDF/CDC/La Poste (19 December 2019, 19-45/747-321)

APMC/GSEZ/TIPSP/Arise (19 December 2019, 19-45/757-326)

Keşan Cement (19 December 2019, 19-45/758-327)

CMLKK Liman 2 (19 December 2019, 19-45/769-331)

FSI/Snam-OLT Offshore (9 January 2020, 20-03/18-8)

HSI/Hilton Sao Paulo Morumbi (16 January 2020, 20-04/33-16)

Mitsubishi/Wallenius Wilhelmsen (16 January 2020, 20-04/35-18)

Alpla Holding/PTT Global (16 January 2020, 20-04/37-19)

Migros/Dörtler (16 January 2020, 20-04/38-20)

Generali/Union-Zaragoza Properties (6 February 2020, 20-08/73-41)

Synthomer/OMNOVA (6 February 2020, 20-89/90-55)

Sumitomo/Toyota (13 February 2020, 20-10/101-59)

Mylan (20 February 2020, 20-11/125-72)

Viacom (26 March 2020, 20-16/233-114)

Superonline/Türk Telekom (16 April 2020, 20-20/267-128)

Brookfield/JCI (30 April 2020, 20-21/278-132)

Botaş (7 May 2020, 20-23/301-147)

Asahi (11 June 2020, 20-28/362-162)

Firmenich International (25 June 2020, 20-31/388-174)

Hegsakon/Unico (25 June 2020, 20-31/393-176)

Baring/Travelex (9 July 2020, 20-33/415-191)

Naturelgaz/Socar Turkey (9 July 2020, 20-33/427-194)

Hitachi/Honda/Keihin/Showa/Nissin (9 July 2020, 20-33/413-189)

SOCAR/BP (9 July 2020, 20-33/426-193)

Batıbeton (24 July 2020, 20-35/453-200)

BMW/Daimler/Ford/Porsche/Ionity (28 July 2020, 20-36/483-211)

Varian/Varinak (28 July 2020, 20-36/491-216)

DIC/BASF (28 July 2020, 20-36/497-222)

Marport/TIL (13 August 2020, 20-37/523-231)

Yıldızlar (13 August 2020, 20-37/525-233)

Güneş Sigorta (27 August 2020, 20-39/539-240)

Pigments (17 September 2020, 20-42/579-259)

Calderys/Haznedar/Durer/Vender (12 November 2020, 20-49/669-293)

Cheplapharm (19 November 2020, 20-50/683-298)

PSA/FCA (30 December 2020, 20-57/794-354)

Mitsui/Honshu (7 January 2021, 21-01/4-3)

Other Cases

Toros Gübre (3 November 2000, 00-43/464-254)

Sodexo (28 April 2006, 06-31/376-99)

Batıçim/Batısöke (26 May 2006, 06-36/474-128)

Antalya Airport (16 May 2007, 07-41/452-174)

Lafarge Beton (9 December 2009, 09-58/1396-364)

Uludağ Electricity Distribution (11 March 2010, 10-22/296-106)

Yeşilırmak Electricity Distribution (11 March 2010, 10-22/297-107)

Çoruh Electricity Distribution (11 March 2010, 10-22/298-108)

Uludağ Electricity Distribution (8 April 2010, 10-29/438-164)

Turkish Pharmacists' Association I (7 July 2015, 15-28/336-108)

Dow (2 August 2015, 15-42/690-259)

Türk Telekomünikasyon (11 May 2016, 16-16/263-115)

Turkcell (18 May 2016, 16-17/285-128)

Dow Turkey (4 August 2016, 16-26/433-192)

Siemens (13 November 2016, 16-36/620-M)

Enerjisa (6 December 2016, 16-42/686-314)

EMDR (10 August 2017, 17-26/396-175)

Mars Sinema (18 January 2018, 18-03/34-21)

Çekok Gıda (8 February 2018, 18-04/56-31)

Warner Bros (17 January 2019, 19-04/36-14)

Ege Gübre (7 February 2019, 19-06/51-18)

Huawei (14 November 2019, 19-40/670-288)

Askaynak (26 December 2019, 19-46/793-346)

Custom Consultants Association (6 February 2020, 20-08/77-44)

Çiçek Sepeti (2 July 2020, 20-32/405-186)

Arslan Nakliyat (28 July 2020, 20-36/485-212)

Unilever (September 3, 2020, 20-40/550-247)

A101 (22 October 2020, 20-47/638-280)

Havaş (5 November 2020, 20-48/655-287)

United Phosphorus/Agromed (14 July 2011, 11-43/938-302)

Court Judgments

1st Chamber of the Council of State (5 July 1984, E. 1984/72, K. 1984/155)

5th Chamber of the Council of State (22 November 1988, E. 1988/2749, K. 1988/2845).

10th Chamber of the Council of State (15 January 2001, E. 2000/1432, K. 2001/54)

10th Chamber of the Council of State (27 February 2001, E. 1998/5517, K. 2001/738)

10th Chamber of Council of State (2 April 2002, E. 1999/3957, K. 2002/894)

10th Chamber of Council of State (7 October 2002, E. 2002/4182, K. 2002/3508))

10th Chamber of the Council of State (7 October 2003, E. 2002/4519, K. 2003/3811)

10th Chamber of the Council of State (4 November 2003, E. 2001/355, K. 2003/4245)

10th Chamber of the Council of State (5 December 2003, E. 2001/4817, K. 2003/4770)

10th Chamber of the Council of State (23 December 2003, E. 2002/693, K. 2003/5295)

10th Chamber of the Council of State (23 December 2003, E. 2002/3686, K. 2003/5292)

10th Chamber of the Council of State (26 April 2004, E. 2001/2004, K. 2004/4070)

11th Civil Chamber of the High Court of Appeals (23 June 2006, E. 2005/3755, K. 2006/7408)

11th Civil Chamber of the High Court of Appeals (10 October 2007, E. 2006/9834, K. 2007/12673)

11th Civil Chamber of the High Court of Appeals (5 October 2009, E. 2008/5575, K. 2009/10045 K)

11th Civil Chamber of the High Court of Appeals, (30 March 2015, E. 2014/13296, K. 2015/4424)

11th Civil Chamber of the High Court of Appeals (13 April 2015, E. 2015/15, K. 2015/5128)

11th Civil Chamber of the High Court of Appeals (8 March 2016, E. 2015/5134, K. 2016/2543)

12th Chamber of the Council of State (13 May1968, E. 1682, K. 1099)

13th Chamber of the Council of State (12 December 2006, E. 2006/313, K. 2006/4716)

13th Chamber of the Council of State (25 September 2007, E. 2006/3356, K. 2007/5248)

13th Chamber of the Council of State (29 January 2008, E. 2006/4192); approved by the decision of the Plenary Session of the Council of State (14 February 2013, E. 2008/2191)

13th Chamber of the Council of State (1 February 2013, E. 2009/109, K. 2013/212)

13th Chamber of the Council of State (2 February 2010, E. 2007/9330, K. 2010/1325)

13th Chamber of the Council of State (15 March 2010, E. 2008/13171, K. 2010/2225)

13th Chamber of the Council of State (14 April 2011, E. 2011/688, K. 2015/1456)

13th Chamber of the Council of State (12 September 2011, E. 2011/2383, K. 2011/3671)

13th Chamber of the Council of State (13 December 2012, E. 2009/1523, K. 2012/3795)

13th Chamber of Council of State (26 March 2013, E. 2009/5890, K. 2013/847)

13th Chamber of the Council of State (3 April 2014, E. 2013/3006, K. 2014/1284)

13th Chamber of the Council of State (30 May 2014, E. 2010/4818, K. 2014/2197)

13th Chamber of the Council of State (12 November 2014, E. 2010/4464, K. 2014/3480)

13th Chamber of the Council of State (14 April 2015, E. 2011/710, K. 2015/1459)

13th Chamber of the Council of State (25 May 2015, E. 2009/5608, K. 2014/2054)

13th Chamber of the Council of State (5 June 2015, E. 2015/698, K. 2015/2125)

13th Chamber of Council of State (22 March 2016, E. 2011/2660, K. 2016/775)

13th Chamber of the Council of State (16 December 2016, E. 2010/4617, K. 2016/4241)

13th Chamber of the Council of State (27 December 2017, E. 2011/3511, K. 2017/4404)

Bibliography

13th Chamber of the Council of State (9 July 2018, E. 2018/1837, K. 2018/232)

13th Chamber of the Council of State (11 December 2019, E. 2015/3353, K. 2019/4244)

13th Chamber of the Council of State (11 December 2019, E. 2019/1035, K. 2019/4253)

13th Chamber of the Council of State (21 May 2019, E. 2016/4058, K. 2019/1782)

13th Chamber of the Council of State (21 May 2019, E. 2016/4069, K. 2019/1783)

13th Chamber of the Council of State (28 July 2020, E. 2014/462, K. 2020/1774)

13th Chamber of the Council of State (13 October 2020, E.2018/706, K.2020/2549)

13th Chamber of the Council of State (2 December 2020, E. 2020/1939, K. 2020/3507)

13th Chamber of the Council of State (2 December 2020, E. 2020/1941, K. 2020/3508)

15th Chamber of the Council of State (11 November 2015, E. 2015/2514, K. 2015/7361)

15th Chamber of the Council of State (13 November 2015, E. 2015/4441, K. 2015/7545)

4th Civil Chamber of the High Court of Appeals, File No. 2016/3818, Judgment No. 2016/6946, dated 25 May 2016

13th Civil Chamber of the High Court of Appeals (25 December 2002, E. 2002/12626, K. 2002/14028)

15th Criminal Chamber of the High Court of Appeals (20 January 2016, E. 2015/14529, K. 2016/634)

19th Civil Chamber of the High Court of Appeals (1 November 1999, E. 99/3350, K. 99/6364)

19th Civil Chamber of the High Court of Appeal decision No. 2002/7580, dated 29 November 2001, File No. 2002/2827

19th Civil Chamber of the High Court of Appeals decision No. 2008/731 dated 4 February 2008, File No. 2007/7136

19th Civil Chamber of the High Court of Appeals decision No. 2008/2858 dated 24 March 2008, File No. 2008/27

19th Civil Chamber of the High Court of Appeals decision No. 2007/8775 dated 9 October 2008, File No. 2007/5290

1st Chamber of Turkish Constitution Court (19 October 1992, E. 1991/1619, K. 1992/1423)

3rd Civil Chamber of the High Court of Appeals, File No. 2009/17737, Judgment No. 2009/18986, dated 23 November 2009

The 4th Administrative Court Ankara (26 November 2014, E. 2013/1811, K. 2014/1609)

4th Chamber of the Council of State (23 May 2011, E. 2009/248, K. 2011/4403)

10th Civil Chamber of Court of Appeals, File No. 2003/835, Judgment No. 2003/1628, dated 6 March 2003.

8th Administrative Chamber of the Ankara Regional Court's *Enerjisa* decision (10 October 2018, E. 2018/658, K. 2018/1236)

8th Administrative Chamber of the Ankara Regional Administrative Court (20 January 2021, E. 2020/699, K. 2021/68)

Ankara 2nd Administrative Court (17 March 2020, E. 2018/2415, K. 2019/2649)

Ankara 2nd Administrative Court (27 June 2019, E. 2018/1292, K. 2019/1292)

Ankara 3th Administrative Court (27 October 2020, E. 2020/1059, K. 2020/2043)

Ankara 6th Administrative Court (18 December 2019, E. 2019/246, K. 2019/2625) reviewed after the annulment decision of the High State Court (8 July 2009, 09-32/703-161)

Ankara 6th Administrative Court (18 December 2019, E. 2019/946, K. 2019/2625)

Ankara 6th Administrative Court (31 December 2014, E. 2013/1839, K. 2014/1727)

Bibliography

Ankara 7th Administrative Court (14 January 2021, E. 2021/60)

Ankara 7th Administrative Court (26 December 2018, M. 2017/203, K. 2018/2471)

Ankara 9th Administrative Court (28 March 2019, E. 2018/2277)

Ankara 9th Administrative Court (21 October 2019, E. 2018/2277, K. 2019/2087)

Ankara 12th Administrative Court (7 March 2019, E. 2018/1145, K. 2019/475)

Ankara 12th Administrative Court (15 June 2020, E. 2018/2099, K. 2019/2342)

Ankara 12th Administrative Court (9 October 2014, E. 2013/1754, K. 2014/1094)

Ankara 13th Administrative Court (17 September 2020, E. 2020/315, K. 2020/1569)

Ankara 13th Administrative Court (24 October 2014, E. 2013/1598, K. 2014/1495)

Ankara 14th Administrative Court (2 October 2014, E. 2012/1803, K. 2014/1065)

Ankara 15th Administrative Court's *Enerjisa* decision (16 November 2017, E. 2017/412, K. 2017/3045)

Ankara Regional Administrative Court (8th Administrative Chamber) (4 March 2020, E. 2019/2944, K. 2020/424 and 20 February 2020, E. 2019/3384, K. 2020/320)

Batman Civil Court of First Instance (acting as the Consumer Court), File No. 2016/463, Judgment No. 2017/147, dated: 21 February 2017

High Court of Appeals decision No. 1999/6364, dated 1 November 1999, File No. 3350

Istanbul 12th Consumer Court (23 May 2017, E. 2016/23, K. 2017/184)

Istanbul 12th Consumer Court, (23 May 2017, E. 2016/979, K. 2017/191)

Istanbul 6th Commercial Court of First Instance (21 October 2018, E. 2017/33, K. 2018/1153)

İstanbul 16th Commercial Court of First Instance (15 March 2019, E. 2017/976, K. 2019/211)

Istanbul 16th Commercial Court of First Instance (4 October 2019, E. 2017/91, K. 2019/845)

İzmir 4th Commercial Court of First Instance decision No. 2004/905, dated 2 December 2004, File No. 2004/466

İzmir 4th Commercial Court of First Instance decision No. 2007/155 dated 12 April 2007, File No. 2006/507

Kadıköy 3. Commercial Court of First Instance decision No. 2006/266, dated 4 April 2006, File No. 2002/793

Marmaris 1st Civil Court of First Instance (14 November 2017, E. 2017/17, K. 2017/494)

Plenary Session of the Administrative Law Chambers (28 September 2001, E. 2001/480, K. 2001/637)

Plenary Session of the Administrative Law Chambers (22 December 2005, E. 2004/106, K. 2005/3262)

Plenary Session of the Administrative Law Chambers (26 September 2012, E. 2012/1266, K. 2007/307)

Plenary Session of the Administrative Law Chambers (20 February 2014, E. 2010/3333, K. 2014/437)

Plenary Session of the Administrative Law Chambers (9 April 2018, E. 2015/3253, K. 2017/3542)

Case Law: Other Jurisdictions
European Union

AG Opinion

AG Jacobs' Opinion in Case C-7/97 *Oscar Bronner GmbH & Co KG v. Mediaprint* [1998] ECR I-7791

AG Wahl's Opinion in Case C-177/16, *AKKA/LAA* [2017] EU:C:2017:286

CJEC/CJEU

Joined Cases 56 and 58-64 *Établissements Consten S.à.R.L. and Grundig-Verkaufs-GmbH v. Commission of the European Economic Community* [1966] ECR 299

Case C-48/69 *Imperial Chemical Industries Ltd. v. Commission of the European Communities* [1972] ECR 619

Case 6-72 *Europemballage Corporation and Continental Can Company Inc. v. Commission of the European Communities* [1973] ECR 215

Joined Cases 6 and 7-73 *Commercial Solvents* [1974] ECR 223

Joined Cases 40 to 48, 50, 54 to 56, 111, 113 and 114-73 *Coöperatieve Vereniging "Suiker Unie" UA and others v. Commission of the European Communities* [1975] ECR 1663

Case 27/76 *United Brands Company v. Commission* [1978] ECR 207

Case 85/76 *Hoffmann-La Roche & Co. AG v. Commission* [1979] ECR 461

Case 155/79 *AM & S Europe Limited v. Commission of the European Communities* [1982] ECR 1575

Case 322/81 *Michelin v. Commission* [1983] ECR 3461

Case 75/84 *Metro SB-Großmärkte GmbH & Co. KG v. Commission of the European Communities* [1986] ECR 3021

Case 118/85 *Commission v. Italian Republic* [1987] ECR 2599

Case 238/87 *AB Volvo* [1988] ECR 6211

Case C-62/86 *AKZO Chemie BV v. Commission* [1991] ECR I-3359

Case C-18/93 *Corsica Ferries Italia Srl v. Corpo dei Piloti del Porto di Genova* [1994] ECR I-1783

Joined Cases C-241/91 P and C-242/91 P *Magill* [1995] ECR I-743

Case C-333/94 P *Tetra Pak International SA v. Commission* [1996] ECR I-5951

Case C-7/97 *Oscar Bronner GmbH & Co KG v. Mediaprint* [1998] ECR I-7791

Case C-163/99 *Portugal v. Commission* [2001] ECR I-2613

Case C-418/01 *IMS Health* [2004] ECR I-5039

Case C-95/04 *British Airways plc v. Commission* [2007] ECR I-2331

Joined Cases C-468/06 to C-478/06 *GlaxoSmithKline* [2008] ECR I-7139

Case C-202/07 P *France Télécom v. Commission* [2009] ECR 2369

Case C-280/08 P *Deutsche Telekom AG v. Commission* [2010] ECR I-9555

Case C-67/13 P *Groupement des Cartes Bancaires v. Commission* [2014] EU:C:2014:2204

Case C-23/14 *Post Danmark A/S v. Konkurrencerådet* [2015] EU:C:2015:651

Case C-177/16 *AKKA/LAA* [2017] EU:C:2017:689

CFIEC/GCEU

Case T-30/89 *Hilti AG v. Commission* [1991] ECR II-1439

Case T-83/91 *Tetra Pak International SA v. Commission* [1994] ECR II-755

Joined Cases T-305/94, T-306/94, T-307/94, T-313/94 to T-316/94, T-318/94, T-325/94, T-328/94, T-329/94 and T-335/94 *Limburgse Vinyl Maatschappi and others v. Commission of the European Communities* [1999] ECR II-931

Case T-41/96 *Bayer AG v. Commission of the European Communities* [2000] ECR II-3383

Case T-203/01 *Manufacture française des pneumatiques Michelin v. Commission* [2003] ECR II-4071

Case T-219/99 *British Airways v. Commission* [2003] ECR II-5917

Joined Cases T-67/00, T-68/00, T-71/00 and T-78/00 *JFE Engineering Corp and others v. Commission of the European Communities* [2004] ECR II-2501

Joined Cases T-125/03 and T-253/03 *Akzo Nobel Chemicals Ltd and Akcros Chemicals Ltd v. Commission of the European Communities* [2007] ECR 3523

Case T-201/04 *Microsoft Corp. v. Commission* [2007] ECR II-3601

Case T-286/09 *Intel Corp. v. Commission* [2014] EU:T:2014:547

Case T-814/17 *Lithuanian Railway v. Commission* [2020] EU:T:2020:545

European Commission

European Sugar Industry (Case IV/26.918) Commission Decision 73/109/EEC [1973] OJ L 140/17

Polypropylene (Case IV/31.149) Commission Decision [1986] OJ L 230/1

Torras/Sarrio (Case No. IV/M.166) Commission Decision [1992] OJ C 58/5

Portuguese Airports (Case No IV/35.703) Commission Decision 1999/199/EC [1999] OJ L 69/31

Virgin British Airways (Case IV/D-2/34.780) Commission Decision 2000/74/EC [2000] OJ L 30/1

Deutsche Post AG – Interception of cross-border mail (Case COMP/C-1/36.91), Commission Decision 2001/892/EC [2001] OJ L 331/40

Microsoft (Case COMP/C-3/37.792) Commission Decision No. C(2004)900 final

Clearstream (Case COMP/38.096) Commission Decision [2009] OJ C 165/5

Intel (Case COMP/C-3/37.990) Commission Decision [2009] O.J. (C 227) 13

Slovak Telekom (Case AT.39.523) Commision Decision No. C(2014) 7465 final

Altice/PT Portugal (Case M.7993) Commission Decision No. C(2018) 2418 final

Google Android (Case AT.40099) Commission Decision No. C(2018) 4761 final

Germany

Bundeskartellamt, 6 February 2019, Case No. B6-22/16

Düsseldorf Court of Appeal (Oberlandesgericht Düsseldorf), 26 August 2019, Case VI-Kart 1/19

German Federal Supreme Court's (Bundesgerichtshof) decision of 23 June 2020, Case KVR 69/19

Düsseldorf Court of Appeal (Oberlandesgericht Düsseldorf), 24 March 2021, Case Kart 9/2021

Netherlands

Cases 04/237 and 04/249 LJN AU8309 *Secon Group and G-Star International v. The Netherlands Competition Authority*, 7 December 2005

Spain

CNMC (Comisión Nacional de los Mercados y la Competencia), 7 April 2016, Case S/DC/0503/14 *Fabricantes de Turrón*

USA

Standard Oil Co. of New Jersey v. United States, 221 U.S. 1 (1911)

Chicago Board of Trade v. United States, 246 U.S. 231 (1918)

United States v. Arnold, Schwinn & Co., 388 U.S. 365 (1967)

Verizon Communications v. Law Offices of Curtis V. Trinko, LLP, 540 US 398 (2004)

Leegin Creative Leather Products, Inc. v. PSKS, Inc., 171 Fed. Appx. 464 (2007)

Leegin Creative Leather Products, Inc. v. PSKS, Inc., 551 U.S. 877, 886, 127 S. Ct. 2705, 168 L.Ed.2d 623 (2007)

United States v. eBay, Inc., 968 F.Supp.2d 1030 (N.D. Cal. 2013)

Concurrences
Competition Laws Review

Concurrences Review

Concurrences is a print and online quarterly peer reviewed journal dedicated to EU and national competitions laws. It has been launched in 2004 as the flagship of the Institute of Competition Law in order to provide a forum for academics, practitioners and enforcers. Concurrences' influence and expertise has garnered contributions or interviews with such figures as Christine Lagarde, Bill Kovacic, Emmanuel Macron, Antonin Scalia and Magrethe Vestager.

CONTENTS

More than 12,000 articles, print and/or online. Quarterly issues provide current coverage with contributions from the EU or national or foreign countries thanks to more than 1,500 authors in Europe and abroad.

FORMAT

In order to balance academic contributions with opinions or legal practice notes, Concurrences provides its insight and analysis in a number of formats:

- Forewords: Opinions by leading academics or enforcers
- Interviews: Interviews of antitrust experts
- On-Topics: 4 to 6 short papers on hot issues
- Law & Economics: Short papers written by economists for a legal audience
- Articles: Long academic papers
- Case Summaries: Case commentary on EU and French case law
- Legal Practice: Short papers for in-house counsels
- International: Medium size papers on international policies
- Books Review: Summaries of recent antitrust books
- Articles Review: Summaries of leading articles published in 45 antitrust journals

BOARDS

The Scientific Committee is headed by Laurence Idot, Professor at Panthéon Assas University. The International Committee is headed by Frederic Jenny, OECD Competition Comitteee Chairman. Boards members include Douglas Ginsburg, Bruno Lasserre, Howard Shelanski, Richard Whish, Wouter Wils, Joshua Wright, etc.

ONLINE VERSION

Concurrences website provides all articles published since its inception, in addition to selected articles published online only in the electronic supplement.

WRITE FOR CONCURRENCES

Concurrences welcome spontaneous contributions. Except in rare circumstances, the journal accepts only unpublished articles, whatever the form and nature of the contribution. The Editorial Board checks the form of the proposals, and then submits these to the Scientific Committee. Selection of the papers is conditional to a peer review by at least two members of the Committee. Within a month, the Committee assesses whether the draft article can be published and notifies the author.

e-Competitions Bulletin

CASE LAW DATABASE

e-Competitions is the only online resource that provides consistent coverage of antitrust cases from 85 jurisdictions, organized into a searchable database structure. e-Competitions concentrates on cases summaries taking into account that in the context of a continuing growing number of sources there is a need for factual information, i.e., case law.

- 18,000 case summaries
- 4,000 authors
- 85 countries covered
- 30,000 subscribers

SOPHISTICATED EDITORIAL AND IT ENRICHMENT

e-Competitions is structured as a database. The editors make a sophisticated technical and legal work on all articles by tagging these with key words, drafting abstracts and writing html code to increase Google ranking. There is a team of antitrust lawyers – PhD and judges clerks - and a team of IT experts. e-Competitions makes comparative law possible. Thanks to this expert editorial work, it is possible to search and compare cases by jurisdiction, legal topics or business sectors.

PRESTIGIOUS BOARDS

e-Competitions draws upon highly distinguished editors, all leading experts in national or international antitrust. Advisory Board Members include: Sir Christopher Bellamy, Ioanis Lianos (UCL), Eleanor Fox (NYU), Frédéric Jenny (OECD), Jacqueline Riffault-Silk (Cour de cassation), Wouter Wils (King's College London), etc.

LEADING PARTNERS

- Association of European Competition Law Judges: The AECLJ is a forum for judges of national Courts specializing in antitrust case law. Members timely feed e-Competitions with just released cases.

- Academics partners: Antitrust research centres from leading universities write regularly in e-Competitions: University College London, King's College London, Queen Mary University, etc.

- Law firms: Global law firms and antitrust niche firms write detailed cases summaries specifically for e-Competitions: Allen & Overy, Baker McKenzie, Cleary Gottlieb Steen & Hamilton, Jones Day, Norton Rose Fulbright, Skadden, White & Case, etc.

The Institute of Competition Law

The Institute of Competition Law is a publishing company, founded in 2004 by Dr. Nicolas Charbit, based in Paris, London and New York. The Institute cultivates scholarship and discussion about antitrust issues though publications and conferences. Each publication and event is supervised by editorial boards and scientific or steering committees to ensure independence, objectivity, and academic rigor. Thanks to this management, the Institute has become one of the few think tanks in Europe to have significant influence on antitrust policies.

AIM

The Institute focuses government, business and academic attention on a broad range of subjects which concern competition laws, regulations and related economics.

BOARDS

To maintain its unique focus, the Institute relies upon highly distinguished editors, all leading experts in national or international antitrust: Bill Kovacic, Mario Monti, Eleanor Fox, Laurence Idot, Frédéric Jenny, Ioannis Lianos, Richard Whish, etc.

AUTHORS

3,800 authors, from 55 jurisdictions.

PARTNERS

- Universities: University College London, King's College London, Queen Mary University, Paris Sorbonne Panthéon-Assas, etc.

- Law firms: Allen & Overy, Cleary Gottlieb Steen & Hamilton, Baker McKenzie, Hogan Lovells, Jones Day, Norton Rose Fulbright, Skadden Arps, White & Case, etc.

EVENTS

Brussels, Dusseldorf, Hong Kong, London, Milan, New York, Paris, Singapore, Warsaw and Washington, DC.

ONLINE VERSION

Concurrences website provides all articles published since its inception.

PUBLICATIONS

The Institute publishes Concurrences Review, a print and online quarterly peer-reviewed journal dedicated to EU and national competitions laws. e-Competitions is a bi-monthly antitrust news bulletin covering 85 countries. The e-Competitions database contains over 18,000 case summaries from 4,000 authors.

17 years of archives
30,000 articles

4 DATABASES

Concurrences
Access to latest issue and archives

- 12,000 articles from 2004 to the present
- European and national doctrine and case law

e-Competitions
Access to latest issue and archives

- 18,000 case summaries from 1911 to the present
- Case law of 85 jurisdictions

Books
Access to all Concurrences books

- 42 e-Books available
- PDF version

Conferences
**Access to the documentation
of all Concurrences events**

- 500 conferences (Brussels, Hong Kong, London, New York, Paris, Singapore and Washington, DC)
- 250 PowerPoint presentations, proceedings and syntheses
- 300 videos
- Verbatim reports

NEW

New search engine
Optimized results to save time

- Search results sorted by date, jurisdiction, keyword, economic sector, author, etc.

New modes of access
IP address recognition

- No need to enter codes: immediate access
- No need to change codes when your team changes: offers increased security and saves time

Mobility

- Responsive design: site optimized for tablets and smartphones